ETHICS
PROBLEMS AND PRINCIPLES

ETHICS
PROBLEMS AND PRINCIPLES

JOHN MARTIN FISCHER

MARK RAVIZZA

Harcourt Brace Jovanovich College Publishers
Fort Worth Philadelphia San Diego
New York Orlando Austin San Antonio
Toronto Montreal London Sydney Tokyo

23463554

Publisher   Ted Buchholz
Acquisitions Editor   Jo-Anne Weaver
Project Editor   Cindy Lavin
Production Manager   J. Montgomery Shaw
Art & Design Supervisor   John Ritland
Text Designer   Wendy Calmenson/The Book Company
Cover Designer   Eva Thornton

"Ethics" by Thomas Nagel from *The View From Nowhere* by Thomas Nagel. Copyright © 1986 by Thomas Nagel. Reprinted by permission of Oxford University Press, Inc.

Library of Congress Cataloging-in-Publication Data

Fischer, John Martin, 1952-
    Ethics: problems and principles/John Martin Fischer, Mark
  Ravizza.
        p.   cm.
    Includes bibliographical references and index.
    ISBN 0-03-047527-9 (pbk.)
    1. Ethics.   2. Social ethics.   I. Ravizza, Mark, 1958–
  II. Title.
  BJ1012.F536   1991
  170—dc20
ISBN: 0-03-047527-9

91-12246
CIP

Address for editorial correspondence:
301 Commerce Street, Suite 3700
Fort Worth, TX 76102

Address for orders:
6277 Sea Harbor Drive
Orlando, Florida 32887
1-800-782-4479, or 1-800-433-0001 (in Florida)

PRINTED IN THE UNITED STATES OF AMERICA

2 3 4 5 016 9 8 7 6 5 4 3 2 1

We dedicate this book to our nieces and nephew:
Jenna, Molly, Anna, Melanie, and Matthew

Preface

This book is designed to assist individuals in thinking about their moral lives. More specifically, it is designed to help people come to understand and refine our moral principles and to see how they apply to various situations.

We begin the Introduction with a number of moral puzzle cases. These puzzles and hypothetical problems are then analyzed in the rest of the Introduction and used for discussion throughout the book. The puzzles and problems help to focus our attention on the variety of contexts in which moral issues emerge and the different aspects of those contexts which are morally important. Thinking about the problem cases helps us to achieve a deeper, more incisive understanding of our own moral convictions and commitments. And we need such an understanding if we are to lead our lives responsibly and participate in the democratic political process.

We believe this book will prove useful to students with varying levels of experience, including beginning students, who should be able to discern the moral dilemmas and puzzles and identify the main options for resolving the problems. Students new to philosophy should make use of the Introduction and the summaries of the articles as guides to reading the articles in this book. These guides should help the student to see our main points and how these points connect with those of other authors. Also, these guides assist the student in carefully reading, interpreting, and critically evaluating the arguments of the authors. The Introduction and summaries are not *substitutes* for the articles, but they are *supplements* to them.

Many of the articles collected here are not easy to read. They involve some intricate and challenging argumentation, certain to benefit intermediate and advanced students of philosophy. Beginning students will be able to see the problems, the main ways of responding to the problems, and the process involved in organizing moral views. More advanced students will see the rich complexity of the problems and the intricacies of the various theoretical options.

We believe this book can stand alone as the single text in a course on ethics. Alternatively, the book can be used in conjunction with other texts. One possibility would be to use this text with a text on contemporary ethical issues (such as abortion, preferential treatment, and so forth). Another possibility would be to use a text with selections from the history of ethics. An excellent historical text is Oliver A. Johnson's *Ethics: Selections from Classical and Contemporary Writers,* published by Holt, Rinehart and Winston, Inc.

John Martin Fischer and Mark Ravizza
University of California, Riverside

Acknowledgments

We are very grateful to many people who have helped us with this project. Charles Young, Robert Hanna, and Alexander Rosenberg have given us careful and insightful comments on the Introduction. Greg Ransom compiled the Bibliography (in consultation with us). The following have provided invaluable assistance with the summaries of the articles: Greg Ransom, Andrew Light, Yoko Arisaka, Sarah Austin, and Ken Dickey. We thank all of you for your help.

Contents

Part I

INTRODUCTION

MORAL PROBLEMS AND PUZZLES

Consider, to begin, the case of Bystander 2.[1] A trolley is hurtling down the tracks. There is an "innocent" person on the track ahead of the trolley, and he will be killed if the trolley continues going straight ahead. There is a spur of track leading to the right. Unfortunately, there are five "innocent" persons on that spur of track. The brakes of the trolley have failed, and you are strolling by the track. You see that you could throw a switch that would cause the trolley to go onto the right spur. You are an "innocent bystander," in the sense that you are not an employee of the railroad, or a member of any public safety agency. You can throw the switch, saving the one person but causing the five to die, or you can do nothing, allowing the one to die. Unfortunately, the only way in which you can save the one person is by causing the five to die. What should you do?

The persons on the tracks have done nothing morally wrong for which they deserve to die, nor have they forfeited their right to life. Moreover—and this is a general assumption in describing all of these puzzle cases—no "special" facts distinguish the persons involved in the cases. For instance, none of the six persons involved in Bystander 2 is a great scientist about to find a cure for cancer, a great musician, or any other type of gifted individual. Furthermore, you have not made special arrangements with any of them.[2]

It seems that it would be at least permissible for you to omit the option of shunting the train to the right and thus allow it to continue going straight ahead. Perhaps it is also obligatory to do this, but it seems at least reasonable that you may allow the trolley to continue. You fail to save the one, but you preserve the lives of the five.

Consider a second case, Transplant.[3] You are a great surgeon—a remarkably great surgeon. There are five persons in the hospital, each of whom needs an organ in order to survive. It just so happens that an innocent visitor has arrived in the hospital, and you know that he is tissue-compatible with all the people who need organs, and that you could cut him up and distribute his parts among the five who need them. Would it be permissible for you to perform the operation without his consent?

Surely, it is uncontroversial that you may *not* proceed. It is impermissible for you to perform the operation, and it seems that this is so even if you could conceal what you had done (for example, if you knew that the visitor is a hermit, and no one would find out that he had been killed). Why is it permissible for you to save the five in Bystander 2, but not in Transplant? In both cases the numbers are the same: you can either act so that one lives or act so that five live. Why exactly may you act so that the five live in the first case, but not in the second? It is interesting to note here that we are not interested only in the outcomes or consequences of our behavior, but we are also deeply interested in how they come about. We are interested in the paths that lead to the outcomes as well as the outcomes themselves.

Consider a third case, Drug. You own a bottle of medicine. Five persons are dying, and each needs one-fifth of the medicine in order to survive. Another person is dying, but he needs all of the medicine in order to survive. What should you do?

Given that you have not promised the medicine to the one person, it is at least permissible for you to give the medicine to the five. Perhaps it is also obligatory to give the medicine to the five (supposing that you do not need it), but it is evidently at least permissible to do so.[4]

Consider now a fourth case, Fat Man.[5] You are standing on a bridge, watching a trolley hurtling down the tracks below you toward five innocent persons. The brakes have failed, and the only way you can stop the train is to impede its progress by throwing a heavy object in its path. There is a fat man standing on the bridge next to you, and you could push him over the railing and onto the tracks below. If you do, the fat man will die, but the five will be saved. (You can imagine that you wouldn't need to push the fat man to get him to topple. Perhaps he is peering over the handrailing watching the lamentable scenario below, and you can simply wobble the handrail . . .)

What should you do? It may seem, upon first thinking about the case, that it is quite clear that you may not push the fat man over the railing. This conclusion, however, raises the question, why is it permissible to save the five in Drug but not in Fat Man? Obviously, this is parallel to the question about Bystander 2 and Transplant. What is it in the pairs of cases, Bystander 2 and Drug, on the one hand, and the pair of Transplant and Fat Man, on the other, that makes these cases similar yet crucially different from each other?

Suppose now that you have a boat. Alarmingly, there are six persons drowning, but in different places. You can save five, who are in the same area, or you can save one, who is in a different area. You cannot save all six drowning swimmers. As in Bystander 2 and Drug, it seems at least permissible to save the five in Boat.

Next, consider Shark. You see a large shark heading toward five swimmers. It is evident to you that the swimmers are in jeopardy, especially since you have just seen the movie "Jaws"! You are on a pier, where there is an innocent fisherman fishing. You happen to have a gun, and while you cannot shoot the shark, you could shoot the fisherman and cause him to fall into the path of the shark.[6] The shark would then eat the fisherman, thus allowing the five swimmers to escape.

What to do? As in Transplant and Fat Man, it does not seem permissible here to save the five. Rather, it seems evident that you may not shoot the innocent fisherman even if, by doing so, you could save the five innocent persons.

The above puzzle cases illustrate the fact that we care not just about outcomes or consequences, but also about the means by which we arrive at these end-states. Our intuitions are thus "path-dependent," or "path-sensitive." What principles can explain this path-sensitivity? What general principles can explain the asymmetries in our intuitive judgments about the puzzle cases? Why do we equate Bystander 2, Drug, and Boat, on the one hand, and Transplant, Fat Man, and Shark, on the other; and why do we distinguish morally between the first three cases and the second three?

Rights Strategy.   It is often tempting to appeal to the idea of rights (moral rights) in trying to resolve moral problems. When you hear the description of Transplant, you might be tempted to say that it is wrong to kill the innocent visitor and use his organs to save the five dying patients because you would be violating some right of his. The claim would be that it is unethical to violate such a right, even in order to save many people's lives.

Which right is it that is (allegedly) being violated? Suppose one says, as surely it is plausible to say, that the right in question is the right to retain one's bodily parts. Presumably, each of us has strong moral rights to retain all of our bodily parts; perhaps these rights are analogous to property rights. In any case, it is reasonable to say that it is wrong to kill the one individual in Transplant because you would be violating his rights to retain his bodily organs; you would be taking things to which a person has rights and giving them to others who have no such rights to those things.

Upon reflection, however, this explanation of the wrongness of killing the one individual in Transplant seems inadequate. To better understand this inadequacy, consider another case, Scan.[7] Again, there are five persons dying. This time they are dying of a disease. Suppose that there is a scanning device that can scan the brain of an individual, and if the individual has certain neurological properties, can generate information that can be used to save the five dying persons. Imagine further that there is an innocent visitor in the hospital who is neurologically suited to the scan. Unfortunately, if you (a great neurologist) do the scan, you kill this innocent person, for the scanning method is lethal. You can save the five if you do the scan, but you will kill the one if you do so, and this is the only way in which you could save the five.

It seems that Transplant and Scan are morally on the same par. If it is morally unacceptable to save the five in Transplant, it is also morally unacceptable to save the five in Scan. However, the explanation suggested above of the wrongness of saving the five in Transplant is clearly irrelevant to Scan: there is no issue of property rights to one's bodily parts or the redistribution of something from someone with a stronger claim (right) to it to others with a weaker—or no—claim (right) to it. Thus, the explanation above developed to explain the wrongness of saving the five in Transplant is unsatisfying insofar as it is not possible to *generalize* it appropriately.

Note that this situation is similar to Fat Man. Here, it was thought to be impermissible to shove the fat man in front of the train, thus saving the five. Unlike Scan, however, there is no issue of rights over bodily parts in Fat Man. One is not proposing to take things to which an individual has rights and give them to others who have no such rights. Thus, the purported explanation in terms of rights over one's bodily organs does not generalize suitably to all of the relevant cases.

Perhaps a rights theorist will fall back on the claim that in Transplant you would be violating an innocent person's right to life. It might be claimed that the pertinent right is the right to life, rather than rights to particular bodily organs. The claim here would be that it is in general wrong to behave so that one individual's right to life is violated, even if by acting so that the right is violated you could save five innocent persons' lives.

Notice, however, that in Bystander 2 you would be behaving so that one innocent person's right to life is violated if you were to refrain from shunting the train to the right. Nevertheless, it is not impermissible to do so. In Drug (if you were to distribute the drug to save the five instead of giving all of it to save the one patient) and Boat (if you were to rescue the five drowning swimmers instead of the lone swimmer), you would also be behaving so that one person's right to life is violated in order to save five. Again, we do not feel that it is impermissible to behave in this way. Thus, we do not see how any simple, straightforward appeal to the right to life can help resolve the moral puzzles presented above.

Some might say, however, that there is a crucial distinction between *violating* a right and merely *not guaranteeing* that an individual have the thing to which he has a right. So, for example, in Bystander 2 you would (allegedly) not violate the one person's right to life by failing to shunt the train away from him; you would merely fail to guarantee that the individual's life be preserved. Taking this approach, one cannot passively violate a right—one cannot violate a right by failing to act (or by "doing nothing"). There would thus be an important distinction between actively violating a right and passively comporting oneself so that a right is allowed to be violated. This approach raises the issue of whether we can appeal to the distinction between action and omission in attempting to generate a solution to our puzzle.

Actions and Omissions. Some think that there is a critical moral difference between actively bringing about an outcome and passively bringing it about, i.e., allowing it to happen. They think that the difference between action and omission in itself is morally significant. Employing the idea that there is such a difference, one might frame principles that explain our moral intuitions in some of the puzzle cases.

If it is wrong, in general, to actively bring about a death (even if by doing so one can prevent five deaths from occurring), then it would be wrong in Transplant to kill the innocent visitor to the hospital, even if by doing so you could use his organs to save five dying patients. Furthermore, a proponent of the moral importance of the distinction between action and omission might say that it would be permissible to allow the one to die in Bystander 2. In Bystander 2 you merely allow the one to die, whereas in Transplant you must kill the one in order to save the five. Similar considerations apply to the other cases. In Fat Man (if you push the fat man in front of the trolley) and Shark (if you shoot the fisherman so that he falls in front of the shark), you would actively bring about the death of the one in order to save the five, whereas in Drug (if you use the drug to save five patients instead of one) and Boat (if you rescue five swimmers instead of one), you would simply refrain from saving the one and thereby save the five.

It is not at all evident, however, that the principle that embodies this distinction between action and omission is suitably generalizable. Suppose that you (for whatever reason) wish that your husband were dead. He is about to have his morning coffee, and you give him a bit of cleaning fluid, claiming that it is cream. He puts it in his coffee and dies. In Cleaning Fluid 1 you actively bring about the death of your husband.

Suppose that in Cleaning Fluid 2 you have exactly the same (regrettable) motivation. In this case the maid has left some cleaning fluid on the kitchen table, and your husband is about to put it into his coffee (thinking that it is cream). You see that he is about to do so, and you can easily warn him. You refrain. He puts the cleaning fluid in his coffee, drinks it, and dies. (We are supposing here that the man uses rather a lot of cream.)

The only difference between the two cases is the difference between action and omission—everything else is held constant. Yet there does not seem to be any moral difference between the two cases. The act of killing your husband is equally wrong in both cases. Thus, the difference between action and omission cannot *in itself* be morally relevant. These two cases are exactly the same factually except for the difference between action and omission, and they are the same morally. Thus, if there are two cases in which there is a difference between action and omission accompanied by a moral difference, the moral difference must come either from some factor other than the difference between action and omission, or from this factor plus some additional factor. This is because if the difference between action and omission is in itself morally significant, then it would be impossible to have the original pair of cases in which there is only a difference between action and omission and no moral difference.[8]

To further emphasize the point, consider Bystander 1. Bystander 1 is just like Bystander 2, except that in Bystander 1 the five persons are on the track straight ahead, and the one person is on the spur of track to the right. (This is Judith Jarvis Thomson's version of "Bystander.") It seems to us that Bystander 2 and Bystander 1 are morally on the same par. It is permissible to behave so that the five are saved in Bystander 2 if and only if it is permissible to behave so that the five are saved in Bystander 1. How can it make a decisive moral difference in these cases whether or not you push a button (which shunts the train to the right)? If these two cases are morally on a par, then there is further reason to think that the difference between action and omission is not in itself always morally significant.

The Doctrine of Double Effect.   In Transplant, the death of the innocent visitor to the hospital is in some fairly clear intuitive sense a means to saving the five. You would be using the innocent person as a means to achieving your (admittedly worthwhile) goal. On the other hand, in a case like Bystander 2 (or for that matter, Bystander 1), the death of the one is in no way a means to saving the five. For example, in Bystander 1, if you press a button that causes the train to go to the right, pushing the button (and thereby reconfiguring the tracks) would be your means to saving the five, and the death of the one would be a mere side-effect of what you did. Similarly, in Fat Man and Shark, the death of the one innocent person would be (in some clear intuitive sense) your means to saving the five, whereas in Drug and Boat the death of the innocent individuals would be mere side-effects (and not means).

The **Doctrine of Double Effect** distinguishes between intended *ends* and necessary *means,* on the one hand, and unintended but foreseen *side-effects* on the other. The doctrine exploits this distinction to claim that whereas it is sometimes permissible to bring about a bad result as a merely foreseen side-effect of what you do, it is in general not permissible to bring about such an effect as an intended end or a necessary means to some intended end. In particular, the doctrine claims that it is sometimes permissible to kill an innocent person as a foreseen (but unintended) side-effect of something you do, but it is in general impermissible to kill an innocent person as an intended end or a necessary means of an intended end. Thus, the doctrine would rule out killing the one in Transplant, Fat Man, and Shark, while leaving it a permissible option to save the five in Bystander 1, Drug, and Boat.

How is it possible to distinguish exactly what constitutes an intended means or a mere side-effect? This is a very difficult project. The difference is that when one intends something as a means to an end-result, then it is appropriate to change one's behavior under certain hypothetical circumstances to bring about the same intended end-result. The same alterations in behavior would not be appropriate if the thing in question were merely foreseen rather than intended as a means. For example, suppose that in Shark, when you shoot the fisherman, he falls away from the path of the shark and lands on a rock. It would then be appropriate to shoot him again, thus causing him to land in the water in the path of the shark (insofar as this is possible). In contrast, if in Boat the one swimmer is able to make it to a rock and thus avoid drowning, it would be inappropriate (and indeed completely gratuitous) to push him off the rock or otherwise cause him to drown. When one intends a bad result, one's behavior must be adjusted to achieve this result; one's behavior "tracks" or is guided by badness. This tracking of badness or "attraction" to badness may seem particularly morally objectionable.

Consider the following case, Hospital.[9] There are five innocent persons in a hospital. They all need some medication in order to live. Unfortunately, the only way to save them is to manufacture a drug right in the hospital. Suppose that the process of manufacturing the drug releases (as a side-effect) a lethal gas that would kill one innocent person in another room in the hospital.

The Doctrine of Double Effect implies that it would not be permissible to cut up an innocent visitor to save the five dying patients in Transplant, but it would be permissible to save the five in Hospital. After all, in Transplant, the death of the one would be an intended means of saving the five, while in Hospital, the death of the one would be a mere side-effect of what one does in order to save the five. This discrimination between the two cases seems implausible, however: Transplant and Hospital seem to be morally equivalent (although plainly factually different in certain respects).[10] To the extent that the doctrine appears to introduce a differentiation not licensed by common sense, it is to that extent implausible. Again, this principle does not appear to generalize in an appropriate fashion.

Suppose, also, that in Bystander 3, the right spur of track loops around and connects with the main track. Thus, if the one person (imagine that he is large enough to stop the train) were not on the track to the right, the train would continue around and eventually run over the five; but someone *is* on the track. Think of Bystander 3 as in all other respects relevantly similar to Bystander 1. Now it would seem that the Doctrine of Double Effect implies that although it would be permissible to shunt the train to the right and thereby save the five in Bystander 1, it would *not* be permissible to do so in Bystander 3. This is because the death of the one in Bystander 1 would be a mere side-effect of what one does in order to save the five, but the probable death of the one in Bystander 3 would be a necessary means of saving the five. It is implausible to say that these two cases should be differentiated morally. Certainly there is a factual difference between the two cases—a bit of track—but this factual difference should not make a moral difference. Again, the Doctrine of Double Effect appears to introduce a normative differentiation that is not compatible with common sense.[11]

Let us go back to the alleged justification (or normative motivation) for the Doctrine of Double Effect. It was claimed that it is particularly morally repugnant to be "guided" or "tugged" by evil—to adjust one's behavior to track badness. Typically, in a case where one intends a death as a means, one has **nested intentions**. Yes, one intends the death; but this intention is a mere proximate intention. One also intends some (apparent) greater good. Why should we focus on the mere proximate (or nested) intention and take it to be morally decisive? Why shouldn't the agent's ultimate intention be relevant (or even decisive)? When one intends evil as a means, one's behavior adjusts to track evil but only as a means to some greater intended good.

Harming and Failing to Benefit. Intuitively, it seems almost inescapable that there is a moral difference between harming someone and merely failing to benefit him. For example, if I were to kill my neighbor's child, I would harm the child in a particularly egregious manner. In contrast, when I fail to send money to feed a starving child in Mozambique, I merely fail to benefit the child. It seems clearly worse to kill my neighbor's child than to fail to save a child in Mozambique.

The distinction between harming and failing to benefit has been employed by those who believe that we have stronger **negative duties** than **positive duties**. A negative duty is a responsibility not to harm, whereas a positive duty is a responsibility to benefit (help or assist) someone.

The factual distinctions discussed above—between action and omission, between intended means and mere side-effects—are (quite apart from their normative uses) tricky and delicate. Similarly, it is difficult to say exactly what it is to harm someone (or even to benefit him).[12] Let us say, however, that harming someone at least involves making him worse off than he otherwise would have been, whereas benefiting someone makes him better off than he otherwise would have been.

Proponents of the claim that we have stronger negative duties than positive duties attach intrinsic moral significance to the distinction between harming and merely failing to benefit. Thus, they can say that in Bystander 2, you would merely fail to benefit the one (if you allowed the train to proceed straight ahead), whereas you would clearly harm the innocent visitor to the hospital in Transplant if you were to cut him up in order to save the five. Similarly, in Fat Man (if you push the fat man) and Shark (if you shoot the fisherman), you would have to harm one in order to save the five, whereas in Drug and Boat you merely fail to benefit one in order to save the five.

Just as Bystander 1 indicated the inadequacy of the claim that the distinction between action and omission is in itself always morally significant, it also points to the inadequacy of the parallel claim with respect to harm and failing to benefit. If Bystander 2 and Bystander 1 are morally on a par, then the distinction between harming and merely failing to benefit cannot in itself be morally significant.

Consider also Random Mechanism. In this case, the tracks are configured in the shape of a Y. On the left track are five innocent persons, and on the right is one. There is a random mechanism at the bifurcation point of the tracks; when the train arrives, the mechanism randomly directs it either to the right or the left. Suppose, however, that you (a bystander) can override the random mechanism by pressing a certain button. If you press the button, the train is definitely shunted to the right—the five are saved, but you cause the death of the one.

The principle asserting stronger negative than positive duties appears to permit you to allow the death of the one in Bystander 2 while not allowing you to save the five in Random Mechanism. This is because in Bystander 2 you would not be harming the one—you would not be making him worse off than he would be "otherwise" (i.e., but for your intervention). In contrast, in Random Mechanism, it seems that you would be making the one worse off than he otherwise might be. You would transform the situation from one where the one had a fifty-fifty chance of living to one where he essentially had no chance of living. Perhaps it is not obvious, but we believe that Bystander 2 and Random Mechanism are morally on a par. If it is permissible to allow the one to die in Bystander 2, thus saving the five, it seems permissible to save the five in Random Mechanism. Again, the principle appears to posit a moral discrimination which is not licensed by our considered intuitive judgments.

Thomson's Strategy.   Let's go back to Bystander 1. Here, it seems permissible to shunt the train to the right, thus saving the five. Notice that, if you were to do so, you would take something that threatens five and deflect it so that it threatens only one. Here you would be doing something to the threat to minimize the incidence of a bad result; you would not be doing something bad to a person to minimize the incidence of a bad result, nor would you be introducing a new threat.

In contrast, in Transplant, if you were to save the five you would (in a clear sense) do something bad to a person (i.e., killing someone for his vital organs) in order to minimize the incidence of a bad result. Also, you would introduce a new threat, not simply redirect an already extant threat.

Judith Jarvis Thomson employs the above insights to suggest the following: whereas it may be permissible to redirect an already extant threat in order to minimize the incidence of a bad result, it is in general impermissible either to redirect an extant threat by acts that themselves violate someone's stringent rights or to introduce a new threat in order to minimize the incidence of a bad result. Note that in Fat Man and Shark, you would clearly violate someone's stringent rights in order to achieve your goals, whereas in Drug and Boat you would not.

The principle suggested by Thomson is different from the Doctrine of Double Effect. The doctrine distinguishes morally between Transplant and Hospital. In contrast, Thomson's principle appears to rule out saving the five in both cases. This is because, in Transplant, you are clearly violating the innocent visitor's stringent rights if you use his organs to save the five dying patients, and in Hospital (if you save five patients by manufacturing a drug that produces a lethal gas that kills one patient), you are introducing a new threat rather than merely redirecting an already extant threat.

Thomson's principle does, however, apparently have some unintuitive implications. Consider first an implication which Thomson recognizes and embraces. Thomson's principle would distinguish the following two cases.

The first case is called Deflect-onto-Pasadena. In this case, China has launched a nuclear weapon toward Los Angeles. The president is informed. He can either allow the bomb to continue on its path, in which case it would hit Los Angeles, or he can employ deflecting missiles that would cause the bomb to be redirected. Unfortunately, the redirected bomb would land in Pasadena. The president cannot cause the bomb to avoid hitting a populous area altogether, but considerably fewer people would die if the bomb were to hit Pasadena.

The second case is Bomb Pasadena. In this case, China has launched a nuclear weapon toward Los Angeles. The president is informed, but this time he does not have any deflecting technology available to him. Rather, he can directly bomb Pasadena. The explosion in Pasadena would cause the bomb to change its trajectory, and the Chinese bomb (heading toward Los Angeles) would then be deflected into a remote desert area. Of course, many people would die as a result of the bombing of Pasadena, but we may plausibly suppose that considerably fewer would die than if Los Angeles were hit by the nuclear weapon.

Thomson's principle implies that the two cases are morally disparate. It implies that, whereas it would be permissible for the president to cause the bomb to be deflected in Deflect-onto-Pasadena, it would *not* be permissible for the president to cause the bomb to be deflected in the manner suggested in Bomb Pasadena. It is not evident, however, that there exists such a moral difference. To see this point, consider the following cases.

Call the first case, Jiggle-the-Tracks 1.[13] A trolley is hurtling down a track toward five innocent persons. As before, the brakes have failed, and there is no way of stopping the trolley. You are a bystander watching the scenario develop. You notice that there is a spur of track leading to the right on which (very close to the bifurcation of the tracks) stands one innocent person. You also notice that there is a button you could push that would cause the tracks to jiggle in such a way as to cause the train to go onto the right fork. If you were to push the button, you would save the five persons but cause the death of the one.

What to do? It seems intuitively permissible to push the button, and Thomson's approach would permit this option. You would deflect a threat that threatens five in such a way that it then threatens only one.

Now imagine a related case, Jiggle-the-Tracks 2. Everything is the same here except for the manner of track-jiggling which would result from your pushing the button. That is, there is a trolley hurtling down the tracks toward five persons with a spur leading to the right on which there stands a man (very close to the point of track bifurcation). This time, if you push the button, the tracks would be jiggled in such a way that the man would be toppled onto the track in front of the train. Suppose that the man is large enough to stop the progress of the train, but if this were to occur, he would be killed.

The two Jiggle cases seem to be morally parallel. It would be morally permissible to push the button in Jiggle 2 if and only if it would be morally permissible to do so in Jiggle 1. Whereas it seems that there is no important moral difference between the two cases, Thomson's approach must distinguish them. She must say that although it is morally permissible to push the button in Jiggle 1, it would not be morally permissible to do so in Jiggle 2. This is because in Jiggle 1, you would deflect a threat without violating anyone's stringent rights, whereas in Jiggle 2 you would violate someone's rights when you jiggle the man onto the track.

Here is a similar pair of cases. Call the first case, Lethal Gas 1. In this case, you can see that lethal gas is proceeding down a hallway toward a room in which there are five innocent persons. You know that there is a trapdoor leading to a small room to the right. If you open the trapdoor, the lethal gas will be directed to the right, killing an innocent man who is sitting in the room.

Lethal Gas 2 is similar except that you know that if you open the trapdoor and do nothing else, the lethal gas will continue proceeding toward the end of the hallway to the room where the five are. (Perhaps there is a different draft of air in Lethal Gas 2 from the one in Lethal Gas 1.) You see, however, that if you open the trapdoor and push the one man (who, again, is sitting in a small room to the right) into the main hallway, he will stop the lethal gas (perhaps he is fat and the hall is narrow). Lamentably, if you push the man into the hallway, the lethal gas will kill him.

In Lethal Gas 1, diverting the gas onto the man redirects a threat without violating anyone's stringent rights. In Lethal Gas 2, pushing the man into the gas violates the man's rights. Thomson must distinguish the two cases. Although there is a clear factual difference between the two cases, it is unclear that this factual difference underwrites a moral difference. It seems that the two Lethal Gas cases are morally equivalent, and yet Thomson's approach must distinguish them.

Participants and Bystanders.   It is very tempting to say about Transplant, for example, that if you were to cut up the visitor in the hospital, you would take someone, for example, who was not a **participant** in the problematic context or situation and force him into the situation. The visitor is not a participant in the original situation; he is a mere outsider or **bystander**. In contrast, in cases such as the Bystander cases, all of the persons involved are participants. Similarly, in Fat Man, you would take a mere outsider and force him into the situation (if you were to push the fat man over the handrail), whereas in Drug, you would simply make a decision between participants (insiders).[14]

This approach distinguishes nicely between cases such as Random Mechanism and Fat Man because the persons on the alternative tracks to which a trolley is randomly directed are all participants in a way that the fat man is not; but what about cases such as Bystander 1 and Fat Man? How can it be established that the one person in Bystander 1 is a participant, whereas the fat man in Fat Man is a mere outsider? It is unclear how this could be established. In Fat Man, the fat man would not be in danger but for the existence of the bystander who can cause him to fall over the handrail. In Bystander 1, the one person would not be in danger but for the existence of the bystander who can cause the train to be shunted to the right. So it is a challenge for the proponent of this approach to distinguish in a useful way between insiders (participants) and outsiders (bystanders).

Non-additivity.   In his contribution to this anthology, John Taurek describes a distinctive way of viewing certain cases. His point is that moral "goods" and "bads" are **non-additive**. That is to say, if five individuals experience some moral bad, it need not follow that this state of affairs is morally worse than one in which one individual experiences the same moral bad. For instance, if five individuals experience a headache of a certain intensity, this is not necessarily a morally worse situation than one in which one individual experiences a headache of the same intensity. One way of arguing for this sort of view (or at least rendering it plausible) is to point out that we cannot simply add up the five separate headaches to get one migraine; there is no single individual who experiences a "mega-headache" composed of the five headaches of the five separate individuals. Similarly, Taurek would argue that the death of one is no worse a situation than the deaths of five.

If one adopts this view, one might be attracted to a certain way of resolving cases such as Bystander 1, Drug, and Boat. For example, in Drug, one might be tempted to flip a coin to determine whether to give the drug to the one or the five. This approach would give each individual an equal chance of surviving. Similarly, one might explore a similar strategy in cases such as Bystander 1 (and Bystander 2) and Boat.

However, this leaves the residual problem of whether one should also employ these strategies in cases such as Transplant, Fat Man, and Shark. Evidently not. Thus, the approach suggested by Taurek does not in itself provide the resources to solve the puzzles set out above. (In all fairness, however, it should be noted that Taurek does not suggest that his approach can be employed to solve this problem, only that it is appropriate in certain contexts.)

Summary.   We have presented a number of cases with puzzling results. We next considered various principles (some of which embody distinctions that seem quite intuitive and natural) that attempt to distinguish the cases in illuminating and satisfying ways. We have seen the strengths and weaknesses of the various principles. None of the proposals seems entirely adequate. None of the proposed principles captures all of our considered judgments about the puzzle cases. Of course, it does not follow from this fact that the proposed principles are worthless. Many of them capture what we want to say about certain situations, even if they don't crystallize what we want to say about all situations. Furthermore, we can learn from their inadequacies, possibly revising them and building upon their insights. The inadequacy of existing proposals might provide reason to continue to seek more refined and morally sensitive principles. Ultimately, we seek a less superficial—and more penetrating—level of understanding.

METHODOLOGY

Although there may be a wide area of agreement on moral matters, reasonable people may disagree about many cases. How can disagreements be resolved in ethics? It is relatively clear how to proceed in order to make progress in mathematics and science, but how can progress be made in ethics? At this point we need to discuss methodology in ethics.

Let us begin by thinking about how we go about practicing a science—physical science or social science. Start with astronomy. There are certain data which must be explained by some general theory. The data here are observations about planetary motion, for example. After collecting a certain number of data, we seek to explain the data by generating a set of principles. These principles need to imply the data and also meet certain other conditions. The principles should be internally consistent, compact (i.e., non-redundant), and (in some sense which is difficult to specify) "explanatory." The principles must help us to systematize and understand the data. Having generated a set of principles that explain the data we have collected, we are in a position to predict future data—astronomical theories will allow us to predict future planetary motions.

Similarly, in a social science such as linguistics, we begin with a set of data that need to be explained. Suppose the data are a collection of judgments concerning which sequences of words in a certain language constitute "well-formed sentences." That is, the data are native speakers' judgments about which sequences of words are syntactically (grammatically) appropriate. For example, in English the sequence of words, "mat lays green slowly dog GNP," is not a well-formed, grammatical sentence. In contrast, "John reads the book," is. Given a collection of such judgments, a linguist develops a set of principles that explain and underlie the data. These principles may be called a "grammar"; they specify the syntactic rules of a language. As above, the principles should imply the data, and they should be internally consistent, compact (i.e., non-redundant), and illuminating. Once the grammar has been generated, we should be able to employ it to make predictions about which sentences will be judged to be acceptable.

In both the case of a natural science and a social science, we seek a certain match between the data and the general principles. We seek a homeostasis or equilibrium—the principles should be in accord with the data. What if our general principles are inconsistent with some of the data? It is clear that, insofar as we wish to attain an equilibrium, we must either alter the principles or reconsider the data. In the natural sciences, for example, we may repeat experiments or gather data again, making sure that the original data can be replicated and that distorting factors are screened out. Once we are sure of the data, we tend to take them as "hard," and we exhibit a propensity to adjust and reformulate our theories. Sometimes, if we are quite confident of our theories, we might temporarily "bracket" some data, assuming that we will be able to see them as distorted or inaccurate in the future; but we presumably feel an obligation to address the situation in the future. In order to achieve a suitable equilibrium in the social sciences, there may be a mutual adjustment between principles and data, but again the data are (it might seem) relatively fixed—one cannot simply alter the data *in order to make them fit with the principles.*

In one approach, ethics is similar to the natural and social sciences to the extent that it seeks a match between data and general principles. Here the data are intuitive judgments about particular cases, both actual and hypothetical, as well as about policies and rules. We seek a set of moral principles that fit suitably with the data. Again, these general principles should imply the data, and they should be internally consistent, compact, and (in some sense, though difficult to specify) illuminating or "explanatory." To be explanatory, the principles should not "latch onto" morally peripheral facts, even if by doing so they can remain consistent with the data; rather, they should pick out morally central and deep facts, facts that not only point us to the right actions, but also to the reasons for their rightness. Having generated a moral theory, this theory can help us to extend our moral judgments to new cases—problems and dilemmas we had not previously considered.

What do we do when certain data and our principles do not fit together? Again, we are faced with a problem of theoretical choice. We can either adjust the data, reconsidering our moral views about a particular matter, or we can retain our moral views about a particular matter and adjust our principles to fit the particular judgment. (Perhaps we can do a bit of both sorts of adjustment.) The "tinkering" and adjustment process in ethics goes both ways. Sometimes we re-think a particular judgment, and sometimes we must re-think our principles. Ultimately, we seek what John Rawls has called a **reflective equilibrium**.[15] We seek a state in which our principles are in accord with our judgments. This, of course, is the sort of project on which we embarked in the first section of this introductory essay; we tried to bring our judgments into alignment with certain general principles.

We should now distinguish between **narrow reflective equilibrium** and **wide reflective equilibrium**.[16] (The distinction is rough and a matter of degree.) When one is in a state of narrow reflective equilibrium, one's actual **intuitive judgments**—the judgments one makes about cases one has considered—are rendered consistent and systematized by a set of general principles. No wide-ranging consideration of hypothetical cases (not already considered by the agent) or the results of social theory is necessary here, and the principles considered may be rather narrow.

In contrast, when one is in a state of wide reflective equilibrium, one's **considered judgments** about a wide range of actual and hypothetical cases are rendered consistent with each other and with the truths of social science, and they are explained and organized by some underlying principles. Here one is obliged to consider a broad array of actual and possible cases, rules, and policies, and to integrate one's views with the truths of the social sciences. Ideally, in ethics (as opposed to more restricted contexts of practical reasoning), we ought to strive to achieve a wide reflective equilibrium.[17]

We have developed a parallel between the methodologies employed in the natural and social sciences and one proposed methodology for ethics. It is now time to consider a possible disanalogy. It might be supposed that, whereas the data in the natural sciences such as physics or astronomy are relatively hard and fixed—imposing a strong obligation to conform the theories to the data—the data in ethics are soft and elastic. That is, in ethics we often re-think a particular intuitive judgment in light of a plausible and powerful theory that organizes and explains our other intuitions. The situation is different in the natural sciences, however; one cannot simply ignore recalcitrant data (or alter them) so as to achieve harmony with the theory. (If one does temporarily bracket some data in science, there is presumably an obligation to address the situation in the future. Until the data are satisfactorily explained or explained away, the theory is not deemed fully adequate.)

One way to explain the apparent asymmetry between science and ethics with respect to the hardness of data is to say that whereas science is naturalistic, ethics is constructive.[18] A **naturalistic theory** would try to capture facts that are in the objective world and exist independently of theories. If science attempts to mirror objective, independent facts, it would be no surprise that the data of science would be relatively hard. A **constructive theory**, on the other hand, attempts not to discover pre-existent facts, but to create or construct the relevant facts. If moral theory does not attempt to capture and mirror an objective, independent world, but rather seeks to construct a consistent set of facts from our beliefs and intuitions, it is not surprising that there would be a certain flexibility in the data. That is, if particular moral judgments are not supposed to correspond to or match particular moral facts that exist in the objective world, then there might be more room to adjust particular moral judgments to fit into a coherent overall moral perspective.[19]

Of course, the alleged asymmetry in the hardness of data need not in any way vitiate the claim that ethics is in certain important respects similar to science. Furthermore, some would argue that the apparent asymmetry vanishes upon adoption of a more refined philosophy of science. These theorists would argue that scientific data are not immune to alteration and adjustment insofar as no data are purely "given" and independent of theory. Taking this holistic view, data are not separable from theories, and thus no data are in principle immune from alteration; the data are not unmediated mirrors of reality, but are always mediated by concepts and more abstract principles. If this is so, then there would be a convergence between the nature of the data in science and the nature of the data in ethics.

It is worth pursuing here another analogy between the methodology of science and the methodology of ethics proposed here (the method of seeking a wide reflective equilibrium). In science, we sometimes must construct elaborate experiments. The point of these experiments is to investigate the effects of changing the value of one variable. That is, we need to make sure that only one thing is varying at a time, in order to find out exactly what is causing the effect (if there is an important effect). In order to screen out distorting effects of other factors and to ensure that the values of only one variable are changing, sometimes it is necessary to construct incredibly elaborate, complex, and even expensive experiments. These experiments sometimes create conditions and circumstances that are quite different from the circumstances that ordinarily exist in the world. The whole purpose of these elaborate set-ups is to achieve a controlled experiment: we isolate one factor and see what its effects are.

Similarly, in ethics we sometimes construct elaborate hypothetical cases (some of which were presented earlier). An important purpose of such examples is to make sure that we have a **controlled ethical thought-experiment**. We wish to make sure that we isolate one factor (say, the difference between action and omission) and ascertain its effects. Of course, sometimes we must imagine conditions and circumstances quite different from what ordinarily exist in the world in order to successfully isolate one factor and screen out other distorting effects. Just as it is reasonable and appropriate to construct controlled experiments in science, it seems to be justified to do so in ethics. Few theorists object to the construction of elaborate scientific experiments that create conditions very different from the ones most frequently occurring in the world. The analogy between ethics and science in this respect would then provide some reason to accept the legitimacy of **hypothetical thought-experiments** in ethics.

It is useful to point out briefly how the method of seeking a wide reflective equilibrium works. We are looking for general principles that meet certain constraints (of consistency, compactness, and so forth) and that match the data in a satisfactory way. A satisfactory match requires that the principles not have (perhaps previously unnoticed) unintuitive consequences, that they be suitably generalizable, and that they neither introduce moral discriminations not found in common sense nor blur distinctions found in common sense. For example, we argued above that the principle which claims that there is intrinsic moral importance in the distinction between actions and omissions introduces a moral discrimination that is finer than what is dictated by common sense. A similar defect was uncovered in the Doctrine of Double Effect. Neither principle generalized satisfactorily. Ultimately we want moral principles that are *both* faithful to our deepest moral convictions *and* comprehensive.

It should be pointed out that the method of seeking a wide reflective equilibrium is not the only methodology that might be employed in ethics. An alternative methodology would claim that substantive moral principles (and judgments about particular cases) can be derived in some way from reason alone. In one such approach, the very structure of practical reasoning and moral agency issues in substantive moral principles. This approach is associated with Immanuel Kant (1724–1804). Another broadly Kantian approach argues that substantive moral principles can be derived from the nature of moral concepts such as "right" and "wrong," and "good" and "bad."[20] A different strategy would argue that substantive moral principles emanate from truths about human nature. This approach is Aristotelian (introduced by Aristotle, 384–322 B.C.).

Another approach to ethical methodology would claim that there are special moral facts in the world to which we have access by a faculty of ethical intuition; with this approach, we are not constructing the moral facts, and the moral facts are also not natural facts. They are special, "non-natural" facts to which we have access via our faculty of ethical intuition. Just as an astronomer might peer into a telescope to detect the planets, with this approach it is as if we peer into special moral telescopes to detect moral facts. This approach is associated with G. E. Moore (1873–1958).[21]

So the methodology which strives to secure a wide reflective equilibrium—sometimes called a **coherence approach** to ethics—is only one approach to methodology in ethics. Here we cannot argue that it is the only suitable methodology, or even the best. We merely present it as a viable approach to thinking about ethical problems, making progress toward understanding our own deepest commitments, and perhaps making progress toward reducing ethical disagreements.

The sort of thinking encouraged by the method of wide reflective equilibrium is particularly useful in coming to understand one's own moral views more fully and satisfactorily. This kind of thinking quite naturally provides guidelines for revising one's provisional moral principles. Thus, engaging in the sort of thinking encouraged by the method of wide reflective equilibrium can help us to generate principles which more faithfully reflect our deepest feelings and convictions. As our principles become more refined and precise, we gain a deeper understanding of the world and, ultimately, of ourselves.

APPLICATIONS

Thus far we have discussed how the Trolley Problem and other similar examples can be used to test and refine our normative principles. Now it is time to illustrate how these principles can be applied to some paradigmatically difficult ethical situations.

The Bombing of London. Consider the following situation that confronted English officials during the Second World War:

> A German "spy ring" in Britain consisted of a double agent on the British side and a string of fictitious people. It was on this supposed network of agents that the German government relied for information about where the V1 and V2 rockets were falling. The aiming was broadly accurate, hitting the target of London. It was proposed that the double agent should send back reports indicating that most of them had fallen well north of London, so that the rocket ranges would correct their aim a number of miles to the south. The result of this would have been to make most of the rockets fall in Kent, Surrey or Sussex, killing far fewer people than they did in London. This proposal is said to have been resisted successfully by Herbert Morrison, on the grounds that the British government was not justified in choosing to sacrifice one lot of citizens in order to save another lot.
>
> I do not know the details of the arguments actually used, but it may have been a reluctance to play a God-like role, deciding who is to live and who is to die, that made the members of the government resist the proposal. [22]

Did the English officials do the right thing in choosing not to divert the bombs? Would it have been permissible to sacrifice a smaller number of citizens in Kent, Surrey, or Sussex in order to save a greater number in London? This difficult case may be used to illustrate how the principles discussed earlier can provide guidance in morally complex situations.

First, consider Morrison's rationale for arguing that it was not permissible to divert the rockets. The suggestion given is that he might have argued for this decision out of a "reluctance to play a God-like role, deciding who is to live and who is to die." When examined more closely, this seems a poor justification for the decision. The Trolley-type examples show that, in the interest of producing the best outcome, sometimes it is permissible to intervene, even when doing so involves making life-and-death choices. Such examples illustrate that there is, as Judith Jarvis Thomson says, no Principle of Moral Inertia: "There is no *prima facie* duty to refrain from interfering with existing states of affairs just because they are existing states of affairs." [23] Simply because the trolley is currently heading for five people on one track, it does not follow that a bystander may not intervene and change its course in order to reduce the number of deaths. Similarly, the fact that the bombs already were aimed at London, did not in itself provide sufficient reason to avoid redirecting them onto a less populated area. The English decision not to divert the missiles needed, therefore, to be supported by something more than a hesitancy to tamper with the present course of events, or a reluctance to make life-and-death decisions.

Yet even if the purported reasons behind Morrison's argument were not the best, many share his intuition that even though it would result in a great many lives being saved, redirecting missiles onto innocent civilians is not permissible. Several of the principles discussed above provide support for this intuition. For example, this case naturally lends itself to the distinction between harming and failing to benefit. Recall that a negative duty (not to harm) is argued to be more stringent than a positive duty (to benefit). According to this principle, the English chose rightly in not diverting the missiles, because their negative duty to avoid harming the people in the outlying towns was greater than any positive duty to assist the people in London. Similarly, the English decision could be justified on the grounds that killing is worse than letting die. Analyzed in this way, the English officials had no choice but to let the people of London die, for to redirect the rockets would have made the officials witting accomplices in the killing of the citizens of Kent, Surrey, or Sussex, and such killing is impermissible even though it would prevent a greater number of deaths in London.

Of course, the general applicability of both the principle concerning positive and negative duties and of **killing and letting die** is challenged by the Trolley examples discussed previously. A principle that has been advanced to improve upon these traditional guidelines is Judith Jarvis Thomson's, which argues that an existing threat may be redirected (as long as this does not infringe the stringent rights of anyone), but a new threat may not be introduced. Accepting this sort of principle provides reason to reassess Morrison's view. Given that the bombs could have been diverted without infringing any stringent rights of the citizens of Kent, Surrey, and Sussex, strict application of Thomson's principle suggests that the English government would have been permitted (and perhaps even obligated) to divert the threat by redirecting the bombs onto the smaller towns.

A similar judgment is reached if the English decision is analyzed using the Doctrine of Double Effect, but for different reasons. Recall that this doctrine depends upon a distinction between foreseen side-effects, on the one hand, and intended ends and necessary means on the other. The Doctrine of Double Effect holds that although it may be permissible to perform an action that leads to some unintended but foreseen bad result, it is not permissible to perform an action that leads to a bad result as an intended end or necessary means to some intended end. According to this doctrine, the morally salient feature of the English decision was whether the deaths of the innocent citizens would have been either a necessary means or intended end of the missile diversion, or whether these deaths would have been merely a side-effect that was foreseen but unintended. Advocates of the plan to divert the missiles could plausibly have argued that only the latter was the case, for the officials' intention surely was to divert the bombs from London, not to kill the citizens of Kent, Surrey, or Sussex. That the deaths of the citizens would have been a foreseen but certainly unintended side-effect is evinced by the fact that even if all the citizens were miraculously to have left the cities on the day of the bombings, the British would still have wanted to redirect the missiles away from London and toward these cities.[24] (The point of redirecting the missiles would have been to protect the London citizens, and not to kill the citizens of the other three cities.) Insofar as the deaths of these citizens were neither an intended end nor necessary means to saving the lives of the people in London, it would have been permissible, according to the Doctrine of Double Effect, to divert the rockets.

Finally, a quite different way to approach this problem is to question why the English should have wanted to divert the bombs in the first place. It is natural to suppose that in such trade-off situations, the relative number of people involved should itself be a significant factor in one's decision. After all, other things being equal, it would seem better to have saved the lives of more people in London than of fewer people in Kent, Surrey, and Sussex combined. As the discussion above illustrated, however, this assumption may not be as self-evident as is first supposed. If Taurek is correct that the comparative number of lives lost is not in itself a morally decisive factor, then the English government would not have had any grounds even to begin justifying a decision to divert the missiles.

What should the English have done? A number of principles discussed earlier disagree about what the right course of action would have been. Others agree, but provide different explanations for their decisions. Surely the fate of large numbers of citizens both in London and in Kent, Surrey, and Sussex could have been radically altered had the English adhered to one or another of these principles in reaching their final decision. Reflecting on this fact underscores how much can be at stake when we choose the ethical principles that ultimately guide our actions.

Terror Bombing vs. Strategic Bombing: Dresden.   Consider another example from World War II. Late in 1940, the situation for England looked grave. Military officials feared that unless drastic measures were taken, Hitler's armies would win the war. In response to this situation, the English shifted the strategy behind their air attacks on Germany. Prior to this point, the English had followed a policy of "strategic bombing." This policy required the Royal Air Force to aim exclusively at identified military targets; indiscriminate bombing of civilian areas was expressly forbidden.[25] After the raid on Coventry, in late 1940, this policy was revised. Now, for the first time, "terror bombing" was permitted. Pilots were instructed to aim for the centers of cities, rather than at military installations only. The intent of this terror bombing was to weaken the German war effort by demoralizing the civilian population. Such bombing soon became the rule rather than the exception:

> What had once been called indiscriminate bombing (and commonly condemned) was now [after the raid on Coventry] required, and by early 1942, aiming at military targets was barred: "the aiming of points are to be the built-up areas, not for instance, the dockyards or aircraft factories." The purpose of the raids was explicitly declared to be the destruction of civilian morale.[26]

The English followed this strategy of indiscriminate bombing until the infamous bombing of Dresden in 1945. It has been estimated that in this attack alone nearly 100,000 people died. By this stage of the war, the tide had changed and the feared Allied defeat which originally gave rise to the bombings no longer seemed a serious threat. Even Churchill began to express hesitation about the continued practice of terror bombing: "It seems to me that the moment has come when the question of bombing German cities simply for the sake of increasing terror, though under other pretexts, should be reviewed. . . . The destruction of Dresden remains a serious query against the conduct of Allied bombing."[27] All told, some 300,000

Germans (most of whom were civilians) died as a result of the terror bombing. Another 780,000 Germans were seriously injured.

Was the English government justified in its decision to attack German cities for the purpose of terrorizing the German people and weakening their morale? Was this terror bombing really worse than the traditionally accepted strategic bombing which preceded it? Certainly, both types of bombings injured, killed, and left homeless large numbers of men, women, and children, many of whom were not directly involved in fighting the war against England. Traditionally it has been considered wrong to attack civilians directly, especially children, unless they were somehow contributing to the war effort.[28] Yet despite the fact that these two types of bombings shared the morally questionable consequence of directly harming non-combatants, many felt that the manner in which this consequence was reached was significantly different in the two cases. How might our principles be used to explain this moral difference?

In this context, distinctions between killing and letting die, or between harming and failing to benefit clearly would have been of little help, since the choice at hand was not between these kinds of alternatives. In both types of bombing, it was a foregone conclusion that civilians would be harmed and killed. What was at issue, rather, was the intention behind the killings and the degree to which such killing was to be pursued. The principle, then, that seems best to suggest a morally relevant difference in this case is the Doctrine of Double Effect.

According to this doctrine, the killing of civilians as a consequence of strategic bombing was permissible because their deaths were merely a foreseen but unintended side-effect of air raids which were themselves permitted because England's war with Germany was a just war. That the deaths were unintended is shown by the fact that the aim of the mission was simply to destroy military targets, and the deaths of the civilians were not, strictly speaking, part of the means that was required to achieve this end. Had the non-combatants been removed from the bomb site, the mission would still have gone as planned, been judged a success, and no further effort would have been made to track down and bomb the civilians. In contrast, in the case of the terror bombing, the deaths of the non-combatants were *intended* by the pilots. The aim of their mission was to weaken the German resistance by demoralizing the civilian population, and the means to accomplish this was to inflict as much suffering as possible upon the German people. Had these civilians been removed from the bomb site, the pilots would have had to re-direct their planes in order to find the people and attack them, if the goal of their mission was to be achieved. Since the harming of civilians (which normally is considered impermissible) was an intended consequence of the terror bombing, such attacks would, in general, be prohibited by the Doctrine of Double Effect. Therefore, in contrast to strategic bombing, terror bombing was not justified (according to the Doctrine of Double Effect) by virtue alone of England's just engagement in a war with Germany. Rather, in order to validate such terror bombing, the English would have had to argue that there were other overriding moral considerations that permitted them, in this particular case, to violate the Doctrine's general injunction against terror bombing.[29]

Craniotomy vs. Hysterectomy. England's shift from strategic bombing to terror bombing offers a clear example of how the intent behind an action can dramatically affect the way in which an action is normatively judged. Parallel considerations apply to a wide variety of cases found both on and off the battlefield. To take one more example, consider a distinction that is sometimes made in situations where a fetus must be killed in order to save the mother's life. According to certain major religions, Catholicism for example, abortion is not permissible because it involves taking the life of the fetus. Strict adherents to this doctrine have argued that the prohibition against killing the fetus applies even in very rare cases where (because of complications at birth) a woman will die unless the head of the fetus she is trying to deliver is crushed. This procedure is called a craniotomy. In such cases, conservatives have argued that it is better to let the woman die than to perform the craniotomy and kill the fetus. (In this case, assume that it is not possible to perform a cesarean section operation to save both mother and child.)

This conservative judgment is reversed, however, in another context in which the mother's life can be saved only at the expense of that of the fetus. In cases where a pregnant woman has cancer of the uterus, it is judged to be permissible for the woman to have a hysterectomy to remove the cancer (a process that also kills the fetus). Some conservatives argue that although the result is the same in both the craniotomy and the hysterectomy—i.e., the fetus dies—the first case is importantly different from the second. The defense of this distinction hinges on the fact that in the craniotomy the crushing of the fetus's head is an intended consequence of the procedure, whereas in the hysterectomy, the death of the fetus is merely an unintended but foreseen side-effect of the hysterectomy. Thus, by appealing to the Doctrine of Double Effect, conservatives can maintain that the craniotomy is impermissible because the physician intends to crush the fetus's skull as a necessary means to save the mother, whereas the hysterectomy is permissible because the physician intends to remove the cancer, and the death of the fetus is merely an unintended but foreseen side-effect of the process.

Euthanasia: Active vs. Passive. The morally complex practice of euthanasia is another area in which the principles discussed above are frequently employed. In these cases, a distinction is often drawn between active euthanasia, in which a patient is killed (usually in order to spare him the suffering of a long, painful death), and passive euthanasia, in which the patient is simply allowed to die, and the medical team makes no effort to keep him alive. Two examples will serve to illustrate this distinction. First, consider a case of passive euthanasia. An eleven-year-old boy with cystic fibrosis was brought to the hospital. Even with the best treatment, he probably had no more than a few months to live. The most immediate danger to his life, however, was a severe bronchial infection, and the doctors felt that without a bronchoscopy the boy would soon be dead. Such a procedure is difficult to perform on children, and is not always successful. After reviewing the available options, the boy's mother insisted that no special effort be made to save her son. "'Just maintain him,' she said, 'and let him die in peace.'"[30]

Contrast this case with an example of active euthanasia based on the "mercy-killing" trial of a doctor. His patient was dying a protracted and painful death of cancer.[31] She had shrunk from her original weight of 140 pounds to a mere 80 pounds, and although her doctor had done all he could, lamentably the patient had no hope for recovery, only the prospect of a long, slow, agonizing death. Listening to his patient's suffering and incessant pleas for relief, the doctor eventually decided to put an end to the unwanted torment, and he injected air into his patient's veins. Within minutes, she was dead. The doctor was later arrested and charged with murder.

Although in both cases, the doctors' overall aims were to hasten the patients' deaths and minimize needless suffering, the two examples differ in that the second doctor actively brought about this death, whereas the doctors in the first case merely withheld treatment that was required to prevent a natural death from occurring. The American Medical Association has endorsed the view that the difference between these types of cases is a morally significant one, and it has stated that whereas passive euthanasia is sometimes permissible, active euthanasia is not. Once again our principles could be used to attempt to explain and justify this judgment. In particular, some ethicists appeal to the distinction between killing and letting die, and argue that although active euthanasia should be prohibited because it requires the doctor to kill the patient, passive euthanasia should be permitted because it only involves letting the patient die. Given this tidy division, the doctor in the second case could be considered to have acted in an unethical fashion, whereas the doctors in the first case should not suffer any moral censure for concurring with the mother's decision to let her child die.

This approach is appealing in that it apparently offers a clear criterion to use in deciding what measures may, and may not, be taken in cases of terminal illness. Unfortunately, the actual cases of euthanasia are not always as easily divided as the distinction may suggest. Consider the following two examples:

> Nancy Cruzan, now 32, has done nothing for the past seven years. She has not hugged her mother or gazed out of the window or played with her nieces. She has neither laughed nor wept, her parents say, nor spoken a word. Since her car crashed on an icy night, she has lain so still for so long that her hands have curled into claws; nurses wedge napkins under her fingers to prevent the nails from piercing her wrists. . . .
>
> . . . Nancy is not dying. She could live 30 years just as she is. And since she is awake but unaware, most doctors agree that she is not suffering. But her parents are suffering, for it is they who live with her living death. They are so convinced Nancy would not want to go on this way that they have asked the courts for authorization to remove her feeding tube and 'let her go.'[32] [Note: Nancy's feeding tubes were eventually removed and she died on December 26, 1990.]

A similar case is that of the unfortunate baby, Betsy Novick:

> Baby girl Betsy Novick had immediately apparent physical malformations when she was born. A diagnosis of Seckel or "bird-headed" dwarfism was made. She had, in addition to low birth weight and length, large eyes, a large beaklike nose, narrow face, receding lower jaw, strabismus, and a club foot. Seckel dwarfism, an autosomal recessive genetic disease,

had affected Mr. Novick's brother as well. Life expectancy is good, but a much simplified gross cerebral structure is related to mental retardation. It was apparent that institutionalization would be necessary. . . .

. . . In the next two months Betsy developed a persistent pyloric stenosis, a narrowing of the pylorus between the stomach and intestines, causing projectile vomiting that did not respond to phenobarbital, atropine, or special diet. If not surgically treated, death by starvation would result. The parents, at first stunned by the additional severe medical problem, considered the alternatives. They envisioned the virtually certain, severe burden and suffering to be placed on the child in any institutions conceivably available in the next decade or two. They decided that it was a burden the child should not bear, even though in principle they knew society should be providing better support for them. They decided against surgery. The child died after two weeks of deterioration.[33]

Both of these cases illustrate that applying distinctions between active and passive euthanasia is not always a non-controversial task. In the case of Nancy Cruzan, it is far from clear whether removing her feeding tube and withholding food should be construed as actively killing her, or merely as passively allowing her to starve to death. Similarly, in Betsy Novick's tragic situation, the question arises whether her family is actively or passively putting her to death when they deny her the surgery that would surely be performed if she did not additionally suffer the regrettable handicaps characteristic of bird-headed dwarfism. The American Medical Association has stated that whereas the intentional termination of life is not permissible, "the cessation of the employment of extraordinary means to prolong the life of the body when there is irrefutable evidence that biological death is imminent is the decision of the patient and/or his immediate family."[34] Cases like that of Nancy Cruzan and Betsy Novick are morally complex in part because they are not indisputably situations in which the patients' lives are actively terminated, but neither are they cases in which death is imminent nor in which extraordinary means are required to sustain life.

Turning to the other principles discussed above does little to dispel the complexities surrounding these sorts of cases. The distinction between negative and positive duties is not of much help here, for it leaves us with the query as to whether withholding food or medical treatment should be classified as failing in a negative duty to avoid harm, or merely failing in a positive duty to provide aid. The Doctrine of Double Effect does not do much better. In both the cases of Nancy Cruzan and Betsy Novick, the parents and physicians intend the death of the patient, and the necessary means to reach this end is the refusal to provide food or necessary treatment. Recall that the doctrine prohibits doing anything that intentionally leads to a bad result. This leaves us with the highly controversial question whether starving a child with few possibilities for any type of normal life should itself be considered to lead to a bad result. Such examples serve as a reminder that we cannot expect that all the situations we encounter will neatly fall into the divisions set by our general normative principles.

Lifeboat Examples.   The fate of a small group of mariners set adrift in a lifeboat is a paradigmatically complex moral situation, one that is often used to exemplify the difficult decisions that arise in contexts of famine relief, scarce medical resources, or any other situation in which people's survival is conditioned by a limited supply of material goods.[35] To illustrate these problems, consider the following account of an actual sea disaster:

> *In 1842, a ship struck an iceberg, and more than 30 survivors were crowded into a lifeboat intended to hold only 7. As a storm threatened, it became obvious that the lifeboat would have to be lightened of its human load if anyone were to survive. The captain reasoned that the right thing to do in this situation was to force some individuals to go over the side and drown. Such an action, he reasoned, was not unjust to those thrown overboard, for they would have drowned anyway. If he did nothing, however, he would be responsible for the deaths of those he could have saved. Some people opposed the captain's decision. They claimed that if nothing were done and everyone died as a result, no one would be responsible for the deaths. On the other hand, if the captain attempted to save some, he would be able to do so only by killing others and their deaths would be his responsibility. It was claimed that this would be worse than doing nothing and letting all die. The captain rejected this reasoning and decided that he must throw some people overboard. Since the only possibility for rescue required great efforts of rowing by survivors, the captain decided that the weakest would have to be sacrificed. In this situation, it would be absurd, he thought, to decide by drawing lots who should be thrown overboard.*
>
> *As it turned out, after days of hard rowing, the survivors were rescued. . . .*[36]

Later the captain was tried for his actions on the lifeboat. Was he morally culpable for the deaths of the people he tossed overboard? Using the various principles we have discussed, how would we determine his guilt or innocence? It might be useful for the reader to explore different strategies (employing the principles presented above, or related principles) for coming to grips with this case.

Famine Relief.   Thus far we have discussed how the various principles that emerged from our examination of the trolley cases can provide guidance in a variety of morally difficult situations. Before leaving this discussion, it is worth noting that the trolley examples can also influence our moral judgments in a quite different way. In the process of helping us to revise our normative principles, the trolley cases call into question previously accepted norms and principles, and this can lead us to reevaluate ethical judgments that we previously took for granted. Here is one example. Ordinarily people think that there is an important difference between murdering a neighbor's child and failing to give money to save an infant starving to death in a distant African nation. This difference is often explained by pointing to distinctions between actions and omissions or between harming and failing to benefit. Thus, one might argue that killing a neighbor's child is importantly different from failing to give to charity (and thereby allowing an infant to starve to death), because in the former case you are actively harming a child, whereas in the latter case you are merely omitting to do something to aid one. (Note that the distinctions between **actions and omissions** and between harming and failing to aid are separate distinctions, although they may overlap in many cases. Presumably, there could be cases in which one harms by omitting to do something, and in which one fails to aid by performing some action.)

Cases like Bystander 1 and Bystander 2, and Cleaning Fluid 1 and Cleaning Fluid 2 dispute the distinctions between actions and omissions, and between harming and failing to benefit. Such cases provide reasons to re-think the accepted view that failing to aid famine victims is morally different from directly harming them. This is not to say that upon further reflection more satisfactory moral reasons will be found which indeed justify this intuitive difference. Rather, the point is merely to underscore that the trolley cases not only help us to refine normative principles that can provide guidance in morally complex situations, but they also afford us the opportunity to reconsider our understanding of situations that might appear to be normatively less complex.

THEORY

The Structure of Ethics. How should one live? What ought one to do? Ethics studies the issues that arise once we begin to reflect on these fundamental questions. To distinguish some of the ways in which these questions may be approached, the study of ethics is commonly grouped into three areas: descriptive ethics, normative ethics, and meta-ethics. The first area, descriptive ethics, explores the ethical practices of people in different societies and in different groups within a society. It seeks to learn how people actually behave and what ethical beliefs they hold. This research is conducted largely by social scientists such as anthropologists, sociologists, and historians.

Whereas **descriptive ethics** is concerned with the way things *are*, the second branch of ethics—**normative ethics**—is concerned with the way things *ought* to be. It asks not how persons *do* behave, but how they *should* behave. This type of inquiry is termed "normative" because it attempts to generate the norms, or standards, of right action. One of the central tasks of normative ethics is to articulate a set of moral principles that prescribe which actions are right and wrong, and to justify these principles as valid for all members of the moral community. This portion of normative ethics is sometimes labeled **general normative ethics**. Another and equally important part of normative ethics (one which is often referred to as **applied normative ethics**) is the study of how the general moral rules should guide actions in specific contexts. As we have just seen, it is not sufficient simply to formulate and defend general principles; one also must be able to apply these principles to morally complex situations, such as abortion, euthanasia, famine relief, preferential treatment, etc. An applied ethicist, for instance, might use a general principle like the Doctrine of Double Effect in order to clarify what a doctor is permitted to do to relieve the suffering of a terminally ill patient.

The third and final branch of ethics is **meta-ethics**. Meta-ethics, or **critical ethics** as it is sometimes called, focuses on more theoretical questions concerning the nature of ethical concepts and the justification of normative theories.[37] In contrast to general normative ethics, which seeks to articulate and defend principles that prescribe what is right and wrong, meta-ethics asks about the forms of argument that are used to justify these principles and the meanings of the ethical terms these principles employ, such as "right," "permissible," and "obligation." Normative ethics focuses on questions of the following sort: "Is killing always worse than letting die?" or "Is it ever permissible to harm one person in order to benefit another?" Meta-ethics turns to questions that deal with the nature of normative theory itself, such as: "What does it mean to say that something is right or obligatory?" "Is there only one true set of normative principles for all persons?" "Are all ethical principles relative to a particular society and context?" "Do ethical principles correspond to some fact in the world, or are they only expressions of feelings and opinions?"

Two Kinds of Theories. The discussion of the problems and principles in this anthology belongs largely to the area of normative ethics. Earlier we discussed how the trolley-type cases can be used to clarify our moral intuitions and revise particular normative principles. However, the trolley cases are more than a useful tool for refining normative principles. They also help to point out a tension between two general ethical intuitions, each of which underlies one of the major approaches to ethical theory. Cases like Bystander 1 (in which you shunt a trolley away from five people and toward one), Drug (in which you distribute a drug to save five persons instead of one), and Boat (in which you rescue five swimmers instead of one lone swimmer) elicit the first type of intuition. These examples suggest that in deciding what is the right thing to do, one should focus on the course of action that will bring about the best available outcome. We think, for example, that the owner of the drug ought to distribute the medication among the five patients who each requires a fifth, because saving five lives is better than saving just one. The thought that what is right depends upon what leads to the best overall outcome finds expression in a group of theories called **consequentialist theories**.[38] In their most general form, consequentialist theories hold that the moral value of an action is entirely a function of the value of its consequences.[39] For instance, **act-utilitarianism**, one of the most familiar consequentialist theories, maintains that an action is right if and only if it produces the greatest possible balance of good over bad. This approach is attractive because it is natural to suppose that the right thing to do is to maximize good results and minimize bad ones. Surely one ought to act in a way that makes things as good as possible.

Still, as compelling as such consequentialist intuitions might seem, other trolley-type examples like Transplant (in which you do not cut up an innocent visitor to use his organs to save five dying patients), Fat Man (in which you do not shove a man in front of the trolley in order to save five), and Shark (in which you do not shoot a fisherman in order to save five swimmers from a shark), underscore a competing set of intuitions that are sharply at odds with these intuitions. These cases suggest that the rightness of action is not solely a function of the outcome to which it leads. For example, even though having one person die seems better than having five die, many people share the intuition that a surgeon should not dissect an innocent visitor and plunder his organs in order to save five dying patients. Such examples suggest that what is right depends not only upon the outcome, but also upon how the outcome is reached. The ends do not, as the saying goes, justify the means. According to these intuitions, there are constraints upon what one may do in trying to reach some desired end. In determining which course of action is right, one cannot simply weigh the overall values that would be produced in each possible outcome; one must also consider the paths that must be traversed in order to reach these ends. Accepting such intuitions leads people to the other main group of ethical theories: **deontologi-cal theories** (from the Greek word *"deon"* meaning "duty"). Deontological theories deny the consequentialist claim that the rightness of an action is solely a function of the outcome produced.

One reason the trolley cases are so perplexing is that, taken as a whole, they graphically pose a formidable question: what constraints, if any, should be placed on the apparently natural imperative to seek the best possible outcome? How, in other words, can we reconcile our deontological intuitions with our consequentialist ones? To shed some light on this question, the next pages briefly look at these two different types of theories, and the roles that ethical principles play in them.

Consequentialist Theories

Two central concepts in any ethical theory are those of **the right and the good**.[40] What typifies consequentialist theories is the way that they relate these two concepts: first they specify what is good, then they define what is right in terms of the good. Let us examine these two steps more closely. First, a consequentialist theory specifies what is good in non-moral terms.[41] That is, it defines what is good without making any reference to what is right, obligatory, or morally valuable. For example, the good might be defined as something like pleasure, happiness, or satisfaction of preferences, but it may not be defined in terms of doing one's duty or fulfilling moral obligations. This first step—specifying the good—provides a measure to compare possible out-comes and to rank them in a hierarchy ranging from best to worst. The second step—defining the right in terms of the good—then provides a principle that speci-fies which of the available outcomes one ought to produce. For example, one of the simplest forms of consequentialism holds that an action is right if and only if it produces the greatest possible balance of good over bad, taking into account the good of everyone affected.

Since the common structure shared by consequentialist theories is general and abstract, consequentialism can come in a variety of forms. Indeed there can be as many different types of consequentialist theories as there are ways of defining the good and the right in terms of the good. To illustrate how this fairly abstract struc-ture can be embodied in a particular set of theories, we will discuss a group of consequentialist theories that come under utilitarianism. First we will look at how these various utilitarian theories define the good, and then we will examine how they define the right in terms of the good.

Defining the Good. [Note: Here the term "the good" means "that which is good," such as "the good of the people." This term is used frequently in this text in both singular and plural forms. Note, therefore, that the term, "the goods" in this text does not refer to possessions or material goods in the usual sense. When cases refer to concrete, material "goods," this will be specified.] In defining the good, utilitarian theories give a particular account of **intrinsic value**. Something has intrinsic value when it is valuable in itself, and is not merely a means to some further end. For example, the daily use of dental floss is not intrinsically good, because we do not value threading waxed string between our molars for its own sake. The regular use of dental floss is good only insofar as it produces certain results, for example, healthy teeth. In turn, these healthy teeth might be valued only insofar as they lead to some other end, and so on. Ultimately, however, an end will be reached that is valued not because of any further consequences to which it might lead, but simply because it is valuable in its own right.[42] Such an end is intrinsically valuable. It is this intrinsic value which is the true measure of utility, but which ends have this intrinsic value? Is there only one thing that is intrinsically valuable, or are there many such goods?

Different utilitarian theories give different answers to these questions. In its classical form, utilitarianism has a monistic conception of intrinsic value; that is, it holds that only one type of thing is valuable as an end in itself. Jeremy Bentham (1748–1832, for example, argues that the intrinsic value of any outcome is solely a function of the amount of pleasure that is experienced.[43] John Stuart Mill (1806–1873) agrees that utility should be understood in terms of the happiness or pleasure experienced. Unlike Bentham, however, he stresses that pleasures associated with the higher faculties in humans have more value than lower, sensual pleasures, like those associated with eating and drinking, which any animal could experience. Mill is careful, therefore, to insist that when comparing the utility produced by various actions, one must heed not only the *quantity* of pleasure produced, but the *quality* as well. From this sentiment comes Mill's famous dictum: "It is better to be a human being dissatisfied than a pig satisfied, better to be Socrates dissatisfied than a fool satisfied."[44] In spite of these differences over how various types of pleasures should be compared, both Bentham and Mill share the fundamental belief that, ultimately, pleasure alone is of intrinsic value. As a result of this similarity their theories are often grouped together under the heading **hedonistic utilitarianism**.

Subsequent utilitarian theories have criticized the view that all intrinsic value can be reduced to pleasurable states of consciousness. One reason behind this criticism is that it seems possible to have pleasurable experiences that are themselves of questionable value. For example, imagine a world just like ours, except for the addition of a deluded sadist who constantly hallucinates that he is surrounded by children, all of whom are being mercilessly tortured.[45] The sadist delights in observing the ceaseless torment of others, and because he falsely believes there are actually toddlers being mistreated, he derives great pleasure from his surroundings. Compare such a world to another one just like it; only in this world, in place of the sadist, there is a deluded, but compassionate fellow who constantly feels great sorrow from observing the sufferings of the fictitious children around him. From the point of view of a hedonistic utilitarian theory like Bentham's, the first world with the deluded sadist is a better world than the other, because it has quantitatively more pleasure. This conclusion has troubled many, however. It goes against commonsense judgment to think that a sadist enjoying the supposed torment of others is somehow better than a compassionate person empathizing with this suffering. Such intuitions have led people to reject hedonistic utilitarian theories on the grounds that utility cannot be measured solely in terms of pleasurable states of consciousness.

As a result of various criticisms leveled against hedonistic utilitarianism, more recent utilitarian theories have investigated other ways to define the good. Some theorists, G. E. Moore (1873–1958), for example, have turned to a pluralistic conception of the good, arguing that other things besides pleasure or happiness could be intrinsically valuable. Among these values, utilitarians have included the experience of beauty, friendship, health, and knowledge. Because these sorts of utilitarian theories recognize a plurality of goods, they compare the outcomes of possible actions by looking at the total sum of intrinsic value that is produced, where intrinsic value includes not just the total pleasure or pain experienced. Another strategy for defining the good is found in **preference-utilitarian theories**. These theories argue that what is intrinsically valuable is the satisfaction of people's preferences, and hence they compare the utility of various outcomes in terms of how successfully the desires and preferences of people are fulfilled.

Defining the Right.   [*Note*: Here the term, "the right," refers to that which is inherently right or correct, and is not to be confused with rights that are privileges or justify a claim to property, etc.] Thus far we have discussed the differences among utilitarian theories that stem from the different ways these theories define the **good**. The other opportunity to introduce variations in utilitarianism comes when these theories define the **right**. Utilitarian theories are characterized by their acceptance of the **principle of utility**. In its broadest form, this principle defines the right as being whatever produces the greatest possible good or utility, when equal consideration is given to the good of all persons affected. Although all utilitarian theories, by definition, must take the principle of utility to be the only fundamental normative principle, these theories may disagree on how to interpret and apply this principle. For example, exactly how is the good of all persons supposed to be maximized? Is an action right if it leads to the highest *total* utility or to the highest *average* utility?[46] Furthermore, in evaluating agents and their actions, should a theory require that people do what objectively has the highest probability of maximizing utility, or merely what they subjectively believe will maximize utility? Here a distinction is sometimes made between assessing the rightness of an action and assessing the rightness of the agent's character or motives. Thus, some utilitarians argue that when evaluating the rightness of an *action*, we should consider whether that action is the one that objectively has the best chance of maximizing utility, but when appraising an agent's *motives*, we should focus only on whether the person does what he has good reason to believe will maximize net utility.

Of course, each of these points is subject to disputes which in turn give rise to different variants of utilitarianism. However, of all these types of questions, the one that leads to the most dramatic differences concerns whether the principle of utility is to be applied to particular acts or to general rules of conduct.[47] In the former case, the theory becomes an **act-utilitarian** theory (also called **direct utilitarianism**). This type of theory seeks to maximize the net utility produced by each individual action. In the latter case, the theory becomes a **rule-utilitarian** theory (also called **indirect utilitarianism**). This type of theory seeks to find general rules that will produce the greatest utility over the long run. We take a closer look at each of these theories in turn.

Act-Utilitarianism.   Act-utilitarians apply the principle of utility to individual actions. They hold that in each case, the right action is the one that produces the greatest possible balance of good over bad, when equal consideration is given to the good of each person affected. In the case of Drug, for example, a hedonistic act-utilitarian would first calculate the net amount of good that would result if he saved five lives by alloting five of the six persons one-fifth of the drug each. He would then compare this amount to the net good resulting from allocating all of the drug to one person, thereby saving only one of the six lives. When each person's pleasure is given equal weight and is considered impartially, it is easily seen that saving five lives rather than one maximizes the net utility. The right thing to do, therefore, is to dispense one-fifth of the drug to each of the five persons who needs this amount.

Act-utilitarianism is distinguished by its claim that the right action in any particular situation is whatever maximizes net utility, given the interests of all persons affected. This is an attractive view for a number of reasons. First, act-utilitarianism is motivated by the simple and plausible idea that it is right to do what maximizes human welfare. Also, act-utilitarianism is a flexible theory that is not bound by rigid rules. Consequently, it does not place agents in moral dilemmas in which they have conflicting obligations that will be violated no matter what they do. Since the right action in any given case is whatever maximizes utility, it will never happen that a person is obligated to do two conflicting things. Thus, the theory supplies a straightforward way to assess what is right or wrong in any context.

Since the principle of utility is all that is required to judge which actions are right and which are wrong, commonsense moral principles—such as "Thou shalt not kill!" or "Never tell a lie!"—might seem to have no place in an act-utilitarian theory. Similarly, the types of principles discussed in this anthology might also appear superfluous. After all, if the principle of utility determines what is right or wrong in each particular situation, what need is there for other moral principles?

Fortunately, act-utilitarians need not take such an extreme position. Nothing in their theory commits them to abolishing the common practice of using moral principles to guide their actions. According to act-utilitarians, such principles still have a role to play in our everyday moral practices, but these principles should not be taken to specify what is right or wrong. Only the principle of utility can do this. Instead these principles serve merely as "rules of thumb." Such "rules" are useful because we do not want to go through the process of calculating how best to maximize utility for each and every action. Indeed, to require persons to take the time and trouble to calculate the utility ramifications of each of their acts would in itself probably reduce utility. In lieu of such tedious calculations, moral principles can serve as guides to indicate which types of actions do, in general, promote or reduce utility. Hence, common moral prohibitions, such as those against lying, adultery, and murder, are interpreted in an act-utilitarian theory merely as useful generalizations specifying that these sorts of actions typically do not lead to the best possible outcome. In a similar way, an act-utilitarian can justify the practice of training children to act in accord with "rules," because such training leads, in general, to actions that produce the best consequences.

What must be kept in mind, however, is that these principles, rules, or habits do not have any independent justification, nor do they make any moral claims, in and of themselves, upon agents to act in certain ways. Actions—even killing another person—have no inherent moral value; the rightness or wrongness of an action is determined solely by the utility it yields in a particular situation. On some occasions the usual rules of thumb may not properly indicate the action that will maximize utility. In these instances, act-utilitarians should realize that the rules they typically follow are not sacrosanct, and they should recognize the need to go through the process of calculating which of their available actions most likely will lead to the best result.[48] If, due to some unusual turn of events, an intuitively wrong action, such as stealing an innocent person's goods or taking his life, produces the best consequences, then this action is the right thing to do, it is obligatory.

This feature of utilitarianism has been thought by many to lead to serious problems for the theory because it seems to require act-utilitarians to make judgments that conflict sharply with considered moral intuitions. Consider a famous example, in which a person must decide between two courses of action, each of which will produce an equal amount of utility.[49] Because these actions result in the same net utility, act-utilitarians must hold that they are morally equivalent. The person may do either one. What if one of the actions involves lying, or stealing, or some other form of apparent injustice, and the other does not? Many think that even though the overall outcomes are the same, the one action is worse simply by virtue of the means employed to reach the end. Act-utilitarians cannot easily accommodate this intuition, however, because according to their theory the only source of moral value is the utility produced, and on this score the two actions are indistinguishable.

One of the main criticisms of act-utilitarianism is that it obligates one to do *any* action that maximizes net utility, no matter how intuitively reprehensible that action might seem. For example, reading a case like Transplant, most people share the intuition that a surgeon should not kill an innocent visitor in order to share his organs with five dying patients. This case, along with other similar cases like Fat Man and Shark, suggest that there are certain things that simply should not be done, even if so doing would bring about the greatest amount of good.[50] It is not readily apparent, however, how this quite natural judgment could be justified on act-utilitarian grounds. Other things being equal, it does seem that saving five lives will lead to more pleasure or happiness than not killing the one. If this is true, then act-utilitarians should say that killing the hospital visitor in Transplant is not only permissible, but obligatory. However, once a theory requires that one do *anything* that maximizes utility, the worry quickly arises that a person will be obliged to do all sorts of seemingly heinous actions that intuitively should not be allowed.[51]

Of course, the act-utilitarian can take some steps to mitigate the force of this traditional objection. One of the most popular strategies is to emphasize that in comparing alternative outcomes, one must weigh the ramifications that the action will have not just on those directly affected in the short term, but also on those more indirectly affected in the future.[52] Remember that a utilitarian theory requires that alternative consequences are compared from an impartial standpoint which gives equal weight to every person that is affected (even those affected in a quite indirect way). Using this type of response, act-utilitarians can argue that dissecting the innocent visitor will not maximize utility. Admittedly, his death would result in large utility increases for the five dying patients, but it could also result in a large amount of disutility once it was discovered that innocent visitors to the hospital were in danger of being used as spare parts. Patients would stop going to the hospital, confidence in the health care system would be undermined, and so on. Once the disutility of all these long-term effects is acknowledged, act-utilitarians contend, it will be obvious that it is not right to kill the visitor even if in the short term this would supply the organs to save five lives.

The difficulty with this response is that it assumes that the physician's murderous surgery will become general knowledge. What if this isn't the case? What if the doctor is certain that the crime cannot possibly be unearthed? (Assume, for example, that the visitor is a homeless transient with no family or friends. The doctor knows this; it is late at night and he is able to perform the surgery alone without anyone discovering it.) In this case, act-utilitarians do seem committed to the judgment that the doctor should kill the visitor. As we said above, however, this conclusion runs afoul of our ordinary moral judgments. What is particularly puzzling about this type of case is that, using the utilitarian approach, the rightness or wrongness of the action seems to depend upon whether the act can be kept a secret, but in a case such as this it does not seem that the moral value of the action would change simply because others find out about it.[53]

Here is another example that further illustrates the problems that can arise when an act-utilitarian theory passes judgment on actions which are intuitively wrong, but which will go unnoticed.[54] Betty is an act-utilitarian living in a suburban community in southern California. Due to a serious drought one summer, water is strictly rationed and the citizens living in Betty's town are forced to drastically curtail their usual water consumption. This rationing is required in order that sufficient water will be available to meet the agricultural needs of the state. This arid situation is intolerable for Betty who relishes taking long, cool showers two and three times a day. When she isn't showering, Betty enjoys lounging in her private garden which is dotted with trickling fountains and artificial ponds, all of which consume vast quantities of the now-precious water supply. The rationing situation is so unpleasant for Betty that she spends hours pondering her fate and her water meter. One day she realizes that it would be quite simple to adjust her meter so that it registers only one third of her actual water consumption. The adjustment leaves no telltale marks on the meter, and Betty is entirely certain that no one will ever learn that she is using more water than she has been rationed. Betty ponders what to do and she reasons as follows: "All the other good citizens in my town will, of course, limit their water usage (especially since they will have to pay stiff penalties if they exceed their allotted amount). Certainly my extra showers and trickling fountains will not make a noticeable difference to the effort to save the water needed for agricultural purposes. It will, however, make a big difference to me. Since the total utility will be maximized if I use more water, it is my *duty* to take long showers and enjoy my trickling fountains."

This example poses two problems for an act-utilitarian theory. First, it illustrates once again how act-utilitarianism can end up endorsing actions that might normally be criticized.[55] Certainly if the people living in southern California must sacrifice for the sake of the agricultural interests of their state, justice seems to demand that all the people should share equally in this hardship. From this point of view, Betty's "free-riding" is unjust and should be condemned.

Second, the story of Betty indicates that in certain cases, if everyone were to follow strict act-utilitarian reasoning, the overall result could be less than optimal. For example, think what would happen if all the residents in Betty's part of the state discovered how to adjust their meters, and they were to privately rationalize their own use of water just as Betty did hers. With everyone in southern California freely using as much water as they pleased, the overall water supply would certainly be depleted, and the state's agriculture placed in jeopardy—a result that presumably would not maximize utility. This suggests the seemingly paradoxical result that in a society where everyone explicitly employed act-utilitarian reasoning and individually worked to maximize utility, the net result might be worse than the outcome that would be produced if the people were not all trying to maximize utility.[56]

Some theorists have argued that objections to act-utilitarianism, of the sort we have been discussing, arise because the principle of utility is used to judge the rightness of particular actions considered in isolation. One way to avoid these types of objections would be to consider one's action by asking not only, "What would be the outcome if I did this?" but also, "What would be the outcome if everyone did this?" This approach more easily handles the examples of intuitively wrong actions that will never be discovered. However, the price of this solution is to abandon the essence of an act-utilitarian theory which holds that one should act in a way that will maximize utility *in this particular case.* A utilitarian theory that focuses not on what the particular outcome will be, but rather on what the outcome would be if everyone acted in the same way, is sometimes called **general utilitarianism**.

Rule-Utilitarianism.   Another approach that attempts to avoid the shortcomings of act-utilitarianism is rule-utilitarianism. Like act-utilitarianism, rule-utilitarianism accepts that the principle of utility is ultimately what determines whether an action is right or wrong. The theories differ, however, in how they apply this principle. Whereas act-utilitarianism applies the principle to particular actions, rule-utilitarianism applies it to general rules. In other words, act-utilitarians consider each particular situation and ask, "Which action will maximize utility in this one instance?" In contrast, rule-utilitarians ask, "What general rules will maximize utility in the long run, assuming that everyone accepts them or complies with them?"[57]

As was the case with act-utilitarianism, rule-utilitarianism comes in a variety of forms. For example, some rule-utilitarian theories evaluate each rule individually; other theories judge the consequences not of single rules, but of entire systems of rules taken as a whole. Advocates of this latter view argue that this approach appreciates the fact that normally morality is thought of in terms of a whole way of life and not in terms of piecemeal rules. Another point at which rule-utilitarian theories differ is whether one should look at actual rules or ideal rules. The former sort of utilitarianism, sometimes called **actual rule-utilitarianism** holds that acts are right or wrong depending upon whether they conform to the prevailing moral rules (which are assumed to be the rules that lead to the greatest net utility). The latter type of theory, **ideal rule-utilitarianism**, holds that the rightness or wrongness of actions is determined by their conformity to an ideal set of rules. These ideal rules are determined either by asking which set of rules would maximize utility if everyone accepted them, or by asking which set of rules would maximize utility if everyone conformed to them.[58] In the discussion that follows, rule-utilitarianism will mean an ideal rule-utilitarian theory in which the rules are evaluated on the assumption that everyone accepts them.

For the rule-utilitarian of this sort, an action is right if and only if it conforms to the set of moral rules that maximizes utility when everyone in the community accepts it. Thus, moral principles or rules have a very different role to play in a rule-utilitarian theory than an act-utilitarian one. Whereas for act-utilitarians, moral principles are simply general guidelines that should be set aside whenever doing so would maximize utility, moral principles for rule-utilitarians cannot be set aside or treated as mere rules of thumb. This is true, even if ignoring a rule in some particular context would lead to the best overall outcome. What is important for rule-utilitarians is not which rules maximize utility in any single case, but which ones maximize utility in the long run when all outcomes are considered. Once these rules are accepted, they become the criteria of right and wrong. In short, an action is right because it conforms to a moral rule, not because it produces the best overall consequence in any particular situation.

As might be expected, the rules proposed by various rule-utilitarian theories often are quite similar to the traditional moral principles found in society, principles such as "Thou shalt not kill," "Thou shalt not lie," etc. In selecting these rules, the rule-utilitarian has to judge which principles would maximize utility if they were accepted by all members of the moral community. This selection process will bear some similarities to the method of reflective equilibrium outlined in Part II. Both methods will consider a range of cases, and try to select the rules that yield the right results when applied over this range. However, the two methods are importantly different. The method of reflective equilibrium measures principles against our intuitions and considered judgments. Ultimately the standard of success is that a given principle withstand our reflective scrutiny and yield conclusions that are in line with our considered judgments over a range of cases. In contrast, a rule-utilitarian theory ultimately evaluates principles not against intuitions and considered judgments, but against the principle of utility. The final measure of success is that the universal acceptance of a particular set of rules maximizes utility over the course of time. Although the rules suggested by rule-utilitarian theories often do closely conform with principles that would intuitively be accepted, there is no theoretical demand for this to be the case. Consequently, before the principles discussed in this anthology would be accepted by a rule-utilitarian, they would have to be shown to lead to the greatest possible utility if everyone in the society accepted them.

By concentrating on general rules, rather than on particular actions, rule-utilitarians hope to avoid the criticisms, discussed above, that utilitarianism requires people to act in ways that conflict sharply with commonsense judgments. One thought here is that a rule-utilitarian theory is less likely to obligate a person to do something that intuitively seems to be terrible, because even though such an action might maximize the good in some particular context, it probably will not do so in the majority of cases. Furthermore, it is argued that since a rule-utilitarian theory considers the good that would result if everyone accepted the same general rules, it does not as readily encounter the difficulties act-utilitarianism does when judging intuitively wrong actions that will go unnoticed. For example, recall that for act-utilitarians, it is right for Betty to tamper with her meter and to take the long, cool showers she adores, because in her particular case this excessive water consumption maximizes utility as long as it goes undetected. Such an action is more easily criticized by rule-utilitarians, because they can argue that acceptance of a rule that allowed such tampering would not, in general, maximize utility. This is demonstrated by the fact that if other citizens were to accept this rule and generally act in accord with it, the water supply soon would be depleted, resulting in a worse situation for everyone. Similarly, in the case of Transplant, even if the surgeon could extract the organs of an innocent visitor to save five dying patients without anyone learning of his murder, he arguably should not do this (on rule-utilitarian grounds), because acceptance of a general rule that allowed such killing would quickly undermine people's trust in the health care professions, resulting in a less than optimal outcome. After all, people would be much more hesitant to visit a doctor, if everyone accepted that a doctor may kill a patient as long as the crime will not be discovered and the patient's organs are needed to save the lives of other patients.

Initially, then, rule-utilitarianism promises to avoid some of the obvious criticisms that are often levelled against act-utilitarian theories. Nevertheless, many have worried that in the end rule-utilitarianism cannot make good on this promise. The reason for this worry is that rule-utilitarianism is feared to be an inherently unstable position. The criticism here can be posed in the form of a dilemma: either a rule-utilitarian theory eventually collapses into act-utilitarianism, or it must face a charge of "rule worship." Let us consider the problem of rule worship first. For rule-utilitarians, moral principles are justified only by the consequences to which they lead; no inherent moral value attaches to the acts themselves. According to this view, crimes like murder, rape, and torture are wrong only because such actions do not, in general, maximize utility. Once the rules are in place, however, a difficult problem emerges. Remember that rule-utilitarianism holds that once moral rules are selected, they become the criteria of right and wrong, and no departure from them is permitted. Yet if rule-utilitarians choose their rules solely out of a concern for maximizing utility, then why should they continue to obey these rules once they become convinced that in a particular context utility would be maximized by ignoring them? The problem of rule worship arises, then, when a rule-utilitarian theory requires one to follow a rule (whose original *raison d'être* is to maximize utility), even though it is obvious that, in the present situation, doing so will not maximize utility.

Consider, for example, Mrs. Olga Hooper, an elderly woman dying a slow, painful death from bone cancer in a small-town hospital. Medical authorities decide there is no possible cure, and at most she will live only a few more agonizing weeks. So severe is her pain that it cannot be relieved without killing her with an overdose of painkillers. Pleading that she can no longer endure the torment and that she is ready to die, Mrs. Hooper begs for the medication that will result in her death. She has no family or friends left in the world, and the physician is confident that he can painlessly put her to sleep without anyone learning that she died from anything other than her terminal cancer. On rule-utilitarian grounds, the doctor should not dispense the lethal dosage of narcotics, because this would violate a general rule that prohibits physicians from killing their patients. If, however, utilitarianism says that right and wrong are based ultimately upon utility—and there is nothing intrinsically wrong with killing—then it seems implausible for the physician to apply the principle of utility at the level of rules rather than actions. Thus, if the physician accepts the basic insight of utilitarianism, it is hard to see why the doctor should not heed the dying woman's request. To adhere to a rule even though it no longer achieves its intended end seems to be rule worship. It does not help to argue that the rule should still be followed because most of the time killing does not maximize utility; nor does it help to argue that things in general are better if everyone refrains from killing. If the doctor is truly concerned to maximize pleasure (and to minimize suffering), and in this case he can do so by giving poor Mrs. Hooper the drug, then why shouldn't he do this? Speaking more generally, if utilitarians justify moral principles on the grounds that what matters is maximizing utility, then it seems strange not to pick the action that will maximize utility simply because to do so would violate a rule.

To avoid the charge of rule worship, rule-utilitarians might argue that if an exception to a rule does indeed maximize utility in a certain situation, then the rule can simply be modified to accommodate this instance. For example, to handle a case like that of Mrs. Hooper, one might modify the rule against killing as follows: "Thou shalt not kill, unless the person wants to die, and is in terrible pain, and is about to die anyway."[59] The problem with this strategy is that once one allows rules to be refined in this way, it is unclear where this process will stop. For regardless of how precisely a rule is formulated, exceptions to it soon appear. For example, the rule revised above would need to be modified again to recognize that killing is permissible to maximize utility in cases like Bystander 1. Critics argue that if this process is continued, rule-utilitarians will end up modifying a rule every time act-utilitarians would break it. Thus, in order to avoid the problem of rule worship, a rule-utilitarian theory will just collapse into a form of act-utilitarianism, or at least the two theories will become extensionally equivalent.[60]

Our discussion of utilitarianism has concentrated thus far on how act- and rule-utilitarians handle one of the most familiar objections to any utilitarian theory, namely that in certain situations, a utilitarian theory says that one ought to do something which seems to be intuitively wrong (or even horrible). Before leaving this brief look at utilitarianism, it is worth noting two other influential objections to this sort of theory. First, critics complain that when comparing the utility of different outcomes, utilitarian theories focus only on the quantity of utility produced, and not on how this utility is *distributed* to the various parties involved. In other words, utilitarianism places no direct value on considerations of justice or fairness in the distribution of goods. Thus, if a society can maximize utility by having a majority of its population suffer in order to increase greatly the pleasure of a few, then a utilitarian theory holds that this is precisely what ought to be done. Imagine, for example, a small society composed of five people choosing between two hypothetical outcomes A and B. In outcome A, the utility is evenly distributed among the five persons affected by the outcome; each person derives 20 units for a net utility gain of 100 units. In outcome B one person enjoys 201 units of utility while the other four suffer minus 25 units each, producing a net utility of 101 units. On strict act-utilitarian grounds, outcome B is better than outcome A, even though the second outcome seems grossly unfair. This situation is comparable to a society in which a small portion of the population derives enormous benefits by exploiting the rest of the community.

The standard utilitarian response to this type of objection argues that given the realities of our world and human nature, outcomes with such inequitable distributions will never be the ones that maximize utility. Yet this response ignores the main point of the objection. At best, a utilitarian theory can value justice and fairness only insofar as these are part of the best possible outcome. Critics of utilitarianism argue that justice is a moral value *independent* of any relationship to the amount of utility produced in the outcome. And this is precisely what utilitarian theories fail to appreciate.[61]

A second objection to utilitarianism stems from its claim that people are obligated to do whatever maximizes the overall utility of the group without giving any special weight to their own projects or interests. This appears to be an overly demanding requirement. It apparently obligates each person to abandon all actions that contribute primarily to his or her own good, whenever an alternative course of action would lead to a greater amount of good given the interests of everyone involved. Since it seems unlikely that people are doing all they could do to maximize the common good, accepting utilitarianism appears to require that most people make radical adjustments in their lifestyle. One might argue, for instance, that the money spent on luxury items would produce much greater utility if it were redistributed to the poor and destitute. After all, the pleasure of sipping a well-aged brandy or enjoying a night at the theater is little compared to the satisfaction a starving child would derive from a long overdue meal or a warm bed. A standard reply to this type of objection insists that making such strict demands on maximization would itself lead to less good in the long run. If each person always felt obliged to devote all his time and energy to working for the common good, people would lose incentive and carry such a burden of obligation that overall utility would be diminished.

This response, however, does not address the real force of the objection. The worry here stems from the utilitarian demand that actions be evaluated solely on the basis of their contribution to the overall, common good, as judged from an impersonal point of view. Such a directive completely ignores the special value we place on our projects and actions simply because they are *ours*. Usually we choose to do things because we care about them, because they matter to us, and not because such action will lead to the best overall outcome for everyone involved. To require that we choose our actions solely by attending to impersonal concerns threatens to alienate us from all the personal interests that are normally thought to play an important role in shaping our lives. Indeed, Bernard Williams, who persuasively raises this type of objection, contends that the utilitarian imperative always to maximize the good can ultimately undermine our integrity by obligating us to undertake any action that leads to the greatest good, even when this compromises the personal values and projects we care about.[62]

For example, if an overweight utilitarian is standing on the bridge as in Fat Man, his moral theory *obligates* him to set aside all his personal interests and throw himself in front of the oncoming trolley in order to save the five helpless people stranded on the tracks. This is true even if saving the people will compromise many of the man's most cherished personal values and goals. For example, imagine the man is an astronomer and environmentalist whose untimely death will come just as he is about to observe a rare comet that will complete his life's work. Further assume that the people on the trolley track are all environmentally insensitive land developers who are finalizing a deal for a new shopping mall which the naturalist despises and has fought for years. In spite of all this, if saving the developers results in even a slight gain in net utility, then the utilitarian must sacrifice his life and interests in order to save theirs.

Both of the preceding objections concerning distributive justice and integrity have been said to derive from the same fundamental problem with utilitarian theory: a failure to take seriously the separate and individual nature of persons.[63] An example of this failure is clearly evinced in a common utilitarian strategy for answering these sorts of objections. The utilitarian argues as follows: "It seems right for a person to accept pain at one stage in his life in order to avoid much greater suffering at another, later stage. If this is right at the intrapersonal level, then why should not the same thing hold at the interpersonal level? That is, why shouldn't one person sacrifice in order to avoid greater harm for some other person?"[64]

This response fails to acknowledge that intrapersonal concerns are importantly different from interpersonal ones. We think of persons as distinct and separate individuals, not merely as component parts of some larger entity. This recognition of the essential individuality of persons fuels the intuition that it matters not just how much net good is produced, but also how this good is distributed to each individual. Similarly, we think of persons as having individual, personal concerns that are distinct from any impersonal concerns for the general good, and because of this we think that the moral value of action cannot be reduced to impersonal concerns alone. In choosing the morally right course of action, a person's individual values and projects may well have an important and proper role to play. Because utilitarianism understands moral value only in terms of the aggregate good realized, it has no resources to appreciate the independent moral significance of concerns either with distributive justice or personal integrity.

Prompted by such worries, many philosophers turn away from utilitarianism and from consequentialist theories in general. Such people argue that the problems encountered by utilitarianism teach us that an adequate moral theory cannot make its conception of the right dependent entirely upon the goodness of the consequences produced. Instead, a moral theory should recognize that there are duties to act in certain ways which are quite independent of any concern for the outcome. As we mentioned earlier, such "duty-based" theories are called deontological theories, and this type of theory is the topic of the next section.

Deontological Theories

Deontological theories oppose the consequentialist dictum that an agent ought always to act in a way that brings about the best overall outcome (where the goodness of the outcome can be defined independently of the rightness of that outcome). This opposition leads to two important differences between consequentialist and deontological theories. First, in some situations a deontological theory may *prohibit* an agent from following a certain course of action, even though that action would lead to the best possible outcome. For example, in Fat Man, a deontological theory might hold that there is a strict prohibition against killing a person as a means to saving others, and that the bystander ought not to topple his chubby companion onto the trolley tracks, even though this would forestall the deaths of five persons. Second, in other situations, a deontological theory may *permit* agents to act in ways that produce the best outcome, but *not obligate* them to do so. For example, consider a case similar to Drug, except that in this scenario the owner of the drug is dying, and he must take all the medication himself in order to live. On strict act-utilitarian grounds, the owner of the drug ought to give up the medication in order to save the lives of five dying persons, each of whom needs one-fifth of the drug to survive. In contrast, a deontological theorist might say that although the owner *may* give up the drug to save the five other people, he is *not obligated* to do so.

Deontologists claim that by having a conception of right and wrong that is not based entirely upon the outcome produced, their theories offer a number of advantages over rival utilitarian views. First, deontological theories purport to avoid many of the counterintuitive conclusions that plague act-utilitarianism. As we saw earlier, act-utilitarianism leads to the troubling conclusion that a person is obligated to do whatever results in the best outcome, even if this means doing things that normally would be considered terrible. For example, in Transplant, if the surgeon is secretly able to dissect the one visitor and redistribute his organs, then on act-utilitarian grounds, the doctor *must* do this. In contrast, a deontological theory recognizes that there are moral duties which cannot generally be violated in the interests of maximizing the good. Such duties and prohibitions constrain what agents may do in order to achieve the best possible results. A deontological theory, therefore, might insist that regardless of whether anyone detects the murder, the moral law simply forbids physicians to kill their patients. Utilitarianism cannot accommodate this natural intuition, because it reduces all moral evaluations to judgments about optimizing the ends. Deontologists argue that, since utilitarianism does not acknowledge that both means and ends have moral significance, it cannot adequately reflect the true nature of our moral judgments.

A second claim that deontological theories make is that they more clearly appreciate the important roles that past actions and commitments should play in moral decisions. Because utilitarianism is a forward-looking theory that places moral value on actions only insofar as they will lead to good consequences in the future, it cannot directly acknowledge the moral weight that past commitments ordinarily have in our deliberations. For instance, an act-utilitarian theory maintains that one should keep one's promises only if this leads to the greatest net utility. Any obligation to keep the promise comes only from considerations of the negative utility that will result in the future if the promise is broken. In contrast, a deontological theory might take the past promise itself to create a moral obligation to perform the promised deed. This obligation would not be based upon any considerations of future utility; rather it would be grounded simply on a recognition that the promise has been made, and that once made, a promise should not be broken. Of course, a utilitarian might complain that in most cases, both a utilitarian and a deontological theory will agree that breaking a promise is wrong; hence, choosing one theory over the other makes no significant practical difference. However, this reply misses the force of the deontologist's objection. His complaint is that utilitarianism understands past actions and commitments as having only a derivative moral value, whereas the deontologist holds that such commitments create obligations that are quite independent from any concerns with future goods.

Finally, deontological theories claim to take the individual nature of persons more seriously than utilitarian theories. Earlier we discussed the objection that utilitarian theories do not adequately take into account the separateness of persons, and as a result they fail to pay sufficient attention to issues like distributive justice. Deontological theories avoid these sorts of objections because they can argue that there is a moral obligation to be just, which places an independent constraint upon how the goods may be distributed. Similarly, deontological theories allow for a greater richness in our understanding of the moral relationships into which people can enter. For the utilitarian there is only one moral relationship: that of benefactor to recipient. In contrast, deontological theories recognize that many other kinds of relationships can give rise to moral obligations—for example, that of promisor and promisee, parent and child, etc.

Types of Deontological Theories.   Since deontological theories do not define the right in terms of the good, they must articulate and defend an independent account of what makes an action right. As might be expected, there are a wide variety of deontological theories, each of which reflects different approaches to meeting this challenge. These theories can be analyzed from a number of different perspectives. First, one can ask whether a theory states that there are general rules that prescribe right and wrong, or whether judgments of right and wrong must be made in each particular case. The former type of theory, called **rule-deontology**, argues that an action is right if and only if it conforms with some duty or moral rule. The latter type of theory, termed **act-deontology**, rejects this appeal to general duties, and instead claims that we are only able to judge what is right and wrong in particular situations. Second, among rule-deontologists, differences arise over whether there is a plurality of moral rules, or whether there is just one fundamental rule from which all the other rules can be derived. A third important difference among deontological theories concerns what they take to be the ultimate justification of our judgments of right or wrong. For example, some theories state that God gives us the moral rules; others, that these rules are based upon some sort of rational contract or can be derived from reason alone; still others propose that obligations follow directly from certain non-natural properties in the world.

To illustrate one form a deontological theory might take, we will briefly consider one of the most famous deontological theories, that of Immanuel Kant (1724–1804). Kant is a rule-deontologist who maintains that there is only one fundamental moral principle, and he argues that it can be justified by rational considerations alone. For Kant, we act rightly if and only if we act in accord with duty and we do so because of duty. But what is our duty? To answer this question, Kant points to what he believes is the supreme principle of morality, the **categorical imperative**. In its most familiar formulation the categorical imperative commands: "Act only according to that maxim by which you can at the same time will that it should become a universal law of nature."[65] To understand the force of the categorical imperative, it is helpful to contrast it with another type of imperative, a **hypothetical imperative**. A hypothetical imperative takes the form: "If conditions AB obtain, then do X." An example of such an imperative is: "If you want to go to the Giants game, then buy a ticket." Obviously an imperative of this sort obligates people only to buy a ticket, if they desire to go to the ball game. Speaking more generally, hypothetical imperatives are not applicable to all persons in all situations, but only to those who satisfy the conditions specified. In contrast, categorical imperatives have the form: "Do X!" Examples of this type of imperative are: "Keep your promises!" or "Tell the truth!" Note that in these cases, the obligation to obey the commands is unconditional: it applies to all people, all the time, in all situations, and it does not depend upon any further end being willed. Since Kant requires that one do one's duty for duty's sake alone, he held that the moral law must be a categorical, and not merely a hypothetical, imperative.

For Kant, the categorical imperative is the basic principle of morality from which all other obligations can be derived.[66] According to the categorical imperative, one should act only on a **maxim** that can be universalized. This deserves a word of explanation. By maxim, Kant means the subjective principle, or rule, that underlies and guides one's action; it is the principle that explains what the person thinks he is doing and the circumstances under which he is doing it. For instance, a jogger who does supine gluteal stretches and straight-leg raises each morning before his run in the park acts on the maxim, "Whenever I go jogging, I stretch my muscles beforehand." According to Kant, if the maxim of an action can be universalized, then that action is permissible; if the maxim of an action cannot be universalized, then the action is morally wrong, and an agent has an obligation not to do it. To be universalizable, a maxim must pass two tests. First it must be able to be *conceived* as a universal law without any contradiction. Second, it must be able to be *willed* as a universal law without any contradiction.[67] Two examples will help to clarify how these tests are supposed to work.

With respect to the first test, Kant says: "Some actions are so constituted that their maxim cannot even be conceived as a universal law of nature without contradiction, let alone be willed as what ought to become one."[68] To illustrate a maxim that fails this test, Kant offers the following sort of example. Audrey desperately needs money and wants a loan. Unfortunately, she has a problem. No one will lend her money unless she promises to repay it, but given her financial straits, Audrey is aware that she will never be able to do this. Still her need is so great that she considers borrowing the money anyway. Thus, Audrey considers acting on the following maxim: "Whenever I am short of money, I shall borrow money and promise to pay it back, even though I know that this will never be done."[69] To test whether acting on this maxim is permissible, the categorical imperative first enjoins her to see whether the maxim can be conceived consistently as a universal law. That is, she must ask,

"How would things stand if my maxim became a universal law?"[70] Or, in more ordinary language, "What if everyone, without exception, acted on the principle: when I am in need, I shall make promises that I have no intention of keeping?" The purpose of this first test is to examine whether it is possible for everyone to act on the maxim in question without contradiction. Clearly in this case, if the world were such that everyone in financial difficulties made promises without having any intention of keeping them, then the entire practice of promising would be undermined. After all, the very idea of a promise is that it is intended to be kept, but this maxim conceives of promises that are never intended to be kept. To conceive of such a maxim as a universal law, therefore, would require that everyone think of promises both as something that may, and may not, be broken, and this leads directly to a contradiction.

The second way in which a maxim may fail to be universalizable is that it cannot be willed without contradiction. In regard to these sorts of maxims Kant writes, "In the case of others we do not find this inner impossibility [i.e., a contradiction in conception], but it is still impossible to will that their maxim should be raised to the universality of a law of nature, because such a will would contradict itself."[71] This test involves asking if we would be able to will consistently that everyone should act on the same principle in all similar circumstances. Kant illustrated this test with the following type of example. Leo is very well off. When he leaves his palatial manor, Leo observes that all his neighbors are struggling with great hardships. Leo could help them if chose to, but he does not. Instead he laughs: "What does it matter to me? Let everyone be as happy as Heaven wills or as he can make himself; I won't deprive him of anything; I won't envy him; only I have no wish to contribute anything to his well-being or to his support in distress!"[72] Could such a maxim be willed as a principle that everyone, without exception, should follow? Unlike the case of promise-breaking, formulating this maxim as a universal law does not immediately involve one in contradictions. That is, it is logically possible that everyone would act in accord with a principle that rejected all forms of assistance to others. Nevertheless, Kant argues that even if a person could *conceive* such a maxim to be a universal law, he could never *will* it to be a law. The reason for this is that Kant thinks that situations could arise in which the person himself would be in need, and in such a case he would not will that everyone act on this maxim of selfishness. As Kant says: "For a will which decided in this way would be in conflict with itself, since many a situation might arise in which the man needed love and sympathy from others, and in which, by such a law of nature sprung from his own will, he would rob himself of all hope of the help he wants for himself."[73]

The success of Kant's project in general, and the content of the categorical imperative in particular have long been debated. Philosophers still argue about how Kant's test of universalizability is supposed to be applied, and whether it does indeed provide necessary and sufficient conditions for establishing the permissibility of an action.[74] Fortunately, we need not enter into this debate here. What is important for our purposes, is to note how Kant's theory attempts to give a definition of the right that is independent from any concern about producing the optimal outcome. To do this, Kant looks to whether the maxims of the acts are universalizable in the sense required by the categorical imperative. Because this right-making characteristic is an intrinsic feature of the action, which is not dependent upon the consequences produced, the principles in Kant's theory have a very different role to play from those in utilitarian theories. For Kant, moral rules are not just helpful rules of thumb, nor does their justification rest upon the claim that they lead to the greatest good. Rather these principles are right because they are derived from the basic moral principle—the categorical imperative. As such, these principles serve as absolute constraints on our actions and they cannot be overridden by considerations of utility. Since actions are held to be right and wrong because of features which are intrinsic to them, Kant's theory is not as easily charged with rule-worship as a rule-utilitarian theory is. In the case of Mrs. Hooper, for example, if there is something intrinsically wrong with a surgeon acting on a maxim to kill a patient, then this will give an independent reason for the doctor not to kill the patient even though his not killing the patient does not yield the best results.

Not all deontological theories, however, claim that our moral rules are absolute, nor do they maintain that these rules may all be derived from just one fundamental moral principle. To illustrate this point, consider one other type of deontological theory, that of W. D. Ross (1877–1940).[75] Although both Kant and Ross are rule-deontologists, they have significantly different views about the status of our moral principles. Whereas Kant insists that there is only one basic moral principle, a categorical imperative, and he argues that it can be justified by appealing to the nature of rational agents, Ross holds that there are several basic moral duties, all of which are self-evident and known directly through intuition. Among these self-evident moral duties, Ross includes duties such as fidelity, beneficence, justice, reparation, and non-maleficence.

One difficulty with such a pluralistic conception of moral rules is that because there is more than one basic principle, it is possible that in some situations the various principles will come into conflict with one another. For example, in Bystander 1, the bystander has two moral duties that are at odds with one another: a duty of beneficence to save the five, and a duty of non-maleficence to refrain from harming the one. Whatever the bystander does in this instance, he cannot avoid violating one duty or the other. In part to avoid this type of worry, Ross distinguishes between actual and *prima facie* duties. An actual duty is what one ought to do in a given situation, all things considered. In contrast, a *prima facie* duty merely obligates one to do something as long as no other stronger moral considerations override it. All of the basic moral duties in Ross's theory are *prima facie* duties. As such they are not absolute, and they can be set aside in situations like Bystander 1 in which another stronger duty takes precedence. A problem that remains for this approach, however, is that it is not always easy to decide, in cases where two or more principles clash, which of the conflicting duties is stronger. Unlike some forms of utilitarianism which offer a decision procedure to determine which action is right or wrong in any given situation, a deontological theory, like that of Ross, must ultimately depend on agents having a direct intuition of what is the right way to resolve a given conflict. Ross does provide some guides to help in these decisions. For example, he says that the duty of non-maleficence is, in general, stronger than the duty of beneficence.[76] However, his theory does not supply a general hierarchy that can be used to rank the various *prima facie* duties, and thus doubts may remain about which duty should be given priority in any particular case.[77]

A Problem for Deontology.   As we saw above, an important attraction of utilitarian theories, and indeed of consequentialist theories in general, is that they offer a very natural explanation of what makes actions right or wrong. It seems reasonable to accept the utilitarian view that, roughly speaking, the right act is the one that leads to the best available outcome. Deontological theories reject this simple definition of the right. They maintain that there are duties and obligations that are not based on consequentialist considerations, and that these duties restrict what persons may do in their efforts to maximize the good. As a result of this claim, deontological theories face a challenge not faced by rival utilitarian theories: they must explain why it is right to adhere to one of these deontological restrictions, even when doing so leads to pain and suffering that would have been avoided had one ignored the prohibition and simply followed the principle of utility. The standard reply to this challenge argues that violating a deontological restriction is inherently wrong, and hence such violations should be avoided even when this results in a less than optimal outcome. For example, the surgeon should not cut up the innocent visitor in Transplant (even though this would lead to more overall utility), because physicians have a duty not to murder innocent people, and they should not compromise this duty for the sake of utility. Explaining deontological restrictions in this way, however, quickly leads to a new and deeper puzzle.

Consider the case of Transplant 2. In this case, imagine that the surgeon has refused to dissect the innocent visitor in order to save the other five patients. One of the dying patients learns of the decision. In a last, desperate attempt to save his own life, the patient threatens that if the doctor does not dissect the visitor, he will do so, *and* slice up two nurses for good measure. Suppose the doctor is convinced that the patient can make good on his desperate threat. Now the deontological doctor is faced with a puzzling situation. Initially she justified her decision on the grounds that murder was wrong, and hence it should be avoided regardless of the outcomes. If it is the case that one murder is wrong, however, then surely three murders would be worse.[78] If the doctor is committed to preventing these sorts of deontological violations, why should she not act in a way that would prevent the *most* violations? In short, if violating deontological restrictions is a wrong to be avoided despite the consequences, then why should a moral theory prohibit one from acting in a way that would minimize these infractions?[79]

Despite this objection, many people share the view that the surgeon should stand by her principles. What seems to lie behind this judgment is the deontologist's basic intuition that the rightness of an action depends not only on the outcome, but also on the path taken to reach that outcome. Philosophers sympathetic to this view point out that "deontological reasons have their full force against *your doing something*—not just against *its happening.*"[80] The intuition here is that it matters not only *what* type of actions are performed, but also *who* performs them. For example, if the surgeon in Transplant 2 were simply to weigh one murder against three others, this would leave out what some take to be an important fact, namely that in the one scenario she does the killing, and in the other scenario someone else does. To ignore this fact would be to make a mistake similar to the one which we charged consequentialist theories with earlier—failing to take seriously the separate and individual nature of persons.

Unfortunately such deontological intuitions appear to stand in need of further explanation and justification. Critics complain that it is irrational to endorse deontological constraints that prohibit an agent from acting in a way that would prevent even greater violations by someone else. Thus, in contrast to consequentialist theories that can defend their conception of the right by appealing to the simple and rational idea that one should maximize good consequences, deontological theories must struggle to find a rational basis for their view that deontological constraints may not be violated even in the service of preventing further such violations.[81]

Faced with the perplexing task of justifying deontological constraints, some philosophers have sought a compromise between our consequentialist and deontological intuitions. Samuel Scheffler argues forcefully that we may think of deontological theories as departing from consequentialism in two ways.[82] First, deontological theories have what he terms **agent-centered prerogatives**. That is, using deontological theory one is often permitted to maximize the good, but, unlike a utilitarian theory, one is not obligated to do so. Second, deontological theories have **agent-centered restrictions**. That is, in certain situations deontological theories restrict the agent from taking a course of action that would maximize the goodness of the outcome. Scheffler points out that it is only the latter difference—the agent-centered restrictions—that give rise to the seeming irrationality of deontological theories. It is these restrictions that prohibit one from acting in a way that minimizes the violations of the rules. Recognizing this, Scheffler argues for a hybrid theory that does away with agent-centered restrictions but leaves agent-centered prerogatives. In such a theory, maximizing utility is always permissible, but it is not required.

OBJECTIONS

We have presented and discussed a variety of puzzling moral situations. Some of these situations are hypothetical and imaginary cases. Furthermore, we have suggested a possible methodology for coming to grips with these cases, the methodology of pursuing the state of wide reflective equilibrium. With this approach, one seeks a match between one's principles and one's views about cases. We have discussed some options regarding sets of principles which might be entertained in seeking a state of wide reflective equilibrium. Some philosophers have objected to this entire approach to ethics, however. They claim that it is not useful or worthwhile to consider hypothetical cases of the sort presented above. It is worth thinking about some of their objections.

Some people object to the use of hypothetical examples in ethics because these examples—many of them, at any rate—are very different from situations in ordinary life. These people argue as follows. We are, presumably, seeking to understand *our lives*, and to generate a deeper understanding of the dilemmas and problems we have in our lives, including the personal and political choices we must make. We need satisfying general principles that can help us sort out the immediate concerns we have. If this is our goal, why should we think about and worry about the unusual and fanciful hypothetical examples of the sort adduced above? Why not focus on ordinary, "real-world" examples, rather than arcane and esoteric hypothetical cases?

It might also be claimed that the hypothetical cases presented earlier are excessively abstract. The objection is as follows. Real-world problems are extremely complex, and their appropriate moral resolution frequently depends on particular details and facts about the situation. The hypothetical cases presented do not contain the pertinent details; rather, they contain abstract, stick-figure characters in highly schematized situations. Given the epigrammatic nature of the descriptions of some of the cases, we don't know what to think about them morally. Using certain ways of resolving the vagueness of the examples we will come to one moral judgment about the situation, and with other ways of resolving the vagueness of the examples we will come to another moral judgment. Details matter morally, and the examples leave out these details, inevitably distorting the richness and complexity of moral life.

Can these concerns about the abstract and hypothetical nature of the examples be answered? Does the methodology of scrutiny of hypothetical examples and seeking a wide reflective equilibrium necessarily distort moral experience and fail to respect the complexity of moral life?

First, note that a consideration of hypothetical cases should not exclude consideration of actual cases and policy issues. Indeed, when one aspires to a state of wide reflective equilibrium, one must consider actual as well as hypothetical examples, and integrate one's views with the truths of the social sciences. Further, the principles generated must be tested against actual examples and are to be employed in guiding one's behavior in the real world. The important point is that consideration of hypothetical examples is entirely compatible with consideration of actual examples, and the analysis of hypothetical situations is just one component of the overall project of attaining a wide reflective equilibrium. We do not argue that one should be exclusively preoccupied with such examples, only that they should not be ignored entirely.

In a book about economic problems one is likely to focus on such issues as unemployment, inflation, inefficiencies of various sorts, pollution, and so forth. This is because the book is about certain economic problems. The solutions to these problems must generalize to other, less problematic contexts; the economic principles and forms of analysis adduced to resolve the problems must apply generally. The process is similar for ethical principles and forms of analysis. It is perhaps not surprising that a book about ethical problems should focus on situations which we find troubling and in some respects unusual. Ultimately, however, the principles and theories adduced to illuminate the problems must apply generally to our ordinary lives.

Why consider hypothetical cases at all? One answer has already been suggested: just as in science where we construct controlled experiments, in ethics we attempt to construct controlled thought-experiments. We try to isolate single factors and ascertain their moral significance. Having done so, we attempt to construct general principles and theories that are sensitive to the true moral importance of these factors.

Without controlled thought-experiments, it would be difficult to generate suitably precise principles that properly reflect the relative moral weights of different particular considerations.

There is another point to abstraction. Insofar as we abstract away from irrelevant details, we gain simplicity and clarity. This is one reason that scientists generally employ abstraction in their theory construction. Take, for example, the social science of economics. Economists build models that inevitably abstract away from many features of the actual world. They create abstract models in which market conditions are assumed to be of a certain sort (admittedly very different from real-world conditions) and in which consumer behavior is assumed to be of a certain sort (admittedly very different from the behavior of real-world consumers). These models do not purport to reflect accurately all of reality; rather, they are pictures of some part of reality, or perhaps they are idealizations of reality. The whole point of model construction in economics is to gain simplicity and clarity by reducing complexity. With irrelevant details stripped away, we gain more insight into the salient features of situations. Of course, great care must be taken when applying the insights gained from the model to reality, and it should never be assumed that the mapping from model to reality will be simple or straightforward. Much can be learned, however, even about complex economic environments by studying the properties of simpler models.

Let us say a few more words making more precise the analogy between the thought-experiments of ethics and economists' models. An economist constructs a model which is really a hypothetical "world." This hypothetical world is characterized by the assumptions of the model and is presumably considerably simpler than our world (or even the part of our world pertinent to the model). Having constructed this simpler world, the economist considers its properties and (ideally) generates conclusions. These conclusions may to some extent illuminate features of our world.

Similarly, when we construct thought-experiments in ethics, we are constructing hypothetical worlds (albeit very small ones). These worlds are characterized by the assumptions of the examples, and they are in many ways simpler than real-world situations. We then scrutinize the hypothetical worlds and (ideally) generate conclusions. Again, these conclusions may to some extent illuminate features of our world. In ethics, hypothetical examples are very much like the models of economics.

If the techniques of model-building and abstraction are useful and worthwhile in economics, then why should these techniques not yield similar benefits in ethics? Why should there be an asymmetry between social sciences (such as economics) and ethics with respect to the usefulness of model-building? Perhaps there is some difference between ethics and economics that makes model-construction in ethics inappropriate, but we have yet to see exactly what this difference is.

We have presented the allegation that the method of seeking a wide reflective equilibrium is insensitive to the subtlety and complexity of moral life. Nothing could be further from the truth. Admittedly, hypothetical examples tend to be abstract in certain respects, but the methodology this text employs invites us to consider various examples and to attempt to isolate those features of them that are morally relevant. Each abstract example is really an invitation to consider whether its description is complete and perspicuous: has the description picked out the morally important features, or have some been left out? If it is suspected that a morally important feature is left out, then there is an invitation to construct a related example that includes the allegedly pertinent feature. Then it can be determined whether the inclusion of this feature really does influence one's moral judgment. The methodology presented takes into consideration the fact that different ways of resolving the vagueness of abstract examples will issue in different moral judgments. Employing this methodology should heighten one's sensitivity to the importance of details and to the extreme complexity of moral life. The use of abstraction does not in itself lead to distortion, unless one confuses the model with reality.

Why focus on *difficult* cases? Can't we learn more about morality from clear, uncontroversial situations? Why worry at all about the unclear, difficult cases? Again, no one is proposing that we focus exclusively on difficult cases, or that we ignore the insights gained from easy, clear cases. Consideration of difficult cases is merely one component of seeking a wide reflective equilibrium. We do not propose that people who think about the problems posed in this book ignore the insights gained from relatively clear cases and morally unambiguous situations. Similarly, no one who presents an anthology composed of articles about practical problems such as abortion, infanticide, euthanasia, preferential treatment, sexual morality, and the like proposes that one ignore the insights gained from relatively clear cases and morally unambiguous contexts.

Certain philosophers are opposed to the use of hypothetical examples in ethics.[83] It is hard to understand the point of their objection or to fit it with the history of philosophy and current philosophical practice, however. Quite simply, thought-experiments of various sorts have played important roles in the history of philosophy, and continue to play a central role in philosophy today.

One of the first great thought-experiments is the example of "Gyges's Ring" in Plato's (428–c.348 B.C.) *Republic*. Here we are asked to imagine if it would still be in our interests to act morally, even if we could wear a ring that would make us invisible. Of course, this sort of technology was not available in Plato's day, and neither is it available today. It is a "science-fiction" example, a hypothetical case involving non-existent technology. Plato employs it to test our intuitions and to screen out certain distorting influences, in this case the influence of conventional sanctions attached to detected wrongdoing. Is Plato's thought-experiment inappropriate? If not—and this thought-experiment has obvious contemporary analogues in cases involving questions of public good—then is there some difference between the sorts of thought-experiments involved in the cases presented above and Plato's thought-experiment?

Plato's thought-experiment pertains to ethics. Consider also a famous thought-experiment in epistemology: Descartes's evil demon hypothesis. René Descartes (1596–1650) was concerned to understand how we can know about the external world on the basis of our experiences. He asked how we can know that we are not being deceived by an evil demon. That is, he pointed out that it would be possible (in some sense) for us to have just the same sort of experiences as we actually have but that these experiences be induced artificially by an evil demon. Given that this is possible, how can we distinguish the actual situation from the hypothetical possibility? Finally, if we cannot distinguish these two sorts of situations, then how can we know anything about the external world?

Again, Descartes's thought-experiment is a hypothetical, fanciful example. The technology required to systematically induce deceptive experiences did not exist in Descartes's day, and it does not exist today. Descartes's point in introducing the example was to help to develop an understanding of our knowledge of the external world. Was this thought-experiment inappropriate? If not, then exactly what is the difference between Descartes's hypothetical example and the kinds of hypothetical examples in ethics presented and discussed in this text?

Not only do thought-experiments figure prominently in the history of philosophy, but they occur frequently in contemporary philosophy. A contemporary analogue of Descartes's evil demon example is developed by Hilary Putnam. This is the problem of: "How can I know that I am not a brain-in-a-vat being electronically stimulated to have the pattern of experiences that I do have?" If I cannot distinguish "from the inside" the situation of being a brain-in-a-vat from being connected to the world in the way in which we ordinarily believe we are, then how can I know anything about the external world?[84]

Also, Hilary Putnam has introduced into current philosophical discussions thought-experiments involving other possible planets exactly like ours except containing certain small changes. We are imagined to have exact duplicates ("doppelgangers") on these other planets, and philosophers debate various points about metaphysics and philosophy of mind employing these "Twin-Earth" thought-experiments.

Now what exactly is the relationship between the thought-experiments in the history of philosophy and contemporary philosophy, on the one hand, and the thought-experiments in ethics presented above? It would seem entirely arbitrary and mysterious to take seriously Plato's thought-experiment, Descartes's thought-experiment, and the various contemporary thought-experiments pertaining to metaphysics and the philosophy of mind, and yet *not* take seriously the examples and moral thought-experiments presented above. What could ground this sort of asymmetry?

Thus there is a dilemma for those who would dismiss the sorts of hypothetical cases discussed above as irrelevant to ethics properly construed. Perhaps they wish to dismiss all consideration of hypothetical examples and thought-experiments in philosophy. This is certainly a consistent position, but it is manifestly a radical position that cannot countenance significant portions of historical and current philosophical practice. Or, they can say that there is some crucial difference between the thought-experiments in the history of philosophy and in current philosophy apart from those in ethics. What exactly could this difference be? We have yet to see this difference spelled out.

It is interesting to note that some philosophers who appear to dismiss the use of hypothetical examples in ethics are in fact committed to their legitimacy. For example, R. M. Hare appears at times to rail against the use of certain hypothetical examples in ethics; typically, these examples are adduced (by other philosophers) to controvert utilitarianism. Upon closer inspection, it emerges that Hare is objecting to the misuse of such examples. Indeed, Hare believes that a moral theory should apply in all possible contexts, and thus he must take seriously any possible example that purports to defeat his proposed theory. He does take seriously all such examples, arguing that these examples do not really (when properly understood) call utilitarianism into question.

Of course, some hypothetical examples *are* irrelevant to our moral concerns. Consider a possible world in which five minutes after a human being is killed, he pops back into existence. In this world, certain basic facts about biology and physics are different from the facts in our world. If someone concluded from the fact that it would not be seriously wrong to kill someone in this imaginary world that it would not be seriously wrong to kill someone in our real world, he would be mistaken. This is because this imaginary world is not relevant to ours (at least in any straightforward way).

Now it would be desirable to have a way of distinguishing those possible situations that are morally relevant to us from those that are not. Regrettably, this is difficult to produce. Suppose one tried the following: "In an imaginary world, certain basic facts of biology and physics are different from the facts in our world, and this is what renders it irrelevant to us." This does not seem to do the trick, since there are surely possible situations in which certain facts about biology and physics are (slightly) different from the facts in our world but are morally relevant to our world. Suppose, for example, that the world in question had frogs with different internal organs from the organs they have in our world or bees which mated in a different way from the way in which they mate in our world. Surely, this world could be morally relevant to ours. And in general, *any* hypothetical example will involve *some* departure from the conditions (either particular or general) that obtain in the actual world. Otherwise, it would not be a *hypothetical* example. So we need to say which departures are relevant, and this is not easy to do. Ascertaining the features in certain possible scenarios that are not morally relevant to our world is an interesting and challenging one.

The objections we have been investigating come from the worry that our methodology is too abstract—that it inappropriately abstracts away from some of the rich details and complexity of our moral lives. There is another possible worry, i.e., that the approach we have suggested is not sufficiently abstract. That is, some might wonder why we need to consider particular examples and cases (actual or hypothetical) at all. Why not simply meditate on general facts about practical reasoning (or perhaps human nature)? Can't moral principles be derived from central facts about human free agency or human nature quite apart from *any* consideration of examples?

We acknowledged the existence of several alternative methodologies above, and we cannot discuss their prospects at length here. It suffices to point out that it is not clear that any of these approaches can successfully reach its goal of providing substantive moral principles. Take, for example, the Kantian project of deriving substantive moral principles from very minimal assumptions about practical reasoning and free agency. The problem is that if the assumptions are genuinely minimal and not morally controversial, it is extremely difficult to generate substantive results. If one does generate such results, it may be from having made substantive, controversial moral assumptions at the beginning; such assumptions would then need to be justified, and it is hard to see how they could be justified apart from testing them against actual and possible cases. There is then a dilemma for the Kantian. Either you stick with very uncontroversial, minimal facts about free agency and practical reasoning, in which case your principles will be empty. Or, you start with more substantive moral claims, in which case it seems fair to ask for justification of these claims. Given that these claims do not embody uncontroversial and deep metaphysical features of ourselves, how else could they be justified except by appeal to the moral data?

Of course, it would be ideal if we could generate substantive moral principles that could help us lead good and satisfying lives from reason alone, or perhaps from deep principles concerning human nature. Presumably it would simplify things greatly if we could be certain that God prescribes a particular set of moral principles. Given the uncertain status and prospects of these alternatives, however, it might be prudent to have available and to employ judiciously the sort of methodology we have outlined above.

Summary.   The methodology of seeking a wide reflective equilibrium (which involves the consideration of hypothetical as well as actual cases, and difficult as well as clear cases) is perhaps not a perfect approach. Nor is it the only approach to achieving clarity and understanding in ethics. All we have proposed here is that it is one approach that is useful and worthwhile in certain respects. Furthermore, we have suggested that the dismissal of the consideration of hypothetical examples cannot be as abrupt or easy as many have supposed. We have pointed out that the method of abstraction and model-building is a legitimate and useful theoretical approach in certain contexts. Also, thought-experiments have a legitimate role in the history of philosophy and contemporary philosophy. Why should the thought-experiments proposed herein be any different?

Notes

[1]A similar case is introduced by Judith Jarvis Thomson in "Killing, Letting Die, and the Trolley Problem," (p. 67). This version of Bystander is different from other versions discussed by Thomson and Fischer ("Thoughts on the Trolley Problem," p. 308); it is for this reason that we call it "Bystander 2." Later in the Introduction, we introduce the version presented by Thomson, and call it "Bystander 1."

[2]We shall engage in schematic and partial descriptions of the various cases, and the reader will certainly need to keep in mind that certain ways of filling in the rest of the details of the cases will affect the moral judgments appropriate to the cases.

[3]Thomson introduces and discusses this case in "Killing, Letting Die and the Trolley Problem," (p. 67), and "The Trolley Problem," (p. 279).

[4]For an alternative approach, according to which you should flip a fair coin, thus giving each person an equal chance of living, see John Taurek, "Should the Numbers Count?" (p. 214).

[5]Again, the case is borrowed from Thomson.

[6]We can imagine that you cannot shoot the shark because the water is too deep.

[7]For a discussion of this case and a further analysis of the proposed strategy for solving the Trolley Problem, see John Martin Fischer, "Tooley and the Trolley," *Philosophical Studies* (1991, forthcoming).

[8]For a discussion of the methodology employed here, see Shelly Kagan, "The Additive Fallacy," (p. 252); and Heidi Malm, "In Defense of the Contrast Strategy," (p. 271).

[9]This example comes from Philippa Foot, "The Problem of Abortion and the Doctrine of the Double Effect," (p. 59).

[10]In saying that two cases are morally equivalent, we do not mean that the two cases are alike in every respect, nor even that there are equally strong moral reasons against killing the

one in each case. Rather, Transplant and Hospital are said to be morally equivalent only in the sense that in both cases it is impermissible to kill the one person in order to save the five.

[11]For a different view of Bystander 3, see Michael Costa, "Another Trip on the Trolley," (p. 303).

[12]For an excellent discussion of the concept of harm, see the four volumes in Joel Feinberg's comprehensive work, *The Moral Limits of the Criminal Law* (Oxford: Oxford University Press).

[13]There is a discussion of this case (and the following cases) in John Martin Fischer, "Thoughts on the Trolley Problem," (p. 308). Thomson's proposed solution is more refined than what is suggested in the text, and there is a more careful discussion of it in Fischer's essay.

[14]For an interesting development of this sort of strategy, see Robert Hanna, "Morality *De Re*: Reflections on the Trolley Problem," (p. 318).

[15]John Rawls, *A Theory of Justice* (Cambridge: Harvard University Press, 1971), 20ff.

[16]These are Rawls's terms.

[17]For interesting discussions of narrow and wide reflective equilibrium, see Norman Daniels, "Two Approaches to Theory Acceptance in Ethics;" and David Copp, "Considered Judgments and Moral Justification: Conservatism in Moral Theory," both of which appear in: David Copp and David Zimmerman, eds., *Morality, Reason, and Truth* (Totowa, New Jersey: Rowman and Allanheld, 1984), 120-140 and 141-168, respectively.

[18]The terms are Dworkin's: Ronald Dworkin, "The Original Position," re-printed in Norman Daniels, ed. *Reading Rawls* (Stanford: Stanford University Press, 1989), 16-50.

[19]A clarification of the above remarks is in order. Kant is interpreted as a "constructivist" in ethics, but he is of course not interested in generating moral principles by considering particular examples. It is best to distinguish Kant's constructivism from other forms of moral constructivism. Kant is a moral constructivist insofar as he believes that moral agents freely give themselves or "construct" the moral law; but, nevertheless, the moral law and "moral facts" are objective because the source of construction—pure practical reason—is objectively real in each moral agent. In contrast, a "constructivist" such as John Rawls does not believe that the moral facts are "objective;" this is the sort of constructivism that is more congenial to the method of wide reflective equilibrium. For a discussion of these issues, see John Rawls, "Dewey Lectures," "Kantian Constructivism in Moral Theory," *Journal of Philosophy* 77 (1980), 515-572.

[20]This is the approach of R. M. Hare. For a recent presentation of Hare's view, see R. M. Hare, *Moral Thinking* (Oxford: Clarendon Press, 1981).

[21]G. E. Moore, *Principia Ethica* (Cambridge: Cambridge University Press, 1903).

[22]Jonathan Glover, *Causing Death and Saving Lives* (Middlesex: Penguin Books Ltd., 1977), 102. Glover considers this sort of justification only to raise criticisms of it later. The example was taken from Sefton Delmer, *The Counterfeit Spy* (London, 1971), Ch. 12.

[23]Judith Jarvis Thomson, "Killing, Letting Die, and the Trolley Problem," (p. 67).

[24]As mentioned above, distinguishing between intended means and mere side-effects is a difficult task. Hence, such counterfactual tests should be applied with caution.

[25]How successfully this policy could be implemented is another question. In the early years of the war most of the English air raids had to be conducted at night. Given the poor quality of the English navigational systems it was estimated in 1941 that no more than a third of the bombs dropped within five miles of their target. See Michael Walzer, *Just and Unjust Wars* (New York: Basic Books, 1977). Much of this discussion follows Walzer's account of the English decision to adopt a policy of terror bombing.

[26]Walzer, 255-256.

[27]Walzer, 261.

[28]That such non-combatants were killed even as a result of strategic bombing was especially true in the early years of the war when most of the English air raids had to be conducted at night. Given the poor quality of the English navigational systems, it was estimated that no more than a third of the bombs dropped within five miles of their targets. Thus, even when the official target of a raid was a military installation located on the outskirts of a city, chances were high that many non-combatants would be killed by bombs that missed their intended marks.

[29]For example, even though the Doctrine of Double Effect prohibits terror bombing in general, the English might have argued that in this particular case, terror bombing was the only means to prevent the disaster of a Nazi victory. Hence there was an overriding moral imperative to harm the civilians in order to prevent the much more serious moral violations that surely would have resulted had the Nazis defeated England. Although this type of defense plausibly could have justified following a policy of terror bombing in the earlier years of the war, it is much less clear that a similar defense could have been used to validate similar bombings, like that of Dresden, in the later years of the war. See Walzer, 261.

[30]Adapted from Robert M. Veatch, *Case Studies in Medical Ethics* (Cambridge: Harvard University Press, 1977), 335.

[31]This example is based on a report of the Sanders case in *Time*, January 9, 1990, 13.

[32]*Time*, March 19, 1990, 62. On June 25, 1990, a U. S. Supreme Court ruling blocked Cruzan's parents from withholding food and water unless sufficient evidence was presented to show that Nancy Cruzan would have wanted to die. After her former co-workers testified that Cruzan had said she never wanted to "live like a vegetable," a state judge ruled that this was sufficient evidence to remove her feeding tubes. Nancy Cruzan died on December 26, 1990, from dehydration.

[33]Tom L. Beauchamp and James F. Childress, *Principles of Biomedical Ethics* (Oxford: Oxford University Press), 309–310.

[34]Statement approved by the House of Delegates of the AMA on December 4, 1973. Cited in James Rachels, "Euthanasia, Killing, and Letting Die," James P. Sterba, ed., *Morality in Practice*, (Belmont: Wadsworth Publishing Company, 1988), 186.

[35]For one example, see Garrett Hardin's highly questionable extension of lifeboat ethics to the issues of aid to developing nations in "Lifeboat Ethics: The Case Against Helping the Poor," *Psychology Today*, no. 4, vol. 8 (September 1974), pp. 38–43, 123–126.

[36]Victor Grassian, *Moral Reasoning* (Englewood Cliffs: Prentice-Hall, Inc., 1981), 7–8.

[37]The prefix "meta" often is used to mean "about." Thus, meta-ethics is about the nature of ethics.

[38]Strictly speaking, consequentialist theories are sometimes understood to be a special class of teleological theories, but this distinction will not be important for the purposes of this introduction. Henceforth, we will simply refer to this general type of theory as being "consequentialist."

[39]Often philosophers specify this point more precisely, saying that consequentialist theories must hold that an action is right if and only if it *maximizes* the value produced. Other philosophers, such as Michael Slote, weaken this condition and suggest that these theories need only claim that the moral value of an action is *some* function of the value realized. See Michael Slote, *Common-sense Morality and Utilitarianism* (Boston: Routledge & Kegan Paul, 1985).

[40]The following explanation of the relationship between consequentialist and deontological theories follows the familiar account found in William K. Frankena, *Ethics* (Englewood Cliffs: Prentice-Hall, Inc., 1973); and John Rawls, *A Theory of Justice*. On this account, all ethical theories are categorized as being either consequentialist or deontological theories. Some

philosophers have objected to this dichotomy, arguing that theories like those of Aristotle which emphasize the development of a certain type of character and virtue are not easily countenanced by this division, and should instead be distinguished as a third type of ethical theory—sometimes called "virtue ethics." The question of whether virtue theories ultimately should be subsumed under the headings of either consequentialism or deontologism, or whether they should be treated as a separate type of theory, is not one to be settled here. For simplicity we will follow the familiar Frankena/Rawls account. For an extended discussion of virtue ethics, see Peter A. French, Theodore E. Uehling, Jr., and Howard K. Wettstein, eds., *Ethical Theory: Character and Virtue, Midwest Studies in Philosophy Vol. XIII* (Notre Dame: University of Notre Dame Press, 1988).

[41]Recently certain philosophers have disputed this requirement, arguing that as long as consequentialist theories are required to hold that rightness consists in maximal goodness, then the right and the good will remain distinct properties, even if the good is not defined independently of the right. For example, see David Brink, "Utilitarianism and the Personal Point of View," *Journal of Philosophy* 83 (1986), 417–438.

[42]Of course some things can have both intrinsic and extrinsic value. Such a good is valued both for its own sake and because it leads to other goods. For example, some people value the activity of running both for its own sake and because it tends to produce a more healthy body.

[43]Jeremy Bentham, *An Introduction to the Principles of Morals and Legislation*, (1789).

[44]John Stuart Mill, *Utilitarianism* (1863), Ch. II.

[45]This example is based on one discussed by J. J. C. Smart, although in presenting the example, Smart is trying to defend a version of hedonistic utilitarianism. See J. J. C. Smart and Bernard Williams, *Utilitarianism: For and Against* (Cambridge: Cambridge University Press, 1973), 25. Smart's example is similar to one used by Moore in his discussion of evil in *Principia Ethica*, 209–210.

[46]Note that when the total number of persons is held fixed, these two approaches converge. Thus, the distinction between maximizing total or average utility only becomes an issue if the population size itself is subject to utilitarian considerations. In this case, the approach that seeks to maximize total utility runs into problems to the extent that it requires people to keep adding to the population as long as this produces any incremental increase in total utility, even if this expanding population leads to a much lower average utility. And the approach that seeks to maximize average utility encounters difficulties, because it seems to demand that people who are deriving the least utility in society should be killed in order to raise the average utility. For an illuminating discussion of such matters, see Derek Parfit, *Reasons and Persons* (Oxford: Clarendon Press, 1984).

[47]A third approach applies the principle of utility to agents' character traits or motives. See Robert Adams, "Motive Utilitarianism," *Journal of Philosophy* 73 (1976), 467–481.

[48]To some, this points to a difficulty with the act-utilitarian's use of rules. How is one supposed to know in any given situation whether to follow the rule or to go through the process of working out which outcome has the best utility? If one is never certain in advance whether a rule of thumb points to morally right action, then it appears one will have to calculate the probable utility consequences for every action—if only to know whether or not to follow the rule of thumb.

[49]This example is based on the "Ross-Butler" examples discussed by Frankena in *Ethics*, 36.

[50]Of course, many thinkers allow that such prohibitions can be set aside in order to avoid catastrophic moral disasters.

[51]For one discussion of this point, see Thomas Nagel, "War and Massacre," *Mortal Questions* (Cambridge: Cambridge University Press, 1979), 53–74.

[52]Another response to this objection argues that not doing the horrible action is wrong, but not blameworthy, because on utilitarian grounds, one should not be disposed to do things that normally do not maximize utility. Since discouraging these traits would reduce utility in the long run, utilitarian theories should not penalize people for having these characters. See Peter Railton, "Alienation, Consequentialism, and the Demands of Morality," *Philosophy and Public Affairs* 13 (Spring 1984), 134–171.

[53]Another case that illustrates this problem, and which is perhaps more plausible, runs as follows. Two persons are shipwrecked on an otherwise deserted island. One of the persons, a wealthy woman, is dying, and she asks the other person to give her friend a large sum of money if he ever gets off the island. As it turns out the man is saved the very next day. He is very poor, and when he goes to meet the friend of the dead woman, he discovers that she is quite wealthy and has no need of money. If it is true, and we will stipulate that it is, that the poor man will derive more pleasure from having the money than the rich person will, then it seems an act-utilitarian should maintain that the man should not give the money to the friend. However, such "back-sliding" is thought by many to be impermissible, regardless of the consequences.

[54]R. B. Brandt discusses a similar example in *Ethical Theory*, (Englewood Cliffs: Prentice-Hall, Inc., 1959), 389–390. For a utilitarian response, see Smart and Williams, *Utilitarianism: For and Against*, 57.

[55]Act-utilitarians respond to these types of objections in a variety of ways. For example, one might argue that even if no one discovered Betty's extra consumption of water, this action would still not produce the best overall outcome, because it would corrupt Betty's character and weaken her regard for the law. If it were true that having developed this type of character, Betty would be more likely in the future to act in a way that harmed others, then one could argue that Betty should not use more water, because by doing so she would develop a character that is considered morally bad on act-utilitarian grounds.

[56]A similar type of worry is often raised against egoistic theories that hold that each person ought to maximize his own welfare. Such difficulties bear a close resemblance to the problems encountered by persons who follow a dominance strategy of maximization in "prisoner's dilemma" games. See R. Duncan Luce and Howard Raifa, *Games and Decisions* (New York: John Wiley and Sons, Inc., 1957); and Derek Parfit, *Reasons and Persons*.

[57]Of course, it makes a difference whether the utility of a rule is evaluated assuming that everyone accepts the rule or that everyone complies with it. The type of rule-utilitarianism one has will vary with how this question is answered.

[58]Here, acceptance of a rule is considered to be a slightly weaker condition than strict compliance with the rule.

[59]Rather than revising the rule, making it ever more specific, one might argue that these types of exceptions can be justified by appealing to some higher moral rule that specifies when exceptions should be made in order to maximize utility. Although this strategy provides a different structure to justify the exceptions, since it allows for ever more specific types of exemptions, it still threatens to collapse into act-utilitarianism.

[60]See David Lyons, *The Forms and Limits of Utilitarianism* (Oxford: Oxford University Press, 1965).

[61]Note that this objection applies specifically to utilitarian theories, insofar as they rank outcomes solely in terms of the quantity of utility produced. Other consequentialist theories can try to accommodate our intuitions about justice by maintaining that in comparing the goodness of various outcomes, one should consider not only the amount of good produced, but also the manner in which this good is distributed. By recognizing that an equitable distribution is itself good, these consequentialist theories hope to avoid the objections concerning distributive justice which have plagued utilitarian theories. See T. M. Scanlon, "Rights,

Goals, and Fairness," in *Public and Private Morality*, ed., Stuart Hampshire (Cambridge: Cambridge University Press, 1978), 93–111; and Samuel Scheffler, *The Rejection of Consequentialism*, (Oxford: Clarendon Press, 1982).

[62]Smart and Williams, *Utilitarianism: For and Against.*

[63]See John Rawls, *A Theory of Justice*; and Samuel Scheffler, *The Rejection of Consequentialism.*

[64]For one example of this argument, see Smart and Williams, *Utilitarianism: For and Against.*

[65]Immanuel Kant, *Groundwork of the Metaphysics of Morals*, translated by H. J. Paton (New York: Harper and Row, 1964), 88.

[66]Kant further argues that the categorical imperative can itself be justified by reflecting on the nature of autonomous, rational agents, but the reasons behind this claim need not concern us in this introduction.

[67]Kant, 91.

[68]*Ibid.* A universal law of nature is a fully general statement that expresses how things are, and it must hold for all cases without exception.

[69]Kant, 90.

[70]*Ibid.*

[71]Kant, 91.

[72]Kant, 90–91.

[73]Kant, 90.

[74]For discussion of some of the problems concerning universalizability see: Paul Dietrichson, "Kant's Criteria of Universalizability," in *Foundations of the Metaphysics of Morals with Critical Essays*, ed. Robert Paul Wolff (New York: The Bobbs-Merrill Company, Inc., 1969), 163–207; J. L. Mackie, *Inventing Right and Wrong* (New York: Penguin Books, 1977); Onora O'Neill, *Acting on Principle: An Essay on Kantian Ethics* (New York: Columbia University Press, 1975).

[75]W. D. Ross, *The Right and the Good* (Oxford: Oxford University Press, 1930).

[76]Yet as an example like Bystander 1 shows, even this intuition may easily be challenged.

[77]One strategy for avoiding some of these problems is to provide a "lexical" ordering of the principles. For example, see Rawls, *A Theory of Justice.*

[78]Of course, such reasoning is challenged by Taurek's article, "Should The Numbers Count?" (p. 214).

[79]This problem is posed by Robert Nozick in *Anarchy, State and Utopia* (New York: Basic Books, Inc., 1974). This same problem can be illustrated by the case of Fat Man. In this example, the person standing on the bridge must decide either (1) to do nothing and allow the trolley driver to kill the five persons on the track, or (2) to push the fat man in front of the trolley, thereby killing him but saving the five. In this case a deontologist is once again faced with a puzzling situation. According to her theory, she should not push the fat man in order to save the five, because to do so would be to violate a duty not to harm, and such violations should generally be avoided. However, if she were to push the fat man, she would prevent the trolley driver from violating an even greater duty not to kill the five innocent persons. (To make the case less controversial, imagine that the trolley driver could stop the trolley if he wanted, but he is intent upon killing the five innocent people on the track.)

[80]Thomas Nagel, *The View from Nowhere* (Oxford: Oxford University Press, 1986), 177. Emphasis added.

[81]Michael Bratman suggests one interesting strategy for explaining these constraints that draws on a parallel between deontological constraints and prior plans. See Michael E.

Bratman, *Intentions, Plans, and Practical Reason* (Cambridge: Harvard University Press, 1987). Whereas some proponents of the analogy between the structure of deliberation in the intrapersonal and interpersonal cases have been concerned to render consequentialism more plausible, Bratman's approach might help to provide some sort of foundation for non-consequentialism.

[82]Scheffler, *The Rejection of Consequentialism* (Oxford: Clarendon Press, 1982).

[83]It is indeed quite fashionable to criticize the use of such examples in ethics. For a classic source of this position, see Elizabeth Anscombe, "Modern Moral Philosophy," *Philosophy* 33 (1958), 1–19.

[84]For illuminating discussions of this issue, see Hilary Putnam, *Reason, Truth and History* (New York: Cambridge University Press, 1981); and Anthony Brueckner, "Brains in a Vat," *Journal of Philosophy* 83 (1986), 148–167. The "moral analogue" of this problem is the problem presented by the "experience machine," which artificially induces various pleasant experiences. For a discussion of the experience machine, see Robert Nozick, *Anarchy, State, and Utopia* (Basic Books, Inc., 1974, pp. 42–45).

 ·*Part II*

PROBLEMS AND PUZZLES

The Problem of Abortion and the Doctrine of the Double Effect

PHILIPPA FOOT ▪ University of California, Los Angeles
Virtues and Vices and Other Essays in Moral Philosophy, 1978

The **Doctrine of the Double Effect (DDE)** is a principle which traditionally has been used to provide guidance in morally complex situations such as abortion, euthanasia, and war (see Introduction). Foot criticizes the DDE because it does not accurately reflect our considered moral intuitions, and she suggests that more important than the distinction between direct and oblique intentions upon which the DDE rests is a distinction between positive duties to provide aid and negative duties to avoid harm.

The DDE places great importance on the distinction between a direct intention (something one *intends* as an end or as a necessary means to an end) and an oblique intention (something one merely *foresees* will happen as an *unintended* side-effect). The DDE maintains that whereas it is sometimes permissible to act in a way that brings about a bad result as an unintended but foreseen side-effect of some greater good, it is in general not permissible to bring about such a bad result as an intended end or as a necessary means to some intended end.

Foot considers several pairs of cases in which the DDE appears to yield judgments that concur with our moral intuitions. For example, it does seem permissible, in a case like Drug (see Introduction) to distribute a drug to save the lives of five persons (each of whom needs one-fifth of the drug) rather than use all of the drug to save the life of a single patient, but it does not seem permissible to save the lives of the five patients by killing a certain individual and then making a serum from his dead body (see also Transplant in Introduction). Similarly, it does seem permissible for the driver of a runaway trolley (which is about to kill five workmen) to shunt the trolley onto a track on which only a single person is working, but it does not seem permissible for a judge to execute an innocent man in order to avert a riot which would claim the lives of many more people. The DDE explains such intuitions as follows: in cases like Drug and the runaway trolley, it is permissible to act so that the five live and the one dies, because in each case the death of the one is merely foreseen, but not directly intended either as an end or as a necessary means to an end. In contrast, it is not permissible to kill the single individual in Transplant or in the riot case, because in these cases the individual's death is not merely a foreseen side-effect; it is directly intended as a necessary means to save the greater number of people.

Foot notes that although the DDE yields results that agree with our ordinary moral judgments in many cases, the strength of the doctrine depends more upon the distinction between what one does and what one allows than upon the distinction between **direct and oblique intentions**. Foot refines this intuition and ultimately argues that the salient moral feature in cases like those mentioned above is a distinction between a **negative duty** to avoid harm and a **positive duty** to provide aid. In addition, she suggests that a duty to avoid harm is, in general, greater than a duty to provide aid, and hence, it is usually not permissible to harm someone even if by so doing you can provide aid to a greater number of persons. Foot believes that this explains why the surgeon in Transplant should not harm the single patient in order to save the lives of five other people, and why the judge should not execute an innocent man in order to save the lives of the people who might die in the ensuing riot. In contrast, in cases in which the same type of duties are in conflict—cases like that of the runaway trolley in which a negative duty to refrain from harming five persons is in conflict with a negative duty to refrain from harming one, or Drug in which a positive duty to aid five patients is in conflict with a positive duty to aid one—then it is permissible to aid (or refrain from harming) the greatest number of persons possible.

In many cases, Foot's principle and the DDE agree on which actions are permissible. There are cases on which these principles disagree, however, and in such cases Foot thinks her view comes closer to capturing our ordinary moral intuitions. To illustrate this point, Foot considers a case like Hospital (see Introduction). In this case, the lives of five persons in a hospital can be saved by a certain drug, but producing this drug will release a deadly gas that will kill a patient who is in another room and who cannot be moved. Foot holds that most people will intuitively think that it is not permissible to produce the gas. The DDE cannot countenance this intuition, however, for it would say that the gas may be manufactured, since the death of the patient would merely be a **foreseen side-effect** and not an **intentional end** or **means to an end**. In contrast, Foot's principle does match our intuition, for it holds that the drug may not be manufactured because the duty to avoid harming the one patient is greater than any duty to provide aid to the five. Thus, Foot rejects the DDE and advocates her principle based on the distinction between positive and negative duties. Finally, Foot illustrates how her principle can guide our judgments concerning abortion by applying the principle to several difficult situations in which either the life of the mother or the fetus (or both) are at stake.

---

*ONE OF THE REASONS WHY MOST OF US FEEL puzzled about the problem of abortion is that we want, and do not want, to allow to the unborn child the rights that belong to adults and children. When we think of a baby about to be born it seems absurd to think that the next few minutes or even hours could make so radical a difference to its status; yet as we go back in the life of the foetus we are more and more reluctant to say that this is a human being and must be treated as such. No doubt this is the deepest source of our dilemma, but it is not the only one. For we are also confused about the general question of what we may and may not do where the interests of human beings conflict. We have strong intuitions about certain cases; saying, for instance, that it is all right to raise the level of education in our country, though statistics allow us to predict that a rise in the suicide rate will follow, while it is not all right to kill the feeble-minded to aid cancer research. It is not easy, however, to see the principles involved, and one way of throwing light on the abortion issue will be by setting up parallels involving adults or children once born. So we will be able to isolate the "equal rights" issue, and should be able to make some advance.

I shall not, of course, discuss all the principles that may be used in deciding what to do where the interests or rights of human beings conflict. What I want to do is to look at one particular theory, known as the "doctrine of the double effect" which is invoked by Catholics in support of their views on abortion but supposed by them to apply elsewhere. As used in the abortion argument this doctrine has often seemed to non-Catholics to be a piece of complete sophistry. In the last number of the *Oxford Review* it was given short shrift by Professor Hart.[1] And yet this principle has seemed to some non-Catholics as well as to Catholics to stand as the only defence against decisions on other issues that are quite unacceptable. It will help us in our difficulty about abortion if this conflict can be resolved.

The doctrine of the double effect is based on a distinction between what a man foresees as a result of his voluntary action and what, in the strict sense, he intends. He intends in the strictest sense both those things that he aims at as ends and those that he aims at as means to his ends. The latter may be regretted in themselves but nevertheless desired for the sake of the end, as we may intend to keep dangerous lunatics confined for the sake of our safety. By contrast a man is said not strictly, or directly, to intend the foreseen consequences of his voluntary actions where these are neither the end at which he is aiming nor the means to this end. Whether the word "intention" should be applied in both cases is not of course what matters: Bentham [1748-1832] spoke of *"oblique intention,"* contrasting it with the *"direct intention"* of ends and means, and we may as well follow his terminology. Everyone must recognize that some such distinction can be made, though it may be made in a number of different ways, and it is the distinction that is crucial to the doctrine of the double effect. The words "double effect" refer to the two effects that an action may produce: the one aimed at, and the one foreseen but in no way desired. By "the doctrine of the double effect" I mean the thesis that it is sometimes permissible to bring about by oblique intention what one may not directly intend. Thus the distinction is held to be relevant to moral decision in certain difficult cases. It is said for instance that the operation of hysterectomy involves the death of the foetus as the foreseen but

not strictly or directly intended consequence of the surgeon's act, while other operations kill the child and count as the direct intention of taking an innocent life, a distinction that has evoked particularly bitter reactions on the part of non-Catholics. If you are permitted to bring about the death of the child, what does it matter how it is done? The doctrine of the double effect is also used to show why in another case, where a woman in labour will die unless a craniotomy operation is performed, the intervention is not to be condoned. There, it is said, we may not operate but must let the mother die. We foresee her death but do not directly intend it, whereas to crush the skull of the child would count as direct intention of its death.[2]

This last application of the doctrine has been queried by Professor Hart on the ground that the child's death is not strictly a means to saving the mother's life and should logically be treated as an unwanted but foreseen consequence by those who make use of the distinction between direct and oblique intention. To interpret the doctrine in this way is perfectly reasonable given the language that has been used; it would, however, make nonsense of it from the beginning. A certain event may be desired under one of its descriptions, unwanted under another, but we cannot treat these as two different events, one of which is aimed at and the other not. And even if it be argued that there are here two different events—the crushing of the child's skull and its death—the two are obviously much too close for an application of the doctrine of the double effect. To see how odd it would be to apply the principle like this we may consider the story, well known to philosophers, of the fat man stuck in the mouth of the cave. A party of potholers have imprudently allowed the fat man to lead them as they make their way out of the cave, and he gets stuck, trapping the others behind him. Obviously the right thing to do is to sit down and wait until the fat man grows thin; but philosophers have arranged that flood waters should be rising within the cave. Luckily (luckily?) the trapped party have with them a stick of dynamite with which they can blast the fat man out of the mouth of the cave. Either they use the dynamite or they drown. In one version the fat man, whose head is *in* the cave, will drown with them; in the other he will be rescued in due course.[3] Problem: may they use the dynamite or not? Later we will find parallels to this example. Here it is introduced for light relief and because it will serve to show how ridiculous one version of the doctrine of the double effect would be. For suppose that the trapped explorers were to argue that the death of the fat man might be taken as a merely foreseen consequence of the act of blowing him up. ("We didn't want to kill him . . . only to blow him into small pieces" or even ". . . only to blast him out of the cave.") I believe that those who use the doctrine of the double effect would rightly reject such a suggestion, though they will, of course, have considerable difficulty in explaining where the line is to be drawn. What is to be the criterion of "closeness" if we say that anything very close to what we are literally aiming at counts as if part of our aim?

Let us leave this difficulty aside and return to the arguments for and against the doctrine, supposing it to be formulated in the way considered most effective by its supporters, and ourselves bypassing the trouble by taking what must on any reasonable definition be clear cases of "direct" or "oblique" intention.

The first point that should be made clear, in fairness to the theory, is that no one is suggesting that it does not matter what you bring about as long as you merely foresee and do not strictly intend the evil that follows. We might think, for instance, of the (actual) case of wicked merchants selling, for cooking, oil they knew to be poisonous and thereby killing a number of innocent people, comparing and contrasting it with that of some unemployed gravediggers, desperate for custom, who got hold of this same oil and sold it (or perhaps *they* secretly gave it away) in order to create orders for graves. They strictly (directly) intend the deaths they cause, while the merchants could say that it was no part of their *plan* that anyone should die. In morality, as in law, the merchants, like the gravediggers, would be considered as murderers; nor are the supporters of the doctrine of the double effect bound to say that there is the least difference between them in respect of moral turpitude. What they are committed to is the thesis that *sometimes* it makes a difference to the permissibility of an action involving harm to others that this harm although foreseen, is not part of the agent's direct intention. An end such as earning one's living is clearly not

such as to justify *either* the direct or oblique intention of the death of innocent people, but in certain cases one is justified in bringing about knowingly what one could not directly intend.

It is now time to say why this doctrine should be taken seriously in spite of the fact that it sounds rather odd, that there are difficulties about the distinction on which it depends, and that it seemed to yield one sophistical conclusion when applied to the problem of abortion. The reason for its appeal is that its opponents have often *seemed* to be committed to quite indefensible views. Thus the controversy has raged around examples such as the following. Suppose that a judge or magistrate is faced with rioters demanding that a culprit be found for a certain crime and threatening otherwise to take their own bloody revenge on a particular section of the community. The real culprit being unknown, the judge sees himself as able to prevent the bloodshed only by framing some innocent person and having him executed. Beside this example is placed another in which a pilot whose aeroplane is about to crash is deciding whether to steer from a more to a less inhabited area. To make the parallel as close as possible it may rather be supposed that he is the driver of a runaway tram which he can only steer from one narrow track on to another; five men are working on one track and one man on the other; anyone on the track he enters is bound to be killed. In the case of the riots the mob have five hostages, so that in both the exchange is supposed to be one man's life for the lives of five. The question is why we should say, without hesitation, that the driver should steer for the less occupied track, while most of us would be appalled at the idea that the innocent man could be framed. It may be suggested that the special feature of the latter case is that it involves the corruption of justice, and this is, of course, very important indeed. But if we remove that special feature, supposing that some private individual is to kill an innocent person and pass him off as the criminal, we still find ourselves horrified by the idea. The doctrine of the double effect offers us a way out of the difficulty, insisting that it is one thing to steer towards someone foreseeing that you will kill him and another to aim at his death as part of your plan. Moreover there is one very important element of good in what is here insisted. In real life it would hardly ever be certain that the man on the narrow track would be killed. Perhaps he might find a foothold on the side of the tunnel and cling on as the vehicle hurtled by. The driver of the tram does *not* then leap off and brain him with a crowbar. The judge, however, needs the death of the innocent man for his (good) purposes. If the victim proves hard to hang he must see to it that he dies another way. To choose to execute him is to choose that this evil *shall come about*, and this must therefore count as a *certainty* in weighing up the good and evil involved. The distinction between direct and oblique intention is crucial here, and is of great importance in an uncertain world. Nevertheless this is no way to defend the doctrine of the double effect. For the question is whether the difference between aiming at something and obliquely intending it is *in itself* relevant to moral decisions; not whether it is important when correlated with a difference of certainty in the balance of good and evil. Moreover we are particularly interested in the application of the doctrine of the double effect to the question of abortion, and no one can deny that in medicine there are sometimes certainties so complete that it would be a mere quibble to speak of the "probable outcome" of this course of action or that. It is not, therefore, with a merely philosophical interest that we should put aside the uncertainty and scrutinize the examples to test the doctrine of the double effect. Why can we not argue from the case of the steering driver to that of the judge?

Another pair of examples poses a similar problem. We are about to give to a patient who needs it to save his life a massive dose of a certain drug in short supply. There arrive, however, five other patients each of whom could be saved by one-fifth of that dose. We say with regret that we cannot spare our whole supply of the drug for a single patient, just as we should say that we could not spare the whole resources of a ward for one dangerously ill individual when ambulances arrive bringing in victims of a multiple crash. We feel bound to let one man die rather than many if that is our only choice. Why then do we not feel justified in killing people in the interests of cancer research or to obtain, let us say, spare parts for grafting on to those who need them? We can suppose, similarly, that several dangerously ill people can be saved only if we kill a certain individual and make a serum from his dead

body. (These examples are not over fanciful considering present controversies about prolonging the life of mortally ill patients whose eyes or kidneys are to be used for others.) Why cannot we argue from the case of the scarce drug to that of the body needed for medical purposes? Once again the doctrine of the double effect comes up with an explanation. In one kind of case but not the other we aim at the death of the innocent man.

A further argument suggests that if the doctrine of the double effect is rejected this has the consequence of putting us hopelessly in the power of bad men. Suppose for example that some tyrant should threaten to torture five men if we ourselves would not torture one. Would it be our duty to do so, supposing we believed him, because this would be no different from choosing to rescue five men from his torturers rather than one? If so, anyone who wants us to do something we think wrong has only to threaten that otherwise he himself will do something we think worse. A mad murderer, known to keep his promises, could thus make it our duty to kill some innocent citizen to prevent him from killing two. From this conclusion we are again rescued by the doctrine of the double effect. If we refuse, we foresee that the greater number will be killed but we do not intend it: it is he who intends (that is strictly or directly intends) the death of innocent persons; we do not.

At one time I thought that these arguments in favour of the doctrine of the double effect were conclusive, but I now believe that the conflict should be solved in another way. The clue that we should follow is that the strength of the doctrine seems to lie in the distinction it makes between what we *do* (equated with direct intention) and what we allow (thought of as obliquely intended). Indeed it is interesting that the disputants tend to argue about whether we are to be held responsible for what we allow as we are for what we do.[4] Yet it is not obvious that this is what they should be discussing, since the distinction between what one does and what one allows to happen is not the same as that between direct and oblique intention. To see this one has only to consider that it is possible *deliberately* to allow something to happen, aiming at it either for its own sake or as part of one's plan for obtaining something else. So one person might want another person dead, and deliberately allow him to die. And again one may be said to *do* things that one does not aim at, as the steering driver would kill the man on the track. Moreover there is a large class of things said to be brought about rather than either done or allowed where either kind of intention is possible. So it is possible to *bring about* a man's death by getting him to go to sea in a leaky boat, and the intention of his death may be either direct or oblique.

Whatever it may, or may not, have to do with the doctrine of the double effect, the idea of *allowing* is worth looking into in this context. I shall leave aside the special case of giving permission, which involves the idea of authority, and consider the two main divisions into which cases of allowing seem to fall. There is firstly the allowing which is forbearing to prevent. For this we need a sequence thought of as somehow already in train, and something that the agent could do to intervene. (The agent must be able to intervene, but does not do so.) So, for instance, he could warn someone, but *allows* him to walk into a trap. He could feed an animal but *allows* it to die for lack of food. He could stop a leaking tap but *allows* the water to go on flowing. This is the case of allowing with which we shall be concerned, but the other should be mentioned. It is the kind of allowing which is roughly equivalent to *enabling*; the root idea being the removal of some obstacle which is, as it were, holding back a train of events. So someone may remove a plug and *allow* water to flow; open a door and *allow* an animal to get out; or give someone money and *allow* him to get back on his feet.

The first kind of allowing requires an omission, but there is no other general correlation between omission and allowing, commission and bringing about or doing. An actor who fails to turn up for a performance will generally spoil it rather than allow it to be spoiled. I mention the distinction between omission and commission only to set it aside.

Thinking of the first kind of allowing (forebearing to prevent), we should ask whether there is any difference, from the moral point of view, between what one does or causes and what one merely allows. It seems clear that on occasions one is just as bad as the other, as is recognized in both morality and law. A man may murder his child or his aged relatives, by allowing them to die of starvation as well as by giving poison; he may also be

convicted of murder on either account. In another case we would, however, make a distinction. Most of us allow people to die of starvation in India and Africa, and there is surely something wrong with us that we do; it would be nonsense, however, to pretend that it is only in law that we make the distinction between allowing people in the underdeveloped countries to die of starvation and sending them poisoned food. There is worked into our moral system a distinction between what we owe people in the form of aid and what we owe them in the way of non-interference. Salmond, in his *Jurisprudence*, expressed as follows the distinction between the two.

> *A positive right corresponds to a positive duty, and is a right that he on whom the duty lies shall do some positive act on behalf of the person entitled. A negative right corresponds to a negative duty, and is a right that the person bound shall refrain from some act which would operate to the prejudice of the person entitled. The former is a right to be positively benefited; the latter is merely a right not to be harmed.* [5]

As a general account of rights and duties this is defective, since not all are so closely connected with benefit and harm. Nevertheless for our purposes it will do well. Let us speak of negative duties when thinking of the obligation to refrain from such things as killing or robbing, and of the positive duty, e.g., to look after children or aged parents. It will be useful, however, to extend the notion of positive duty beyond the range of things that are strictly called duties, bringing acts of charity under this heading. These are owed only in a rather loose sense, and some acts of charity could hardly be said to be *owed* at all, so I am not following ordinary usage at this point.

Let us now see whether the distinction of negative and positive duties explains why we see differently the action of the steering driver and that of the judge, of the doctors who withhold the scarce drug and those who obtain a body for medical purposes, of those who choose to rescue the five men rather than one man from torture and those who are ready to torture the one man themselves in order to save five. In each case we have a conflict of duties, but what kind of duties are they? Are we, in each case, weighing positive duties against positive, negative against negative, or one against the other? Is the duty to refrain from injury, or rather to bring aid?

The steering driver faces a conflict of negative duties, since it is his duty to avoid injuring five men and also his duty to avoid injuring one. In the circumstances he is not able to avoid both, and it seems clear that he should do the least injury he can. The judge, however, is weighing the duty of not inflicting injury against the duty of bringing aid. He wants to rescue the innocent people threatened with death but can do so only by inflicting injury himself. Since one does not *in general* have the same duty to help people as to refrain from injuring them, it is not possible to argue to a conclusion about what he should do from the steering driver case. It is interesting that, even where the strictest duty of positive aid exists, this still does not weigh as if a negative duty were involved. It is not, for instance, permissible to commit a murder to bring one's starving children food. If the choice is between inflicting injury on one or many there seems only one rational course of action; if the choice is between aid to some at the cost of injury to others, and refusing to inflict the injury to bring the aid, the whole matter is open to dispute. So it is not inconsistent of us to think that the driver must steer for the road on which only one man stands while the judge (or his equivalent) may not kill the innocent person in order to stop the riots. Let us now consider the second pair of examples, which concern the scarce drug on the one hand and on the other the body needed to save lives. Once again we find a difference based on the distinction between the duty to avoid injury and the duty to provide aid. Where one man needs a massive dose of the drug and we withhold it from him in order to save five men, we are weighing aid against aid. But if we consider killing a man in order to use his body to save others, we are thinking of doing him an injury to bring others aid. In an interesting variant of the model, we may suppose that instead of killing someone we deliberately let him die. (Perhaps he is a beggar to whom we are thinking of giving food, but then we say "No, they need bodies for medical research.") Here it does seem relevant that in allowing him to die we are aiming at his death, but presumably we are inclined to see this as a violation of negative rather than positive duty. If this is right, we see why we are unable in either case

to argue to a conclusion from the case of the scarce drug.

In the examples involving the torturing of one man or five men, the principle seems to be the same as for the last pair. If we are bringing aid (rescuing people about to be tortured by the tyrant), we must obviously rescue the larger rather than the smaller group. It does not follow, however, that we would be justified in inflicting the injury, or getting a third person to do so, in order to save the five. We may therefore refuse to be forced into acting by the threats of bad men. To refrain from inflicting injury ourselves is a stricter duty than to prevent other people from inflicting injury, which is not to say that the other is not a very strict duty indeed.

So far the conclusions are the same as those at which we might arrive following the doctrine of the double effect, but in others they will be different, and the advantage seems to be all on the side of the alternative. Suppose, for instance, that there are five patients in a hospital whose lives could be saved by the manufacture of a certain gas, but that this inevitably releases lethal fumes into the room of another patient whom for some reason we are unable to move. His death, being of no use to us, is clearly a side effect, and not directly intended. Why then is the case different from that of the scarce drug, if the point about that is that we foresaw but did not strictly intend the death of the single patient? Yet it surely is different. The relatives of the gassed patient would presumably be successful if they sued the hospital and the whole story came out. We may find it particularly revolting that someone should be *used* as in the case where he is killed or allowed to die in the interest of medical research, and the fact of *using* may even determine what we would decide to do in some cases, but the principle seems unimportant compared with our reluctance to bring such injury for the sake of giving aid.

My conclusion is that the distinction between direct and oblique intention plays only a quite subsidiary role in determining what we say in these cases, while the distinction between avoiding injury and bringing aid is very important indeed. I have not, of course, argued that there are no other principles. For instance it clearly makes a difference whether our positive duty is a strict duty or rather an act of charity: feeding our own children or feeding those in faraway countries. It may also make a difference whether the person about to suffer is one thought of as uninvolved in the threatened disaster, and whether it is his presence that constitutes the threat to the others. In many cases we find it very hard to know what to say, and I have not been arguing for any general conclusion such as that we may never, whatever the balance of good and evil, bring injury to one for the sake of aid to others, even when this injury amounts to death. I have only tried to show that even if we reject the doctrine of the double effect we are not forced to the conclusion that the size of the evil must always be our guide.

Let us now return to the problem of abortion, carrying out our plan of finding parallels involving adults or children rather than the unborn. We must say something about the different cases in which abortion might be considered on medical grounds.

First of all there is the situation in which nothing that can be done will save the life of child and mother, but where the life of the mother can be saved by killing the child. This is parallel to the case of the fat man in the mouth of the cave who is bound to be drowned with the others if nothing is done. Given the certainty of the outcome, as it was postulated, there is no serious conflict of interests here, since the fat man will perish in either case, and it is reasonable that the action that will save someone should be done. It is a great objection to those who argue that the direct intention of the death of an innocent person is never justifiable that the edict will apply even in this case. The Catholic doctrine on abortion must here conflict with that of most reasonable men. Moreover we would be justified in performing the operation whatever the method used, and it is neither a necessary nor a good justification of the special case of hysterectomy that the child's death is not directly intended, being rather a foreseen consequence of what is done. What difference could it make as to how the death is brought about?

Secondly we have the case in which it is possible to perform an operation which will save the mother and kill the child or kill the mother and save the child. This is parallel to the famous case of the shipwrecked mariners who believed that they must throw someone overboard if their boat was not to founder in a storm, and to the other famous case of the two sailors, Dudley and Stephens, who

killed and ate the cabin boy when adrift on the sea without food. Here again there is no conflict of interests so far as the decision to act is concerned; only in deciding whom to save. Once again it would be reasonable to act, though one would respect someone who held back from the appalling action either because he preferred to perish rather than do such a thing or because he held on past the limits of reasonable hope. In real life the certainties postulated by philosophers hardly ever exist, and Dudley and Stephens were rescued not long after their ghastly meal. Nevertheless if the certainty were absolute, as it might be in the abortion case, it would seem better to save one than none. Probably we should decide in favour of the mother when weighing her life against that of the unborn child, but it is interesting that, a few years later, we might easily decide it the other way.

The worst dilemma comes in the third kind of example where to save the mother we must kill the child, say by crushing its skull, while if nothing is done the mother will perish but the child can be safely delivered after her death. Here the doctrine of the double effect has been invoked to show that we may not intervene, since the child's death would be directly intended while the mother's would not. On a strict parallel with cases not involving the unborn we might find the conclusion correct though the reason given was wrong. Suppose, for instance, that in later life the presence of a child was certain to bring death to the mother. We would surely not think ourselves justified in ridding her of it by a process that involved its death. For in general we do not think that we can kill one innocent person to rescue another, quite apart from the special care that we feel is due to children once they have prudently got themselves born. What we would be prepared to do when a great many people were involved is another matter, and this is probably the key to one quite common view of abortion on the part of those who take quite seriously the rights of the unborn child. They probably feel that if *enough* people were involved one must be sacrificed, and they think of the mother's life against the unborn child's life as if it were many against one. But of course many people do not view it like this at all, having no inclination to accord to the foetus or unborn child anything like ordinary human status in the matter of rights. I have not been arguing for or against these points of view but only trying to discern some of the currents that are pulling us back and forth. The levity of the examples is not meant to offend.

Notes

*"The Problem of Abortion and the Doctrine of the Double Effect" originally appeared in the *Oxford Review*, Number 5, 1967.

[1]H. L. A. Hart, "Intention and Punishment," *Oxford Review*, 4, Hilary 1967. I owe much to this article and to a conversation with Professor Hart, though I do not know whether he will approve of what follows.

[2]For discussions of the Catholic doctrine on abortion, see Glanville Williams, *The Sanctity of Life and the Criminal Law* (New York, 1957); also N. St. John Stevas, *The Right to Life* (London, 1963).

[3]It was Professor Hart who drew my attention to this distinction.

[4]See, e.g., J. Bennett, "Whatever the Consequences," *Analysis*, January 1966, and G. E. M. Anscombe's reply in *Analysis*, June 1966. See also Miss Anscombe's "Modern Moral Philosophy" in *Philosophy*, January 1958.

[5]J. Salmond, *Jurisprudence*, 11th edition, p. 283.

Killing, Letting Die, and the Trolley Problem

JUDITH JARVIS THOMSON ▪ Massachusetts Institute of Technology
The Monist, 1976

Judith Jarvis Thomson discusses the thesis that **killing** is worse than **letting die**. She presents a series of cases in which it intuitively seems that one *may* choose to kill rather than to let die. She also offers some suggestions to explain our intuitions about these cases.

The first section begins by asking what it means to say that killing is worse than letting die. Thomson argues that this cannot mean that for any pair of acts which are the same in every respect except that the first involves killing and the second involves letting die, the first is worse than the second. A more plausible interpretation of the thesis that killing is worse than letting die is that it applies only to cases like Transplant (see Introduction) in which an agent has a *choice* between killing and letting die. The intuition to which proponents of the thesis appeal is that in Transplant, the surgeon may not kill one person in order to save five dying patients, and the reason he may not do so is that killing one person is worse than letting five die. Even given this charitable interpretation, however, the killing/letting die thesis fails to match our moral intuitions in some circumstances. To illustrate this point, Thomson considers two situations discussed by Foot: Transplant and Trolley Driver (in which a trolley driver whose brakes have failed must choose between letting the trolley continue its course, killing five persons or shunting the trolley to the right, killing one). Thomson rejects Foot's explanation of the difference between these cases. Thomson proceeds by presenting Bystander 1 (see Introduction), which is similar to Foot's trolley case except that the relevant decision-making agent is a bystander rather than the trolley driver. In Bystander 1 it seems permissible for the agent to cause the train to turn to the right. Thus

Foot's solution to the moral puzzle is inadequate: the explanation of the wrongness of saving the five in Transplant cannot be that one's **negative duty** to refrain from killing is more stringent than one's **positive duty** to save the lives, for in Bystander 1 it does seem permissible to shunt the trolley, and in so doing the bystander would be killing one person in order to save the lives of five.

In Section II, Thomson notes that the most striking difference between cases in which an agent may act and those in which he may not is that in the former, the act merely deflects a **threat** from a larger group onto a smaller one, whereas in the latter, the act brings a new threat to bear on the smaller group. As a first step in explaining when and how threats may permissibly be distributed, Thomson considers cases that involve the distribution of goods. According to Thomson, persons can have or fail to have claims in relation to *evils* just as they can have or fail to have claims in relation to *goods*. Thomson's intuitions about claims on goods derive from the common notion of property ownership. **Goods** and **evils** are things to be distributed unless particular parties have claims for or against those goods and evils. To illustrate some of the ways prior claims can influence the distribution of a good, Thomson imagines a Health-Pebble floating toward the beach. This Health-Pebble bestows health upon the sick. If someone owns the Health-Pebble, that person has a claim on it, and he is entitled to it. If the Health-Pebble is not owned, the moral thing to do is to distribute it most justly—i.e., to the greatest number of persons possible. Analogously, in Bystander 1, if the one man has a greater claim against being killed by a trolley than do the five (perhaps he has been guaranteed safety by the mayor), then the trolley may not be shunted onto him. In contrast, if all six persons on the tracks have equal claims against being harmed by the trolley, then the moral thing to do is to bring about the least bad distribution of the threat—i.e., direct the trolley so that the least number of people are harmed.

In the third section Thomson extends the previous discussion of claims in order to explain the difference between cases like Bystander 1 and Transplant. She argues that in contrast to Bystander 1 (in which the one man does not have any greater claim against being killed by a runaway trolley than do the five) in Transplant, the one patient does have more of a claim to his body parts than do the five dying patients. Therefore, it is not permissible to redistribute his organs. Thomson further refines this suggestion to explain the intuition that in Fat Man (see Introduction), one cannot save the five persons by pushing the fat man into the path of the oncoming trolley. Thomson's idea is that if one person has no more claim against the bad (or for the good) than other people do, then it is permissible to do something to the bad (or good) in order to redistribute it in the most just manner possible; it is not permissible, however, to do something *to a person* in order to bring about this better **distribution**. Thus, it is permissible to shunt the trolley (assuming that the one has no greater claim against this threat than do the five) because in this case the redistribution is accomplished by doing something *to the threat*. In contrast, it is not permissible to push the fat man because in this case, one would need to do something *to a person* in order to bring about a better distribution of the threat.

I.

MORALLY SPEAKING IT MAY MATTER A GREAT DEAL how a death comes about, whether from natural causes, or at the hands of another, for example. Does it matter whether a man was killed or only let die? A great many people think it does: they think that killing is worse than letting die. And they draw conclusions from this for abortion, euthanasia, and the distribution of scarce medical resources. Others think it doesn't, and they think this shown by what we see when we construct a pair of cases which are so far as possible in all other respects alike, except that in the one case the agent kills, in the other he only lets die. So, for example, imagine that

(1)   Alfred hates his wife and wants her dead. He puts cleaning fluid in her coffee, thereby killing her,

and that

(2)   Bert hates his wife and wants her dead. She puts cleaning fluid in her coffee (being muddled, thinking it's cream). Bert happens to have the antidote to cleaning fluid, but he does not give it to her; he lets her die.[1]

Alfred kills his wife out of a desire for her death; Bert lets his wife die out of a desire for her death. But what Bert does is surely every bit as bad as what Alfred does. So killing isn't worse than letting die.

But I am now inclined to think that this argument is a bad one. Compare the following argument for the thesis that cutting off a man's head is no worse than punching a man in the nose. "Alfrieda knows that if she cuts off Alfred's head he will die, and, wanting him to die, cuts it off; Bertha knows that if she punches Bert in the nose he will die—Bert is in peculiar physical condition—and [Bertha], wanting him to die, punches him in the nose. But what Bertha does is surely every bit as bad as what Alfrieda does. So cutting off a man's head isn't worse than punching a man in the nose." It's not easy to say just exactly what goes wrong in this argument, because it's not clear what we mean when we say, as we do, such things as that cutting off a man's head is worse than punching a man in the nose. The argument brings out

that we don't mean by it anything which entails that for every pair of acts, actual or possible, one of which is a nose-punching, the other of which is a head-cutting-off, but which are so far as possible in all other respects alike, the second is worse than the first. Or at least the argument brings out that we can't mean anything which entails this by "Cutting off a man's head is worse than punching a man in the nose" if we want to go on taking it for true. Choice is presumably in question, and the language which comes most readily is perhaps this: if you can cut off a man's head or punch him in the nose, then if he is in 'normal' condition—and if other things are equal—you had better not choose cutting off his head. But there is no need to go into any of this for present purposes. Whatever precisely we do mean by "Cutting off a man's head is worse than punching a man in the nose," it surely (a) is not disconfirmed by the cases of Alfrieda and Bertha, and (b) is confirmed by the fact that if you can now either cut off my head, or punch me in the nose, you had better not choose cutting off my head. This latter is a fact. I don't say that you had better choose punching me in the nose: best would be to do neither. Nor do I say it couldn't have been the case that it would be permissible to choose cutting off my head. But things being as they are, you had better not choose it.

I'm not going to hazard a guess as to what precisely people mean by saying "Killing is worse than letting die." I think the argument of the first paragraph brings out that they can't mean by it anything which entails that for every pair of acts, actual or possible, one of which is a letting die, the other of which is a killing, but which are so far as possible in all other respects alike, the second is worse than the first—i.e., they can't if they want to go on taking it for true. I think here too that choice is in question, and that what they mean by it is something which is not disconfirmed by the cases of Alfred and Bert. And isn't what they mean by it confirmed by the fact—isn't it a fact?—that in the following case, Charles must not kill, that he must instead let die:

(3)   Charles is a great transplant surgeon. One of his patients needs a new heart, but is of a relatively rare blood-type. By chance, Charles

learns of a healthy specimen with that very blood-type. Charles can take the healthy specimen's heart, killing him, and install it in his patient, saving him. Or he can refrain from taking the healthy specimen's heart, letting his patient die.

I should imagine that most people would agree that Charles must not choose to take out the one man's heart to save the other: he must let his patient die.

And isn't what they mean by it further confirmed by the fact—isn't it a fact?—that in the following case, David must not kill, that he must instead let die:

(4) David is a great transplant surgeon. Five of his patients need new parts—one needs a heart, the others need, respectively, liver, stomach, spleen, and spinal cord—but all are of the same, relatively rare, blood-type. By chance, David learns of a healthy specimen with that very blood-type. David can take the healthy specimen's parts, killing him, and install them in his patients, saving them. Or he can refrain from taking the healthy specimen's parts, letting his patients die.

If David may not even choose to cut up one where *five* will thereby be saved, surely what people who say "Killing is worse than letting die" mean by it must be right!

On the other hand, there is a lovely, nasty difficulty which confronts us at this point. Philippa Foot says[2]—and seems right to say—that it is permissible for Edward, in the following case, to kill:

(5) Edward is the driver of a trolley, whose brakes have just failed. On the track ahead of him are five people; the banks are so steep that they will not be able to get off the track in time. The track has a spur leading off to the right, and Edward can turn the trolley onto it. Unfortunately there is one person on the right-hand track. Edward can turn the trolley, killing the one; or he can refrain from turning the trolley, killing the five.

If what people who say "Killing is worse than letting die" mean by it is true, how is it that Edward may choose to turn that trolley?

Killing and letting die apart, in fact, it's a lovely, nasty difficulty: why is it that Edward may turn that trolley to save his five, but David may not cut up his healthy specimen to save his five? I like to call this the trolley problem, in honor of Mrs. Foot's example.

Mrs. Foot's own solution to the trolley problem is this. We must accept that our "negative duties," such as the duty to refrain from killing, are more stringent than our "positive duties," such as the duty to save lives. If David does nothing, he violates a positive duty to save five lives; if he cuts up the healthy specimen, he violates a negative duty to refrain from killing one. Now the negative duty to refrain from killing one is not merely more stringent than the positive duty to save one, it is more stringent even than the positive duty to save five. So of course Charles may not cut up his one to save one; and David may not cut up his one even to save five. But Edward's case is different. For if Edward "does nothing," he doesn't do nothing; he kills the five on the track ahead, for he drives right into them with his trolley. Whichever Edward does, turn or not turn, he kills. There is, for Edward, then, not a conflict between a positive duty to save five and a negative duty to refrain from killing one; there is, for Edward, a conflict between a negative duty to refrain from killing five and a negative duty to refrain from killing one. But this is no real conflict: a negative duty to refrain from killing five is surely more stringent than a negative duty to refrain from killing one. So Edward may, indeed must, turn that trolley.

Now I am inclined to think that Mrs. Foot is mistaken about why Edward may turn his trolley, but David may not cut up his healthy specimen. I say only that Edward "may" turn his trolley, and not that he must: my intuition tells me that it is not required that he turn it, but only that it is permissible for him to do so. But this isn't important now: it is, at any rate, permissible for him to do so. Why? Compare (5) with

(6) Frank is a passenger on a trolley whose driver has just shouted that the trolley's brakes have failed, and who then died of the shock. On the track ahead are five people; the banks are so steep that they will not be able to get off the track in time. The track has a spur leading off to the right, and Frank can turn the trolley

onto it. Unfortunately there is one person on the right-hand track. Frank can turn the trolley, killing the one; or he can refrain from turning the trolley, letting the five die.

If Frank turns his trolley, he plainly kills his one, just as if Edward turns his trolley, he kills his one: anyone who turns a trolley onto a man presumably kills him. Mrs. Foot thinks that if Edward does nothing, he kills his five, and I agree with this: if a driver of a trolley drives it full speed into five people, he kills them, even if he only drives it into them because his brakes have failed. But it seems to me that if Frank does nothing, he kills no one. He at worst lets the trolley kill the five; he does not himself kill them, but only lets them die.

But then by Mrs. Foot's principles, the conflict for Frank is between the negative duty to refrain from killing one, and the positive duty to save five, just as it was for David. On her view, the former duty is the more stringent: its being more stringent was supposed to explain why David could not cut up his healthy specimen. So by her principles, Frank may no more turn that trolley than David may cut up his healthy specimen. Yet I take it that anyone who thinks Edward may turn his trolley will also think that Frank may turn his. Certainly the fact that Edward is driver, and Frank only passenger could not explain so large a difference.

So we stand in need, still, of a solution: why can Edward and Frank turn their trolleys, whereas David cannot cut up his healthy specimen? One's intuitions are, I think, fairly sharp on these matters. Suppose, for a further example, that

(7) George is on a footbridge over the trolley tracks. He knows trolleys, and can see that the one approaching the bridge is out of control. On the track back of the bridge there are five people; the banks are so steep that they will not be able to get off the track in time. George knows that the only way to stop an out-of-control trolley is to drop a very heavy weight into its path. But the only available, sufficiently heavy weight is a fat man, also watching the trolley from the footbridge. George can shove the fat man onto the track in the path of the trolley, killing the fat man; or he can refrain from doing this, letting the five die.

Presumably George may not shove the fat man into the path of the trolley; he must let the five die. Why may Edward and Frank turn their trolleys to save their fives, whereas George must let his five die? George's shoving the fat man into the path of the trolley seems to be very like David's cutting up his healthy specimen. But what is the relevant likeness?

Further examples come from all sides. Compare, for example, the following two cases:

(8) Harry is President, and has just been told that the Russians have launched an atom bomb towards New York. The only way in which the bomb can be prevented from reaching New York is by deflecting it; but the only deflection-path available will take the bomb onto Worcester. Harry can do nothing, letting all of New York die; or he can press a button, deflecting the bomb, killing all of Worcester.

(9) Irving is President, and has just been told that the Russians have launched an atom bomb towards New York. The only way in which the bomb can be prevented from reaching New York is by dropping one of our own atom bombs on Worcester: the blast of the American bomb will pulverize the Russian bomb. Irving can do nothing, letting all of New York die; or he can press a button, which launches an American bomb onto Worcester, killing all of Worcester.

Most people, I think, would feel that Harry may act in (8): he may deflect the Russian bomb from its New York path onto Worcester, in order to minimize the damage it does. (Notice that if Harry doesn't deflect that bomb, he kills no one—just as Frank kills no one if he doesn't turn his trolley.) But I think most people would feel that Irving may not drop an American bomb onto Worcester: a President simply may not launch an atomic attack on one of his own cities, even to save a larger one from a similar attack.

Why? I think it is the same problem.

II.

Perhaps the most striking difference between the cases I mentioned in which the agent may act, and the cases I mentioned in which he may not, is this: in the former what is in question is deflecting a threat from a larger group onto a smaller group, in the latter what is in question is bringing a different threat to bear on the smaller group. But it is not easy to see why this should matter so crucially. I think it does, and have a suggestion as to why, but it is no more than a suggestion.

I think we may be helped if we turn from evils to goods. Suppose there are six men who are dying. Five are standing in one clump on the beach, one is standing further along. Floating in on the tide is a marvelous pebble, the Health-Pebble, I'll call it: it cures what ails you. The one needs for cure the whole Health-Pebble; each of the five needs only a fifth of it. Now in fact that Health-Pebble is drifting towards the one, so that if nothing is done to alter its course, the one will get it. We happen to be swimming nearby, and are in a position to deflect it towards the five. Is it permissible for us to do this? It seems to me that it is permissible for us to deflect the Health-Pebble if and only if the one has no more claim on it than any of the five does.

What could make it be the case that the one has more claim on it than any of the five does? One thing that I think *doesn't* is the fact that the pebble is headed for the one, and that he will get it if we do nothing. There is no Principle of Moral Inertia: there is no prima facie duty to refrain from interfering with existing states of affairs just because they are existing states of affairs. A burglar whose burgling we interfere with cannot say that since, but for our interference, he would have got the goods, he had a claim on them; it is not as if we weigh the burglar's claim on the goods against the owner's claim on them, and find the owner's claim weightier, and therefore interfere—the burglar has no claim on the goods to be weighed.

Well, the Health-Pebble might actually belong to the one. (It fell off his boat.) Or it might belong to us, and we had promised it to the one. If either of these is the case, the one has a claim on it in the sense of a right to it. If the one alone owns it, or if we have promised it only to the one, then he plainly has more claim on it than any of the five do; and we may not deflect it away from him.

But I mean to be using the word "claim" more loosely. So, for example, suppose that the five are villains who had intentionally caused the one's fatal illness, hoping he would die. (Then they became ill themselves.) It doesn't seem to me obvious that a

history like this gives the one a *right* to that pebble; yet it does seem obvious that in some sense it gives the one a claim on it—anyway, more of a claim on it than any of the five has. Certainly anyway one feels that if it comes to a choice between them and him, he ought to get it. Again, suppose the six had played pebble-roulette: they had seen the pebble floating in, and agreed to flip a coin for positions on the beach and take their chances. And now the pebble is floating in towards the one. It doesn't seem to me that a history like this gives the one a *right* to that pebble; yet it does seem obvious that in some sense it gives him a claim on it, anyway, more claim on it than any of the five has. (While the fact that a pebble is floating towards one does not give him more claim on it, the compound fact that a pebble is floating towards him and that there was a background of pebble-roulette does, I think, give him more claim. If two groups have agreed to take what comes, and have acted in good faith in accordance with that agreement, I think we cannot intervene.)

I leave it open just precisely what sorts of things might give the one more claim on that Health-Pebble than any of the five has. What seems clear enough, however, is this: if the one has no more claim on it than any of the five has, we may deflect it away from him and towards the five. If the one has no more claim on it than any of the five has, it is permissible for us to deflect it in order to bring about that it saves more lives than it would do if we did not act.

Now that Health-Pebble is a good to those dying men on the beach: if they get to eat it, they live. The trolley is an evil to the living men on the tracks: if they get run down by it, they die. And deflecting the Health-Pebble away from one and towards five is like deflecting the trolley away from five and towards one. For if the pebble is defected, one life is lost and five are saved; and if the trolley is deflected, so also is one life lost and five saved. The analogy suggests a thesis: that Edward (or Frank) may deflect his trolley if and only if the one has no more claim against the trolley than any of the five has—i.e., that under these circumstances he may deflect it in order to bring about that it takes fewer lives than it would do if he did not.

But while it was at least relatively clear what sorts of things might give the one more of a claim *on* the Health-Pebble, it is less clear what could give the one more of a claim *against* a trolley. Nevertheless there are examples in which it is clear enough that the one has more of a claim against the trolley than any of the five does. Suppose that

(i)　The five on the track ahead are regular track workmen, repairing the track—they have been warned of the dangers of their job, and are paid specially high salaries to compensate. The right-hand track is a dead end, unused in ten years. The Mayor, representing the City, has set out picnic tables on it, and invited the convalescents at the nearby City Hospital to have lunch there, guaranteeing them safety from trolleys. The one on the right-hand track is a convalescent having his lunch there; it would never have occurred to him to have his lunch there but for the Mayor's invitation and guarantee of safety. And Edward (Frank) is the Mayor.

The situation if (i) is true is very like the situation if we own the Health-Pebble which is floating in on the tide, and have promised it to the one. If we have promised the Health-Pebble to the one and not to the five, the one has more claim on it than any of the five does, and we therefore may not deflect it away from him; if Edward (Frank) has promised that no trolley shall run down the one, and has not made this promise to the five, the one has more claim against it—more claim to not be run down by it—than any of the five does, and Edward therefore may not deflect it onto him.

So in fact I cheated: it isn't permissible for Edward and Frank to turn their trolleys in *every* possible instance of (5) and (6). Why did it seem as if it would be? The cases were underdescribed, and what you supplied as filler was that the six on the tracks are on a par: that there was nothing further true of any of them which had a bearing on the question whether or not it was permissible to turn the trolleys. In particular, then, you were assuming that it was not the case that the one had more claim against the trolleys than any of the five did.

Compare, by contrast, the situation if

(ii)　All six on the tracks are regular track workmen, repairing the tracks. As they do everyday, they drew straws for their assignments for the day. The one who is on the right-hand

track just happened to draw the straw tagged "Right-hand track."

Or if

(iii)　All six are innocent people whom villains have tied to the trolley tracks, five on one track, one on the other.

If (ii) or (iii) is true, all six are on a par in the relevant respect: the one has no more claim against the trolley than any of the five has and so the trolley may be turned.

Again, consider the situation if

(iv)　The five on the track ahead are regular track workmen, repairing the track. The one on the right-hand track is a schoolboy, collecting pebbles on the track. He knows he doesn't belong there: he climbed the fence to get onto the track, ignoring all warning signs, thinking, "Who could find it in his heart to turn a trolley onto a schoolboy?"

At the risk of seeming hardhearted about schoolboys, I have to say I think that if (iv) is true, the trolley not only may be, but must be turned. So it seems to me arguable that if—as I take to be the case if (iv) is true—the five have more claim against the trolley than the one does, the trolley not only may be, but must be turned. But for present purposes what counts is only what makes it permissible to turn it where it is permissible to turn it.

President Harry's case, (8), is of course like the cases of Edward and Frank. Harry also deflects something which will harm away from a larger group onto a smaller group. And my proposal is that he may do this because (as we may presume) the Worcesters have no more claim against a Russian bomb than the New Yorkers do.

The situation could have been different. Suppose an avalanche is descending towards a large city. It is possible to deflect it onto a small one. May we? Not if the following is the case. Large City is in avalanche country—the risk of an avalanche is very high there. The founders of Large City were warned of this risk when they built there, and all settlers in it were warned of it before settling there. But lots and lots of people did accept the risk and settle there, because of the beauty of the countryside and the money to be made there. Small

City, however, is not in avalanche country—it's flat for miles around; and settlers in Small City settled for a less lovely city, and less money, precisely because they did not wish to run the risk of being overrun by an avalanche. Here it seems plain we may not deflect that avalanche onto Small City to save Large City: the Small Cityers have more claim against it than the Large Cityers do. And it could have been the case that New York was settled in the teeth of Russian-bomb-risk.

The fact that it is permissible for President Harry in (8) to deflect that atom bomb onto Worcester brings out something of interest. Mrs. Foot had asked us to suppose "that some tyrant should threaten to torture five men if we ourselves would not torture one." She then asked: "Would it be our duty to do so, supposing we believed him . . . ?" Surely not, she implies: for "if so anyone who wants us to do something we think wrong has only to threaten that otherwise he himself will do something we think worse. A mad murderer, known to keep his promises, could thus make it our duty to kill some innocent citizen to prevent him from killing two."[3] Mrs. Foot is surely right. But it would be unfair to Mrs. Foot to summarize her point in this way: we must not do a villain's dirty work for him. And wrong, in any case, for suppose the Russians don't really care about New York. The city they really want to destroy is Worcester. But for some reason they can only aim their bomb at New York, which they do in the hope that President Harry will himself deflect it onto Worcester. It seems to me it makes no difference what their aim is: whether they want Worcester or not, Harry can still deflect their bomb onto Worcester. But in doing so, he does the villains' dirty work for them: for if he deflects their bomb, he kills Worcester for them.

Similarly, it doesn't matter whether or not the villains in (iii) want the one on the right-hand track dead: Edward and Frank can all the same turn their trolleys onto him. That a villain wants a group dead gives them no more claim against a bomb or a trolley than these in the other group have.

Mrs. Foot's examples in the passages I quoted are of villains who have not yet launched their threat against anyone, but only threaten to: they have not yet set in train any sequence of events—e.g., by launching a bomb, or by starting a trolley

down a track—such that if we don't act, a group will be harmed. The villains have as yet only *said* they would set such a sequence of events in train. I don't object to our acting on the ground of uncertainties: one may, as Mrs. Foot supposes, be perfectly certain that a villain will do exactly what he says he will do. There are two things that make it impermissible to act in this kind of case. In the first place, there are straightforward utilitarian objections to doing so: the last thing we need is to give further villains reason to think they'll succeed if they too say such things.[4] But this doesn't take us very far, for as I said, we may deflect an already launched threat away from one group and onto another, and we don't want further villains thinking they'll succeed if they only manage to get such a sequence of events set in train. So the second point is more important: in such cases, to act is *not* to deflect a threat away from one group and onto another, but instead to bring a different threat to bear on the other group. It is to these cases we should now turn.

III.

Edward and Frank may turn their trolleys if and only if the one has no more claim against the trolleys than any of the five do. Why is it impermissible for David to cut up his healthy specimen?

I think the Health-Pebble helps here. I said earlier that we might suppose that the one actually owns the Health-Pebble which is floating in on the tide. (It fell off his boat.) And I said that in that case, he has more claim on it than any of the five has, so that we may not deflect it away from him and towards the five. Let's suppose that deflecting isn't in question any more: the pebble has already floated in, and the one has it. Let's suppose he's already put it in his mouth. Or that he's already swallowed it. We certainly may not cut him open to get it out—even if it's not yet digested, and can still be used to save five. Analogously, David may not cut up his healthy specimen to give his parts to five. One doesn't come to own one's parts in the way in which one comes to own a pebble, or a car, or one's grandfather's desk, but a man's parts are his all the same. And therefore that healthy specimen has more claim on those parts than any of the five has—just as if the one owns the

Health-Pebble, he has more claim on it than any of the five do.

I do not, and did not, mean to say that we may *never* take from one what belongs to him to give to five. Perhaps there are situations in which we may even take from one something that he needs for life itself in order to give to five. Suppose, for example, that that healthy specimen had caused the five to catch the ailments because of which they need new parts—he deliberately did this in hope the five would die. No doubt a legal code which permitted a surgeon to transplant in situations such as this would be open to abuses, and bad for that reason; but it seems to me it would not be unjust.

So perhaps we can bring David's case in line with Edward's and Frank's, and put the matter like this: David may cut up his healthy specimen and give his parts to the five if and only if the healthy specimen has no more claim on his parts than any of the five do. This leaves it open that in some instances of (4), David may act.

But I am inclined to think there is more to be said of David's case than this. I suggested earlier that if George, in (7), shoves the fat man into the path of the trolley, he does something very like what David does if David cuts up his healthy specimen. Yet George wouldn't be taking anything away from the one in order to give it to the five. George would be "taking" the fat man's life, of course; but what this means is only that George would be killing the fat man, and Edward and Frank kill someone too. And similarly for Irving, in (9): if he bombs Worcester, he doesn't take anything away from the Worcesters in order to give it to the New Yorkers.

Moreover, consider the following variant on David's case:

(4′) Donald is a great diagnostician. Five of his patients are dying. By chance Donald learns of a healthy specimen such that if Donald cuts him up into bits, a peculiar physiological process will be initiated in the five, curing them. Donald can cut his healthy specimen up into bits, killing him, thereby saving his patients. Or he can refrain from doing this, letting his patients die.

In (4′), Donald does not need to give anything which belongs to his healthy specimen to his five; unlike David, he need only cut his healthy specimen up into

bits, which can then be thrown out. Yet presumably in whatever circumstances David may not act, Donald may not act either.

So something else is involved in George's, Irving's, and Donald's cases than I drew attention to in David's; and perhaps this other thing is present in David's too.

Suppose that in the original story, where the pebble is floating in on the tide, we are for some reason unable to deflect the pebble away from the one and towards the five. All we can do, if we want the five to get it instead of the one, is to shove the one away, off the beach, out of reach of where the pebble will land; or all we can do is to drop a bomb on the one; or all we can do is to cut the one up into bits.

I suppose that there might be circumstances in which it would be permissible for us to do one or another of these things to the one—even circumstances which include that the one owns the pebble. Perhaps it would be permissible to do them if the one had caused the five to catch the ailments because of which they need the pebble, and did this deliberately, in hope the five would die. The important point, however, is this. The fact that the one has no more claim on the pebble than any of the five do does make it permissible for us to deflect the pebble away from the one and towards the five; it does not make it permissible for us to shove the one away, bomb him, or cut him to bits in order to bring about that the five get it.

Why? Here is a good, up for distribution, a Health-Pebble. If we do nothing, one will get it, and five will not; so one will live and five will die. It strikes us that it would be better for five to live and one die than for one to live and five die, and therefore that a better distribution of the good would be for the five to get it, and the one not to. If the one has no more claim on the good than any of the five has, he cannot complain if we do something to *it* in order to bring about that it is better distributed; but he can complain if we do something to *him* in order to bring about that it is better distributed.

If there is a pretty shell on the beach and it is unowned, I cannot complain if you pocket it to give to another person who would get more pleasure from it than I would. But I can complain if you shove me aside so as to be able to pocket it to give to another person who would get more pleasure from it than I would. It's unowned; so you can do to it whatever would be necessary to bring about a better distribution of it. But a *person* is not something unowned, to be knocked about in order to bring about a better distribution of something else.

Here is something bad, up for distribution, a speeding trolley. If nothing is done, five will get it, and one will not; so five will die and one will live. It strikes us that it would be better for five to live and one die than for one to live and five die, and therefore that a better distribution of the bad thing would be for the one to get it, and the five not to. If the one has no more claim against the bad thing than any of the five has, he cannot complain if we do something to *it* in order to bring about that it is better distributed: i.e., it is permissible for Edward and Frank to turn their trolleys. But even if the one has no more claim against the bad thing than any of the five has, he can complain if we do something to *him* in order to bring about that the bad thing is better distributed: i.e., it is not permissible for George to shove his fat man off the bridge into the path of the trolley.

It is true that if Edward and Frank turn their trolleys, they don't merely turn their trolleys: they turn their trolleys onto the one, they run down and thereby kill him. And if you turn a trolley onto a man, if you run him down and thereby kill him, you certainly do something to *him*. (I don't know whether or not it should be said that if you deflect a Health-Pebble away from one who needs it for life, and would get it if you didn't act, you have killed him; perhaps it would be said that you killed him, perhaps it would be said that you didn't kill him, but only caused his death. It doesn't matter: even if you only caused his death, you certainly did something to him.) So haven't their ones as much ground for complaint as George's fat man? No, for Edward's (Frank's) turning his trolley onto the one, his running the one down and thereby killing him, isn't something he does to the one to bring about that the trolley is better distributed. The trolley's being better distributed *is* its getting onto the one, it *is* running the one down and thereby killing him; and Edward doesn't turn his trolley onto the one, he doesn't run the one down and thereby kill him, in order to bring this about—what he does to bring it about is to turn his trolley. You don't bring about that a thing melts or breaks by melting or breaking

it; you bring about that it melts or breaks by (as it might be) putting it on the stove or hitting it with a brick. Similarly, you don't bring about that a thing gets to a man by getting it to him; you bring about that it gets to him by (as it might be) deflecting it, turning it, throwing it—whatever it is you do, by the doing of which you will have got it to the man.

By contrast, George, if he acts, does something to the fat man (shoves him off the bridge into the path of the trolley) to bring about the better distribution of the trolley, viz., that the one (the fat man) gets it instead of the five.

A good bit more would have to be said about the distinction I appeal to here if my suggestion is to go through. In part we are hampered by the lack of a theory of action, which should explain, in particular, what it is to bring something about by doing something. But perhaps the intuition is something to take off from: that what matters in these cases in which a threat is to be distributed is whether the agent distributes it by doing something to it, or whether he distributes it by doing something to a person.

The difference between Harry's case and Irving's is, I think, the same. Harry, if he acts, does something to the Russian bomb (deflect it), in order to bring about that it is better distributed: the few Worcesters get it instead of the many New Yorkers. Irving, however, does something to the Worcesters (drops one of our own bombs on them) in order to bring about that the Russian bomb is better distributed: instead of the many New Yorkers getting it, nobody does. Hence the fact that the Worcesters have no more claim against the Russian bomb than the New Yorkers do makes it permissible for Harry to act; but not for Irving to.

If we can speak of making a better distribution of an ailment, we can say of Donald too that if he acts, he does something to his healthy specimen (cut him up into bits) in order to bring about a better distribution of the ailments threatening his five patients: instead of the five patients getting killed by them, nobody is.

And then the special nastiness in David, if he acts, lies in this: in the first place, he gives to five what belongs to the one (viz., bodily parts), *and* in the second place, in order to bring about a better distribution of the ailments threatening his five— i.e., in order to bring about that instead of the five patients getting killed by them, nobody is—he does something to the one (viz., cuts him up).

IV.

Is killing worse than letting die? I suppose that what those who say it is have in mind may well be true. But this is because I suspect that they do not have in mind anything which is disconfirmed by the fact that there are pairs of acts containing a killing and a letting die in which the first is no worse than the second (e.g., the pair containing Alfred's and Bert's) *and* also do not have in mind anything which is disconfirmed by the fact that there are cases in which an agent may kill instead of letting die (e.g., Frank's and Harry's). What I suspect they have in mind is something which is confirmed by certain cases in which an agent may not kill instead of letting die (e.g., David's and Donald's). So as I say, I think they may be right. More generally, I suspect that Mrs. Foot and others may be right to say that negative duties are more stringent than positive duties. But we shan't be able to decide until we get clearer what these things come to. I think it's no special worry for them, however. For example, I take it most people think that cutting a man's head off is worse than punching a man in the nose, and I think we aren't

any clearer about what this means than they are about their theses. The larger question is a question for all of us.

Meanwhile, however, the thesis that killing is worse than letting die cannot be used in any simple, mechanical way in order to yield conclusions about abortion, euthanasia, and the distribution of scarce medical resources. The cases have to be looked at individually. If nothing else comes out of the preceding discussion, it may anyway serve as a reminder of this: that there are circumstances in which—even if it is true that killing is worse than letting die—one may choose to kill instead of letting die.

Notes

[1] Cf. Judith Jarvis Thomson, "Rights and Deaths" (p. 190); also Michael Tooley, "Abortion and Infanticide," *Philosophy and Public Affairs* (Fall 1972), sec. 5, and James Rachels, "Active and Passive Euthanasia" (p. 111).

[2] In her very rich article, "Abortion and the Doctrine of the Double Effect" (p. 59). Most of my examples are more or less long-winded expansions of hers. See also G. E. M. Anscombe's brief reply, "Who Is Wronged?" in the same issue of the *Oxford Review*.

[3] Foot, "Abortion and the Doctrine," p. 59.

[4] Cf. D. H. Hodgson, *Consequences of Utilitarianism: A Study in Normative Ethics & Legal Theory* (New York: Oxford University Press, 1967), pp. 77ff.

Ducking Harm

CHRISTOPHER BOORSE AND
ROY A. SORENSEN ▪ University of Delaware/New York University
The Journal of Philosophy, 1988

Boorse and Sorensen discuss "ducking," where Person A, in avoiding harm to himself, leaves Person B in a position where he may be harmed. They compare and contrast ducking harm to "sacrificing," where A places B in harm's way to avoid harm to himself.

Here are two of the cases of **ducking/sacrificing** presented in this selection: Mall Gunman: (a1) Angela, who is at the end of a line, sees someone about to shoot at her. She knows that the bullet can kill only one person. She leaps aside, and the bullet kills Brenda, who is next in line. (a2) is the same as (a1), but Angela grabs Brenda and moves her in front as a shield; the bullet kills Brenda. Speeding Truck: (b1) Arthur, at the end of a line of stopped cars, sees a runaway truck in his rearview mirror. He changes lanes; the truck crushes into Brian's car, injuring him. (b2) is the same as (b1), but Arthur beckons to a new driver (Brian) to join the line behind him; Brian is injured by the truck.

The moral puzzle in these cases is to explain why we are inclined to view A as less blameworthy in the type-1 but not in the type-2 cases, even when A knows that B will be harmed in each case. The legal puzzle is to determine what principles make A less civilly or criminally liable in the type-1 than in the type-2 cases.

The ducking puzzle cannot be solved by mere appeal to self-defense, which is involved in both ducking and sacrificing. At least seven factors may change our evaluation of the morality of ducking. At first sight, each alters either the absolute acceptability of ducking or its comparative acceptability with sacrificing.

(i)   *Responsibility for threat.* A may lose ducking rights to the extent that he (at least partially) created the danger.
(ii) *Innocence of act.* A's duck is less acceptable the more it involves intrinsically wrong acts, such as escaping by lying or stealing rather than by merely running away.
(iii) *Equal quantity of harm.* A's duck is worse if, in avoiding mere property damage to himself, B is killed or severely injured.
(iv) *Equal probability of harm.* A is less justified in ducking insofar as he is less likely to be injured than B.
(v)   *Benefit or cost to A.* A may have more right to duck if he has paid a prior cost for being able to do so. Conversely, ducking is criticized when the ducker benefits from the harm's befalling someone (i.e., benefits beyond avoiding it himself).
(vi) *Voluntariness.* The more voluntarily B assumes risk, the clearer it is that A may duck the risked harm to B.
(vii) *Identifiability of victim.* If the victim of a duck can be named in advance, it seems worse to duck than if the victim is anonymous.

Boorse and Sorensen point out that quantity (iii) and probability (iv) of harm have an easy utilitarian justification, but it is hard to see factor (vii), identifiability of victim, as serious. If the right to a pure duck is clear, (v) and (vi) cannot make duckers more justified in doing it, only more comfortable.

Boorse and Sorensen consider six ways of solving the basic puzzle.

(1) *Fair competition.* In sacrificing (but not ducking), one unfairly shifts the odds of the competition.
(2) *Included wrong (innocence factor).* Acts of sacrifice tend to be wrong per se, whereas acts of ducking are innocent per se.
(3) *Act versus omission.* Sacrifices tend to be acts; ducks tend to be omissions.
(4) *Causation.* Ducking does not cause death; sacrificing does.
(5) *Double effect.* There is a difference in intent in ducking versus sacrificing.

(6)   *Kant.* According to the Kantian view, in sacrificing, one uses a person as a means, whereas in ducking one does not.

None of these is deemed acceptable. Boorse and Sorensen also consider the view that the distinction in question (between ducking harm and sacrificing others) does not have moral significance after all. They reject this skepticism.

This essay aims to state a puzzle and survey possible solutions. It is worth noting that ducking and sacrificing occur in the national and international arenas, especially in war, distribution of harms and benefits, and so forth.

---

*OFTEN A PERSON A CAN TRANSFER A THREATENED harm to another person B. Often too there are two ways A can achieve this result, one more acceptable than the other. One way is for A merely to exit the threatening situation, leaving B behind to suffer the injury. The other way is for A directly to place B in harm's way as A's shield. This distinction between *ducking* harm to B and *using B as a shield* — or, as we shall often call it, "sacrificing"[1] B — is neglected in law and moral philosophy.[2] It is an analogue to the act/omission distinction, arousing similar intuitions, but wholly within the realm of acts. If accepted, it is a new nonconsequentialist constraint on distributing harm, and its explanation may be an adequacy condition on solutions to the act/omission problem.

I.

In a recent joke two campers, Alex and Bruce, meet a ravenous bear. As Alex grabs his running shoes, Bruce points out that no one can outrun a bear. "I don't have to outrun him," Alex replies. "I only have to outrun you." Few contemporary Western-ers[3] will criticize Alex for running away full tilt, or even for using his new Sauconys® [a type of athletic footwear]. But suppose Alex instead ties Bruce's ankles, or knocks Bruce unconscious and throws him to the bear. Alex is now blameworthy in ethics and in law. The result is the same in both cases: Bruce's death. Further, Alex may know the result to be the same if he knows he can outrun Bruce. Nonetheless most people sharply distinguish the two acts.

The bear example has unusual features—e.g., that Alex survives *by* Bruce's death—and so we will usually discuss purer examples of ducking. A standard pure case is this one:

Mall Gunman:

(a1) Angela, at the end of a movie ticket line, sees X about to shoot a .22 automatic at her. Angela knows that a .22 bullet will kill one person but not two. Angela leaps aside; the bullet kills Brenda, who is next in line.

(a2) Same as (a1), but Angela grabs Brenda and moves her in front as a shield; the bullet kills Brenda.

A slight variant which is useful later is a line of cars:

Speeding Truck:

(b1) Arthur, at the end of a line of stopped traffic, sees a runaway truck in his rearview mirror. Arthur changes lanes; the truck crashes into Brian's car, injuring him.

(b2) Same as (b1), but Arthur beckons to a new driver, Brian, to join the line behind him; Brian does so and is injured by the truck.

Other situations offer more subtle examples of the duck/sacrifice distinction.

Terrorists:

(c1) Alison is one of 25 U.S. government officials on an airplane, each with a briefcase bearing an official seal. Terrorist hijackers announce they will kill one American per hour until their demands are met. Surreptitiously Alison covers her seal with a Libya Air sticker. The terrorists pass her briefcase and shoot Beatrice, the next American.

(c2) Same as (c1), but Alison has no Libyan sticker. Instead, she switches briefcases with Babette, a French novelist, while she is in the bathroom. The terrorists shoot Babette.

Such cases raise moral and legal puzzles. The moral puzzle, like that posed by parallel acts and omissions, is to explain why we are strongly inclined to view A as blameless in the 1 but not in the 2 cases. At a minimum, we find A *less* blameworthy in 1. What morally relevant difference is there between ducking and forced shielding, when both are acts of A that A knows will lead to B's death? Similarly, the legal puzzle is what principles can assign A lower civil and criminal liability for ducking. What makes the legal puzzle especially acute, however, is the remarkable fact that, on standard accounts of homicide, A seems to have no defense to murder or manslaughter even for ducking. This surprising claim is explained in section III.

There is no doubt that ducking is approved in a wide range of cases. It is usually conceded that anyone has the right to escape disaster even when not everyone can escape. One may rush to the exit of a burning theater, though one will be criticized for trampling others in one's flight. It is equally clear to most people that forced shielding is wrong, and felons are often convicted of murder for the death of their human shields.[4] B's self-defense rights are symmetrical: B may forcibly resist being sacrificed, but he may not prevent A from ducking, since that would be to sacrifice A. Likewise, a similar distinction can be drawn in aggressive competition for scarce resources. One may rush to buy food in a famine or to sell stock on bad news. In a variant of the camper tale, Alex races Bruce for a single dose of rattlesnake antidote; the shift from escaping a threat to securing a benefit has no effect on intuition.

An important difference is that in scarce-resource situations, "sacrificing" B is not enshielding B, but merely wrongful direct interference with him. The previous examples illustrate this point, as well as the following case:

Sinking Boats

(d1) Arnold's only escape from his sinking boat is a rescue helicopter equidistant from him and Ben's sinking boat. Given the fog, the rescuers will follow the stronger distress signal. Arnold improvises a large aerial to strengthen his signal; he is saved and Ben drowns.

(d2) Same as (d1), but Arnold makes his signal stronger by jamming Ben's signal; the rescuers are diverted to Arnold.

Because sacrificing here lacks the element of enshielding, the duck/sacrifice distinction may be different or less clear. Our discussion will concentrate on the active-threat type (a)-(c); but the scarce-resource variety should be kept in mind, especially regarding solutions that employ the concept of using B as a means.

It is important to see that the ducking puzzle cannot be solved by mere appeal to "self-defense." Self-defense cannot distinguish ducking from sacrificing; the puzzle is how to distinguish among acts of self-defense. In case (a), A escapes the gunman's bullet exactly as much by ducking as by using B as a shield, and both the situation and the effect on B are the same. Legally, none of the acts falls under self-defense anyway, since the death caused is of B, an innocent bystander. Many ethical writers on abortion endorse killing the innocent in self-defense. Often what they endorse, however, is killing an innocent "assailant," whereas in our examples the innocent victim is not the threat. Among other objections, a blanket endorsement of all killing to save one's life violates the widespread expectation that people on waiting lists for organ transplants will let themselves die rather than remove rivals higher on the list, or kill healthy persons to expand the organ pool.

Also, the moral and legal issues are not restricted to defense of self or defense of body. The same puzzle arises for non-self victims and non-death harms. With the mall gunman, Y may be standing outside the line and save A either by pushing A aside or by pushing B in front of A. Morally speaking, Y is likely to be criticized for pushing B into the path of a bullet but not for pushing A out of it. Legally, it seems obvious that pushing A out of death's path should not subject Y to criminal charges or civil liability to B's relatives. The puzzle also survives changing the harm from death to bodily injury or property damage. Doubtless A may wall in his property against a coming flood, even if the water is thereby diverted to the home of B; but he may not build his wall out of the bricks of *B*'s doomed home. In an era of faculty cutbacks, one may save one's job by writing faster, but not by burning one's colleagues' manuscripts, even if they are worthless.

II.

At least seven factors can change our evaluation of the morality of ducking. At first sight, each alters either the absolute acceptability of ducking or its comparative acceptability with sacrificing.

(i) Responsibility for threat. *A* may lose ducking rights to the extent that he created the danger or has complicity in its creation. *A*'s duck is clearly wrong if he hired the gunman or rented the bear.[5] If *A* is only accidentally or negligently, not intentionally, responsible for the threat, his rights are less clear. How much does it matter if the bear was lured by *A*'s odor or that of the food cooler *A* forgot to close, or if the enraged gunman is *A*'s dismissed employee?

(ii) Innocence of act. Presumably *A*'s duck is less acceptable the more it involves intrinsically wrong acts. *A* is more blameworthy if he can escape only by lying or stealing than if he merely runs away. This factor is considered in section IV as a solution to the basic puzzle.

(iii) Equal quantity of harm. *A*'s duck is worse insofar as the injury *A* avoids is less than the injury *B* suffers. In (b1), if *A*'s vehicle is a heavy truck and *B*'s a small car, surely *A* must not prefer *B*'s death to his own property damage.

(iv) Equal probability of harm. *A* is less justified in ducking insofar as he is less likely to be injured than *B*. In (a1), if *A* has an invisible bulletproof vest, his fear of a head shot may not justify him in ducking the bullet to unprotected *B*.

(v) Benefit or cost to A. *A* may have more right to duck if he has paid a prior cost for being able to do so. This idea explains the morality of queues when those first in line have waited the longest. Similarly, contributors to blood banks win priority in a blood shortage. Conversely, ducking is criticized when the ducker benefits from the harm's befalling someone (i.e., benefits beyond avoiding it

himself). Thus the strong denunciation of wartime draft dodgers: as citizens they unfairly benefit from others' injuries in saving the common nation.

(vi) Voluntariness. The more voluntarily *B* assumes risk, the clearer it is that *A* may duck the risked harm to *B*. Drivers in fog are shamelessly guided by the lights of more reckless drivers who pass them. *A* feels better running from the bear on a safari than on a camping trip.

(vii) Identifiability of victim. Another familiar factor from the act/omission debate is whether the victim of a duck can be named in advance. The fleeing resistance fighter feels less guilty knowing the Gestapo will arrest someone else than knowing it will arrest his housemate. In the famous "squib" [firecracker] case,[6] one prefers throwing the lighted firecracker randomly into the crowd to placing it in a specific person's lap.

Although these factors affect our feelings about the morality of ducking, not all survive analysis. Factors (iii) and (iv), quantity and probability of harm, have an easy utilitarian justification. But it is hard to see factor (vii), identifiability of victim, as serious ethics. And, if the right to a pure duck is clear, factors (v) and (vi) cannot make duckers more justified, only more comfortable, in exercising it.

III.

To focus moral discussion further, we now analyze ducking according to standard legal principles.[7] To avoid confusion by the gunman's guilt, let us consider (a1) with a nonhuman danger: say, a boulder rolling with just enough momentum to crush one person. *A*'s leap is a voluntary act. *A* thus satisfies the first legal requirement for a crime: a *voluntary act* or *omission* where there is a special duty to act. *A*'s leap also satisfies both prongs of the standard test for legal *causation* of *B*'s death. First, *A*'s leap is a *necessary condition* of *B*'s death ("cause in fact"), since, if *A* remains, *A* dies and *B* lives. Second, no *unforeseeable intervening cause* deprives *A*'s act of legal responsibility. No cause temporally intervenes, since the boulder was in motion before *A* leaped; furthermore, *A* foresees the chain of causation before acting. Thus, *A*'s leap is a legal cause of *B*'s death.[8] Finally, because *A* foresees this result, he intends it in law. That is, in a philosophically preferable formulation, A has the state of intent *or* knowledge that suffices for murder.

These points suggest that A by leaping knowingly kills B, and, therefore, A is guilty of homicide unless A has a recognized defense. *Self-defense* covers injury only to assailants, whereas B is an innocent backstander. In theory the defense of *necessity* applies to any choice of a lesser evil under constraint of natural forces. It is here unavailable to A because A does not choose a lesser evil, merely substituting one death for another. *Duress*, the only other relevant possibility, is traditionally restricted to human threats, with natural dangers left to necessity. Also, duress is traditionally held not to excuse homicide. On this description, duress is doubly inapplicable to A, since the boulder is a natural evil and A's act is homicide.

In sum, A's duck, a voluntary act, is a known necessary condition of B's death, with no unforeseen intervening causes; and no classical defense seems to apply. If A is to escape criminal liability, legal theory must somehow locate him in 1-5 on the total list of possibilities:

(1) A does not act.
(2) A acts, but not voluntarily.[9]
(3) A acts voluntarily, but does not cause B's death.
(4) A's act is justified homicide.
(5) A's act is excused homicide.[10]
(6) A's act is criminal homicide:
   (a) involuntary manslaughter.
   (b) voluntary manslaughter.
   (c) second-degree murder.

Several possible innovations in legal doctrine are discussed in section IV. The most promising line suggested by standard accounts of criminal law is as follows. One discards the artificial distinction between duress and necessity; one also adopts a modern trend to excuse acts under duress that a "person of reasonable firmness" would find irresistible. A's duck can then be held to be excusable homicide under thus unified and liberalized duress/necessity. This line frees A from criminal guilt, with the residual oddity of leaving him a killer. But it does nothing to distinguish ducking from forced shielding. The point of the "reasonable firmness" test is precisely to excuse killing under threat of being killed, to recognize that people of ordinary firmness will sacrifice others' lives to save their own. A does this equally in duck and shield cases. So the legal puzzle that remains is the same as the moral one: A is still either legally guilty or legally innocent in both acts.

IV.

We now consider six ways of solving the basic puzzle. The first two, fair competition and included wrong, are common-sense ideas with no ties to any particular moral theory. Two more belong to action theory, the basic legal metaphysics of action and causation. The last two, the psychological approach of double effect and Kantian exploitation, use specific moral traditions. A skeptical seventh solution is discussed in part V.

1. Fair competition. A natural (if obscure) proposal is that, by sacrificing B, but not by ducking, A unfairly shifts the odds of the competition. Two campers fleeing a bear run a fair race, but perhaps hobbling one's tentmate is as unfair in life as in sport. Everyone in the theater line has an equal chance to notice the gunman and escape, unless shoved directly into the bullet's path. The underlying idea here may be that, if B falls to bullet or bear, B's fate is his fault rather than A's. Fairness explains the profit factor (v): the draft dodger shares the benefits of war, but unjustly avoids the cost of the struggle.

The problem with this proposal is that often B has no chance of escape at all; therefore he has no fair chance; therefore A's using him as a shield cannot deprive him of a fair chance. If A is a champion sprinter, B never had a chance to win the race. Nor did B ever have a fair chance to become a champion sprinter, since athletic ability is partly genetic. To say that B may escape by superior intellect only replicates the problem on the intellectual level. In queue examples, order in line and timing of threat are random, but only the last person in line may be able to escape. A may be taller than B and block his view; only the last car in line may be maneuverable. In these cases the very situation, so to speak, is unfair to B. It is hard to see, however, how A's act increases the unfairness of a competition that B is certain to lose anyway.[11]

2. Included wrong (innocence factor). Another idea is that factor (ii) solves the whole puzzle. Tying B's legs and shoving him are wrongs *per se* —moral offenses under normal circumstances, and crimes of battery. Running or leaping is an act innocent in itself. Perhaps one may escape from harm at B's expense if and only if one does not commit an intrinsically wrong act in doing so.

This proposal has several serious independent defects. First, hobbling and shoving are trivial wrongs and, as batteries, mere misdemeanors. It is implausible to hold that the difference between no wrong and a trivial wrong escalates, when each leads to death, into the moral difference between justified act and criminal homicide. No such multiplier effect is recognized in other contexts. It is no worse—surely not significantly worse—for Judas to betray Jesus with a pinch than with a kiss. It is no worse to frighten B over a cliff by screaming a racial epithet than "$E = MC^2$." It is no worse to feed one's diabetic wife cyanide than placebo insulin.

It is true that traditional law contains at least two examples of multiplier effects, but each is a perennial target of criticism. The first example is the felony-murder and misdemeanor-manslaughter rules.[12] The felony-murder rule at common law— now abolished in England, but surviving in almost all American states—held that a person who causes an unintended death in the commission of a felony is guilty of murder. A similar rule made death caused in a misdemeanor or other unlawful act manslaughter. The moral objection to these rules was well stated by Oliver Wendell Holmes when he suggested that shooting at another's chickens is no more blameworthy when the bullet accidentally hits a person. Holmes wrote:

> If the object of the rule is to prevent such accidents, it should make accidental killing with firearms murder, not accidental killing in the effort to steal; while, if its object is to prevent stealing, it would do better to hang one thief in every thousand by lot.[13]

After heavy criticism by theorists, the rules were abolished in the English Homicide Act of 1957 and the American Model Penal Code.

A second multiplier effect is the traditional "eggshell skull" rule that criminals and tortfeasors "take their victims as they find them."[14] This is the doctrine that one is the legal cause of death resulting from one's light blow to a hemophiliac or other unforeseeably fragile victim. In American criminal law, the eggshell-skull rule is normally combined with felony murder or misdemeanor manslaughter; it supplies causation while they supply *mens rea*. The tort counterpart holds one liable for all damage resulting from negligent conduct acting on existing (but not subsequent) conditions, however bizarre. These doctrines find liability for unforeseeable harm and thus magnify small faults into large ones. To view abnormal subsequent events as excuses, but not abnormal existing conditions, seems irrational, and the eggshell-skull doctrine is not explicitly preserved in the Model Penal Code. Since duck and sacrifice deaths are foreseen, the relevance of these legal multiplier rules is dubious in any case.

Apart from multiplier effects, the included-wrong view of ducking makes a distinctly false prediction: that, when ducking involves a greater intrinsic harm than forced shielding, ducking is worse. Suppose that A's flight must damage C's valuable flowerbeds; it surely does not follow that A should instead shove B or tie his legs. Finally, our intuitions about forced shielding seem largely unchanged when the included act is innocuous. Suppose A uses no force on B, but summons him into a bullet's path by a greeting or a handshake.[15] Or suppose A forcibly moves B not by a shove, but by a friendly arm around his shoulders. Should one then say that A is guiltless, and also guiltless if B ordinarily does not mind being shoved? These examples suggest that to seize on included wrongs is an act of theoretical desperation in the attempt to explain firm but mysterious intuitions.

3. Act versus omission. Some philosophers and jurists will wish to subsume the sacrifice/duck distinction under the act/omission distinction, or related ones such as doing/allowing.[16] If ducking is an omission, the desired contrast follows from standard legal principles:

> Generally one has no legal duty to aid another person in peril, even when that aid can be rendered without danger or inconvenience to himself. He need not shout a warning to a blind man headed for a precipice or to an absent-minded one walking into a gunpowder room with a lighted candle in hand. He need not pull a neighbor's baby out of a pool of

water or rescue an unconscious person stretched across the railroad tracks, though the baby is drowning or the whistle of an approaching train is heard in the distance (LaFave and Scott, 183).

Admittedly it is odd to describe running for dear life, or violent leaping, as nonacts. But the suggestion is not absurd, because typical omissive conduct is also an act, the act of doing something else.[17] In the Samaritan tale, priest and Levite do something, viz., walk on; the pool lizard sips his Margarita while the baby drowns. Conversely, on one classical legal conception of an act as willed muscular contraction, standing still is an act: it requires many muscles and, in the face of a bear or bullet, a will of steel.[18] Thus, one might view running or leaping as an omission, the failure to stand still. Certainly ethicists and judges often prove flexible in adjusting their act/omission distinctions to yield favored results.[19]

An especially tempting precedent may be the law's treatment of "pulling the plug" on terminal patients as an omission. In an influential article,[20] George P. Fletcher proposed to view disconnecting a respirator as ceasing treatment, and ceasing treatment as nontreatment. If pulling the plug is an omission, it is nonculpable if consistent with the special duty of care imposed by the doctor-patient relationship, which in turn might depend on common practice. One difficulty with Fletcher's position is that a bystander's or intruder's disconnecting the respirator is murder, so that the same conduct is act or omission depending on who engages in it. Another difficulty is that the law normally views ceasing aid more harshly than failure to begin aid.[21] The former difficulty would not affect the omission theory of ducking, but the latter might.

A more serious problem is that ducking is clearly intermediate between act and true omission. In the gunman case, the true omission is failure of A, standing outside the line, to run *into* the bullet's path, i.e., to make himself a shield. Thus, the omission theory recognizes two omissions, which may be problematic if one is worse than the other—a possibility illustrated below. One might reply that it is no worse to recognize two omissions than two acts of homicide, as ethics and law already do. In the gunman case there are four possibilities:

(1)   A shoots B himself.
(2)   A shoves B into the bullet's path.
(3)   A ducks the bullet to B.
(4)   A fails to run into the bullet's path to shield B.

Perhaps this is a list of two acts (1, 2) and two omissions (3, 4) in order of decreasing culpability. There are other possibilities: A may duck under B's legs (2.5), using B as a shield without laying violent hands upon him. These and other cases[22] may suggest a continuum between pure act and pure omission, with various forms of shields, ducks, and duck-shield combinations in between, and moral culpability varying continuously. A continuum of guilt is a truism in ethics, and, although legal offenses are discrete, there is a continuum in punishment.

Unfortunately for this lovely theory, some ducks clearly are culpable homicides. Suppose A's car is parked between a rolling rock and a helpless child. A sees the child in the rock's path, but drives off to avoid an ugly dent. A can be convicted of murder or manslaughter in any American court.[23] On the other hand, had A merely failed to interpose his car between rock and child, he would be innocent in both Anglo-American law and, presumably, an ethics that takes the act/omission distinction seriously.[24] As regards action and causation, in the first case A kills the child by the familiar method of unblocking a hazard. One can kill a man by tampering with his parachute, stripping insulation from his power tool, puncturing his sterile suit in a biological warfare lab, or blasting his submarine hull. A, by moving his car, enables[25] the rock to hit the child, and so, in principle, he also does so when the block is A's own body or body part.

The existence of duck homicides is a fatal objection to the omission view of ducking reminiscent of the first problem with Fletcher's view. The same conduct must be act or omission depending on how much harm it avoids. When A ducks to save his life, it is to be an innocent omission; when A ducks to save his car, it is culpable homicide. But how can a life-saving duck be *less an action* than a car-saving duck? Quantity of harm ill-suits the basic legal metaphysics of action; surely it belongs rather to the moral calculus of criminal defenses.

4. Causation. Another approach via legal metaphysics appeals to causation: to deny that ducking causes death. Attacking the standard necessary-condition view of causation in law, Fletcher pursues this new line on omission cases in a more recent discussion.[26] It is independent of act/omission in that one may cause death by omission (starving a child). Instead, Fletcher tentatively correlates cause/no cause with killing/letting die, the distinction he likes best for law. Common sense is indeed less inclined to say A kills B by ducking than by forcibly making him a shield. One feels that to grab B is to do something to B, while in ducking A does not *act on* B at all. Fletcher observes that similar concepts of interference or intrusion are basic to the ethical frameworks of John Rawls and Robert Nozick.[27]

How to define this "relational theory of action" . . . is one major challenge to Fletcher's view. In grabbing or hobbling, A makes physical contact with B, but A may also summon B by greeting or gesturing without contact. Greeting B pushes sound waves upon him, but so does leaping aside. No doubt the sound waves of a greeting are part of a direct causal chain leading to B's death, whereas the sound waves of A's leap are not even physically necessary conditions for it. Yet in (c2) Alison acted only on Babette's briefcase, not directly on Babette. Our cases suggest that the concept of *acting on*, even if ultimately physical, is not easy to analyze.

Another grave problem is the same objection made to the act/omission theory. It is unclear how the unblocked-hazard kind of killing fits Fletcher's approach. If one can kill by unblocking another force and if killing requires acting on, then unblocking a force that acts on B *is* acting on B. Thus, in the same cases, whether a duck causes death must depend on the amount of harm A avoids. To solve the puzzle, the causal theory must say that a car-saving duck causes B's death, but a life-saving duck does not, which is as implausible as calling only the former an act. Again, such quantitative considerations belong in criminal defense, not in basic law of act and causation.

5. Double effect (psychological solution).

A difference in A's intent in duck versus sacrifice could solve the puzzle for both ethics and law. Perhaps, in sacrificing, A intends B's death, whereas in ducking, A foresees it but does not intend it. The most famous doctrine of this sort is the doctrine of double effect, used in Thomistic ethics but not in Western law. In current form this doctrine states that an act with both good and bad effects is permitted if four conditions hold:

(i)   The act is not wrong in itself.
(ii) The good effects are proportionate to the bad.
(iii) Only the good effects are intended.
(iv) The bad effects are not the means to the good.[28]

Condition (iv) is a gloss on (iii), saying that whoever intends the end intends the means. In some formulations, condition (iii) says that only the good effects are "desired."

In some ways double effect is more successful with ducking than other views. It handles the gunman case, since, if B is a human shield, B's death is A's means (iv). When A leaps aside, B's death cannot be the means to A's survival, since leaping saves A's life even if no B is behind him. This does not hold in the bear story, however, since the bear is faster than both A and B, and therefore A survives only by B's death. So one would expect Thomistic ethics to approve ducking bullets but not bears,[29] except that Catholic applications of double effect are often capricious. Double effect also easily condemns a fatal car-saving duck as violating proportionality (ii): a property value is not proportionate to a child's life. On the other hand, in scarce-resource cases, to "sacrifice" B is not to enshield him, and therefore the means concept may fail to explain the distinction.

In other cases double effect definitely diverges from intuition, simply yielding a strange classification. A's total plan in ducking a bullet can include B's death, if A's wife C is behind B. In this situation A must desire B's death (or injury) as a means to his wife's survival, which violates at least the desire version of (iii) and perhaps (iv). Nevertheless it is hard to feel very indignant at such a duck. Conversely, as Charles Fried observes,[30] double effect may justify shoving people to their deaths in one's headlong flight. Since one would have acted the same if they were not in the way, one passes a standard Catholic test of intent. Clearest and most counterintuitive is the case of ducking under B's legs. Here B's death or injury is again A's means of survival, violating (iv). Yet it seems preposterous to claim that leaping sideways is innocent but leaping over or under B is murder.

In three-person cases it is debatable whether double effect's judgments are correct. When Y shoves A out of danger that strikes B, Y's motive is crucial. If Y's intention is to save A, the act is permissible; if his intention is to harm B, the act is wrong. In the latter case, pushing A aside is just as bad as pushing B in front—i.e., the duck/sacrifice distinction disappears. In general, double effect approves benevolent and condemns malevolent victim selection. Perhaps that is right. Or perhaps an alternative consequentialist view is better: that, if the act is right, bad motives cannot make it wrong. On that view, in some happy situations one may exercise evil impulses without moral cost. Such is the law's view, insofar as one who knows he has a valid defense may kill out of hatred with impunity. One may lawfully delight in killing one's archenemy in self-defense or by judicial execution:

> Whenever the circumstances of the killing would not amount to murder, the proof even of express malice will not make it so. One may harbor the most intense hatred toward another; he may court an opportunity to take his life; may rejoice while he is imbruing his hands in his heart's blood; and yet, if, to save his own life, . . . he was fully justified in slaying his adversary, his malice shall not be taken into the account. The principle is too plain to need amplification. Golden v. State, 25 Ga. 527, 532 (1858).

This view simply illustrates the law's general tendency to reject motive in favor of other factors, e.g., intent. Since Catholic ethics now admits the intent to kill in these cases, however, such cases are not strictly analogous to the double-effect view of ducking.

6. Kant. A sixth solution, which overlaps the Catholic approach, is to employ the Kantian concept of "using a person as a means." Kant's second version of the categorical imperative holds that rational beings must always be treated as ends, never merely as means. As in double effect, if B is a shield, his body is the means to A's survival. Kant would say that this act denies B's humanity, that it uses or exploits him. Nancy Davis suggests this explanation for many of our intuitions about act/omission cases.

Like double effect, a Kantian view of exploitation condemns ducking under B's legs. It may also have the extra drawback of condemning ducking behind B in a two-shooter case. Suppose two gunmen are each about to fire at A and B respectively. It seems obvious that (at least if A can and B cannot) A may rightly save his life by ducking behind B, who will die anyway. In thriller argot, B is dead on his feet. But this action treats B's body as a means to survival. Perhaps one can reply that here B's body is a means, but not B's death, which will occur anyway, and therefore not B himself. This reply may excuse a two-shooter duck. In the one-shooter case, however, if the choice is between ducking and sacrificing, then B's death is also inevitable *relative* to this choice—B is relatively dead on his feet. Therefore, one ought to be allowed to exploit B's body, as in the two-shooter case; therefore, sacrificing should be as moral as ducking. Insofar as this argument succeeds, Kantians avoid the wrong two-shooter result at the cost of destroying the duck/sacrifice distinction in the one-shooter case.

Another objection to the Kantian solution is its restriction to harm to persons. One is forbidden to exploit persons but not objects. On the Kantian view, the duck/sacrifice distinction should disappear when the harm is to an object—or to a nonrational being, like an animal. This seems to violate intuition, except that all intuitions weaken as values shrink. Smith may move his car from the path of a rockslide, but may not shield it with Jones' car. Smith may spray his beans with Japanese-beetle repellent, but may not spray Jones's beans with Japanese-beetle attractant, even if the same beetles end up on the same beans. Kantians will say that to invade a person's property is to exploit the person. This move is necessary anyway to condemn theft; so Kantian ethics is no worse off for these examples. But does the distinction vanish with unowned objects, such as wild animals? Is there a difference between pulling one's dog away from a bear, diverting his appetite to a wild dog, and throwing the wild dog to the bear? If there is, a Kantian view of exploitation fails to solve the puzzle. The problem equally plagues a Kantian approach to act/omission, where it is clear that our intuitions survive a switch to animals.

V.

A final solution is the skeptical one: to deny that the duck/sacrifice distinction *per se* has any moral significance. At least four arguments might attack the distinction. First is the failure of all six theories to match intuition. If no theory handles all ducks and sacrifices, perhaps our intuitions are irrational. Such a judgment might be reasonable after a long history of failed analyses, but is now, to say the least, premature.

A second reason for skepticism is our thesis that ducking is not always innocent. If some ducks are culpable homicides, but corresponding pure omissions are not, then one might argue that ducking is not *per se* significant in the way omission is. But that is to argue that, because our distinction is not always important, it is never important—a non sequitur. Defenders of act/omission also find their distinction sometimes unimportant. It is true that the culpable (nonstatutory) omissions of traditional law involve special relationships, not degree of harm as in the rock-child case. But European Good-Samaritan laws and some ethicists (e.g., Richard Trammell) do classify omissions by degree of harm. Furthermore, even for culpable ducks, the distinction may be important. Many people would judge more harshly a man who guards his car by throwing a child into a rock's path than one who only drives his car away, exposing the child. Thus, the duck/sacrifice distinction may remain as a matter of degree.

A third argument for skepticism is the duck/shield continuum imagined in section IV. Somewhat artificially, a continuum can be constructed, and one of a type that inspires a sorites.* One way to do so in the bear story is for Alex to pour water on Bruce's boots, the camp being in rugged terrain. If Alex soaks Bruce's boots so thoroughly that Bruce cannot run at all, his act is pure sacrifice. If he leaves the boots alone and runs, it is pure duck. In between he can drip one drop on the boots, or two drops, or three drops, and so on.

Still, a similar continuum can be constructed between pure act and pure omission. Suppose *B* bleeds to death from two wounds, *A*'s stab and a tiger bite, and, as *B* bleeds to death, *A* refrains from carrying him to a doctor. If *A*'s stab is so violent that *B* bleeds too fast to be saved, *A* kills him by pure act. If *A* does not stab *B* at all, *A*'s conduct is pure omission. In between, *A*'s stab wound can bleed one drop, or two drops, and so on. The conditions for a sorites are met here by the legal maxim *de minimis non curat lex* [the law takes no account of trifles], which implies that accelerating *B*'s death by one drop is not killing, but at some indeterminate point *A* becomes a killer.[31] Another example is the way Gulag prisoners die from combined starvation and overwork. The fact is that many distinctions, like day/night, survive a continuum; to think otherwise is an instance of the twilight fallacy. A continuum no more refutes the duck/sacrifice distinction than it refutes act/omission or any other ordinary distinction; it merely shows them to be vague, like all distinctions in ethics and law.

The fourth argument for rejection would be to supplement the first by explaining our intuitions away. This could be done in either of two ways. One might ascribe them to irrational features of human moral psychology—e.g., the superstition about identifiable victims. Or one might explain them as due to other genuine factors with which the duck/sacrifice distinction usually covaries. The latter is the main line of writers who deny significance to the act/omission distinction.[32] They hold that cases where act/omission seems important really hang on factors such as motive, intent, certainty of result, ease of avoidance, and number of omitters.

Of these factors, certainty, intent, and motive are relevant to ducking. As to certainty, one stipulates hypothetically that Alex is sure to outrun Bruce, but such certainty quickly evaporates from the mind. In real life Alex is not sure; he may not even think the problem through, merely running

---

*Note: A sorites argument exploits a continuum. "Slippery-slope" arguments are a kind of sorites. Here is a simple example of such an argument. Consider a heap of sand. If you take away one grain, it is still a heap. If you take away another, it is still a heap. And, for any N, if you have a heap of N grains and you take away one grain, you still have a heap. But employing these premises one can get to the conclusion that one grain of sand is a heap. This argument has an implausible conclusion, but it is a puzzle to pinpoint the problem with the argument.

as hard as he would if camping alone, but, thanks to Bruce, with greater success. Panic and uncertainty negate intention. If we produce certainty by making Bruce a helpless quadriplegic, common sense wavers. Now hobbling Bruce is no worse than outrunning him, and it may be heartless of Alex not to knock Bruce unconscious before running away, to spare his agony. As to intent and motive, whenever A chooses sacrificing *over* ducking, A's intent to kill is clear and his motive suspect. But, if A must sacrifice B or die—e.g., the gunman scenario in a narrow corridor—the wrongness of sacrificing is less obvious.

Nevertheless we are unready to embrace the skeptical solution. Unless one is a doctrinaire utilitarian, intuitions so firm and prevalent should not be surrendered without a struggle. What we claim is that the duck/sacrifice distinction is a package deal with act/omission—an act/omission analogue within the realm of acts. As with act/omission, moreover, to reject a distinction in ethics may not be to reject it for law. In general, criminal law should approximate social moral consensus, if only to avoid capricious enforcement and the chaos of jury nullifications of law in mercy killing and insanity cases. Other nonmoral policy considerations supporting act/omission may support duck/sacrifice as well. Thus, it may be that criminal law must treat ducks more kindly than sacrifices even if ethical theorists disagree.

Our aim in this paper has been to state a puzzle and survey possible solutions. We have focused throughout on two-person or three-person cases, leaving multiparty cases and social policy aside. It is worth noting that ducking and sacrificing occur in the national and international arenas, especially in war. The history of World War II is one long series of ducks and sacrifices by allies and enemies.[33] In domestic policy, distribution of harms and benefits—which, unlike our simple examples, come in countless types and magnitudes—often involves choices between *direct* and *indirect* injuries to various groups. The issue whether government penalties on a constitutionally protected choice (abortion) are equivalent to rewards for choosing the alternative (maternity care funds) might be seen as a duck/sacrifice choice by a third party, government.[34] Many defenders of affirmative-action quotas seem convinced that racially reserved places, as

in *Bakke*,* directly benefit minorities but only indirectly harm whites. We invite other writers to explore social applications of the distinction.

Notes

*We thank Julia Driver, Leslie Friedman Goldstein, David Haslett, Douglas Stalker, and Roslyn Weiss for helpful conversations, and Paul Robinson and Stephen Schulhofer for advice on law. We do not duck final responsibility.

[1]We regret our lack of a term as simple and natural as 'duck' for the other side of the distinction. 'Enshield' is accurate but artificial; as noted below, it fails in scarce-resource cases. The lack of a natural term may suggest the existence of several subdistinctions that more detailed analysis would reveal.

[2]Ducking is an occasional literary theme. Canadian novelist Robertson Davies' Deptford trilogy (*Fifth Business*, *The Manticore*, and *World of Wonders*) deals at length with the psychological effects of a childhood ducking incident on Dunstan Ramsay. In Orwell's *1984*, Winston Smith's final degradation, as he faces the rat torture, is his cry: "Do it to Julia!"

[3]Possibly in other times and cultures, prevailing ethics has condemned ducking harm as not only unheroic, but impermissible. Medieval chivalry is one Western tradition where some heroic self-sacrifice was obligatory, especially when A was a knight and B a woman or child. Similar attitudes characterized feudal Japan and ancient Rome, to name only two. The orderly and gracious self-sacrifice of male *Titanic* passengers will be long remembered.

For good or ill, contemporary support for the duck/sacrifice distinction is strong. Of 283 Delaware ethics students, before discussion, 84 per cent said that ducking the bullet or the bear was not immoral and that the sacrificial alternative was immoral. If we exclude those who gave different verdicts on ducking bullets and bears, support for the distinction rises to 91 per cent.

[4]Wayne R. LaFave and Austin W. Scott, Jr., *Handbook on Criminal Law* (St. Paul, MN: West, 1972), p. 550. Their explanation: "When the robber intentionally places the victim in danger of being shot, the latter's death is clearly the foreseeable consequence of the former's

*Note: This is a reference to *Regents of the University of California v. Bakke* (1978), a case involving a white man who applied to a state medical school and was denied admission because the university had a racial quota policy. The U.S. Supreme Court upheld the use of affirmative action programs, but prohibited any policies involving a specific racial quota. In effect, this is designed to protect whites from reverse discrimination.

actions." Such convictions may be had on ordinary causal and *mens rea* principles alone, without the felony-murder doctrine; e.g., *R. v. Pagett* (London *Times*, Feb. 4, 1983) (manslaughter); *Pizano v. Superior Court of Tulare County*, 577 P.2d 659 (1978) (murder).

[5]These acts make *A* guilty of murder if *B* dies, and they justify *B*'s sacrificing *A* in self-defense, as Marlowe does at the end of the movie *The Big Sleep*.

[6]*Scott v. Shepherd*, 2 Wm. Blackstone 892, 96 Eng. Rep. 525 (1773). "Shepherd threw a lighted squib into a crowded marketplace and it fell near Willis who, to protect himself, threw it away and it landed near Ryal who also threw it for his protection. It then fell upon Scott and exploded at that instant putting out one of his eyes. It was held that Shepherd had put out Scott's eye" [Rollin M. Perkins and Ronald N. Boyce, *Criminal Law* (Mineola, NY: Foundation Press, 1982), p. 809].

The point of this case is that Shepherd is not excused from causing the harm, since the acts of Willis and Ryal were normal reactions. Perkins and Boyce write: "It is a normal human response for one threatened by harmful force, deadly or non-deadly, to take action in the effort to avoid the impending harm." Because Willis and Ryal acted predictably, their acts are not superseding causes, and Shepherd remains responsible. Our question is: Why are not Willis and Ryal also guilty? To call their behavior normal does not explain their defense. A common-sense causal chain can run through a foreseeable criminal act, as in soliciting crime or lying to a jealous husband. Then both parties are guilty, although the law calls the procurer's guilt complicity rather than causation.

[7]For standard expositions of the concepts in this section, see LaFave and Scott, *op. cit.* (2e 1986); Perkins and Boyce, *op. cit.*; Jerome Hall, *General Principles of Criminal Law* (New York: Bobbs-Merrill, 2nd ed., 1960); Glanville Williams, *Criminal Law: The General Part* (London: Stevens, 2nd ed., 1961); George Fletcher, *Rethinking Criminal Law* (Boston: Little, Brown, 1978); and H. L. A. Hart and A. M. Honore, *Causation in the Law* (New York: Oxford, 2nd ed., 1985). None of these sources discusses ducking in "self-defense;" so perhaps no Anglo-American defendant has ever been charged with ducking. But for the most part unblocked-hazard murders are not discussed either.

[8]A Model Penal Code rule on legal cause finds no causation if "the result was too remote or too accidental in its occurrence to have a [just] bearing on the actor's liability or on the gravity of his offense" [2.03.3(b)]. As a full test of causation, this "rule" (an appeal to jury conscience) might be vague enough for a duck to fail to cause death. But in the MPC it is only an exception to an exception, for harm of a foreseen type caused in an unforeseen way. The Explanatory Comment (p. 262) reiterates the standard rule that one is liable for completely foreseen results, i.e., when "events transpire as the actor intended or knew that they would." That is the situation in ducking. See also Hart and Honore, *op. cit.*, pp. 170–172, on the maxim "Intended consequences can never be too remote."

[9]When *A* ducks to avoid a peril caused by $\mathfrak{X}$, as in the squib case, *A*'s act is often called nonvoluntary, in the sense of either "instinctive" or "compelled." See Hart and Honore, *op. cit.*, pp. 146–162, 329–340. This description is used to explain why $\mathfrak{X}$ is still a cause of the harm to *B*; hence it might employ different criteria from a voluntariness test for *A*'s own liability. In any case, we ignore "instinctive" ducks (and sacrifices) because the puzzle arises equally for deliberate ones. We assume that nonvoluntariness in the sense of "compulsion" amounts to the defense of necessity or duress.

[10]Criminal defenses are traditionally divided into justifications and excuses, although some defenses are hard to classify. Necessity and public duty are examples of justifications; duress, and mistake of fact are excuses. The justification/excuse distinction sometimes has practical effects: a justified, but not an excused, act may be assisted or repeated by other agents; an excused, but not a justified, act of violence may be properly resisted. See, for example, Paul H. Robinson, *Criminal Law Defenses* (St. Paul, MN: West, 1984), vol. 1, p. 165.

[11]One may object that this criticism proves too much: that no one ever loses a fair race. But, even in sport, contests are only considered fair to the degree that there is some possibility any contestant can win. A heavyweight vs. bantamweight wrestling match is not a fair bout. So, if *A* is a track Olympian and *B* an arthritic one-legged cripple, even by sport standards the race is unfair, and *A* scarcely makes it more unfair by hobbling *B* more. In line examples, the race analogy fails anyway.

[12]LaFave and Scott, *op. cit.*, pp. 545–561, 594–602. The felony-murder rule is often presented as a theory of an "implied" intent to kill, but this is an unconvincing legal fiction. It seems better to regard the rule as a frank multiplier effect.

[13]*The Common Law* (Boston: Little, Brown, 1881), p. 58.

[14]Hart and Honore, *op. cit.*, pp. 172–176, 342–347; Hall, *op. cit.*, pp. 254, 257–261. William L. Prosser, *Handbook of the Law of Torts* (St. Paul, MN: West, 4th ed., 1971), pp. 261/2. When death is foreseeable, any degree of homicide can be committed by an act that is *per se* lawful (lawful in circumstances where it does not unjustifiably cause death). One can murder by lying to a blind man approaching a cliff, opening a window in a sickroom, throwing a main power switch, etc.

[15]One might object that a greeting or handshake is not innocent here because it is an act of betrayal. But the betrayal must be either *A*'s insincerity or the death of *B*. Handshakes are so conventional that "insincerity" is hardly

a wrong; and to appeal to B's death makes the explanation circular and destroys the contrast with ducking.

[16]The doing/allowing distinction (e.g., killing/allowing to die) is discussed by Philippa Foot in "The Problem of Abortion and the Doctrine of the Double Effect," *Oxford Review*, V (1967), p. 59. Foot suggests that allowing is not the same as omission, since one can allow by acting (removing a plug allows water to flow) and do by omitting (a missing actor spoils a performance). As shown by Nancy Davis, exactly what distinction Foot thinks has moral force is unclear, since she seems to hold that allowing one's child to starve is a kind of murder ["The Priority of Avoiding Harm," in Bonnie Steinbock, ed., *Killing and Letting Die* (Englewood Cliffs, NJ: Prentice-Hall, 1980), pp. 172-214].

[17]Because omissive conduct is almost an act or acts, the basic concept is not *omission*, but *causing result R by omission* (during time period P). A simple test that usually works well is the following: A causes R by omission if and only if (i) A could have acted in such a way that R would not have occurred, but did not; and (ii) R would also have occurred if A had done no action at all. (Doing nothing is not behaving, e.g., sleeping or falling unconscious.) This test is too narrow when A's inaction would cause others to act (e.g., they notice A's fall).

[18]See Holmes, *op. cit.*, p. 91: "An act is always a voluntary muscular contraction, and nothing else." Although Holmes is in the tradition of John Austin, *Lectures on Jurisprudence* (London: Murray, 1863), Austin and other writers usually speak of willed bodily *movements*, which would not cover standing still. It being agreed that there are no purely mental crimes, the issue usually discussed is whether "act" includes effects and circumstances (killing by firing a gun) or only bodily movement (crooking the forefinger). Standing still as an act is left undiscussed.

[19]Foot's construal of starving one's child as murder by allowing has already been mentioned. In law, Fletcher cites *Rex v. Smith*, 2 Car. and P. 448, 172 E. R. 203 (Gloucester Assizes, 1826), involving the three Smiths' injurious confinement of their idiot brother. The court won its way to an acquittal by finding both that keeping the brother locked up was an omission and that the Smiths had no duty of aid. The case antedates, however, modern rules on omissive crime.

[20]George P. Fletcher, "Prolonging Life: Some Legal Considerations," *Washington Law Review*, XLII (1967): 999-1016.

[21]Although one "may have no duty to pick an unconscious person off the railroad tracks as a train is approaching around the bend, yet if he once lifts him off the track, he cannot thereafter lay him down again in his original position; if he should do so, and the train should kill him, he would be criminally liable for the homicide"

(LaFave and Scott, *op. cit.*, p. 185). See also Prosser, *op. cit.*, pp. 343/4.

The first difficulty mentioned in the text is cited by Steinbock in her introduction to *Killing and Letting Die* (*op. cit.*, p. 6).

[22]Another possibility occurred in an Oklahoma post office massacre on August 20, 1986. One employee fleeing the gunman locked himself in a spacious vault and survived, but others who were locked out died. This is a case of hogging a refuge. Hogs are worse than ducks, even if one is unbearably cowed.

[23]The fact that the car is A's property is no excuse; one cannot use one's property to kill. Suppose A and B are mountaineers, and B borrows A's pitons without permission. Clearly A cannot repossess them while B is hanging from the rockface. As mentioned above, an otherwise lawful act that foreseeably causes death without justification or excuse is criminal homicide.

Besides such rare situations, to deny that moving a car aside is an act causing death allows the following ready murder method. Induce B, your enemy, to drive behind your van in the left lane of a divided highway with occasional crossroads, such as route 1 south of Media, PA. When a car ahead stops for a left turn, delay changing lanes until the last second. B, whose view is blocked by your van, will crash and die.

[24]Of course, one can assign moral significance to act/omission in some cases, but not in all cases. Richard Trammell discusses the possibility that acts are worse than omissions only when the omitted act requires more than minimal effort. See "Saving Life and Taking Life," *The Journal of Philosophy*, LXXII, 5 (March 13, 1975): 131-137. Fixing a dent requires more than minimal effort and expense; what guides intuition in the rock-child case is not the absolute cost to A, but the relative value of car and child.

[25]This is Foot's term for a type of allowing that is removing an "obstacle which is . . . holding back a train of events" (Foot, *op. cit.*, reprinted in Steinbock, *op. cit.*, p. 161).

[26]*Rethinking Criminal Law* (Boston: Little, Brown, 1978), esp. pp. 588-610.

[27]*Ibid.*, pp. 603/4. According to Fletcher, Rawls requires a concept of interference to explain the first principle of justice and to distinguish it from the second. One may restrict conduct that interferes with the liberty of others (e.g., religious persecution but not religious liberty); but nonallocation of resources to a person is not an interference, hence not a restriction of his liberty [Rawls, *A Theory of Justice* (Cambridge, MA: Harvard, 1971), pp. 60, 195-257]. Nozick uses "impinge" in discussing boundary crossings [*Anarchy, State, and Utopia* (New York: Basic Books, 1974), pp. 57-87].

[28]See, for example, "The Principle of Double Effect," *The New Catholic Encyclopedia* (1967); Germain Grisez,

Abortion: The Myths, the Realities, and the Arguments (New York: Corpus Books, 1970). Some major disagreements about double effect occur among contemporary Catholic writers, especially over the means condition. On the concept of means, see Grisez, p. 330 ff., and Nancy Davis, "The Doctrine of Double Effect: Problems of Interpretation," *Pacific Philosophical Quarterly,* LXV, 2 (April 1984): 107–123.

[29]Grisez's new theory (*op. cit.*) of double effect loosens the orthodox tests for unintended side effects, accommodating Aquinas's original thesis (*Summa Theologiae, Treatise on Justice,* question 64, article 7) that self-defense is unintended killing (not justified intentional killing). Grisez holds that any foreseen effect can be unintended if it is physically inevitable, i.e., "humanly indivisible" from the good effect. Grisez thus applies Aquinas's self-defense view to all cases, even suction abortion, relaxing a few traditional prohibitions and redescribing many cases of evil means as failures of proportionality. In particular, he holds (334) that, without violating the ban on suicide, a mother may "save her child by purposely interposing her body as a shield against an attacking animal." So Grisez's version of double effect probably approves ducking bears as well as bullets.

[30]Charles Fried, *Right and Wrong* (Cambridge, MA: Harvard, 1978), p. 39.

[31]Perkins and Boyce, *op. cit.*, pp. 779/80. Hart and Honore (*op. cit.*, pp. 351/2) express some uncertainty about this application of *de minimis.*

[32]For example, Michael Tooley, "An Irrelevant Consideration: Killing vs. Letting Die," p. 106; Peter Singer, *Practical Ethics* (New York: Cambridge, 1979).

[33]As an example of a duck, the United States was criticized for adopting strategies that maximized Russian casualties. An example of a sacrifice is the radio communication deliberately initiated with a shipping convoy near Gibraltar in fall 1942 to divert German submarines from attacking Patton's North African *Torch* invasion fleet. The examples are interesting in that usual moral judgments are reversed: the duck is condemned, the sacrifice approved.

[34]This was the issue in the abortion funding cases (*Harris v. McRae,* 448 U.S. 297, 1980; *Maher v. Roe,* 432 U.S. 464, 1977). Comparing abortion to private schools, the Supreme Court ruled that government cannot prohibit abortion, but need not fund it equally with maternity.

Part III

KILLING VS. LETTING DIE

Whatever the Consequences

JONATHAN BENNETT ▪ Syracuse University
Analysis, 1966

Is it always wrong to kill the innocent? A conservative argues that it is always wrong to kill the innocent. In this essay Jonathan Bennett wishes to show that it is not. Instead, the killing of the innocent must be weighed against the consequences of not killing the innocent. The consequences of concern to Bennett are those in which the failure to kill the innocent will lead to the deaths of others.

Bennett addresses the case of the distinction between killing an unborn child by crushing its skull (operating) or allowing a mother to die during labor (not operating)—which he calls "the obstetrical example." Although both possibilities involve the death of an innocent human being, some would say that there is an asymmetry between these two deaths because these deaths come about in a different manner. (This alleged asymmetry permits the conservative to argue that whereas it is always wrong to kill the innocent, it may be permissible to allow the innocent to die.) The difference is supposed to be between what someone *does* and the *consequences* of what someone does. Killing the child is alleged to be an *action;* the death of the mother in the case in which one does not operate is supposed to be a *consequence* of what one does (in this case, not operating).

Can the distinction between act and consequence be drawn in a way that makes the alleged moral difference plausible? Bennett argues that it cannot be. Bennett points out that it is frequently the case that the **act/consequence distinction** correlates with differences in (a) expectation, (b) inevitability, (c) intention, (d) independently formed moral judgments, (e) immediacy, and (f) acting/refraining. Bennett then argues that factors (a) through (e) are present in both cases in the obstetrical example; since they are symmetrically present, appealing to such features cannot help the conservative to draw the relevant distinction in a morally plausible way. Furthermore, Bennett argues that although factors (e) and (f) are present asymmetrically, they are not a morally plausible basis on which to draw the distinction.

For Bennett the only distinction of significance between killing and letting die in the obstetrical example is as follows. Relatively few bodily movements of the doctor of all the possible movements the doctor might make would result in the death of the child. In contrast, a relatively large number of bodily movements the doctor might make out of all bodily movements possible would lead to the death of the mother. And this, Bennett argues, is no plausible basis for making a moral distinction. Thus, Bennett concludes that the conservative's distinction between act and consequence cannot be drawn in a plausible manner, and thus that the claim that it is always wrong to kill (whereas it is sometimes permissible to allow an innocent to die) is cast into doubt.

THE FOLLOWING KIND OF THING CAN OCCUR.[1] A woman in labour will certainly die unless an operation is performed in which the head of her unborn child is crushed or dissected; while if it is not performed the child can be delivered, alive, by post-mortem Caesarian section. This presents a straight choice between the woman's life and the child's.

In a particular instance of this kind, some people would argue for securing the woman's survival on the basis of the special facts of the case: the woman's terror, or her place in an established network of affections and dependences, or the child's physical defects, and so on. For them, the argument could go the other way in another instance, even if only in a very special one—*e.g.* where the child is well formed and the woman has cancer which will kill her within a month anyway.

Others would favour the woman's survival in any instance of the kind presented in my opening paragraph, on the grounds that women are human while unborn children are not. This dubious argument does not need to be attacked here, and I shall ignore it.

Others again would say, just on the facts as stated in my first paragraph, that the *child* must be allowed to survive. Their objection to any operation in which an unborn child's head is crushed, whatever the special features of the case, goes like this:

> To do the operation would be to kill the child, while to refrain from doing it would not be to kill the woman but merely to conduct oneself in such a way that—as a foreseen but unwanted consequence—the woman died. The question we should ask is not: "The woman's life or the child's?," but rather: "To kill, or not to kill, an innocent human?" The answer to that is that it is always absolutely wrong to kill an innocent human, even in such dismal circumstances as these.

This line of thought needs to be attacked. Some able people find it acceptable; it is presupposed by the Principle of Double Effect[2] which permeates Roman Catholic writing on morals; and I cannot find any published statement of the extremely strong philosophical case for its rejection.

I shall state that case as best I can. My presentation of it owes much to certain allies and opponents who have commented on earlier drafts. I

gratefully acknowledge my debt to Miss G. E. M. Anscombe, A. G. N. Flew, A. Kenny and T. J. Smiley; and to a number of Cambridge research students, especially D. F. Wallace.

The Plan of Attack

There is no way of disproving the principle: "It would always be wrong to kill an innocent human, whatever the consequences of not doing so." The principle is consistent and reasonably clear; it can be fed into moral syllogisms to yield practical conclusions; and although its application to borderline cases may raise disturbing problems, this is true of any moral principle. Someone who thinks that the principle is laid down by a moral authority whose deliverances are to be accepted without question, without *any* testing against the dictates of the individual conscience, is vulnerable only to arguments about the credentials of his alleged authority; and these are not my present concern. So I have no reply to make to anyone who is prepared to say: "I shall obey God's command never to kill an innocent human. I shall make no independent moral assessment of this command—whether to test the reasonableness of obeying it, or to test my belief that it *is* God's command, or for any other purpose." My concern is solely with those who accept the principle: "It would always be wrong to kill an innocent human, whatever the consequences of not doing so," not just because it occurs in some received list of moral principles but also because they think that it can in some degree be recommended to the normal conscience. Against this, I shall argue that a normal person who accepts the principle must either have failed to see what it involves or be passively and unquestioningly obedient to an authority.

I do not equate "the normal conscience" with "the 'liberal' conscience." Of course, the principle *is* rejected by the "liberal" majority; but I shall argue for the stronger and less obvious thesis that the principle is in the last resort on a par with "It would always be wrong to shout, whatever the consequences of not doing so," or "It would always be wrong to leave a bucket in a hall-way, whatever *etc.*" It is sometimes said that we "should not understand" someone who claimed to accept such wild eccentricities as these as fundamental moral truths—that he would be making a logical mistake, perhaps about what it is for something to be a "moral" principle. I need not claim so much. It is enough to say that such a person, if he was sincere and in his right mind, could safely be assumed to have delivered himself over to a moral authority and to have opted out of moral thinking altogether. The same could be said of anyone who accepted *and really understood* the principle: "It would always be wrong to kill an innocent human, whatever the consequences of not doing so." This principle is accepted by reasonable people who, though many of them give weight to some moral authority, have not abdicated from independent moral thinking. Clearly, they regard the principle as one which others might be led to accept, or at least to take seriously, on grounds other than subservience to an authority. From this fact, together with the thesis for which I shall argue, it follows that those who accept the principle (like others who at least treat it with respect) have not thought it through, have not seen what it comes to in concrete cases where it yields a different practical conclusion from that yielded by "It is wrong to kill an innocent human unless there are very powerful reasons for doing so." I aim to show what the principle comes to in these cases, and so to expose it for what it is.

My arguments will tell equally against any principle of the form "It would always be wrong to . . . , whatever the consequences of not doing so," but I shall concentrate on the one principle about killing, and indeed on its application to the kind of obstetrical situation described in my opening paragraph.

I need a label for someone who accepts principles of the form: "It would always be wrong to . . . , whatever the consequences of not doing so." "Roman Catholic" is at once too wide and too narrow; "intrinsicalist" is nasty; "absolutist" is misleading; "deontologist" means too many other things as well. Reluctantly, I settle for "conservative." This use has precedents, but I offer it as a stipulative definition—an expository convenience and not a claim about "conservatism" in any ordinary sense.

Well then: When the conservative condemns the operation described in my opening paragraph, he does so *partly* because the operation involves the

death of an innocent human. So does its nonperformance; but for the conservative the dilemma is asymmetrical because the two alternatives involve human deaths in different ways: in one case the death is part of a killing, in the other there is no killing and a death occurs only as a consequence of what is done. From the premiss that operating would be killing an innocent human, together with the principle: "It would always be wrong to kill an innocent human, whatever *etc.*," it does follow that it would be wrong to operate. But the usual conservative—the one I plan to attack—thinks that his principle has *some* measure of acceptability on grounds other than unquestioning obedience to an authority. He must therefore think that the premiss: "In this case, operating would be killing an innocent human while not-operating would involve the death of an innocent human only as a consequence" gives *some* reason for the conclusion: "In this case, operating would be wrong." I shall argue that it gives no reason at all: once the muddles have been cleared away, it is just not humanly possible to see the premiss as supporting the conclusion, however weakly, except by accepting the principle "It would always be wrong *etc.*" as an unquestionable *donnée* [given].

The Action/Consequence Distinction

When James killed Henry, what happened was this: James contracted his fingers round the handle of a knife, and moved his hand in such a way that the knife penetrated Henry's body and severed an artery; blood escaped from the wound, the rate of oxygen-transfer to Henry's body-cells fell drastically, and Henry died. In general, someone's performing a physical action includes his moving some part or parts of his body. (The difference between "He moved his hand" and "His hand moved" is not in question here: I am referring to movements which he *makes*.) He does this in a physical environment, and other things happen in consequence. A description of what he *did* will ordinarily entail something not only about his movements but also, *inter alia*, about some of their upshots. Other upshots will not ordinarily be covered by any description of "what he did," but will be counted amongst "the consequences of what he did." There are various criteria for drawing the line between what someone did and the consequences of what he did; and there can be several proper ways of drawing it in a given case.

This last point notwithstanding, there are wrong ways of dividing a set of happenings into action and consequences. Even where it is not positively wrong to give a very parsimonious account of "what he did," it may be preferable to be more inclusive. If in my chosen example the obstetrician does the operation, it is true that he crushes the child's head with the consequence that the child dies, but a better account, perhaps, would say that he *kills* the child by crushing its head. There can certainly be outright wrongness at the other end of the scale: we cannot be as inclusive as we like in our account of "what he did." If at the last time when the operation could save the woman's life the obstetrician is resignedly writing up his notes, it is just not true that, as he sits at his desk, he is killing the woman; nor, indeed, is he killing her at any other time.

The use of the action/consequence distinction in the conservative premiss is, therefore, perfectly correct. Operating *is* killing; not-operating is not. What are we saying when we say this? By what criteria is the action/consequence distinction drawn in the present case? I shall try, by answering this, to show that in this case one cannot attach moral significance to the fact that the line drawn by the distinction falls where it does. Briefly, the criteria for the action/consequence distinction fall into two groups: those which could support a moral conclusion but which do not apply to every instance of the obstetrical example; and those which do apply to the example but which it would be wildly eccentric to think relevant to the moral assessment of courses of action. There is no overlap between the two groups.

Aspects of the Distinction: First Group

Some differences which tend to go with the action/consequence distinction, and are perhaps to be counted amongst the criteria for it, clearly do have moral significance. None of them, however, is generally present in the obstetrical example.

Given a question about whether some particular upshot of a movement I made is to be covered by the description of what I *did*:

(a) The answer may depend in part upon whether in making the movement I was entirely confident that that upshot would ensue; and this could reasonably be thought relevant to the moral assessment of my conduct. This aspect of the action/consequence distinction, however, is absent from most instances of the obstetrical example. The classification of not-operating as something other than killing does not imply that the obstetrician rates the woman's chance of survival (if the operation is not performed) higher than the child's chance of survival (if it is performed). If it did imply this then, by contraposition, not-operating would in many such cases have to be classified as killing after all.

(b) The answer may depend in part upon how certain or inevitable it was that that upshot would ensue from my movement, or upon how confidently I ought to have expected it to ensue; and that too may have a strong bearing on the moral assessment of my conduct. But it gets no grip on the obstetrical example, for in many cases of that kind there is moral certainty on both sides of the dilemma. If the conservative says that the action/consequence distinction, when correctly drawn, is always associated with morally significant differences in the inevitability of upshots of movements, then he is vulnerable to an argument by contraposition like the one in (a). He is vulnerable in other ways as well, which I shall discuss in my next section.

(c) The answer may depend in part upon whether I made the movement partly or wholly for the sake of achieving that upshot; and this is a morally significant matter. But the obstetrical example is symmetrical in that respect also: if the obstetrician crushes the child's head he does so not because this will lead to the child's death or because it constitutes killing the child, but because that is his only way of removing the child's body from the woman's.

To summarize: moral conclusions may be supported by facts (a) about what is expected, but in the example each upshot is confidently expected; (b) about what is inevitable, but in the example each upshot is inevitable; or (c) about what is ultimately aimed at, but in the example neither upshot is aimed at.

An Aside: Degrees of Inevitability

I have suggested that a conservative might say: "The action-consequence distinction is always associated with a morally significant difference in the degree to which upshots are certain or inevitable." This is false; but let us grant it in order to see whether it can help the conservative on the obstetrical example. I concede, for purposes of argument, that if the operation is not performed the woman will pretty certainly die, while if it is performed the child will even more certainly die.

What use can the conservative make of this concession? Will he say that the practical decision is to be based on a weighing of the comparative desirability of upshots against the comparative certainty of their achievement? If so, then he must allow that there *could* be a case in which it was right to kill the child—perhaps a case where a healthy young widow with four children is bearing a hydrocephalic child, and where her chance of survival if the operation is not performed is *nearly* as bad as the child's chance of survival if it is performed. If a professed "conservative" allows that there could, however improbably, be such a case, then he is not a conservative but a consequentialist; he does after all base his final judgment on the special features of the case; and he has misrepresented his position by using the language of action and consequence to express his implausible views about the comparative inevitability of upshots. On the other hand, if the conservative still absolutely rules out the killing of the child, whatever the details of the particular case, then what could be his point in claiming that there is a difference in degree of inevitability? The moral significance of this supposed difference would, at best, have to be conceded to be an obscure one which threw no light on why anyone should adopt the conservative view.

A certain conservative tactic is at issue here. Miss G. E. M. Anscombe has said:

> If someone really thinks, in advance, *that it is open to question whether such an action as procuring the judicial execution of the innocent should be quite excluded from consideration*—I do not want to argue with him; he shows a corrupt mind. [3]

The phrase "quite excluded from consideration" clearly places Miss Anscombe as what I am calling a "conservative." (The phrase "a corrupt mind," incidentally, tends to confirm my view that conservatives think their position can stand the light of day, i.e. that they do not see it as tenable only by those

who passively obey some moral authority.) Now, in the course of a footnote to this passage Miss Anscombe remarks:

> In discussion when this paper was read, as was perhaps to be expected, this case was produced: a government is required to have an innocent man tried, sentenced and executed under threat of a "hydrogen bomb war." It would seem strange to me to have much hope of averting a war threatened by such men as made this demand. But the most important thing about the way in which cases like this are invented in discussions, is the assumption that only two courses are open: here, compliance and open defiance. No one can say in advance of such a situation what the possibilities are going to be— e.g. that there is none of stalling by a feigned willingness to comply, accompanied by a skilfully arranged "escape" of the victim.

This makes two points about the case as described: there might be nothing we could do which would have a good chance of averting a war; and if there were one such thing we could do there might be several. The consequentialist might meet this by trying yet again to describe a case in which judicially executing an innocent man *is* the only thing we could do which would have a good chance of averting a war. When he has added the details which block off the other alternatives, his invented case may well be far removed from present political likelihood; it may even be quite fantastic. Still, what does the conservative say about it?

Here is Miss Anscombe, at her most gamesome, on the subject of "fantastic" examples:

> A point of method I would recommend to the corrupter of the youth would be this: concentrate on examples which are either banal: you have promised to return a book, but . . . and so on, or fantastic: what you ought to do if you had to move forward, and stepping with your right foot meant killing twenty-five young men, while stepping with your left foot would kill fifty drooling old ones. (Obviously the right thing to do would be to jump and polish off the lot.) [4]

The cards are now well stacked; but this is a game in which a conservative should not be taking a hand at all. Someone may say (i): "In no situation could it be right to procure the judicial execution of the innocent: political probability aside, the judicial execution of the innocent is absolutely impermissible in any possible circumstances." Or someone may say (ii): "It is never right to procure the judicial execution of the innocent: a situation in which this would be right has never arisen, isn't going to arise, and cannot even be described without entering into the realm of political fantasy." These are different. The former is conservatism, according to which "the judicial execution of the innocent should be quite excluded from consideration." The latter is not conservatism: according to it, the judicial execution of the innocent is taken into consideration, assessed in the light of the political probabilities of the world we live in, and excluded on that basis. The former is Miss Anscombe's large type; the latter, apparently, is her footnote. The difference between (i) "In no situation could it be right . . ." and (ii) "No situation is even remotely likely to occur in which it would be right . . ." can be masked by dismissing what is relevant but unlikely as "fantastic" and therefore negligible. But the difference between the two positions is crucial, even if in the first instance it can be brought out only by considering "fantastic" possibilities. The two may yield the same real-life practical conclusions, but (ii) can be understood and argued with in a way in which (i) cannot. If someone accepts (ii), and is not afraid to discuss a "fantastic" but possible situation in which he would approve the judicial execution of an innocent man, he can be challenged to square this with his contrary judgment in regard to some less fantastic situation. Whether he could meet the challenge would depend on the details of his moral position and of the situations in question. The point is that we should know where we stood with him: for example, we should know that it was *relevant* to adduce evidence about how good the chances would be of averting war in this way in this situation, or in that way in that. It is just this sort of thing which the unwavering conservative must regard as irrelevant; and that is what is wrong with his position. Miss Anscombe says: "No one can say in advance of such a situation what the possibilities are going to be;" but the central objection to conservatism is, precisely, that it says in advance that for the judging of the proposed course of action it *does not matter* what the possibilities are going to be. Why, then, go on about them—if not to disguise conservatism as something else when the going gets tough?

I have based this paper on the obstetrical example in the hope that, without being jeered at for having "invented" an example which is "fantastic," I could present a kind of case in which a conservative principle would yield a practical conclusion different from any likely to be arrived at by consequentialist arguments. The claim that in these cases there would always be a morally significant difference between the woman's chance of survival and the child's could only be another attempt to get the spotlight off conservatism altogether— to get the consequentialist to accept the conservative's conclusion and forget about his principle. In the obstetrical example, the attempt is pretty desperate (though, with the aid of judiciously selected statistics, it is made often enough); with other kinds of example, used to examine this or other conservative principles, it might be easier for the conservative to make a show of insisting on the addition of details which render the examples "fantastic." But this does not mean that the case against conservatism is stronger here than elsewhere. It means only that the obstetrical example gives less scope than most for the "there-might-be-another-way-out" move, or protective-coloration gambit, which some conservatives sometimes use when they shelter their position by giving the impression that it does not really exist.

A conservative might invoke inevitability, without comparing degrees of it in the consequentialist manner, by saying that if the operation is not performed the woman still has *some* chance of survival while if it is performed the child has *none*. Barring miracles, this is wrong about the woman; not barring miracles, it is wrong about the child. It could seem plausible only to someone who did not bar miracles but took a peculiar view of how they operate. Some people do attach importance in this regard to the fact that if the operation is not performed the woman may take some time to die: they seem to think—perhaps encouraged by an eccentric view of God as powerful but *slow*—that the longer an upshot is delayed the more room there is for a miraculous intervention. This belief, whatever the assumptions which underlie it, gives no help to the conservative position. For suppose the obstetrician decides to try, after operating and delivering the child, to repair its head by micro-surgery. The woman's supposed "some chance" of survival if the child's head is not crushed is of the same kind as the obstetrician's "some chance" of saving the child after crushing its head: in each case there is what the well-informed plain man would call "no chance," but in each case it will take a little time for the matter to be finally settled by the events themselves—for the woman to die or the obstetrician to admit failure. Would the conservative say that the obstetrician's intention to try to save the child in this way, though hopeless, completely alters the shape of the problem and perhaps makes it all right for the obstetrician to crush the child's head? If so, then what we have here is a morality of gestures and poses.

Aspects of the Distinction: Second Group

I return to the main thread of my argument. Of the remaining three aspects of the action/consequence distinction, it was not quite true to say that all are present in (every instance of) the obstetrical example; for the first of them has not even that merit. The main point, however, is that even if it were always present it would not help the conservative—though it might help us to diagnose his trouble.

(d) Someone's decision whether an upshot of a movement of mine is to be covered by his description of what I *did* may depend partly on his moral assessment of my role in the total situation. Your condemnation of me, or perhaps your approval, may be reflected in your putting on the "action" side of the line an upshot which an indifferent on-looker would count as merely a "consequence." This aspect of the action-consequence distinction—if indeed it is one independently of those already discussed—cannot help the conservative who believes that a premiss using the distinction tends to *support* a moral conclusion. That belief demands a relevance relation which slopes the other way.

There seem to be just two remaining aspects to the action/consequence distinction. Certainly, there are only two which do appear in all instances of the obstetrical example. These two must be the sole justification for saying that operating would be killing while not-operating would not be killing;

and so they must bear the whole weight of any conservative but non-authoritarian case against killing the child.

(e) Operating is killing-the-child because if the obstetrician operates there is a high degree of *immediacy* between what he does with his hands and the child's dying. This immediacy consists in the brevity or absence of time-lag, spatial nearness, simplicity of causal connexions, and paucity of intervening physical objects. The relations amongst these are complex; but they are severally relevant to the action/consequence distinction, and in the obstetrical example they all pull together, creating an overwhelming case for calling the performance of the operation the *killing* of the child.

(f) Not-operating is not killing-the-woman because it is not *doing* anything at all but is merely *refraining* from doing something.

Since (e) and (f) are so central to the action/consequence distinction generally, it is appropriate that they should sometimes bear its whole weight, as they do in the conservative's (correct) application of the distinction to the obstetrical example. But if (e) and (f) are all there is to the premiss: "In this case, operating would be killing an innocent human while not-operating would involve the death of an innocent human only as a consequence," then this premiss offers no support at all to the conclusion: "In this case, operating would be wrong."

The matters which I group under "immediacy" in (e) may borrow moral significance from their loose association with facts about whether and in what degree upshots are (a) expected, (b) inevitable or (c) aimed at. In none of these respects, however, is there a relevant asymmetry in the obstetrical example. The question is: why should a difference in degree of immediacy, unaccompanied by other relevant differences, be taken to support a moral discrimination? I cannot think of a remotely plausible answer which does not consist solely in an appeal to an authority.[5]

Suggestions come to mind about "not getting one's hands dirty;" and the notion of what I call "immediacy" does help to show how the literal and the metaphorical are mingled in some uses of that phrase. In so doing, however, it exposes the desire to "keep one's hands clean," in cases like the obstetrical example, as a symptom of muddle or primness or, worst of all, a moral egoism like Pilate's. (To be fair: I do not think that many conservatives would answer in this way. If they used similar words it would probably not be to express the nasty sentiment I have mentioned but rather to say something like: "I must obey God's law; and the rest is up to God." Because this suggests a purely authoritarian basis, and because it certainly has nothing to do with immediacy, it lies beyond my present scope.)

Similarly with the acting/refraining distinction in (f). I shall argue in my next section that our criteria for this distinction do not invest it with any moral significance whatever—except when the distinction is drawn on the basis of independently formed moral judgments, and then it cannot help the conservative case for the reason given in (d). And if neither (e) immediacy nor (f) acting/refraining separately has moral significance, then clearly they cannot acquire any by being taken together.

Acting and Refraining

Suppose the obstetrician does not operate, and the woman dies. He does not kill her, but he *lets her die*. The reproach suggested by these words is just an unavoidable nuisance, and I shall not argue from it. When I say "he lets her die," I mean only that he knowingly refrains from preventing her death which he alone could prevent, and he cannot say that her survival is in a general way "none of my business" or "not [even *prima facie*] my concern." If my arguments so far are correct, then this one fact—the fact that the non-operating obstetrician *lets the woman die* but does not *kill her*—is the only remaining feature of the situation which the conservative can hope to adduce as supporting his judgment about what ought to be done in every instance of the obstetrical example.[6] Let us examine the difference between "X killed Y" and "X let Y die."

Some cases of letting-die are also cases of killing. If on a dark night X knows that Y's next step will take him over the edge of a high cliff, and he refrains from uttering a simple word of warning because he doesn't care or because he wants Y dead, then it is natural to say not only that X lets Y die but also that he kills him—even if it was not X who suggested the route, removed the fence from the cliff-top, *etc.* Cases like this, where a failure-to-prevent is described as a doing partly *because* it is

judged to be wicked or indefensible, are beside my present point; for I want to see what difference there is between killing and letting-die which might be a *basis for* a moral judgment. Anyway, the letting-die which is also killing must involve malice or wanton indifference, and there is nothing like that in the obstetrical example. In short, to count these cases as relevant to the obstetrical example would be to suggest that not-operating would after all be killing the woman—a plainly false suggestion which I have disavowed. I wish to criticise the conservative's argument, not to deny his premiss. So from now on I shall ignore cases of letting-die which are also cases of killing; and it will make for brevity to pretend that they do not exist. For example, I shall say that killing involves moving one's body—which is false of some of these cases, but true of all others.

One more preliminary point: the purposes of the present enquiry do not demand that a full analysis be given either of "X killed Y" or of "X let Y die." We can ignore any implications either may have about what X (a) expected, (b) should have expected, or (c) was aiming at; for the obstetrical example is symmetrical in all those respects. We can also ignore the fact that "X killed Y" loosely implies something about (e) immediacy which is not implied by "X let Y die," for immediacy in itself has no moral significance.

Consider the statement that *Joe killed the calf*. A certain aspect of the analysis of this will help us to see how it relates to *Joe let the calf die*. To say that Joe killed the calf is to say that

(1)   Joe moved his body:

and

(2)   the calf died;

but it is also to say something about how Joe's moving was connected with the calf's dying—something to the effect that:

(3)   if Joe had not moved as he did, the calf would not have died.

How is (3) to be interpreted? We might take it, rather strictly, as saying

(3′): If Joe had moved in *any* other way, the calf would not have died.

This, however, is too strong to be a necessary condition of Joe's having killed the calf. Joe may have killed the calf even if he could have moved in other ways which would equally have involved the calf's dying. Suppose that Joe cut the calf's throat, but could have shot it instead: in that case he clearly killed it; but (3′) denies that he killed it, because the calf might still have died even if Joe had not moved in just the way he did.

We might adopt a weaker reading of (3), namely as saying

(3″): Joe could have moved in *some* other way without the calf's dying.

But where (3′) was too strong to be necessary, (3″) is too weak to express a sufficient connexion between Joe's moving and the calf's dying. It counts Joe as having killed the calf not only in cases where we should ordinarily say that he killed it but also in cases where the most we should say is that he let it die.

The truth lies somewhere between (3′), which is appropriate to "Joe killed the calf in the only way open to him," and (3″), which is appropriate to "Joe killed the calf or let it die." Specifically, the connexion between Joe's moving and the calf's dying which is appropriate to "Joe killed the calf" but not to "Joe let the calf die" is expressed by

(3‴): Of all the other ways in which Joe might have moved, *relatively few* satisfy the condition: if Joe had moved like that, the calf would have died.

And the connexion which is appropriate to "Joe let the calf die" but not to "Joe killed the calf" is expressed by

(4):   Of all the other ways in which Joe might have moved, *almost all* satisfy the condition: if Joe had moved like that, the calf would have died.

This brings me to the main thesis of the present section: apart from the factors I have excluded as already dealt with, the difference between "X killed Y" and "X let Y die" *is* the difference between (3‴) and (4). When the killing/letting-die distinction is stripped of its implications regarding immediacy, intention *etc.* —which lack moral significance or don't apply to the example— all that remains is a distinction having to do with where a set of movements lies on the scale which

has "the only set of movements which would have produced that upshot" at one end and "movements other than the only set which would have produced that upshot" at the other.

This, then, is the conservative's residual basis for a moral discrimination between operating and not-operating. Operating would be killing: if the obstetrician makes movements which constitute operating, then the child will die; and there are very few other movements he could make which would also involve the child's dying. Not-operating would only be letting-die: if throughout the time when he could be operating the obstetrician makes movements which constitute not-operating, then the woman will die; but the vast majority of alternative movements he could make during that time would equally involve the woman's dying. I do not see how anyone doing his own moral thinking about the matter could find the least shred of moral significance in *this* difference between operating and not-operating.

Suppose you are told that X killed Y in the only way possible in the circumstances; and this, perhaps together with certain other details of the case, leads you to judge X's conduct adversely. Then you are told: "You have been misled: there is another way in which X could have killed Y." Then a third informant says: "That is wrong too: there are two other ways . . . *etc.*" Then a fourth: "No: there are three other ways . . . *etc.*" Clearly, these successive corrections put no pressure at all on your original judgment: you will not think it relevant to your judgment on X's killing of Y that it could have been carried out in any one of n different ways. But the move from "X killed Y in the only possible way" to "X killed Y in one of the only five possible ways" is of the same *kind* as the move from "X killed Y" to "X let Y die" (except for the latter's implications about immediacy); and the moral insignificance of the former move is evidence for the moral insignificance of the latter move also.

The difference between "X killed Y" and "X let Y die" is the sum-total of a vast number of differences such as that between "X killed Y in one of the only n possible ways" and "X killed Y in one of the only $n + 1$ possible ways." If the difference between ". . . n . . ." and ". . . $n + 1$ . . ." were morally insignificant only because it was *too small* for any moral discrimination to be based upon it, then the sum-total of millions of such differences might still have moral significance. But in fact the differences in question, whatever their size, are of the *wrong kind* for any moral discrimination to be based upon them. Suppose you have judged X adversely, on the basis of the misinformation: "X killed Y in the only way possible in the circumstances;" and this is then replaced, in one swoop, by the true report: "X did not kill Y at all, though he did knowingly let Y die." Other things being equal, would this give you the slightest reason to retract your adverse judgment? Not a bit of it! It would be perfectly reasonable for you to reply: "The fact remains that X chose to conduct himself in a way which he knew would involve Y's death. At first I thought his choice could encompass Y's death only by being the choice of some rather specific course of conduct; whereas the revised report shows me that X's choice could have encompassed Y's death while committing X to very little. At first I thought it had to be a choice to act; I now realize that it could have been a choice to refrain. What of it?"

There are several things a conservative is likely to say at this point—all equivalent. "When we know that the crucial choice could have been a choice to refrain from something, we can begin to allow for the possibility that it may have been a choice to refrain from doing something wrong, such as killing an innocent human." Or: "You say 'other things being equal,' but in the obstetrical example they aren't equal. By representing letting-die as a kind of wide-optioned killing you suppress the fact that the alternative to letting the woman die is killing the child."

Replies like these are available to the conservative only if he does not need them and can break through at some other point; for they assume the very point which is at issue, namely that in every instance of the obstetrical example it would be wrong to kill the child. I think that in some cases it would indeed be wrong—(I do not press for a blanket judgment on all instances of the example—quite the contrary); and in such a case the obstetrician, if he rightly let the woman die, could defend his doing so on the basis of the details of the particular case. Furthermore, he might wish to begin his defence by explaining: "I let the woman die, but I did not kill her;" for letting-die is in general likely to be more defensible than killing. My analysis incidentally

shows one reason why: the alternatives to killing are always very numerous, and the odds are that at least one of them provides an acceptable way out of the impasse; whereas the alternative to letting-die is always some fairly specific course of conduct, and if there are conclusive objections to *that* then there's an end of the matter. All this, though, is a matter of likelihoods. It is no help in the rare cases where the alternatives to killing, numerous as they are, arguably do *not* include an acceptable way out of the impasse because they all involve something of the same order of gravity as a killing, namely a letting-die. The conservative may say: "Where innocent humans are in question, letting-die is not of the same order of gravity as killing: for one of them is not, and the other is, absolutely wrong in all possible circumstances." But this, like the rejoinders out of which this paragraph grew, assumes the very point which is at issue. All these conservative moves come down to just one thing: "At this point your argument fails; for the wrongness of killing the child, in any instance of the obstetrical example, *can* be defended on the basis of your own analysis of the acting/refraining distinction—plus the extra premiss that it would always be wrong to kill the child."

The Stress on the Specific

My argument is finished; but its strategy might be thought to be open to a certain criticism which I want to discuss.

The obstetrical example is a *kind* of situation, on every instance of which the conservative makes a certain judgment. I have argued that this judgment, as applied to many instances of the example, cannot be defended except by the unquestioning invocation of authority. This would have been damaging to the conservative position even if I had appealed only to "fantastic" kinds of instance such as seldom or never occur; but in fact my claims have been true of many real-life instances of the obstetrical example. Still, a conservative might resist my drive towards the relatively specific, my insistence upon asking: "What is there about *this* kind of instance which justifies your judgment upon it?" He might claim that even my opening paragraph presents so special a kind of situation that he cannot fairly be asked to find in *it* something which supports his judgment other than by a blanket appeal to his general principle that it would always be wrong to kill an innocent human. There are two ways in which he might defend this stand: they look alike, but their fatal defects are very different.

The first is by the use of a sub-Wittgensteinian argument from the nature of language. Although I have never encountered it, it is a possible and plausible objection to my strategy of argument. The conservative might say: "Granted that facts about (a) expectation, (b) inevitability and (c) intention are irrelevant to the way the action/consequence distinction applies to the obstetrical example; it does not follow that when we apply the distinction to the example *all* we are doing—apart from (d) reflecting our already-formed moral judgments—is to report facts about (e) immediacy and (f) acting/refraining. Language and thought don't work like this. When we say: 'Operating would be killing; not-operating would not be killing though it would have death as a consequence,' we are not *just* talking about immediacy and specificity of options. We are using words which, *qua* [as] words in the language, are laden with associations having to do with (a)-(d); and these associations of the words cannot simply be ignored or forgotten in a particular case. Language is not atomic in that way, and it would be at best a clumsy instrument if it were."

I agree that we often do, and perhaps must sometimes, decide our conduct in one situation partly through verbal carry-overs from others in which similar conduct could be justified more directly. But I think that everyone will agree that the more serious a practical problem is, the greater is our obligation to resist such verbal carry-overs and scrutinize the particular problem in order to see what there is about *it* which would justify this or that solution to it. A practical problem in which human lives are at stake is a deeply serious one, and it would be an abdication from all moral seriousness to settle it by verbal carry-overs. I am not saying: "Take pity on the poor woman, and never mind what the correct description of the situation is." I am opposing someone who says: "This is the correct description of the situation—never mind what its force is in this particular case."

The second objection to my stress on the particular case, or the specific kind of case, is one which conservatives do sometimes use; and it connects with a muddle which is not special to conservatives. It

goes like this: "We must have rules. If every practical problem had to be solved on the spot, on the basis of the fine details of the particular case, the results would be disastrous. Take a situation which falls under some rule which I know to be justified in most situations. There may not be time or means for me to learn much more about the present situation than just that it does fall under the rule; the details of the case, even if I can discover them, may be too complex for me to handle; my handling of them, even if intellectually efficient, may without my knowing it be self-interested or corrupt; by deciding, however uncorruptly, not to follow the rule on this occasion, I may weaken its hold on me in other situations where it clearly ought to be followed; and even if I could be sure that I was in no such danger, I might help others into it by publicly breaking the rule."[7]

This is all true, but it does not help the conservative. Notice first that it tells against undue attention to individual cases rather than against undue attention to limited kinds of case: its target is not the specific but the particular. Still, it could be developed into an attack on over-stressing very specifically detailed kinds of case: its opening words would then have to be replaced by: "We must have rather general rules." This is true too, but it is still no help to the conservative.

This argument for our bringing practical problems under rather general rules is based on the consequences of our not doing so: it points to the dangers attendant on suspending a general rule and considering whether one's practical problem might be better resolved by applying a less general one. But sometimes these dangers will be far too slight to justify doing what a given general rule enjoins in a particular situation. If the thesis under discussion is to have any practical upshot which is not ludicrous ("Never break any general rule which would enjoin the right action in more cases than not"), or vague to the point of vacuity ("Always apply some fairly general rule"), or merely question-begging ("Never break a rule forbidding an action which really is absolutely impermissible"), then it must allow us to raise questions of the form: "Need we be deterred by the dangers attendant on suspending *this* rule in favour of *this* more specific rule in *this* kind of situation?" The answer will depend upon what the challenged general rule is, what the proposed substitute for it is, the intelligence and character of the agent, and the likelihood that his breaking the rule (if it comes to that) would become generally known and, if known, demoralizing to others. These matters need not be so complex as to defeat finite intelligence, or so primrose-strewn that fallen man dare not venture among them. Furthermore, they can themselves be embodied in rules carefully formulated in advance—meta-rules about the kinds of situation in which this or that ground-level general rule may be suspended in favour of this or that more specific one.

Here is a possible case. A certain obstetrician accepts the rule, "Do not kill innocent humans," as applicable in every kind of situation he has thought of except the kind described in my opening paragraph. He wants a rule for this kind too, as a shield against the confusions, temptations and pressures of the concrete situation; and after reflection he adopts the following: "If the child is not hydrocephalic it is not to be killed. If it is hydrocephalic it is to be killed unless either (a) the woman is bound to die within a month anyway, or (b) the woman has no other children under eighteen and she is known to be a chronic acute depressive. If (a) or (b) or both are true, the child is not to be killed."

By preferring this rule to the more general one for instances of the obstetrical example, the obstetrician is not rendering it likely that in some situations he will flounder around not knowing what rule about killing to apply. For he has a clear enough meta-rule: "If the only way to save a woman's life is to kill the child she is bearing, apply this rule: . . . ; otherwise apply the rule: Do not kill innocent humans."

The obstetrician is not satisfied with his ground-level rule for instances of the obstetrical example, and he hopes to be able to improve it. Still, he is resigned to his rule's ignoring various matters which, though they are relevant to what the ideally right action would be, would involve him in the dangers of over-specificity mentioned above. "Is the woman a potential murderess or the child a mongol?"—the answers are probably unobtainable. "In what ways would the woman's death represent a real loss to others?"—the answer, even if discoverable, could be so complex as to elude any manageable rule. "Would either course of action bring the medical profession into undeserved but seriously damaging

disrepute?"—it would be too easy for that to be unconsciously conflated with the question of which course would best further the obstetrician's own career. "Would the child, if delivered alive, be especially helpful to students of hydrocephalus?"—asking that could be the first step on a downward path: by allowing one woman to die partly because her child will be medically interesting if alive, even an uncorrupt man may ease the way towards allowing some other woman to die partly because *she* will be medically interesting when dead.

Although he pays heed—neurotically pays far too much heed—to the conservative's warnings against over-specificity, this obstetrician arrives at a conclusion quite different from the conservative's. That is the crux. The conservative who warns against the dangers of over-specifying is trying to find a consequentialist basis for his whole position. Unlike the 'protective-coloration gambit' discussed earlier, this is legitimate enough in itself; but it simply does not yield the conservative position on the matter under discussion. For it to do so, the conservative would have to show that our obstetrician's more specific rule is *too* dangerous in the ways mentioned above; and he would have to do this without applying danger-inflating standards which would commit him also to condemning as too dangerous the suspension of the general rule: "Never leave a bucket in a hall-way." He may object: "Buckets in hall-ways are not important enough to provide a fair analogy. Where something as grave as killing is in question, we should be especially sensitive to the dangers of suspending a general rule." But then when something as grave as letting someone die is involved in applying the rule, we should be especially reluctant to accept, without good empirical evidence, popular clichés about the dangers of suspending general rules. The two points cancel out.

Of course, there are these dangers, and we should guard against them. To assess them at all precisely, though, would require more than we know of sociology, psychology and the philosophy of mind; and so our guarding against them can consist only in our keeping the urge towards specificity under some restraint, our remembering that in this matter it is not always true that the sky is the limit. The conservative who hopes to secure his position by pointing out these dangers must claim that he *can* assess them, and can discover in them a simple, sweeping pattern which picks out a certain list of general rules as the ones which ought never to be suspended by anyone in any circumstances. No-one would explicitly make so preposterous a claim.

"So you do at any rate retreat from act- to rule-utilitarianism?" No. Rule-utilitarianism can be presented (1) as a quasi-mystical doctrine about the importance of rule-following *"per se,"* or (2) as a doctrine about the importance of rule-following because of what rule-following empirically *is*, because of what happens when people follow rules and what happens when they don't. In version (1), rule-utilitarianism is a distinct doctrine which has nothing to recommend it. In version (2), it is just part of a thorough act-utilitarianism. (In most actual presentations, there is a cloudy attempt to combine (2)'s reasonableness with (1)'s rejection of act-utilitarianism.) In this section I have been discussing what the consequences might be, for myself or others, of my suspending or breaking a given general rule. These are among, not additional to, the consequential factors whose relevance I have been urging all through the paper. There has been no retreat.

Conclusion

Principles of the form: "It would always be wrong to . . . , whatever the consequences of not doing so" seem defensible because the action/consequence distinction does often have a certain kind of moral significance. But in proportion as a situation gives real work to the rider " . . . whatever the consequences of not doing so," in proportion as it puts pressure on this rider, in proportion as the "consequences of not doing so" give some moral reason for "doing so"—to that extent the action/consequence distinction lacks moral significance in that situation. The obstetrical example is just an extreme case: there the rider serves to dismiss the entire moral case against applying the principle; and, proportionately, the action/consequence distinction carries no moral weight at all.

The phenomenon of conservatism, then, can be explained as follows. The conservative naturally thinks that the action/consequence distinction has great moral significance because of its frequent connexion with differences concerning (a) expectation, (b) inevitability, (c) intention and (d) independently formed moral judgments. He then encounters cases like the obstetrical example, where (a)–(d) are irrelevant but where the distinction can still be applied because of facts about (e) immediacy and (f) acting/refraining. Failing to see that in these cases the distinction has lost absolutely all its moral bite, and perhaps encouraged by a mistake about "rule-following *per se*," he still applies his principle in the usual way. Those who do not follow him in this he finds lax or opportunist or corrupt; and many of them half agree, by conceding to his position a certain hard and unfeeling uprightness. Both are wrong. Conservatism, when it is not mere obedience, is mere muddle.

Notes

[1] J. K. Feeney and A. P. Barry in *Journal of Obstetrics and Gynaecology of the British Empire* (1954), p. 61. R. L. Cecil and H. F. Conn (eds.), *The Specialties in General Practice* (Philadelphia, 1957), p. 410.

[2] See G. Kelly, *Medico-Moral Problems* (Dublin, 1955), p. 20; C. J. McFadden, *Medical Ethics* (London, 1962), pp. 27–33; T. J. O'Donnell, *Morals in Medicine* (London, 1959), pp. 39–44; N. St. John-Stevas, *The Right to Life* (London, 1963), p. 71.

[3] G. E. M. Anscombe, "Modern Moral Philosophy," *Philosophy*, vol. 33 (1958), p. 17.

[4] G. E. M. Anscombe, "Does Oxford Moral Philosophy Corrupt the Youth?" *The Listener*, February 14, 1957, p. 267. See also the correspondence in ensuing numbers, and Michael Tanner, "Examples in Moral Philosophy," *Proceedings of the Aristotelian Society*, vol. 65 (1964–5).

[5] Conservatives use words like "direct" to cover a jumble of factors of which immediacy is the most prominent. Pius XII has said that a pain-killing, life-shortening drug may be used "if there exists no direct causal link, either through the will of interested parties or by the nature of things, between the induced consciousness [*sic*] and the shortening of life . . ." (Quoted in St. John-Stevas.)

[6] In a case where the child cannot survive anyway: 'It is a question of the *direct taking* of one innocent life or merely *permitting* two deaths. In other words, there is question of one *murder* against two deaths . . .' Kelly, *op. cit.*, p. 181.

[7] For a gesture in this direction, see St. John-Stevas, *op. cit.*, pp. 14–16. See also McFadden, *op. cit.*, p. 133.

An Irrelevant Consideration: Killing Versus Letting Die

MICHAEL TOOLEY ▪ The Australian National University
Killing and Letting Die, 1980

Like Bennett, Michael Tooley claims that the distinction between intentionally killing and intentionally letting die is not *in itself* morally significant. To support this position he appeals to a principle he terms the **moral symmetry principle**. Roughly stated, this principle holds that "it is as wrong to intentionally refrain from interfering with a causal process leading to some morally significant result as it is to initiate the process." Tooley discusses an example in which two sons independently decide to kill their rich father. One of the sons covertly places poison in his father's drink; just as he does so, the second son arrives on the scene intending to do the same thing. The second son then permits his father to sip the poisoned drink and refrains from giving him an antidote. Tooley asks whether one son did something more wrong than the other, and answers, no. Applying the moral symmetry principle to this case, Tooley contends that since both sons have morally equivalent motives (to have their father dead), it is just as wrong for the second son intentionally to refrain from giving his father the antidote as it is for the first son to poison the father. Thus, despite the fact that one son killed his father while the other merely let his father die, the acts are morally equivalent in Tooley's view.

To help clarify his version of the moral symmetry principle, Tooley considers a possible objection. The objection compares two cases. In the first case (Action M), an individual refrains from divulging information to an enemy even though he is aware that this refusal will result in the enemy torturing an innocent child. In the second case (Action N), an individual tortures a child in order to force the enemy to divulge the pertinent information. The objector's strategy is to argue that anyone who accepts Tooley's moral symmetry principle also should accept a generalized form of this principle that maintains that Actions M and N are morally equivalent. The objector will argue, however, that Actions M and N are *not* morally equivalent; therefore, Tooley's moral symmetry principle ought to be rejected.

In response to this objection, Tooley first emphasizes that his original formulation of the moral symmetry principle does not imply that Actions M and N are morally equivalent. Moreover, he argues that one can accept the moral symmetry principle without accepting a generalized form of the principle that would judge the two actions to be morally equivalent. In Tooley's view, acceptance of the moral symmetry principle is compatible with acknowledging that there is an important intuitive difference between intentionally preventing someone else from performing an action and refraining from performing that action oneself. The moral difference between Actions M and N, then, does not undermine the moral symmetry principle; it "merely reflects the fact that one's obligations to prevent others from doing something may not be as great as one's obligation to refrain from doing it oneself." Tooley claims that the above objection confuses the moral symmetry principle with a form of consequentialist reasoning (see Introduction), and he stresses that although accepting consequentialism does commit one to adopting the moral symmetry principle, accepting the moral symmetry principle does not require one to adopt consequentialism.

Tooley intends to show that the distinction between killing and letting die is not *in itself* morally significant. He does not deny, however, that there are other factors that *generally* make it the case that killing is worse than letting die. He mentions three such factors: motive, cost to the agent and/or society, and the probability that death will result from one's actions. Tooley's point is that the differences in these factors, and *not* the distinction between killing and letting die, make killing worse in general than letting die. To support this claim, Tooley offers an example that isolates these three factors to show that the difference between acting and intentionally refraining from acting is not in itself morally significant. He imagines a machine holding two children—John and Mary. If one pushes a button, John is killed and Mary is saved; if one does not push the button, then John is saved and the machine automatically kills Mary. Tooley argues that there is no significant moral difference between these two options even though in the first scenario, one's action kills John, and in the other, one's refraining from action lets Mary die. (For a discussion of this example, see Heidi Malm's "Killing, Letting Die, and Simple Conflicts," p. 133.) Tooley concludes that "there is no intrinsic distinction between killing and letting die."

In closing, Tooley asks what bearing his criticisms of the distinction between killing and letting die should have on the distinction between active and passive euthanasia. After dismissing several possible answers, Tooley ultimately argues that "it is far from clear that the commonly accepted distinction between active and passive euthanasia is morally significant."

MANY PEOPLE HOLD THAT THERE IS AN IMPORTANT moral distinction between passive euthanasia and active euthanasia. Thus, while the AMA maintains that people have a right "to die with dignity," so that it is morally permissible for a doctor to allow someone to die if that person wants to and is suffering from an incurable illness causing pain that cannot be sufficiently alleviated, the AMA is unwilling to countenance active euthanasia for a person who is in similar straits, but who has the misfortune not to be suffering from an illness that will result in a speedy death.

A similar distinction with respect to infanticide has become a commonplace of medical thinking and practice. If an infant is a mongoloid, or a microcephalic, and happens also to have some other defect requiring corrective surgery if the infant is to live, many doctors and hospitals believe that the parents have the right to decide whether the surgery will be performed, and thus whether the infant will survive. But if the child does not have any other defect, it is believed that the parents do not have the right to terminate its life.[1]

The rationale underlying these distinctions between active and passive euthanasia, and between active and passive infanticide, is the same: the idea that there is a crucial moral difference between intentionally killing and intentionally letting die. This idea is admittedly very common. But I believe that it can be shown to reflect either confused thinking or a moral point of view unrelated to the interests of individuals.

Two sons are looking forward to the death of their nasty but very wealthy father. Tired of waiting, they decide, independently of one another, to kill their father. The one puts some poison in his father's whiskey, and is discovered doing so by his brother, who was just about to do the same thing. The latter then allows his father to imbibe the deadly drink, and refrains from administering an antidote which he happens to have. The one son killed his father. The other merely allowed him to die. Did the former do something significantly more wrong than the latter?

My own view is that the actions are morally equivalent, since I think that the following general principle—which may be referred to as the moral symmetry principle—is sound.[2]

> Let C be a causal process that normally leads to an outcome E. Let A be an action that initiates process C, and B be an action that stops process C before outcome E occurs. Assume further that actions A and B do not have any other morally significant consequences, and that E is the only part or outcome of C which is morally significant in itself. Then there is no moral difference between performing action A, and intentionally refraining from performing action B, assuming identical motivation in the two cases.

This principle implies that, other things being equal, it is just as wrong intentionally to refrain from administering an antidote to someone who is dying of poisoning as it is to administer the poison, provided that the same motive is operative in both cases. And, more generally, it follows that the distinction between killing and intentionally letting die is not in itself a morally significant one.

Some people find this hard to accept. However, it has been my experience that those who are inclined to reject the moral symmetry principle often do so because of a failure to understand exactly what it does and does not imply. Let me begin by considering an objection which, though badly confused, helps to clarify the principle.[3] The criticism in question claims that the moral symmetry principle can be shown to be mistaken by the following counterexample. It involves considering these two actions:

> Action M: An individual refrains from giving information to the enemy even though he knows that the enemy will torture a child as long as he refuses to divulge the information.

> Action N: An individual tortures a child in order to induce the enemy to give him information.

The contention is that it is "surely monstrous" to view these two actions as morally equivalent. The intuitive appeal of this position is obvious. Whether it will stand up under critical reflection is quite another matter. The crucial point, however, is that this example is just not relevant to the moral symmetry principle. That principle states, very roughly, that it is as wrong intentionally to refrain from interfering with a causal process leading to some morally significant result as it is to initiate the process. It does not assert that it is as wrong to refrain from preventing someone else from initiating a causal process as it is to initiate it oneself. So it does not imply that actions M and N are morally equivalent.

One might try to argue that although the moral symmetry principle does not imply that actions such as M and N are morally equivalent, one can formulate a generalized moral symmetry principle which does have this implication, and which ought to be accepted by anyone who is willing to accept the original principle. One can certainly formulate such a principle. The difficulty is to justify the claim that anyone who accepts the original principle ought to accept the generalization of it. For it would seem that if intentionally refraining from preventing someone else from doing something and doing it oneself are morally equivalent actions, then preventing someone else from doing something and intentionally refraining from doing it oneself are also morally equivalent actions.[4] But the intuitive feeling of most people would surely be that the mere fact that when one prevents someone else from doing something one is interfering with someone's action, whereas when one merely refrains from doing something oneself one is not, is a morally relevant difference. Thus there is a *prima facie* case against any extension of the moral symmetry principle that would have the consequence that intentionally refraining from preventing someone else from doing something is morally equivalent to doing it oneself. I certainly do not wish to assert that this *prima facie* case cannot be overcome. However, any argument that succeeded in overthrowing it would *ipso facto* give one reason to reject the contention that it is "monstrous" to treat actions M and N as morally equivalent.

What the objection to the moral symmetry principle has in effect done is to confuse that principle with *consequentialism* in ethics. If consequentialism is true, then so is the moral symmetry principle. But the converse is emphatically not the case. It is very important to realize that one can accept the moral symmetry principle without committing oneself to a consequentialist position.[5]

In order to reinforce my contention that any moral difference between actions M and N, rather than counting against the moral symmetry principle, merely reflects the fact that one's obligation to prevent others from doing something may not be as great as one's obligation to refrain from doing it oneself, consider actions that are similar to M and N except that the relevant effects are achieved *directly* rather than by influencing someone else's action:

Action M*:   *One is confronted with a machine that contains a child and a military secret. The machine is so constructed that unless one pushes a button, the child will be tortured and the secret will be destroyed. If one pushes the button, the child will emerge unharmed, but the secret will be transmitted to the enemy. One refrains from pushing the button.*

Action N*:   *One is confronted with a similar machine. This time, however, it is so constructed that unless one pushes a button, a secret will be transmitted to the enemy, while a child will emerge unharmed. If one pushes the button, the secret will be destroyed, but the child will be tortured. One pushes the button.*

Although the moral symmetry principle does not quite entail that actions M* and N* are morally equivalent, I believe that anyone who accepts that principle would agree that there is no moral difference between M* and N*. Doubtless there are *some* philosophers who would also characterize this view as "monstrous." And some philosophers have tried to argue that there is, at least, significant moral difference between acting and refraining from acting; however, all the arguments that I have seen in support of this contention seem to me to be either

unsound or else not relevant to the claim that the distinction is significant *in itself.*[6]

But what is one to say about the feeling—which is admittedly fairly widespread—that there is a morally significant difference between acting and refraining from acting? I do not want simply to dismiss this feeling, even though I would maintain that appeal to such "moral intuitions" does not constitute a good way of arriving at sound moral principles. What I want to do is to try to show how the feelings in question may rest upon certain confusions.

The place to begin is by distinguishing the following two questions:

(1)   Is the distinction between killing and intentionally letting die morally significant *in itself?*

(2)   Are there *other factors* which make it *generally* the case that killing someone is more seriously wrong than intentionally letting someone die?

The answer to the second question is surely yes. In the first place, the *motive* of a person who kills someone is generally more evil than the motive of a person who merely lets someone die. A person may let someone die out of laziness or apathy, and though I would insist that such inaction is seriously wrong, it is surely not as seriously wrong as the action of a person who kills someone else because he *wants* him dead. Secondly, the alternative to letting someone die—saving his life—may involve considerable risk to the agent, or a very large expenditure of society's resources. This will rarely be true of refraining from killing someone. Thirdly, if one performs an action that normally results in the death of a person, there is little likelihood that the person will survive. While if one merely refrains from saving someone's life, there is often a substantial chance that he will survive in some other way.

These three factors—motive, cost to the agent and/or society, and the probability that death will result from one's action or inaction—all tend to make it the case that an attempt to kill someone will generally be more seriously wrong than intentionally refraining from saving someone's life. It is these factors that make the difference, rather than the difference between killing and letting die. People are right in thinking that killing is generally morally worse than merely letting someone die. Where they go wrong is in failing to notice that there are factors involved that can explain this difference in a perfectly satisfactory fashion. And, as a result, they mistakenly conclude that the difference between killing and letting die must be morally significant *in itself*.

Let me conclude my case against the distinction by mentioning an example which isolates the interfering variables, and thus raises in a vivid way the issue of whether there really is any significant moral difference between acting and intentionally refraining from acting. Imagine a machine containing two children, John and Mary. If one pushes a button, John will be killed, but Mary will emerge unharmed. If one does not push the button, John will emerge unharmed, but Mary will be killed. In the first case one kills John, while in the second case one merely lets Mary die. Does one really wish to say that the action of intentionally refraining from pushing the button is morally preferable to the action of pushing it, even though exactly one person perishes in either case? The best action, it would seem to me, would be to flip a coin to decide which action to perform, thus giving each person an equal chance of surviving. But if that isn't possible, it seems to me a matter of indifference whether one pushes the button or not.

If there is no intrinsic difference between killing and intentionally letting die, where does this leave the distinction between active and passive euthanasia? There are two possibilities that need to be considered. The first is that even if neither active nor passive euthanasia is wrong in itself, it may be that legalizing the former would have undesirable consequences, as Yale Kamisar and others have contended.[7] I do not think that this line of argument is sound; however it is certainly one that deserves very serious consideration.

The second possibility is one that arises if one holds both that there is no intrinsic difference between active and passive euthanasia and that euthanasia is, nevertheless, wrong in itself, on the grounds, say, that a person does not have a right to kill even himself in order to put an end to unbearable suffering. Such a view would be compatible with the acceptance of passive euthanasia in some cases, though not in all. For while one would be committed to holding that passive euthanasia, like active euthanasia, was wrong in itself, there might be circumstances in which the former was morally justified. The cost of keeping a person alive, for example, might be so great that allowing him to die would be the lesser of evils.

My response to this second attempt to ascribe at least limited moral significance, albeit of a derived variety, to the distinction between active and passive euthanasia, is to reject the view that active euthanasia is wrong in itself. What I should argue, ultimately, is that there must surely be some justification for the institution of morality, some reason for society to accept moral rules. And what reason more plausible than that the acceptance of a certain set of moral rules accords better with the interests of people than the acceptance of some other set of moral rules, or none at all? But some moral rules that people accept, or have accepted, are clearly such as do not serve the interests of individuals—*e.g.*, various sexual prohibitions, such as that against masturbation. The prohibition of active euthanasia seems to be another case of a moral point of view which does not further the interests of individuals living together in society. Why, then, has this moral point of view been accepted? The answer here, as in the case of the traditional sexual outlook of Western society, is found in the powerful influence of the Christian churches.[8] This historical point deserves to be kept firmly in view when one is reflecting upon the morality of euthanasia. Many otherwise thoughtful people somehow lose sight of the fact that what they refer to as "moral intuitions" regarding euthanasia sprang originally from a certain theological outlook, one that is no longer taken seriously by most people who have taken the trouble to examine its credentials carefully and impartially.

In conclusion, then, it is far from clear that the commonly accepted distinction between active and passive euthanasia is morally significant. This has been, admittedly, a very brief survey of the relevant issues. In some cases I have been able to do little more than touch upon them in passing. However, I have tried to argue, in some detail, that the distinction between killing and letting die is not morally significant in itself. If this is right, then the reason that is most commonly offered for holding that there is a morally significant difference between active and passive euthanasia is in fact unsound.

Notes

[1]See, for example, "Moral and Ethical Dilemmas in the Special-Care Nursery," by Raymond S. Duff and A. G. M. Campbell in *The New England Journal of Medicine*, 289 (Oct. 25, 1973), 890–94, and "Dilemmas of 'Informed Consent' in Children," by Anthony Shaw in *The New England Journal of Medicine*, 289 (Oct. 25, 1973), p. 886.

[2]I appealed to a closely related principle in my papers discussing abortion and infanticide. See pages 58–60 of "Abortion and Infanticide," *Philosophy & Public Affairs*, 2 (Fall 1972), 37–65, and pages 84–86 of "A Defense of Abortion and Infanticide" in J. Feinberg, ed., *The Problem of Abortion* (Belmont, CA: Wadsworth Publishing Co., 1973), 51–92, for some remarks that are relevant to the present principle as well. My view is that when actions A and B are related in the way indicated, it is true both that performing A is morally equivalent to intentionally refraining from performing B, and that performing B is morally equivalent to intentionally refraining from performing A, assuming the same motivation in both cases.

[3]This objection was advanced by Philip E. Devine in his paper "Tooley on Infanticide," read at the Eastern Meeting of the American Philosophical Association in Atlanta, December 1973.

[4]This is surely very reasonable. But if justification is wanted, one can argue that (1) if actions Q and R are morally equivalent, then so are the actions of intentionally refraining from Q and intentionally refraining from R, and that (2) the action of intentionally refraining from performing some action Q is equivalent to performing action Q.

[5]There is some relevant discussion by Bernard Williams in *Utilitarianism: For and Against*, by J. J. C. Smart and Bernard Williams (Cambridge: Cambridge University Press, 1973) pp. 82–100.

[6]The argument offered by Daniel Dinello in his article "On Killing and Letting Die" seems simply unsound. The argument advanced by P. J. Fitzgerald, on the other hand, in his article "Acting and Refraining," [see bibliography for publishing information] appears irrelevant to the contention that the distinction is morally significant in itself. For a vigorous defense of the view that the distinction is not in itself morally significant, see Jonathan Bennett's paper, "Whatever the Consequences," [p. 93] Bennett's article is slightly marred by an inadequate analysis of the distinction between acting and refraining, but this does not affect his central contentions.

[7]Yale Kamisar, "Euthanasia Legislation: Some Non-Religious Objections," in *Euthanasia and the Right to Death*, ed. A. B. Downing, (Los Angeles: Nash Publishing Co., 1969).

[8]For a discussion that helps to bring out the extent to which contemporary Western aversion to voluntary euthanasia reflects the influence of the Christian church, see Raanan Gillon's article, "Suicide and Voluntary Euthanasia: Historical Perspective," in *Euthanasia and the Right to Death*, ed. A. B. Downing (Los Angeles: Nash Publishing Co., 1969). Also very helpful in this regard is the discussion by Glanville Williams in Chapter VIII of his book, *The Sanctity of Life and the Criminal Law*.

Active and Passive Euthanasia

JAMES RACHELS ▪ University of Alabama, Birmingham
The New England Journal of Medicine, 1975

In this essay, James Rachels argues that in those situations in which *passive* euthanasia is already held to be morally permissible, there can be no morally sound reasons for disallowing *active* euthanasia. For Rachels, the larger moral principle at issue in the presumed moral distinction between active and passive euthanasia is whether killing is in itself worse than letting die. He believes this latter issue can be decided by comparing cases of **killing** and cases of **letting die** that are exactly alike in all aspects except for this distinction. If Rachels can draw a negative conclusion to the broader question of the relative morality of killing and letting die, then a negative answer to the narrower question of the relative morality of active and passive euthanasia would follow. Rachels offers a pair of cases that are exactly alike except that one describes a killing and the other a letting die. He believes that these cases show that killing and letting die are not morally distinguishable. (Rachels thus agrees with Tooley.)

The paired examples Rachels offers are called the Bathtub Cases. (These cases are similar to Tooley's example of the two sons.) In the first scenario, there is a killing by Smith, who, wanting his cousin dead, deliberately drowns the young child as it takes a bath. In the second scenario there is a letting die by Jones, who, wanting his cousin dead, knowingly allows the young child to drown from an accidental fall into the bathtub. In both cases, Smith and Jones are equally motivated to kill or let die by the opportunity to inherit the fortune of their young cousin. This shows, according to Rachels, that although the first death involving Smith is a killing and the second death involving Jones is a letting die, from a moral point of view the actions of Smith and Jones are equally reprehensible. (For a discussion of this methodology, see Kagan, p. 252, and Malm, p. 271.)

Returning to the issue of active and passive euthanasia, Rachels concludes that the crucial mistake made by those who favor passive euthanasia but oppose active euthanasia is to overlook the equivalent motivation on the part of relatives and doctors in cases of both active and passive euthanasia. He argues that only if the responsible parties did not share a humanitarian motivation in their respective decisions to kill or let die, could active euthanasia be worse than passive euthanasia because, as we have seen, killing is in itself not worse than letting die. When the responsible parties do share the same humanitarian concerns in their decisions, active euthanasia is not worse than passive euthanasia. In fact, Rachels argues, active euthanasia is often far more humane than passive euthanasia, because passive euthanasia often involves far more suffering. Rachels concludes that the question of whether a Down's syndrome child should be allowed to live or die can have nothing to do with whether or not the intestinal tract of such a child is blocked. The only relevant question must be whether the life of such a child is or is not worth preserving. If it is, then a simple operation is always demanded. If it is not, then a lethal injection is preferred to a slow death from the complications of the child's physical pathologies.

Abstract. The traditional distinction between active and passive euthanasia requires critical analysis. The conventional doctrine is that there is such an important moral difference between the two that, although the latter is sometimes permissible, the former is always forbidden. This doctrine may be challenged for several reasons. First of all, active euthanasia is in many cases more humane than passive euthanasia. Secondly, the conventional doctrine leads to decisions concerning life and death on irrelevant grounds. Thirdly, the doctrine rests on a distinction between killing and letting die that itself has no moral importance. Fourthly, the most common arguments in favor of the doctrine are invalid. I therefore suggest that the American Medical Association policy statement that endorses this doctrine is unsound. (N Engl J Med 292:78–80, 1975)

THE DISTINCTION BETWEEN ACTIVE AND PASSIVE euthanasia is thought to be crucial for medical ethics. The idea is that it is permissible, at least in some cases, to withhold treatment and allow a patient to die, but it is never permissible to take any direct action designed to kill the patient. This doctrine seems to be accepted by most doctors, and it is endorsed in a statement adopted by the House of

Delegates of the American Medical Association on December 4, 1973:

> The intentional termination of the life of one human being by another—mercy killing—is contrary to that for which the medical profession stands and is contrary to the policy of the American Medical Association.
>
> The cessation of the employment of extraordinary means to prolong the life of the body when there is irrefutable evidence that biological death is imminent is the decision of the patient and/or his immediate family. The advice and judgment of the physician should be freely available to the patient and/or his immediate family.

However, a strong case can be made against this doctrine. In what follows I will set out some of the relevant arguments, and urge doctors to reconsider their views on this matter.

To begin with a familiar type of situation, a patient who is dying of incurable cancer of the throat is in terrible pain, which can no longer be satisfactorily alleviated. He is certain to die within a few days, even if present treatment is continued, but he does not want to go on living for those days since the pain is unbearable. So he asks the doctor for an end to it, and his family joins in the request.

Suppose the doctor agrees to withhold treatment, as the conventional doctrine says he may. The justification for his doing so is that the patient is in terrible agony, and since he is going to die anyway, it would be wrong to prolong his suffering needlessly. But now notice this. If one simply withholds treatment, it may take the patient longer to die, and so he may suffer more than he would if more direct action were taken and a lethal injection given. This fact provides strong reason for thinking that, once the initial decision not to prolong his agony has been made, active euthanasia is actually preferable to passive euthanasia, rather than the reverse. To say otherwise is to endorse the option that leads to more suffering rather than less, and is contrary to the humanitarian impulse that prompts the decision not to prolong his life in the first place.

Part of my point is that the process of being "allowed to die" can be relatively slow and painful, whereas being given a lethal injection is relatively quick and painless. Let me give a different sort of example. In the United States about one in 600

babies is born with Down's syndrome. Most of these babies are otherwise healthy—that is, with only the usual pediatric care, they will proceed to an otherwise normal infancy. Some, however, are born with congenital defects such as intestinal obstructions that require operations if they are to live. Sometimes, the parents and the doctor will decide not to operate, and let the infant die. Anthony Shaw describes what happens then:

> . . . When surgery is denied [the doctor] must try to keep the infant from suffering while natural forces sap the baby's life away. As a surgeon whose natural inclination is to use the scalpel to fight off death, standing by and watching a salvageable baby die is the most emotionally exhausting experience I know. It is easy at a conference, in a theoretical discussion, to decide that such infants should be allowed to die. It is altogether different to stand by in the nursery and watch as dehydration and infection wither a tiny being over hours and days. This is a terrible ordeal for me and the hospital staff—much more so than for the parents who never set foot in the nursery.*

I can understand why some people are opposed to all euthanasia, and insist that such infants must be allowed to live. I think I can also understand why other people favor destroying these babies quickly and painlessly. But why should anyone favor letting "dehydration and infection wither a tiny being over hours and days?" The doctrine that says that a baby may be allowed to dehydrate and wither, but may not be given an injection that would end its life without suffering, seems so patently cruel as to require no further refutation. The strong language is not intended to offend, but only to put the point in the clearest possible way.

My second argument is that the conventional doctrine leads to decisions concerning life and death made on irrelevant grounds.

Consider again the case of the infants with Down's syndrome who need operations for congenital defects unrelated to the syndrome to live. Sometimes, there is no operation, and the baby dies, but when there is no such defect, the baby lives on. Now, an operation such as that to remove an intestinal obstruction is not prohibitively difficult. The reason why such operations are not performed in these

---

*Shaw A: "Doctor, Do We Have a Choice?" The New York Times Magazine, January 30, 1972, p. 54

cases is, clearly, that the child has Down's syndrome and the parents and doctor judge that because of that fact it is better for the child to die.

But notice that this situation is absurd, no matter what view one takes of the lives and potentials of such babies. If the life of such an infant is worth preserving, what does it matter if it needs a simple operation? Or, if one thinks it better that such a baby should not live on, what difference does it make that it happens to have an unobstructed intestinal tract? In either case, the matter of life and death is being decided on irrelevant grounds. It is the Down's syndrome, and not the intestines, that is the issue. The matter should be decided, if at all, on that basis, and not be allowed to depend on the essentially irrelevant question of whether the intestinal tract is blocked.

What makes this situation possible, of course, is the idea that when there is an intestinal blockage, one can "let the baby die," but when there is no such defect there is nothing that can be done, for one must not "kill" it. The fact that this idea leads to such results as deciding life or death on irrelevant grounds is another good reason why the doctrine should be rejected.

One reason why so many people think that there is an important moral difference between active and passive euthanasia is that they think killing someone is morally worse than letting someone die. But is it? Is killing, in itself, worse than letting die? To investigate this issue, two cases may be considered that are exactly alike except that one involves killing whereas the other involves letting someone die. Then, it can be asked whether this difference makes any difference to the moral assessments. It is important that the cases be exactly alike, except for this one difference, since otherwise one cannot be confident that it is this difference and not some other that accounts for any variation in the assessments of the two cases. So, let us consider this pair of cases:

In the first, Smith stands to gain a large inheritance if anything should happen to his six-year-old cousin. One evening while the child is taking his bath, Smith sneaks into the bathroom and drowns the child, and then arranges things so that it will look like an accident.

In the second, Jones also stands to gain if anything should happen to his six-year-old cousin.

Like Smith, Jones sneaks in planning to drown the child in his bath. However, just as he enters the bathroom Jones sees the child slip and hit his head, and fall face down in the water. Jones is delighted; he stands by, ready to push the child's head back under if it is necessary, but it is not necessary. With only a little thrashing about, the child drowns all by himself, "accidentally," as Jones watches and does nothing.

Now Smith killed the child, whereas Jones "merely" let the child die. That is the only difference between them. Did either man behave better, from a moral point of view? If the difference between killing and letting die were in itself a morally important matter, one should say that Jones's behavior was less reprehensible than Smith's. But does one really want to say that? I think not. In the first place, both men acted from the same motive, personal gain, and both had exactly the same end in view when they acted. It may be inferred from Smith's conduct that he is a bad man, although that judgment may be withdrawn or modified if certain further facts are learned about him—for example, that he is mentally deranged. But would not the very same thing be inferred about Jones from his conduct? And would not the same further considerations also be relevant to any modification of this judgment? Moreover, suppose Jones pleaded, in his own defense, "After all, I didn't do anything except just stand there and watch the child drown. I didn't kill him; I only let him die." Again, if letting die were in itself less bad than killing, this defense should have at least some weight. But it does not. Such a "defense" can only be regarded as a grotesque perversion of moral reasoning. Morally speaking, it is no defense at all.

Now, it may be pointed out, quite properly, that the cases of euthanasia with which doctors are concerned are not like this at all. They do not involve personal gain or the destruction of normal healthy children. Doctors are concerned only with cases in which the patient's life is of no further use to him [the patient], or in which the patient's life has become or will soon become a terrible burden. However, the point is the same in these cases: the bare difference between killing and letting die does not, in itself, make a moral difference. If a doctor lets a patient die, for humane reasons, he is in the same moral position as if he had given the patient a lethal injection for humane reasons. If his decision was wrong—if, for example, the patient's illness was in fact curable—the decision would be equally regrettable no matter which method was used to carry it out. And if the doctor's decision was the right one, the method used is not in itself important.

The AMA policy statement isolates the crucial issue very well; the crucial issue is "the intentional termination of the life of one human being by another." But after identifying this issue, and forbidding "mercy killing," the statement goes on to deny that the cessation of treatment is the intentional termination of a life. This is where the mistake comes in, for what is the cessation of treatment, in these circumstances, if it is not "the intentional termination of the life of one human being by another?" Of course it is exactly that, and if it were not, there would be no point to it.

Many people will find this judgment hard to accept. One reason, I think, is that it is very easy to conflate the question of whether killing is, in itself, worse than letting die, with the very different question of whether most actual cases of killing are more reprehensible than most actual cases of letting die. Most actual cases of killing are clearly terrible (think, for example, of all the murders reported in the newspapers), and one hears of such cases every day. On the other hand, one hardly ever hears of a case of letting die, except for the actions of doctors who are motivated by humanitarian reasons. So one learns to think of killing in a much worse light than of letting die. But this does not mean that there is something about killing that makes it in itself worse than letting die, for it is not the bare difference between killing and letting die that makes the difference in these cases. Rather, the other factors—the murderer's motive of personal gain, for example, contrasted with the doctor's humanitarian motivation—account for different reactions to the different cases.

I have argued that killing is not in itself any worse than letting die; if my contention is right, it follows that active euthanasia is not any worse than passive euthanasia. What arguments can be given on the other side? The most common, I believe, is the following:

"The important difference between active and passive euthanasia is that, in passive euthanasia, the doctor does not do anything to bring about the patient's death. The doctor does nothing, and the patient dies of whatever ills already afflict him. In active euthanasia, however, the doctor does something to bring about the patient's death: he kills him. The doctor who gives the patient with cancer a lethal injection has himself caused his patient's death; whereas if he merely ceases treatment, the cancer is the cause of the death."

A number of points need to be made here. The first is that it is not exactly correct to say that in passive euthanasia the doctor does nothing, for he does do one thing that is very important: he lets the patient die. "Letting someone die" is certainly different, in some respects, from other types of action—mainly in that it is a kind of action that one may perform by way of not performing certain other actions. For example, one may let a patient die by way of not giving medication, just as one may insult someone by way of not shaking his hand. But for any purpose of moral assessment, it is a type of action nonetheless. The decision to let a patient die is subject to moral appraisal in the same way that a decision to kill him would be subject to moral appraisal: it may be assessed as wise or unwise, compassionate or sadistic, right or wrong. If a doctor deliberately let a patient die who was suffering from a routinely curable illness, the doctor would certainly be to blame for what he had done, just as he would be to blame if he had needlessly killed the patient. Charges against him would then be appropriate. If so, it would be no defense at all for him to insist that he didn't "do anything." He would have done something very serious indeed, for he let his patient die.

Fixing the cause of death may be very important from a legal point of view, for it may determine whether criminal charges are brought against the doctor. But I do not think that this notion can be used to show a moral difference between active and passive euthanasia. The reason why it is considered bad to be the cause of someone's death is that death is regarded as a great evil—and so it is. However, if it has been decided that euthanasia—even passive euthanasia—is desirable in a given case, it has also been decided that in this instance death is no greater an evil than the patient's continued existence. And if this is true, the usual reason for not wanting to be the cause of someone's death simply does not apply.

Finally, doctors may think that all of this is only of academic interest—the sort of thing that philosophers may worry about but that has no practical bearing on their own work. After all, doctors must be concerned about the legal consequences of what they do, and active euthanasia is clearly forbidden by the law. But even so, doctors should also be concerned with the fact that the law is forcing upon them a moral doctrine that may well be indefensible, and has a considerable effect on their practices. Of course, most doctors are not now in the position of being coerced in this matter, for they do not regard themselves as merely going along with what the law requires. Rather, in statements such as the AMA policy statement that I have quoted, they are endorsing this doctrine as a central point of medical ethics. In that statement, active euthanasia is condemned not merely as illegal but as "contrary to that for which the medical profession stands," whereas passive euthanasia is approved. However, the preceding considerations suggest that there is really no moral difference between the two, considered in themselves (there may be important moral differences in some cases in their *consequences*, but, as I pointed out, these differences may make active euthanasia, and not passive euthanasia, the morally preferable option). So, whereas doctors may have to discriminate between active and passive euthanasia to satisfy the law, they should not do any more than that. In particular, they should not give the distinction any added authority and weight by writing it into official statements of medical ethics.

Saving Life and Taking Life

RICHARD TRAMMELL ▪ Grove City College
The Journal of Philosophy, 1975

Richard Trammell argues that we have a greater obligation to refrain from killing another person than we do to save someone from dying. Trammell presents a pair of situations where the efforts and motivations directed toward a stranger are assumed to be the same. In the first case, a gunman demands that you shoot a stranger and kill him or he will steal $1000 from you. In the second case, someone asks you to give $1000 to save the life of a stranger who will die without the monetary aid. Trammell believes that it is certainly wrong in the first instance to kill the stranger to save the $1000, and that we have a strong obligation not to shoot him; while in the second instance we have a lesser obligation to give away $1000 to a stranger to save his life.

Trammell argues that the moral distinction between **avoiding killing** and **acting to save a life** is a distinction between a negative duty and a positive duty. There are several factors that, Trammell argues, underlie the **negative/positive duty distinction**. The first among these is the relative ability to **discharge** one or the other kind of duty. Trammell argues that there is clear and complete asymmetry in the ability any person has to fulfill the requirements of positive and negative duties. In the case of a positive duty to help those in need, it is never possible for a person to come to the aid of every person who is in fact in need. By contrast, in the case of the positive duty not to seriously injure others, it is in most every situation possible for a person not to seriously injure others. In other words, negative duties can be successfully discharged while positive duties cannot—an empirical distinction that may underlie the positive duty/negative duty distinction. Trammell asks us to imagine making the choice of spending our next dollar on car safety as part of a negative duty not to kill others or giving that dollar to charity as part of our positive duty to save others. If they were morally equivalent actions, then we might just as well always spend the next dollar on charity rather than on repairing our car—leaving us always with an unrepaired car. Indeed, due to the untold numbers of poor who could be helped by our next dollar, we would be quickly reduced to having no more dollars than the poorest other person. Trammell implies that an ethic that requires such moral asceticism is so strenuous in its demands on the individual that it must be implausible.

The second factor which Trammell finds underlying the positive/negative distinction is the contrast between those actions that close the options to act left available to other persons and those actions that leave open the options to act available to other persons. This **optionality principle** can be illustrated by the example of a person who comes across someone in need. If that person kills the person in need, he shuts off the good which is the continuation of that life. If he merely passes the person in need by, he allows some other person to come along and provide the person in need the aid he needs to survive. In other words, killing is an action that closes off all options for realizing a good, while merely not saving leaves open many options for realizing a good.

The third factor which Trammell sees as underlying the positive/negative duty distinction concerns the notion of **individual responsibility**. Trammell's argument here is that those who put others in a situation of needing to be saved share a greater responsibility for going to the aid of those they have placed in jeopardy than someone who shares no such responsibility for creating such problems. Trammell applies the underlying factor of responsibility to help account for the asymmetry in his earlier examples involving the $1000 cost to not kill or to save and the $1 cost (at the margin) to repair the car or to aid charity. Trammell points out that to kill a stranger by shooting him would make one responsible for his death, but by contrast there is no basis for believing one is responsible for a stranger's need to be saved. Similarly, you would be responsible for hurting someone with your car, but you are clearly not responsible for the fact that the persons in need of charity are in that unfortunate situation.

THE PURPOSE OF THIS PAPER IS TO EXAMINE THE distinction between "negative" and "positive" duties. Special attention will be given to certain criticisms raised against this distinction by Michael Tooley.

A Paradigm Case

If someone threatened to steal $1000 from a person if he did not take a gun and shoot a stranger between the eyes, it would be very wrong for him to kill the stranger to save his $1000. But if someone asked from that person $1000 to save a stranger, it would seem that his obligation to grant this request would not be as great as his obligation to refuse the first demand—even if he had good reason for believing that without his $1000 the stranger would certainly die. Refraining from the action of killing is a kind of "inaction" which it seems appropriate to call a "negative" duty. Saving is a kind of "action" which it seems appropriate to call a "positive" duty.[1] In this particular example, it seems plausible to say that a person has a greater obligation to refrain from killing someone than to save someone, even though the effort required of him ($1000) and his motivation toward the stranger be assumed identical in both cases. None of this is meant as exact analysis, but rather as an initial indication of what seems to be a plausible view.

According to Tooley, one reason we intuitively feel greater responsibility not to intervene harmfully than to aid is that harmful intervention usually implies a malicious motive whereas failure to aid often involves only indifference. Also it usually requires greater effort to perform positive action to save someone than to refrain from killing. Tooley[2] asks us to consider the following illustration:

> (1) Jones sees that Smith will be killed by a bomb unless he warns him. Jones's reaction is: "How lucky, it will save me the trouble of killing Smith myself." So Jones allows Smith to be killed by the bomb, even though he could easily have warned him. (2) Jones wants Smith dead, and therefore shoots him. Is one to say there is a significant difference between the wrongness of Jones's behavior in these two cases? Surely not. This shows the mistake of drawing a distinction between positive and negative duties and holding that the latter impose stricter obligations than the former (59/60).

In some respects Tooley's illustration is misleading. For example, Jones's extreme hatred for Smith and his cynical joy at seeing Smith blown to bits, have a "masking" or "sledgehammer" effect, which makes it difficult to evaluate the significance of the distinction between negative and positive duties. The fact that one cannot distinguish the taste of two wines when both are mixed with green persimmon juice, does not imply that there is no distinction between the wines.

In addition, Tooley sets up his procedures in such a way that he arbitrarily excludes consideration of those cases where the prima facie claim for the moral relevance of the distinction between negative and positive duties is strongest. He stipulates that the cases of negative and positive duties considered must involve "minimal effort," thus eliminating from consideration cases in which effort is more than minimal *but still a constant* (60).

Suppose Tooley's example is modified as follows: Jones's attitude toward Smith is neutral in both cases. It costs Jones $1000 to save Smith from the bomb. It costs Jones $1000 to avoid shooting Smith. *Without introducing any new variables,* we have made Tooley's example parallel to the paradigm case; and now it ceases to appear that Jones has the same obligation to save Smith as not to kill Smith.

The paradigm case (or Tooley's, as modified above) provides prima facie justification for the claim that in some cases we are under greater obligation to avoid taking a life than to save a life, even though effort and motivation are constants. Anyone wishing to defend the moral equivalence of negative and positive duties should avoid introducing the ad hoc requirement of "minimal effort," since precisely one of the reasons for doubting the universal moral equivalence of negative and positive duties is that we feel obligated to go to almost any length to avoid killing someone, but not under equally great obligation to save someone.

Suppose it is granted that, in cases involving great effort, we are under greater obligation not to kill than to save—i.e., the distinction between positive and negative duties is morally significant. But it is also held that this distinction does not apply in cases of minimal effort. (This is perhaps Tooley's position, although he does not explicitly say so.) Then the following questions need to be answered. Does the distinction cease to hold gradually or suddenly? If suddenly, at what point in decrease of effort does the distinction cease to hold, and why? If gradually, why should the distinction cease to hold altogether at any point?

Dischargeability of a Duty

A number of factors underlie the distinction between negative and positive duties, one of which is the dischargeability of a duty. It is an empirical fact that in most cases it is possible for a person not to inflict serious physical injury on any other person. It is also an empirical fact that in no case is it possible for a person to aid everyone who needs help. The positive duty to love one's neighbor or help those in need sets a maximum ethic which would never let us rest except to gather strength to resume the battle. But it is a rare case when we must really exert ourselves to keep from killing a person.

In short, the negative duty of not killing can be discharged completely. The statement, "For every x, if x is a person, then y does not kill x," is true for many y's. But the positive duty of saving can never be discharged completely. The statement, "For every x, if x is a person and x needs aid, y aids x," is not true for any y in the world.

Denial of the distinction between negative and positive duties leads straight to an ethic so strenuous that it might give pause even to a philosophical John the Baptist. Compare the following two cases: (1) by spending a dollar (say to make a minor but essential repair on his car) Smith can avoid harming a person *(x)*; (2) by giving a dollar to charity, Smith can help a person *(y)* avoid harm. Suppose that Smith's motivation toward the people is the same, the effort is minimal and identical in amount, and each person will be saved from an equivalent amount of harm. Now suppose that Tooley is right and that Smith is as obligated to spend the dollar to help y as he is to spend the dollar to avoid hurting x. So Smith gives a dollar to charity. But the poor are always with Smith. Before he has a chance to fix his car, Smith notes that another dollar to this charity would have the same beneficial effect. Now perhaps giving this second dollar would come harder than the first. But still it would come no harder than the unspent dollar for the car repair; and thus Smith gives his second dollar to charity. Bit by bit, Smith gives away all his resources— reminding himself from time to time that he is just as obligated to give another dollar to charity as to fix his car. The problem is that, even though fulfillment of one particular act of aid involves only minimal effort, it sets a precedent for millions of such efforts. If one maintains as a general principle that we have equal duty not to kill as to save, then either one must uphold an ethic so strenuous that asceticism is the only morally defensible way of life; or else one must be willing to allow Smith to harm someone with his car for lack of a simple repair.

P. J. Fitzgerald, in his article "Acting and Refraining,"[3] makes a point related to what has been said above. Fitzgerald says that the duty to refrain from a certain action "merely closes off one avenue of activity," whereas the duty to perform a certain action "closes off all activities but one." Now it might seem that Fitzgerald is overlooking an essential point. Even though a negative duty is something we should not do, and hence involves a kind of inaction, there may be great effort involved in carrying out this inactivity. For example, someone may have to wreck his car to avoid running over someone else. The inaction involved in a negative duty does not necessarily imply freedom to do whatever we please. Sometimes to avoid killing someone might close off "all activities but one."

However, this apparent exception really proves the rule. There are billions of people whom we have a duty not to kill. It is an exceptional case indeed when fulfillment of this duty for any particular person imposes one specific action (like swerving a car to avoid hitting a pedestrian). Even in such exceptional cases, the specific action required can usually be quickly discharged, without recurrent obligation. As a rule, fulfilling the duty not to kill leaves us free to carry out a vast range of activities without constraint. The case is very different when it comes to the duty to save. The duty to save is "distractive" (Santayana's [1863-1952] term) and demands of us the "one thing needful," preventing us from doing anything else. Thus P. J. Fitzgerald's formulation, even though there are various kinds of exceptional situations, gives overwhelming statistical support to the distinction between negative and positive duties.

The Optionality Principle

"Optionality" is a second important factor underlying the distinction between negative and positive duties. Some actions either destroy a good or make it impossible for anyone else to realize a certain good; whereas other actions do not destroy and perhaps leave open to others the option of realizing the good in question. Suppose that the continuation of x's life is good. Then obviously if someone kills x, not only does the killer fail to contribute toward the realization of this good; he also closes everyone else's option to do so. But if a Levite or priest merely passes by on the other side of x, then at least the option is left open for some Good Samaritan to come along and provide x the aid he needs to live.

A negative duty is a duty not to do an action that closes all options, not only for oneself but for everyone else, to realize a certain good that would (or might) have been realized if one had done nothing. A positive duty is the duty to do an action to bring about a certain good, which someone else might also have the option to bring about.

It should be noted that there is an essential difference between negative and positive duties in regard to the probability of the good being realized in case the duty is not met. There is a logical equivalence between y failing to meet the negative duty of not causing x to suffer at time z, and a probability of 1 that x suffer at time z; whereas there is no logical equivalence between y failing to meet the positive duty of relieving x from suffering at time z, and a probability of 1 that x suffer at time z. If x kills y, it is certain that y will not live; but if x fails to save y, someone else may still have the option of saving y.

Responsibility

Still another factor underlying the distinction between negative and positive duties is responsibility. To illustrate this factor, consider the following case. A fire is started by Miller. Both Miller and Thompson, who also happens on the scene, witness a woman on the third floor crying for help. According to the responsibility factor, if everything else is equal, Miller is more obligated to try to save the woman than Thompson, because Miller is responsible for the woman being in the situation of needing to be saved, whereas Thompson is not. In general, if x kills y, then x is responsible for y's death.[4] But if x fails to save y, then x may or may not be responsible for y being in the situation in which y needs to be saved. The more directly involved x is for y's needing to be saved, the more responsible x is for helping to rescue y. If, for example, x accidentally gave y poison, we might expect x to spend as much effort to save y as we would expect x to spend to avoid poisoning y to begin with. Certainly more would be required from x to save y than from uninvolved neighbor z. In the paradigm case, it was clear that, if the person shot the stranger between the eyes, he would be responsible for the stranger's death. But there was no reason for believing that the person was responsible for the other stranger's being in a position of needing to be saved. In the charity-versus-car-repair case, x is clearly responsible for hurting someone

with his car through negligence; but x may very well not be responsible for the plight of the unfortunate administered to by charity.

To summarize, we have suggested three factors that underlie the distinction between negative and positive duties. The negative duty not to kill can be fully discharged, whereas the duty to save cannot. Failure to meet the duty of not killing cuts off any possibility of realizing the good connected with the life in question, whereas failure to save leaves open the option for someone else to save. Finally, a person is not necessarily responsible for someone else's needing to be saved; but he is responsible for the life of anyone he kills.

Tooley Again

In order to test the analysis developed in this paper, two additional illustrations from Tooley will be considered, beginning with his diabolical-machine[5] example:

> Imagine a machine which contains two children, John and Mary. If one pushes a button, John will be killed, but Mary will emerge unharmed. If one does not push the button, John will emerge unharmed, but Mary will be killed. In the first case one kills John, while in the second case one merely lets Mary die. Does one really wish to say that the action of intentionally refraining from pushing the button is morally preferable to the action of pushing it, even though exactly one person perishes in either case?

Failure to meet a negative duty makes the realization of some good impossible which would have been realized if one had not acted at all. But in evaluating whether or not an action prevents the realization of a "good," one must consider the overall results of the action. In the case given by Tooley, whether one does or does not push the button, one person lives and one person dies. Therefore regardless of which action one chooses, there is no overall good to be realized and no negative nor positive duty involved.

Tooley also raises the question why killing an infant is wrong, if refraining from conception is not wrong, since in both cases a potential human being is kept from coming to maturity. For x to kill an infant is to act in such a way that it closes out all options for anyone to realize the good involved in the infant's continued life. But if x acts to prevent his conceiving children, x does not take away any good the world would have had if x had done nothing.[6] Also, the duty to have all the children potentially involved in one's genes is a nondischargeable duty, since, regardless of how many children one had, one would be obligated to try to have some more. But the duty not to kill infants is a duty that can in the great majority of cases be easily discharged. No doubt other important principles differentiate the morality of contraception from infanticide. The distinction between negative and positive duties is one of these principles.

Notes

[1]Philippa Foot defends the view that we are more obligated to meet negative duties of not injuring people than to meet positive duties of helping them. See "The Problem of Abortion and the Doctrine of the Double Effect," *The Oxford Review*, v (1967): 5–15, p. 59.

[2]Michael Tooley, "Abortion and Infanticide," *Philosophy & Public Affairs*, II, 1 (Fall 1972).

[3]*Analysis*, xxvii. 4 (March 1967): 133–139.

[4]If y's death was unforeseeable and unavoidable, then x is not responsible in a moral sense. In this case one might wish to say that no negative duty has been violated, just as no positive duty would be violated if x had no way of knowing that y needed to be saved, or knew it but had no way of helping x.

[5]Taken from a paper delivered by Michael Tooley at the American Philosophical Association Meeting, Eastern Division, held in Atlanta, Georgia, December 27–29, 1973. The paper is entitled "Abortion and Infanticide Revisited." The example is from pages 19–20. Tooley's original article "Abortion and Infanticide," has been revised and published in a collection of essays entitled *The Problem of Abortion*, edited by Joel Feinberg (Belmont, Calif.: Wadsworth, 1973).

[6]The case would be different if x had donated sperm for artificial insemination and then without justification tried to interfere with the conception process afterward.

On the Relative Strictness of Negative and Positive Duties

BRUCE RUSSELL ▪ Wayne State University
American Philosophical Quarterly, 1977

Russell examines whether the duty to refrain from killing someone is stricter than the duty to save someone. His conclusion is that **negative duties** are not stricter than positive duties. Russell first presents various examples (like those offered by Philippa Foot and Richard Trammell) that support the claim that the **killing/letting die distinction** *has* moral significance in itself. He then examines cases (like Michael Tooley's diabolical-machine) that support the claim that the killing/letting die distinction *has no* moral significance in itself. In the previous essay, Trammell argues in favor of the moral significance of the killing/letting die distinction and offers three reasons in support of the greater duty not to kill than to save life (**optionality, responsibility, and dischargeability of duty**). Russell argues *against* these considerations.

Russell offers a principle which he claims can account for most of the considered judgments in the relevant conflict-of-interest cases. The principle is that, other things being equal, it is worse (morally) to adopt a plan that calls for harming some in order to aid others than it is to let those others be harmed regardless of whether: (a) the harm to some is brought about through an action or an omission; and/or whether (b) the harm is logically necessary or only physically inevitable, given the successful execution of the plan.

In closing, Russell applies his principle to a number of the cases he considered earlier (such as Tooley's diabolical-machine example), and he argues that his principle is attractive not only because it accounts for most of our considered judgments, but also because it connects with concepts of the worth and dignity of persons.

RECENTLY A NUMBER OF PHILOSOPHICAL DISCUSsions have appeared in which the question of whether we have a greater duty to refrain from injuring people than to bring them aid is considered. In particular, they have centered about the question whether we have a greater duty to refrain from taking life than we have to save life. In this discussion I will consider in what sense (if any) it could be said that negative duties are stricter than positive duties and, more specifically, whether there is any sense in which the duty to refrain from killing someone is stricter than the duty to save someone.

I will conclude that in an important sense negative duties are not stricter than positive duties. I will consider various examples and arguments that would seem to count against my conclusion. It can be shown, I think, that absurd consequences result if the refraining from injuring/bringing aid distinction is taken to have moral significance in itself. Other principles are available to account for the intuitive judgments we make in those cases generally thought to support the claim that negative duties are stricter than positive ones. Not only will such principles be offered but arguments in support of the claim that negative duties are stricter than positive duties will be criticized and found wanting.

I. THE KILLING/LETTING DIE DISTINCTION

To determine if the difference between killing and letting die is morally relevant, we must carefully distinguish between the two. Jonathan Bennett's argument to the effect that the distinction has no moral relevance has been vitiated by Daniel Dinello's criticism of the way in which he draws it.[1] In this discussion I will adopt a modified version of Dinello's characterization of that distinction.

(A) x killed y if x caused y's death by performing movements which affect y's body such that y dies as a result of these movements.

(B) x let y die if

    (a) there are conditions (C) affecting y, such that if they are not altered, y will die.

    (b) there are certain movements (M) which, if performed by x, will prevent y from dying.

    (c) x is in a position to perform such movements (i.e., if x tries to perform such movements, he will succeed in performing them and x is able to try to perform them).

    (d) x fails to perform these movements.

    (e) y dies as a result of (C).[2]

Now the above account of letting die does not imply that x is morally responsible if he lets y die. It may not be reasonable to expect x to be aware of (a) or (b). If that were true and if x was not in fact aware of (a) or (b), then he could not be accused of negligence even if (a)-(e) obtained. In addition, even if x were aware of (a) and (b), there could be good moral reasons for him to abstain from performing the movements that would save y. For instance, x might have to take the heart from a healthy z and transplant it in y in order to save him in a case where x would not be morally culpable for failing to do this. Perhaps it is because when we speak of letting die it is often in the context of accusation that some have thought that, in cases like the above, it would be incorrect to say that x let y die.[3] Though the use of the words "letting die" often carries with it the ascription of (moral) responsibility, it need not. We can correctly say, "x let y die" and add, "for good (moral) reasons" (reasons which may include reference to contravening duties or non-culpable ignorance) thereby avoiding any ascription of (moral) responsibility.

(e) is needed since, if (a)-(d) are satisfied, it does not necessarily follow that x let y die. Someone else might intervene and save y while x stands idly by. In that case, x would not let y die. But not only must y die if x lets him die, he must also die as a result of the conditions which endanger his life and about which x is able to do something. If x fails to perform (M) while someone else shoots y in the head and as a result no one is able to save y, then x does not let y die. Given (a)-(d), it is only if y dies as a result of (C) that x can be charged with letting him die.[4]

Given the above account of the distinction between killing and letting die, I will argue that that distinction has no moral significance in itself, i.e., if other things are equal (including considerations about intentions, contravening duties, etc.), there are no cases in which the killing/letting die distinction has moral significance.

If the above account is broadened by replacing "killed," "dies," etc. by appropriate versions of "harmed," "is harmed," etc., an account of the distinction between harming and allowing harm will result.

II. THE STRICTNESS OF DUTIES

There are (at least) three senses in which one duty can be said to be stricter than another.

(1) *Moral Culpability:* Duty S is stricter than duty T if, and only if, other things being equal, one is more culpable for not having performed S than for not having performed T.

For example, the duty to save a life is stricter in this sense than the duty to relieve discomfort and the duty to refrain from taking life is stricter than the duty to refrain from causing discomfort.

(2) *Utilitarian Overrides:* Duty S is stricter than duty T if, and only if, other things being equal, a greater amount of non-moral good (e.g., pleasure, freedom from pain and suffering, etc.) is required to justify non-compliance with S than with T.

(1) and (2) are not equivalent for one might hold that of two duties, S and T, no amount of non-moral good could justify non-compliance with either of the duties. Thus it would not be the case that a greater amount of non-moral good would be required to justify non-compliance with S than with T (or vice versa) in sense (2). Nevertheless, one might wish to maintain that S was a stricter duty than T in sense (1). Some would hold that if S were the duty to

refrain from killing someone in order to save others and T were the duty to refrain from torturing someone to prevent someone else from torturing others, then S would be stricter than T in sense (1) but not in sense (2). This might also be held to be the case if S and T were not both negative duties but if S were a negative duty and T a positive duty. For instance, let S remain as above and let T be the duty to save life.

(3) *Perfect vs. Imperfect Duties:* Duty S is stricter than duty T if, and only if, other things being equal, the amount of sacrifice owed to relevant individuals in the performance of S is greater than that for T.

To say that the amount of sacrifice owed to relevant individuals is greater in the case of one duty than in the case of another means either that one would be more culpable for non-performance in the one case than in the other or that a greater amount of non-moral good would be required to override the one duty than the other. (3) applies the senses of strictness defined in (1) and (2) to considerations about the amount of sacrifice owed to individuals. The duty to save life might be just as strict in sense (1) or (2) as the duty to refrain from taking life when the first kind of duty is taken to be owed to people in general or to some group of people, while the second duty might be stricter than the first if the first is taken to be owed to specific individuals. Why this should be so will be discussed below (VB, 3).

III. CASES IN SUPPORT OF THE CLAIM THAT THE KILLING/ LETTING DIE DISTINCTION HAS MORAL SIGNIFICANCE IN ITSELF

Dinello gives a case which lends support to the claim that the killing/letting die distinction (when correctly drawn) has moral significance.

C_1: Consider the following example: Jones and Smith are in a hospital. Jones cannot live longer than two hours unless he gets a heart transplant. Smith, who had one kidney removed, is dying of an infection in the other kidney. If he does not get a kidney transplant, he will die in about four hours. When Jones dies, his one good kidney can be transplanted to Smith, or Smith could be killed and his heart transplanted to Jones. Circumstances are such that there are no other hearts or kidneys available within the time necessary to save either one. Further, the consequences of either alternative are approximately equivalent, that is, heart transplants have been perfected, both have a wife and no children, *etc.*[5]

Dinello then goes on to claim that there is a greater duty to refrain from killing Smith than there is to save Jones (by killing Smith). This is a difficult case for anyone who would hold that in itself the killing/letting die distinction has no moral significance. In order to maintain that position and accept Dinello's judgment on (C₁), some morally relevant aspect of this case must be found which is not essentially related to the killing/letting die distinction but that is covertly introduced along with the other aspects of the case. Another alternative would be to present reasons to show that Dinello's intuitions are not well-founded here.

Richard L. Trammell presents another difficult case for those who deny the killing/letting die distinction has moral significance.

C₂: If someone threatened to steal $1000 from a person if he did not take a gun and shoot a stranger between the eyes, it would be very wrong for him to kill the stranger to save his $1000. But if someone asked from that person $1000 to save a stranger, it would seem that his obligation to grant this request would not be as great as his obligation to refuse the first demand—even if he had good reason for believing that without his $1000 the stranger would certainly die.[6]

Philippa Foot presents a number of examples that are meant to support the claim that in general we have a greater duty to refrain from injuring than to bring aid. I will give three of her examples because I think they contain important differences.

C₃: Suppose that a judge or magistrate is faced with rioters demanding that a culprit be found for a certain crime and threatening otherwise to take their own bloody revenge on a particular section of the community. The real culprit being unknown, the judge sees himself as able to

prevent the bloodshed only by framing some innocent person and having him executed.[7]

To make this case symmetrical with others she presents, Foot later alters it slightly so that the rioters threaten to take the lives of five hostages rather than the lives of certain members of some community. A family of similar cases can be generated from this example. All of them will involve the choice between helping some by *injuring* or *killing* others or letting those in need of help be injured or killed by refusing to kill or injure others.

C₄: A person can help others by deliberately letting someone die (e.g., by letting a starving beggar die) and then using that person's vital bodily parts (heart, kidneys, etc.) in order to save others.[8]

(C₄) differs from (C₃) in that *both* alternatives involve *letting* someone *die.* In (C₃) one of the alternatives involves *killing* someone to aid others; the other, letting some persons die.

C₅: Suppose, for instance, that there are five patients in a hospital whose lives could be saved by the manufacture of a certain gas, but that this inevitably releases lethal fumes into the room of another patient whom for some reason we are unable to move.[9]

This case is significant because Foot thinks that defenders of the doctrine of double effect must conclude that it is morally permissible to produce the gas which she claims runs counter to our moral intuitions. Defenders of the moral significance of the killing/letting die distinction have no difficulty with this case since producing the gas would amount to *killing* the immobile patient while not producing it would only be *letting* the other patient *die.*[10]

In an essay entitled "The Survival Lottery," John Harris defends a kind of lottery where people are chosen at random to supply vital organs "whenever doctors have two or more dying patients who could be saved by transplants, and no suitable organs have come to hand through 'natural' deaths."[11] We will call this case (C₆) where the vital organs of some healthy person are taken in order to save others. Harris argues that such an action is morally permissible while indicating that he believes it is contrary to our moral intuitions to claim such.[12] Because this example has significant features in common with (C_1-C_5), it must be placed in the same class with them whatever the final ruling might be as to the moral permissibility of the envisioned actions.

IV. CASES IN SUPPORT OF THE CLAIM THAT THE KILLING/ LETTING DIE DISTINCTION HAS NO MORAL SIGNIFICANCE IN ITSELF

Trammell cites two examples given in different papers by Michael Tooley that seem to count against those who hold that the killing/letting die distinction has moral significance in itself. I will give Tooley's case of a diabolical-machine and alter Trammell's (C_2) so that it appears to count against those who maintain that the killing/letting die distinction has moral significance.

D_1: Imagine a machine which contains two children, John and Mary. If one pushes a button, John will be killed, but Mary will emerge unharmed. If one does not push the button, John will emerge unharmed, but Mary will be killed. In the first case one kills John, while in the second case one merely lets Mary die. Does one really wish to say that the action of intentionally refraining from pushing the button is morally preferable to the action of pushing it, even though exactly one person perishes in either case?[13]

D_2: If someone threatened to steal \$1 from a person if he did not take a gun and shoot a stranger between the eyes, it would be very wrong for him to kill the stranger to save his \$1. If someone asked from a person \$1 to save a stranger, it would seem that his obligation to grant this request would be just as great as his obligation to refuse the first demand—given that he had good reason for believing that without his \$1 the stranger would certainly die.

I have modified Foot's (C_3) along the lines of her (C_4) in order to show that there is not always a greater duty to refrain from injuring than to bring aid.

D_3: Suppose that the innocent man the judge has in his custody is a diabetic. Now he can obtain the release of the five hostages by (i) *letting* the diabetic die through refusing him insulin or by (ii) *killing* him through hanging, shooting, etc. On the other hand, he can (iii) refuse to either kill the diabetic or let him die and thereby let the hostages be killed.

If the killing/letting die distinction is in itself morally significant, then the judge would have a stricter duty (in one of the three senses of "strictness") to let the diabetic die than to kill him. But what difference could it make whether the judge killed the innocent man or let him die by refusing him insulin, other things being equal? If the distinction is taken to have moral significance in itself, when applied to this modified judge-rioters case it leads to absurd consequences.

V. ARGUMENTS IN FAVOR OF THE MORAL SIGNIFICANCE OF THE KILLING/LETTING DIE DISTINCTION

A. *Harman*

In a discussion whose purpose is to show that "morality arises when a group of people reach an implicit agreement or come to a tacit understanding about their relations with one another," Gilbert Harman attempts to explain what he assumes to be the case, viz., that "our morality takes it to be worse to harm someone than to refuse to help someone."[14] His hypothesis is that moral agreement results from bargaining with conditional intentions. Applying these considerations to the harming/helping distinction, Harman reasons that everyone (the rich, the poor, the strong, the weak) would agree to avoid harming one another since that would benefit all. However, "the rich and the strong would not benefit from an arrangement whereby everyone would try to do as much as possible to help those in need."[15] Given this situation, the weak and the poor hold out for the strong principle of mutual aid while the rich and the strong favor only a very weak one, perhaps one that requires everyone to do something (perhaps very minimal) to help those in need.

Harman suggests that the result is a compromise between the strong version of the principle of mutual assistance offered by the weak and the poor and the weak version offered by the rich and the strong. On the other hand, the principle of refraining from harming has unanimous support and is thus very strong. This account is meant to explain why we (purportedly) take it to be worse to harm someone than to refuse him aid. If Harman's bargaining hypothesis about how we come to adopt certain moral attitudes were correct, we might use it to support the claim that any group of people that contained rich and strong, weak and poor, *ought* to bargain for a stronger duty to refrain from harming than to bring aid since that would be the best bargain to strike, even if they did not in fact realize it.

But the bargaining procedure Harman proposes is insufficient for determining *moral* principles. We can imagine agreement on all sorts of principles of etiquette being reached as a result of the kind of bargaining process Harman offers and other clearly immoral bargains being struck on the basis of race, sex, religion, etc. To rule out agreements based on bargains of the latter sort, Harman would have to introduce something comparable to Rawls' veil of ignorance.[16] When that is done, it is not clear that the parties would see the duty to refrain from injuring as stricter than the duty to bring aid since from behind the veil of ignorance they would not be able to tell whether, as people in ordinary life, they would need aid or not. As it stands, Harman's account of the bargaining process is not an adequate account of a procedure for determining moral principles since it makes no provision for fairness or impartiality between the bargaining parties. Thus, his conclusion concerning the relative strictness of negative and positive duties is not well founded.

B. *Trammell*

In his discussion, Richard L. Trammell offers three reasons why he thinks there is a greater obligation not to kill than to save life.

(1) *Optionality*

Trammell notes that certain kinds of action destroy the possibility of other people's intervening to prevent evil from occurring while others do not. He then says (correctly, I believe) that killing someone closes off everyone's options to realize a good (viz., to keep the dead person alive) but that passing a dying person by, when one can help to prevent his death, leaves open the possibility of others coming to his assistance. Given that it is better to adopt an alternative that has less chance than some other of producing the same amount of non-moral evil (e.g., pain, physical disability, death, etc.), it would be better to pass a dying person by than to kill someone (other things being equal, of course).

While this conclusion holds, I think, when killing is compared with passing a dying person by, it does not hold when killing is compared with letting someone die. Whether a person adopts a plan to kill someone or to let him die, the death is logically necessary given successful execution of the relevant plan. On the other hand, if the relevant omission involves passing by a dying person without offering assistance and the relevant act, shooting someone in the head at close range, then in neither case is the death of that person logically necessary. It might even be the case that the probability of death given the relevant omission is greater than that given the relevant act.[17] If one gives equivalent descriptions of corresponding negative and positive duties, then optionality either becomes an accidental feature or necessarily not a feature of non-compliance with either kind of duty. So any moral significance optionality may have cannot be used to account for the moral significance (if any) of the refraining from injuring/bringing aid distinction.

(2) *Responsibility*

An argument can be constructed from Trammell's discussion of responsibility that seems to support the claim that there is a greater duty to refrain from injuring than to bring aid.[18] It rests on a premise that connects non-moral responsibility for states of affairs with the strictness of moral obligations. It seems that for Trammell a person is non-morally responsible for a state of affairs if, and only if, he has either caused or somehow brought about that state of affairs. He argues that if a person is non-morally responsible for a state of affairs that injures or endangers someone else, that person is under a greater obligation to aid the injured or endangered person than are those who are not so responsible. He claims that the obligation to bring aid that the person who is responsible has incurred is just as great (or nearly as great) as his obligation to refrain from causing the injury or danger in the first place.

If we let X = the strictness of the duty to bring aid on the part of those who are *not* non-morally responsible for some injury or danger, Y = the strictness of the duty to bring aid on the part of those who *are* non-morally responsible for some injury or danger, and Z = the strictness of the obligation not to injure or endanger in the first place, then the argument has the following structure:

(1) $X < Y$
(2) $Y = Z$
(3) $X < Z$

From this one can conclude that, in general, (except where one has caused the injury) the duty to bring aid is not as strict as the duty to refrain from injuring.

This argument fails on two counts. First, (1) is not obviously true. If someone accidentally (and non-negligently) nudged another person (a non-swimmer) into the water, he would be non-morally responsible for the resulting predicament. But if both he and another man knowingly let the non-swimmer drown when they could easily have saved him, it would be beside the point should the other man plead for a lighter sentence on the grounds that *he* did not accidentally nudge the drowned man, i.e., on the grounds that he was not non-morally responsible for the drowned man's predicament. If the cause that sent the non-swimmer into the water was truly accidental (and non-negligent), then what moral difference could it make whether the cause was an unintended nudge rather than merely a slippery deck? To call the act accidental and non-negligent is to imply that the relevant person is completely absolved of moral responsibility for the resulting situation. If the person has no moral responsibility for the situation, there would seem to be no grounds for assigning him a greater duty for changing it than others similarly situated.

Let us now suppose that someone intentionally or negligently nudged a non-swimmer into the water. Would he have a greater duty to bring aid to the non-swimmer than an innocent bystander [would]?

I think that he would, at least if strictness is understood in the third sense given above. In order to right the wrong he has done, this man might be required to jump into shark-infested waters to save the drowning non-swimmer while the innocent bystander would not be morally blameworthy should he refrain from taking the plunge under these circumstances. But in this case it is plausible to maintain $Y > Z$, i.e., that (2) is false. In general, no one has a duty to refrain from injuring someone where that duty is so great that it would require one to endanger oneself in a way comparable to that which would result from jumping into shark-infested waters.[19] But if initially a person cannot be required to sacrifice so much in order to be morally blameless but can be required to sacrifice that much if he is to be blameless after intentionally (or negligently) injuring or endangering another, it makes sense to say that the duty to bring aid under those circumstances is stricter than the initial duty to refrain from injuring or endangering. Thus $Y > Z$.

In summary, if a person is non-morally responsible but *not* morally responsible for the injury or danger to another, then (1) is false. On the other hand, if a person is non-morally responsible *and* morally responsible for the injury or danger to another, then (2) is false. Thus, in any case, the argument that I have presented and that can be gleaned from Trammell's discussion fails to support the desired conclusion.

(3) Dischargeability of a Duty

Trammell rightly points out that given the world as it is, it is impossible for one person "to aid everyone who needs help."[20] Yet it is infrequent that we need expend great effort or incur great risk to avoid harming people. His point seems to be that the continuous and substantial effort required, if it were a duty to aid everyone who needs help, would be too much to expect of people. It would be unreasonable to require people to forgo their own interests so completely. However, the sacrifice needed to fulfill the negative duty of refraining from killing is generally slight and easily discharged. Thus it is reasonable to require people to refrain from killing others but not reasonable to require them to save everyone.

One might well grant Trammell his point if the positive duty to bring aid is understood as a duty "to aid *everyone* who needs help" or even to aid everyone whose life can be saved. But suppose there are duties to bring aid that are not so general, duties whose formulation contains reference to limits upon the effort or risk that can be reasonably required of those who are to fulfill them. For instance, one might claim that there was a duty to save those whose [lives were] in danger provided one did not have to risk one's own basic interests. We must now see why the principle that limits the amount of sacrifice required to perform what would otherwise be morally obligatory acts leads to the conclusion that negative duties are, in one sense, no stricter than positive duties.[21]

Suppose there is a person who is in need of aid and that we can bring aid to him. Suppose we can assign a number that represents the amount of effort or risk we would have to assume in order to give the person the aid he needs. Let this number be represented by "e." Now also suppose there are $(n - 1)$ people who are in relevantly similar situations to the person who needs our help. Next, suppose that "B" represents the greatest sacrifice or effort we can offer without endangering our basic interests. Now given the formal principle of justice that enjoins treating relevantly similar cases in similar ways, we would have the same degree of duty to all the n people. But given that in general we cannot be required to forgo our basic interests, it follows that $n \times e \leq B$. Whenever the effort or risk (e) and/or the number of similarly situated people (n) becomes so great that if we had a duty to any one individual, our obligations would become so great as to jeopardize our basic interests, then, barring overwhelming utilitarian considerations, we have no obligation to any particular individual in the relevant circumstances. So if there are a large number of needy people similarly situated, we will not owe each individual very much effort or be required to incur anything but minimal risks. If we did owe any one individual very much, then given the formal principle of justice and the large number of similarly situated people, we would be required to perform what would more properly be called supererogatory acts.[22]

But these considerations do not show that the refraining from injuring/bringing aid distinction has moral significance *in itself*. On the contrary, one would think that in certain situations where the sacrifice required to aid someone was slight and/or the number of relevantly similar cases was small, the duty to bring aid in these cases would be just as strict (in the third sense of "strictness") as the duty to refrain from injuring. (Think of a case where all one need do to save a drowning man is throw him a life preserver.) Whether the effort or risk required to bring aid in a particular case is great or small is not of paramount importance.[23] What is important is the total amount of effort or risk required if one is to treat all relevantly similar cases in the same manner. The fact that we are generally required to expend greater effort and incur greater risks to avoid harming any particular individual than we are to bring him aid can be explained on the basis of the fact that there are relatively few individuals situated in such a way that we must go to great lengths to avoid harming them while there are relatively many individuals who would benefit from even slight effort on our part to bring them aid.[24]

The apparent difference between (C_2) and (D_2) can now be accounted for. Depending upon the amount of relevantly situated people in the world and depending upon one's own financial resources, it might or might not be a stricter duty (in sense 3) to refrain from injuring than to bring aid in each of the respective cases. The reason we tend to think that it would not be a stricter duty in (D_2) is because $1 represents a rather small drain on the financial resources of most people. Given that there are relatively few people in the world whose lives could be saved by the expenditure of $1, the total burden of treating relevantly similar cases in the same way (viz., by giving a dollar) would not exceed reasonable limits. But $1000 represents a considerable drain on the financial resources of most people. Given that there are relatively many people in the world whose lives could be saved by the expenditure of $1000, the total burden of treating relevantly similar cases in the same way (viz., by giving $1000) would exceed reasonable limits—even for a Rockefeller. However, for many people a onetime expenditure of $1 (or even of $1000) would not require them to forgo their basic interests. And, for the most part, one need not risk $1 or $1000 to avoid killing someone. The apparent difference between (D_2) and (C_2) and between the alternatives in (C_2) and (D_2) are a result of important contingencies in the world. But these contingencies are not essentially attached to the refraining from injuring/bringing aid distinction.

VI. ASYMMETRIES

So far I have criticized arguments offered in support of the claim that negative duties are stricter than positive ones. I have concluded that as long as the fulfillment of positive duties does not jeopardize a person's basic interests, his duty to fulfill them is as strict as his duty to fulfill negative duties, i.e., just as much effort and risk is required in the one case as in the other. But what about cases where to bring aid would require someone to forgo his basic interests while failure to do so would have the consequence that others would be required to forgo theirs? All the cases listed above (with perhaps the exception of C_2 and D_2) appear to be symmetrical with respect to the neglect of basic interests since all the alternatives within each particular case require that someone give up his basic interests. In these cases there is no need to consider how many people are similarly situated and no need to appeal to the formal principle of justice to determine whether, in the relevant circumstances, someone's basic interests will be jeopardized. The adoption of the relevant alternative will by itself result in the death of some person and thus will require him to forgo his basic interests (if he has any).

To account for our considered judgments, which tell us that it is not morally indifferent which alternative is adopted in such cases, some have appealed to the principle that, other things being equal, it is worse (morally) to kill than to let die. This principle accounts nicely for our judgments in certain hostage (e.g., C_3) and "hospital" (e.g., C_1, C_5, C_6) cases. But there are other "hospital" (e.g., C_4) and hostage (e.g., D_3 (i) and (iii)) cases where the principle gives no guidance since both alternatives involve letting someone die. In other cases, the principle seems to give us improper guidance since D_3 (i) (an alternative that involves letting die) would be preferable to D_3 (ii) (an alternative that involves killing) by that principle. In a case similar to (D_3) but involving a runaway railway train, if the driver has to *do* something (e.g., turn a wheel, pull a lever, etc.) to steer down track A upon which one person is tied, but can remain on track B, where one person is also tied, *without doing* anything (e.g., by keeping his hands off a wheel, a lever, etc.), then by the principle under consideration he would have a greater duty to stay on B than to steer down A (other things being equal). However, I think most of us would judge that it is morally indifferent which alternative the driver adopts and that D_3 (i) deserves the same moral judgment as D_3 (ii), whatever that may be. These examples show, I think, that the killing/letting die distinction has no moral significance in itself.

However, there is another asymmetry that exists between the alternatives in all of the examples which, I believe, can account for the moral judgments we make in these cases. The asymmetry is that the death of some person will contribute to the well-being of others while the death of those others will not contribute to the well-being of the relevant person. This is easily seen in the hostage cases where it is assumed that the death of the man in the judge's custody is needed to save the hostages but the reverse is not true.[25] In these cases it seems appropriate to say that killing the man (or letting him die) is a means to saving the hostages.

But in the hospital cases (especially C_5) it is not so clear that the death of the relevant patient is a means to saving the others. In (C_1, C_4 and C_6) all one needs are the vital organs of some donor, not his death. In (C_5) all one needs is to produce a gas, the production of which happens to release lethal fumes into the room of an immobile patient, not the death of that patient. The difference between the relevant alternatives in the hostage case and those in the hospital cases is that in the former the death of some person is needed to save others while in the latter all that is needed is some act (or omission) that will inevitably lead to someone's death if performed (or permitted). To say the death, the acts or the omissions are needed means that it is only through them that there is any likelihood the relevant persons can be saved. In none of the cases is the death of someone *logically* necessary to save those whose lives are in jeopardy. The rioters could all faint and the hostages walk away unharmed, and it is possible for the needy patients to make miraculous recoveries. But in the hostage case it is a logically necessary component of a plan that must (in a non-logical sense) be adopted if the relevant people are to be saved. In the hospital cases not only is the death of someone not logically necessary to save those in need, it is not even a logically necessary component of the plan needed (in a non-logical sense) to save the dying patients. To say that something is a logically necessary component of some plan means that any proper description of that plan must be formulated in terms of that something.

Defenders of the doctrine of double effect try to exploit the kinds of differences that appear between the hostage and the hospital cases. When they do so, they rule cases like the hostage ones to be morally impermissible on the grounds that the death (or harm) to the relevant persons would be directly intended while ruling that some cases that have features in common with the hospital ones are morally permissible on the grounds that in those cases death is foreseen but not directly intended. While the doctrine of double effect can account for some of our considered judgments,[26] it can be shown to lead to absurd consequences. We can show this by modifying the hostage case. Suppose the rioters condition the release of the hostages upon the removal of all the vital organs from the body of the relevant person, rather than upon his death. Given the choice, would it be morally preferable to meet that demand rather than the one requiring the man's death? I do not see how it would or how one could even bring about the death without adopting some plan comparable to one that calls for the removal of vital organs. This modification of the hostage case suggests that there is no morally relevant difference between adopting a plan where death is logically necessary and one where it is only physically inevitable, given the successful execution of the relevant plan.

We are now in a position to formulate a principle which, I think, can account for most of our considered judgments in the relevant conflict of interest cases. The principle is that, other things being equal, it is worse (morally) to adopt a plan where the death of someone is needed (in a non-logical sense) to save another than it is to let that other die regardless of whether (a) the death is brought about through an action or an omission and whether (b) it is logically necessary or only physically inevitable, given the successful execution of the plan. While it may be the case that only where death is a logically necessary component of the relevant plan is it proper to call it a means to saving those in need,[27] given the examples offered

above, I think it is proper to say that even when death is not a logically necessary component it can nevertheless be treated *as if* it were a means to the appropriate end. In any case, it seems proper to say that *the people*, for whom death is a certain outcome upon successful execution of the relevant plan, are being used as means (only), even if their deaths are not strictly speaking means to the relevant end. To adopt a plan where someone is killed or let die for the sake of others is to treat the relevant person as a means only. To use people in that way is an affront to their worth and dignity in a way that simply letting someone die is not, given there are no means available (short of bringing about the death of another) for saving that person. This is an important consequence since it shows that not only does the principle I have offered account for most of our considered judgments, but that it also connects with important moral concepts, concepts concerning the worth and dignity of persons.

There are several ways in which the principle can be broadened. First, a more general principle concerning harming and allowing harm instead of killing and letting die can be formulated. Second, it is not really important whether the death of someone is needed to save another or not. There would not be much point in adopting a plan which called for the death of someone as a "means" to saving others if there were other plans available that would accomplish the same end without that cost (assuming complete knowledge of alternatives). Nevertheless, should a person adopt such a plan in those circumstances, it would be worse than letting the relevant person die, though, of course, the best alternative would be to adopt the plan that promised to save the dying person at little or no cost to others. We need not require that the relevant plan be the only one with any likelihood of saving the relevant people. One could be led to that conclusion because that feature happens to belong to the relevant alternatives in most conflict of interest cases involving the lives of various people. Given these considerations, the following more general formulation of the principle seems more appropriate: other things being equal, it is worse (morally) to adopt a plan which calls for harming some in order to aid others than it is to let those others be harmed regardless of whether (a) the harm to some is brought about through an action or an omission and whether (b) the harm is logically necessary or only physically inevitable, given the successful execution of the plan.

All that remains is to check the application of the principle against our considered judgments in the diabolical-machine case (D_1) and in the double-transplant case (C_1). As it stands, (D_1) is inconclusive. What our judgments would be and what the application of the above principle would yield depends on the inner workings of the machine. If pushing the button releases lethal fumes into John's chamber while not pushing it allows an already dying Mary to succumb, then I think our considered judgments would be the same as those in (C_5) and application of the principle would yield the same results. On the other hand, if pushing the button causes a railway train to steer down track A upon which John is tied, while not pushing it allows it to proceed down track B upon which Mary is tied, then I think our intuitions would tell us it makes no difference which alternative is adopted. Again, application of the principle prohibiting the use of people as a means would yield the same conclusion.

(C_1) presents a slightly more difficult case since it seems that the only thing that could account for our judgment that Jones ought to be allowed to die rather than killing Smith is that the one alternative involves letting die while the other involves killing. But I have given reasons to discount the moral relevance of the killing/letting die distinction and have explicitly discounted it in the formulation of my principle. On closer examination, though, we find that there is a relevant asymmetry in this case since it would not be proper to say Jones was let die *in order to* save Smith while it would be proper to say Smith was killed in order to save Jones should the respective alternatives be adopted. The principle I have offered says, in its more specific formulation, that it is worse to kill or let die *in order to* save others than it is to simply let those others die, other things being equal. Thus, there is an asymmetry between the alternatives in (C_1) that allows my principle to take hold and yield judgments that square with our moral intuitions.

This discussion is now complete. I have tried to show that positive duties are as strict as negative duties as long as complete fulfillment of them does not infringe upon a person's basic interests and that there is a principle available which will offer guidance where there is a conflict of basic interests. This principle has none of the disadvantages of either the doctrine of double effect or of the killing/letting die distinction. Besides yielding judgments that square with our moral intuitions, it is essentially connected to notions of personal dignity and worth. As such, it should be doubly difficult to unseat.[28]

Notes

[1]Bennett's discussion is in "'Whatever the Consequences'," p. 93.

Dinello's discussion is in "On Killing and Letting Die," *Analysis*, vol. 31 (1971), pp. 83–86. For Dinello's criticism of the way Bennett draws the killing/letting die distinction, see pp. 84–85.

[2]This account of letting die differs from Dinello's (p. 85) in that it makes no reference to what x has reason to believe, it contains a parenthetical remark explaining (c) and it includes (e). I am indebted to Fred Berger for discussions which led to this formulation and which concerned points discussed in the following paragraph.

[3]David H. Sanford has claimed that a doctor cannot be accused of letting someone die if he fails to kill a healthy person to obtain a needed heart; cp. "Killing and Letting Die," p. 3, delivered at the Western Division Meeting of the American Philosophical Association, April 30, 1976. John Casey has tried to present reasons why it would be improper to say that the doctor lets the patient die in cases of this type; cp. "Actions and Consequences" in *Morality and Moral Reasoning* (London, 1971), pp. 154–205, esp. Parks II and III (pp. 165–89). All Casey has shown, I believe, is that because of conversational or contextual implicature it is misleading or even improper to claim that the doctor lets the patient die in the relevant circumstances. But this does not show that it is incorrect to claim that, nor need such a claim be misleading if the proper qualifications are made (*e.g.*, in terms of good moral reasons).

[4]Sanford (*op cit.*, p. 4) gives reasons for requiring that y die (if x lets him die) but fails to note that y must die as a result of the relevant causes.

[5]Dinello, *op cit.*, pp. 85–86.

[6]Richard L. Trammell, "Saving Life and Taking Life," p. 116.

[7]Philippa Foot, "The Problem of Abortion and the Doctrine of Double Effect," p. 59.

[8]Foot, *ibid.*, p. 59.

[9]Foot, *op cit.*, p. 65.

[10]James Hanink fails to deal with this case in his article in defense of the Doctrine of Double Effect. To be consistent he would have to treat it as he does the case where a fat man is trapped (face pointing outward) in the only exit from a cave. We can suppose just one person (instead of several) is trapped inside the cave, which is rapidly filling with water, and that he will drown if a stick of dynamite is not discharged to blow the fat man out of the exit. For Hanink, blowing the man free does not seem intuitively wrong. Given this, I suspect his intuitions in the gas/lethal fumes case would be that it was morally permissible to produce the gas. To judge the case in that way would seem to be counter-intuitive.

See James Hanink, "Some Light on Double Effect," *Analysis*, vol. 35 (1975), pp. 147–151. See p. 149 for the case of the trapped fat man, a case that also appears in Foot, *op. cit.*, pp. 61, 69. For criticism of Hanink's position, see R. A. Duff, "Absolute Principles and Double Effect," *Analysis*, vol. 36 (1976), esp. pp. 68–69.

[11]John Harris, "The Survival Lottery," *Philosophy*, vol. 50 (1975), p. 83.

[12]Harris, *ibid.*, pp. 81, 87.

[13]Cited in Trammell, *op. cit.*, p. 120. Taken from Michael Tooley's "Abortion and Infanticide Revisited," delivered at the American Philosophical Association Meeting, Eastern Division, held in Atlanta, Georgia, December 27–29, 1973.

[14]Gilbert Harman, "Moral Relativism Defended," *The Philosophical Review*, vol. 84 (1975), pp. 3, 13.

[15]Harman, *ibid.*, p. 12.

[16]See John Rawls, *A Theory of Justice* (Cambridge, 1971), p. 139 where he points out bargaining in "the usual sense" is ruled out by the veil of ignorance.

[17]Jonathan Bennett has noted the moral significance of inevitabilities and expected inevitabilities. He has argued that the greater inevitability of harm does not *necessarily* attach to violations of negative rather than positive duties (Bennett, *op. cit.*).

[18]I say "constructed" because the argument as it stands is confused. It is not always clear whether Trammell is using "responsible" in a moral or a non-moral sense. Also Trammell's conclusion that "a person is not necessarily responsible for someone else's needing to be saved; but he is responsible for the life of anyone he kills" (p. 120) is either false, irrelevant or suffers from ambiguity depending respectively on whether "responsible" is being used morally or non-morally throughout or morally in one place and non-morally in the other.

[19]See the next section of the dischargeability of duty where legitimate limitations on moral obligations are discussed.

[20] Trammell, *op. cit.*, p. 118.

[21]Cp. Rawls's account of supererogatory acts as those that would normally be required "if not for the loss or risk involved for the agent himself," *A Theory of Justice, op. cit.*, p. 117. Cp., also, p. 439.

[22]I believe it is these three factors, *viz.*, the formal principle of justice, a large number of needy persons similarly situated, and the principle of legitimate limitations on moral obligations, that led Kant and Mill to distinguish between perfect and imperfect duties. It is not that people are not morally required to expend as much effort or incur as much risk to help the needy as to avoid injuring anyone. It is rather that the amount of effort can be distributed with a certain amount of leeway when it comes to aiding the needy, given that to try to aid everyone would lead one beyond the bounds of moral obligation. See *Utilitarianism* (New York, 1948), pp. 61–62, and for Kant's distinction between perfect and imperfect duties see *Groundwork of the Metaphysic of Morals*, tr. by H. J. Paton (New York, 1964), p. 89n.

[23]Trammell allows (p. 118) that where only minimal effort is required either to bring aid or to avoid injuring there may be no morally relevant difference between violating the respective duties. But whether there is a morally relevant difference or not can only be determined by looking beyond the particular case to other relevantly similar ones.

[24]These considerations can form the basis of an argument for moving beyond what Robert Nozick has called "the minimal state." If individuals have positive as well as negative rights (or the correlative duties), then there is no reason the state should not protect these as well. Since no individual can be required to aid all the needy people in the world, each needy person cannot have a right against any particular individual among the better-off to meet all his needs. But each needy person might have a right to have the better-off as a group meet his needs, *i.e.*, each needy person would be entitled to have his needs met by the people who comprise the better-off class, while, of course, there ought to be a fair distribution of the total burden among the members of the better-off group. See Nozick's *Anarchy, State, and Utopia* (New York, 1974), esp. pp. ix and 10 where his narrow, Lockean conception of rights is offered.

[25]Foot, *op. cit.*, p. 62.

[26]Foot, *op. cit.*, pp. 62–63.

[27]Warren Quinn criticized a point in an earlier paper of mine on the grounds that it is not strictly proper to call something a means to a given end just because, in the circumstances, it is an empirically inevitable consequence of something which is, strictly speaking, a means to that end.

[28]I would like to express my indebtedness to Fred Berger, Warren Quinn, Tom Shillock and Bonnie Steinbock whose comments on the earlier paper I delivered at the Pacific Division Meeting of the APA have helped to make this discussion better than it otherwise would have

been. Special thanks are due my ex-colleague Murdith McLean. It was he who first suggested to me that the notion of using people as means was important in the relevant conflict of interest cases. I have benefited in untold ways from the discussions we have had on this and other philosophical topics. Finally, I would like to thank Hugh Fitzpatrick for helping me to pare down to size a longer version of this paper. Of course, none of these people are responsible for any errors that may remain.

Killing, Letting Die, and Simple Conflicts

HEIDI MALM ▪ Loyola University of Chicago
Philosophy and Public Affairs, 1989

Heidi Malm considers a simple conflict case, suggested by Michael Tooley, in which a diabolical-machine contains two children, John and Mary. If one pushes a button, John will be killed but Mary will emerge unharmed; if one does not push the button, John will emerge unharmed but Mary will be killed. In this paper, Malm seeks to establish that the agent's alternatives are *not* **morally equivalent** in this case or in similar cases. The paper contains three sections.

In the first section, Malm argues that (i) in cases such as the above (in which other things are equal), killing and letting die are not morally equivalent, even though (ii) killing is not in itself worse than letting die. She suggests that (ii) can be established if there is at least one case in which other things are equal and the alternatives of killing and letting die deserve equivalent moral assessments. To this end, Malm compares Smith and Jones. Smith pushes a machine button, which he knows will result in a child's being crushed, solely because he is curious about how flat a person can be. Jones fails to push a machine button, which he knows will result in a child's being crushed, solely because he is curious about how flat a person can be. She judges that Jones deserves as much moral approbation as Smith, and concludes that killing is not in itself worse than letting die.

However, Malm maintains that killing and letting die are morally equivalent *only* if, in *every* case in which other things are equal, the options of killing and letting die deserve equivalent moral assessments. She draws attention to the distinction between the **comparison case** involving the two agents Smith and Jones and the **conflict case** (above) involving a single deciding agent who must choose between two or more alternative courses of action (killing John or letting Mary die). Malm notes that it is a necessary condition of a conflict between killing and letting die that killing changes who lives and who dies, while letting die does not. Given this claim, **killing and letting die** are "dependently morally equivalent" (i.e., equivalent in cases of simple conflict) only if the following principle (LC) is correct: "An agent is at liberty to change who lives and who dies when other things are equal." Malm claims that LC is not correct. To prove this point she argues by example that it is impermissible for an agent to change who lives and who dies unless the agent has a good reason for doing so. Based on this argument, she concludes that killing and letting die do *not* deserve equivalent moral assessments in every case. The section concludes with her suggestion that the intuition that it is impermissible for an agent to change who lives and who dies without a good reason for doing so rests on a conception of persons as noninterchangeable and on an agent's obligation to respect them as such.

In the second section, Malm seeks to undermine the suggestion that in a case involving a conflict between killing and letting die, one ought to flip a coin to decide what to do. Malm points out that in the conflict between killing John and letting Mary die, if the agent does nothing, Mary has no chance of living whereas John has every chance of living. If the agent flips a coin to decide what to do, he thereby increases Mary's chances of living but decreases John's chances of living, but doing this seems inappropriate. It treats the children unequally, and there are no moral grounds for the coin flip.

Finally, Malm argues that the **morally significant difference** between killing and letting die does not entail that the difference between acting and refraining is a morally important matter. She emphasizes that the source of the difference between killing and letting die in the conflict case described above is the impermissibility of substituting one person's death for another's, and not simply the difference between acting and refraining. She concludes by considering conflict cases in which killing and letting die do not correlate with acting and refraining, respectively, judging that the moral difference between killing and letting die remains even when the difference between acting and refraining does not.

CONSIDER THE FOLLOWING EXAMPLES:

Imagine a machine containing two children, John and Mary. If one pushes a button, John will be killed, but Mary will emerge unharmed. If one does not push the button, John will emerge unharmed, but Mary will be killed.[1]

A railway train whose brakes have just failed is headed down track A. Smith, a bystander, can divert the train onto track B by pulling a nearby lever. If Smith pulls the lever, John, who is tied on track B, will be hit by the train and killed. If Smith does not pull the lever, Mary, who is tied on track A, will be hit by the train and killed.[2]

In each of these cases the agent must either perform a positive act and kill one person, or not perform that act and allow another person to die. If we grant that other things are equal (for example, that neither person deserves to die and that each person's death would lead to the same amount of sadness in the world), then it should be clear that the agent's alternatives are morally equivalent—or so the proponents of the moral equivalence of killing and letting die seem to believe. Indeed, it is the assumed clarity of this judgment that allows these cases to be offered as evidence for that view.

But is it really clear? I once thought that it was. But I now think that the judgment that the agent's alternatives are morally equivalent is not only not intuitively obvious, but, in fact, false. Further, I think it is false for reasons other than those one would typically expect. I develop this view in Section I, arguing that in cases such as the above, other things are equal and the acts of killing and letting die are morally different. I also argue that killing is not in itself worse than letting die. In Section II I consider the suggestion that the agent ought to flip a coin to decide between the two alternatives. I argue that even if this option is available it should not be taken. In Section III, I discuss the implications of the developed view for claims about the moral significance of the difference between killing and letting die and the difference between acting and refraining. I argue that while cases such as the above require us to recognize a morally significant difference between killing and letting die, they do not require us to recognize a morally significant difference between acting and refraining.[3]

I.

The above examples are instances of what I will call "simple conflict examples." They are *conflict* examples in that they involve one situation, one agent, and a choice between two (or more) prima facie wrong acts. They are *simple,* as opposed to complex, in that unlike many other examples used in the killing—letting die debate, they lack complications that can arise from an agent's prior intention to kill or let die, heinous motives, special responsibilities, risks of harm to the agent, and the use of one person's body as a means to save another's life. In each case we need only determine whether there is a morally significant difference between performing a rather trivial positive act (such as pushing a button) that kills one person, and not performing that act and allowing another person to die. It is this factual simplicity that allows these cases to be good *test cases* for claims about the moral significance of the difference between killing and letting die.

Before discussing simple conflict examples further, I need to clarify the view that there is no morally significant difference between killing and letting die, and discuss a type of example which, I think, clearly does provide it with support.[4]

Let us call the view that there is no morally significant difference between killing and letting die the *moral equivalence principle.* It entails that acts of killing and letting die deserve equivalent moral assessments when other things are equal: the acts will be both wrong, both permissible, or both right, and the agents will be equally blameworthy, praise-worthy, or excused. One typical way to defend this view is to offer pairs of cases that are similar except that the agent in one case kills a person, while the agent in the other case lets a person die. The aim of these examples is to show that killing a person is not *in itself worse* than letting a person die.[5] Consider the following modified version of the machine example offered above:

(a) Smith walks into a room and discovers that a machine that has been set up to crush the child inside has malfunctioned. Smith knows

that he could restart the machine by pushing a nearby button, and he does so solely because he is curious to see how flat a person can be.

(b) Jones walks into a room and discovers that a machine that has been set up to crush the child inside is about to do so. Jones knows that he could stop the machine by pushing a nearby button, but he does not do so solely because he is curious to see how flat a person can be.

I will call this the "comparison version of the machine example." Comparison examples in general involve two situations and two agents, each of whom performs a prima facie wrong act. In the above example Smith pushes a button and kills a person, while Jones refrains from pushing a button and allows a person to die. All other considerations (such as the agents' motives, their lack of prior intentions, their subjective certainty of the deaths, and the risks to the agents) have been equalized. Were killing a person in itself worse than letting a person die, then we should see a difference in the moral status of Smith's and Jones's behaviors. But we do not. The acts are clearly both wrong, and Jones, it seems to me, deserves as much moral disapprobation as Smith. Thus I think that this example provides strong grounds for holding that killing is not in itself worse than letting die. I will assume throughout this discussion that this claim is correct.

An argument that is sufficient to show that killing is not in itself worse than letting die, however, is not sufficient to show that the moral equivalence principle is correct—and this is true regardless of whether we ignore, as I will throughout, the highly implausible view that letting a person die is in itself worse than killing. The former claim (that killing is not in itself worse than letting die) can be established by showing that there is at least one case in which other things are equal and the acts of killing and letting die deserve equivalent moral assessments.[6] The latter claim, on the other hand—the moral equivalence principle—entails that acts of killing and letting die deserve equivalent moral assessments in every case in which other things are equal. Thus in the absence of an argument establishing that, other things being equal, acts of killing and letting die can deserve different moral assessments only if killing is in itself worse than letting die (or letting die is in itself worse than killing),[7] the proponent of the moral equivalence principle is left to defend his view by showing that it accords with our judgments in a variety of cases in which other things are equal. With this in mind, let us return to simple conflict examples, and in particular to the conflict version of the machine example. This example was first offered by Michael Tooley in an article defending the moral equivalence of killing and letting die.

> Imagine a machine containing two children, John and Mary. If one pushes a button, John will be killed, but Mary will emerge unharmed. If one does not push the button, John will emerge unharmed, but Mary will be killed.

The agent in this case must either push a button and kill John, or not push a button and allow Mary to die. All other considerations, we can assume, are equal—neither child deserves to die, neither child was the cause of the other's being in the machine, each child's death would lead to the same amount of sadness in the world, each child would have performed the same number of good works, and so on. I will refer to this set of equivalences by saying that one child's death is "as regrettable" as the other's. If our judgments indicate that the agent's alternatives are morally equivalent, then we have further evidence that the moral equivalence principle is correct. If not, we have evidence against that view.

Before addressing this issue I need to distinguish the sorts of assessments made in conflict and comparison examples and introduce some terminology. The structural differences between conflict and comparison examples (such as the presence of one situation on the one hand and two on the other) necessitate an important *evaluative* difference, that is, a difference in the sorts of evaluations they require us to make. Comparison examples require us to assess the acts in question *independently* of one another. The task is to determine whether the acts, which are occurring in similar situations, deserve equivalent moral assessments. Conflict examples, on the other hand, require us to assess the acts in question in light of their being the *alternatives* of an agent. The task here is to determine whether there are moral grounds for preferring one act to the other given that one act must occur. This evaluative

difference suggests the following terminology regarding the moral status of acts. Let us say that two acts are *independently morally equivalent* (or "morally equivalent$_i$") if and only if those acts would deserve equivalent moral assessments were they to occur in similar situations. Let us also say that two acts are *dependently morally equivalent* (or "morally equivalent$_d$") if and only if those acts would deserve equivalent moral assessments were they the alternatives of one agent. In other words, two acts are dependently morally equivalent if and only if an agent's choice between those acts would be a morally indifferent choice.

This notion of "dependently morally equivalent" will be used frequently in the discussion that follows. It is thus worth clarifying with an example.

> John and Mary are drowning on opposite sides of a pier. Agent Smith, who cannot swim, is standing on top of the pier and has access to one life preserver. If Smith throws the life preserver to the left, John's death will be prevented and Mary will die. If Smith throws the life preserver to the right, Mary's death will be prevented and John will die. If Smith does not throw the life preserver at all, both Mary and John will die.

In this example, which, for our purposes, may be described as a conflict between letting die and letting die, the acts of throwing the life preserver to the left and throwing it to the right are dependently morally equivalent: provided that the agent performs one of these two acts, it is morally indifferent which one he performs.

Returning to the conflict version of the machine example, the question before us is this: Are the agent's alternatives of pushing the button and not pushing the button dependently morally equivalent? Tooley thinks that they are:

> In the first case one kills John, while in the second case one merely lets Mary die. Does one really wish to say that the action of intentionally refraining from pushing the button is morally preferable to the action of pushing it, even though exactly one person perishes in either case? . . . It seems to me a matter of indifference whether one pushes the button or not.[8]

(Tooley also suggests that the "best action," should the circumstances allow, would be to flip a coin to decide between the two alternatives. I will set that option aside for now, as it seems to presuppose that the acts of pushing the button and not pushing the button are dependently morally equivalent.)

At one time I thought Tooley was correct. After all, "one person perishes in either case," Mary's death is no less regrettable than John's death, and we have already seen that killing a person is not in itself worse than letting a person die. But I now think that the judgment that the agent's alternatives are morally equivalent$_d$ arises from either of two faulty approaches to the situation, and that once we see what is at stake in this example (and in simple conflicts in general) we will judge that the agent's alternatives are morally different—he ought *not* push the button.

We might arrive at the judgment that the agent's alternatives are morally equivalent$_d$ by assessing the example as if it were a comparison example. That is, we might first assess the act of pushing a button and killing a person, then assess the act of not pushing a button and allowing a person to die, and then compare those assessments to determine whether they are equivalent or different. Since neither act is independently worse than the other (as we saw in the comparison version of the machine example) we might then assume that the agent's choice between them must be a morally indifferent choice. But this approach is faulty on two grounds. First, it rests on an assumption that has not been adequately tested, namely, that two acts that are independently morally equivalent must be dependently morally equivalent as well. Second, by assessing the acts independently of one another we run the risk of ignoring considerations that arise *because* the acts conflict. This prevents us from answering, with any confidence, the central question of whether there are moral grounds for preferring one act to the other given that one act must occur.

We might also arrive at the judgment that the agent's alternatives are morally equivalent$_d$ by focusing more on the *outcomes* of the agent's alternatives than on the agent's alternatives themselves. By the "outcomes" of the agent's alternatives I mean the states of affairs in which Mary lives and John dies, and John lives and Mary dies. These outcomes are certainly morally equivalent in that neither state of affairs is morally preferable, in and

of itself, to the other. (This is entailed by the assumption that other things are equal.) It is not the moral equivalence of these outcomes that is at issue, however, but the moral equivalence$_d$ of the agent's alternatives themselves—the acts by which he produces one state of affairs rather than the other. And it does not follow, at least by logic alone, that if two acts produce morally equivalent states of affairs then those acts must themselves be dependently morally equivalent.

Let us take a closer look at the machine example. The relevant facts are (1) one child will live and one child will die regardless of what the agent does, (2) Mary is currently under a threat of death and John is not (though it is not important that Mary began in this position rather than John), and (3) the agent has it in his power to change fact 2: he can push a button and transfer the impending death from Mary to John. Fact 3 brings to the fore a point that has thus far been ignored. It is a necessary condition of a conflict between killing and letting die that the act of killing (or the act by which the agent kills) *changes who lives and who dies*, while the act of letting die does not.[9]

Once this point is noticed we see that the agent's alternatives are morally equivalent$_d$ only if his choice between pushing a button and changing who lives and who dies, and not pushing a button and leaving the situation as it is, is a morally indifferent choice. More generally, we see that in a simple conflict between killing and letting die, the agent's alternatives are morally equivalent$_d$ only if the following principle is correct:

LC: **An agent is at liberty to change who lives and who dies when other things are equal.**

If this principle is not correct, then even though killing is not in itself worse than letting die, and even though Mary's death is no less regrettable than John's death, the agent is still not permitted to transfer the impending death from Mary to John. (By an act's being "permitted" I mean that it is not the case that the agent ought not perform the act, all things considered. Were the agent's choice indifferent, then the acts of pushing the button and not pushing the button would each be permissible in this sense.)

Is this principle correct? It is not, I think, obviously so. But if it is not *obviously* correct, then this example, and simple conflicts in general, cannot do the work they were originally thought to do: they cannot support the moral equivalence principle by being cases in which it is intuitively clear that the acts of killing and letting die deserve equivalent moral assessments. Moreover, it seems to me that this principle is, in fact, *counter*intuitive.

To test LC, consider the following scenarios, in which agent Smith tries to defend his decision to you, the victim's parent. For the first scenario (which will provide contrast for the important second scenario) suppose that Smith decided not to push the button, with the result that Mary was killed in the machine and John lived. Smith now walks up to you and tells you that your daughter, Mary, is dead. When you ask what happened, he tells you about the machine and explains that while he regrets having allowed your daughter to die, he did not push the button to save her because that would have just killed another child instead. How would you react towards the agent, assuming you are not irrational with grief? Would you claim that the agent acted wrongly—that he *ought* to have pushed the button and saved your daughter? I don't think so. I think you would recognize that the agent has a morally satisfactory defense of what he did: given that one child's death is as regrettable as the other's, he had no good reason to push the button, and you have no reasonable grounds for complaint.

Now consider the alternate scenario in which you are John's parent and Smith decided to push the button, with the result that John was killed in the machine and Mary lived. Smith now walks up to you and tells you that your son, John, is dead. When you ask what happened, he tells you about the machine and explains that while he regrets having killed your son, he pushed the button and killed him because had he not done so, some other child would have died instead. Would your reaction towards the agent be the same in this case, assuming again that you are not irrational with grief? I don't think so. Your first response, I think, would be to ask the agent *why* he chose to substitute your son's death for some other child's. That is, you would demand of the agent (and I think rightly so) a justification—a good reason—for transferring the death from Mary to John. But since other things are equal, the agent cannot have a good

reason. The most he can say is that he had no good reason not to. Yet few of us would regard this as a morally satisfactory defense of what he did, and in the absence of such a defense we would judge his act to be impermissible.

The point thus far is that, in the first scenario, the fact that there was no good reason *to push* the button, because one equally regrettable death would occur in either case, provides the agent with an adequate defense of what he did. Given that fact, there are no moral grounds for arguing that the agent *ought* to have pushed the button, nor is there a need for any further defense of his not having done so. (I will return to this latter point in a moment.) In short, his act was permissible. But in the second scenario, the parallel claim that there was no good reason *not to push* the button, again because one equally regrettable death would occur in either case, does not provide the agent with an adequate defense of what he did.[10] Our judgments indicate that the agent needs a good reason *to* transfer the death from Mary to John, and not merely no good reason not to, if that act is to be permissible.

Having noted our demand for a justification (good reason) in the second scenario, we might wonder whether we should have demanded a justification in the first scenario as well. In other words, might we maintain, reasonably, that an agent needs a good reason for *not* transferring a death from one person to another if such an act is to be permissible? I don't think so. In making such a demand we would be subscribing to the principle that an agent ought to change who lives and who dies unless he has a good reason for not doing so. But that principle entails that an agent ought to change who lives and who dies when other things are equal. It is thus both inconsistent with LC (as LC permits the nonchange) and counterintuitive in its own right. It would entail that Smith ought to have killed John and saved Mary, and more generally that an agent is morally *obliged* to perform an act which, given the assumption that other things are equal, there seems to be no morally good reason to perform. Let us grant, then, that our initial judgments in the first scenario are correct: the fact that there was no good reason to push the button, because one equally regrettable death would occur in either case, renders the act of not pushing the button permissible.

It is our judgments in the second scenario that cause the problem for LC. According to those judgments, an agent needs a good reason for changing who lives and who dies if such an act is to be permissible. But when other things are equal there cannot be a good reason. Thus when other things are equal an agent is not permitted to change who lives and who dies. This is inconsistent with LC, as that principle entails that an agent is permitted to change who lives and who dies when other things are equal.

Our judgments are thus inconsistent with LC and in accordance with the following principle:

NC: It is morally impermissible to substitute one person's death for another's (change who lives and who dies) without a good reason for doing so.[11]

NC is not a very demanding principle. Though it requires that there *be* a good reason for changing who lives and who dies, it is consistent with a variety of views about what would count as a good reason. Thus a consequentialist might maintain that one extra unit of happiness is enough to permit (or even oblige) an agent to change who lives and who dies,[12] while a nonconsequentialist might demand a more justice-oriented reason (for example, A's strangling B might provide agent C with a good reason for killing A and preventing B's death). But if NC is correct, then the agent's alternative in the present case (and in simple conflicts in general) are not morally equivalent$_d$. For from the fact that other things are equal it follows that (a) the agent has no justification for transferring the death from Mary to John, and consequently (b) he *ought not do so*.

To sum up thus far, in order to maintain that an agent's alternatives are morally equivalent$_d$ in a simple conflict situation, one must hold more than that killing a person is not in itself worse than letting a person die. One must also hold that an agent is at liberty to change who lives and who dies when other things are equal—that is, that LC is correct. I have argued that LC is not only not intuitively obvious but in fact counterintuitive, in that its implications are inconsistent with our considered moral judgments. In the remainder of this section I would like to suggest why we are drawn away from LC and towards NC.[13]

As I see it, the problem with LC is not simply that it allows a change in the world that there is no good reason for making. In other words, I am not suggesting that "being the status quo" carries moral weight. If a gust of wind, or a dog's wagging tail, caused the button to be pushed, then the situation would not have gotten worse from a moral point of view. Nor am I suggesting that *an agent* needs a justification any time he makes a change in the world. Were there two rocks in the machine, or perhaps two goldfish, then I think we would judge that an agent is permitted to have the one rock crushed, or the one fish crushed, rather than the other (other things being equal).[14] Instead, the problem with LC is that it permits an agent to treat *other persons* in the same way he may treat rocks, or fish, or things in general (with respect to the present issue). LC grants agents a power or control over other persons' lives by granting agents the right to redistribute death when other things are equal. Thus an agent may redistribute death among persons because he finds one person aesthetically more pleasing than another, because he thinks one person will benefit him more than another (even though the total objective benefit would remain the same), or simply because he is bored. But an agent who redistributes death among persons for these or a variety of other nonmoral reasons[15] seems to me to be an agent who is not *respecting* those persons, each one individually, as *persons*—as moral agents in their own right. He is treating them as things that *he* may rightfully interchange, and thus as things over which he may exercise control.

LC, then, permits an agent to treat other persons as things that he may rightfully interchange. But treating other persons in this way is at best only a small step, and at worst no step at all, above treating other persons as mere objects. And since treating other persons as mere objects is inconsistent with even the vaguest understanding of "respecting other persons as persons," we have some grounds for thinking that LC is inconsistent with an obligation to respect other persons as persons: whereas LC permits an agent to treat other persons as things that he may rightfully interchange, this obligation, most likely, prohibits it. I have not, however, offered an analysis of "respect for persons" that can prove the point I am here suggesting, nor have I argued that an agent's treating other persons as things that he may rightfully interchange is in fact on a par with treating them as mere objects. So let us weaken the above claim to say that LC is inconsistent with an obligation to respect other persons as *individuals*, where by this I mean only an obligation not to treat other persons as things that an agent may rightfully interchange.

Given the above, our rejection of LC and acceptance of NC can be said to rest on a conception of persons as noninterchangeable and an agent's obligation to respect them as such. I will discuss the implications of NC for claims about the moral significance of the difference between killing and letting die in Section III.

II.

I previously set aside the agent's option to flip a coin on the grounds that as a random way to decide between two alternatives it presupposes that those alternatives are morally equivalent$_d$. I have now argued that the agent's alternatives are not morally equivalent$_d$, because the agent needs a justification for changing who lives and who dies, and no justification is available. However, if a case can be made that flipping a coin is in fact the best option—that is, if it can be argued that flipping a coin is *morally better* than not flipping it—then this argument would provide the agent with a justification for changing who lives and who dies should the flip favor that alternative. I think that no such case can be made.

When Tooley suggests that flipping a coin would be the "best" option, he adds that it would give each child an "equal chance of surviving."[16] He does not tell us just *why* it would be best, morally, to give each child an equal chance of surviving, but the most likely answer is that it would treat Mary and John equally and fairly. I think that flipping a coin does neither of these.

First, flipping a coin does not treat the children equally, for in the process of giving them equal chances for surviving, it increases Mary's chances (as she initially had no chance) and decreases John's (as he initially had every chance). In short, flipping a coin benefits Mary at John's expense. Second, flipping a coin does not treat the children fairly, for while there are cases in which it is fair to benefit one person at another's expense (for example,

progressive taxation to fund welfare programs), we expect, in such cases, a justification for treating them unequally (for example, the benefit to A is great and the cost to B small, or B was the cause of A's need). Yet in the present case there seems to be no justification for treating the children unequally. Granted, Mary does not deserve to die, nor to be where she is, but John does not deserve to die, nor to be where he is either (namely, in a position which is such that Mary lives only if he dies). Moreover, John is not at fault for Mary's peril, the cost to John is high, and the benefit to Mary is no greater than the cost to John. Thus to the degree to which flipping a coin seems fair to Mary, it seems unfair to John.

Are there any other grounds? It might be argued that flipping a coin is morally better than not flipping it because the former act makes the death a random event, at least among the current class of potential victims, Mary and John. But this argument will not succeed, because the death is a random event (at least from the moral point of view) even if the agent does not flip a coin. The initial assumption that other things are equal guarantees that either (a) the children were placed in their respective positions randomly, so that the death was a random event to begin with, or (b) whatever it was that led to Mary's being placed on one side of the machine and John on the other was morally irrelevant (for example, Mary was closer to one side of the machine than the other). If (b) is the case, then even though the death was not truly random to begin with, it was at least "morally random," in that it was random from a moral point of view, and nothing moral is to be gained by making it truly random.[17]

The preceding point can be put in terms of flipping a coin. If other things are equal then Mary and John already underwent a sort of flip of the coin (they were placed in the machine in at least a morally random way), and John won that flip. Since subjecting them to another flip of the coin cannot make a death that was morally random to begin with any more morally random (given the independence of the flips), we do not as yet have grounds for holding that the agent ought to flip a coin.

Moreover, by looking at the case in this way we see the difficulty of finding any other grounds. In order to provide such grounds one would have to show that the initial flip of the coin (that is, the initial placement of the children) was itself morally objectionable. Yet one cannot object to the occurrence of that flip, since that would imply that John *should have* been placed on one side of the machine and Mary on the other (assuming that they had to be placed in the machine at all). This is either prejudicial against John, or entails that other things are not equal. Nor can one object to the outcome of that flip, since that too would show a prejudice against John by implying that he should have *ended up* on the one side of the machine rather than the other. The only other option, it seems to me, is to argue that one flip of the coin is objectionable when two flips are possible. But this option seems to commit us to an infinite regress. For whatever would favor two flips over one should also favor three flips over two, four over three, and so on.

In summary, the decision to flip a coin and risk changing who lives and who dies is as much in need of justification as the decision to push the button. But when other things are equal, there are no moral grounds for holding that the agent ought to flip a coin, and thus no moral grounds for changing who lives and who dies.

III.

If agents are not at liberty to change who lives and who dies when other things are equal, then there is a morally significant difference between killing and letting die because there are some situations in which other things are equal and letting die is permissible but killing is not.[18] Yet this difference between killing and letting die, a difference in the effect that another moral value can have on the permissibility of the acts, does not entail that killing is *in itself worse* than letting die, in the sense of being intrinsically more evil. It is consistent with holding that when acts of killing and letting die are considered independently and with no moral reason in favor of either act (as in the comparison version of the machine example) one is as bad as the other.[19]

Nor does the present account entail that the difference between acting and refraining is in itself a morally important matter. For while the alternative of killing requires an action in the machine example, so that the action can be said to be

"worse" than the refraining (it is impermissible and the refraining is permissible), the source of the difference is the impermissibility of substituting one person's death for another's, and not the bare difference between acting and refraining. Moreover, there are other conflict situations in which the alternatives of killing and letting die *inversely* correlate with the alternatives of acting and refraining. In these cases the refraining will be worse than the action.

To show this, I need to construct a conflict example out of two separate examples. For the first example, consider the following situation, in which the agent allows a person to die only if she performs a positive act:

> *Sue is in her rowboat in the middle of the river. Because of the current she can row only downstream or to the shore. She is done fishing for the day and is about to row to shore when she looks upstream and notices a boat capsized in the distance and a tired person, Mary, swimming towards her. Sue realizes that if she stays where she is for ten more minutes (that is, if she does not row), Mary will be able to swim up to the boat and grab onto the side. This will prevent Mary's death. (Sue does not need to row Mary to shore, since a short rest will enable Mary to swim in on her own.) Sue also realizes that if she rows to shore now, or even downstream, Mary will be unable to catch up to the boat and will surely drown. Sue rows to shore and Mary dies.*

In this case Sue lets Mary die (she fails to prevent a death when she has the ability, the opportunity, and the knowledge of the ability and opportunity to prevent that death) by performing a positive act rather than by the more common means of refraining from a positive act. Now consider the following example, in which Sue kills John by refraining from a positive act rather than by the more common means of performing a positive act:

> *Sue is in her rowboat on the river. Quite some time ago she decided to quit rowing for a while so that she could read and sunbathe. Now, as she looks up from her book, she notices that her boat is drifting towards John, who is floating peacefully on a sailboard in front of her. Sue realizes that unless she rows to the right or to the left, her boat will crash into John and he will die. Sue does nothing, John is struck, and he dies.*

Though this case easily fits the standard description of "letting die," in that the agent refrained from a positive act that would have prevented the victim's death, it is, I think, a case of killing. It parallels a case in which a driver who has not had to steer or brake for some time must now do so in order to avoid running over and killing a person.[20] What distinguishes it, at least in part, from a case of letting die is the agent's contribution to the existence of the initial peril. Had Sue stayed home for the day, then John would not have been in his perilous situation, whereas Mary would have been in hers.[21] When this example is combined with the preceding one, we get the following conflict example, in which the alternatives of killing and letting die inversely correlate with the alternatives of acting and refraining:

> Sue is in her boat on the river. Because of the current, she can row only downstream or to the right. As she looks behind her and to her left, she notices a boat capsized in the distance and a tired person, Mary, swimming towards her. Sue realizes that if she refrains from rowing for ten more minutes, Mary will be able to swim up to the boat and grab onto the side. This will prevent Mary's death. Sue also realizes that if she refrains from rowing for ten more minutes her boat will drift into John, who is floating peacefully on a sailboard in front of her. This will kill John.

In this example, as in the machine example, the agent must either kill John or allow Mary to die. But here, unlike in the machine example, the alternative of killing correlates with refraining, and the alternative of letting die correlates with acting. The point of this example is to show, first, that in conflict situations in general, the alternatives of killing and letting die do not necessarily correlate, respectively, with the alternatives of acting and refraining, and second, that the fact that they do so correlate in the machine example is a morally irrelevant coincidence.

It might be objected that this second point is fully established only if the agent's alternatives are *morally* different in the rowboat example, and that it is not clear that they are. Granted, this example is more difficult to assess than the machine example because the fact that the boat is drifting towards John suggests that his life is, to some degree, already

in peril. Still, I think the moral difference between the agent's alternatives will become clear if, for each alternative, we place ourselves in the role of the victim's parent. Though Sue has a prima facie duty to prevent Mary's death, this does not provide her with a sufficient reason for killing John.

Moreover, there are other conflict situations in which (a) John's life is not already in peril, (b) the alternatives of killing and letting die are morally different, yet (c) the alternatives of killing and letting die do not correlate with alternatives of acting and refraining because both alternatives require the agent to act. Consider the following case:

> Sue is in her boat on the river on a very cold day. Having been drenched by a wake of water, she must head to either shore immediately or else she will lose all four limbs to frostbite. In the path towards the shore on her left is John (in a wetsuit) floating peacefully on his sailboard. Behind her and to her left is a boat capsized in the distance and tired Mary swimming towards her. In the path towards the shore on her right is nothing.

Sue has the following three alternatives: (1) She can row towards the shore on her right, thereby not killing John and allowing Mary to die (as Mary was unable to catch up to the boat). (2) She can row towards the shore on her left, thereby killing John but preventing Mary's death (as Mary was able to catch up to the boat). Or (3) she can refrain from rowing altogether, thereby neither killing John nor allowing Mary to die, but incurring a serious harm to her own welfare.

Were there no moral difference between killing and letting die, there would be no moral difference between alternatives 1 and 2. In each case Sue would suffer no harm and one other person would perish. But these alternatives are not morally equivalent$_d$. On the one hand, in rowing to the right Sue prevents her own harm and allows Mary to die. This alternative is morally permissible, at least given the standard view that an agent is not obliged to prevent a death when doing so would result in a significant harm to herself (and she is not the cause of the other's peril). On the other hand, in rowing to the left, Sue prevents her own harm as well as Mary's death, but she kills John in the process. This alternative is impermissible on two grounds. First, the need to prevent a serious harm to oneself does not justify the infliction of an even greater harm on an innocent other. Second, in rowing to the left, Sue is substituting John's death for Mary's with no justification for doing so. But since each alternative requires the agent to act, the moral difference between them cannot rest on the difference between acting and refraining.[22]

In summary, neither the factual difference nor the moral difference between killing and letting die rests on the difference between acting and refraining. Thus while there is a morally significant difference between killing and letting die because there are some situations in which other things are equal and letting die is permissible but killing is not, this difference is independent of the difference between acting and refraining.

Notes

I would like to thank the Editors of *Philosophy & Public Affairs* for their comments on an earlier draft of this article.

[1]Michael Tooley, "An Irrelevant Consideration: Killing versus Letting Die," p. 106. This example also plays a central role in chapter 6 of his book *Abortion and Infanticide* (Oxford: Clarendon Press, 1983).

[2]Bruce Russell discusses a similar case in "On the Relative Strictness of Negative and Positive Duties." Runaway train examples are also discussed in Philippa Foot, "Abortion and the Doctrine of the Double Effect," p. 59; Judith Thomson, "Killing, Letting Die, and the Trolley Problem," p. 67; and Nancy Davis, "The Priority of Avoiding Harm," in *Killing and Letting Die.*

[3]By "refraining" I mean the intentional nonperformance of a positive act. Also, though I will speak of *acts* of killing and letting die, I do not mean to suggest that either type of act necessarily involves the performance of positive acts. I discuss this below.

[4]"Simple conflict examples" will henceforth refer to simple conflicts between killing and letting die. There are other conflict examples that are simple, with respect to the absence of complications, but are not conflicts between killing and letting die.

[5]See, for example, James Rachels, "Active and Passive Euthanasia," p. 111.

[6]This needs to be modified. The case must be one that lacks *canceling* considerations, and should be one that lacks *sledgehammer* considerations. (I borrow the latter term from Richard Trammell, "Saving Life and Taking Life," p. 116.) For example, suppose that one agent kills a person, another agent lets a person die, and both agents are insane. Such a case cannot fairly be used to show that killing is not in itself worse than letting die, because the insanity of the agents cancels (or precludes) any difference in blameworthiness. Similarly, suppose that one agent kills a person, another agent lets a person die, both agents act from the most heinous motives imaginable, and both victims die extremely gruesome deaths. Here the heinousness of the agents' motives and the gruesomeness of the deaths may have a "sledgehammer" effect on our intuitions which prevents us from discerning a difference in the moral status of the acts or agents. I will assume throughout this discussion that these considerations are not present.

[7]James Rachels seems to assume this claim in "Reasoning about Killing and Letting Die," *The Southern Journal of Philosophy* 19 (1981). I think it is false, however, as the argument herein will show. I discuss the claim in more detail in "Directions of Justification in the Negative-Positive Duty Debate," presented at the Pacific Division meeting of the American Philosophical Association, Portland, Oregon, March 1988, and in "In Itself," manuscript.

[8]Tooley, "An Irrelevant Consideration," p. 106. It is worth noting that Tooley does not *argue* that the agent's alternatives are morally equivalent$_d$. Rather, he takes it to be intuitively obvious that they are and then uses this point to argue that there is no moral difference between killing and letting die. The success of his argument is thus dependent on the degree to which we share Tooley's intuitive judgment.

[9]One might object to this claim by offering a case in which there is only one potential victim (for example, a case in which I could shoot you while you are drowning). But in order for a case to involve an act of letting die, there must be something the agent could do to prevent the death (such as throw you a life preserver). Thus cases involving only one potential victim either do not involve (or potentially involve) an act of letting die, because there is nothing the agent could do to prevent the death, or do not involve a *conflict* between killing and letting die, because there is something the agent could do that neither kills nor lets die, namely, the act that would prevent the victim's death.

[10]I am not suggesting that there is in *fact* no good reason not to push the button, but only considering the claim that there is no good reason *because* one equally regrettable death would occur in either case. The principle I will present shortly entails that if there is not a good reason *to push* the button, then there *is* a good reason not to push the button.

[11]I use "substitute one person's death for another's" to emphasize that in order for an agent to change who lives and who dies there must be a particular person who would die, and some way for an agent to make it the case that another person dies instead. Thus NC would not be applicable to the following case. A gunman takes two

hostages. He intends to shoot hostage A, but changes his mind and shoots hostage B. Here the gunman does not change who lives and who dies, because prior to his pulling the trigger, there is no particular person who would die (a mental state alone cannot put A in a death-leading train of events), and after his pulling the trigger, no change in who lives and who dies has been made. (Martin Gunderson offered this example while commenting on a draft of this article at the Pacific Division meeting of the American Philosophical Association, San Francisco, California, March 1987). In contrast, NC would be applicable to the following case. A gunman takes two hostages. He shoots hostage A, but while the bullet is in the air, agent Smith (who is not the gunman) pushes B in front of A, so that the bullet kills B instead of A. (The reason for making Smith distinct from the gunman is to prevent our assessment of the act of shooting at a hostage from coloring our assessment of the act that changes who lives and who dies.)

[12]At least some of the less sophisticated versions of consequentialism, it seems, are inconsistent with NC and entail LC. If all that matters, for example, are the total units of pleasure and pain, then it should not matter whether an agent redistributes those units.

[13]I am not entirely satisfied with the explanation that follows. Little will rest on it, however, in the remaining sections.

[14]Of course, we may wonder why the agent would *want* to do this, but any inquiry here would, I think, be one of curiosity. It would not be a search for a moral justification. If the agent responded that he found one rock, or one fish, aesthetically more pleasing than the other, then I think we would rest content (and rest content even if, after bothering to conduct a survey, we found that for every person who had an aesthetic preference for one rock or one fish there was another person who had an aesthetic preference for the other rock or the other fish).

[15]I am assuming here that these are not morally relevant reasons. However, were it argued that they are, then "other things" would not be equal if an agent found one person aesthetically more pleasing than another, for example.

[16]Tooley, "An Irrelevant Consideration," p. 106. Tooley is a bit misleading here, since nothing can give the children *equal* chances of surviving. The facts of the case dictate that one child will have a 100 percent chance and the other no chance at any given moment. What flipping a coin can do (with the resolve to act on the flip) is give each child an equal chance *for being* the one that survives. (I will assume that that is what Tooley meant.) The difference between these two is illustrated in the following case. Three persons are stranded at sea, and it is known that a rescue boat will arrive in a week. One person, the agent, can survive another week without food. The other two, Mary and John, will die if they do not eat before the week is up. The agent has some food at his disposal, and he knows

that if he divides it between Mary and John, each will have a 50 percent chance of surviving the week. He also knows that if, and only if, he gives all the food to either Mary or John, that person will have a 100 percent chance of surviving the week. Thus the agent can (a) give Mary and John equal chances of surviving by splitting the food between them or (b) give them equal chances for being the one that survives by flipping a coin to decide which of the two receives all the food. In a conflict between killing and letting die, only option (b) is possible.

[17]Warren Quinn suggested the notion of "morally random." It is needed because the "other things being equal" clause guarantees equivalences only in morally relevant considerations. It is unproblematic because considerations that are not morally relevant are, obviously, not relevant. Thus there is no reason to prefer a truly random death to a morally random death. As an example of a case in which the death was not (at least) morally random to begin with, suppose that Mary was placed where she is because she is a little girl and whoever set up the machine wanted to kill a little girl, and John was placed where he is because the machine would not function without a counterbalancing weight. Here Mary, but not John, would be the victim of undeserved prejudice, and the moral benefit of countering this prejudice would make the option of flipping a coin (or even the option of pushing the button) morally more attractive than it would be were Mary and John either (a) equally the victims of prejudice (for example, had they been chosen from a larger group because of their race and then randomly placed in the machine) or (b) not the victims of prejudice at all (for example, had an electrical storm caused a pair of adjacent tanning booths to malfunction in such a way that freeing Mary from her booth would lock John in his).

[18]It cannot reasonably be objected that other things are not equal in the machine example because one act changes who lives and who dies and the other does not. First, this difference is a necessary condition for a conflict between killing and letting die. It is not on par with, say, a difference in risks to the agent, a difference that could be equalized but was not. Second, I have argued that *one* morally relevant consideration (the obligation to act from respect for persons as individuals), which is *equally present* with respect to both acts, effects a difference in the moral permissibility of those acts. If this entails that other things are not equal, then the claim that "other things being equal, there is no morally significant difference between killing and letting die" is trivial. It would entail that acts of killing and letting die deserve equivalent moral assessments only when there is no moral reason for giving them different assessments.

[19]The present account thus suggests that killing and letting die are morally different types of acts in that they are prohibited by nonidentical duties. The evidence for the difference between the duties is that there are some

situations in which other things are equal and a violation of one is permissible while a violation of the other is not. The source of the difference, at least for conflict cases, is a moral value external to the acts. (I develop this view in detail in "Between the Horns of the Negative-Positive Duty Debate," forthcoming in *Philosophical Studies.*)

Philippa Foot defends a similar view, though with a different basis, when she argues: "It is not that killing is *worse* than allowing to die, but that the two are contrary to distinct virtues, which gives the possibility that in some circumstances one is impermissible and the other permissible" ("Euthanasia," *Philosophy & Public Affairs* 6, no. 2 [Winter 1977]: 101). The virtues Foot has in mind are justice and charity.

[20]Of course we can *find* a positive act on which to hang the killing by tracing the agent's responsibility for the death back to her positive act of taking the boat onto the river. But we would be inclined to do this only if we already believed that Sue killed John rather than allowed him to die, and assumed that killings had to be associated with positive acts. Further, Sue took her boat onto the river in the previous case of letting die as well. Thus it is not the presence or absence of a positive act that distinguishes (or helps us distinguish) an act of killing from an act of letting die.

[21]The agent need not have *intended* to create the peril. In the present case it was the current that brought John and Sue into line. What I am suggesting is that it is a necessary condition of killing (but not of letting die) that the agent contributed to the *existence* of the peril, and a necessary condition of letting die (but not of killing) that some peril be already in existence.

There are problems, however, with saying that it is a necessary condition of letting die that the agent did *not* contribute to the existence of the peril. Suppose that Smith gives Jones poison and stands by and watches him die even though he knows that he has an antidote in his pocket and that he could easily give it to Jones. In this case Smith contributes to the existence of the peril and, it

seems, lets Jones die. One way to explain this case is to say that Smith both kills Jones and lets him die, noting that the act (or series of acts) that does each is distinct. Thus we might treat the case as if there were two agents, with Smith₁ killing Jones by giving him the poison, and Smith₂ letting Jones die by not administering the antidote. (We could then explain why we would judge Smith to be more blameworthy than an agent who starts a death-leading train of events [for example, by pulling a trigger], but then has no means to stop it.) If this is plausible then we can say that it is a necessary condition of letting die that the act (or series of acts) by which the agent lets die did not contribute to the existence of the initial peril.

[22]It might be objected that if we grant that Sue may row to shore to save her limbs, then it is her *not rowing* to the left (a refraining) that allows Mary to die, and her *rowing* to the left (an action) that kills John. Thus the example *is* one in which the alternatives of killing and letting die correlate with the alternatives of acting and refraining. In response, there are three things to notice about this example. First, in this example, unlike typical cases of letting die, the agent lets a person die *only if* she acts, and her range of options is rather limited. In typical cases, the agent may or may not act; she may stand on her head or she may do nothing, provided that she does not perform the one positive act (or one of the set of positive acts) that would prevent the victim's death. Second, while it is true that we can *describe* Sue's act of rowing to the right as her "not rowing to the left," the description we use does not determine the actual active or passive character of the act. (Consider, for example, "Bill stood up" and "Bill refrained from staying seated.") Third, an objection based on an evaluative claim about what Sue *may* do (that is, given that Sue may row to shore, and so on) does not undercut the central factual claim that Sue *has to act* if she is to let die and *has to act* if she is to kill. Thus I think this example does show that killing and letting die need not correlate with acting and refraining.

Actions, Intentions, and Consequences: The Doctrine of Doing and Allowing

Warren S. Quinn ▪ University of California, Los Angeles
The Philosophical Review, 1989

In this essay, Warren S. Quinn undertakes a discussion of the **Doctrine of Doing and Allowing (DDA)**. His aims are: 1) to find the formulation of the distinction between doing and allowing that best fits our intuitions, and 2) to find a theoretical rationale for thinking the distinction morally significant.

In the first section, Quinn illustrates the distinction between doing and allow-ing by considering two rescue cases. In Rescue I, you can save either five people who are in danger of drowning in one location or a single person who is in danger of drowning somewhere else, but you cannot save all six. In Rescue II, you can save five people who are drowning, but to do so you must drive over (and thereby kill) someone who is trapped on the road, someone who could otherwise be freed later. Quinn maintains that you are perfectly justified in saving the five in Rescue I, but that it is far from obvious that you are justified in saving the five in Rescue II. The DDA must account for these intuitions. In particular, the DDA must discriminate against one kind of agency—which Quinn calls **positive** agency—and in favor of another kind of agency—which he calls **negative** agency. Quinn warns that the distinction between positive and negative agency may or may not fall in line exactly with the traditional distinction between doing and allowing, or action and inaction. This section concludes with Quinn's consideration and rejection of proposals (like those offered by Bennett and Foot) for formulating the distinction between positive and negative agency.

In the second section, Quinn clarifies his distinction between positive and negative agency by considering two more rescue cases. In Rescue III, you are traveling on a train to rescue five who are in imminent danger of death. The driver has left you in charge of the train, and you can stop it by pulling on the brakes. You suddenly see someone ahead, trapped on the track. Unless you act, he will be killed; but if you stop the train and free the man, the rescue mission will be aborted. In Rescue IV, you are on a train on which there has just been an explosion. Since stopping the train is a complicated business that would take time, you set the train on automatic forward and rush back to the five badly wounded passengers. While attending to them, you learn that a man is trapped on the track far ahead. You must decide whether to return to the cab to save him or stay with the passengers and save them.

Quinn judges that you must stop the train in Rescue III, but that you may stay with the five passengers in Rescue IV. He identifies the difference in the two cases as one of intention: in Rescue III, and but not in Rescue IV, the train kills the man *because* of your intention that it continue forward.

Next, Quinn defines an agent's **most direct contribution** to a harmful conse-quence of his agency as the contribution that most directly explains the harm. For example, in Rescue I, our most direct contribution to the death of the one is our failure to save him (our saving the five explains the death of the one less directly), whereas in Rescue II, our act of running over the one most directly explains his death. Employing this definition, Quinn defines harmful *positive* agency as agency in which the agent's most direct contribution to the harm is an action of his own or that of some object. He defines harmful *negative* agency as agency in which the agent's most direct contribution to the harm is an inaction, or a failure to prevent the harm. Thus, allowing the single individual to drown in Rescue I is an example of negative agency, whereas driving over the single individual in Rescue II is an example of positive agency.

In the third section, Quinn applies his version of the DDA to a number of test cases. He considers several situations in which the DDA might need to be qualified to bring it in line with commonsense morality. Of particular interest is Quinn's application of the DDA to a version of the Trolley Problem in which a driver of the trolley must choose between letting the trolley run over five persons who are trapped on the track ahead, or shunting the trolley onto a different track on which there is only one person. Initially it appears that the Trolley Problem presents a counterexample to the DDA. This is because intuitively it seems permissible for the driver to shunt the trolley, but the DDA does not yield this result (since switching appears to be positive agency, whereas doing nothing seems to be negative agency). To avoid this result, Quinn argues that the driver's choice is actually between two different *positive* options, and thus the driver may act in a way that produces the lesser harm. Failing to switch the trolley is argued to be a form of positive agency, because by not switching the trolley, the driver intends that it continue forward, and ultimately this leads to the death of the five. Since the driver's most direct contribution to the death of the five can be traced to the action of an object which he controls (i.e., the trolley that he intends to continue forward), letting the trolley continue its present course is a form of positive agency.

Having thus defined harmful positive and negative agency, and having argued that our intuitions discriminate against harmful positive agency as compared to harmful negative agency, Quinn concludes by seeking a defensible rationale to support the intuitions. Citing Philippa Foot, Quinn distinguishes between **negative and positive rights**. Negative rights are rights against harmful intervention and therefore seem to proscribe harmful positive agency; positive rights are claim-rights to aid or support and therefore seem to proscribe harmful negative agency. Foot's idea is to explain the distinction between harmful positive and negative agencies by noting that, other things being equal, negative rights are harder to override than positive rights. Quinn agrees with Foot's judgment, but seeks to explain why it should be the case that negative rights are harder to override than positive rights.

After noting various possible positions concerning the strength of the precedence of negative rights over positive rights, Quinn suggests that negative rights are especially important because they protect the authority of an individual to make decisions about the things most important to him—his mind, body, and life. Positive rights are also important, but negative rights take precedence because they define the terms of moral possibility; their precedence is essential to the moral fact of our lives, minds, and bodies truly being ours. Quinn concludes by noting that this rationale is anti-consequentialist because, according to consequentialism, the main point of morality is to increase the average or total welfare within the human community whereas in Quinn's view, an equally important moral task is to specify the mutual authority and respect that are the basic terms of voluntary human association.

---

[1]SOMETIMES WE CANNOT BENEFIT ONE PERSON without harming, or failing to help, another; and where the cost to the other would be serious— where, for example, he would die—a substantial moral question is raised: would the benefit justify the harm? Some moralists would answer this question by balancing the good against the evil. But others deny that consequences are the only things of moral relevance. To them it also matters whether

the harm comes from action, for example, from killing someone, or from inaction, for example, from not saving someone. They hold that for some good ends we might properly allow a certain evil to befall someone, even though we could not actively bring that evil about. Some people also see moral significance in the distinction between what we intend as a means or an end and what we merely foresee will result incidentally from our choice. They hold that in some situations we might properly bring about a certain evil if it were merely foreseen but not if it were intended.

Those who find these distinctions morally relevant think that a benefit sufficient to justify harmful choices of one sort may fail to justify choices no more harmful, but of the other sort.[2] In the case of the distinction between the intentional and the merely foreseen, this view is central to what is usually called the Doctrine of Double Effect (DDE). In the case of the distinction between action and inaction, the view has no common name, so for convenience we may call it the Doctrine of Doing and Allowing (DDA). (Because harm resulting from intentional inaction has, typically, been allowed to occur.) Absolutist forms of either doctrine would simply rule out certain choices (for example, murder or torture) no matter what might be gained from them. Nonabsolutist forms would simply demand more offsetting benefit as a minimum justification for choices of one sort than for equally harmful choices of the other sort.

In this paper I shall examine the Doctrine of Doing and Allowing.[3] My aim is twofold: first, to find the formulation of the distinction that best fits our moral intuitions and second, to find a theoretical rationale for thinking the distinction, and the intuitions, morally significant. Both tasks are difficult, but the former will prove especially complex. What we find in the historical and contemporary literature on this topic is not a single clearly drawn distinction, but several rather different distinctions conforming roughly but not exactly to the distinction between what someone does and what he does not do. Special cases of inaction may be treated by an author as belonging, morally speaking, with the doings, and special cases of doing as belonging with the inactions. So in searching for the proper intuitive fit, we shall have to be alert to the possibility that the distinction between action and inaction (or

between doing and allowing) is only a first approximation to the distinction we really want.

In evaluating various formulations of the doctrine I shall need special test cases. These will often involve improbable scenarios and repetitive structural elements. This is likely to try the reader's patience (he or she may begin to wonder, for example, whether we are discussing the morality of public transportation). But it may help to recall that such artificialities can hardly be avoided anywhere in philosophy.[4] As in science, the odd sharp focus of the test cases is perfectly compatible with the general importance of the ideas being tested. And the DDA is, I think, of the greatest general significance, both because it enters as a strand into many real moral issues and because it stands in apparent opposition to that most general of all moral theories, consequentialism.

Before beginning, I should emphasize that both the DDE and, especially, the DDA apply more directly to moral justification than to other forms of moral evaluation. It is therefore open to a defender of the DDA to admit that two *unjustified* choices that cause the same degree of harm are equally *bad*, even though one choice is to harm and the other not to save. I note this only because some writers have looked for such pairs in hope of refuting the doctrine.[5] Take the well-known example of an adult who deliberately lets a child cousin drown in order to inherit a family fortune.[6] The act seems so wicked that we understand the point of saying that it is no better than drowning the child. But if so, how can we hold that the difference between killing and letting die matters morally?

This objection seems to presuppose that if letting someone die is ever more acceptable, *ceteris paribus* [other things being equal], than killing someone, it must be because some intrinsic moral disvalue attaches to killing but not to letting die. And if so, this intrinsic difference must show up in all such cases.[7] But the doctrine may, and I shall argue should, be understood in a quite different way. The basic thing is not that killing is intrinsically worse than letting die, or more generally that harming is worse than failing to save from harm, but that these different choices run up against different kinds of rights—one of which is stronger than the other in the sense that it is less easily defeated. But its greater strength in this sense does not entail that its *violation* need be noticeably worse.

Such relations between rights are possible because moral blame for the violation of a right depends very much more on motive and expected harm than on the degree to which the right is defeasible. Your right of privacy that the police not enter your home without permission, for example, is more easily defeated than your right that I, an ordinary citizen, not do so. But it seems morally no better, and perhaps even worse, for the police to violate this right than for me to. So there is nothing absurd in saying that the adult acts as badly when he lets the child drown as when he drowns the child, while insisting that there are contexts in which the child would retain the right not to be killed but not the right to be saved.

I.

The Doctrine of Doing and Allowing has been most notably defended in recent moral philosophy by Philippa Foot.[8] It will be convenient, therefore, to begin with two of the examples she uses to show the intuitive force of the doctrine.[9] In Rescue I, we can save either five people in danger of drowning at one place or a single person in danger of drowning somewhere else. We cannot save all six. In Rescue II, we can save the five only by driving over and thereby killing someone who (for an unspecified reason) is trapped on the road. If we do not undertake the rescue, the trapped person can later be freed. In Rescue I, we seem perfectly justified in proceeding to save the five even though we thereby fail to save the one. In Rescue II, however, it is far from obvious that we may proceed. The doctrine is meant to capture and explain pairs of cases like these in which consequential considerations are apparently held constant (for example, five lives versus one) but in which we are inclined to sharply divergent moral verdicts.

The first order of business is to get clearer on the crucial distinction that the doctrine invokes. In effect, the DDA discriminates between two kinds of agency in which harm comes to somebody. It discriminates *in favor of* one kind of agency (for example, letting someone drown in Rescue I) and it discriminates *against* the other kind (for example, running over someone in Rescue II).[10] That is, it

makes these discriminations in the sense of allowing that the pursuit of certain goods can justify the first kind of harmful agency but not the second. I shall call the favored kind of agency *negative*, since on any plausible account it is usually a matter of what the agent does *not* do. For parallel reasons, I shall call the disfavored kind of agency *positive*. But, as indicated earlier, the distinction between positive and negative agency may or may not line up exactly with the ordinary distinction between doing and allowing or action and inaction. We may discover, as we consider various special circumstances, that certain actions function morally as allowings and certain inactions as doings. So let us begin by sifting various proposals for spelling out the nonmoral difference between the two kinds of agency.

One such proposal comes from some brief passages in the *Summa Theologiae* where Aquinas could be taken to suggest that the difference between the two forms of agency is one of voluntariness.[11] In harmful positive agency, the harm proceeds from the will of the agent while in harmful negative agency it does not.[12] St. Thomas seems to think that foreseeable harm that comes from action is automatically voluntary. But he thinks that foreseeable harm coming from inaction is voluntary only when the agent could and *should* have acted to prevent it. Positive agency would therefore include all foreseeably harmful actions and those foreseeably harmful inactions that could and should have been avoided. And negative agency would include the foreseeably harmful inactions that could not or need not have been avoided.

But what kind of "should" (or "need") is this? If we take it to be moral, the doctrine becomes circular.[13] Inactions falling under positive agency are harder to justify than inactions falling under negative agency. Why? Because by definition the latter need not have been avoided while the former, if possible, should have been.

We could, however, avoid the circularity by taking the "should" to be premoral, reflecting social and legal conventions that assign various tasks to different persons. And we might think that these conventions play a central role in an important premoral, but morally relevant, notion of causality.[14] The helmsman's job is to steer the ship, and this is why we say that it foundered *because of* his careless inaction. The loss of the ship would thus be like the death in Rescue II, which happens because of what we do. And both cases would contrast with the death in Rescue I, which we do not, in the relevant sense, bring about. Voluntariness would thus be seen as a distinctive kind of causal relation linking agency and its harmful upshots in the cases of action and conventionally proscribed inaction (positive agency), but not in the case of conventionally permitted inaction (negative agency). So formulated, the doctrine would not only be clear but would have an obvious rationale. Harmful negative agency is easier to justify because in such cases the harm cannot, in the relevant causal sense, be laid at the agent's door.

I have two objections to this proposal. First, there is little reason to treat most instances of the neglect of conventional duty as positive agency. We can usually explain in other ways just why morality takes these tasks so seriously. If human communities are to thrive, people will have to perform their social roles. That is why, in a variant of Rescue I, the private lifeguard of the lone individual might not be morally permitted to go off to save the five, even though a mere bystander would be. To explain this difference, we would not also need to suppose that the private lifeguard and bystander stand in different causal relations to the person's death. There is, moreover, room to think that the special duty of the private lifeguard should be put aside, especially if his employer is a pampered rich man, and the five are too poor to afford personal attendants. But this kind of circumstance would have no justificatory force where death was the upshot of clearly positive agency. In Rescue II, for example, it would not matter that the man trapped on the road was rich and spoiled while the five were poor and worthy.

My second objection is more general. The type of proposal we are examining relationalizes the special moral opprobrium attaching to positive agency by reference to its special causal properties. Since negative agency is not, in the intended sense, the cause of its unfortunate upshots, the moral barriers against it are lower. But this leaves the doctrine open to a serious criticism. For there are other conceptions of causality according to which we are in (the original) Rescue I every bit as much a cause of death as in Rescue II. What matters, according to

these conceptions, is whether a nonoccurrence necessary for a given effect was, relative to a certain standard background, surprising or noteworthy. In this sense, we may say that a building burns down because its sprinklers failed to work, even though their failure was traceable to the diversion of water to another more important fire. That the diversion was quite proper is nothing against the claim that the failure of the sprinklers helped cause the loss of the building. And something similar holds for Rescue I. The fact that we did not save the one because we quite properly saved the others would not show that his death was not in part due to our choice.

So even if there is a causal notion that corresponds to Aquinas's idea of the voluntary, it is in competition with other causal notions that may seem better to capture what is empirically important in scientific and ordinary explanation. And it is arguable that the defense of the doctrine should not depend on a causal conception that we would otherwise do without. If the doctrine is sound it ought to remain plausible on an independently plausible theory of causation. In any case, this is what I shall assume here. So I shall grant opponents of the doctrine that the permissible inactions we are considering, no less than the impermissible actions, are partial causes of their harmful upshots. This will force me to try to make sense of the doctrine on other grounds.

But this still leaves the task of stating the nonmoral content of the distinction between harmful positive and harmful negative agency. Perhaps the difference should, after all, be put in the most simple and straightforward way, as the difference between action that produces harm and inaction that produces harm. If we think of action along the lines proposed by Elizabeth Anscombe and taken up by Donald Davidson—a conception whose basic outline I propose to adopt—individual actions are concrete particulars that may be variously described.[15] To say that John hit Bill yesterday is to say that there was a hitting, done by John to Bill, that occurred yesterday. To say that John did not hit Bill, on the other hand, is to say that there was no such hitting. Taking things this way, the distinction between harmful positive agency and harmful negative agency would be the distinction between harm occurring because of what the agent does (because of the existence of one of his actions) and harm occurring because of what the agent did not do but might have done (because of the noninstantiation of some kind of action that he might have performed).[16]

Surprisingly, most moral philosophers who write on these matters reject this way of drawing the distinction. Jonathan Bennett, a severe critic of the DDA, dismisses Davidson's conception of action without argument.[17] Most likely he minds its failure to provide a clear criterion for distinguishing action from inaction in all cases, one that would tell us, for example, whether observing a boycott (by not buying grapes) or snubbing someone (by not acknowledging his greeting) consists in doing something by way of inaction or simply in deliberately not doing something. Bennett is reluctant to assign moral work to any distinction that leaves some cases unclear, especially where there is no theoretically compelling reductionistic theory for the clear cases. But I am disinclined to adopt such a standard. Almost no familiar distinction that applies to real objects is clear in all cases, and theoretical reducibility is a virtue only where things really are reducible. In any case, the imposition of such a standard would shut down moral theory at once, dependent as it is on the as yet unreduced and potentially vague distinctions between what is and is not a person, a promise, an informed consent, etc.

But Bennett is not simply negative. He proposes an ingenious and, for limited applications, clearly drawn distinction between positive and negative *facts* about agency as a respectable way of formulating the doctrine.[18] (Not of course to save it, but to expose it.) Roughly speaking, an event is brought about by someone's positive instrumentality, as Bennett calls it, when the event is explained by a relatively strong fact about the agent's behavior—for example, that he moved in one of a limited number of ways. Negative instrumentality, on the other hand, explains by reference to relatively weak facts about behavior—for example, that the agent moved in any one of a vast number of ways.

The trouble is that this distinction gets certain cases intuitively wrong. Bennett imagines a situation in which if Henry does nothing, just stays where he is, dust will settle and close a tiny electric circuit which will cause something bad—for example, an explosion that will kill Bill.[19] If Henry does nothing, he is by Bennett's criterion positively

instrumental in Bill's death. (For only one of Henry's physical actions, staying still, will cause the death, while indefinitely many will prevent the death.) But suppose Henry could save five only by staying where he is—suppose he is holding a net into which five are falling. Surely he might then properly refuse to move even though it means not saving Bill. For his agency in Bill's death would in that case seem negative, much like that in Rescue I.

Bennett also misses the opposite case. Suppose the device will go off only if Henry makes some move or other. In that case his instrumentality in the death would, for Bennett, be negative. But those who would rule out Rescue II would surely not allow Henry to go to the rescue of five if that meant setting off the device. For his agency in the death of Bill would in that case seem positive.[20] Bennett's distinction, however admirable in other ways, is not the one we seem to want. Perhaps this is already clear when we reflect that, according to him, the instrumentality of someone who intentionally moves his body (in, for example, following the command "Move in some way or other—any way you like!") is negative.

Philippa Foot also rejects the idea that the distinction between positive and negative agency is that between action and inaction.[21] She claims that it would not make any interesting moral difference if respirators (presumably sustaining patients who would otherwise die) had to be turned on again each day. Active turning off and passive not turning on would be morally the same. To be relevant to the present issues, her idea must be that this would not make a difference even in cases where some great good could come about only if a particular respirator were not running. Let us see whether this is right. Suppose there are temporary electrical problems in a hospital such that the five respirators in Ward B can be kept going only if the one in Ward A is off. On Foot's view it should not matter whether a hospital attendant keeps the five going by shutting down the one or, in case it is the kind that needs to be restarted, by simply not restarting it.

It would be very odd to think that if the single respirator were already off, the attendant would be required to restart it even if that meant shutting down the five in Ward B. So Foot's idea must imply that if the single respirator were running, the attendant could just as properly shut it down to keep the others running. Now while there seems something more objectionable about shutting the respirator down, I think that all things considered it might be permitted. One reason is that we could perhaps see it as a matter of the hospital's allocating something that belongs to it, a special kind of circumstance that we shall consider later. But suppose the hospital is an unusual one in which each patient must provide his own equipment and private nursing care. Suppose further that you are an outsider who happens for some reason to be the only person on the scene when the electrical problem arises. In this case, it seems to matter whether you keep the respirators in Ward B going by not restarting the one in Ward A (it being of the type that needs restarting and the private nurse having failed to show up that day) or whether you actually shut it down. The first case seems rather like Rescue I and the second uncomfortably like Rescue II.

Foot goes on to offer what she takes to be a different and better interpretation of the distinction. She thinks what matters is not the difference between action and inaction but the difference between two relations an agent can have to a sequence of events that leads to harm. It is one thing to *initiate* such a sequence or to *keep it going*, but quite another to *allow it to complete itself* when it is already in train.[22] Agency of the first two kinds is positive, while agency that merely allows is negative. One problem with this account arises when we try to explain the difference between allowing a sequence to complete itself and keeping it going when it would otherwise have stopped. We might have thought that the former was a matter of doing nothing to stop it and the latter was a matter of doing something to continue it. But that would seem to take us back to the rejected distinction between action and inaction.

Another problem concerns forms of help and support which do not seem to consist in keeping already existing dangerous sequences at bay. Suppose I have always fired up my aged neighbor's furnace before it runs out of fuel. I haven't promised to do it, but I have always done it and intend to continue. Now suppose that an emergency arises involving five other equally close and needy friends who live far away, and that I can save them only by going off immediately and letting my

neighbor freeze. This seems to be more like Rescue I than Rescue II, but it doesn't appear to be a case in which I merely allow an already existing fatal sequence to finish my neighbor off. For he was not already freezing or even, in some familiar sense, in danger of freezing before the emergency arose. Or if we think he was in danger, that danger was partly constituted by what I might fail to do. We might simply stipulate, of course, that any fatal sequence that appears to arise from a *failure* to help someone is really the continuation of a preexisting sequence. But then we seem to be falling back on the notion of inaction as fundamental.

II.

I am therefore inclined to reject Bennett's and Foot's positive suggestions, despite their obvious attractions. May we then return to the simple and straightforward way of drawing the distinction, as between harm that comes from action and harm that comes from inaction? I think not. Cases involving the harmful *action of objects or forces* over which we have certain powers of control seem to demand a more complex treatment.[23] Consider, for example, the following variant of Rescue II (call it Rescue III). We are off by special train to save five who are in imminent danger of death. Every second counts. You have just taken over from the driver, who has left the locomotive to attend to something. Since the train is on automatic control you need do nothing to keep it going. But you can stop it by putting on the brakes. You suddenly see someone trapped ahead on the track. Unless you act he will be killed. But if you do stop, and then free the man, the rescue mission will be aborted. So you let the train continue.

In this case it seems to me that you make the wrong choice. You must stop the train. It might seem at first that this is because you occupy, if only temporarily, the role of driver and have therefore assumed a driver's special responsibility to drive the train safely. But, upon reflection, it would not make much moral difference whether you were actually driving the train or merely had access to its brake. Nor would it much matter whether you were in the train or had happened upon a trackside braking device.[24] The important thing from the standpoint of your agency is that you *can* stop the train and thereby prevent it from killing the one.

But this is not the only thing that matters, as can be seen in a different kind of case. Suppose, in a variant of Rescue I (Rescue IV), you are on a train on which there has just been an explosion. You can stop the train, but that is a complicated business that would take time. So you set it on automatic forward and rush back to the five badly wounded passengers. While attending to them, you learn that a man is trapped far ahead on the track. You must decide whether to return to the cabin to save him or stay with the passengers and save them.

May you stay? I think you may.[25] We would be more tolerant of inaction here than in Rescue III. And this is because of your intentions. In Rescue III you intend, in a strong sense that implies desire for and not merely toleration of, an action of the train that in fact causes the man's death, its passing over the spot where he is trapped.[26] Not, of course, because he is trapped there. But because the train must pass that spot if the five are to be saved. In Rescue IV, however, things are different. In that case you do not in that strong sense intend any action of the train that leads to the man's death. The purposes for which you act would be just as well served if the train's brakes were accidentally to apply themselves.

In Rescue III, but not in Rescue IV, the train kills the man *because* of your intention that it continue forward. This implicates you, I believe, in the fatal action of the train itself. If you had no control, but merely wished that the rescue would continue—or if, as in Rescue IV, you had control but no such wish—you would not be party to the action of the train. But the combination of control and intention in Rescue III makes for a certain kind of complicity. Your choice to let the train continue forward is strategic and deliberate. Since you clearly *would* have it continue for the sake of the five, there is a sense in which, by deliberately not stopping it, you *do* have it continue. For these reasons your agency counts as positive.

The surprise in this is that we must bring the distinction between what is intended and merely foreseen into the DDA. But the two doctrines do not therefore merge. As I shall try to show in another paper, the DDE depends on something different—on whether or not a victim is *himself*

an intentional object, someone whose manipulation or elimination will be useful. But the victim is not in that way involved in the special kind of positive agency we find in Rescue III. What is intended there is not something for him—that he be affected in a certain way—but some action of an object that (foreseeably but quite unintentionally) leads to his death.

To the idea of positive agency by action, we must therefore add positive agency by this special kind of inaction. But this is, I think, the only complication we need to build into the doctrine itself. (Other more minor qualifications will be discussed in the next section.) We may now construct the doctrine in stages, starting with some definitions. An agent's *most direct contribution* to a harmful upshot of his agency is the contribution that most directly explains the harm. And one contribution explains harm more directly than another if the explanatory value of the second is exhausted in the way it explains the first.

In the absence of special circumstances involving the actions of objects, an agent's contributions to various effects in the world are those of his voluntary actions and inactions that help produce the effects. So in ordinary cases, his most direct contribution to any effect is the action or inaction that most directly explains the effect. In Rescue I, for example, our most direct contribution to the death of the one is our failure to save him. Our going off to save the five contributes less directly. For it explains the death precisely by explaining the failure to save.[27] In Rescue II, on the other hand, our most direct contribution to the death of the man trapped on the road is our act of running him over.

In special circumstances, that is, where harm comes from an active object or force, an agent at the controls may by inaction contribute [to] the harmful action of the object itself. This, as we have seen, happens just in case the object harms because the agent deliberately fails to control it and he fails to control it because he wants some action of the object that in fact leads to the harm. Having defined this much, the rest is straightforward. Harmful positive agency is that in which an agent's most direct contribution to the harm is an action, whether his own or that of some object. Harmful negative agency is that in which the most direct contribution is an inaction, a failure to prevent the harm.

III.

We should now look briefly at certain kinds of cases in which common-sense morality seems to qualify the doctrine as I have just described it, permitting us to harm or even kill someone in order to help others. I am not thinking here of the avoidance of great catastrophes. The doctrine, as already indicated, need not be absolutist. And even in its nonabsolutist form, it cannot contain everything of moral relevance. Special rights to do that which produces harm and special duties to prevent harm must also be factored in. In this way the doctrine has the force of one important *prima facie* principle among others. Rights of competition, to give a familiar example, legitimate certain kinds of harmful positive agency—such as the shrewd but honest competition in which you take away another person's customers. The right to punish is another familiar example. On the other side, special duties to aid may arise from jobs, contracts, natural relations, or from the fact that someone's present predicament was of your making.[28] These special duties explain why some instances of negative agency seem no easier to justify than active harmings.

These familiar rights and duties do not require that the doctrine be qualified. They merely oppose it in particular cases. But other situations seem either to require special amendments to my definitions of positive and negative agency or to show that in certain situations the doctrine lacks its usual *prima facie* force. Qualifications of the first sort sometimes seem required where harm arises from the active *withdrawal* of aid. In one kind of case you actively abort a project of rescuing or helping that, knowing what you now know, it would have been wrong to undertake. For example, you stop the train in Rescue III, and the five therefore die. In another kind of case, you remove something from where it would help fewer to where it would help more, for example, a raft that is presently within the reach of one drowning victim but that could be moved to the vicinity of several other victims.[29] The object might be your body. You might, for example, cushion the fall of one baby if you stay where you are, but cushion the fall of several others if you move. In all these cases harm comes to someone because you decide to act rather than to do nothing. But because your action is a certain kind of withdrawing of aid, it naturally enough seems to count as negative agency.

In other cases, harmful positive agency seems to lack some of the *prima facie* opprobrium that usually attaches to it. Sometimes this is because the harm would have been avoided but for some blameable fault of the person harmed. Suppose, for example, that the person in Rescue II who blocks the road had been repeatedly warned not to stray where he might interfere with important rescue efforts. If so, we might feel somewhat more justified in proceeding with the rescue (although never, I think, as justified as we feel in Rescue I). People must, after all, accept some responsibility for the predicaments they stupidly and wrongly bring upon themselves.[30]

In a quite different kind of case, someone may have a special liability to be harmed by a physical or psychological interaction that is generally innocuous and, therefore, of no general moral significance. He might have a rare disease that makes any kind of physical contact very harmful to him. Or he might become dangerously hysterical if we yell in his presence. In such cases we might feel that we could try to save other people from some serious danger even if it would mean brushing up against him or yelling. For, unlike standard instances of harmful positive agency, the attempt would not seem to count as an aggression against the victim, since he does not suffer because of any *general or typical* liability to harm. And this seems sensible. Morality must to some degree reflect the standard human condition. In particular, it must be capable of defining a class of presumptively innocent actions.[31]

Another qualification concerns large public and private objects, like the building of skyscrapers, highways, and dams. We are clearly permitted to help initiate such projects even though we know that in their course some deaths or injuries are practically inevitable. For one thing, the harm is usually remote from what we do. And, more important, the actual harm will generally have been preventable, and its occurrence will be much more directly traceable to the wrongful agency of persons more immediately concerned. It is of course essential that we do not in any way intend the harm that may occur, and take reasonable precautions to prevent it.

In the celebrated Trolley Problem, we seem to find yet another exception to the doctrine's strictures against harmful positive agency.[32] In this case a runaway trolley threatens five who are trapped on the track where it is now moving. If the driver does nothing the five will die. But he can switch to a side-track where only one person is trapped. Most people think the driver may switch tracks. But switching is positive agency while doing nothing appears to be negative agency. So the case looks like a counterexample.

But if we look again, we can see that the driver's passive option, letting the train continue on the main track, is really a form of positive agency. This is because the only possibly acceptable reasons for him not to switch would be to prevent the death of the man on the side-track or to keep clean hands. But the clean-hands motive begs the question; it presupposes that the doctrine does not also speak against not switching. So in deciding the status of his possible inaction we must put this motive aside. This leaves the aim of preventing the death of the man on the side-track. But if the driver fails to switch for this reason, it is because he intends that the train continue in a way that will save the man. But then he intends that the train continue forward past the switch, and this leads to the death of the five. So, by my earlier definitions, his choice is really between two different positive options—one passive and one active.[33] And that is why he may pick the alternative that does less harm. Properly understood, Trolley Cases are no exception to the doctrine.

IV.

Perhaps we have found the basic form of the doctrine and the natural qualifications that, when combined with other plausible moral principles, accurately map our moral intuitions. But someone will surely object that intuitiveness and correctness are different things and that intuitions about particular kinds of cases may reflect nothing more than conditioning or prejudice. What we need, therefore, is a more philosophical defense of the doctrine, a rationale that can be called upon to support the intuitions. Foot locates a kind of rationale in the

distinction, borrowed from the law but applied to morality, between negative and positive rights. Negative rights are claim rights against harmful intervention, interference, assault, aggression, etc. and might therefore naturally seem to proscribe harmful positive agency, whether by action of the agent himself or by action of some object to which, by strategic inaction, he lends a hand. Positive rights, on the other hand, are claim rights to aid or support, and would therefore seem to proscribe harmful negative agency. Foot's idea seems to be that general negative rights are, *ceteris paribus*, harder to override than general positive rights.[34] And while this seems intuitively correct, it is not obvious why it should be so.

The thesis that negative rights are harder to override immediately implies that negative rights take precedence over positive rights. And it is the thesis of precedence that matters most to us, since it applies directly to circumstances, such as the ones we have been considering, in which the two kinds of rights compete with each other—situations in which the positive rights of one person or group can be honored just in case the negative rights of another person or group are infringed. In Rescue II, for example, the positive rights of the five to be saved from death compete in this way with the negative right of the trapped person not to be killed.

The weakest thesis of precedence would hold that in such oppositions the negative rights prevail just in case the goods they protect (the goods that would be lost if they were overridden) are at least as great as the goods protected by the positive rights (the goods that would be lost if they were overridden). The goods in question are life, health, freedom from injury, pleasure, *de facto* liberty, etc.—goods that do not include or presuppose the moral good of respect for any of the rights in conflict.[35] All other things being equal, the weakest thesis of precedence would forbid us to kill one person to save another, but would permit us to kill one in order to save two.

A very strong thesis of precedence, on the other hand, would rule out any infringement of certain very important negative rights (for example the right not to be killed or the right not to be tortured) no matter what positive rights were in competition with them. This would still allow positive rights protecting more important goods to prevail over negative rights protecting less important goods—would permit us, for example, to knock one person down in order to save another from serious injury. But it would not permit us, for example, to kill or torture one to save any number of others even from death or torture.

A perhaps more plausible intermediate thesis would hold that no negative rights are absolute, but would accord to the most important ones considerably more force than they have on the weakest thesis. Such a view might well accommodate the ordinary thought that while someone may not be killed to save five, he might be killed to stave off the kinds of disasters that consequentialists dream up. It might go on to state some kind of criterion for when negative rights must give way; or it might, in Aristotelian fashion, leave the matter to moral perception.[36]

If, on the other hand, negative rights do not take precedence over positive rights then either the reverse is true or neither takes precedence over the other. If positive rights actually take precedence, then we might, as seems absurd, kill two to save one. Suppose one person is drowning and two are trapped on the road. A morality that permitted us to run over and kill the two in order to save the one seems not only odious but incoherent. For once we have decided to kill the two, we have placed them in at least as much danger as the one was in originally. And that would presumably activate their positive rights to be saved from their predicament—rights that would collectively outweigh the positive rights of the one who is drowning.

If there is going to be precedence, it clearly has to be precedence of negative rights. But this leaves open the possibility that neither kind of right takes precedence over the other, that is, that in the competitions we are considering the rights protecting the greater balance of good should, *ceteris paribus*, prevail. In such a moral system the person trapped on the road in Rescue II could not with moral authority object to our running over and killing him. For we shall be saving five others each of whom values his life just as much as he values his. This moral system is perfectly coherent. But it has unappealing aspects.

In such a morality the person trapped on the road has a moral say about whether his body may be destroyed only if what he stands to lose is greater than what others stand to gain. But then surely he has no real say at all. For, in cases where

his loss would be greater than the gain to others, the fact that he could not be killed would be sufficiently explained not by his authority in the matter but simply by the balance of overall costs. And if this is how it is in general—if we may rightly injure or kill him whenever others stand to gain more than he stands to lose—then surely his body (one might say his person) is not in any interesting moral sense *his*. It seems rather to belong to the human community, to be dealt with according to its best overall interests.

If it is morally his, then we go wrong if, against his will, we destroy or injure it simply on the ground that his loss will be less than the gains of others. The same is true of his mind. If we may rightly lobotomize or brainwash him whenever others will gain more than he will lose, then his mind seems to belong not to him but to the community. There is an obvious parallel here with his different, and much less important, relation to his property. An object does not belong to him if he may have and use it, and others may not take it from him, only as long as his keeping it would be better for him than his losing it would be for them.[37] Whether we are speaking of ownership or more fundamental forms of possession, something is, morally speaking, his only if his say over what may be done to it (and thereby to him) can override the greater needs of others.[38]

A person is constituted by his body and mind. They are parts or aspects of him. For that very reason, it is fitting that he have primary say over what may be done to them—not because such an arrangement best promotes overall human welfare, but because any arrangement that denied him that say would be a grave indignity. In giving him this authority, morality recognizes his existence as an individual with ends of his own—an independent *being*.[39] Since that is what he is, he deserves this recognition. Were morality to withhold it, were it to allow us to kill or injure him whenever that would be collectively best, it would picture him not as a being in his own right but as a cell in the collective whole.[40]

This last point can be illustrated not by thinking of bodies or minds but of lives. The moral sense in which your mind or body is yours seems to be the same as that in which your life is yours. And if your life is yours then there must be decisions concerning it that are yours to make—decisions protected by negative rights. One such matter is the choice of work or vocation. We think there is something morally amiss when people are forced to be farmers or flute players just because the balance of social needs tips in that direction. Barring great emergencies, we think people's lives must be theirs to lead. Not because that makes things go best in some independent sense but because the alternative seems to obliterate them as individuals. This obliteration, and not social inefficiency, is one of the things that strikes us as appalling in totalitarian social projects—for example, in the Great Cultural Revolution [China, 1965–68].

None of this, of course, denies the legitimate force of positive rights. They too are essential to the status we want as persons who matter, and they must be satisfied when it is morally possible to do so. But negative rights, for the reasons I have been giving, define the terms of moral possibility. Their precedence is essential to the moral fact of our lives, minds, and bodies really being ours.

But it might be objected that the weakest thesis of precedence would give us some degree of moral independence, and at the same time would let us do the maximum good, honoring as many positive rights as possible. On that thesis, it would not be proper to kill one person to save another who is equally happy and useful—it would not be proper, say, to flip a coin. But it could be right to kill one to save two or even five to save six. Why then adopt a stronger thesis? The answer, I think, depends on how important the relevant forms of legitimate control are to us—the extent to which we wish to belong, in the sense under discussion, to ourselves.[41] And this might depend on the aspect of ourselves in question.

We feel, I believe, most strongly about assaults on our minds. Here most of us are far from minimalists about the precedence of negative rights. The idea that against our will we could justifiably be brainwashed or lobotomized in order to help others cuts deeply against our sense of who and what we are. Here it seems the sense of our own rightful say leads almost to absolutism. We feel less strongly about our persons (at least those parts that do not directly affect our minds) and labor. But even here we wish, I think, to have a kind of defensive say that goes far beyond the weakest thesis of

precedence. A system that gave you some authority over what might be done to you but allowed us to kill or injure you whenever that would even slightly maximize the overall good would seem a form of tokenism.

It must be said that something like the precedence of negative rights can be accepted by a certain kind of consequentialist—one who thinks that a person's having an effective say over what is done to him (but not over what is done to others) is, in itself, a kind of good that can be added to the more familiar goods of life or happiness.[42] This kind of consequentialism would grant each of us a kind of special authority against interference. But it is unclear that it would thereby give us the moral image of ourselves we think fitting. For it locates the ultimate ground of proper deference to a person's will in the fact that such deference maximizes the general balance of good. In such a system, it is not so much his right to have his way that really matters as the general goodness of letting him have his way.

A consequentialist might reply that anything other than a consequentially grounded system of rights leads to absurdities, and that in praising the virtues of a rights-based morality I can be saying no more than that there is value in the social influence of such a system—that it is good if people's rights are respected and bad if they are violated. But circumstances can arise in which respecting someone's negative rights will lead to an abuse of the negative rights of others. And in at least this kind of case it would be incoherent, the consequentialist will insist, to suppose that negative rights can override their positive counterparts.[43] Suppose B and C will be murdered unless we murder A. A has a negative right against our murdering him, and B and C have positive rights that we help prevent their being murdered. If the ground of the system of rights lies in the value of respect for (or at least nonviolation of) rights, then surely the positive rights of B and C must prevail. For only by murdering A can we maximize the value that the entire system aims at.

But this objection misses the mark. The value that lies at the heart of my argument—the appropriateness of morality's recognizing us as independent beings—is in the first instance a virtue of the moral design *itself*. The fittingness of this recognition is not a goal of action, and therefore not something that we could be tempted to serve by violating or infringing anybody's rights. It is also true, of course, that we think it good if people actually respect each other's rights. But this value depends on the goodness of the moral design that assigns these rights. It is not that we think it fitting to ascribe rights because we think it a good thing that rights be respected. Rather we think respect for rights a good thing precisely because we think people actually have them—and, if my account is correct, that they have them because it is fitting that they should. So there is no way in which the basic rationale of a system of rights rules it out that a person might have a right not to be harmed even when harming him would prevent many others from being harmed in similar ways.

The rationale that I have proposed is anticonsequentialist not only in its assignment of priority to negative rights, but also, and more fundamentally, in its conception of the basic social function of morality. For consequentialism, it seems fair to say, the chief point of morality is to make things go better overall—to increase average or total welfare within the human community. But on the view presented here, an equally basic and urgent moral task is to define our proper powers and immunities with respect to one another, to specify the mutual authority and respect that are the basic terms of voluntary human association. The doctrine we have been discussing addresses this task directly. And this is why it is far more than a casuistical curiosity. Whether we ultimately agree with it or not, we should recognize that, in giving each person substantial authority over what can rightly be done to him, the doctrine conveys an important and attractive idea of what it is to be a citizen rather than a subject in the moral world.

Notes

[1] Thanks to Rogers Albritton, Tyler Burge, Philippa Foot, Matthew Hanser, Thomas Nagel, Michael Thompson, Derek Parfit, T. M. Scanlon, and to the editors of *The Philosophical Review* for valuable suggestions and criticisms.

[2] Harm here is meant to include any evil that can be the upshot of choice, for example, the loss of privacy, property, or control. But to keep matters simple, my examples will generally involve physical harm, and the harm in question will generally be death.

[3] I shall examine the DDE in a subsequent paper, "Actions, Intentions, and Consequences: The Doctrine of Double Effect."

[4] Think of Gettier cases, brain transplants, teletransporters, etc.

[5] For example, Michael Tooley in "Abortion and Infanticide," *Philosophy and Public Affairs* 2 (1972), p. 59.

[6] From James Rachels, "Active and Passive Euthanasia," p. 111.

[7] In "Harming, Not Aiding, and Positive Rights," *Philosophy and Public Affairs* 15 (1986), pp. 5–11, Frances Kamm rightly makes us distinguish between two ways in which killing might be intrinsically worse than letting die: a) killing might have some bad essential feature that cannot attach to letting die or b) killing might have some bad essential feature that, while not essential to letting die, can nevertheless be present in cases of letting die. If (b) is true then the moral equivalence of the two cases in which the child drowns would not establish a general moral equivalence between killing and letting die. For letting the child drown might be a special case in which letting die has the bad feature essential to killings but not to lettings die. And even apart from Kamm's point, the idea that intrinsically nonequivalent parts must always make an overall evaluative difference when embedded in identical contexts seems wrong. Consider aesthetics. There may certainly be important intrinsic aesthetic differences between two lampshades even though they create an equally bad overall impression when placed on a certain lamp.

[8] In "The Problem of Abortion and the Doctrine of the Double Effect," p. 59, Foot argued that the distinction between doing and allowing could do all the work usually credited to the distinction between the intentional and the merely foreseen. In "Killing and Letting Die," Jay Garfield, ed., *Abortion: Moral and Legal Perspectives* (Amherst, Mass.: University of Massachusetts Press, 1984), pp. 178–185 and even later in "Morality, Action and Outcome," in Ted Honderich, ed., *Morality and Objectivity* (London, England: Routledge and Kegan Paul, 1985), pp. 23–38, she withdraws this claim, arguing instead that any intuitively adequate morality must assign an independent moral significance to the distinction between doing and allowing.

[9] From "Killing and Letting Die."

[10] It seems clear that an agent's *not* doing something (for example, not saving someone from drowning) can be morally evaluated as justified, unjustified, right, or wrong, in precisely the sense in which these terms apply to actions. I shall therefore speak of assessing the justification or the rightness of someone's *agency* in some matter, meaning by this an evaluation of his knowingly acting or not acting.

[11] *Summa Theologiae* XVII (Cambridge, England: Blackfriars, 1970), la2ae Q. 6 article 3, pp. 15–16. The

terms "positive agency" and "negative agency" are not, of course, St. Thomas's. This is the interpretation that he might give to them.

[12]In speaking of an inaction as harmful or as producing harm (or in speaking of harm as coming from it) I am not begging the question against Aquinas. For I mean these expressions only in the weak sense of connecting the inaction with a harmful upshot, and not in any sense that would imply that the harm was voluntary.

[13]It may be, of course, the Aquinas's account of the voluntary is not meant as part of the theory of justification and is therefore not directed to the distinction between positive and negative agency. It might instead be part of the theory of praiseworthiness and blameworthiness, which presupposes an independent account of what can and cannot be justified. If so, there could be no charge of circularity. For harmful inaction clearly does deserve blame only if it could and should, morally speaking, have been avoided.

[14]I am indebted here to Michael Thompson, who thinks that something like this is suggested in the work of Elizabeth Anscombe.

[15]G. M. A. Anscombe, *Intention* (second edition) (Oxford, England: Blackwell, 1963), especially sec. 26, pp. 45–47. See also Donald Davison, *Essays on Actions and Events* (Oxford, England: Clarendon Press, 1980). See there "The Logical Form of Action Sentences," pp. 105–122; "Criticism, Comment and Defence," pp. 122–144, esp.pp. 135–137; and "The Individuation of Events," pp. 163–180.

[16]What I see as right in the Anscombe-Davidson view is the suggested metaphysics—the claim that action is a matter of the presence of something and inaction a matter of its absence. And I think that our intuitions about whether something is an action or inaction as we think about it morally are metaphysically relevant. So I am not greatly worried that someone pursuing the Anscombe-Davidson line might discover criteria of action and inaction that would radically conflict with our judgments in moral thought.

[17]"Morality and Consequences," *The Tanner Lectures on Human Values* II (Salt Lake City, Utah: University of Utah Press, 1981), pp. 54–55.

[18]*Ibid.* pp. 55–69.

[19]*Ibid.* pp. 66–68. If Henry's body were *activating* the device—if he were depressing a trigger or conducting a current—we might see his agency as positive despite his motionlessness. But Bennett doesn't assign any such role to Henry's body.

[20]That Bill's death would in this case be a side-effect of the rescue does not distinguish it from Rescue II. For in neither case is the death of the one intended. It might be objected that here but not in Rescue II the killing would not be *part* of the rescue. But if Henry's movement

sets off the explosion (for example, by triggering a fuse sensitive to movement) then Henry's killing Bill does seem part of the rescue, at least in the sense that he kills Bill by the very movements that form part of the rescue attempt. Of course there could be circumstances in which Henry's movement would not so much set off the explosion as allow it to be set off. Suppose, for example, Henry's remaining where he is prevents dust from settling upon and thereby triggering an explosive device below him. In such a case, I agree that he might go off to save the five. For although he will be active in Bill's death, his agency will involve taking his body from where it would save Bill to where he can make use of it to save the five, a special circumstance that I shall discuss later.

[21]"Morality, Action and Outcome," p. 24.

[22]*Ibid.*, p. 24, including footnote 2 on p. 37.

[23]I have in mind machines or devices (e.g., guns, x-ray machines, and vehicles) and natural objects or forces that are now usefully tamed by having been brought under man-made positive and negative controls (e.g., dams with flood-gates). The leading idea here is that of objects or forces of which it can be said that *we are in fact at their controls*, or at least at one of their controls. In such cases this *de facto* relation can make the objects into something like our agents, thereby opening the possibility of inactive positive agency through the deliberate failure to restrain them. This way of looking at things does not seem apt to me in the case of natural forces that, in a particular instance, we *merely* have the power to stop or prevent. And this comes out in the oddness of saying that, e.g., a doctor who can give a remedy is at (one of) the controls of the disease he can thereby cure. I also have in mind institutional mechanisms (e.g., the Federal Government, the World Bank, and the Federal Reserve System) in which *we can occupy institutional offices with institutional powers*. In these cases the powers can, in an extended sense, be thought of as our agents, and the possibility arises of positive agency by the deliberate failure to exercise them (e.g., to let a bill be enacted by *not* signing it in a timely fashion).

[24]Suppose that you and a friend are off, by car, on a rescue mission that unexpectedly turns into Rescue II. You are sitting in the passenger seat, and your friend is driving. For some reason he hasn't noticed the trapped person, but you have. If you do nothing, your friend will inadvertently run over and kill the man. Can you really think that the end of rescuing the five would *not* justify your friend the driver in deliberately killing the man, but *would* justify you in keeping silent (or in not pulling up the hand brake)? I find this implausible. And it seems equally implausible to suppose that your obligation to yell or pull the brake comes from your having, temporarily, assumed the role of driver. What matters is that the mission has become illicit precisely because, as you can see, it

requires that someone be killed. So it has also become illicit to try to *further* the mission, whether by deliberate action or omission.

[25]At least if you are not the driver or his designated replacement—that is, someone charged with a special moral responsibility to see to it that the train kills no one. If you have that responsibility but lack a special duty toward the injured people (you are not also their doctor), then there would be something extra on the moral balance in favor of stopping. But we should not build this complication into our account of the difference between positive and negative agency. For the force of this extra factor seems independent of facts about agency. It does not seem to derive from any supposition that, if you stay with the passengers, you will really be taking the train forward or will somehow be party to the fatal action of the train itself.

[26]In Rescue III you intend an action of the train that immediately kills the man. But it would make no difference if, in a variant of the case, you did not intend that the train pass over the spot where the man was trapped, but merely intended that it pass over some nearer part of the track (where that would foreseeably lead to its passing over the fatal spot). Nor would it matter, in a further variant of the case, if the intended action of the train would lead to the man's being killed by some immediate cause other than the train. All that is essential is that you intend some action of the train that you can foresee will cause the man's death.

[27]We fail to rescue the one *because* we rescue the five instead. But notice that this account implies, in the previously mentioned puzzle cases of boycotting and snubbing (cases where we are unsure whether there is a genuine action by way of an inaction or merely a deliberate inaction), that the agent's most direct contribution to the upshot is an inaction. Grape sales decline because we don't buy grapes, and we don't buy them *because* we are boycotting. Happily, this means that we do not have to decide whether boycotting is a genuine action in order to determine the boycotter's agency in the intended upshot. It will turn out on either hypothesis to be negative.

[28]If you have advertently or inadvertently poisoned someone who can yet be saved by an antidote that you actually have, then you seem to be in no moral position to go to the rescue of five others rather than staying to save him.

[29]It seems important in this kind of case that those who are saved by your action have just as much right to the raft as the one who suffers. Removing it from the reach of its owner would, for example, be very questionable. It also seems important that the person from whom the raft is taken is not already using the raft to save himself. It is one thing to remove it from his reach and quite another to push him off it.

[30]The responsibility of others also comes in when we know that an action will occasion aggression by a third party—for example, if I know that Jones will murder you if I rescue five of his enemies who are drowning. If it seems that I may proceed with the rescue in this case it is because we shall, quite sensibly, attribute the blame for your death to Jones and not to me. In this kind of situation it is important that the action I undertake is morally pressing. Had Jones threatened to murder you in case I mowed my lawn, my ignoring the threat might well seem a kind of active provocation.

[31]But this qualification does not apply to special liabilities created by *external* features of a situation. If driving by Smith's house would set off an explosive device that would blow him up, then driving by, even when it would be necessary to rescue five others, would count as an aggression rather than a failure to help. And this also makes sense. For there seems to be no way in which we can define the class of presumptively innocent actions by prescinding from unusual external circumstances. Removing a ladder is not presumptively innocent when someone is high up on it. And driving down a public road is not presumptively innocent when someone is trapped on it. But entering someone's field of vision (where that sets off no devices, etc.) seems quite different, even where the person will, because of a rare mental illness, be harmed by it.

[32]I believe the case was introduced by Foot in "The Problem of Abortion and the Doctrine of the Double Effect," p. 59. See also Judith Jarvis Thomson, "The Trolley Problem," p. 279. And Jonathan Glover discusses a fascinating real-life trolley case in *Causing Death and Saving Lives* (Harmondsworth, England: Penguin Books, 1977), pp. 102–103. During World War II British intelligence apparently had the power to deceive the German command about the accuracy of rocket attacks on London. Had they chosen to do so—and they did not—they could have redirected the rockets to less densely populated areas outside the city.

[33]This solution to the trolley problem works equally well for versions in which the choice belongs to someone who happens upon a trackside switch.

[34]See "The Problem of Abortion and the Doctrine of the Double Effect," p. 59. Foot does not actually speak of "general" positive and negative rights. But I think that is what she means. For natural or contractually acquired "special" positive rights may sometimes bind as strongly as general negative rights: We saw, for example, that a private lifeguard in Rescue I might not be permitted to leave to save the five.

[35]In presenting versions of the precedence thesis, I am supposing (*contra* John Taurek in "Should the Numbers Count?" p. 214) that the numbers do count—for example, that saving two lives generally does twice as much

good as saving one. I am also supposing that goods of different kinds (for example, preservation of life and relief from suffering) can be compared and at least roughly summed up, and that in cases of conflicting rights we can make at least a rough comparison of the overall good protected by the rights on each side of the conflict.

[36]Or it might include a criterion that itself requires intuition to apply—by claiming, for example, that a negative right may be justifiably infringed just in case it would be contemptible of its possessor to insist on it. That is the kind of criterion that I find attractive.

[37]And something similar holds for damage. You don't own something if others may damage it whenever that is best for all concerned.

[38]Reference to the specific moral relation that I have in mind (in saying that someone's body and mind are his and not the community's) is made most naturally by a particular moral use of the possessive pronoun. This makes repeated reference awkward, and tempts me to talk in ways that are potentially misleading. I have spoken of a person's mind as belonging to him and have drawn an analogy with property. But both moves are dangerous. The intended sense of "belong" derives from the special use of the possessive. And the analogy with property is, as indicated, inexact. Both relations ground rights of say in what is to be done, but a person's mind or body are definitely not property—not even his property.

[39]I mean here to invoke the ordinary sense of "being," in which human persons, gods, angels, and probably the higher animals—but not plants, cells, rocks, computers, etc.—count as beings.

[40]It would make no difference, I think, if the overall good of the whole were thought to be a mere sum of the good of its parts—that is, if the whole were regarded as a mere colony without a morally significant higher-order function of its own. To deny the precedence of negative rights would still be to limit a person's moral protections precisely by this test: whether or not granting the protections would best serve the collective good. It would be to suppose that he may rightly be killed or injured if the cost to him does not outweigh the sum of the benefits to others. And this seems to me a clear enough way in which he would be regarded, morally, as a cell in the collective whole.

[41]I am not claiming that any person or persons have actually designed morality with an eye to giving themselves the degree of say they find fitting. But I do think that light can be shed on the (timeless) content of morality by considering the importance to us of what would be realized or unrealized in the design of various moral systems.

[42]Amartya Sen makes room for what he calls goal rights in "Rights and Agency," *Philosophy and Public Affairs* 11 (1982), pp. 3–39.

[43]Samuel Scheffler develops such an argument in *The Rejection of Consequentialism* (Oxford, England: Clarendon Press of Oxford University Press, 1982), pp. 80–114. Sen, in "Rights and Agency," Section VI and VII, tries to make room within a consequentialist framework for kinds of agent-relativity that would undermine the argument. But I find these agent-relative features poorly motivated as elements of a possible consequentialism.

Part IV

THE DOCTRINE
OF DOUBLE EFFECT

Ethics

THOMAS NAGEL ▪ New York University
The View From Nowhere, 1986

This essay is a chapter from Thomas Nagel's book, *The View From Nowhere*. A theme running through the book is the division in human perspectives between the external or objective point of view and the internal or subjective point of view, which Nagel considers a fact of our nature. In the realm of ethics, Nagel associates the first perspective, an **objective point of view**, with considerations of *what should happen in the world* as a matter of consequences. He associates the second perspective, a **subjective point of view**, with *what a person should do* as a matter of rights, claims, and duties. According to Nagel, moral reasoning looks very different from these two points of view. The task of his essay is to give a plausible account of the relationship between these distinct moral perspectives.

Nagel suggests that the objective perspective presents an individual with "neutral reasons" for action evaluated in terms of **agent-neutral values**. For example, utilitarianism might be said to provide impersonal hedonistic values which are to be maximized in a neutral way among the relative interests of particular individuals situated in the world. We might say then that utilitarianism is an impersonal morality in which value is perspective-free. By contrast, the subjective perspective considers values that are **agent-relative** in that they are sensitive to particular personal projects and relationships. These provide agent-relative reasons.

Nagel distinguishes among three types of agent-relative reasons: reasons of autonomy (coming from individual preferences, projects, and so forth); reasons of duty (deontological constraints); and reasons of obligation (coming from special commitments and associations). His focus here is on the second of these—reasons that support deontological constraints. Deontological constraints limit the ways others may be treated in the service of either the personal goals of others or of objective moral values. Deontological constraints are naturally thought of as moral rights.

For Nagel, the existence of agent-relative deontological constraints is a paradoxical phenomenon which must be accounted for. For instance, how is it rational for me to be required to refrain from violating a certain right of yours, if my refraining will result in five others' violating similar rights? If I can prevent the violation of *many* rights, why shouldn't I be permitted to violate one right? According to Nagel, the existence of deontological reasons is a "phenomenological" fact, a fact of moral experience, which must be explained or accounted for.

The subjective point of view is traditionally thought of as the personal point of view which considers the individual perspective and interests of a particular person. When adopting the subjective point of view, reasons are thought to be relative to the interests of the person who has those reasons. Yet deontological constraints are reasons that are relative to the interests of particular persons other than the person

who has those reasons. Nagel wants to know why it makes sense to override impersonal values (that do not benefit the self, but benefit others irrespective of who they
are) for deontological constraints (that neither benefit the self nor maximize the
benefit of others, but instead benefit only particular other persons).

For Nagel, this is a paradoxical situation. He illustrates the paradox with a story.
In the story, a man needs to twist the arm of a child in order to save the lives of the
victims of an auto accident. If the child's arm is twisted, then the child's cry of alarm
will prompt the child's grandmother to cooperate in the saving of the crash victims.
Nagel believes that our moral intuitions tell us that it is impermissible to twist the
child's arm—despite the fact that far worse consequences lie ahead for the auto
accident victims as a result of his failure to twist the arm, consequences far worse
than would ever be experienced by the child if the man in fact did twist his arm.

Why should this be so? According to Nagel, the Doctrine of Double Effect can
(very roughly) capture our intuitions here. As Nagel characterizes it, the doctrine tells
us that we must not choose or act to maltreat someone as an intended end or as a
means to some other end, but we are permitted to cause or merely fail to prevent
harms which we do not aim at as an end or as a means to another end. In relation to
our story, then, the moral intuition we have that the child's arm must not be twisted
is reflected in the Doctrine of Double Effect as the prohibition against intentionally
maltreating someone as a means to some other end. For Nagel, the challenge is to
explain this paradox: the agent-relative perspective of the doctrine that prohibits
arm-twisting exerts a stronger pull over the agent-neutral perspective that considers
the larger consequences of the action for the victims of the auto accident.

Nagel sees this as a collision of perspectives, causing a conflict between the reasons associated with the objective point of view and the reasons associated with the
subjective point of view. The collision occurs when Nagel calls the "subjective self" is
forced to aim at evil in order to achieve the good aimed at by the "objective self." The
intuitive primacy of the evil aims of the subjective self is due to the structure of the
internal perspective. For Nagel, the nerve of deontological constraints is the fact that
intentional actions that have harm as their ends or means are actions which are *guided
by* that evil aim. The man in our story is not allowed to twist the child's arm because the
immediate aim guiding this action would be the production of the child's pain. According to Nagel, from the subjective point of view this reflects a strongly perceived relation
between evil and intentional aiming. It is the intentional character of such aiming to
produce an evil that differentiates such an action from one which merely produces a
known evil result. It is "the intensifying beam of our intentions" that magnifies the
moral importance of an agent's evil aims. Nagel holds that, from the personal perspective, moral value must always be considered as internal to an agent's aim. As Nagel puts
it, "When I twist the child's arm intentionally I incorporate that evil into what I do: it is
my deliberate creation." And by twisting the child's arm, "You are pushing directly and
essentially against the intrinsic normative force of your goal."

Because neither the subjective nor the objective perspective is more basic, Nagel
concludes that neither agent-relative nor agent-neutral reasons are dominant. There
is an irreducible moral complexity that is grounded in the irreducible multiplicity of
perspectives involved in personhood.

1. THREE KINDS OF AGENT-RELATIVITY

. . . I WANT TO TAKE UP SOME OF THE PROBLEMS that must be faced by any defender of the objectivity of ethics who wishes to make sense of the actual complexity of the subject. The treatment will be general and very incomplete. Essentially I shall discuss some examples in order to suggest that the enterprise is not hopeless.

The discussion will revolve around the distinction between agent-relative and agent-neutral values. I won't try to set forth a full ethical theory, even in outline, but I will try to say something in this chapter and the next about the central problem of ethics: how the lives, interests, and welfare of others make claims on us and how these claims, of various forms, are to be reconciled with the aim of living our own lives. My assumption is that the shape of a moral theory depends on the interplay of forces in the psychic economy of complex rational beings. (I shall not say anything about aesthetic values, whose relation to human interests is obscure, though they are revealed to us by the capacity of certain things outside us to command our interest and respect.)

There is one important component of ethics that is consequentialist and impersonal. If what I said in the last chapter is right, some kind of hedonistic, agent-neutral consequentialism describes a significant form of concern that we owe to others. Life is filled with basic pleasures and pains, and they matter. Perhaps other basic human goods, such as health and survival, have the same status, but let me put that aside for the moment. I want now to examine other sorts of objective reasons that complicate the picture. Ethics is concerned not only with what should happen, but also independently with what people should or may *do*. Neutral reasons underlie the former; but relative reasons can affect the latter. In philosophical discussion, the hegemony of neutral reasons and impersonal values is typically challenged by three broad types of reasons that are relative in form, and whose existence seems to be independent of impersonal values.

The first type of reason stems from the desires, projects, commitments, and personal ties of the individual agent, all of which give him reasons to act in the pursuit of ends that are his own. These I shall collect under the general heading of reasons of autonomy (not to be confused with the autonomy of free will).

The second type of reason stems from the claims of other persons not to be maltreated in certain ways. What I have in mind are not neutral reasons for everyone to bring it about that no one is maltreated, but relative reasons for each individual not to maltreat others himself, in his dealings with them (for example by violating their rights, breaking his promises to them, etc.). These I shall collect under the general, ugly, and familiar heading of deontology. Autonomous reasons would limit what we are obliged to do in the service of impersonal values. Deontological reasons would limit what we are *permitted* to do in the service of either impersonal or autonomous ones.

The third type of reason stems from the special obligations we have toward those to whom we are closely related; parents, children, spouses, siblings, fellow members of a community or even a nation. Most people would acknowledge a noncontractual obligation to show special concern for some of these others—though there would be disagreement about the strength of the reasons and the width of the net. I'll refer to them as reasons of obligation, even though they don't include a great many obligations that are voluntarily undertaken. I mention them here only for completeness and won't discuss them in detail. I have less confidence here than with regard to the other two categories that in ordinary thought they resist agent-neutral justification.

I am not sure whether all these agent-relative reasons actually exist. The autonomous ones and perhaps the obligatory ones are fairly intelligible; but while the idea behind the deontological ones can, I think, be explained, it is an explanation which throws some doubt on their validity. The only way to find out what limits there are to what we may or must do in the service of impersonal values is to see what sense can be made of the apparent limits, and to accept or reject them according to whether the maximum sense is good enough.

Taken together, autonomous, obligatory, neutral, deontological reasons cover much of the territory of unreflective bourgeois morality. Common sense suggests that each of us should live his own life (autonomy), give special consideration to certain others (obligation), have some significant concern for the general good (neutral values), and treat the people he deals with decently (deontology). It also suggests that these aims may produce serious inner conflict. Common sense doesn't have the last word in ethics or anywhere else, but it has, as J. L. Austin said about ordinary language, the first word: it should be examined before it is discarded.

Attempts have been made to find room for some version of all three types of apparent exception to impersonal ethics in a more complex impersonal system, using developments of consequentialism like rule-utilitarianism and motive-utilitarianism. A recent example is Hare's two-level version of utilitarianism in *Moral Thinking*. And T. M. Scanlon offers a consequentialist but nonutilitarian justification of deontological rights in "Rights, Goals, and Fairness." I shall not try to show that these reductions of the agent-relative to the agent-neutral fail, since I believe they are partly correct. They just aren't the whole truth. I shall try to present an alternative account of how the exceptions might make sense independently. My aim is to explain what it is that eludes justification in neutral terms. Since this is most conspicuous with regard to autonomy and deontology, I shall concentrate on them. The account in both cases depends on certain discrepancies between what can be valued from an objective standpoint and what can be seen from an objective standpoint to have value from a less objective standpoint.

2. REASONS OF AUTONOMY

Not all the sources of subjective reasons are as simple as sensory pleasure and pain. I believe that the most reasonable objectification of the value that we all recognize in our own encounter with these experiences is an impersonal one. Difficult as it may be to carry out, each of us has reason to give significant weight to the simple sensory pleasure or pain of others as well as to his own. When these values occur in isolation, the results can be demanding. If you and a stranger have both been injured, you have one dose of painkiller, and his pain is much more severe than yours, you should give him the painkiller—not for any complicated reasons, but simply because of the relative severity of the two pains, which provides a neutral reason to prefer the relief of the more severe. The same may be said of other basic elements of human good and ill.

But many values are not like this. Though some human interests (and not only pleasure and pain) give rise to impersonal values, I now want to argue that not all of them do. If I have a bad headache, anyone has a reason to want it to stop. But if I badly want to climb to the top of Mount Kilimanjaro, not everyone has a reason to want me to succeed. I have a reason to try to get to the top, and it may be much stronger than my reason for wanting a headache to go away, but other people have very little reason, if any, to care whether I climb the mountain or not. Or suppose I want to become a pianist. Then I have a reason to practice, but other people have little or no reason to care if I practice or not. Why is this?

Why shouldn't the satisfaction of my desire to climb the mountain have impersonal value comparable to the value it has for me—just like the elimination of my headache? As it happens, you may have to put up with severe altitude headaches and nausea to get to the top of a mountain that high: it has to be worth it to you. Why doesn't the objectification of these values preserve the relation among them that exists in the perspective of the climber? This problem was originally formulated by Scanlon. He makes a strong case against the view that the satisfaction of preferences as such provides the raw material for ethics—the basis of our claims to the concern of others. The impersonal value of things that matter to an individual need not correspond to their personal value to him. "The fact that someone would be willing to forgo a decent diet in order to build a monument to his god does not mean that his claim on others for aid in his project has the same strength as a claim for aid in obtaining enough to eat"(Scanlon (1), pp. 659-60).

There are two ways in which a value may be conditional on a desire: the value may lie either outside or inside the conditional, so to speak. In the former case, a person's having X if he desires X has neutral value: satisfaction of the desire has objective utility that everyone has reason to promote. In the latter case, if a person desires X, his having X has relative value for him: susceptibility to the value is conditional on having the desire, and satisfaction of the desire does not have impersonal utility.

It isn't easy to state a general rule for assigning desires to one category or the other. I have claimed that sensory experiences which we strongly like or dislike simply in themselves have agent-neutral value because of those desires. Such immediate likes and dislikes, not resulting from any choice or underlying reason, are very different from the desires that define our broader aims and ambitions. The former result in mental states that are transparently good or bad, because the attitude of the subject is decisive. The latter require more complicated evaluation.

Most of the things we pursue, if not most of the things we avoid, are optional. Their value to us depends on our individual aims, projects, and concerns, including particular concerns for other people that reflect our relations with them; they acquire value only because of the interest we develop in them and the place this gives them in our lives, rather than evoking interest because of their value. When we look at such desires objectively, from outside, we can acknowledge the validity of the reasons they give for action without judging that there is a neutral reason for any of those things to be done. That is because when we move to the objective standpoint, we leave behind the perspective from which the values have to be accepted.

The crucial question is how far the authority of each individual runs in determining the objective value of the satisfaction of his own desires and preferences. From the objective standpoint we see a world which contains multiple individual perspectives. Some of the appearances of value from within those perspectives can just be taken over by the objective self. But I believe that others must remain essentially perspectival—appearances of value only *to the subject*, and valid only from within his life. Their value is not impersonally detachable, because it is too bound up with idiosyncratic attitudes and aims of the subject, and can't be subsumed under a more universal value of comparable importance, like that of pleasure and pain.

Anyone may of course make the ends of another person his own, but that is a different matter: a matter of personal sympathy rather than of objective acknowledgment. So long as I truly occupy the objective standpoint, I can recognize the value of one of these optional ends only vicariously, through the perspective of the person who has chosen it, and not in its own right.

This is true even if the person is myself. When I regard my life from outside, integration of the two standpoints cannot overcome a certain form of detachment. I can't directly appreciate the value of my climbing Mount Kilimanjaro just because I want to, as I appreciate the value of my being adequately fed and clothed. The *fact* that I want to, viewed from outside, has none of the importance of *wanting to*, experienced from within. I can see a reason here only through the perspective of TN [Thomas Nagel], who has chosen an optional goal which adds to the values operating within his life something beyond the reasons that simply come at him independently of his choices. I cannot see it except as a value for him, and I cannot therefore take it on without qualification as an impersonal value.

While this seems to me true, there is a natural way to dispute it. I have acknowledged that in the case of sensations, a strong desire or aversion can confer agent-neutral value, and it doesn't require that I have the desire or even fully understand it. Even if, for example, I don't mind the sound of squeaking chalk, I can acknowledge that it is impersonally bad for someone who hates it to be subjected to that sound. The impersonal badness attaches not to the experience conceived merely as a certain sound, but to someone's *having an experience he hates*. The evident awfulness is enough. Now someone might ask, why shouldn't a comparable impersonal value attach to someone's *having (or doing) something he wants*—whatever the desire is? Even if I can't objectively identify with the desire, and therefore can't assign any value to the achievement as such, why can't I judge it to have impersonal value under this more complex description? This would be the universal value under which one could objectively favor all preference-satisfaction.

It isn't easy to make the case convincingly, but I don't believe there is such a universal value. One reason is that the personal projects we are talking about generally involve things happening in the world outside our minds. It seems too much to allow an individual's desires to confer impersonal value on something outside himself, even if he is to some extent involved in it. The impersonal authority of the individual's values diminishes with distance from his inner condition. We can see this clearly, I think, in the limiting case of a personal desire for something which will never impinge on his consciousness: posthumous fame, for example. If someone wants posthumous fame, he may have a reason to do what he thinks will achieve it but one cannot see it as anything but a good *for him*. There is no agent-neutral value whatever in the realization of his hope: the only reason anyone else could have for caring about it would be a specific personal concern for him and his ambitions.

On the other hand, the more a desire has as its object the quality of the subject's experience, and the more immediate and independent of his other values it is, the more it will tend to generate impersonal as well as personal reasons. But to the extent that it transcends his own experience, the achievement of a typical personal project or ambition has no value except from the perspective of its subject—at least none in any way comparable to the value reasonably placed on it by the person whose ambition it is. (I am assuming here that we can abstract from any intrinsic value the achievement may have which does not depend on his interest at all—or else that we are dealing with projects whose actual value, whatever it is, derives entirely from the interest of the subject.) Whereas one clearly can find value in the occurrence/ nonoccurrence of a sensory experience that is strongly liked/disliked for itself, whether or not one has or even empathizes with the reaction. To put it in a way that sounds paradoxical: the more subjective the object of the desire, the more impersonal the value of its satisfaction.

If this is right, then a certain amount of dissociation is inevitable when we bring the two standpoints together. From within I am directly subject to certain agent-relative reasons. From without all I can do is to acknowledge the reasonableness for the person I am of being motivated by those reasons— without being motivated by them myself, qua [as] objective self. My objectivity shows up in the acknowledgment that these relative reasons are examples of something general, and could arise for any other agent with optional goals of his own. From a point of view outside the perspective of the ambition to climb Kilimanjaro or become a pianist, it is possible to recognize and understand that perspective and so to acknowledge the reasons that arise inside it; but it is not possible to accept those reasons as one's own, unless one occupies the perspective rather than merely recognizing it.

There is nothing incoherent in wanting to be able to climb Kilimanjaro or play all the Beethoven piano sonatas, while thinking that impersonally it doesn't matter whether one can do this. In fact one would have to be dotty to think it did matter impersonally. It doesn't even matter much impersonally that *if* someone wants to play all the Beethoven sonatas by heart, he should be able to. It matters a little, so that if he is incapable of achieving it, it might be better if he didn't want to—leaving aside whatever value there may be in the ambition itself. The neutral values of pleasure and pain come into effect here. But even that is a rather weak neutral value, since it is not the neutral correlate of the agent-relative reasons deriving directly from the ambition, whose object is not pleasure. If an interest is developed by the agent himself through his choices and actions, then the objective reasons it provides are primarily relative.

Any neutral reasons stemming from it must express values that are independent of the particular perspective and system of preferences of the agent. The general values of pleasure and pain, satisfaction and frustration, fill this role to some extent, as I have said, though only to the extent that they can be detached from the value of the object of desire whose acquisition or loss produces the feeling. (This, incidentally, explains the appeal of hedonism to consequentialists: it reduces all value to the impersonal common denominator of pleasure and pain.) But what there is not, I believe, is a completely general impersonal value of the satisfaction of desires and preferences. The strength of an individual's personal preferences in general determines what they give him reason to do, but it does not determine the impersonal value of his getting what he wants. There is no independent value of preference-satisfaction per se, which preserves its force even from an impersonal standpoint.

3. PERSONAL VALUES AND IMPARTIALITY

This may seem harsh, and if we left it at that, it would be. For if agent-neutral reasons derived only from pleasure and pain, we would have no reason to care about many fundamental aspects of other people's welfare which cannot easily be given a hedonistic interpretation—their freedom, their self-respect, their access to opportunities and resources that enable them to live fulfilling lives.

But I believe there is another way in which these things can be seen as having impersonal value—without giving carte blanche to individual preferences. These very general human goods share with the much more specific goods of pleasure and freedom from pain a characteristic that generates neutral reasons. Their value does not have to be seen through the particular values of the individual who has or lacks them, or through the particular preferences or projects he has performed.[1] Also, though they do not involve solely the contents of consciousness, such goods are very "close to home:" they determine the character of life from the inside, and this lends authority to the value placed on them by the subject. For both these reasons, when we contemplate our own lives and those of others from outside, the most plausible objectification of these very general goods is not agent-relative.

From the objective standpoint, the fundamental thing leading to the recognition of agent-neutral reasons is a sense that no one is more important than anyone else. The question then is whether we are all equally unimportant or all equally important, and the answer, I think, is somewhere in between. The areas in which we must continue to be concerned about ourselves and others from outside are those whose value comes as close as possible to being universal. If impersonal value is going to be admitted at all, it will naturally attach to liberty, general opportunities, and the basic resources of life, as well as to pleasure and the absence of suffering. This is not equivalent to assigning impersonal value to each person's getting whatever he wants.

The hypothesis of two levels of objectification implies that there is not a significant reason for something to happen corresponding to every reason for someone to do something. Each person has reasons stemming from the perspective of his own life which, though they can be publicly recognized, do not in general provide reasons for others and do not correspond to reasons that the interests of others provide for him. Since the relative reasons are general and not purely subjective, he must acknowledge that the same is true of others with respect to

him. A certain objective distance from his own aims is unavoidable; there will be some dissociation of the two standpoints with respect to his individual concerns. The ethical results will depend on the size of the impersonal demands made on him and others by the actual circumstances, and how strongly they weigh against more personal reasons.

One difficult question is whether such a two-tier system implies a significant limit to the degree to which ethics requires us to be impartial between ourselves and others.[2] It would imply this if the agent-relative reasons coming from our personal aims were simply added on to the neutral reasons derived from more universal values. For then I would be permitted to pursue my personal projects in preference to the impersonal good of others just as I can pursue those projects in preference to my own health, comfort, etc.; and I wouldn't have to sacrifice myself in return for the furtherance of *their* personal projects—only for their impersonal good. So it looks as though each person's agent-relative reasons would give him a margin of protection against the claims of others—though of course it could be overridden by sufficiently strong impersonal reasons.

However, there is some reason to doubt that the result will be this straightforward. In weighing our agent-relative reasons against the impersonal claims of others, we may not be able to use the same standards we use within our own lives. To take Scanlon's example again: just as we have more reason to help someone get enough to eat than to help him build a monument to his god—even if he is willing to forgo the food for the monument—so he may have more reason to help feed others than to build the monument, even if he cannot be faulted for starving himself. In other words, we have to give basic impersonal goods more weight when they come from other people's needs than when they compete with personal reasons within our own lives.

I am not sure of the best account of this, or how far it would go toward requiring impartiality. Full impartiality would seem to demand that any tendency toward self-favoritism on the basis of personal reasons be offset by a corresponding decrease in the weight given in one's interpersonal decisions to impersonal reasons deriving from one's own basic needs—so that one's total is not increased, so to speak. All reasons would have to be weighted so that everyone was equally important. But I don't know whether a credible system of this kind could be described, at any rate for the purposes of individual decision making. It seems more likely that interpersonal impartiality, both among others and between oneself and others, would have to be defined in terms of agent-neutral values, and that this would leave room for some partiality toward oneself and one's personal concerns and attachments, the extent of it depending on the comparative importance of relative and neutral reasons in the overall system. A stronger form of impartiality, if one is required, would have to appear at a higher level, in the application of practical reason to the social and political institutions that provide a background to individual choice.

There is one objection to this approach which ought to be mentioned, though probably few people would make it. I have claimed that a neutral objectification of the bulk of individualistic subjective reasons does not make sense. But of course that doesn't entail that a relative objectification is correct instead. There is a radical alternative: it could be that these reasons have no objective validity at all, relative or neutral. That is, it might be said by an uncompromising utilitarian that if there isn't a neutral reason for me to climb Kilimanjaro or learn the Beethoven sonatas—if it wouldn't be a good thing in itself, if the world wouldn't be a better place for my getting to the top of the mountain or being able to play the sonatas—then I have no reason of any kind to do those things, and I had better get rid of my desire to do them as soon as possible. I may not, in other words, accord more personal value to anything in my life than is justified by its impersonal value.

That is a logically possible move, but not a plausible one. It results from the aim of eliminating perspective from the domain of real value to the greatest possible extent, and that aim is not required of us by objectivity, so far as I can see. We should certainly try to harmonize our lives to some extent with how we think the world should be. But there is no necessity, I now believe, to abandon all values that do not correspond to anything desirable from an impersonal standpoint, even though this may be possible as a personal choice—a choice of self-transcendence.

If there are, objectively, both relative and neutral reasons, this raises a problem about how life is to be organized so that both can be given their due. One way of dealing with the problem is to put much of the responsibility for securing impersonal values into the hands of an impersonal institution like the state. A well designed set of political and social institutions should function as a moral buffer to protect personal life against the ravenous claims of impersonal good, and vice versa. I shall say a bit more about the relation between ethics and political theory later.

Before leaving the subject of autonomy, let me compare what I have said with another recent treatment of the relation between personal and impersonal values in ethical theory: Samuel Scheffler's *The Rejection of Consequentialism.* He proposes an "agent-centred prerogative," which would permit each individual to accord extra weight to all of his interests in deciding what to do, above that which they contribute to the neutral value of the total outcome of his actions, impersonally viewed.

> *More specifically, I believe that a plausible agent-centred prerogative would allow each agent to assign a certain proportionately greater weight to his own interests than to the interests of other people. It would then allow the agent to promote the non-optimal outcome of his own choosing, provided only that the degree of its inferiority to each of the superior outcomes he could instead promote in no case exceeded, by more than the specified proportion, the degree of sacrifice necessary for him to promote the superior outcome.*

This proposal is different from mine but not strictly incompatible with it. Scheffler does not make the distinction I have made between those interests and desires that do and those that do not generate impersonal values. He is not committed to a particular method of ranking the impersonal value of states of affairs, but his discussion suggests that he believes the satisfaction of most types of human preferences could be counted in determining whether one state of affairs or outcome was impersonally better than another. But whether or not he would accept my distinction, one could accept it and still formulate the proposal of an agent-centered prerogative; for that proposal describes a limit on the requirement always to produce the impersonally best outcome, which is independent of how the comparative impersonal value of outcomes is determined. It might be determined not by all interests but only by some. Then the prerogative would allow an individual to give those interests extra weight if they were his.

The trouble is that on the autonomy view I have put forward, he may already have some unopposed reasons which favor himself, arising from those desires whose satisfaction yields personal but not impersonal value. Perhaps it's going too far in moral indulgence to add to these a further prerogative of favoring himself with respect to the fundamental goods and evils whose impersonal value is clear.

An alternative position, which combines aspects of Scheffler's and mine, might be this. The division between interests that give rise to impersonal values and interests that don't is not sharp; it is a matter of degree. Some interests generate only relative reasons and no neutral ones; some generate neutral reasons that are just as strong as the relative ones; but some generate both relative reasons and somewhat weaker neutral ones. An individual is permitted to favor himself with respect to an interest to the degree to which the agent-relative reason generated by that interest exceeds the corresponding agent-neutral reason. There is no uniform prerogative of assigning a single proportionately greater weight to the cure of one's headaches, the realization of one's musical or athletic ambitions, and the happiness of one's children.

A variable prerogative of this kind would accord better than a uniform prerogative with Scheffler's account of the motivation behind it: the wish to give moral significance to the personal point of view by permitting morality to reflect the way in which concerns and commitments are naturally generated from within a particular point of view. If some interests are more dependent on a particular normative point of view than others, they will more naturally resist assimilation to the unifying claims of impersonal value in the construction of morality. All this emerges from the attempt to combine subjective and objective standpoints toward action and its motives.

On the other hand, even after such adjustments there will still be claims of impersonal morality that seem from an individual point of view

excessive, and it may be that the response to this will have to include a more general agent-centered prerogative. I shall take up the problem in the next chapter.

4. DEONTOLOGY

Let me turn now to the obscure topic of deontological constraints. These are agent-relative reasons which depend not on the aims or projects of the agent but on the claims of others. Unlike autonomous reasons, they are not optional. If they exist, they restrict what we may do in the service of either relative or neutral goals.

They complicate an already complicated picture. If there are agent-relative reasons of autonomy that do not give rise to agent-neutral interpersonal claims, then the claims of others must compete with these personal reasons in determining what one should do. Deontological constraints add further agent-relative reasons to the system—reasons not to treat others in certain ways. They are not impersonal claims derived from the interest of others, but personal demands governing one's relations with others.

Whatever their explanation, they are conspicuous among the moral appearances. Here is an example to focus your intuitions.

You have an auto accident one winter night on a lonely road. The other passengers are badly injured, the car is out of commission, and the road is deserted, so you run along it till you find an isolated house. The house turns out to be occupied by an old woman who is looking after her small grandchild. There is no phone, but there is a car in the garage, and you ask desperately to borrow it, and explain the situation. She doesn't believe you. Terrified by your desperation she runs upstairs and locks herself in the bathroom, leaving you alone with the child. You pound ineffectively on the door and search without success for the car keys. Then it occurs to you that she might be persuaded to tell you where they are if you were to twist the child's arm outside the bathroom door. Should you do it?

It is difficult not to see this as a dilemma, even though the child's getting its arm twisted is a minor evil compared with your friends' not getting to the hospital. The dilemma must be due to a special reason against *doing* such a thing. Otherwise it would be obvious that you should choose the lesser evil and twist the child's arm.

Common moral intuition recognizes several types of deontological reasons—limits on what one may do to people or how one may treat them. There are the special obligations created by promises and agreements; the restrictions against lying and betrayal; the prohibitions against violating various individual rights, rights not to be killed, injured, imprisoned, threatened, tortured, coerced, robbed; the restrictions against imposing certain sacrifices on someone simply as means to an end; and perhaps the special claim of immediacy, which makes distress at a distance so different from distress in the same room. There may also be a deontological requirement of fairness, of even-handedness or equality in one's treatment of people. (This is to be distinguished from an impersonal value thought to attach to equality in the distribution of benefits, considered as an aspect of the assessment of states of affairs.)

In all these cases it appears that the special reasons, if they exist, cannot be explained simply in terms of neutral values, because the particular relation of the agent to the outcome is essential. Deontological constraints may be overridden by neutral reasons of sufficient strength, but they are not themselves to be understood as the expression of neutral values of any kind. It is clear from the way such reasons work that they cannot be explained by the hypothesis that the violation of a deontological constraint has high negative impersonal value. Deontological reasons have their full force against your doing something—not just against its happening.

For example, if there really are such constraints the following things seem to be true. It seems that you shouldn't break a promise or tell a lie for the sake of some benefit, even though you would not be required to forgo a comparable benefit in order to prevent someone else from breaking a promise or telling a lie. And it seems that you shouldn't twist the arm of a small child to get its grandmother to do something, even something important enough so that you would not be required to forgo a comparable benefit in order to prevent someone else from twisting a child's arm. And it may be that you shouldn't engage in certain kinds of unfair discriminatory treatment (in an official role, for example) even to produce a good result

which you would not be required to forgo in order to prevent similar unfairness by others.

Some may simply deny the plausibility of such moral intuitions. Others may say that their plausibility can be subtly accounted for in terms of impersonal values, and that they appear to involve a fundamentally different type of reason for action only if they are inadequately analyzed. As I have said, I don't want to take up these alternative accounts here. They may provide the best hope of rationally justifying something that has the rough shape of a set of deontological restrictions; but offered as complete accounts they seem to me essentially revisionist. Even if from that point of view they contain a good deal of truth, they do not shed light on the independent deontological conceptions they are intended to replace. Those conceptions still have to be understood, even if they will eventually be rejected.

Sometimes, particularly when institutions and general practices are involved in the case, there is a neutral justification for what looks initially like an agent-relative restriction on action. And it is certainly a help to the acceptance of deontological constraints that general adherence to them does not produce disastrous results in the long run. Rules against the direct infliction of harm and against the violation of widely accepted rights have considerable social utility, and if it ceased to be so, those rules would lose much of their moral attractiveness.

But I am convinced that a less indirect, non-statistical form of evaluation is also at work in support of deontological constraints, and that it underlies the central, most puzzling intuitions in this area. This is what would produce a sense of dilemma if it turned out that general adherence to deontological restrictions worked consistently contrary to impersonal utility. Right or wrong, it is this type of view that I want to explore and understand. There is no point in trying to show in advance that such dilemmas cannot arise.

One reason for the resistance to deontological constraints is that they are formally puzzling, in a way that the other reasons we have discussed are not. We can understand how autonomous agent-relative reasons might derive from the specific projects and concerns of the agent, and we can understand how neutral reasons might derive from the interest of others, giving each of us reason to take them into account. But how can there be relative reasons to respect the claims of others? How can there be a reason not to twist someone's arm which is not equally a reason to prevent his arm from being twisted by someone else?

The relative character of the reason cannot come simply from the character of the interest that is being respected, for that alone would justify only a neutral reason to protect the interest. And the relative reason does not come from an aim or project of the individual agent, for it is not conditional on what the agent wants. Deontological restrictions, if they exist, apply to everyone: they are mandatory and may not be given up like personal ambitions or commitments.

It is hard to understand how there could be such a thing. One would expect that reasons stemming from the interests of others would be neutral and not relative. How can a claim based on the interests of others apply to those who may infringe it directly or intentionally in a way that it does not apply to those whose actions may damage that same interest just as much indirectly? After all, it is no worse *for the victim* to be killed or injured deliberately than accidentally, or as an unavoidable side-effect of the dangerous rescue operation. In fact the special features of action that bring these reasons into effect may not add to the impersonal badness of the occurrence at all. To use an example of T. M. Scanlon, if you have to choose between saving someone from being murdered and saving someone else from being killed in a similar manner accidentally, and you have no special relation to either of them, it seems that your choice should depend only on which one you're more likely to succeed in saving. Admittedly the wickedness of a murder is in some sense a bad thing; but when it is a matter of deciding which of them there is more reason to prevent, a murder does not seem to be a significantly worse event, impersonally considered, than an accidental or incidental death. Some entirely different kind of value must be brought in to explain the idea that one should not kill one person even to prevent a number of accidental deaths: murder is not just an evil that everyone has reason to prevent but an act that everyone has reason to *avoid*.

In any case, even if a murder were a worse event, impersonally considered, than an accidental death, this could not be used to explain the deontological constraint against murder. For that constraint prohibits murder even if it is necessary to prevent other *murders* — not only other deaths.

There is no doubt that ideas of this kind form an important part of common moral phenomenology. Yet their paradoxical flavor tempts one to think that the whole thing is a kind of moral illusion resulting either from innate psychological dispositions or from crude but useful moral indoctrination. Before debunking the intuition, however, we ought to have a better grasp of what it is. No doubt it's a good thing for people to have a deep inhibition against torturing children even for very strong reasons, and the same might be said of other deontological constraints. But that does not explain why we find it almost impossible to regard it as a merely useful inhibition. An illusion involves a judgment or a disposition to judge, and not a mere motivational impulse. The phenomenological fact to be accounted for is that we seem to apprehend in each individual case an extremely powerful agent-relative *reason* not to harm an innocent person. This presents itself as the apprehension of a normative truth, not just as a psychological inhibition. It needs to be analyzed and accounted for, and accepted or rejected according to whether the account gives it an adequate justification.

I believe that the traditional principle of double effect, despite problems of application, provides a rough guide to the extension and character of deontological constraints, and that even after the volumes that have been written on the subject in recent years, this remains the right point of convergence for efforts to capture our intuitions.[3] The principle says that to violate deontological constraints one must maltreat someone else intentionally. The maltreatment must be something that one does or chooses, either as an end or as a means, rather than something one's actions merely cause or fail to prevent but that one doesn't aim at.

It is also possible to foresee that one's actions will cause or fail to prevent a harm that one does not intend to bring about or permit. In that case it does not come under a deontological constraint, though it may still be objectionable for neutral reasons. The precise way to draw this distinction has been the subject of extensive debate, sometimes involving ingenious examples of a runaway trolley which will kill five people unless you . . . , where the dots are filled in by different ways of saving the five, all of which in some way involve one other person's death. I won't try to draw the exact boundaries of the principle. Though I say it with trepidation, I believe that for my purposes they don't matter too much, and I suspect they can't be drawn more than roughly: my deontological intuitions, at least, begin to fail above a certain level of complexity. But one point worth mentioning is that the constraints apply to intentionally permitting as well as to intentionally doing harm. Thus in our example there would be the same kind of objection if with the same end in view you permitted someone else to twist the child's arm. You would have let it happen intentionally, and that would be different from a failure to prevent such an occurrence because you were too engaged in doing something else, which was more important.

5. AGENTS AND VICTIMS

So far this is just moral phenomenology: it does not remove the paradox. Why should we consider ourselves far more responsible for what we do (or permit) intentionally than for consequences of action that we foresee and decide to accept but that do not form part of our aims (intermediate or final)? How can the connection of ends and means conduct responsibility so much more effectively than the connection of foresight and avoidability?

It is as if each action produced a unique normative perspective on the world, determined by intention. When I twist the child's arm intentionally I incorporate that evil into what I do: it is my deliberate creation and the reasons stemming from it are magnified and lit up from my point of view. They overshadow reasons stemming from greater evils that are more "faint" from this perspective, because they do not fail within the intensifying beam of my intentions even though they are consequences of what I do.

That is the picture, but can it be correct? Isn't it a normatively distorted picture?

This problem is an instance of the collision between subjective and objective points of view. The issue is whether the special, personal perspective of agency has legitimate significance in determining what people have reason to do—whether,

because of this perspective, I can have sufficient reason not to do something which, considered from an external standpoint, it would be better if I did. That is, *things* will be better, what *happens* will be better, if I twist the child's arm than if I do not. But I will have done something worse. If considerations of what I may do, and the correlative claims of my victim against me, can outweigh the substantial impersonal value of what will happen, that can only be because the perspective of the agent has an importance in practical reasoning that resists domination by a conception of the world as a place where good and bad things happen whose value is perspective-free.

I have already claimed that the dominance of this neutral conception of value is not complete. It does not swallow up or overwhelm the relative reasons arising from those individual ambitions, commitments, and attachments that are in some sense chosen. But the admission of what I have called autonomous reasons does not imply the possibility of deontological reasons.[4] The two are very different. The peculiarity of deontological reasons is that although they are agent-relative, they do not express the subjective autonomy of the agent at all. They are demands, not options. The paradox is that this partial, perspectival respect for the interests of others should not give way to an agent-neutral respect free of perspective. The deontological perspective seems primitive, even superstitious, by comparison: merely a stage on the way to full objectivity. How can what we *do* in this narrow sense be so important?

Let me try to say where the strength of the deontological view lies. We may begin by considering a curious feature of deontological reasons on which I have not yet remarked. Intention appears to magnify the importance of evil aims by comparison with evil side-effects in a way that it does not magnify the importance of good aims by comparison with good side-effects. We are supposed to avoid using evil means to produce a good end, even though it would be permissible to produce that good end by neutral means with comparably evil side-effects. On the other hand, given two routes to a legitimate end, one of which involves good means and neutral side-effects and the other of which involves neutral means and equally good side-effects, there is no reason to choose the first route. Deontological reasons tell us only not to aim at evil; they don't tell us to aim at good, as a means. Why should this be? What is the relation between evil and intention, or aiming, that makes them clash with such force?

The answer emerges if we ask ourselves what it is to aim at something, what differentiates it from merely producing the result knowingly.

The difference is that action intentionally aimed at a goal is guided by that goal. Whether the goal is an end in itself or only a means, action aimed at it must follow it and be prepared to adjust its pursuit if deflected by altered circumstances— whereas an act that merely produces an effect does not follow it, is not *guided* by it, even if the effect is foreseen.

What does this mean? It means that to aim at evil, even as a means, is to have one's action guided by evil. One must be prepared to adjust it to insure the production of evil: a falling-off in the level of the desired evil becomes a reason for altering what one does so that the evil is restored and maintained. But the essence of evil is that it should *repel* us. If something is evil, our actions should be guided, if they are guided by it at all, toward its elimination rather than toward it maintenance. That is what evil *means*. So when we aim at evil we are swimming head-on against the normative current. Our action is guided by the goal at every point in the direction diametrically opposite to that in which the value of that goal points. To put it another way, if we aim at evil we make what we do in the first instance a positive rather than a negative function of it. At every point, the intentional function is simply the normative function reversed, and from the point of view of the agent, this produces an acute sense of moral dislocation.

If you twist the child's arm, your aim is to produce pain. So when the child cries, "Stop, it hurts!" his objection corresponds in perfect diametrical opposition to your intention. What he is pleading as your reason to stop is precisely your reason to go on. If it didn't hurt you would twist harder, or try the other arm. There may be cases (e.g. of justified punishment or obloquy) when pain is not intrinsically evil, but this is not one of them: the victim is innocent. You are pushing directly and essentially against the intrinsic normative force of your goal, for it is the production of his pain that guides you. It seems to me that this is the phenomenological nerve of

deontological constraints. What feels peculiarly wrong about doing evil intentionally even that good may come of it is the headlong striving against value that is internal to one's aim.

I have discussed a simple case, but naturally there can be complications. One is the possibility of someone volunteering to be subjected to some kind of pain or damage, either for his own good or for some other end which is important to him. In that case the particular evil that you aim at is swallowed up in the larger aim for deontological purposes. So the evil at which we are constrained not to aim is *our victim's evil*, rather than just a particular bad thing, and each individual has considerable authority in defining what will count as harming him for the purpose of this restriction.[5]

All this still leaves unsettled the question of justification. For it will be objected that if one aims at evil as a means only, then even if several people's interests are involved one's action is really being guided not by evil but by overall good, which includes a balance of goods and evils. So when you twist the child's arm, you are guided by the aim of rescuing your injured friends, and the good of that aim dominates the evil of the child's pain. The immediacy of the fact that you must try to produce evil as a subsidiary aim is phenomenologically important, but why should it be morally important? Even though it adds to the personal cost to you, why should it result in a prohibition?

I don't believe there is a decisive answer here. The question is whether to disregard the resistance encountered by my immediate pursuit of what is evil for my victim, in favor of the overall value of the results of what I do. When I view my act from outside and think of it as resulting from a choice of the impersonally considered state of the world in which it occurs, this seems rational. In thinking of the matter this way, I abstract my will and its choices from my person, as it were, and even from my actions, and decide directly among states of the world, as if I were taking a multiple choice test. If the choice is determined by what on balance is impersonally best, then I am guided by good and not by evil.

But the self that is so guided is the objective self, which regards the world impersonally, as a place containing TN and his actions, among other things. It is detached from the perspective of TN, for it views the world from nowhere within it. It chooses, and TN, its instrument, or perhaps one could say its agent, carries out the instructions as best he can. *He* may have to aim at evil, for the impersonally best alternative may involve the production of good ends by evil means. But he is only following orders.

To see the matter in this light is to see both the appeal of agent-neutral, consequentialist ethics and the contrary force of agent-relative, deontological ethics. The detached, objective view takes in everything and provides a standpoint of choice from which all choosers can agree about what should happen. But each of us is not only an objective self but a particular person with a particular perspective; we act in the world from that perspective, and not only from the point of view of a detached will, selecting and rejecting world-states. So our choices are not merely choices of states of the world, but of actions. Every choice is two choices, and from the internal point of view, the pursuit of evil in twisting the child's arm looms large. The production of pain is the immediate aim, and the fact that from an external perspective you are choosing a balance of good over evil does not cover up the fact that this is the intrinsic character of your action.

I have concentrated on the point of view of the agent, as seems suitable in the investigation of an agent-relative constraint. But there is also something to be said about the point of view of the victim. There too we encounter problems having to do with the integration of the two standpoints, and further support for the analysis. Moral principles don't simply tell agents what they may and may not do. They also tell victims what sort of treatment they may and may not object to, resist, or demand.

If I were justified in killing one innocent person to save five others, then he would have no right to object, and on a fully consequentialist view he would have no right to resist. The other five, by contrast, would have the right to object if I *didn't* kill him to save them. A thoroughly impersonal morality would require that victims as well as actors be dominated by impersonal, agent-neutral values in their judgments about how others treat them.

But this seems an excessive demand to make of individuals whose perspective on the world is inherently complex and includes a strong subjective component. Of course none of the six people in

this dilemma wants to die, but only one of them is faced with me trying to kill him. This person is not permitted, on a purely agent-neutral consequentialist view, to appeal for his life against my deliberate attempt to take it from him. His special position as my victim doesn't give him any special standing to appeal to me.

Of course the deontological position has a parallel feature. On a deontological view, the five people I could save by killing the one cannot appeal to me for their lives, against my refusal to save them. (They may appeal against *their* killers, if that's the nature of the death threat, but not against me.) But this does not make the two positions symmetrical, for there is a difference. The deontological constraint permits a victim always to object to those who aim at his harm, and this relation has the same special character or normative magnification when seen from the personal perspective of the victim that it has when seen from the personal perspective of the agent. Such a constraint expresses the direct appeal to the point of view of the agent from the point of view of the person on whom he is acting. It operates through that relation. The victim feels outrage when he is deliberately harmed even for the greater good of others, not simply because of the quantity of the harm but because of the assault on his value of having my actions guided by his evil. What I do is immediately directed against his good: it doesn't just in fact harm him.

The five people I could save by killing him can't say the same, if I refrain. They can appeal only to my objective acknowledgment of the impersonal value of their lives. That is not trivial, of course, but it still seems less pressing than the protest available to my victim—a protest he can make not to them but to me, as the possessor of the life I am aiming to destroy.

This merely corroborates the importance of the internal perspective in accounting for the content of deontological intuitions. It does not prove the correctness of those intuitions. But it confirms that a purely impersonal morality requires the general suppression of the personal perspective in moral motivation, not only in its rejection of relative reasons of autonomy but also in its refusal to accept agent-relative deontological restrictions. Such restrictions need not be absolute: they can be thought of as relative reasons with a certain weight, that are among the sources of morality but do not exhaust it. When we regard human relations objectively, it does not seem irrational to admit such reasons at the basic level into the perspective of both agents and victims.

6. MORAL PROGRESS

This account of the force of deontological reasons applies with special clarity to the constraint against doing harm as a means to your ends. A fuller deontological theory would have to explain the different types of normative grain against which one acts in breaking promises, lying, discriminating unfairly, and denying immediate emergency aid. It would also have to deal with problems about what exactly is being aimed at, in cases of action that can be described in several different ways. But I believe that the key to understanding any of these moral intuitions is the distinction between the internal viewpoint of the agent or victim and an external, objective viewpoint which both agent and victim can also adopt. Reasons for action look different from the first two points of view than from the third.

We are faced with a choice. For the purposes of ethics, should we identify with the detached, impersonal will that chooses total outcomes, and act on reasons that are determined accordingly? Or is this a denial of what we are really doing and an avoidance of the full range of reasons that apply to creatures like us? This is a true philosophical dilemma; it arises out of our nature, which includes different points of view on the world. When we ask ourselves how to live, the complexity of what we are makes a unified answer difficult. I believe the human duality of perspectives is too deep for us reasonably to hope to overcome it. A fully agent-neutral morality is not a plausible human goal.

On the other hand, it is conceivable that deontological restrictions now widely accepted may be modified under the pressure of conflict with the impersonal standpoint. Some degree of skepticism about our current moral intuitions is not unreasonable, in light of the importance to moral belief of our starting points, the social influences pressing on us, and the confusion of our thought. If we aspire to objective truth in this area—that is, truth that is independent of our beliefs—we would be

wise to hold many of our views more tentatively than we are naturally inclined to do. In ethics, even without the benefit of many clear examples, we should be open to the possibility of progress as we are in other areas, with a consequent effect of reduced confidence in the finality of our current understanding.[6]

It is evident that we are at a primitive stage of moral development. Even the most civilized human beings have only a haphazard understanding of how to live, how to treat others, how to organize their societies. The idea that the basic principles of morality are *known*, and that the problems all come in their interpretation and application, is one of the most fantastic conceits to which our conceited species has been drawn. (The idea that if we cannot easily know it, there is no truth here is no less conceited.) Not all of our ignorance in these areas is ethical, but a lot of it is. And the idea of the possibility of moral progress is an essential condition of moral progress. None of it is inevitable.

The pursuit of objectivity is only a method of getting closer to the truth. It is not guaranteed to succeed, and there is room for skepticism about its specific results in ethics as elsewhere. How far it can take us from the appearances is not clear. The truth here could not be radically inaccessible in the way that the truth about the physical world might be. It is more closely tied to the human perspective and the human motivational capacity because its point is the regulation of human conduct. It has to be suited to govern our lives day by day, in a way in which theoretical understanding of the physical world does not. And to do its work it must be far more widely accepted and internalized than in areas where the public is willing to defer to expert opinion.

There might be forms of morality incommensurable with our own that are appropriate for Martians but to which we do not have access for the same reason that we do not have access to the minds of such creatures. Unless we can understand their lives, experiences, and motives from inside, we will be unable to appreciate the values to which they respond in a way that allows us to objectify them accurately. Objectivity needs subjective material to work on, and for human morality this is found in human life.

How far outside ourselves we can go without losing contact with this essential material—with the forms of life in which values and justifications are rooted—is not certain. But I believe that ethics, unlike aesthetics, requires more than the purification and intensification of internal human perspectives. It requires a detachment from particular perspectives and transcendence of one's time and place. If we did not have this capacity then there would be no alternative to relativism in ethics. But I believe we do have it, and that it is not inevitably a form of false consciousness.

Even the very primitive stage of moral development we have reached was arrived at only by a long and difficult journey. I assume a much longer one lies ahead of us, if we survive. It would be foolish to try to lay down in advance the outlines of a correct method for ethical progress, but it seems reasonable at present to continue the awkward pursuit of objectivity described here. This does not mean that greater detachment always takes us closer to the truth. Sometimes, to be sure, objectivity will lead us to regard our original inclinations as mistaken, and then we will try to replace them or bracket them as ineliminable but illusory. But it would be a mistake to try to eliminate perspective from our conception of ethics entirely—as much of a mistake as it would be to try to eliminate perspective from the universe. This itself must be objectively recognized. Though it may be equally tempting, it would be no more reasonable to eliminate all those reasons for action that cannot be assimilated to the most external, impersonal system of value than it would be to eliminate all facts that cannot be assimilated to physics.

Yet in defending the legitimacy of agent-relative principles, we must guard against self-deception and the escalation of personal claims simply to resist burdensome moral demands. It is not always easy to tell, for example, whether a morality that leaves extensive free space in each individual life for the pursuit of personal interests is not just a disguise for the simplest form of badness: selfishness in the face of the legitimate claims of others. It is hard to be good, as we all know.

I suspect that if we try to develop a system of reasons which harmonizes personal and impersonal claims, then even if it is acknowledged that each of us must live in part from his own point of view,

there will be a tendency for the personal components to be altered. As the claims of objectivity are recognized, they may come to form a larger and larger part of each individual's conception of himself, and will influence the range of personal aims and ambitions and the ideas of his particular relations to others and the claims they justify. I do not think it is utopian to look forward to the gradual development of a greater universality of moral respect, an internalization of moral objectivity analogous to the gradual internalization of scientific progress that seems to be a feature of modern culture.

On the other hand there is no reason to expect progress to be reductive, though here as elsewhere progress is too easily identified with reduction and simplification. Distinct individuals are still the clients of ethics, and their variety guarantees that pluralism will be an essential aspect of any adequate morality, however advanced.

There have to be principles of practical reason that allow us to take into account values that we do not share but whose force for others we must acknowledge. In general, the problem of how to combine the enormous and disparate wealth of reasons that practical objectivity generates, together with the subjective reasons that remain, by a method that will allow us to act and choose in the world, is dauntingly difficult.

This brings us to a final point. There can be no ethics without politics. A theory of how individuals should act requires a theory—an ethical theory, not just an empirical one—of the institutions under which they should live: institutions which substantially determine their starting points, the choices they can make, the consequences of what they do, and their relations to one another. Since the standpoint of political theory is necessarily objective and detached, it offers strong temptations to simplify, which it is important to resist. A society must in some sense be organized in accordance with a single set of principles, even though people are very different.

This is inconvenient: it may seem that political theory must be based on a universal human nature, and that if we cannot discover such a thing we have to invent it, for political theory must exist. To avoid such folly, it is necessary to take on the much more difficult task of devising fair uniform social principles for beings whose nature is not uniform and whose values are legitimately diverse. If they were diverse enough, the task might be impossible—there may be no such thing as intergalactic political theory—but within the human species the variation seems to fall within bounds that do not rule out the possibility of at least a partial solution. This would have to be something acceptable from a standpoint external to that of each particular individual, which at the same time acknowledges the plurality of values and reasons arising within all those perspectives. Even though the morality of politics is rightly more impersonal than the morality of private life, the acknowledgment of personal values and autonomy is essential even at the level that requires the greatest impersonality.

There is no telling what kinds of transcendence of individuality will result over the long term from the combined influence of moral and political progress, or decline. A general takeover of individual life from the perspective of the universe, or even from the perspective of humanity, seems premature—even if some saints or mystics can manage it. Reasons for action have to be reasons for individuals, and individual perspectives can be expected to retain their moral importance so long as diverse human individuals continue to exist.

Notes

[1] This is the rationale behind the choice of primary goods as the common measure of welfare for distributive justice in Rawls (1). See Rawls (2) for a much fuller treatment. That essay, Scanlon (1), and the present discussion are all treatments of the "deep problem" described in Rawls (1), pp. 173–5. Dworkin's defense of resources rather than welfare as the correct measure of equality is also in part a response to this problem.

[2] Impartiality should not be confused with equality. Nothing I say here bears on the question of how much equality is required in the allocation of what has impersonal value. Absolute impartiality is consistent with a denial that equality should be an independent factor at all in settling distributive questions.

[3] A good statement of a view of this type is found in Fried.

[4] This is emphasized by Scheffler, who has a cautiously skeptical discussion of deontological constraints under the heading of "agent-centred restrictions."

[5] The same seems to apply even when informed consent is impossible, as when we cause suffering or damage to a young child for its own greater good—though here there may be a residual inhibition: if we imagine in the case described that the *child's* safety depends on getting the car keys, it doesn't altogether remove the revulsion against twisting his arm to get them.

[6] See Parfit (2), pt. 1, for discussion of some ways commonsense morality might be revised to bring it closer to consequentialism.

Actions, Intentions, and Consequences: The Doctrine of Double Effect

WARREN S. QUINN ▪ University of California, Los Angeles
Philosophy and Public Affairs, 1989

In this essay, Warren S. Quinn looks at three paired cases: SB (Strategic Bomber) and TB (Terror Bomber), which involve wartime bombing; DR (Direction of Resources) and GP (Guinea Pig), which deal with the medical response to a disease; and CC (Craniotomy Case) and HC (Hysterectomy Case), which concern the fate of an unborn fetus. According to Quinn, these paired cases are similar in that in each case, agents bring about the same good consequences at the same cost in harm, although each case in the paired cases differs in the moral and behavioral character of the actions displayed by the agents involved. Quinn examines these cases in order to clarify the two sorts of agency between which the DDE (Doctrine of Double Effect) is taken to discriminate. His purpose is to become clear on which discrimination the proponents of the DDE must really be relying upon.

After discussing (and rejecting) various approaches, Quinn claims that the moral force of the DDE "ought to be capturable on any plausible theory of the intentional." For Quinn, the intentional structure of a situation is revealed when we see what effects are required for an agent to further his goals, or when we see that some effects fail to serve an agent's purposes. According to Quinn, when we look at our paired cases in this way, we will see that the DDE actually discriminates between two kinds of agency that differ slightly from the "intentional" and "foreseen" distinction. These two kinds of agency are what Quinn calls **harmful direct agency** and **harmful indirect agency**. Harmful direct agency is "agency in which harm comes to some victims . . . from the agent's deliberately involving them in something in order to further his purpose precisely by way of their being so involved." Harmful indirect agency is "harmful agency in which either nothing is in that way intended for the victims or what is so intended does not contribute to their harm." According to Quinn, this way of characterizing the DDE successfully draws a difference in intentional structure between the paired cases without making an appeal to what he calls the troublesome notion of "closeness" (which is needed to give an account of "means").

The DDE discriminates against harmful direct agency, even though people may figure as intentional objects not only of a choice to act but also of a choice not to act. Thus, the DDE cuts across the distinction between harming and allowing harm (embodied in the Doctrine of Doing and Allowing discussed in Quinn, p. 145).

Quinn closes his essay with a discussion of what he calls "the question of rationale." For Quinn, in the case of the DDE, this means providing a deeper reason for accepting the moral difference which intuition senses between harmful direct agency and harmful indirect agency. In Quinn's view, the rationale behind the DDE is a Kantian ideal that reflects the sort of respect we feel others are owed as free and equal human agents capable of voluntary action. We can see this deeper ideal when we notice that the distinction between direct and indirect agency is grounded in a concern about the attitude which agents have toward victims. It is objectionable if a victim is "viewed strategically" by an agent, or if a victim enters an agent's strategic thinking as material for his purposes, or as cast in a role serving the agent's ends.

SITUATIONS IN WHICH GOOD CAN BE SECURED for some people only if others suffer harm are of great significance to moral theory.[1] Consequentialists typically hold that the right thing to do in such cases is to maximize overall welfare. But nonconsequentialists think that many other factors matter. Some, for example, think that in situations of conflict it is often more acceptable to let a certain harm befall someone than actively to bring the harm about. I believe that this view, which I call the Doctrine of Doing and Allowing, is correct, and I defend it elsewhere.[2] But there is a different and even better known anticonsequentialist principle in the Doctrine of Double Effect (for short, the DDE).[3] According to one of the common readings of this principle, the pursuit of a good tends to be less acceptable where a resulting harm is intended as a means than where it is merely foreseen.[4] It is this controversial idea that I wish to examine here.

There are two major problems with the DDE. First, there is a difficulty in formulating it so that it succeeds in discriminating between cases that, intuitively speaking, should be distinguished. In particular, I will need to find a formulation that escapes the disturbing objection that under a strict enough interpretation the doctrine fails to rule against many or most of the choices commonly taken to illustrate its negative force. Second, there is a question of rationale. What, apart from its agreeing with our particular intuitions, can be said in favor of the doctrine? Indeed, why should we accept the intuitions that support it? In answer, I shall suggest a rationale with clear Kantian echoes.

I.

Like the Doctrine of Doing and Allowing, the DDE discriminates between two kinds of morally problematic agency. It discriminates against agency in which there is some kind of intending of an objectionable outcome as conducive to the agent's end, and it discriminates in favor of agency that involves only foreseeing, but not that kind of intending, of an objectionable outcome. That is, it favors and disfavors these forms of agency in allowing that, *ceteris paribus* [other things being equal], the pursuit of a great enough good might justify one but not the other. The doctrine is meant to capture certain kinds of fairly common moral intuitions about pairs of cases which have the *same* consequential profile—in which agents bring about the same good result at the same cost in lives lost and harm suffered—but in which the character of the intention differs in the indicated way.

One such pair of contrasting cases is drawn from modern warfare: In the Case of the Strategic Bomber (SB), a pilot bombs an enemy factory in order to destroy its productive capacity. But in doing this he foresees that he will kill innocent civilians who live nearby. Many of us see this kind of military action as much easier to justify than that in the Case of the Terror Bomber (TB), who deliberately kills innocent civilians in order to demoralize the enemy. Another pair of cases involves medicine: In both there is a shortage of resources for the investigation and proper treatment of a new,

life-threatening disease. In the first scenario doctors decide to cope by selectively treating only those who can be cured most easily, leaving the more stubborn cases untreated. Call this the Direction of Resources Case (DR). In the contrasting and intuitively more problematic example, doctors decide on a crash experimental program in which they deliberately leave the stubborn cases untreated in order to learn more about the nature of the disease. By this strategy they reasonably expect to do as much long-term medical good as they would in DR. Call this the Guinea Pig Case (GP). In neither case do the nontreated know about or consent to the decision against treating them.

Another pair of medical examples is found in most discussions of double effect. In the Craniotomy Case (CC) a woman will die unless the head of the fetus she is trying to deliver is crushed. But the fetus may be safely removed if the mother is allowed to die. In the Hysterectomy Case (HC), a pregnant mother's uterus is cancerous and must be removed if she is to be saved. This will, given the limits of available medical technology, kill the fetus. But if no operation is performed the mother will eventually die after giving birth to a healthy infant. Many people see less of a moral difference between these two cases than between the other pairs. This might be for a variety of reasons extraneous to the doctrine: because the fetus is not yet a person and therefore not yet within the moral framework, because the craniotomy is seen as a way of defending the mother against the fetus, because the fetus's position within the mother's body gives her special rights over it, and so on. But the relative weakness of the intuitive contrast here might also signal something important about the doctrine's central distinction. I shall say more about this later. But for the present it will be useful to include this pair of cases under the DDE, if only because it naturally illustrates the objection mentioned earlier.

According to that objection, the doctor in CC does not intend, at least not strictly speaking, that the fetus actually die.[5] On the contrary, we would expect the doctor to be glad if, by some miracle, it survived unharmed. It is not death itself, or even harm itself, that is strictly intended, but rather an immediately physical effect on the fetus that will allow its removal.[6] That effect will of course be fatal to the fetus, but it is not intended *as* fatal. The intentions in CC are therefore really no different from those in HC.

It might seem that this kind of point cannot be made about the bombing and nontreatment cases. In GP the doctors seem to need the disease to continue so that they can observe its effects. And in TB the pilot seems to need the deaths of the civilians to lower enemy morale. But Jonathan Bennett suggests a way of extending the objection to the bombing case.[7] The terror bomber does not, he argues, need the civilians actually to be dead. He only needs them to be as good as dead and to seem dead until the war ends. If by some miracle they "came back to life" after the war was over, he would not object. And something similar might be said about the doctors in GP. While they need the disease to continue its course, they do not need the victims actually to be harmed by it. If by some miracle the victims developed special ways of withstanding the disease so that they remained comfortable and well-functioning despite its progress, the doctors would be glad.[8]

This line of objection clearly threatens to deprive the doctrine of most of its natural applications. One reply is to say that it surely matters how *close* the connection is between that which is, strictly speaking, intended and the resulting foreseen harm. If the connection is close enough, then the doctrine should treat the harm as if it were strictly intended.[9] And, the reply might go on, the connection is close enough in the cases I have used to illustrate the doctrine's negative force. But what does this idea of closeness amount to? H.L.A. Hart suggests a possible answer by way of the example of someone violently striking a glass just in order to hear the sound of the initial impact. In such a case the further outcome, the shattering of the glass, is "so immediately and invariably" connected with the intended impact that the connection seems conceptual rather than contingent.[10] The death of the fetus in CC is, arguably, connected with the intended impact on its skull in just this immediate and invariable way. And the deaths, or at lease some harms, in TB and GP seem just as closely connected with what is strictly intended in those cases.

But what of the contrasting cases? Since hysterectomies are rarely performed on pregnant women, they rarely result in the death of the fetus. So we might say that what is strictly intended in HC (that the uterus be removed) is not, in the relevant sense, closely connected with the fetus's death. And we might hope to find something similar to say in SB and DR. But in taking this way of preserving the contrasts, we would be making everything depend on which strictly intended outcomes of the various choices we fasten upon.

This leads to a new problem. For certain things that the doctor in CC strictly intends for the fetus lack an invariable fatal upshot. Indeed, if craniotomies are ever performed on fetuses that are already dead, then a craniotomy is already such a thing. Even more obviously, the doctor in HC might strictly intend something that is invariably fatal to a fetus. Suppose, for example, that hysterectomies performed on patients who are in the early months of pregnancy are distinguished by the use of a special anesthetic that is safer for the patient and, in itself, harmless to the fetus. This peculiarity could hardly make the operation in HC more difficult to justify, but it would imply that the strictly intended medical means were immediately and invariably connected with the death of a fetus.[11] Perhaps similar things can be said about the other cases. A strategic bomber might have as his mission the bombing of automotive factories. This would not make him a terror bomber, for he would still not aim at civilian casualties. But, for obvious reasons, no automobile factories have ever existed completely apart from civilian populations. So the kind of thing the bomber strictly intends immediately and invariably results in some innocent deaths.

Two problems have emerged. First, since more than one thing may be strictly intended in a given choice, the pronouncements of the doctrine may depend on how the choice happens to be described. This relativity is embarrassing. We would like the doctrine to speak with one voice in any given case. Second, if we try to get around this problem by saying that the doctrine discriminates against a choice in which anything that is strictly intended is also closely connected with death or harm, the doctrine will make uninviting moral distinctions. As we have seen, it will speak against HC if hysterectomies performed on pregnant patients have some distinguishing surgical feature. Otherwise it will speak in favor. And it will speak against the strategic bomber's attack on an urban factory if he was looking specifically for an automotive plant but not, perhaps, if he was looking for a strategically important productive facility.[12] Another approach clearly seems called for.

Instead of looking for a way to identify intrinsically bad effects that are "close enough" to what is intended, we might look instead for a way to identify choices that are intended under some intrinsically negative description. We might then find a way to show that the actions in TB and CC, but not in SB or HC, are intentional *as killings* and that the inaction in GP, but not in DR, is intentional *as a letting die*. Elizabeth Anscombe gives us one such criterion.[13] If we ask a man why he is pushing a mower, he will perhaps say "to cut the grass"; if we ask why he is cutting the grass, he may say "to get things spruced up around here," and so on. The "to . . ." answers, or answers that can be understood in terms of them, give further intentions with which the agent acts. If, his choice being described in a certain way, he accepts the 'why' question and replies with a "to . . ." answer, then his choice is intentional under that description. But if he rejects the question in a certain familiar way, his choice is unintentional. If asked why he is cutting the grass he replies, for example, "I don't care about that, I'm just out to annoy the neighbors" or "Can't be helped—it goes with this terrific form of exercise," his cutting the grass is not, as such, intentional.

This seems to give the desired result when applied to our cases. If we ask the doctor in CC why he is killing the fetus, he will naturally say "to save the mother." If we ask the pilot in TB why he is killing the civilians, he will say "to help with the war." And if we ask the doctors in GP why they withhold treatment, they will say "to observe the progress of the disease." And it might be thought that if we ask similar questions in the other cases, the 'why' question will be rejected in a way that shows the choices to be unintentional. Thus, if asked why he is killing the fetus, the doctor in HC will avoid a "to . . ." answer, saying instead something like "It can't be helped if I am to save the mother."

Actually, this seems not quite right. If the doctors in DR were asked why they weren't treating the group in question, they might naturally reply "*to save our resources for more easily treated cases.*" And this, by Anscombe's criterion, would seem to make the nontreatment intentional. But waiving this difficulty, there is another worry. What if the

agents in the problematic cases (TB, GP, and CC) become philosophically sophisticated? Perhaps they will then come to reject the "why" questions in the manner of their counterparts. The terror bomber, for example, might respond by saying, "The actual deaths can't be helped if I am to create the realistic appearance of death and destruction." By giving such answers, he and the others will be opting for a more demanding criterion of the intentional. All aspects of an action or inaction that do not in the strictest sense contribute to an agent's goal will be trimmed away as unintentional. By this criterion, the action in CC is intentional as a crushing and that in TB is intentional as an apparent killing. But neither is intentional as a killing. And in GP the inaction is intentional as a way of facilitating medical research, but not as a letting die.

Now it would be very natural to object that the ordinary, more relaxed criterion of the intentional is the right one, and that the stricter criterion is specious. But how is this to be made out? We might try to introduce a form of essentialism here, claiming that the surgery in CC and the bombing in TB are essentially killings or harmings, while the surgery in HC and the bombing in SB are not. But surely the ground of this essentialism would be the prior conviction that the killings in CC and TB are intentional while those in HC and SB are not. The issue about intentionality seems to be the basic one. And what would we say about the inaction in GP—that it was essentially a failure to prevent harm? But then this would also seem true of the inaction in DR.

On the one side we have Anscombe's criterion of the intentional, which pretty well maps our ordinary ways of speaking, while on the other we have a criterion that is structurally similar but stricter. The problem here about intention is reminiscent of a problem about causality that arises in connection with the Doctrine of Doing and Allowing. Certain defenses of that doctrine (which discriminates against active harming and in favor of allowing harm) appeal to a familiar conception of causality according to which active harming *causes* harm while inactively allowing harm does not. But opponents counter that according to other, philosophically superior conceptions of causality, inaction can be every bit as much a cause of harm. Now I have argued that if DDA is sound theory, it ought to have force on any plausible conception of causality.[14] And I feel much the same here. If the DDE is sound, its force ought to be capturable on any plausible theory of the intentional, even one that would revise ordinary ways of speaking. So, for purposes of argument, I shall grant opponents of the doctrine the greatest latitude in paring back intentional actions to their indisputably intentional cores.

II.

We must therefore find a different reply to the difficulty with which we started. And I think I see a way. For we have been neglecting one striking respect in which members of our contrasting pairs differ. Take TB and SB. In the former case, but not the latter, the bomber undeniably intends in the strictest sense that the civilians be involved in a certain explosion, which he produces, precisely because their involvement in it serves his goal. He may not, if Bennett is right, intend their deaths. But his purpose requires at least this—that they be violently impacted by the explosion of his bombs. That this undeniably intended effect can be specified in a way that does not strictly entail their deaths is, on the view I am proposing, beside the point. What matters is that the effect serves the agent's end precisely because it is an effect *on civilians*. The case with SB is quite different. The bomber in that case intends an explosion, but not in order that any civilians be affected by it. Of course he is well aware that his bombs will kill many of them, and perhaps he cannot honestly say that this effect will be "unintentional" in any standard sense, or that he "does not mean to" kill them. But he can honestly deny that their involvement in the explosion is anything to his purpose.

The same contrast is found in the medical cases. The doctor in CC strictly intends to produce an effect on the fetus so that the mother can be saved by that effect. But the doctor in HC has, as we have seen, no such intention. Even if he cannot deny that, in some ordinary sense, he "intends" the fetus's death, he can rightly insist that the effects on the fetus of his surgery are nothing toward his medical purpose. Similarly, the doctors in GP intend, as something toward their futher goal, that the disease in the untreated patients work its course. And this could be true even if, wishing to

investigate only the effects of the disease within cells, they had no interest in the pain and loss of function it also causes. But in DR nothing that happens to the untreated patients serves the doctors' further goal.[15]

The important way in which the cases differ should not be obscured by the following complication. We have seen that a doctor in HC might intend to use the special anesthetic "safest for a *pregnant* patient." Would it follow from this allusion to the fetus that the doctor does, after all, strictly intend something for it? No. The medical relevance of the patient's pregnancy does not mean that any of the surgical effects on the fetus are medically useful. Something similar holds in SB. Suppose the bomber wants, for moral reasons, to target factories in the least populated district of a certain city. If so, the formulation of his strictly intended means contains an indirect reference to the civilians whom he may kill. But this hardly turns him into a terror bomber. The impact of his bombs on those civilians is still nothing to his military purpose.

This clear distinction between the intentional structures of the contrasting cases is the key to a new and better formulation of the doctrine. To put things in the most general way, we should say that it distinguishes between agency in which harm comes to some victims, at least in part, from the agent's deliberately involving them in something in order to further his purpose precisely by way of their being so involved (agency in which they figure as *intentional objects*)[16] and harmful agency in which either nothing is in that way intended for the victims or what is so intended does not contribute to their harm.[17] Let us call the first kind of agency in the production of harm *direct* and the second kind *indirect*. According to this version of the doctrine, we need, *ceteris paribus*, a stronger case to justify harmful direct agency than to justify equally harmful indirect agency.[18] Put this way, the doctrine solves the original problem of showing a genuine difference in the intentional structures of our contrasting cases, even under a strict interpretation of what is intended. And it makes no appeal to the problematic notion of "closeness." For direct agency requires neither that harm itself be useful nor that what is useful be casually connected in some especially close way with the harm it helps bring about.[19] There is another, related advantage. With this version of the doctrine, we can sidestep all potentially controversial questions about whether the agents in our various cases kill or harm intentionally. It is enough that we can identify the things they controversially intend as contributing to their goal.

Our further bit of line-drawing remains. We have not yet defined the difference between the more pronounced moral asymmetry of DR and GP, or SB and TB, and the apparently weaker asymmetry of HC and CC. This difference may partly depend on whether the agent, in his strategy, sees the victim as an advantage or as a difficulty. In CC the doctor wants the fetus removed from the birth canal. Its presence there is the problem. In GP and TB, on the other hand, the availability of potential victims presents an opportunity. By bringing it about that certain things are true of them, the agents positively further their goals. Perhaps it would not be surprising if we regarded fatal or harmful exploitation as more difficult to justify than fatal or harmful elimination. If so, we might say that the doctrine strongly discriminates against direct agency that benefits from the presence of the victim (direct *opportunistic* agency) and more weakly discriminates against direct agency that aims to remove an obstacle or difficulty that the victim presents (direct *eliminative* agency).

III.

The DDE, of course, has only prima facie moral force. Special rights may allow us to harm someone's interests by way of direct (and even direct opportunistic) agency. Various rights of competition and the right to punish seem to be examples. Certain other cases may prompt qualifications or special interpretations of the doctrine. Suppose that the doctor in HC needs to alter, harmlessly, the position of the fetus before the womb can be safely removed. Whether the overall surgical procedure would still count as indirect harming seems a matter of interpretation. If we saw the manipulation of the fetus as a partial cause of its later removal, we would presumably count the harming as direct. If we saw the manipulation as a precondition, but not a partial cause, of the removal, we would count the harming as indirect.

Another problematic kind of case involves innocent hostages or other persons who physically get in the way of our otherwise legitimate targets or projects. Does our shooting through or running over them involve a direct intention to affect them? I think not. It is to our purpose, in the kind of case I am imagining, that a bullet or car move through a certain space, but it is not to our purpose that it in fact move through or over someone occupying that space. The victims in such cases are of no use to us and do not constitute empirical obstacles (since they will not deflect the missile or vehicle in question). If we act despite their presence, we act exactly as we would if they were not there. If, on the other hand, we needed to aim at someone in order to hit a target, that person would clearly figure as an intentional object. Another tricky case is one in which we could, and would if we had to, accomplish our end by harmful indirect agency; but it is better, perhaps safer for those to be benefited, to pursue the end by harmful agency that is direct. It seems clear why we might wish to make this kind of case an exception.

Before we turn to the defense of the doctrine, we should briefly consider the way in which it interacts with the distinction, mentioned in connection with the Doctrine of Doing and Allowing, between what is actively brought about and what is merely allowed to happen. I have claimed that DDE, with the exceptions noted, discriminates against harmful direct agency. But, as we have seen, people may figure as intentional objects not only of a choice to act but also of a choice not to act. DDE therefore cuts across the distinction between harming and allowing harm. Sometimes, as in TB and CC, it discriminates against direct agency in which harm is done. And sometimes, as in GP, it discriminates against direct agency in which harm is allowed.

In all of these cases we seem to find an original negative or positive right that, while opposed by other rights, seems to be strengthened by the fact that harm will come via direct agency.[20] Civilians in wartime have negative rights not to be killed. But if their government is waging an unjust war, these rights may conflict with the strong rights of self-defense. A sufficiently developed fetus *in utero* might also have some negative right not to be killed. But this right may not prevail, either because the fetus is not yet fully one of us or because its mother has strong rights over her body. In TB and CC, the directness of the threatening agency apparently serves to strengthen these negative rights, perhaps giving them a power to stand against moral forces to which they would otherwise give way. Something similar happens in GP. The untreated people have, presumably, some positive right to medical aid. This right might not be binding if doctors could cure more people by directing aid elsewhere. But it stands against any attempt to maximize medical benefit by deliberately letting the people deteriorate. Again, the directness of the intention strengthens the force of the opposing right or claim.

It is interesting to consider whether DDE might also come into play where no independent negative or positive right is present. Suppose, in an act of pure supererogation, I am about to aid you but am checked by the realization that your difficulty can be turned either to my advantage or to that of someone I care more for. Does my change of mind, for that reason, violate any of your rights? I am inclined to think not. It might be bad of me to be checked by such a reason, but its appearance cannot create an obligation where none existed before. Rights not to be caught up, to one's disadvantage, in the direct agency of others seem to exist only where some positive or negative right already applies. Their effect always seems to be that of strengthening some other right.

The effect of the doctrine is therefore to *raise* rather than to lower moral barriers. So we should not expect a proponent of DDE to be more tolerant of harmful indirect agency than those who reject the doctrine but share the rest of his moral outlook. We should rather expect him to be *less* tolerant of harmful direct agency. This point is important. For casual critics of the doctrine sometimes seem to suppose that its defenders must be ready to allow killings or harmings simply on the ground that the agency is indirect. But nothing could be further from the truth. The doctrine in no way lessens the constraining force of any independent moral right or duty.

IV.

We must now turn to the question of rationale. At first glance, harmful direct agency might seem harder to justify because it requires that the agent welcome something bad for the victim. The terror bomber, for example, must welcome the news that the innocent civilians are blown up, even if he is not glad that they won't be miraculously resurrected after the war. The trouble is that it also seems the strategic bomber must, in some sense, welcome the same news, since if the civilians had been unharmed the factory would not in fact have been destroyed.[21] Of course the news is good for different reasons. It is good news for the terror bomber because it announces the very thing that he intended, while it is good news for the strategic bomber because it announces the thing that he foresaw would be evidence of what he intended. But this difference does little more than register what we already knew—that the terror bomber strictly intended the deaths while the strategic bomber merely foresaw them as necessary costs. So it is hard to see how it could be used to explain the moral difference between direct and indirect agency.

Nor is it the case that harms of direct agency need be worse than those of indirect agency. If someone threatened by a terror bomber and someone equally threatened by a strategic bomber both needed rescuing, the former would not seem to have the stronger claim to help. Indeed, there would seem to be no reason to rescue either in preference to someone threatened by purely natural causes.[22] And if we sometimes think that the first rescue must have priority, it seems to be only because we are tempted to regard the violation of a special right against harmful direct agency as a distinctive and additional kind of moral evil. But then it would be circular simply to appeal to the evil in order to explain the existence or force of the right.

Perhaps the following rationale is more promising. Someone who unwillingly suffers because of what we intend for him as a way of getting our larger goal seems to fall under our power and control in a distinctive way. And there may be something morally problematic in this special relation— something over and above what is morally objectionable in the simpler relation of bringing about or not preventing harm. If this is right, then harmful direct agency must have two things against it, while equally harmful indirect agency need have only one. This additional negative element can be seen most clearly in the contrast between the doctor's attitudes in GP and DR. In the former, but not the latter, they show a shocking failure of respect for the persons who are harmed; they treat their victims as they would treat laboratory animals. DDE might therefore seem to rest on special duties of respect for persons, duties over and above any duty not to harm or to prevent harm.

While this is surely on the right track, we must proceed with caution. For there is also a kind of disrespect in typical cases of wrongful indirect agency. A strategic bomber who ought to have refrained from destroying a rather unimportant target because of likely civilian casualties has failed to treat his victims with the consideration that they and their interests deserve. So we must look for a kind of disrespect that is peculiar to wrongful direct agency—a kind different from that shown in wrongly giving a victim's interests too little weight.

What seems specifically amiss in relations of direct harmful agency is the particular way in which victims enter into an agent's strategic thinking. An indirect agent may be certain that his pursuit of a goal will leave victims in its wake. But this is not because their involvement in what he does or does not do will be useful to his end. The agent of direct harm, on the other hand, has something in mind for his victims—he proposes to involve them in some circumstance that will be useful to him precisely because it involves them. He sees them as material to be strategically shaped or framed by his agency.

Someone who harms by direct agency must therefore take up a distinctive attitude toward his victims. He must treat them as if they were then and there *for* his purposes. But indirect harming is different. Those who simply stand unwillingly to be harmed by a strategy—those who will be incidentally rather than usefully affected—are not viewed strategically at all and therefore not treated as for the agent's purposes rather than their own. They may, it is true, be treated as beings whose harm or death does not much matter—at least not as much as the achievement of the agent's goals. And that presumption is morally questionable. But in a counterpart case of direct agency there is the *additional* presumption that the victim may be cast in some role that serves the agent's goal.

The civilians in TB serve the bomber's goal by becoming casualties, and the infected people in GP serve the doctors' goal by becoming guinea pigs. If things were different, the victims might become these things only voluntarily. Suppose, for example, the civilians had effective bomb shelters and the sick people medicines of their own. Then the bomber or doctors could succeed only with the cooperation of the victims. The service exacted would then be voluntary. But in cases of indirect agency the victims make *no* contribution. If the civilians in SB had shelters and if the sick people in DR had medicines, the bomber and the doctors would see no point in their refusing to use them.

The DDE rests on the strong moral presumption that those who can be usefully involved in the promotion of a goal only at the cost of something protected by their independent moral rights (such as their life, their bodily integrity, or their freedom) ought, prima facie, to serve the goal only voluntarily.[23] The chief exceptions to this strong presumption are cases in which people have or would have strong moral obligations to give themselves to the service of a goal even at such personal costs—especially cases in which it would be indecent of them to refuse. But surely there is not, or may not be, any such obligation in the cases we have been considering: noncombatants (even those on the wrong side) are not morally obligated to serve the right side by accepting the role of demoralizing civilian casualties, victims of dangerous diseases are not typically obligated to become guinea pigs for the sake of others, and I suppose it is at least open to question whether the fetus in CC, if it could grasp its predicament, would have to accept, for the sake of its mother, the sacrifice of its life.

In these cases, but not in their indirect counterparts, the victims are made to play a role in the service of the agent's goal that is not (or may not be) morally required of them. And this aspect of direct agency adds its own negative moral force—a force over and above that provided by the fact of harming or failing to prevent harm.[24] This additional force seems intuitively clearest in direct opportunistic agency, such as TB and GP, where unwilling victims are not only harmed but, in some sense, used. And this must be why the doctrine seems most plausible when it discriminates against opportunistic direct agency. It must also help explain why some of the most perverse forms of opportunistic agency, like torture, can seem absolutely unjustifiable.

It is less plausible, on the other hand, to think of the victims of direct eliminative agency as used. This may be why the doctrine seems to discriminate against eliminative agency less forcefully. And it may therefore help explain why some people feel that the direct agency of CC is not much harder to justify than the indirect agency of HC. But something of the questionable character of direct opportunistic agency also seems present in direct eliminative agency. Someone who gets in your way presents a strategic problem—a casual obstacle whose removal will be a service to your goals. And this is quite unlike what we find in harmful indirect agency, where victims can be obstacles only in a moral sense.

In discriminating to some extent against both forms of direct agency, the doctrine reflects a Kantian ideal of human community and interaction.[25] Each person is to be treated, so far as possible, as existing only for purposes that he can share. This ideal is given one natural expression in the language of rights. People have a strong prima facie right not to be sacrificed in strategic roles over which they have no say. They have a right not to be pressed, in apparent violation of their prior rights, into the service of other people's purposes. Sometimes these additional rights may be justifiably infringed, especially when the prior right is not terribly important and the harm is limited, but in all cases they add their own burden to the opposing moral argument.

The Doctrine of Double Effect thus gives each person some veto power over a certain kind of attempt to make the world a better place at his expense. This would be absurd if the entire point of morality were to maximize overall happiness or welfare. But that is not its entire point. An equally urgent basic task is to define the forms of respect that we owe to one another, and the resulting limits that we may not presume to exceed. The doctrine embodies our sense that certain forms of forced strategic subordination are especially inappropriate among free and equal agents.

Notes

I am grateful for very helpful suggestions from Rogers Albritton, Philippa Foot, Matthew Hanser, and many others; and for criticism from audiences at New York University, the University of California at Irvine, and Princeton University.

[1]Harm is meant in a very broad sense that includes the loss of life, rightful property, privacy, and so on. In my examples, the relevant harm will usually be the loss of life.

[2]Warren S. Quinn, "Actions, Intentions, and Consequences: The Doctrine of Doing and Allowing," p.145.

[3]The doctrine, which is usually traced to Thomas Aquinas, *Summa Theologiae*, II-II, Q. 64, art. 7, is typically put as a set of necessary conditions on morally permissible agency in which a morally questionable bad upshot is foreseen: (a) the intended final end must be good, (b) the intended means to it must be morally acceptable, (c) the foreseen bad upshot must *not* itself be willed (that is, must not be, in some sense, intended), and (d) the good end must be proportionate to the bad upshot (that is, must be important enough to justify the bad upshot). The principle that follows in the text, which I henceforth treat as if it were itself the doctrine, is really what I find most important and plausible in its first three conditions. I ignore the fourth condition both because it is probably best understood in a way that makes it noncontroversial and because I am concerned here not so much with how choices with a "second effect" can be justified as with whether, *ceteris paribus*, the structure of intention makes a justificatory difference. That seems to me the fundamental question.

[4]The principle is sometimes put in terms of the difference between a harmful *result* that is "directly" intended and one that is "indirectly" (or "obliquely") intended. But it also might be put in terms of the difference between a directly and an indirectly intended *act* of harming. In either variant, the point of calling the merely foreseen result or action "indirectly *intended*" is to mark a species of linguistic impropriety in an agent's asserting, with a completely straight face, that a clearly foreseen harm or harming is quite *un*intended. If I have no desire to wake you but simply do not care that my fiddling will have that effect I cannot say that your waking or my waking you is purely unintentional. Whether there is any natural sense in which they are intentional is a debated point. In the final analysis, I shall sidestep this controversy, concerning myself with a species of intention that an agent clearly does not have toward a merely foreseen result of his agency—namely, the intention that the result occur, or that he bring it about, as a means of achieving his purpose.

[5]See Herbert L. A. Hart, "Intention and Punishment," in *Punishment and Responsibility* (Oxford: Clarendon Press, 1968), p. 123. Hart finds the intentions in CC and HC to be parallel. But he does not argue, and does not seem to think, that a similar point can be made about most other cases that the doctrine might seem to distinguish. Nancy Davis finds more general problems along

these lines in "The Doctrine of Double Effect: Problems of Interpretation," p. 199.

[6]If the miracle happened, and after its removal the fetus were quickly restored to its previous healthy condition, we would say that the craniotomy had done no real harm. In the actual case, the harm done to the fetus by the craniotomy consists in the *combination* of the desired immediate effect on it (which permits its removal) and the further natural effects that flow from that first effect. Since these further effects are not strictly intended, the objection holds that the harm itself is not strictly intended. See Jonathan Bennett, *Morality and Consequences*, The Tanner Lectures on Human Values II (Salt Lake City: University of Utah Press, 1981), pp. 110–11.

[7]Ibid., p. 111.

[8]Perhaps then it would not really be, at least in these people, a disease. But then it might be said that the doctors don't really need it to be a disease in *them*. It would be good enough if, due to their special powers of compensation, it is for them a harmless condition very much like a disease in others.

[9]Philippa Foot perhaps suggests this kind of reply in "The Problem of Abortion and the Doctrine of Double Effect," p. 59.

[10]Hart, "Intention and Punishment," p. 120.

[11]Of course this special operation could, however inappropriately, be performed on patients who were not pregnant. And this might lead someone to speculate that the doctrine speaks against a strictly intended and invariably harmful kind of action or omission only if the harm is an empirically necessary consequence. But this cannot be right. Suppose there is some good that will arise immediately upon your being injected with a certain fatal poison. The good does not require that you actually die. But that is what will happen, since the very real and naturally abundant antidote that could save you has not been, and in fact never will be, discovered. In such a case, the doctrine should certainly speak against my poisoning you. But the directly and invariably connected harm would not follow of empirical necessity.

[12]If the latter intention sometimes gets fulfilled, for example, by bombing electric power facilities built into remote and isolated dams.

[13]G.M.A. Anscombe, *Intention*, 2d ed. (Oxford: Blackwell, 1963), sec. 25, pp. 41–45.

[14]See Quinn, "Actions, Intentions, and Consequences: The Doctrine of Doing and Allowing," p. 145.

[15]Not even, I would argue, the fact of their not receiving the treatment. What really furthers the goal is the treatment received by the other, more tractable cases. The nontreatment of the first group contributes, at most, in an odd and secondary sense. This point applies, I think, to a wide range of intentional expressions. Suppose we decide to combat a disease by spending our limited resources on education rather than on inoculation. Education, and not noninoculation, will then be our *means* of combat; and the *way* we fight the disease will be by educating, not by not inoculating.

[16]I might instead have said "agency in which harm comes to victims . . . from the agent's deliberately producing some *effect on them* in order to further his purpose precisely by way of their being so affected." But there is a certain kind of ingenious case, attributed to David Lewis, that such a formulation might seem to miss. Suppose that another terror bomber wishes to demoralize enemy leaders by bombing a major center of population, and suppose he knows that these leaders will be convinced that the city is destroyed by seeing, from afar, the explosion of his bombs over it. The explosion occurs an instant before the fatal effects below. So in this case the bomber does not, strictly speaking, intend to blow up the civilians, or produce any *physical* effects on them, as a means to his end. Yet the case seems, morally speaking, to be like TB rather than SB. But notice that while such a strategy does not aim at *physically* affecting its victims, it does strictly aim at exploding bombs in their vicinity. Whether or not this change in their situation could be counted as an effect on them, as I think it could, the bomber strictly intends to involve them in something (to make his bombs explode over them) in order to further his purpose precisely by way of their being involved.

[17]This way of drawing the distinction excludes a pair of cases sometimes used to illustrate double effect: in one we give powerful analgesics to lessen the terrible pain of a dying patient, where we foresee that he will die as a side-effect. In the other we relieve his suffering by intentionally killing him with the same or other drugs. In both cases we are to suppose that life is no longer a good and that we act with his explicit or correctly presumed consent. So we cannot see ourselves as infringing, justifiably or unjustifiably, any of his moral rights. For this reason I see these cases as really quite different from the others, in which there is conflict between the moral claims of different people. Indeed, I think that the doctrine in misapplied in nonconflict cases. I see, for example, no difference between amputating someone's leg to save him and proceeding with some life-saving treatment that, as a side-effect, results in the loss of the limb. And by parity of reasoning it seems to me that if stopping pain is urgent enough from the patient's perspective to make death acceptable as a side-effect, it ought to make death acceptable as a means.

[18]A terminological point: something counts as "harmful direct agency" only insofar as harm comes to the very people who are deliberately affected by the agency. Insofar as harm comes to others, the agency also counts as "indirectly harmful." A single act or omission can thus be both directly and indirectly harmful.

[19]Nor, of course, does it require that the agent have *particular* victims in mind. It is enough, as in the case of a terrorist's car bomb, that he intends something for someone or other.

[20]Positive rights are rights to aid while negative rights are rights to noninterference. While borrowed originally from the law, these terms are here used in a moral sense.

[21]See Bennett, *Morality and Consequences*, pp. 102–3.

[22]Samuel Scheffler makes a similar point in *The Rejection of Consequentialism* (Oxford: Clarendon Press, 1982), p. 109.

[23]I am deliberately not considering cases where the sacrifice is financial. What to think in such cases partly depends on the sorts of moral rights people really have to keep money or property that is legally or conventionally theirs when others have more pressing material needs. It is quite consistent with everything I say here to deny that the doctrine speaks against liberal schemes of redistributing wealth.

[24]Although it is, as we have seen, a kind of negative moral force that is activated only when other rights are present.

[25]But there is a way in which the rationale I have provided is not Kantian. For it draws a sharp moral line between adversely affecting someone in the pursuit of an end that he does not share (not treating as an end in itself) and adversely affecting someone because his being so affected is strategically important to achieving an end that he does not share (very roughly, treating him as a means). Neither the terror bomber nor the strategic bomber treats his victims as ends in themselves, but only the former treats them as something like means. And I have argued that this difference is significant—that morality erects an extra barrier against the strategic posture of harmful direct agency. Kant might disagree, focused as he is on the alleged status of people as ends in themselves. But I have difficulty attaching any sense to that idea except via intuitions that certain forms of treatment are unacceptably disrespectful of rational beings. And the intuition that is more disrespectful, all other things being equal, to treat someone as if he existed for purposes he does not share than simply not to be constrained by his purposes, seems to me plausible enough to be worth incorporating in a proper idea of what it means for persons to be ends in themselves. On this conception, one aspect of being an end in itself would be to have, *ceteris paribus*, a stronger right against directly harmful agency than against indirectly harmful agency.

Rights and Deaths

JUDITH JARVIS THOMSON ▪ Massachusetts Institute of Technology
Philosophy and Public Affairs, 1973

This essay is a response to an article by John Finnis, "The Rights and Wrongs of Abortion," which discusses an earlier work by Judith Jarvis Thomson, "A Defense of Abortion." In that work, Thomsom imagines a situation in which an ailing violinist's body has been attached to your own (without your prior knowledge or approval) in order to provide life support for the violinist. In Thomson's view, in such a situation it is perfectly permissible to unplug the violinist even though it would result in his death.

In his article, Finnis argues that we can understand the permissibility of unplugging the violinist only if we distinguish between what he calls **direct and indirect killing**. According to Finnis, a direct killing would be a choice against life, whereas an indirect killing would not be a choice directed against life. The character of choice here is determined by the ends (or the necessary means to these ends) at which an agent aims. In a direct killing, an agent makes a choice against life because he chooses to kill in order to bring about a death either as an end in itself or as a means to some further end. In an indirect killing, an agent does not make a choice against life because he makes his choice without intending the death as either a means or an end even though such a choice will inevitably lead to the death of another individual. The death in this situation is one which is merely foreseen but not intended. As Thomson puts the point, "You directly kill a person if your choice in acting is a choice to bring about death, either as an end or a means. By contrast, you only indirectly kill a person if, though you foresee his death will be a consequence of what you do, your choice in acting is not a choice to bring about his death, either as end or means."

Finnis believes that the unplugging of the violinist is permissible because the unplugging is an indirect killing rather than a direct killing. The unplugging counts as an indirect killing because the death of the violinist is neither your aim in unplugging the violinist nor a means to that aim. For Finnis, what is always impermissible is the direct killing of the innocent.

Thomson raises two questions about Finnis's position. First, she asks why Finnis's distinction between direct killing and indirect killing makes any difference for moral purposes. As Thomson puts it, "What we need to know is why it should matter so crucially whether the death a man foresees is, on the one hand, his end or means, or on the other hand, a merely foreseen consequence." Second, she wants to know whether or not any moral difference involved in direct and indirect killing is the moral difference which Finnis really has in mind.

Thomson explores this conflict, testing Finnis's contradictory claims with case comparisons. In Thomson's view the way to show which differences make a moral difference is to test the distinction by isolating the difference as far as is possible in a pair of parallel cases. This can be done, for example, by coming up with the clearest case of a direct killing we can think of and comparing that case to the clearest case of indirect killing we can imagine, while making sure that the two cases differ, as far as is possible, only in that one respect. (This methodology is also employed and discussed previously by Tooley, Rachels, Malm, and by Kagan and Malm in essays that follow.)

Thomson imagines two scenarios. In the first scenario, Case (4), an enemy nation threatening attack possesses one missile launcher that can reach our shores. It will take at least two years to produce another. As a necessary technical feature of the launcher, the rockets which it fires can be triggered only by very small children who can easily be trained in less than a day to do this. In the second scenario, Case (5), there is again an enemy nation threatening attack with one missile launcher that can reach our shores. Again, this launcher can be triggered only by very small children. However, in this case the children must work in a team and can be adequately trained only over a two-year period. By contrast with our other scenario, rather than taking two years to be replaced, in this scenario a missile launcher can be easily built in less than a day. That is to say, Case (5) differs from Case (4) in that it is the launcher which the enemy can easily replace, rather than the small children who must be trained to fire the missiles.

Thomson argues that our reasons for attacking the missile site will make any bombing we might do in Case (5) count as a direct killing of the children. Here, we would have every reason to aim at the death of the children, using them as a means to our own survival. In contrast, our bombing the missile site in Case (4) would count only as an indirect killing of the children. In this case we would not be using the deaths as a means to our own survival, or as an end. Rather, we merely foresee the deaths of the children as a regrettable consequence of taking out the missile launcher. Thomson claims that bombing in Cases (4) and (5) would be morally equivalent, but since (4) involves indirect killing and (5) involves direct killing, the distinction between indirect and direct killing cannot make a moral difference (by the method of case comparison).

In closing, Thomson responds to Finnis's objection that she has inappropriately equated certain cases in which a woman allows a pregnancy to continue to cases in which one person is a Good Samaritan to another. Thomson claims that although there may be certain factual differences between these two types of cases, from a moral point of view they are equivalent. In support of this point, she argues that Finnis's objection depends upon the claim that the difference between killing and not saving makes a moral difference, and she presents several examples that call this claim into question.

IN . . . [HIS] ARTICLE ["THE RIGHTS AND WRONGS of Abortion,"*Philosophy and Public Affairs* (2, Winter 1973).], John Finnis makes a great many adverse remarks about my article on abortion.[1] I cannot take them all up: there are too many. I shall instead concentrate on certain of his positive proposals. One of them (I take it up in section II) would, if true, make abortion impermissible in cases in which I think it permissible; and another (I take up in section III) would, if true, undercut an argument I had used to support the permissibility of abortion in those cases, and in others as well. Both proposals have consequences well beyond the abortion issue, and so on any view call for close attention.

I.

But first, some things Finnis says about rights. I *think* his main complaint against me in the part of his paper which deals with rights is that I was wrong to discuss them at all—my doing so "needlessly complicates and confuses the issue." I find this puzzling. My aim was to raise doubts about the argument that abortion is impermissible because the fetus is a person, and all persons have a right to life; and how is one to do that without attending to rights? But this is merely by the way. More interesting, I think, is this: I had said that the right to life was not unproblematic—that a man's having a right to life does not guarantee either that he has

a right to be given the use of whatever he needs for life, or that he has a right to continued use of whatever he is currently using, and needs for life. So, I said, the right to life will not serve the opponents of abortion in the very simple and clear way in which they seem to have thought it would. Finnis thinks my point about the right to life is correct and familiar enough: he has an explanation of it. He says that he will call, for example, one man's right to slit another's throat a "Hohfeldian right;" presumably one man's right to hit another on the nose is also a Hohfeldian right. Hohfeldian rights have the same "logical structure," he says: "to assert a Hohfeldian right is to assert a three-term relation between two persons and the action of one of those persons insofar as that action concerns the other person." So (I suppose) to assert:

(1)   Alfred has a right to hit Bill on the nose,

is to assert that a three-term relation holds between Alfred, Bill, and a certain action. By contrast, to assert:

(2)   Charles has a right to life,

is to assert that a two-term relation holds between Charles and a certain thing ("or state of affairs"). Rights such as are attributed by assertions of (2) "cannot be completely analyzed in terms of some unique combination of Hohfeldian rights"—i.e. (if I have understood this), sentences such as (2) are not analyzable into any function of sentences such as (1). And (he says) this fact is, though I did not recognize it, the explanation of what I drew attention to in the right to life.

Now I am inclined to think that this account of what one asserts when one asserts (1) and (2) has no future. Finnis has simply not noticed the difficulties which lie in wait for it.[2] What precisely is supposed to be the third term in the case of (1)? An actual, particular action of Alfred's, viz., his hitting of Bill on the nose? But what if there never is any such action, since Alfred never exercises his right? Or perhaps, instead, the third term is an act-kind? But if so, which? And what precisely is supposed to be the second term in the case of (2)? Life? Charles's continuing to live? And what if his continuing to live does not exist, since he does not continue to live, since he gets killed? The mind reels.

I suspect that what lurks behind Finnis's account is a grammatical difference: in (1), the phrase "right to" is followed by a verb phrase, and indeed a verb phrase whose main verb ("hit") is what some philosophers call an "action verb." By contrast, in (2), the phrase "right to" is followed by a noun phrase ("life"). And perhaps his point, then, is this: that sentences like (2) in this respect are not analyzable into sentences like (1) in this respect. ("He has a right to life" is presumably equivalent to "He has a right to live;" but I suppose it would be said that the verb "live" is not an "action verb.") If this is his point, he may for all I know be right—we should need to be told how to recognize an "action verb" when we meet one, but perhaps Finnis could tell us this.

But for present purposes, it doesn't matter whether he can or not, or even whether this is his point or not: for his aim was to explain what I drew attention to in the right to life, and *that* is not explainable by *any* difference between the logic or grammar of (2) on the one hand, and sentences such as (1) on the other.

For the fact is, I was simply over-fascinated by the example currently on the table. I said that a man's having a right to life does not guarantee either that he has a right to be given the use of whatever he needs for life, or that he has a right to continued use of whatever he is currently using, and needs for life. The right to life is a natural right; and being fascinated by the right to life, I noticed only that analogous points hold of all the natural rights. I should have noticed that analogous points hold of *all* rights. If Alfred very much wants to hit Bill on the nose, Bill might well sell him the right to do so—Bill sells, Alfred buys, and then has the right. Does he have a right to be given the use of whatever it is he needs if he is to hit Bill on the nose? If Bill has been carried off by an eagle, and can only be reached by helicopter, does Alfred have a right to be given a helicopter? Hardly. If Alfred steals your helicopter, and is on his way to Bill, does he have a right to continued use of your helicopter? Scarcely.

The situation about rights, it seems to me, is really this: *all* of them are problematic in the way I mentioned—none of them will serve anybody in the very simple and clear way in which opponents of abortion have seemed to think the right to life would serve them. Unlike Mr. Finnis, I think there does not exist any even remotely plausible theory of the logic of rights. And yet, again unlike Mr. Finnis, I think there does not exist any issue of importance in ethics in which we can avoid or sidestep them.

II.

I had suggested in my article that it is morally permissible for you to unplug the ailing violinist from yourself to save your life, even though to unplug him is to kill him. "Quite so," says Finnis. I had then asked: so why not abortion in analogous circumstances? What if a woman is pregnant due to rape, and allowing the child to remain inside her endangers her life? May she not arrange for an abortion to save her life? Finnis replies: (1) That would be *direct* killing of the innocent, and direct killing of the innocent is always impermissible. (2) Your unplugging the violinist from yourself to save your life is only *indirect* killing. Indirect killing is not always impermissible, but it sometimes is—in particular, indirectly killing that violinist is.

A very important difference, then, this difference between direct and indirect killing: it bears a heavy moral weight. And I am not convinced that Finnis has made clear how it is able to carry that weight.

He puts it like this. Your killing of someone is direct if your choice in acting is "a choice against life;" and he says—anyway, I *think* he means to say[3]—that a choice is a choice against life where it is a choice to bring about a death, either as an end in itself, or as a means to some further end. You directly kill a person if your choice in acting is a choice to bring about a death, either as end or means. By contrast, you only indirectly kill a person if, though you foresee his death will be a consequence of what you do, your choice in acting is not a choice to bring about his death, either as end or means. (I had said in a footnote in my article that what matters is whether or not the *killing* is the agent's end or means; Finnis says that what matters is whether or not the *death* is the agent's end or means. There are reasons to prefer my account, but I am content to adopt his in what follows.)

Two questions present themselves: (1) Why should it be thought that this difference makes a moral difference? (2) If it makes a moral difference, does it make the moral difference Finnis wants it to?

The difficulties to which question (2) points are familiar enough, and I shall not spend much time over them.[4] I suppose Finnis is right to say that if you unplug the violinist, you only indirectly kill him: since you unplug him to save your life, his death is not your end (your end is the saving of your life), and it is not your means either (your means to the saving of your life is the unplugging you do). But what if a woman is pregnant due to rape, and allowing the child to remain inside her endangers her life? Suppose she takes a medicine known to cause miscarriage,[5] and takes it in order to cause miscarriage in order to save her life? The child's death is not her end (her end is the saving of her life), and it is not her means either (her means to the saving of her life is the medicine she takes and the miscarriage it causes). So here too the killing should be indirect. But if it is indirect, it should be permissible, for just as you unplug the violinist to save your life, she takes the medicine to save her life. Yet on Finnis's view *she* acts wrongly, she does the impermissible.

Finnis needs to have the woman's killing of the child turn out to be direct killing, and your killing of the violinist to be indirect killing. And I am afraid he has not succeeded in getting what he needs. He mentions four questions we should ask about a putative indirect killing. (a) "Would the chosen action have been chosen if the victim had not been present?" If so, there is reason to say the killing is

indirect: the death is not the agent's end, but is a mere (foreseen) side-effect of the action he takes to reach his end. But as Finnis himself grants, *this* will not distinguish between the cases we are looking at: "in both situations, the oppressive presence of the victim is what makes one minded to do the act in question." (b) "Is the person making the choice the one whose life is threatened by the presence of the victim?" Yes, in both cases. (c) "Does the chosen action involve not merely a denial of aid and succor to someone but an actual intervention that amounts to an assault on the body of that person?" No more in the one case than in the other. What Finnis has in mind in raising this question is that we should contrast with your unplugging the violinist, not a woman's neatly and cleanly taking a teaspoon of medicine, but rather a craniotomy, i.e. an operation in which the child's skull is crushed to make it possible to get it out of its mother. (And a craniotomy, of course, the mother is not likely to be limber enough to perform herself.) You can unplug the violinist, thereby killing him, while wearing white gloves; in a craniotomy you have actually to take hold, and it is far too messy for that. But I cannot think that Finnis means us to take this point very seriously. Abortifacients one could take by teaspoon would then be morally safe, and the existing procedure for a late abortion (the use of saline solution) only slightly less so. Jonathan Bennett [p. 93] poured scorn on this kind of consideration in the article which Finnis cites, and I think he was quite right to do so. (d) "But is the action against someone who had a duty not to be doing what he is doing, or not to be present where he is present?" I think Finnis supposes there is more fault in the case of you and the violinist than in the case of the woman and child: in the former case, "the whole affair is a gross injustice." I should have thought there was no need to remind anyone of the injustice in rape. But more important, it is hard to see how anyone could think that this question has any bearing at all on the question whether a given death is, on the one hand, an agent's end or means, or on the other hand, a mere foreseen consequence of what he does to save his life.

Still, it might be said that perhaps the killing in the case of woman and child (but not in the case of you and the violinist) really is a direct killing, even though Finnis has just not argued very well for it. Or again, it might be said (Professor Grisez, for example, [whom Finnis cites] would say) that the killings in both cases are indirect, and Finnis has simply been wrong in thinking that while one is permissible, the other is not. So it seems to me that we should turn back to question (1), and ask— Mr. Finnis, his arguments, his moral views apart— why it should be thought that this difference which we are now looking at makes a moral difference.

Some people may think that Finnis has already sufficiently answered this question when he asked us to notice that a direct killing involves a choice "against life." Isn't that bad? And isn't it plain that a man's choices, intentions, reasons have a bearing on the moral evaluation proper to what he does?

Of course they do. But a man who kills only indirectly foresees perfectly clearly that he will bring about a death, and chooses the act he knows will bring it about. What we need to know is why it should matter so crucially whether the death a man foresees is, on the one hand, his end or means, or on the other hand, a merely foreseen consequence.

Sometimes what is done for us is just this: we are given sample acts in which a death is a man's end or means. Here a man kills for nothing further, he kills merely out of hate; there a man kills for money. And the acts are indeed horrendous. Alongside these are set acts in which though a man kills, and the death he brings about is foreseen, it is neither his end nor his means. Here is a bombardier, assigned the task of destroying a missile site which has been launching a rain of deadly missiles onto his country. Unfortunately there is a child on the site, the sick two-year-old daughter of the missile site's commanding officer. If the bombardier drops his bombs, that child will be killed. Most regrettable that the thing has to be done, yet plainly not a horrendous act if he goes ahead.

But this enterprise, fascinating though it may be, proves nothing at all. A man may perform a dreadful deed while wearing boots, and a permitted, even a quite good deed, while barefoot. This hardly establishes the (hitherto unnoticed) moral significance of boots.

What is needed is to show that the difference *makes* the moral difference, or at least contributes to it. And the best way to test such a claim is to isolate the difference so far as possible. We should try to get as clear a direct killing and as clear an indirect killing as we can, which so far as possible differ only in that respect, and then look to see if a moral difference emerges.

Imagine the following:

(3) A violent aggressor nation has threatened us with death unless we allow ourselves to be enslaved by it. It has, ready and waiting, a monster missile launcher, which it will use on us unless we surrender.

So far, so good. Nothing bizarre yet. Unfortunately, while I think the missile launcher it has trained on us is perfectly possible, it is not such as the average violent aggressor nation has as yet aspired to.

(3) (continued): The missile launcher has interior tunnels, each leading to a missile. For technical reasons, the tunnels had to be very small; for technical reasons also, each missile has to be triggered by a human hand. Midgets are too large. So it was necessary to train a team of very young children, two-year-olds in fact, to crawl through and trigger the missiles.

There are two possible continuations of this story. We might imagine two worlds, in both of which (3) is true, but in one of which (4) is, and in the other of which (5) is:

(4) Their technology being what it is, they were able to build only one missile launcher; it will take at least two years to produce another. (By contrast, training the team of children was easy, indeed, was done in a day.) We are capable of bombing the site. Unfortunately, if we bomb to destroy the launcher to save our lives, we kill the children.

(5) Their psychology being what it is, they were able to train only one team of children; it will take at least two years to train another. (By contrast, building the launcher was easy, indeed, was done in a day.) We are capable of bombing the site. Unfortunately, bombing the site will save our lives only if by bombing we kill the children.

Now I take it that if (4) is true, and we act, we only indirectly kill the children: their deaths are not our end, nor do we need their deaths if we are to achieve our end—our end would be just as well achieved if by some miracle the children survive the bombing. Cases such as this have standardly been regarded as cases of indirect killing in the literature on this topic. By contrast, if (5) is true, and we act, we directly kill the children: their deaths are necessary to the achieving of our end, and if, by a miracle, they survive the bombing, we must bomb again.

Of course some very high-minded people may say we must not bomb in either case: after all, the children are innocent! Lower-minded people, like me, will say we can bomb in either case: after all, it is the violent aggressor nation which itself imposed that risk on the children. But what I think no one can say is that we may bomb if (4) is true, but not if (5) is. If that were true, a violent aggressor nation would do well to aspire to such a missile launcher. Careful engineering of tasks and supplies so as to insure the truth of (5) would guarantee it could swallow the virtuous at leisure.

I suspect that the most likely response to what I have said is: those children are not really innocent in the sense intended in the principle, "Direct killing of the innocent is always impermissible." "Innocent" here does not mean "free of guilt," but has a technical sense:[6] perhaps "not currently doing harm, or about to do harm in the immediate future," perhaps "not part of the threat directed at others." The children on the launching team are no doubt free of guilt (they mean no one any harm), but they are part of the threat to us, for they are precisely the ones who will launch the missiles against us.

But how is this supposed to bear on the issue at hand? Finnis seemed to think that the innocence or lack of innocence of the victim has a bearing on the question whether he is killed directly or indirectly—see his question (d) above. But then were we misled as to the difference between direct and indirect killing? We were told it was a matter of whether the victim's death is end or means, or merely a foreseen consequence; and how could the victim's innocence, in the technical, or perhaps in any other, sense bear on *that?* After all, the children are not innocent in the technical sense in either (4) or (5); yet the one killing is indirect, the other direct.

I did indeed take a liberty when I said, above, that cases such as our act in (4) have standardly been regarded as cases of indirect killing in the literature on this topic. What we have standardly been offered are cases in which the victims are innocent in this technical sense. (Compare the sick daughter of the missile site's commanding officer in the case of the bombardier, cited above.) Whereas the children in (4) are not innocent in the technical sense. Nevertheless it was appropriate to take that liberty, for our act in (4) is exactly like the cases we have standardly been offered in those respects which define "indirect killing." It is unlike them in other respects—which only makes clear that the cases we have been offered did not isolate the difference whose moral significance they were intended to convince us of.

In the absence of a new account of the difference between direct and indirect killing, I suspect that innocence is best seen as having a bearing, not on whether a killing is direct or indirect, but rather on whether or not a given direct killing is permissible. Anyone who accepts this is then in a position to explain why the act in (5) is permitted, just as the act in (4) is: though the act in (5) is, unlike the act in (4), a direct killing, still its victims are not innocent in the technical sense, and it is only direct killing of *the innocent* in the technical sense which is categorically ruled out.

But on the other hand, to accept this is also to grant that the difference between direct and indirect killing does not have the moral significance which has been claimed for it. The acts in both (4) and (5) are both permitted, though one is a direct, the other an indirect killing.

And to accept it is also to open the door for abortions in cases in which the child itself is part of the threat to the mother, and hence is not in the technical sense innocent. Such abortions no longer fall under the categorical ban, it having been only a play on the word "innocent" which made it seem that they did fall under it.

III.

Finnis rightly says that it was my intention to assimilate certain cases in which a woman allows a pregnancy to continue to cases in which a man is a Good Samaritan to another; and similarly, to assimilate her refusing to allow the pregnancy to continue, to cases in which a man refuses to be a Good Samaritan to another. My further intention was to draw attention to the fact that there are circumstances in which it is morally acceptable for a man—and so similarly, for the woman—to refuse, to say, "No, the cost is too great, and I will not pay it."

Finnis believes he has a crushing proof I was wrong to do this. "And here," he says, "we have perhaps the decisive reason why abortion cannot be assimilated to the range of Samaritan problems and why Thomson's location of it within that range is a mere (ingenious) novelty." So we should look where he points.

What we find is this: "The child, like his mother,[7] has a 'just prior claim to his own body,' and abortion involves laying hand on, manipulating, that body." I *think* his point is this. A man who refuses to be a Good Samaritan, lays hands on no one, he manipulates no one, he does harm to no one; he merely refrains from giving aid. By contrast, the woman who aborts herself (if she can) does lay hands on and manipulate the child. Well, perhaps she does not actually *touch* it. But she certainly does it a harm: she kills it, in fact. So the decisive reason why I am wrong in making the assimilation is this: a reluctant Samaritan merely does not save a life, whereas the mother actually kills the child.

Now it had not actually escaped my notice that the mother who aborts herself kills the child, whereas a man who refuses to be a Good Samaritan—on the traditional understanding of Good Samaritanism—merely does not save. My suggestion was that from a moral point of view these cases should be assimilated: the woman who allows the pregnancy to continue, at great cost to herself, is entitled to praise in the same amount, and, more important, of the same kind, as is the man who sets forth, at great cost to himself, to give aid. That is why I proposed we attend to the case of you and the violinist: surely if you allow the violinist to remain plugged into you, at great cost to yourself, you deserve praise in the same amount, and of the same kind, as any traditional Good Samaritan— and how does this differ from the case of woman and child? To say "Ah, but if she refuses, she kills, whereas a man who refuses to set forth to give aid merely refrains from saving" is not only not decisive against my assimilation, it is *no* reason at all to think it improper—in the absence of a showing that (a) the difference between killing and not saving makes a moral difference, and indeed that (b) the

difference between killing and not saving makes a sufficiently profound moral difference as to make the assimilation improper, and of course also that (c) the truth of (b) does not conflict with its being permissible for you to refuse to sustain the violinist, i.e. with its being permissible for you to unplug him, thereby killing him.[8]

Finnis has not only not produced these showings, he seems not to have seen they are needed. This *may* be because he thinks that not saving is the same as indirect killing, and therefore already shown to differ morally from real (read: direct) killing. Why else, after all, would he have advised us that if we want to know whether an agent kills directly or indirectly, we should ask whether he makes an assault, or merely denies aid? (Compare question [c] of the preceding section.) But it is, simply, a *mistake* to think that not saving is indirect killing. An indirect killing is perforce a killing, whereas it is quite possible that a man has never killed, and yet that there are many lives he did not save.

Or, alternatively, it *may* be because he thinks (a), (b), and (c) so obvious as to need no argument. My own view is that none of them is obvious. It seems to me to be an interesting, and open, question whether or not (a) is true, and I want to make a few brief suggestions about it below. However (b) strikes me as false, and in fact as shown to be false by the story of you and the violinist; so as is plain, I think (c) false too. As I cannot see that any reasons have been advanced to think (b) true, I shall from here on ignore it, and therefore (c) as well.

Is (a) true? Once again it is noteworthy that the sample acts offered to convince us of the moral significance of the difference do not isolate it.[9] Here is a man who commits a gross and bloody murder; horrendous, isn't it? There is a man who is asleep, and therefore is not saving lives; scarcely horrendous, surely permissible for a man to sleep! But of course there are other things at work here besides the fact that one kills and the other does not save. For one thing, the sleeper does not know he is not saving, whereas the murderer knows he kills. So let us instead compare:

(6) David is walking across a field. Unbeknownst to him, a sick baby has burrowed its way under a clump of hay ahead of him. He steps on the clump, thereby killing it.

(7) Edward is walking across a field. Unbeknownst to him, a sick baby has burrowed
its way under a clump of hay alongside his
path. He walks on; the baby dies; he did not
save it.

Is there a moral difference here? This brings me to
the first point I wished to make about (a): its defenders will have to make a decision. Do they wish
to say that although neither David nor Edward is at
fault or to blame for what they do, or for what
happens, still their acts differ morally? Or do they
wish to say that the acts do not differ morally, that
the important difference is not between killing and
not saving, but between knowingly killing and
knowingly not saving?

I propose we side-step this, and restrict ourselves to cases in which both men act knowingly. A
second difference between committing murder, and
not saving while asleep, is that the murderer aims at
a death whereas the sleeper does not, and this too
contributes to the moral difference between them.
So let us instead compare:

(8) Frank hates his wife and wants her dead. He
puts cleaning fluid in her coffee, thereby
killing her.

(9) George hates his wife and wants her dead. She
puts cleaning fluid in her coffee (being muddled, thinking it's cream). George happens to
have the antidote to cleaning fluid, but he
does not give it to her; he does not save her
life, and she dies.

Horrendous, both!—but if (a) is true, what Frank
did should be worse than what George did, and is
it? I suspect that if anyone feels that it is, this is
because he thinks of Frank as having done *two*
morally significant things: first he imposed a risk
on his wife by poisoning her coffee, and then, like
George, he did not save her. (Maybe he did not
have an antidote, but surely he could have called
for an ambulance.) So he and George both did not
save; but Frank had imposed the risk because of
which his wife needed saving, and it is plainly bad
to impose risks on people even if no harm actually
comes to them. I suspect that it may, ultimately, be
this[10] which inclines people to opt for (a). But
should we? What if there were no room at all for
saving once the agent had made his move?

Whatever we think about Frank and George,
it does seem to be very difficult to construct a clear
and convincing pair of cases in which the difference is isolated (knowledge, intentions, and reasons
are so far as possible the same), but in which the
one who kills acts badly, and the one who refrains
from saving does not. I suppose that (a) could be
true, even if this could not be done; but it does cast
doubt on it.

What does seem plain is just this: the question
of (a)'s truth is so far an open one. It needs attention of a kind which Mr. Finnis has certainly not
paid it, and in the absence of which his objection to
the assimilation I made is merely so much hand
waving.

Notes

[1]"A Defence of Abortion," *Philosophy & Public Affairs* I, no. 1 (Fall 1971).

[2]Actually, a rather dark footnote (10) suggests that
Finnis may not really mean what he said. For in the footnote it appears that "inadequate specification" of the action someone had a right to have done for him may not
make for trouble. Whereas if a relation holds amongst
three things, it holds amongst them however they are
specified.

[3]Because on p. 135 he asks himself: "When *should*
one say that the expected bad effect or aspect of an action
is not intended either as end or as means and hence does
not determine the moral character of the act as a choice
not to respect one of the basic human values?" I take it
that if an expected bad effect, say a death, is *not* intended
as end or as means, then the act which causes the death
does not issue from a choice against life, and hence the
agent does not directly kill.

[4]See, for example, Philippa Foot, "The Problem of
Abortion and the Doctrine of the Double Effect," p. 59,
and Thomas Nagel, "War and Massacre," *Philosophy &
Public Affairs* I, no. 2 (Winter 1972). I should at this place
mention how much I have learned about the matters dealt
with in this section, not merely from these two articles,
but from the discussions of them at the Society for Ethical and Legal Philosophy.

[5]I had not known there were such medicines. But
Finnis tells us that if a pregnant woman's life is threatened
by fever, it is permissible for her to take or be given a
medicine to reduce the fever, even though it is known
that the medicine causes miscarriage. (In *this* case, then,
the killing must be indirect.) So perhaps there are.

[6]Thomas Nagel, *op. cit.*, draws attention to this.

[7]Here I feel the waters rising. Finnis had said in a
footnote that a right to decide what happens in and to

one's body is "to be equated, apparently" with a just prior claim to one's own body; so here he is saying that both child and mother have a right to decide what happens in and to their bodies. Earlier, however, he had said, with *éclat*, that "traditional Western ethics simply does not accept that a person has 'a right to decide what shall happen in and to his body.'" Has traditional Western ethics changed its mind? and so quickly?

[8]Finnis must show (c) as well as (a) and (b), since he agrees with me that you may unplug the violinist. It *may* be that Baruch Brody ("Thomson on Abortion," *Philosophy & Public Affairs* I, no. 3 [Spring 1972]) does not have to show (c) as well as (a) and (b). Brody puts forward the

same ground for rejecting the assimilation as Finnis does, but unlike Finnis, does not say you may unplug the violinist. On the other hand, he does not explicitly say you may not. All he explicitly says on the matter is that my "account of the violinist" is "very problematic."

[9]Michael Tooley ("Abortion and Infanticide," *Philosophy & Public Affairs* 2, no. 1 [Fall 1972]) also draws attention to this, and tries to isolate the difference in order to show it is not morally significant.

[10]And the connected point that a man who wants not to save, and did not impose the risk, can always ask that fascinating question, "Why me?"

The Doctrine of Double Effect: Problems of Interpretation

NANCY (ANN) DAVIS ▪ University of Colorado, Boulder
Pacific Philosophical Quarterly, 1984

Davis points out that the Doctrine of Double Effect (DDE) is a sort of deontological constraint. She states that the DDE requires that: "The bad consequence is not pursued either as an end in itself or as a means to the realization of the agent's good end."

According to Davis, Nagel's position on the DDE is that: "to violate deontological constraints one must maltreat someone intentionally. The maltreatment must be something that one does or chooses, either as an end or as a means, rather than something one's actions merely cause or fail to prevent."

She claims that this view presents problems in application due to problems of interpretation, and the unresolved questions of interpretation are important enough to impugn the DDE.

Davis wants to explore the notions of **means, ends, and intention**. She begins by giving the following cases:

Case 1

A woman's life is endangered by uterine cancer. She will die unless a hysterectomy is performed. The woman is pregnant; hence—on the assumption that the fetus is a person—the surgical removal of the woman's uterus will result in the death of an innocent person.

Case 2

A woman will die in childbirth unless the skull of the fetus is crushed. The fetus will die if its skull is crushed; hence, performing the craniotomy upon the fetus will result in the death of an innocent person.

According to the defenders of the DDE, there is a morally significant asymmetry between Cases 1 and 2. Opponents of the DDE challenge this alleged asymmetry and claim that *if* it is permissible to take action to save a pregnant woman's life by performing a hysterectomy, then it is permissible to take action to save a woman's life by performing a craniotomy upon the fetus. The main disputes between the defenders and opponents of the DDE surround two of the defenders' claims: (i) that the death of the fetus is a *means* to the preserving of the woman's life in Case 2, but is *not a means* in Case 1; and (ii) that the doctor must be said to *intend* the death of the fetus in Case 2, but can be regarded as *merely foreseeing* the death of the fetus in Case 1.

Davis claims that the real controversy between defenders and opponents of the DDE concerns the determination of when something is an intended means (or end) rather than a merely foreseen effect. She discusses rival conceptions of means adopted by opponents and traditional defenders of the DDE. Davis explores various attempts to characterize the distinction between intended means and merely foreseen effects. In particular, Davis distinguishes between the **agent-interpretation** and **event-interpretation** of the means-end relation. The agent-interpretation takes into account the plans and subjective states of the agent, whereas the event-interpretation is more objective, focussing on objective features of sequences of events. Davis argues that the asymmetry between Cases 1 and 2 can be maintained on neither interpretation. Given the difficulty of making the crucial distinction between means and ends, the DDE is impugned.

IN RECENT YEARS THERE HAS BEEN A REVIVAL OF interest in deontology. A number of prominent secular moral theorists—among them Alan Donagan, Charles Fried, and, most recently, Thomas Nagel—have advanced arguments for deontological views that are quite traditional in content and structure.[1] The particular deontological constraints favored are ones that come from the inventory of Hebrew-Christian commonsense morality (for example, constraints on lying, breaking faith, and killing the innocent). And the theoretical apparatus that is employed to systematize what Donagan has called "that part of common morality according to the Hebrew-Christian tradition which does not depend upon any theistic belief"[2] is modeled on that part of common morality which—at least historically—did depend upon various theistic beliefs. In fashioning and defending their secular deontological views, contemporary moral theorists have drawn heavily upon principles and doctrines of theological ethics. A doctrine that has quite recently reappeared in the secular context, one that plays a part in Fried's thinking and a larger part in Nagel's, is the Doctrine of Double Effect (the DDE).

Although the DDE has been sharply criticized by secular philosophers, moralists, and legal theorists,[3] it continues to exercise a powerful attraction, especially for moral theorists with strong non-consequentialist leanings. It is testimony to the great intuitive power of the doctrine that, in spite of the criticisms that have been leveled against it, it has again resurfaced, expanding its base of operations from the theological to the secular, and its role from casuistical principle to deontological bedrock. Says Nagel

> I believe that the traditional principle of double effect, despite problems of application, provides a rough guide to the extension and character of deontological constraints, and that even after the volumes that have been written on the subject in recent years, this remains the right point of convergence for efforts to capture our intuitions.[4]

For the deontologist who holds that there are limits on what agents may do to one another that function as constraints on the agents' pursuit of the optimal outcome, it is essential to distinguish the things that agents are said to *do* from the things that agents merely cause, or allow to happen, or fail to prevent.[5] Even though there are bound to be cases in which it is possible for us to minimize the number of deaths, and even the number of killings of innocent people, by killing one innocent person ourselves, the deontological constraint on the killing of the innocent neither enjoins nor permits such conduct. Deontological constraints attach quite narrowly to an agent's choices and actions rather than to the wider (perhaps purely causal) consequences of them. Many deontologists— though until quite recently, primarily those working in theological ethics, and in the Catholic tradition—have appealed to a distinction between intention and mere foresight in order to distinguish between the things that an agent does and the things that an agent is properly said only to have caused or to have failed to prevent. What an agent *does*, in the relevant sense, is a function of what the agent *intends*: one violates the deontological constraint against lying or the constraint against killing the innocent only if one utters a falsehood or causes a death intentionally. As Nagel has put it

> . . . *to violate deontological constraints one must maltreat someone intentionally. The maltreatment must be something that one does or chooses, either as an end or as a means, rather than something one's actions merely cause or fail to prevent.*
>
> *[Although] it is possible to foresee that one's actions will cause or fail to prevent a harm that one does not intend to bring about or permit . . . [this] is not, in the relevant sense, something that one does and [it] does not come under a deontological constraint . . . .*[6]

The view that it may be morally relevant whether an agent intended to realize a certain result or merely foresaw that that result would come about as a consequence of pursuing some other course of action is one that has great intuitive appeal, and a long history. It is often articulated and defended through the DDE, which is traceable to Aquinas.[7] The DDE allows that it may be permissible for agents to pursue a course of action that they foresee will produce a bad consequence as a side effect (or "second effect") even though it would not

be permissible for agents to pursue that course of action with the intention of producing that consequence. There are four important qualifications that attach to this permission (though it is only the third that will directly concern us here).[8]

(1)　The agent acts with a good intention and seeks to realize a good end (or, at least, one that is morally permissible);

(2)　The agent does not seek or will the bad consequence that he or she foresees will come about, and when this is feasible, tries to mitigate it, or prevent its coming about;

(3)　The bad consequence is not pursued either as an end in itself or as a means to the realization of the agent's good end;

(4)　The good end that the agent seeks to realize is not morally disproportionate to the bad consequence that the agent's pursuing that end will foreseeably bring about.

I shall argue that the problems of application that Nagel alludes to (and dismisses) should not be taken so lightly. Such problems of application arise because of problems of interpretation: the DDE is more difficult to interpret than philosophers like Fried and Nagel have appreciated, and the unresolved questions of interpretation are important enough to impugn their reliance upon the Doctrine.[9] More careful attention to some of the central notions and distinctions embodied in the DDE shows that they require more systematic investigation and defense than they have been given. Some of the distinctions embodied in the DDE are ones that moral theorists have built into their very characterization of deontological constraints. And some of the notions that figure in the DDE—particularly the notions of means, ends, and intention—are likely to be important elements in any deontological theory, and perhaps in any plausible theory of agency. The criticisms that I shall raise are thus potentially very damaging ones.

I.

Much discussion of the DDE has focused on the following two cases:

Case 1

A woman's life is endangered by uterine cancer. She will die unless a hysterectomy is performed. The woman is pregnant, hence—on the assumption that the fetus is a person (an assumption that I shall make for the purpose of this discussion)—the surgical removal of the woman's uterus will result in the death of an innocent person, the fetus.

Case 2

A woman will die in childbirth unless the skull of the fetus is crushed. The fetus will die if its skull is crushed, hence the performance of the craniotomy upon the fetus will result in the death of an innocent person, the fetus.

Many of those who defend the DDE in its application to the deontological constraint on the killing of the innocent maintain that these two cases are not morally on a par. They think that it may be permissible to perform the hysterectomy, but that it is impermissible to perform the craniotomy. In the case of hysterectomy, it is maintained, the death of the fetus is foreseen but not intended: the death is a concomitant effect of preserving the woman's life rather than a means to its preservation. In the case of craniotomy, the death of the fetus is held to be sought as a means to saving the woman's life, and so, although presumably regretted, it is intended. Thus, according to these defenders of the DDE, there is a morally significant asymmetry between cases 1 and 2.

Although the DDE has frequently been invoked in the discussion of these cases, it has not been altogether clear what its role is supposed to be in defending the claim that cases like the first—those in which a death is thought to be merely a foreseen concomitant of saving a life—should be treated differently from cases like the second—those in which a death is thought to be intended as a means to saving a life. Although commentators themselves have not generally made such distinctions, the DDE can figure in the argument in several different ways.

First, it may be called upon to help *distinguish* cases of killing from cases of letting die. Thus it is often said that we have not killed someone when we have "done nothing" unless we intended the person's death to result from our inaction, and refrained from action in the hope of securing that result. When we have merely foreseen that the death will come about, we have killed no one, but

have (at most) merely let a person die. Catholic moralists and philosophers have often employed the DDE in this way (especially in medical ethics textbook discussions of abortion and euthanasia).[10]

Second, the DDE may be called upon to help *explain* our interest in distinguishing between killing and letting die in many of the cases in which we do, in fact, think it is important to distinguish them. Thus it might be thought that the difference between killing and letting die has moral significance when it corresponds to a difference in the agent's intentions.[11]

Third, the DDE may be called upon to play a more ambitious role. It might figure in a proposed *justification* for treating cases in which a death is an intended means differently from cases in which a death is merely a foreseen concomitant. On this interpretation, the distinction between intending something and merely foreseeing it is regarded as one that is morally significant in itself and not merely one that serves as a device for organizing our various intuitions about cases in which agents pursue a course of action that they know will result in the death of an innocent person.[12]

I shall not be concerned here with the possible moral significance of the distinction between intention and mere foresight or with the defensibility of the DDE's projected normative results. Nor shall I undertake to clarify just how the various commentators on the DDE have supposed that it figures in the argument that Case 1 and Case 2 should be treated differently, though I shall begin by considering these traditional applications of the DDE. I believe that it is important to understand why questions of application cannot simply be ignored by those who—like Fried and Nagel—seek to defend the DDE while rejecting the traditional applications. And I believe that considering these cases will help us come to see that some of the problems of interpretation that confront the Doctrine itself—in particular, problems concerning how the notions of an agent's means and an agent's ends are to be understood—are more pressing (and less tractable) than either traditional or modern defenders of the DDE have recognized. My focus will thus be on questions of interpretation: for if the technical details of the Doctrine cannot be satisfactorily worked out, or if the Doctrine emerges from such scrutiny as confused or incoherent, then there is likely to be considerably less interest in the question of whether it may also be rejected on other grounds.

II.

Let us return to cases 1 and 2.

Traditional defenders of the DDE have maintained that the two cases are not morally on a par. They claim that it may be permissible to perform the hysterectomy, but that it is impermissible to perform the craniotomy. Opponents of the DDE have challenged this alleged asymmetry and claimed that *if* it is permissible to take action to save a pregnant woman's life by performing a hysterectomy, then it is permissible to take action to save a woman's life by performing a craniotomy upon the fetus. The principal disputes between traditional defenders and opponents have been over two of the defenders' claims: first, that the death of the fetus is a *means* to the preserving of the woman's life in case 2, the case of craniotomy, but it is *not a means* in case 1, the case of hysterectomy, and second, that the doctor must be said to *intend* the death of the fetus in case 2, but can be regarded as *merely foreseeing* the death of the fetus in case 1. Both opponents and defenders treat these two claims as closely related.

Elizabeth Anscombe, who vigorously defends the DDE, holds the view that it is never permissible to kill the innocent, and she appears to believe that the prohibition of killing the innocent rules out the performance of craniotomy but not the performance of hysterectomy. In the case of craniotomy, but not in the case of hysterectomy, the death of the fetus is a means to the saving of the woman. And, according to Anscombe:

> It is nonsense to pretend that you do not intend what is the means you take to your chosen end. Otherwise there is no substance to the Pauline [of or relating to the apostle Paul] teaching that we may not do evil that good may come of it.[13]

Herbert Hart attacks the DDE, and holds that the hysterectomy and the craniotomy are on a par: in neither case is the death of the fetus unproblematically regarded as a means to the saving of the woman. Says Hart:

> . . . in such cases it could be argued that it is not the death of the foetus but its removal from the body of the mother which is required to save her life; in both cases alike the death of the foetus is . . . foreseen but not used as a means to an end, or an end.[14]

So Hart would allow craniotomy as well as hysterectomy while Anscombe would not. But it is important to note that the principle that Anscombe seems to be advancing—that it must be supposed that agents intend the means that they pursue to realize their chosen ends—is one that Hart could also espouse, for it is consistent with, and quite in the spirit of, his remarks.[15] Presumably, then, since there is agreement on the closeness of the two questions: whether the death of the fetus is a *means*, and whether the death of the fetus in *intended*, and agreement, perhaps, on what the nature of the connection is between the two questions, the real controversy between Hart and Anscombe concerns the determination of *when* something is a means, or when something is *intended*. The disagreement between Hart and Anscombe may thus perhaps be most perspicuously represented as a disagreement about what it is for something to be a means (or an agent's means). The question facing us, then, is this: what rival conceptions of means (or of an agent's means) might opponents of the DDE and its traditional defenders be adopting?

Those who have claimed that the death of the fetus is not a means to the saving of the woman in either case 1 or case 2 have sometimes suggested that this is because the connection between the death of the fetus and the saving of the woman is, in both cases, too tenuous. As Hart says, the death of the fetus is not *required*. But this cannot be treated as obvious, for Anscombe would simply disagree. And indeed, there is considerable room for disagreement, for it is not easy to see just what is being claimed by Hart and others when they say that the death of the fetus is not required in the case of craniotomy (case 2).[16]

Sometimes it is said that what is meant by the claim is that it is *possible* for the fetus to survive the crushing of its skull (and possible for the woman to survive if the fetus does survive the crushing of its skull).[17] But this is not, as it stands, a very helpful suggestion. In what sense is it possible? Given the current state of medical technology and the facts of the case, it is not possible for the woman to survive if the craniotomy is not performed, and it is not possible for the fetus to survive if it is. It may someday be feasible to perform a craniotomy upon a fetus and have it survive. But this does not seem to be relevant to the question of whether the death of this fetus is here and now required for the saving of this woman's life. It may someday be possible to make an omelette without breaking eggshells. But we do not believe, here and now, that someone who breaks eggs in the course of preparing an omelette does not use eggshell-breaking as a means in omelette-making.

It might be objected that I have simply appealed to the wrong notion or test of possibility. Perhaps what people mean who say that the connection is too tenuous, even in the case of craniotomy, is that there is not a *logical or conceptual* connection between the craniotomy and the death of the fetus: for the performance of the craniotomy does not *logically necessitate* the death of the fetus.[18]

No doubt this is true: the craniotomy and the death of the fetus are not logically connected. Logical or conceptual possibility being what it is, the supposition that the fetus survives the assault upon it will be intelligible unless there is a conceptual connection between the death of the fetus and the survival of the woman. The survival of the fetus will be inconceivable just in case the woman *cannot* be saved unless the fetus dies, just in case the doctor cannot intelligibly be thought to be trying to save the woman if he is not regarded as trying to bring about the death of the fetus. On the proposed interpretation of possibility, then, the death of a person will not count as a means unless it is thought to be conceptually connected to an agent's end.

This interpretation of the claim that a means must be *required* for the realization of an agent's end—an interpretation that has it that the death of a person will not count as a means unless it is conceptually connected to the agent's ends—yields some rather bizarre results. One of these is that the performance of the craniotomy is not required to save the woman's life, and so is not a means to preserving her. For there is no conceptual connection between the nonperformance of the craniotomy on the fetus and the death of the woman (or between the performance of the craniotomy and the

woman's surviving). Another is that my shooting you at point blank range is not a means of securing your death, since it is conceivable that you should survive such an assault (even if, in fact, you do not survive). This strategy of attacking the DDE—attacking the claim that there is an asymmetry between cases 1 and 2 by maintaining that the connection between an agent's means and an agent's end is a conceptual connection, and thus tighter than traditional defenders of the DDE have supposed—thus seems unsuccessful, since it leads to such implausible conclusions.

In response it could be pointed out that there are cases in which the supposition that there is a conceptual connection between an agent's means and an agent's end is not so problematic. By and large, these are cases that employ narrow, highly-structured, conventional (often legal) notions. They are the exception rather than the rule. Consider the following case:

Case 3

Ben is heir to the throne in a country which has strict inheritance laws. He believes in the validity of these laws, and he also believes (as do his compatriots) in the divine right of kings. Though he is impatient and anxious to assume the throne, he wishes to do so only on condition that he be the rightful king of the land. This can happen only when the current ruler, Alice, dies. Ben arranges to poison her surreptitiously, and thus bring about her death. Alice dies, and Ben becomes king.[19]

This case is one in which there appears to be a conceptual connection between means and end. Though Ben may imprison Alice or usurp the throne by force, and thus (provided he has influential friends and a powerful army) effectively become the *ruler* of the land, doing this would not achieve his end. What Ben wants is to be the *rightful* king, and this he can become only if Alice dies. Alice's death is required for the realization of Ben's end.[20]

Though we can construct cases in which it can be maintained that there is a conceptual connection between means and end, it is more difficult to construct them than it may appear. Consider the following case, one that may seem to be parallel to (though less artificial and restricted than) case 3.

Case 4

Martha is Fred's niece. Fred is a wealthy man, and his will names Martha as sole beneficiary. Martha longs to inherit the property that Fred plans to leave her, and she is growing impatient. She thus seeks to bring about his death: Martha poisons Fred, and Fred dies.

It might be claimed that case 4 is an example of conceptual connection, for Martha surely seeks Fred's death as a means to inheriting his property, and—as in case 3—there seems to be a conceptual connection between Fred's dying and Martha's inheriting: one can only *inherit* property if the bequeather dies.

But this analysis of case 4 is something less than compelling. It is true that Martha cannot be said to inherit property unless the person bequeathing it to her is dead. But Martha can come into her inheritance—that is, she can gain possession of the property that is her inheritance—without Fred's dying. Indeed, Martha might secure Fred's cooperation in this by making an impassioned plea for funds, and thereby receive the property she covets. Or she might succeed in convincing other people that Fred is dead (while knowing herself that he is not), and thus get hold of the property. Fred's death is not required for the realization of Martha's end.

In light of this, I do not think that reflection on cases like case 3 should inspire us to pursue further refinements of the interpretation of the DDE that holds that the connection between means and end must be a logical or conceptual connection. Case 3 can hardly be regarded as a paradigm case of seeking death as a means, and it should not be used as a model (still less a template) for characterizing the notions of an agent's means, or the relations between an agent's means and an agent's end.

An appeal to cases like case 4 is only slightly less problematic. At best, such cases might lend credence to the view that there must be some description of the means and some description of the end that allow us to see them as conceptually connected (and that are intuitively natural, or otherwise appropriate descriptions).[21] They do not lend support to the claim that the means and the end themselves must be so connected.

Moreover, when we think of a means as a sort of mechanism employed to realize the end—to bring about the end, or to cause it to come into being—then not only is it true that the means and the end *need* not be conceptually connected, there may be reason to suppose that they *cannot* be. On a familiar view—Hume's—cause and effect must be "distinct existences," and distinct existences cannot be conceptually connected in the relevant way.

Perhaps what underlies our unease with the conceptual connection view is the belief that the means-end relation is a species of causal relation, and one that is—on a plausible interpretation of event-causation—extensional. If my doing *a* realizes *b* and *b* is also describable as *c*, then my doing *a* realizes *c*. If Harold's end is Jane's demise, and his chosen means is shooting her, then if Jane is the fastest runner in town, Harold's means of killing Jane is also the means of killing the fastest runner in town.

But things are not this simple. We often make use of a somewhat different notion of means and end, what I shall call an *agent's means* and an *agent's end*. And these notions seem to be intensional: we cannot infer that Harold aimed at the death of the fastest runner in town when we know that his end was Jane's death, and know that Jane is the fastest runner in town. When we describe Harold's end as an *agent's end*, we describe it as *his* end, and thus employ, in so far as we are able, the kinds of descriptions we think that the agent would employ in thinking about it (and perhaps in choosing to aim at it).[22] The same applies to the notion of an agent's means. The characterizations of the agent's means which we employ are ones that in some way connect *Harold's* pursuing the course of action that is his means with his pursuit of, or desire for the realization of, *his* end.

There is, then, a sort of tension. From one perspective, we see the means-end relation as a kind of causal relation between events, and (perhaps) as extensional. From another perspective, we recognise that the notions of an agent's means and an agent's end may stand in no straightforward causal relationship, and we see them as intensional. Disagreement about which of these is the means-end relation embodied in the DDE—or more likely, failure to note that there are two rather different interpretations of the means-end relation—is, I suspect, one of the main sources of the confusion that surrounds the discussion of the DDE. If we consider the means and end from the point of view of the agent—adopt what I shall call the *agent-interpretation*—we may find that the death of the fetus is in no way part of the plan of the doctor who undertakes the craniotomy on the fetus in order to save the woman's life (in case 2). The doctor's purposes, desires, and actions are not framed in terms of this, or directed toward it, and they are intelligible, and intelligible as *his* purposes, desires, and actions, without the supposition that the fetus dies, or that he wants it to die. And so, on the agent-interpretation, it is not true that the death of the fetus is a means to the saving of the woman in case 2.

When our focus is on sequences of events in the world, however, we tend to reason differently. On what I shall call the *event-interpretation*, we understand that crushing the skull of the fetus does, in the circumstances, bring about its death: once the doctor has crushed the skull of the fetus, there is nothing else that need be done to cause the death, and nothing that can be done to prevent it. To perform the craniotomy on the fetus is, on the event-interpretation, to bring about its death, and the performance of the craniotomy is required to save the woman's life. On the event-interpretation, then, the death of the fetus is a means to the saving of the woman in case 2.

Thus we seem to reach the conclusion that the death of the fetus is and is not a means. It is a means to saving the woman's life according to the event-interpretation, but it is not the doctor's means according to the agent-interpretation.[23] Both of the notions seem to underwrite results that are problematic. Recall case 1:

A woman's life is endangered by uterine cancer. She will die unless hysterectomy is performed. The woman is pregnant, hence the surgical removal of the woman's uterus will result in the death of an innocent person, the fetus.

On the event-interpretation, the doctor who performs the hysterectomy on the woman uses the death of the fetus as a means to saving the woman's life. To perform such an operation is, in the circumstances, to bring about the death of the fetus. And this is true whether or not the doctor knows that the woman is pregnant; or thinks that performing the hysterectomy will kill the fetus; or wants the fetus dead. But surely there is something wrong with

a view that allows the possibility that a doctor who does not even know that the woman is pregnant, or does not believe that performing the hysterectomy will kill the fetus, seeks the death of the fetus as a *means* to saving the woman's life. For the death of the fetus is in no way part of such a doctor's plan.

The agent-interpretation does not fare much better. On this interpretation, a doctor who removes a vital organ from a healthy patient to transplant it to another unhealthy patient has not brought about the death of the first as a means to saving the second. For it may be no part of the doctor's plan that the first patient should die from the surgery.

What this discussion makes clear is that there are some difficulties in interpreting the notions of means and end: these notions are neither straightforward nor unproblematic. This poses a problem for DDE opponents as well as for DDE defenders; indeed, it poses the same problem for both of them. For neither defenders nor opponents have undertaken to support their positions with an account of the notions of means, end, or intention, though an understanding of the details of such an account seems crucial for interpreting the DDE. But there is a special problem facing defenders of the Doctrine.

Traditional defenders of the DDE have wished to maintain that there is a morally significant asymmetry between case 1 and case 2: the performance of hysterectomy is permissible, but the performance of craniotomy is not. What reasoning supports the claim that the DDE rules out the performance of craniotomy? It might be something like the following:

(1)   The performance of craniotomy on the fetus is required to save the woman's life.
(2)   So the craniotomy is a means to saving the woman's life.
(3)   The craniotomy brings about the death of the fetus.
(4)   So the death of the fetus is a means to saving the woman's life. [(2), (3)]
(5)   The DDE forbids pursuing a bad means (even) to realize a good end.
(6)   The death of an innocent person is a bad means.
(7)   So the DDE forbids bringing about the death of the fetus [(5), (6)], and hence the craniotomy [(3)].

If this is—at least in general outline—the sort of argument that traditional defenders of the DDE mean to advance to rule out the craniotomy, then they must be endorsing (something like) the event-interpretation of the means-end relation, rather than the agent-interpretation. For the move from (2) and (3) to (4) would not be admissible on the agent-interpretation. So either the DDE defenders' argument does not rule out craniotomy, or else it employs something like the event-interpretation of the means-end relation.

A problem remains either way. It is only reasonable to ask that the same interpretation of the means-end relation be employed in assessing both case 1 and case 2. But it is doubtful that the defenders of the DDE can satisfy this request. If the event-interpretation is applied to case 1, and we construct an argument parallel to the one just presented, substituting "hysterectomy" for "craniotomy," then the conclusion we reach is that the hysterectomy is also forbidden. It thus appears traditional defenders of the DDE must adopt something like the event-interpretation to support the strict prohibition of craniotomy, but that the adoption of this interpretation vitiates the claim that there is a significant asymmetry between cases 1 and 2.

Nor would it help if they were to adopt the agent-interpretation. For on this interpretation it cannot be assumed that the death of the fetus is a means in *either* case 1 or case 2. It thus appears that the asymmetry between these cases cannot be secured on either the event- or the agent-interpretation.

These considerations do quite a lot to undermine the position of traditional defenders of the DDE. But before we rush to join the ranks of the opposition, we should recall that the DDE opponents' characterization of means and end was itself rather less than satisfactory. The problems here seem to stem from the conceptual connection view, which involves an overly restrictive or narrow characterization of means and ends. But perhaps opponents of the DDE—and those defenders of the DDE who, like Fried and Nagel, wish to disassociate themselves from its traditional applications—can make essentially the same criticisms even if they abandon this narrow characterization. For there may be an alternative account that does not employ the troublesome requirement of conceptual connection

between means and end. A number of people have proposed some sort of counterfactual test, among them Philippa Foot and Susan Nicholson. Nicholson employs such a test to try to show that the death of the fetus is not a means to the saving of the woman in case 2 (the case of craniotomy). She says

> That the narrowing of the head and not the death of the fetus is the means to the end of saving the woman is demonstrated by the fact that the fetus would not be killed should it somehow survive the force applied to its skull and be removed alive from the birth canal. [24]

This counterfactual test has the advantage of being less restrictive than the method of asking whether it was, in fact, part of the doctor's plan that the fetus should die. Yet it seems to be precise enough to focus on the particular aspects or descriptions of the plan that we are interested in.

But in fact it will not do. The suggested test does not provide a way of determining whether or not something is a means: it confuses the notion of a means with the notion of (what I shall call) a *supplementary end*. Consideration of two variants of case 4 may help clarify the difference.

Variant 1

Martha[1] is Fred's niece and intended beneficiary. Martha[1] is quite fond of her uncle, but, alas, still fonder of his property. She wants the property so desperately that she decides to kill him to get it. Martha[1] poisons Fred.

Variant 2

Martha[2] is Fred's niece and intended beneficiary. She detests her uncle, and she covets his property. She wants him dead *and* she wants his property, and so she decides to kill him. Martha[2] poisons Fred.

Let us suppose that Fred survives being poisoned, but he suffers amnesia in consequence, and (for reasons undoubtedly best known to himself) travels clandestinely to some unlikely place. Only Martha knows that he is alive, and she is confident that his identity will not be discovered (by him or by anyone else). Everyone supposes that Fred is dead, and so Martha receives the property that is her inheritance.

Martha[1] of (variant 1) would not have been frustrated in the pursuit of her end, and she would have no reason to seek Fred's death once she came into possession of his property. Martha[1] sought Fred's death merely as a means to obtaining the property, not as an end in itself.

Things are different with Martha[2] (of variant 2). She would have been frustrated in part, and she would thus still have a reason to seek Fred's death even if she finds herself in secure possession of his property. (To the question: "Would Martha[2] have a reason to go on to kill Fred if the poison failed, but she assumed secure possession of the property anyway?" the answer would seem to be "yes.") But this is not, as is suggested by Foot's discussion and Nicholson's characterization, a test of whether the death of Fred was sought as a *means* to inheriting his property. It is a test of whether the agent sought the death of Fred *both* as a means to an end—the inheriting of his property—and as a supplementary end in itself.

So the counterfactual test will not do as a test of whether something is a means.[25] Yet there seems to be something to it. Once agents have formed a plan to realize their end, then (other things being equal), if they do not accomplish their means, they must persist in trying to do so (or else abandon that end). If Martha has chosen to poison her uncle in order to inherit his property, and she believes that unless she manages to kill him with the poison she will not succeed in getting hold of the property (for some combination of moral and forensic reasons, Martha thinks that poisoning Fred is the "only way" to kill him), then if the first dose of poison fails to kill Fred, and she is lucky enough to have a second one handy, Martha must keep at it. Similarly, once the doctor has chosen to try to save the woman's life by performing the craniotomy on the fetus, he must persevere if he is to realize his end of saving the woman.

Defenders of the DDE—and we—may find these remarks rather less than satisfying. They appear to presuppose the view that could try to determine whether something is a means (or an agent's means) by determining whether it is part of the agent's plan. But this does not seem to get us anywhere, for it does not seem easier to determine precisely what is (and what is not) part of an agent's plan than it is to determine what is (and what is not) the agent's means.

This criticism may be developed a bit further. The discussion of the notions of means and agent's means arose in the context of trying to spell out when a bad consequence is intended and when that bad consequence is merely foreseen. The guiding supposition seemed to be that if we could, for example, say whether the death of the fetus is a means to the saving of the woman in the case of craniotomy, then we could say whether the death of the fetus is intended or merely foreseen. If the opponents of the DDE now offer the suggestion that the death of the fetus is a means only if it is a part of the doctor's plan, then it looks as if they are reversing the direction of the argument, or else merely arguing in a circle. In either case, there is little progress. We do not seem to be clearer on when something is part of an agent's plan than we are on when it is a means. We are probably no clearer either on when something is a part of an agent's plan than we are on when the agent intends it.

These worries may appear to be procedural rather than substantive. But defenders of the DDE might seek to underscore these worries with a more substantive criticism. According to Anscombe, many of those who discuss the DDE employ an overly crude notion of what it is for an agent to have the intention to do something. What she thinks is that people who suppose that the doctor who performs the craniotomy on the fetus need not intend its death are regarding intention as if it were "an interior act of the mind which could be produced at will."[26] According to Anscombe, such a view of intention is fundamentally mistaken. Agents may be said to intend a death whether or not they have formulated to themselves (anything like) the expression of intention "I will kill."

There is surely something in this. Those who maintain that the doctor who performs craniotomy does not intend the death of the fetus have often spoken as if he could simply decide what his intentions were to be with respect to the death of the fetus. And they have often spoken as if the doctor's report on his state of mind provides the final word in the determination of his intentions (provided he is sincere in what he says). In so far as Anscombe is pointing out that such views are mistaken, I believe that she is correct. The correct ascription to an agent of the intention to do *a* is not based on (nor does it presuppose) the belief that the agent has an occurrent intention to do a, or on the belief that an agent's intention to do a is something that the agent must be able to uncover by introspection, or even on the view that the agents themselves are the sole or final arbiters of what their intentions are. But it is not clear that Anscombe's criticism has force, for it is not clear that the point that she is making is one that the opponents of the DDE must fail to recognize. No one need suppose that the reconstruction of an agent's plan is an attempt to produce a *catalogue* of the agent's *actual* train of thought.

I believe that the opponents of the DDE can accommodate Anscombe's criticism, but—ironically enough—it is not clear that Anscombe herself and other traditional defenders of the DDE can adequately accommodate it. This will be made clearer by considering two more cases, cases which—along with case 1 and case 2—form the *locus classicus* [something that has become a standard for the elucidation of a word or subject] of discussions of the DDE that have taken place in medical ethics texts.

Case 5

A doctor administers what she knows will be a lethal dose of an analgesic drug *(d)* to a patient who is in terrible pain. Any smaller dose will not be effective in relieving the pain. The doctor administers *d* intending thereby to ease the patient's pain, knowing (though regretting) that administering the drug will bring about the death of the patient.

Case 6

A doctor administers what she knows will be a lethal dose of an analgesic drug *d* to a patient who is in terrible pain. The patient's pain cannot be relieved without his dying: only if the patient dies will his pain cease. The doctor regrets the death of the patient, but she administers the lethal dose of *d* to the patient to bring about his death, and thereby relieve his pain.

According to defenders of the DDE, it may be permissible for the doctor in case 5 to administer the drug, but it is impermissible for the doctor in case 6 to do so. In case 5, it is alleged, the death of the patient may be a foreseen but unwanted consequence of relieving the patient's pain. It is not a means (nor is it "sought as a means"); it is merely a "second effect." In case 6, it is alleged, the death of

the patient is intended as a means to relieving his pain.

But what can be the ground of *this* alleged asymmetry? We are to suppose that the causal chains are identical; the behavior of the two doctors is identical, and their behavior would be identical if it were to happen that the patient did not die after receiving the injection (supposing that each doctor believes that it is not possible that this patient be alive and not suffering). Furthermore, each doctor regrets the death of her patient, and each acts with humanitarian motives.[27] Only if something like the occurrent intention or (actual) mental inventory of the doctors is allowed to be the determinant (of whether a course of action is *intended* or whether a certain course of action is to count as the agent's *means)* can there be the required difference between the two cases.[28]

Here traditional defenders of the DDE face an uncomfortable choice. If they refuse to allow that the agent's occurrent intention or mental state is the determinant of whether something is a means, then they can perhaps sustain the claim that there is a significant difference between cases 1 and 2. But then they cannot happily maintain that there is a significant difference between cases 5 and 6. If they allow that an occurrent intention may determine whether something is a means, then they can perhaps sustain the claim that there is a significant difference between cases 5 and 6. But then they cannot happily maintain that there is a significant difference between cases 1 and 2.

It thus appears that the DDE cannot be called upon to give a coherent defense of the view that there is a morally significant difference between both cases 1 and 2 and cases 5 and 6. So traditional defenders of the DDE must make yet another choice. If their intuitions are that there is a morally significant asymmetry between cases 1 and 2 *and* cases 5 and 6, they would do well to give up on the DDE and seek some other casuistical principle. For the DDE cannot accomplish their purpose. Or, at least, it cannot reasonably be supposed that it can do so until and unless it is further examined, and buttressed by an account of means, ends, and intention. If, of the other hand, defenders of the DDE see it as something more than a casuistical principle, then they would do well to abandon the traditional assessment of the four cases, and choose other cases to illustrate the operation of the DDE.

It is the second path that is of greater interest to secular moral philosophy, and it is surely this path that nontraditional defenders of the DDE—secular theorists like Fried and Nagel—would prefer to follow: like traditional defenders of the DDE, they wish to maintain that the distinction between intention and mere foresight is morally and ethically important; yet like opponents of the Doctrine, they doubt that the application of the DDE to the four cases produces the results that traditional defenders have endorsed. But the path is neither a clear nor an easy one. Nontraditional defenders of the DDE cannot hope to demonstrate its tenability simply by choosing new cases to illustrate its application, and appealing to our normative intuitions about such cases. Since what is problematic is how the DDE is to be interpreted, and how it can be applied to cases, this simply begs the question. Nor can they hope to shore up these normative intuitions by appealing to our ordinary understanding of the notions of means, ends, and intention. As I hope to have shown, our ordinary understanding of such notions is neither clear nor unproblematic. Until the notions of means, ends, and intention are more carefully scrutinized, and their various strands untangled, their application to cases cannot yield verdicts that are authoritative.

For the sake of encouraging constructive dialogue, we may allow the following to be understood as the deontologists' credo: "Agents do not violate deontological constraints unless they maltreat other people intentionally." We should not then require that deontologists undertake to supply us with an argument to convince us of its truth. But we cannot reasonably be expected to adopt this stance if, in addition, intention is to be left (in Fried's words) "unanalyzed, a primitive term."[29] Until deontologists provide us with an account of what (they think) it is for an agent to act with a particular intention (rather than with mere foresight), we cannot hope to be able to assess the soundness of deontological views as a class, or the plausibility of any particular proposed deontological constraint.

If, as Fried and Nagel suppose, the distinction between intention and mere foresight is something that is built into the very notion of a deontological constraint, then those who have deontological sympathies must undertake to resolve some of the problems that I have raised in considering the Doctrine of Double Effect. If they are to make progress in this, then it is quite likely that they will have to devote considerably more time and effort to the relevant portions of metaphysics and the philosophy of mind and action than they have thus far thought it necessary to do. I am not here reiterating Anscombe's twenty-five-year-old complaint that it is futile to hope for any progress in moral philosophy until we have resolved the fundamental issues in the philosophy of psychology.[30] (I am more optimistic about moral philosophy and less optimistic about the autonomy of the philosophy of mind than she is.) Rather, what I am pointing out is that, if my line of argument is correct, then the success of the deontologists' moral theoretic endeavor hinges on the tenability of some of their metaphysical claims. Yet deontologists have often been quite cavalier in their attitudes toward metaphysics and the philosophy of action. Two examples would suffice to underscore this point.

Alan Donagan has said that, "In constructing a moral theory no more is necessary than to identify and state any controversial metaphysical presuppositions that distinguish it from its rivals."[31] And Charles Fried has maintained that "in moral philosophy, we may often be forced to swallow some quite unchewed metaphysical morsels, and we should be prepared to do so, provided only that the morsels have a strong intuitive grounding."[32] I believe that this is not a healthy stance to take with respect to the connections between metaphysics and moral philosophy, and that consideration of secular deontologists' problems with the DDE gives us a fair understanding of why this is so. Contra Donagan, moral philosophers cannot really be confident that they can identify which of their metaphysical presuppositions are problematic until they have done a fair bit of metaphysics. And contra Fried, even if we suppose (as we may well not suppose) that the appeal to intuitions represents a good strategy in moral philosophy, it is certainly not obvious that it is a good one to follow in doing metaphysics. For—as I hope my discussion has shown—strong intuitive grounding is, by itself, a poor sort of foundation. The indiscriminate ingestion of "unchewed metaphysical morsels" is thus something we should condemn as an unsound practice. Unless we are more careful, we may find that, like Scrooge's bit of undigested beef, these metaphysical morsels come back in quite terrible forms to haunt us.[33]

Notes

[1]Alan Donagan, *The Theory of Morality* (Chicago: Univ. of Chicago Press, 1977); Charles Fried, *Right and Wrong* (Cambridge, Mass.: Harvard Univ. Press, 1978); Thomas Nagel, "The Limits of Objectivity," in S. McMurrin, ed., *The Tanner Lectures on Human Values*, vol. 1 (Cambridge: Cambridge Univ. Press, 1980) pp. 76–139.

[2]Donagan, p. 29.

[3]Critics include Jonathan Bennett, "Whatever the Consequences," p. 93, and "Morality and Consequences," in S. McMurrin, ed., *The Tanner Lectures on Human Values*, vol. 2 (Cambridge: Cambridge Univ. Press, 1981), pp. 45–116, especially lecture III; Philippa Foot, "The Problem of Abortion and the Doctrine of the Double Effect," p. 59; Jonathan Glover, *Causing Death and Saving Lives* (Harmondsworth: Penguin, 1977), chap. 3; H. L. A. Hart, "Intention and Punishment," *The Oxford Review* 4 (1967), reprinted with modifications in H. L. A. Hart, *Punishment and Responsibility* (Oxford: Oxford Univ. Press, 1968), pp. 113–135; Susan Teft Nicholson, *Abortion and the Roman Catholic Church* (Knoxville, Tenn.: Journal of Religious Ethics Monograph, 1978), chapters 2 and 3; Glanville Williams, *The Sanctity of Life and the Criminal Law* (London: Faber and Faber, 1958), pp. 85–86.

[4]Nagel, p. 129.

[5]See Elizabeth Anscombe, "War and Murder," in Richard Wasserstrom, ed., *War and Morality* (Belmont, Ca.: Wadsworth, 1970), p. 50; Nagel, esp. pp. 131 ff.; Fried, chap. 1; Philip E. Devine, *The Ethics of Homicide* (Ithaca: Cornell Univ. Press, 1978), p. 106.

[6]Nagel, p. 130.

[7]Thomas Aquinas, *Summa Theologica*, II-II, Q. 64, art. 7.

[8]Different commentators offer subtly (but essentially similar) formulations of the four traditional qualifications of the DDE. Mine is a somewhat modified version of that given in *The Catholic Encyclopedia* (1907 edition) in the entry on abortion. Compare the formulations given in "The Principle of Double Effect" in *The New Catholic Encyclopedia* (1967), and in Joseph Mangan, S. J., "An Historical Analysis of the Principle of Double Effect," *Theological Studies* 10 (1949), 60–61.

It is important to recognize that the DDE functions merely as a test of whether a proposed course of action is impermissible, and not as a recipe for right action: if a proposed action fails to satisfy any of the four qualifications, then it is wrong to undertake it; but if it satisfies the four conditions, it does not follow that the action is permissible, let alone good. (From a deontological standpoint, good actions are a subset of permissible ones.)

Failure to recognize that the DDE is not meant to be sufficient for the determination of an action's moral acceptability has, I believe, misled a number of commentators, for example, R. G. Frey. "Some Aspects to the Doctrine of Double Effect," *Canadian Journal of Philosophy* 5 (1975), 259–283, esp. 260, and Michael Walzer, *Just and Unjust Wars* (New York: Basic Books, 1977), pp. 152–157.

[9]Their reliance is not altogether uncritical: Nagel concedes that there are "problems of application," and Fried recognizes that there are difficulties in "identifying the results we intend and distinguishing them from those we merely allow to happen," p. 24. What I wish to suggest is that the problems are less tractable, and more serious, than Nagel and Fried have supposed. They may not accept the applications endorsed by traditional defenders of the DDE, but they do not explain what is problematic about those applications, nor do they offer any guidelines for generating new (correct) ones.

[10]See, for example, Gerald Kelly, S. J., *Medico-Moral Problems* (St. Louis: Catholic Hospital Association, 1958) and Thomas J. O. Donnell, S. J., *Medicine and Christian Morality* (New York: Alba House, 1976).

[11]Philippa Foot considers the fitness of the DDE for this purpose in "Abortion and the Problem of the Double Effect," p. 59.

[12]See, for example, Joseph M. Boyle, Jr., "Towards Understanding the Principle of Double Effect," *Ethics* 90 (1980), 527–538.

[13]Anscombe, p. 51.

[14]Hart, p. 123.

[15]It is also a principle that Fried appears to endorse: "one intends a result if that result is chosen either as one's ultimate end or as one's means to that end," p. 22.

[16]I find it especially difficult to work out what Hart means, for he contrasts Cases 1 and 2 with the following case, in which he thinks the death of the fetus *is* a means:

> ". . . if a doctor found it necessary to kill the foetus while still attached to the wall of the womb by altering the chemical composition of the amniotic fluid with a saline solution in order to avoid the risks of surgery, this would be a clear case of direct intention rather than mere foresight (since the death of the foetus would in this case be a means to an end) . . . ." p. 124.

Why this case would involve intention rather than mere foresight, while the case of the craniotomy would not, is not explained.

[17]See, for example, Leonard Geddes, "On the In-trinsic Wrongness of Killing Innocent People," *Analysis* 33 (1973), 93–97.

[18]For discussion relevant to the conceptual connec-tion question see: Foot; Devine, pp. 122–124; Frey; Geddes; R. A. Duff, "Intentionally Killing the Innocent," *Analysis* 33 (1933), 166–19, and "Absolute Principles and Double Effect," *Analysis* 36 (1976); James Hanink, "Some Light on Double Effect," *Analysis* 35 (1975), 147–151, and "On 'The Survival Lottery,'" *Philosophy* 51 (1976), 223–225; and John Mackie, *Ethics* (Harmondsworth: Penguin, 1977), pp. 160–163.

[19]I owe the substance of this example to Derek Parfit.

[20]Even in this narrow, carefully circumscribed case, there remains room to question whether there is a con-ceptual connection. Couldn't someone brainwash Ben— that is, is it not logically possible to brainwash Ben—to get him to come round to the view that "might makes right" and then execute a coup? Mightn't this suggest that Alice's death is not *required* for the realization of Ben's end?

[21]See Elizabeth Anscombe, *Intention*, 2nd edition, (Oxford: Oxford Univ. Press, 1963), sections 25–27.

[22]Even if Harold knows that Jane is the fastest run-ner in town, it may not be part of his plan to shoot the fastest runner in town. It is certainly intelligible to sup-pose that he regrets killing the town's best runner, but is glad to put an end to Jane.

A caveat is needed to make it clear that the descrip-tions an agent *would* use are not necessarily identical to the descriptions the agent *did* use. For agents sometimes act without due care and attention, and are sometimes guilty of bad faith, and thus avoid facing up to some of the less attractive aspects of their deeds.

[23]It is worth pointing out that discussion of the DDE has been made more confusing than it might have been because people have failed to distinguish the ques-tion of whether the *death* of the fetus is a means and the question of whether the *killing* of the fetus is a means. This has led some to infer that the killing of the fetus is not required to save the woman (or: that performing the craniotomy is not killing the fetus) from the fact that it is not the death of the fetus that is required to save the woman's life. See, for example, Geddes, p. 94: "But in the obstetrical example the *killing* of the infant cannot plausibly be thought of as having any effects desired by the surgeon; the death of the unborn child is not respon-sible, in any way, for the fact that the mother is now alive." See also Hanink, "Some Light on Double Effect," p. 150. Even if the *death* of the fetus is not needed to ensure the woman's survival, the *killing* of the fetus may well be; even if one supposes that the *death* is not a means, one may not be warranted in supposing that the *killing* is not. (Perhaps a killing can be intentional even

when a death is not intended.) I believe that there are two different notions of "means" at work here. What the rela-tions are between them, and what turns on distinguishing them, is far from clear. I hope to discuss this topic further on another occasion.

[24]Nicholson, p. 26.

[25]Judith Thomson pointed our that defenders of the DDE might wish to claim that the notion of means em-ployed in the DDE is not our everyday notion, but is, instead a technical notion, and to maintain that the coun-terfactual test applies only to this technical notion.

Whatever the merits of such a strategy, I believe that it would vindicate neither those defenders of the DDE who, like Anscombe, claim that the DDE is properly ap-plied to distinguish Case 1 and Case 2, nor those who, like Fried and Nagel, reject that application. For they do not profess to be making use of a special, technical notion of means, and none of them offers anything by way of an account of such a notion.

[26]Anscombe, "War and Murder," p. 51.

[27]Of course it is unlikely to be true that the same drug would have the effects described in cases 5 and 6; thus one would usually be able to determine whether the doctor intended to kill or merely foresaw the death as a consequence by looking to see which drug she chose to administer. Similarly, in real life there are likely differ-ences in the doctors' motivations, and, more generally, in their characters. But these differences cannot be called upon as support for the DDE. The DDE is supposed to apply to particular acts, and to treat the agent's intention as critical to the moral assessment of the particular act. And so supposed differences in character or in motivation are irrelevant.

[28]There are other alternatives. We could adopt a constructive and defeasible test, according to which cer-tain intentions are to be attributed to agents unless specific presuppositions can be shown not to apply. (Compare the "rational man" test from law.) This strategy is hardly unproblematic, however, and it (too) requires a substantive account of intention before it can be got off the ground.

[29]Fried, p. 24.

[30]"Modern Moral Philosophy," *Philosophy* 33 (1958), reprinted in J. J. Thomson and Gerald Dworkin, eds., *Ethics* (New York: Harper and Row, 1968), pp. 186–210; p. 186.

[31]Donagan, p. 28.

[32]Fried, p. 20.

[33]This paper has undergone a number of drafts and reformulations. I am grateful to Derek Parfit, Paolo Dau, and T. M. Scanlon for responses to earlier versions. Bar-bara Herman's stylistic suggestions, Judith Thomson's comments, and Dale Jamieson's detailed and patient criti-cism have greatly improved the present version.

Part V

SHOULD NUMBERS COUNT?

Should the Numbers Count?

JOHN TAUREK
Philosophy and Public Affairs, 1977

John Taurek's essay challenges the position that in certain moral trade-off situations involving our ability to bestow benefits or prevent harms, we should consider the numbers of people involved as significant. Taurek begins his discussion with versions of Drug (see Introduction), in which a person who has a lifesaving drug has the option of using this drug to save one person who requires all of it or five others who each require one-fifth of it.

Rejecting the utilitarian approach that says that all things being equal, we should try to save the greater number of people, Taurek takes the position that doing this is inconsistent with other convictions we may hold "with even greater tenacity," such as the view that all persons ought to be given equal concern and respect.

Taurek argues that there are no grounds for a moral requirement that we should always save the five (apart from any special obligations arising from prior promises, etc.). Taurek claims that if the owner of the drug in the hypothetical case is the one person who needs the entire portion in order to be saved, then it would be morally permissible for that person to save his own life and let the other five die. Going through different utilitarian considerations, such as the greater potential for happiness and intrinsic value of the five over the one, Taurek suggests that *none* of these ought to persuade the owner of the drug not to save himself. Simply put, the owner of the drug values his own life more than the lives of the five others, and this is not unreasonable.

Taurek then points out that if this is a reasonable position, then it would seem to be morally permissible for a *third* party to do the same, i.e., to save the one. If there is no special obligation to the five, then it cannot be wrong to save (say) a friend, given that the drug really is owned by the person who has the power to distribute it. Thus, no third party, special obligations aside, would be morally required to save the five instead of the friend. Similarly, Taurek argues that if it would be morally permissible for an individual to save his own arm rather than another's life, then it would be permissible for a third party to save a person's arm rather than another's life.

Turning next to the case where there is no special concern for *any* of the parties involved, Taurek suggests that they each ought to be given an equal chance of surviving. Flipping a coin would be one way to express equal concern and respect for each person. Who could complain that he is treated wrongly under this arrangement? Which option is worse seems to depend on where you stand. If you are one of the five, then clearly it is worse that the one is saved. If you are the one, then it is worse that the five are saved. Taurek suggests that there is no independent or impersonal viewpoint from which it can be seen that the loss of five lives is a worse outcome than the loss of one. (Similarly, the suggestion is that there is no impersonal viewpoint from which it can be seen that the suffering of five persons is *worse* than the suffering of one.)

Taurek concludes the article by answering in advance a counterargument that would show potentially dangerous "real-world" ramifications of his analysis. In this example, the captain of a Coast Guard evacuation ship has time to save only one group of people on an island where a catastrophe has occurred. At one end of the island is a large group of people and at the other end is a smaller group. Using Taurek's analysis, the captain would flip a coin and save the smaller group, but in this case the situation is different, according to Taurek. When a third party is deploying a resource that is *not his own*, it is different from a case where an individual is deciding what to do with his own resources. In this case each person may have an equal claim to the resources of the evacuation ship, and thus some contractual duty may dictate what the captain's policy in all such cases must be. Such a position, Taurek says, is consistent with the fact that the numbers should not count. In such a case no claim is made that it is intrinsically a better thing to save the many rather than the few.

---

*WE HAVE RESOURCES FOR BESTOWING BENEFITS and for preventing harms. But there are limitations. There are many people we are not in a position to help at all. That is one kind of limitation. But there is another kind of limitation we encounter. Often we must choose between bestowing benefits on certain people, or preventing certain harms from befalling them, and bestowing benefits on or preventing harms from befalling certain others. We cannot do both. The general question discussed here is whether we should, in such trade-off situations, consider the relative numbers of people involved as something in itself of significance in determining our course of action.[1] The conclusion I reach is that we should not. I approach this general question by focusing on a particular hypothetical case in which we find ourselves in a position of being able to prevent a certain harm from befalling one person or to prevent a like harm from befalling each of five others, but unable to spare all six from harm.

The situation is that I have a supply of some life-saving drug.[2] Six people will all certainly die if they are not treated with the drug. But one of the six requires all of the drug if he is to survive. Each of the other five requires only one-fifth of the drug. What ought I to do?

To many if seems obvious that in such cases, special considerations apart, one ought to save the greater number. I cannot accept this view. I believe

that at least some of those who do accept it fail to appreciate the difficulty of reconciling their thinking here with other convictions they are inclined to hold with even greater tenacity. First, I want to delineate some of these difficulties. I hope that, in view of them, others might be brought to reflect more critically on the intuitions that underlie this position. I shall then present what seems to me a more appropriate and appealing way of viewing trade-off situations of the kind in question.

Those who think that I ought to distribute my drug in fifths to the five people usually qualify their position. They maintain that "other things being equal, or special considerations apart, one ought to save the greater number." What sort of special considerations to the contrary do they have in mind? What is being ruled out by the "other things being equal" clause?

One thing they have in mind, I think, is the possibility of special facts about the one person that would, in their view, make his death a far worse thing than one might otherwise have supposed. Perhaps he is close to discovering some wonder drug or is on the verge of negotiating a lasting peace in the world's perennial trouble spot. The idea is that it could happen that this one person's continued existence is in some way crucial to the welfare of an unusually large number of people. This would make his death a far worse thing in the minds of some than it would otherwise be. Of course, they also have in mind the possibility that special facts about these five persons could make their deaths not nearly so bad a thing after all. They might be five driveling old people or five idiot infants, loved by no one. In light of such facts as these it may well be permissible, perhaps even obligatory in the view of some, to save the one wholesome person instead of the five others. So when people say, "other things being equal, one ought to save the greater number," they mean to rule out such special considerations as these. The thinking here is that, apart from some such considerations, the death of five innocent persons is a worse thing, a greater evil, a greater loss, than the death of one innocent person. Since I am in a position to prevent either of these bad things from happening, but not both, I am morally required to prevent the worst.

Such reasoning seems appealing to many. I find it difficult to understand and even more difficult to see how it is to be reconciled with certain other convictions widely shared by these same people. Suppose this one person, call him David, is someone I know and like, and the others are strangers to me. I might well give all of my drug to him. And I am inclined to think that were I to do so, I would not be acting immorally. I suspect that many share this view with me.

Of course, some people do think that I would be acting immorally. They think it would be wrong to give all the drug to David while the five others die just because David is someone I know and like. They may allow that this could make my action excusable, but on their view it would not make it right.

For the moment, I address myself to those who, while subscribing to the general position, nevertheless share my view that it would not be wrong for me to use my drug to save a person I know and like. They must deny that the original claim, together with the thinking that lies behind it, commits them to the view that I ought to save the five strangers in this case. Perhaps they will object that, in introducing David as someone I know and like, I have introduced another of those special considerations that were meant to be excluded by the "other things being equal" clause. But if this is one of the special considerations meant to be ruled out, it is of a different sort from

the special considerations previously mentioned. These were facts about the five persons in light of which it was thought their deaths would not be so bad, after all; or facts about David that would make his death a worse thing than the death of a person of more ordinary credentials. The idea was that these considerations would make a difference to what I ought to do, because in light of them the death of the one person would in fact be a worse thing to have happen than would be the deaths of these five.

But I would not think that the fact that David happens to be someone I know and like would make his death a worse thing in comparison to the deaths of these others than it would be if, by chance, I didn't know him or knew him but happened not to like him. So it is not clear to me how this fact is to make a difference in what I am *morally required* to do in this situation. It is not clear to me how it is to make a difference in the view of those who think that, apart from it, I would have a moral obligation to save the five, an obligation deriving from the fact that it is a worse thing, other things being equal, that these five innocent persons should die than it is that this one should.

Perhaps there are special considerations of a kind different from those described thus far. Suppose that one person had contracted with me in advance to have just this quantity of the drug administered to him at this particular time. It could be thought that such a special obligation to the one party arising out of a contract would override the fact that I would be preventing a far worse thing from happening were I to give the drug to the five. An explicit contract or promise may not be the only source of such special obligations to another person. Perhaps a parent is thought to be thus specially obligated to his child, or a child to his parents. Perhaps a doctor has such a special obligation to his regular patients. Perhaps one might think one has such a special obligation to a benefactor, and so on. It seems reasonable to suppose that the existence of such special obligations to specific individuals involved were also meant to be excluded by the "other things being equal" clause. But can this be helpful to those who wish to reconcile their feeling that I do not do wrong when I give all my drug to a friend with an adherence to the original contention?

This does not seem to be a very promising line. Are we to suppose that I have in this situation an overriding obligation to save this one person, deriving from the fact that he is someone I know and like? Such a supposition does not appear to capture my thinking here at all. The fact is that I would act to save David's life because, knowing him and liking him, my concern for his well-being is simply greater than my concern for the well-being of those others, not because I recognize some overriding obligation to him. Imagine that the situation involved David and only one other person, a stranger. In the absence of any special claim of right possessed by the stranger, I would save David. If asked to explain or justify my choice, I would not think to say that I was *morally required* to give my drug to David in virtue of the fact that I happen to know and like him. The fact that David is a friend explains, naturally enough, my preference for saving him rather than this other person. It is the absence of any moral obligation to save this other person rather than David that makes my choice morally permissible. And, rightly or wrongly, that is how I think of my conduct in the situation under discussion. In securing David's survival I am acting on a purely personal preference. It is the absence of any moral requirement to save these others rather than David that makes my doing so morally permissible.

However, this talk of a special duty to the one person, arising not from any promise, contract or quasi-contractual relationship between us, but somehow from the mere fact that I know and like him, would appear to go too far. For, on such a view, it would be more than simply permissible for me to save David, it would be morally obligatory that I save him rather than these five others. And this is not the thinking of those who feel only that it would not be wrong of me to save David.

On the view in question, one is morally required to save the five instead of the one, other things being equal, because, other things being equal, it is a very much worse thing that these five innocent people should die than it is that this one should. But if this fact constitutes a compelling ground for a moral obligation to give the drug to these five rather than to this one, then I too shall have to acknowledge its moral force. The problem, then, is to explain, especially perhaps to these five

people, how it is that merely because I know and like David and am unacquainted with them I can so easily escape the moral requirement to save their lives that would fall on most anyone else in my position. The only relevant consideration here is that I happen to like David more than I like any of them. Imagine my saying to them, "Admittedly, the facts are such that I would be morally obligated to give you this drug, if it didn't happen that I prefer to give it to him." The moral force of such facts must be feeble indeed to be overridden by an appeal as feeble as this.

Contrast this situation with almost any other in which we would be prepared to acknowledge the existence of grounds for a moral requirement to give the drug to these five people. Suppose, for example, that these five had contracted with me in advance to deliver this drug to them at this time and place. It would not seem likely that anyone would think that the fact that I would prefer to give it to someone else instead would alter in any way what I was morally required to do. But of course it might make it harder, psychologically, for me to do what I ought to do. Again, suppose that these five are American soldiers and I am an army doctor with what little is left of the issue of this drug. And let us suppose that this other person is someone I know and like but is a citizen of some other country. Would anyone imagine that the fact that I would prefer to use the drug to save this one person could somehow nullify or lift my obligation to distribute the drug to the five soldiers?

The point is this. Generally, when the facts are such that any impartial person would recognize a moral obligation to do something as important to people as giving this drug to these five would be to them, then an appeal to the fact that one happens to be partial to the interests of some others would do nothing to override the moral obligation. Yet this is the position of those who maintain that in this situation any impartial person would be *morally required* to distribute his drug in fifths to the five. But because I, personally, would prefer to give it to someone else, it is permissible for me to do so.[3]

I am inclined to think, then, that we should either agree that it would be wrong for me to save David in this situation or admit that there are no grounds for a moral requirement on anyone, special obligations apart, to save the five instead of David.

Now as I said earlier there are those who will take the view that I do wrong when I give preference to David in this situation. They may feel that what has been said so far only proves the point. So now I would like to say something in support of the opinion that it would be morally permissible for a person in such circumstances to save a friend rather than the five strangers.

Suppose the drug belongs to your friend David. It is his drug, his required dosage. Now there are these five strangers, strangers to David as well as to you. Would you try to persuade David to give his drug to these five people? Do you think you should? Suppose you were to try. How would you begin? You are asking him to give up his life so that each of the five others, all strangers to him, might continue to live.

Imagine trying to reason with David as you would, presumably, have reasoned with yourself were the drug yours. "David, to be sure it is a bad thing, a very bad thing, that you should die. But don't you see it is a far worse thing that these five people should die? Now you are in a position to prevent either of these bad things from happening. Unfortunately you cannot prevent them both. So you ought to insure that the worst thing doesn't happen."

Don't you think that David might demur? Isn't he likely to ask: "Worse for whom?" And it seems natural and relevant that he should continue to put his case in some such way as this: "It is a far worse thing for me that I should die than that they should. I allow that for each of them it would be a worse thing were they all to die while I continue to live than it would be were I to die and they to continue to live. Indeed I wouldn't ask, nor would I expect, any one of them to give up his life so that I, a perfect stranger, might continue to live mine. But why should you, or any one of them, expect me to give up my life so that each of them might continue to live his?"

I think David's question deserves an answer. What could there be about these strangers that might induce David to think it worth giving up his life so that they might continue to live theirs? The usual sort of utilitarian reasoning would be comical if it were not so outrageous. Imagine any one of these five entreating David, "Look here David. Here I am but one person. If you give me one-fifth of your drug I will continue to live. I am confident that I will garner over the long haul a net balance of pleasure over pain, happiness over misery. Admittedly, if this were all that would be realized by your death I should not expect that you would give up your life for it. I mean, it may not be unreasonable to think that you yourself, were you to continue to live, might succeed in realizing at least as favorable a balance of happiness. But here, don't you see, is a second person. If he continues to live he too will accumulate a nice balance of pleasure over pain. And here is yet a third, a fourth, and finally a fifth person. Now, we would not ask you to die to make possible the net happiness realized in the life of any one of us five. For you might well suppose that you could realize as much in your own lifetime. But it would be most unreasonable for you to think that you could realize in your one lifetime anything like as much happiness as we get when we add together our five distinct favorable balances."

Such reasoning coming from some disinterested outside party might be a little less contemptible, but surely not a bit less foolish. But if we recognize the absurdity of trying to sell David on the idea that it would be a worse thing were these five persons to die than it would be were he to die by suggesting he focus on the large sum of their added happinesses as compared to his own, just what kind of reasoning would sound less absurd? Is it less absurd to ask him to focus on the large sum of intrinsic value possessed by five human beings, quite apart from considerations of their happiness, as compared to the value of himself alone?

I cannot imagine that I could give David any reason why *he* should think it better that these five strangers should continue to live than that he should. In using his drug to preserve his own life he acts to preserve what is, understandably, more important to him. He values his own life more than he values any of theirs. This is, of course, not to say that he thinks he is more valuable, period, than any one of them, or than all of them taken together. (Whatever could such a remark mean?) Moreover, and this I would like to stress, in not giving this drug to these five people he does not wrong any of them. He violates no one's rights. None of these five has a legitimate claim on David's drug in this situation, and so the five together have no such claim. Were they to attack David and to take his drug, they would be murderers. Both you and David would be wholly within your rights to defend against any such attempt to deprive him of his drug.

Such, in any case, is my view. I hope that most people would agree with me. But if it is morally permissible for David in this situation to give himself all of his drug, why should it be morally impermissible for me to do the same? It is my drug. It is more important to me that David should continue to live than it is that these five strangers should. I value his life more than I value theirs. None of these five has any special claim to my drug in this situation. None of them can legitimately demand of me that I give him the drug instead of giving it to David. And so the five together have no such special claim. I violate no one's rights when I use my drug to save David's life. Were these five, realizing that I was about to give my drug to David, to attempt to take it from me, I would think myself wholly justified in resisting.

Thus far I have argued that, since it would not be morally impermissible for the one person, David, to use all of his drug to save himself instead of these five others, it cannot be morally impermissible for me, were the drug mine and given that I am under no special obligations to any of these five, to use it all to save David instead of these other five. In so arguing I have committed myself to a view that may strike some as counterintuitive. On my view, if one party, A, must decide whether to spare another party, B, some loss or harm H, or to spare a third party, C, some loss or harm H', it cannot be A's moral duty, special obligations apart, to spare C harm H' unless it would be B's duty, in the absence of special obligations to the contrary, to spare C harm H' if he could, even at the expense of suffering H himself. To put it another way, my thinking here is simply this. If it would be morally permissible for B to choose to spare himself a certain loss, H, instead of sparing another person, C, a loss, H', in a situation where he cannot spare C and himself as well, then it must be permissible for someone else, not under any relevant special obligations to the contrary, to take B's perspective, that is, to choose to secure the outcome most favorable to B instead of the outcome most favorable to C, if he cannot secure what would be best for each.

The following kind of case might be raised as a counterexample. Many of us, perhaps most of us, might agree that were B somehow situated so that he could spare C the loss of his life, or spare himself the loss of an arm, but could not do both, it would not be morally required, special obligations apart, that he choose to spare C the loss of his life. "But," it will be asked, "suppose you are the one who must choose? You can either spare this person, C, the loss of his life, or spare B the loss of his arm. Even apart from any special obligations to C, wouldn't you acknowledge that you ought to spare C the loss of his life? Wouldn't it be wrong for you to spare B his loss and let C die?"

Well, I do not think it would be morally impermissible for me to spare B the loss of his arm in such a situation. What exactly would be the ground for such a moral requirement? I am to choose which of two possible outcomes is to be realized: in the one, B retains his arm intact and C dies; in the other, B loses his arm and C does not die. If the choice were B's it would be permissible for him to choose the first outcome. But it is not permissible for me to make this same choice? Why exactly is this? By hypothesis, I am under no relevant special obligations in this situation. So what is the difference between B and me in virtue of which I am morally required to secure the outcome most favored by C, though B would not be? Unless it is for some reason morally impermissible for one person to take the same interest in another's welfare as he himself takes in it, it must be permissible for me, in the absence of special obligations to the contrary, to choose the outcome that is in B's best interest. And, of course, this is what I would do if B's welfare were more important to me than C's.

There may well come a point, however, at which the difference between what B stands to lose and C stands to lose is such that I would spare C his loss. But in just these situations I am inclined to think that even if the choice were B's he too should prefer that C be spared his loss. For some people such a point of difference may already have been reached in the case where B stands to lose an arm, while C stands to lose his life. There are profoundly important differences in attitude among people here that I do not know how to reconcile. I personally do not think that anyone should be moved, in the absence of special considerations, to spare me the loss of my life rather than sparing themselves the loss of an arm. Others seem to think that they should.

I suspect that many of those who see in the purported counterexample a forceful objection to my view are people who more than half believe that (ideally) they really should be prepared to spare me the loss of my life even at the expense of losing their arms. Yet they are doubtful that they could bring themselves to make such a choice were it actually to come to that. Sensing this about themselves they are understandably reluctant to openly place such a demand on another. However when they imagine themselves in the role of a third party, who is not especially concerned about B, they feel less conflict about sparing C the loss of his life. They, after all, will not have to lose their arms. But if this is their thinking, then they are not raising a serious objection to the view I have taken.

Let me return now to a further discussion of the original trade-off situation. It is my conviction that were the drug David's to use, he would do nothing wrong, special obligations apart, were he to use it to save himself instead of giving it up to the five strangers. For the same reasons, I believe that were the drug mine and David someone I know and like, it would not be wrong of me, special obligations apart, to save him rather than the five strangers. And so I feel compelled to deny that any third party, relevant special obligations apart, would be *morally required* to save the five persons and let David die. So what do I think one should do in such a situation in the absence of any special concern for any of the parties involved?

First, let me suggest what I would do in many such cases. Here are six human beings. I can empathize with each of them. I would not like to see any of them die. But I cannot save everyone. Why not give each person an equal chance to survive? Perhaps I could flip a coin. Heads, I give my drug to these five. Tails, I give it to this one. In this way I give each of the six persons a fifty-fifty chance of surviving. Where such an option is open to me it would seem to best express my equal concern and respect for each person. Who among them could complain that I have done wrong? And on what grounds?[4]

The claim that one ought to save the many instead of the few was made to rest on the claim that, other things being equal, it is a worse thing that these five persons should die than that this one should. It is this evaluative judgment that I cannot accept. I do not wish to say in this situation that it is or would be a worse thing were these five persons to die and David to live than it is or would be were David to die and these five to continue to live. I do not wish to say this unless I am prepared to qualify it by explaining to whom or for whom or relative to what purpose it is or would be a worse thing.

I grant that for each one of the five persons, it would be worse were David to survive and they to die than it would be if David were to die and the five to survive. But, of course, from David's perspective the matter is otherwise. For him it would be a worse thing were he to die. From my perspective, I am supposing in this situation that it does not really matter who lives and who dies. My situation is not worsened or bettered by either outcome. No doubt others will be affected differently by what happens. For those who love or need David it would be a better thing were the others to die. But for those especially attached to or dependent on one or the other of these five, it would be better were David to die and these five to live.

Some will be impatient with all this. They will say it is true, no doubt, but irrelevant. They will insist that I say what would be a worse (or a better) thing, period. It seems obvious to them that from the moral point of view, since there is nothing special about any of these six persons, it is a worse thing that these five should die while this one continues to live than for this one to die while these five continue to live. It is a worse thing, not necessarily for anyone in particular, or relative to anyone's particular ends, but just a worse thing in itself.

I cannot give a satisfactory account of the meaning of judgments of this kind. But there are important differences between them and those judgments which relativize the value ascribed to some particular person or group, purpose or end. When I judge of two possible outcomes that the one would be worse (or better) for this person or this group, I do not, typically, thereby express a preference between these outcomes. Typically, I do not feel constrained to admit that I or anyone *should* prefer the one outcome to the other. But when I evaluate outcomes from an impersonal perspective (perhaps we may say from a moral perspective), matters are importantly different. When I judge that it would be a worse thing, period, were this to happen than were that to happen, then I do, typically, thereby express a preference between these outcomes. Moreover, at the very least, I feel constrained to admit that I *should* have such a preference, even if I do not. It is a moral shortcoming not to prefer what is admittedly in itself a better thing to what is in itself a worse thing.

Hence, I cannot give such an impersonal evaluative judgment as the ground for a decision to give the drug to the five instead of to the one. I could not bring myself to say to this one person, "I give my drug to these five and let you die because, don't you see, it is a worse thing, a far worse thing, that they should die than that you should." I do not expect that David, or anyone in his position, should think it a better thing were he to die and these five others to survive than it would be were he to survive and they to die. I do not think him morally deficient in any way because he prefers the outcome in which he survives and the others die to the outcome in which they survive and he dies.

In a situation where the one person, David, is a friend of mine and the others strangers to me, I do have a preference for the one outcome as against the other, to me a natural and acceptable preference. But since I do not expect everyone to share such a preference I will not elevate its expression to the status of a universally binding evaluation. I do not say to the five strangers that I give all of my drug to my friend because it is a better thing in itself that he should survive than that they should. I do not believe any such thing. Rather, I simply explain that David is my friend. His survival is more important to me than theirs. I would expect them to understand this, provided they were members of a moral community acceptable to me, just as I would were our roles reversed. Further, in securing David's survival I violate no one's rights. No further justification of my action is needed, just as no further justification is needed in a situation where the drug belongs to the one person. He need not, and plainly should not, give as the ground for his decision to use his drug to secure his own survival the judgment that it is better in itself that he should survive than that they should. Who could expect any of them to accept that? He need only

point out, as if this really needed remarking, that it is more important to him that he survive than it is to him that they should. Furthermore, in thus securing his own survival he violates none of their rights. What more need be said?

In the trade-off situation as presently conceived, all six persons are strangers to me. I have no special affection for any one of them, no greater concern for one than for any of the others. Further, by hypothesis, my situation will be made neither worse nor better by either outcome. Any preference I might show, therefore, if it is not to be thought arbitrary, would require grounding. Of course this is precisely what an impersonal evaluative judgment of the kind discussed would do. It would provide a reason for the preference I show should I give the drug to the five. But for the reasons given, I cannot subscribe to such an evaluation of these outcomes. Hence, in this situation I have absolutely no reason for showing preference to them as against him, and no reason for showing preference to him as against them. Thus I am inclined to treat each person equally by giving each an equal chance to survive.

Yet I can imagine it will still be said, despite everything, "But surely the numbers must count for something." I can hear the incredulous tones: "Would you flip a coin were it a question of saving fifty persons or saving one? Surely in situations where the numbers are this disproportionate you must admit that one ought to save the many rather than the few or the one."

I would flip a coin even in such a case, special considerations apart. I cannot see how or why the mere addition of numbers should change anything. It seems to me that those who, in situations of the kind in question, would have me count the relative numbers of people involved as something in itself of significance, would have me attach importance to human beings and what happens to them in merely the way I would to objects which I valued. If six objects are threatened by fire and I am in a position to retrieve the five in this room or the one in that room, but unable to get out all six, I would decide what to do in just the way I am told I should when it is human beings who are threatened. Each object will have a certain value in my eyes. If it happens that all six are of equal value, I will naturally preserve the many rather than the one. Why?

Because the five objects are together five times more valuable in my eyes than the one.

But when I am moved to rescue human beings from harm in situations of the kind described, I cannot bring myself to think of them in just this way. I empathize with them. My concern for what happens to them is grounded chiefly in the realization that each of them is, as I would be in his place, terribly concerned about what happens to him. It is not my way to think of them as each having a certain *objective* value, determined however it is we determine the objective value of things, and then to make some estimate of the combined value of the five as against the one. If it were not for the fact that these objects were creatures much like me, for whom what happens to them is of great importance, I doubt that I would take much interest in their preservation. As merely intact objects they would mean very little to me, being, as such, nearly as common as toadstools. The loss of an arm of the *Pietà* means something to me not because the *Pietà* will miss it. But the loss of an arm of a creature like me means something to me only because I know he will miss it, just as I would miss mine. It is the loss *to this person* that I focus on. I lose nothing of value to me should he lose his arm. But if I have a concern for him, I shall wish he might be spared his loss.

And so it is in the original situation. I cannot but think of the situation in this way. For each of these six persons it is no doubt a terrible thing to die. Each faces the loss of something among the things he values most. His loss means something to me only, or chiefly, because of what it means to him. It is the loss to the individual that matters to me, not the loss of the individual. But should any one of these five lose his life, his loss is no greater a loss to him because, as it happens, four others (or forty-nine others) lose theirs as well. And neither he nor anyone else loses anything of greater value to him than does David, should David lose his life. Five individuals each losing his life does not add up to anyone's experiencing a loss five times greater than the loss suffered by any one of the five.

If I gave my drug to the five persons and let David die I cannot see that I would thereby have preserved anyone from suffering a loss greater than that I let David suffer. And, similarly, were I to give my drug to David and let the five die I cannot see that I would thereby have allowed anyone to suffer

a loss greater than the loss I spared David. Each person's potential loss has the same significance to me, only as a loss to that person alone. Because, by hypothesis, I have an equal concern for each person involved, I am moved to give each of them an equal chance to be spared his loss.

My way of thinking about these trade-off situations consists, essentially, in seriously considering what will be lost or suffered by this one person if I do not prevent it, and in comparing the significance of that *for him* with what would be lost or suffered by anyone else if I do not prevent it. This reflects a refusal to take seriously in these situations any notion of the sum of two persons' separate losses. To me this appears a quite natural extension of the way in which most would view analogous trade-off situations involving differential losses to those involved, indeed even most of those who find my treatment of the cases thus far described paradoxical. Perhaps then, in one last effort to persuade them, it may be helpful to think about a trade-off situation of this kind.

Suppose I am told that if you, a stranger to me, agree to submit to some pain of significant intensity I will be spared a lesser one. Special circumstances apart, I can see no reason whatever why you should be willing to make such a sacrifice. It would be cowardly of me to ask it of you. Now add a second person, also a stranger to you. Again we are told that if you volunteer to undergo this same considerable pain each of us will be spared a lesser one. I feel it would be no less contemptible of me to ask you to make such a sacrifice in this situation. There is no reason you should be willing to undergo such a pain to spare me mine. There is no reason you should be willing to undergo such a pain to spare this other person his. And that is all there is to it.

Now, adding still others to our number, not one of whom will suffer as much as you are asked to bear, will not change things for me. It ought not to change things for any of us. If not one of us can give you a good reason why you should be willing to undergo a greater suffering so that he might be spared a lesser one, then there is simply no good reason why you should be asked to suffer so that the group may be spared. Suffering is not additive in this way. The discomfort of each of a large number of individuals experiencing a minor headache does not add up to anyone's experiencing a migraine. In such a trade-off situation as this we are to compare your pain or your loss, not to our collective or total pain, whatever exactly that is supposed to be, but to what will be suffered or lost by *any given single one of us*.

Perhaps it would not be unseemly for a stranger who will suffer some great agony or terrible loss unless you willingly submit to some relatively minor pain to ask you to consider this carefully, to ask you to empathize with him in what he will have to go through. But to my way of thinking it would be contemptible for any one of us in this crowd to ask you to consider carefully, "not, of course, what I personally will have to suffer. None of us is thinking of himself here! But contemplate, if you will, what *we* the group, will suffer. Think of the awful sum of pain that is in the balance here! There are so very many more of us." At best such thinking seems confused. Typically, I think, it is outrageous.

Yet, just such thinking is engaged in by those who, in situations of the kind described earlier, would be moved to a course of action by a *mere consideration* of the relative numbers of people involved. If the numbers should not be given any significance by those involved in these trade-off situations, why should they count for anyone? Suppose that I am in a position either to spare you your pain or to spare this large number of individuals each his lesser pain, but unable to spare both you and them. Why should I attach any significance to their numbers if none of those involved should? I cannot understand how I am supposed to add up their separate pains and attach significance to that alleged sum in a way that would be inappropriate were any of those involved to do it. If, by allowing you to suffer your pain, I do not see that I can thereby spare a single person any greater pain or, in this case, even as much pain. I do not see why calling my attention to the numbers should move me to spare them instead of you, any more than focusing on the numbers should move you to sacrifice for them collectively when you have no reason to sacrifice for them individually.

It is not my intention to argue that in this situation I ought to spare you rather than them just because your pain is "greater" than would be the pain of any one of them. Rather, I want to make it clear that in reaching a decision in such a case it is

natural to focus on a comparison of the pain you will suffer, if I do not prevent it, with the pain that would be suffered by any given individual in this group, if I do not prevent it. I want to stress that it does not seem natural in such a case to attempt to add up their separate pains. I would like to combat the apparent tendency of some people to react to the thought of each of fifty individuals suffering a pain of some given intensity in the same way as they might to the thought of some individual suffering a pain many or fifty times more intense. I cannot but think that some such tendency is at work in the minds of those who attribute significance to the numbers in these trade-off situations.

In the original situation we were to imagine that I must choose between sparing David the loss of his life and sparing five others the loss of their lives. In making my decision I am not to compare his loss, on the one hand, to the collective or total loss to these five, on the other, whatever exactly that is supposed to be. Rather, I should compare what David stands to suffer or lose, if I do not prevent it, to what will be suffered or lost by any other person, if I do not prevent that. Calling my attention to the numbers should not move me to spare them instead of him, any more than focusing on the numbers should move him to sacrifice his life for the group when he has no reason to sacrifice for any individual in the group. The numbers, in themselves, simply do not count for me. I think they should not count for any of us.

I suppose that some will take the apparent absurdity of the following scene as constituting a formidable embarrassment to the opinions I have stated thus far. Volcanic eruptions have placed the lives of many in immediate jeopardy. A large number are gathered at the north end of the island, awaiting evacuation. A handful find themselves on the southern tip. Imagine the captain of the only Coast Guard evacuation ship in the area finding himself midway between. Where shall he head first? Having been persuaded by my argument, to the amazement of his crew and fellow officers, the consternation of the government, and the subsequent outrage in the press, he flips a coin and makes for the south.

Admittedly, it will seem obvious to many people in our moral culture that it is the captain's duty to direct his ship to the north end of the island straightaway with no preliminary coin toss. And I don't wish to deny that this may indeed be his duty. But we must ask what is the source or derivation of his duty? If it is said, simply, that it is the captain's duty to save the many rather than the few because, other things begin equal, it is a worse thing that this handful should survive while the many perish than it would be were those few to die and these many to survive, then I would protest. I have said why I think such thinking is unreflective and unacceptable. But I doubt that it is this simple sort of thinking that lies behind the quick and certain judgments of most who, when presented with this case, declare that the captain would be in violation of his duty were he to flip a coin, and then, perhaps, proceed south.

This situation is different in certain important respects from the kind of case I've been discussing up to this point. In this situation, the captain is seen as deploying a resource that is not his own, not exclusively anyway. And though it is not made explicit in the description of the situation, I suspect that in the minds of those who are so quick to judge it is assumed that each of those in jeopardy has a citizen's equal claim to the use or benefit of that resource. For these reasons the Coast Guard captain is seen as *duty-bound* in the situation; duty-bound to behave in accordance with a policy for the use of that resource agreeable to those whose resource it is. Hence the considerations operative here are quite different from those relevant to the decision of a private citizen captaining his own ship or dispensing his own drug or reaching out his hand under no moral constraints but those that would fall on any man.

The recognition of these differences quite obviously colors the judgments of those to whom such a case is presented. Contrast, for example, the way in which most people would judge the Coast Guard captain's conduct with their judgment on the conduct of a private citizen. Were a private citizen to make first for the south end of the island because among the few are some dear to him while among the many are only strangers, most would not raise a hue and cry. Although some might urge that it would have been a better thing had this person gone north to rescue a large number, they are not likely to think of his action as a violation of his duty to these people. But even if, tragically

enough, the Coast Guard captain had friends among the few and none among the many, it will be seen as a breach of his duty should he first see to the safety of his friends. Here it seems that people think of his action as a violation of the rights of those who have a legitimate claim on the resource. How could the Coast Guard captain justify his decision to go first to the south end of the island? How could he justify it to those many at the north end? A justification is owed to them in this case. Personal preferences won't do. For those in the north are seen as having each an equal claim on that resource.

So this case is different from those previously discussed. Still, it may be urged, the point is that the captain *is* thought to be required to secure the safety of the large number first. It would be wrong of him to flip a coin to decide his course of action. And so isn't this a case of the numbers counting? For what other justification could be given to the handful left to die at the south end of the island except to say: "It would be a worse thing were those many in the north to perish than it would be should only the few of you die."

I think there is a possible alternative justification of the captain's action in this situation that involves no appeal to any such claim as that. It is a more attractive justification. I suspect it comes closer to what most people think (perhaps wrongly) is available in this sort of case. I believe we are inclined to think of the situation in this way. A number of people have joined to invest in a resource, the chief purpose of which is to serve the interests of those who have invested. Whether each has invested an absolutely equal amount, or whether individual investments are scaled to individual resources, is neither here nor there. Theoretically at least, each person's investment (or status) is seen as entitling him to an equal share, an equal claim on the use of that resource or on the benefits from its use. Now a policy for the employment of that resource in just such contingencies as this present trade-off situation must be adopted. And it must be a policy agreeable in advance to all those who are supposed to see their interests as equally served. The captain's duty, then, whatever it is, is seen as deriving from this agreement. Thus, to justify his action to those left behind we need only cite the policy to which they, along with the others, have agreed in advance (theoretically, anyway).

Into the formation of such an agreement or policy, a consideration of the relative numbers in possible future trade-off situations may enter in a way to which I would find no objection; in a way that commits no one to the impersonal, comparative evaluation of the outcomes appealed to in the previous justification of the captain's action. It could well be agreed to by all, in advance, that should a trade-off situation arise the resource is to be used to save the maximum number of those who have equal claims. For we may suppose that none of these people knows, at the time the resource is purchased in their collective name, where in the future he may find himself should a trade-off situation arise, whether among the few or among the many. Hence such a policy might be found acceptable to all these people simply on the ground that such a policy maximizes each individual's chances of benefiting from the resource.

Against the background supposition of such an agreement, a justification of the claim that it is the captain's duty to proceed straightaway to the north end of the island could be given. It would be wholly compatible with my views on how the numbers should *not* count. For in such a justification no appeal is made to any claim that it is, or would be, in itself, a better thing that those few should die and these many survive than it would be were these few to survive and the many to perish. Such a justification requires no one to acknowledge that his life, or that he himself is, from some impersonal, objective (moral?) perspective, worth less than two or three or three hundred others.

I believe that most people would prefer to think that this sort of justification is available in most cases like the one under discussion. Unfortunately, in many cases it is not. For it may happen that the facts are such that a policy of using a resource to benefit the larger number when not all can be benefited could not plausibly be justified by an appeal to each claimant's desire to maximize his chances of benefiting—on the understanding, of course, that equal chances go to each other claim holder. Imagine, for example, that on this island the majority live around the north end while the southern portion is inhabited by relatively few. It is now proposed that everyone on the island invest in

an evacuation ship. A policy of using the ship to save the larger number when not all can be saved could not easily be sold to those in the south on the ground that it provides each person with an equal and maximized chance of survival. It will be clear to them that with such a policy an equal investment does not purchase in the south a benefit equal to what it brings in the north. Still, of course, they might be induced to invest equally. Given their circumstances, it may be the best they can do for themselves. But they would not see this as a policy that gives equal weight to the interests of every would-be share holder.

If the bargaining position of the few were sufficiently strong, I believe these southerners might hold out for a more equitable policy, for genuinely equal shares in the benefits of the proposed resource, or for some reduction on their premiums, or for some compensating benefits from elsewhere. Now can we imagine those in the north at this point appealing to morality? "Look here, you are all decent people. Don't you see, if it comes down to it, that it would be a better thing if a larger number of us in the north survive while you perish than it would be were you relatively few to survive while we, the larger number, perish? So be sensible and faithful to the principles of true morality and let us agree that, should a trade-off situation arise, the evacuation ship will be used to save the larger number." Who could waste his time with such sophistries? It might be easier simply to compel the minority to go along with the policy. It would be less hypocritical anyway.[5]

Thus far we have been thinking about a situation in which these people who live on this island have, or are proposing to invest in, an evacuation ship. Each person is supposed to see himself as having an equal claim on this resource, for whatever reasons, whether because he is asked to invest or because of his status as an inhabitant of this island. Since the resource is limited, a situation may develop in which not all of them can be served by it. Hence the need for a policy, some method for determining who will be benefited. Plainly there are many possible policies. But not every policy will allow these people to retain their sense of each having an equal claim on the resource. For example, imagine that it is suggested that medical researchers, high-powered managerial types, and people with IQs over 120, be given first priority. Such a policy, whatever the reasons for adopting it, manifestly does not treat everyone on the island equally. It does not reflect a genuinely equal concern for the survival of each person on this island. Thus, if equal concern is what the inhabitants think they are entitled to, they will reject such a policy.

But under certain conditions, they will reject the policy of using the ship to save the larger number in the event of a trade-off situation, and for the same reasons. The minority who live on the southern tip will not see such a policy as according to each islander an equal claim on the collective resource. Imagine that those in the south know that on the north end there are already more people than the evacuation ship can hold. It is proposed that in the event of a trade-off, the ship is to be used to secure the safety of the larger number. You could hardly expect to convince the southerners that such a policy reflects a genuinely equal concern for the survival of each person on the island, that it accords to them a genuinely equal claim on the resource. You may as well try to convince workers with IQs under 100 that the policy of giving priority to researchers, managers, and to people with IQs over 120 reflects an equal concern for their survival.

Now I think this is how most people will think about these matters when asked to judge a policy governing the use of a resource meant for their benefit. Yet it is curious that many of these same people will not think this way when setting out a policy for using their resource to benefit others. Suppose, for example, that the people on this island have purchased their evacuation ship. On a nearby island, also volcanic, lives another group of people. These people have no means of evacuation because they are too poor, perhaps. The islanders who own the ship are willing, when they themselves are in no danger, to extend aid to those on the other island. Again the question of policy arises. They could, of course, without violating anyone's rights, decide to rescue the other islanders in order of IQ or social importance. But perhaps they want a policy that will treat all equally, that will truly reflect their professedly equal concern for each person's survival. They will then reject a policy that gives preference to those who happen to

have higher IQs or more prestigious social positions. It would be incompatible with their desire to show an equal concern for each person's survival. And yet if it happens that most of these inhabitants live around the north end, while a minority dwells in the south, our islanders, if they are like most of us, will adopt the policy of sending their mercy ship first to the north port to evacuate from among the many. True, those who live in the south cannot complain of any violation of their property rights in the vessel. But can such a policy be thought, any more in this case than in the former, to reflect an equal concern for the survival of each, northerner and southerner alike?

Notes

*I owe a large debt to Rita V. Lewis, whose views on the issues dealt with in this paper have had a pervasive influence on both its content and style. I should also like to thank Herbert Morris for helpful comments made on an earlier version of this essay.

[1] The trade-off situations I am focusing on have relatively simple structures. They present us with three relevant options: (1) We may aid a certain person or group of persons. (2) We may aid an entirely different group of persons. (3) We may do nothing at all to aid anyone. (I exclude from consideration this last option, though I do not argue that doing nothing for anyone is impermissible. Whether, why or in what sense it is, are questions best left to another occasion.) Robert Schwartz has caused me some worries about trade-off situations that are as aptly styled as these simpler ones, and that involve different but overlapping groups of possible beneficiaries. For example, perhaps the exercise of one option would bring aid to A but none to either B or C. A second option might bring aid to both A and B but none to C. Yet a third option might be available that would bring aid to C but none to either A or B. It will be seen that it is not completely obvious how one holding the views I present on the simpler trade-off situations would deal with this case and with cases of still greater complexity. After having caused me the worries, Schwartz had the decency to think out an approach to these decision problems that would appear compatible with my thinking about the simpler ones. But I fear that a discussion of these complications would obscure my main argument here, so I have avoided it.

[2] This is the case described by Phillippa Foot in her paper on "Abortion and the Doctrine of Double Effect," p. 59.

[3] There are a number of possible contortions that one might go through in an attempt to reconcile these views. I cannot consider them all here. What I am chiefly

interested in stressing is that there are serious difficulties involved in any attempt to reconcile these positions. My hope is that, in view of these difficulties, those who would maintain the original position might be brought to reconsider with an open mind the alleged grounds for the moral requirement to save the greater number in cases where one is in fact impartial in one's concern for those involved.

[4]After I had written this paper, my attention was called to Miss Anscombe's note of some years back on this case as put originally by Mrs. Foot. She too was impressed by the fact that in the event a person gave his drug to the one, none of the five others could complain that he had been wronged. Her note is entitled, "Who is Wronged?" *The Oxford Review*, no. 5, 1967.

[5]To be sure, matters may be far more complex than is supposed here. Perhaps this particular investment in an evacuation ship is but one of many investments made by the entire people of this island through their central government for, as it is commonly put, "the common good."

Perhaps, then, it could be said to the southerners that although in this instance the proposed policy for the use of the evacuation ship does not accord to them an equal claim on its benefits, they should not complain. They may well have enjoyed advantages at the expense of the northerners in past instances of "social action," and may look forward, through the intrigues of legislative politics, to yet further advantages in the future. Perhaps it could be argued that somehow it all works out in the long run to everyone's advantage. Maybe even some version of the "majority-rule" principle for policy making could be trotted out in such a context. I despair of finding a clear line of argument in this mare's nest. But if one sets the problem against such a background, the search for a justification of the claim that it is the captain's duty to make straight for the north end of the island will lead back to the general moral underpinnings of government and its functions. And these issues, though related, go beyond the scope of this paper.

Innumerate Ethics

DEREK PARFIT ▪ All Saints' College, University of Oxford
Philosophy and Public Affairs, 1978

Parfit begins by summarizing Taurek's argument that it is permissible to save someone's arm rather than another person's life. Taurek begins by supposing that it would be permissible for someone to save his *own* arm rather than save someone else's life. According to Taurek, we can then assume that a *third* party could also save someone else's arm rather than save yet another person's life. Therefore, it cannot be the case that there is some overriding moral principle that prohibits us from saving someone's arm rather than another person's life. Similarly, Taurek reasons that it would be permissible to save one rather than five persons. Again, Taurek begins with the supposition that it would be permissible for one to save one's own life rather than five others. And given that what a third party can do is the same as what a participant can do, then it would be permissible for a third party to save one rather than five.

The problem with this sort of reasoning, according to Parfit, is that it assumes that the relevant moral reasons are **agent-neutral**. (See Nagel, p. 163.) Parfit holds that some moral reasons are **agent-relative**—they give agents moral permissions that are **agent-specific** in certain ways. So, *I* may be permitted to save *my* arm rather than your life, but a *third party* may *not* be permitted to save my arm rather than your life. Similarly, Parfit points out that the choice of the one to save her own life may come from an agent-relative permission. The reason she would choose her own life over five others is because she has a justifiable *self-interest* in staying alive. According to Parfit, it would not follow that a third party may save the life of one other rather than five others unless the relevant moral reason is agent-neutral. Parfit's point is that Taurek's form of argumentation presupposes the controversial claim that the relevant moral reasons are agent-neutral.

Parfit also explores whether it is a worse thing when more people die. Taurek does not take seriously the proposition that we can reasonably add different individuals' losses. Thus, in Taurek's view, there is no way of saying that the deaths of more people is a worse thing than the death of one. By the same reasoning, Taurek says that the minor suffering of many individuals cannot add up to something as bad as one very terrible experience. (The example he uses is that many people experiencing slight headaches does not add up to a migraine.) Parfit believes that Taurek's position here is fundamentally misguided. Parfit claims that people who believe in the additive quality of suffering do not believe that the sum of lesser pains is the same thing as the greater pain, but that together the lesser pains may be as bad as a greater pain.

First, Parfit points out that in cases where all of the pains under discussion are felt by the same person, it could be the case that the sum of the suffering of the many lesser pains is as terrible for the individual experiencing them as it would be for the same person to endure one big pain. In a similar fashion, Parfit points out, we can speak of the suffering involved in fifty individuals experiencing a slight pain. This involves the analogy between various pains being felt by one individual over time and various individuals having pain at one time. Just as it is not required that the different pains experienced by one individual be experienced in *one episode*, it seems it need not be the case that all pains are experienced by *one person* (in order for there to be a sum of pain). Thus, Parfit concludes that Taurek has not offered good reason to suppose that the numbers should not count.

SUPPOSE THAT WE CAN HELP EITHER ONE PERSON or many others. Is it a reason to help the many that we should thus be helping more people? John Taurek thinks not. We may learn from his arguments.[1]

I.

Taurek understates his conclusion. At one point he is aware of this. Let this be our starting point.

Suppose that we could easily save either the life of one stranger or the arm of another. Call these strangers X and Y. Taurek argues:

> *First Premise*: If the choice were Y's, he would be morally permitted to save his arm rather than X's life.
>
> *Second Premise*: What we ought to do must be the same as what Y ought to do.

Conclusion: It cannot be true that we ought to save X's life rather than Y's arm.[2]

Could it be true that we, but not Y, ought to save X's life? Is there a difference between us and Y in virtue of which this could be true? Some would answer: "Yes. While it would cost us nothing to save X's life, it would cost Y his own arm." Taurek rejects this answer. His argument can be restated in a way which makes this clear. It is aimed at those who believe

(A) If we could save either one stranger's life or another stranger's arm, and it would cost us nothing to do either, we ought to save the first stranger's life.

Taurek assumes

(B) It would not be true that we ought to save this stranger's life at the cost of our own arm, and

(C) Whether we ought to save this stranger's life cannot depend on whether it would cost us nothing, or our own arm.

If we accept both (B) and (C), we must reject (A).

Ought we to accept both (B) and (C)? Only if we find both more plausible than (A). There are some who would accept (C)—such as Godwin and the sterner Utilitarians. These must choose between (A) and (B). Most would choose (A). They would think we ought to save a stranger's life at the cost of our own arm. Suppose that we cannot believe this. Suppose that we find (B) more plausible than (A). We must then choose between (A) and (C). Unless there is some further argument, few would choose (C).

Is there a further argument? Return to the choice between X's life and Y's arm. After claiming that Y would be permitted to save his arm; Taurek writes: "Unless it is for some reason morally impermissible for one person to take the same interest in another's welfare as he himself [permissibly] takes in it, it must be permissible for me, in the absence of special obligations to the contrary, to choose the outcome that is in [Y's] best interest." If "take the same interest in" means "care as much about," this sentence is irrelevant. We *would* be permitted to care about Y's welfare just as much as Y himself (permissibly) cares. But Y would then be someone whom we love deeply. We shall return to such a case. In the case that we are now discussing, Y is a stranger. We must therefore reinterpret Taurek's sentence. It must mean: "Unless we are not permitted to give to the welfare of any stranger just as much priority as he may give to his own welfare. . . ."

Are we so permitted? There are three views. According to some, we ought to give equal weight to everyone's welfare. We may not give priority to a stranger's welfare. Nor may he.

Most of us take a different view. We believe that we may give priority to our own welfare. This priority should not be absolute. Perhaps Y could save his arm rather than X's life; but he ought to save X rather than his own umbrella. May we give priority to the welfare of others? Most of us think we sometimes may, and sometimes ought to do so. Thus we ought to give priority to the welfare of our own children. This is what Taurek calls a "special obligation."

These obligations are "agent-relative." It is to *my* children that I ought to give priority. Taurek would agree. And he agrees that we may give priority to ourselves. The question is, Are these permissions agent-relative? Is it to *myself* that I may give priority?

We would answer yes. That is why we should reject Taurek's argument. If Y could save his arm rather than X's life, so could we. But this would not show that *we* could save Y's arm rather than X's life. None of us would then be saving *his own* arm.

Taurek gives a different answer. He believes that Y's permission cannot be agent-relative. It cannot be a permission to save *his own* arm. It must be a permission to save *anyone's* arm. That is why Taurek draws his conclusion. If Y could save anyone's arm rather than X's life, so could we.

Taurek's view is entirely general. Suppose that I must choose whether to save you from losing *p* or to save some stranger from losing *q*. Taurek thinks I ought to help the stranger only if you, given the choice, ought to do so too. It makes no difference that it would cost me nothing to help the stranger, while it would cost you *p*. This is so whatever *p* may be. Taurek thus assumes:

(D) Whether we ought to help strangers cannot depend upon how much we in particular[3] would thereby lose.

This is believed by some Utilitarians. But Taurek combines (D) with a more popular belief. He assumes that we may give priority to our own welfare. We are permitted to save ourselves from lesser harms rather than saving strangers from greater harms. For example:

(E) It would not be true that we ought to relieve a stranger's agony rather than our own minor pain.[4]

According to (D), whether we ought to help the stranger cannot depend on whether we in particular would undergo the minor pain. The permission claimed by (E) cannot be agent-relative. Hence:

(F) It would not be true that we ought to relieve the agony of one stranger rather than the minor pain of another.

Ought we to accept Taurek's view? Ought we to believe both that we may give priority to our own welfare and that these permissions cannot be agent-relative? I can think of no one else who accepts this view. Since it is not defended by Taurek,[5] I suggest that it should be rejected. When it would cost us nothing to do either, we ought to relieve one stranger's agony rather than another's minor pain. And we ought to save lives rather than limbs.

II.

Ought we to save many lives rather than one? Suppose that we could easily save either one stranger or five others. Call the one stranger David. Taurek argues:

> *First Premise*: If the choice were David's, he would be morally permitted to save himself rather than the five.
>
> *Second Premise*: If this is permissible for David, it must be permissible for us.
>
> *Conclusion*: It cannot be true that we ought to save the five rather than David.

David's permission would be agent-relative.

III.

Taurek argues:

> *First Premise*: If David was our friend, we would be morally permitted to save him rather than the five.
>
> *Second Premise*: That David was our friend would be a fact too trivial to affect our obligations.
>
> *Conclusion*: Even though David is not our friend, we are permitted to save him rather than the five.

Are we to imagine David as a mere acquaintance? Would he just be someone whom we would prefer to save? The argument would then be this. Given

(G) It would not be true that we ought to save the five if we preferred to save someone else,

and

(H) Whether we ought to save the five cannot depend on what we prefer,

we must reject

(I) If we have no preference either way, we ought to save the five.

Taurek defends (H) with a question. If we really ought to save the five, how could we "so easily escape" this obligation? How could it be overridden by a mere preference? A real obligation to save five people's lives surely cannot be as weak as this. We might agree. We must then choose (G) and (I). Few would choose (G).

What if David was more than a mere acquaintance? What if he was someone we love? The argument would now be this. Given

(J) It would not be true that we ought to save the five rather than someone we love,

and

(K) Whether we ought to save the five cannot depend on whether we would thereby lose nothing, or someone we love,

we must reject

(L) If we would lose nothing either way, we ought to save the five.

Taurek's defence of (H) does not apply to (K). Our own death may be the greatest loss, but it would be terrible to lose someone we love. Taurek could not say, "How could you so easily escape your obligation?" Are there other arguments for (K)? Taurek suggests the following. If we were contractually obliged to save the five, or it was our military duty, it would make no difference whether we would thereby lose someone we love. Why should it make a difference in the present case? We might answer: "Contracts and military duties give rise to special obligations. Perhaps we ought to carry out these even at a heavy cost to ourselves. But this need not be true of everything we ought to do. It may not be true of saving the lives of strangers." Taurek has one other reason for rejecting (K). He believes there cannot be agent-relative permissions. Whether we ought to save the five cannot depend upon how much we in particular would thereby lose. Some Utilitarians would agree. But they would reject (J).

In the absence of a further argument, ought we to accept both (J) and (K)? Only if we find both more plausible than (L). Few will.

IV.

Taurek argues:

> *First Premise:* In the absence of special obligations, the only moral reason to prevent an outcome is that it would be worse than its alternative.
>
> *Second Premise:* The deaths of the five would not be a worse outcome than the death of David.
>
> *Conclusion:* We have no moral reason to save the five rather than David.[6]

Why should we accept the second premise? Why would the deaths of the five not be a worse outcome than the death of David?

At certain points, Taurek suggests that no outcome can be worse than its alternative. One of two outcomes may be worse *for particular people,* but it cannot be simply "worse."[7] On this suggestion, Taurek's first premise becomes implausible. It implies that, in the absence of special obligations, we have no moral reason to prevent anything. We have no reason even to prevent those outcomes which are worse for everyone. Even Taurek would not accept this. If he keeps the suggestion that no outcome can be "worse" than its alternative, he must therefore abandon his first premise.

He might instead abandon this suggestion. He must then support his second premise in a different way. He must claim that, while some outcomes can be worse than others, the deaths of the five would not be a worse outcome than the death of David.

Taurek does defend this claim. He argues:

> *First Premise:* If we prefer the worse of two outcomes we are morally deficient.
>
> *Second Premise:* David would not be morally deficient if he preferred that we save him rather than the five.
>
> *Conclusion:* The deaths of the five cannot be a worse outcome than the death of David.[8]

If we accept the second premise, we can reject the first. We might say: "We can prefer the worse of two outcomes without being morally deficient. This would be so if the better outcome would impose on us too great a sacrifice." Taurek gives no argument against this view. Is it less plausible than his conclusion?

V.

Why do we think it worse if more people die? If David dies, he would lose as much as any of the five. But they together would lose more. Their combined losses would outweigh his.

Taurek rejects this reasoning. he does not "take seriously . . . any notion of the sum of two persons' separate losses." He rejects this notion for two reasons.

One is that he cannot understand it. He refers to "our collective or total pain, whatever exactly that is supposed to be." And he writes, "I cannot understand how I am supposed to add up their separate pains and attach significance to that alleged sum. . . ."

What does Taurek not understand? A puzzling passage reads: "Suffering is not additive in this way. The discomfort of each of a large number of individuals experiencing a minor headache does not add up to anyone's experiencing a migraine." If "add up to" meant "be the same as," this would be true. But it would not be relevant. Those who believe that suffering is "additive" do not believe that many lesser pains might be the same thing as one greater pain. What they believe is that the lesser pains might together be as bad.

Consider first pains that are felt by one person. I might decide that fifty minor headaches would be worse than a single migraine. If I had to endure the fifty headaches, I would suffer more. In other words, my "sum of suffering" would be greater. Such comparisons are, even in principle, rough. There is only partial comparability. But that does not make the comparisons senseless. And this use of the phrase "sum of suffering" would, I believe, be understood by Taurek. At any rate, he says nothing against it.

Suppose, next, that each of fifty headaches would be had by a different person. If these headaches were about as bad, they would again together involve about as much suffering. The "sum of suffering" would be about as great. This is not a different use of this phrase. It is the same use. Since he understands this use when applied within one life, Taurek thereby understands it when applied to different lives. So what can his problem be?

There is a well-known problem here. If two headaches come in different lives, it is harder to tell which, if either, is the worse. Certain people, notably some economists, make a bolder claim. On their (official) view, such comparisons are senseless. It makes no sense to suppose that one of the headaches could either be, or not be, worse than the other. More generally, no one can be worse off than anyone else. If I lose an arm and you lose a finger, it makes no sense to suppose that my loss could be greater than yours.

If this were Taurek's view, it would explain his problem. If none of the fifty headaches could be either less bad than a migraine, or at least as bad, we cannot suppose that they together might be worse. We cannot suppose they might involve a greater "sum of suffering." But this is not Taurek's view. He writes of different people undergoing "differential losses," and even contrasts "fifty individuals suffering a pain of some given intensity" with "some individual suffering a pain many or fifty times more intense." Taurek's problem is not about interpersonal comparisons.

What can it be? It may help to quote another passage:

> . . . To my way of thinking it would be contemptible for any one of us in this crowd to ask you to consider carefully, "not, of course, what I personally will have to suffer. None of us is thinking of himself here! But contemplate, if you will, what we, the group, will suffer. Think of the awful sum of pain that is in the balance here! There are so many more of us." At best such thinking seems confused. Typically, I think, it is outrageous.

This recalls a paragraph in C. S. Lewis:

> We must never make the problem of pain worse than it is by vague talk bout "the unimaginable sum of human misery." Suppose that I have a toothache of intensity x: and suppose that you, who are seated beside me, also begin to have a toothache of intensity x. You may, if you choose, say that the total amount of pain in the room is now 2x. But you must remember that no one is suffering 2x: search all time and space and you will not find that composite pain in anyone's consciousness. There is no such thing as a sum of suffering, for no one suffers it. When we have reached the maximum that a single person can suffer, we have, no doubt, reached something very horrible, but we have reached all the suffering there can ever be in the

universe. The addition of a million fellow-sufferers adds no more pain. [9]

Like Taurek, Lewis assumes that any "sum of suffering" must be felt by a single person. Why not add that it must be felt at a single time? That would reduce still further the Problem of Pain. It might even offer a solution. We might not mind a pain, however intense, if it lasted a short enough time. The maximum possible "sum of suffering" would then be something no one minds.

This would not be a true solution. Suffering at other times is more suffering. So is the suffering of other people. Lewis must have known this. I suggest that he confused two different claims. He makes the factual claim that the suffering of more people cannot be more suffering. He may have meant the moral claim that it cannot matter more. He may have thought the suffering of one person to be as great an evil as the suffering of a million.

This provides a second way of understanding Taurek. When he says that "suffering is not additive," he too may not mean that the pains of different people cannot be more pain. He may mean that these pains cannot be *morally* summed—that they cannot together make an outcome worse. If fifty people each have a headache, that would be no worse than if one person does. More generally:

(M) If one person is harmed, that would be just as bad as if any number are each equally harmed.

Whether this is all that Taurek means, it appears to be his view. [10]

Apart from C. S. Lewis, I can think of no one else who accepts this view. Taurek calls it a "natural extension" of

(N) We ought to save one person from harm rather than saving any number from smaller harms. [11]

If the harms to the many would be only *slightly* smaller, few would accept (N). But we might accept

(O) We ought to save one person from harm rather than saving any number from *much* smaller harms.

Is Taurek's view a "natural extension" of (O)? He might say: "Unless you accept (M), how can you explain (O)? Why should we prevent the greater harm rather than *any number* of the smaller harms?

The explanation must be that the smaller harms cannot be morally summed. And this must be because they are harms to different people."

We might give a different explanation. If the single person faces a much greater harm, he may be the person who would be worst off. We may think that we should give priority to helping such people. We should then be appealing to a well-known principle of justice. Call this "Maximin."[12]

What if the single person would not be worst off? Ought we to save one arthritic from blindness rather than saving any number of the blind from arthritis? Ought we to save one deaf person from paralysis rather than any number of the paralysed from deafness? If we answer no, (O) is not our real view. We do not believe that we should always save the single person from the one much greater harm. We would at most believe this if the harm would make this person worst off. We would then accept (O) only when it coincides with Maximin. That would be our real view.[13]

Here is a third example. For each of many people, yesterday was agony. For some other single person, it was a day of minor pain. Ought we now to save this person from a day of agony rather than saving each of the many from a day of minor pain? Would this be so whatever the number of the many?

Suppose that we answer yes. How could we explain our view? We might appeal to Maximin. Call the single person Z. We might claim

(P) Z is the person who would be worst off.

Is this true? If we do not intervene, Z would be worst off throughout the coming day. But the many were as much worse off throughout yesterday. Counting both days, Z would not have suffered more than any of them. Someone might say: "It is irrelevant that, for the many, yesterday was agony. Pain no longer matters when it is over." This objection seems to me invalid. When we are discussing distribution, past pains count. Those who have suffered more have more claim to be spared future pain. In deciding who would be worst off, we must think in terms of lives—we must ask whose life would have gone worst. I conclude that, in this case, Z would not be worst off. If we help the many, he will have had one day of agony and one day of minor pain. But if we help him this will be true of each of them.

If Z would not be worst off, why should we help him rather than them? Why should we prevent his day of agony rather than their days of minor pain? We might claim

(Q) We would be preventing the greater sum of suffering.

Is this true? Taurek might say: "Their pains cannot be summed. Whatever the number of the many, their 'sum of suffering' would be the same. It would be a single day of minor pain." We have rejected this view. If more people are in pain, there is more pain.

There is another way of defending (Q). We might claim

(R) Agony is infinitely worse than minor pain.

Is this true? Perhaps we can imagine pains to which it would apply.[14] But these are not what Taurek has in mind. The pain of his single person is not infinitely worse than the pains of the many. Taurek calls it "fifty times more intense." That means this. Fifty of the lesser pains would be as bad to undergo. No one's judgments would be so precise. But we can assume the following. A thousand of the lesser pains would be worse. They would involve more suffering. (That is not a different claim. It is just another way of saying that they would be worse to undergo.)

If this is the difference between the pains, we cannot appeal to (R). The agony of Z would not be infinitely worse than the pains of the many. So we must abandon (Q). We cannot claim that, in helping Z, we should be preventing the greater sum of suffering. Within one life, a thousand of the lesser pains would involve more suffering. If they came in different lives, each might be easier to bear. Each might involve less suffering. But some number of these pains would involve a greater sum of suffering.

If we cannot appeal to (Q), how could we explain our view? Why should we prevent Z's agony rather than their lesser pains? We might claim

(S) We would be preventing the worse of two outcomes.

Is this true? We might say: "Below some threshold, pain is not morally significant. It is bad for the sufferer. But it cannot make the outcome worse. It is not an evil." This assumption is quite common. It can be challenged. But I shall not present this challenge here.[15] If the assumption is correct, (S) might be trivially true. The agony of Z would be morally significant. It would be, if undeserved, an evil. But the pains of the many might have no significance. In that case, they could not amount to as great an evil. No number of zeroes could amount to one.

Let us make this explanation unavailable. Let each lesser pain be morally significant. Each would be a minor evil. Could we now defend (S)? We might claim

(T) No number of these lesser evils could together be as great an evil.

This would be like Newman's view about pain and sin. He believed that both were bad, but that sin was infinitely worse. If all mankind suffered "extremest agony," that would be less bad than if one venial sin was committed.[16]

Is (T) plausible? Surely not. A thousand of the lesser pains would be worse for Z. He would prefer the agony. If they would be worse for Z, they would surely be a worse outcome. They would be, if undeserved, a greater evil.

If we cannot appeal to (T), how could we explain our view? Why should we help Z rather than any number of the many? Taurek might say: "You must now accept *my* explanation. Pains in different lives cannot be morally summed."

If we are consequentialists, we may have to agree. We must then accept (S). We must think that, in helping Z, we would be preventing the worse of two outcomes. How could this be true? If they came within one life, a thousand of the lesser pains would be a worse outcome. How could there be *no* such number when they come in different lives? We may have to accept Taurek's view. Perhaps pains in different lives cannot be morally summed. Even if a million people suffer, that may be no worse than if one person does.

There is an alternative. We need not be consequentialists. We might say: "We ought to prevent one much greater harm rather than any number of much smaller harms. But this is not because we should be preventing the worse of two outcomes. The urgency of moral claims does not always correspond to the badness of outcomes." On this alternative we avoid Taurek's view. We could still

believe that, if a million people suffer, that is worse than if one person does. And we could still believe that, in the case of equal harms, numbers count. If we could save from equal harm one or a million, we should help the million.

Which alternative is the more plausible?

VI.

Return to David and the five. We have discussed three arguments for Taurek's view. The first assumes

(U) We would be morally permitted to save ourselves rather than the five, but this could not be because we would be saving ourselves.

The second assumes

(V) We would be morally permitted to save a friend rather than the five, but this could not be because we would be saving a friend.

The third assumes

(W) It would not be worse if more people die.

I have questioned these assumptions.

Taurek gives one other argument. Suppose the five invest in a rescue service. They tell David: "You should pay your share. The rescuer should then save us rather than you." This would be unfair. If David pays, he should have a chance of benefiting. Taurek suggests that a coin be flipped.

The argument supports more extreme conclusions. Suppose that David stands to lose, not his life, but his umbrella. The five say: "You should pay your share. The rescuer should then save us rather than your umbrella." This would also be unfair. But should another coin be flipped? Should there be a random choice between five lives and one umbrella?

There is a better solution. The five should pay David's share.[17]

VII.

Taurek ends with this remark. Suppose we save the larger number. This would not "reflect an equal concern for the survival of each." It would be like giving priority to saving the rich.

This is not so. If we give the rich priority, we do not give equal weight to saving each. Why do we save the larger number? Because we *do* give equal weight to saving each. Each counts for one. That is why more count for more.

Notes

[1]John M. Taurek, "Should the Numbers Count?" p. 214.

[2]Taurek, p. 214. Here, and throughout, I summarize Taurek's argument in my own words.

[3]These words matter. Whether we ought to help strangers may depend upon how much we would thereby lose. We ought to save a stranger's umbrella if it would cost us nothing, but not at the cost of our own life. Taurek would agree. But it would make no difference here whether we in *particular* would lose the life. We ought not to save umbrellas at the cost of *anyone's* life.

[4]This is surely implied by [the 46th paragraph].

[5]Curiously, Taurek never mentions agent-relative permissions.

[6]I take this argument to be implied by these two passages: "The claim that one ought to save the many instead of the few was made to rest on the claim that, other things being equal, it is a worse thing that these five persons should die than that this one should." ". . . For the reasons given, I cannot subscribe to such an evaluation of these outcomes. Hence, in this situation, I have absolutely no reason for showing preference to them as against him . . ."

[7]Taurek, op cit. G. E. Moore claimed the reverse (*Principia Ethica*, Cambridge, 1903, pp. 98–99). Taurek's claim seems the more plausible.

[8]Taurek, op cit. Taurek here assumes that some outcomes can be worse than others.

[9]*The Problem of Pain* (London, 1957), pp. 103–104.

[10]More exactly, it would be his view if he abandons the suggestion that no outcome can be "worse" than its alternative. If he keeps that suggestion, his view must be expressed in a different way. For the phrase "just as bad as" we might substitute "something which we have just as strong moral reasons to prevent." For convenience, I shall use "bad" and "worse."

[11]Taurek writes: ". . . a refusal to take seriously . . . any notion of the sum of two persons' separate losses. . . . appears a quite natural extension of the way

in which most would view analogous trade-off situations involving differential losses to those involved". Taurek stops short of accepting (N)—perhaps because of the argument that I discussed in Section I. . . .

[12]Rawls would not apply this principle to individuals (see, for example, John Rawls, "Some Reasons for the Maximin Criterion," *American Economic Review,* 64, Papers & Proc., May 1974, p. 142).

[13]I owe this idea to James Griffin. In an unpublished paper, Griffin argues that the intuitions behind Negative Utilitarianism are, when freed from confusions, intuitions about Justice. I am just extending this idea.

[14]See the footnote on p. 132 of Sidgwick's *The Methods of Ethics,* 7th ed. (London: Macmillan, 1963. To be reprinted by Oxford University Press). See also James Griffin, "Are There Incommensurable Values?" *Philosophy & Public Affairs* 7, no. I (Fall 1977): 44–47.

[15]See Jonathan Glover, "It Makes No Difference Whether Or Not I Do It," *Proceedings of the Aristotelian Society,* Supplementary Volume 49 (1975), pp. 172–176. (In Chapters 16 and 17 of his book *Causing Death and Saving Lives,* London: Penguin Books, 1977, Glover discusses the kind of case with which Taurek is concerned.)

[16]*Certain difficulties felt by Anglicans in Catholic Teaching* (London, 1885), vol. I, p. 204.

[17]Suppose the rights of property are not involved. We are the rescuers, and have not been hired. Taurek might say: "There is still a case for flipping coins. Only then would each person have an equal chance." There would be something in this argument. Would there be enough? Consider three examples: (1) We can save X or Y. Nothing could be lost by flipping coins. Something would be gained. (2) We can save X's life or Y's arm. Something would again be gained. We would give Y a chance. But if Y wins, X would die. The case for flipping coins seems here to be outweighed. (3) We can save David or the five. There is again a case for flipping coins. But I believe it is again outweighed. (Much more needs to be said. I will add this. David's death is undeserved. So is the loss of Y's arm. It is simply their misfortune that their claims are outweighed. In a way, this is unfair. It involves a kind of natural injustice. But such injustice cannot be removed by flipping coins. It could only be transferred. Natural injustice is bad luck. Making more depend on luck will not abolish bad luck.)

The Numbers Should Count

GREGORY S. KAVKA ▪ University of California, Irvine
Philosophical Studies, 1979

Like Parfit, Gregory S. Kavka argues that John Taurek's "Should the Numbers Count?" offers no convincing reason for thinking that the numbers should not count. In the first section of the essay, Kavka looks at Taurek's hypothetical cases. In the first case, the person who owns the drug is the one person who needs all of the drug, and it is deemed permissible for that person to save his own life. The second case stipulates that the person who owns the drug is a friend of the one who needs it, and it is permissible for that person to save his friend. For these two cases, Kavka agrees that the moral intuitions which Taurek asserts are probably correct. However, Kavka argues that given an analysis of the underlying principles at work here, these cases do little to answer the question of whether the numbers should count. The reason why Kavka holds that Taurek's views about Cases 1 and 2 are intuitively correct yet do not necessarily imply that the numbers do not count, is connected to Kavka's analysis of partiality.

Moral systems, he says, are held to be impartial because they apply equally to all and because such systems are supposed to equally protect and promote the interests of everyone. However, there are two good reasons why moral rules allow **partiality** under certain conditions. Such conditions obtain in the first two cases. In the first case, it is considered permissible for the person to save himself because people are disposed to be partial to themselves. Moral rules that require people not to follow this disposition would be hard to enforce and would possibly lead people to disregard the rules. In the second case, the ability to be partial to others to whom one is close is likely to strengthen the relationships (like love and friendship) that serve as foundations of important social institutions such as the family. So moral systems that allow partiality for certain kinds of individual conduct will aid the interests of groups governed by those rules.

Given this view of morality, it is easy to arrive at Taurek's conclusions in the first two cases without necessarily coming to his decision that the numbers do not count. One can instead maintain that while it is possible that the numbers count, they do not count enough in these cases to displace the partiality one would feel towards his own welfare or that of a friend. Therefore, a real test case of whether the numbers should count would instead be found in situations where all involved are strangers.

Kavka extends his critique by pointing out that Taurek is using a "libertarian account of moral obligation" in his analysis of the test cases. Specifically, Kavka argues that Taurek is presupposing something like a Libertarian Aid Principle which stipulates that a person only has an obligation to aid someone else if he is bound by some form of contract or if he is responsible for the fact that the other person needs aid. According to Kavka, the idea that the numbers should not count only follows if the

Libertarian Aid Principle is combined with another principle that our reasons for coming to a decision in such cases are exhausted by our moral *obligations*. This is counterintuitive, however, because there must be something more to morality than moral obligations (as construed in libertarianism). Otherwise, says Kavka, the owner of the drug could merely drink it because it tastes good and not because he actually needs it to be saved.

The second part of the article looks at Taurek's argument that in cases where all parties are strangers, it is recommended that the owner of the drug flip a coin, thus giving everyone who needs the drug an equal chance. Kavka reformulates the problem of the five strangers and the owner of the drug. The choices Taurek gives us are to either give all of the drug to the one who needs it all or to give one-fifth of it to each of the five people who need that amount. Kavka asserts that there are other choices that we could make. For instance, we could give one-fifth of the drug to four of the five people who need one-fifth of the dose, but pour the rest of it down the drain. In this case, one of the five would die and the one who needed all of the drug would die. According to Taurek's analysis, we should be indifferent between this new choice and the first of the original choices which had us saving the one person who needed all of the drug. Because indifference is considered to be a transitive relation, it follows that we would also be indifferent between this new choice and the choice of saving all of the five who need one-fifth of the drug. Here Kavka argues that it seems obvious that we should *not* be indifferent to saving all of the five or most of the five, when we have the capability to save all of the five.

Kavka finishes the argument by suggesting that there may be some middle ground in which a solution could be found to this problem, which would take the relative size of the groups into account.

IMAGINE THAT YOU ARE IN A POSITION TO SAVE the lives of the members of either (but not both) of two non-overlapping groups of people. Knowing that those in the other group will surely die, how should you decide which group to save? One plausible view is that you should consider the numbers of people in each group, and count the fact that more lives would be saved as a significant reason for saving the larger group. In a recent article, John Taurek challenges this view.[1] He argues that in such situations (and, more generally, in situations involving bestowing benefits on, or preventing harm to, non-overlapping groups) one should *not even take into account* the numbers of persons in the two groups.

Taurek's discussion focuses on three hypothetical cases. In each, a person owning a dose of a drug (hereafter called the owner) must decide to give it either to one person who needs it all to survive, or to five other people, each of whom needs one-fifth of it to survive. In each case the five people are strangers to the owner. What distinguishes the cases is the relationship between the one person who needs the full dose and the owner. In case 1 this person is the owner himself, in case 2 he is a friend of the owner, and in case 3 he is a stranger to the owner. Taurek contends that it is morally permissible for the owner to keep the drug for himself in case 1, and to give it to his friend in case 2. He holds that, special circumstances (e.g. relevant contractual obligations) aside, in case 3 the owner has no moral reason to prefer either course of action to the other. He suggests flipping a coin to determine whether to save the one stranger or the five.

I contend that Taurek does not offer us any good reason for supposing that the numbers should not count in arriving at decisions in such situations. In Section I, I argue that while Taurek's judgments about cases 1 and 2 have some intuitive appeal, the principles underlying these judgments have no direct bearing on the numbers question. In Section II, two major flaws in Taurek's treatment of case 3 are pointed out. First, Taurek's method for dealing with such cases violates a very plausible transitivity requirement. Second, Taurek's account ignores the significance of an important analogy between morality and prudential rationality. I conclude that while Taurek's discussion poses an interesting challenge to some pure utilitarian positions, it fails to demonstrate that the numbers should not count.

I.

Taurek presents two arguments in support of his claim that it is permissible for the owner to use the drug to save his own life. First, if the owner saves himself, he violates no one's rights. He does not wrong the five who die, as they have no legitimate claim to the drug. Second, one could not give the owner a reason he could reasonably be expected to accept for surrendering the drug, and his life. In particular, one has no adequate reply if the owner says he would not ask any of the five strangers to make such a sacrifice if their positions were reversed. (Presumably what Taurek has in mind is that such an owner is acting consistently with the Golden Rule in refusing to give up the drug, hence is not acting in a biased or arbitrary way.) In arguing for the permissibility of the owner giving the drug to a friend, Taurek relies again on the observation that the owner would be violating no one's rights in so acting. He also claims that cases 1 and 2 are analogous, so that if the owner using the drug to save himself is permissible, then his using it to save his friend is also permissible.

I admit that insofar as we have clear intuitions about what is permissible in these cases, they are likely to agree with Taurek's. Further, I will not quarrel with the arguments Taurek offers. Rather, I shall try to uncover the principles that underlie our intuitions and Taurek's arguments. Once this is done, it shall become evident that the question of whether the numbers should count has been left untouched by what Taurek says about these cases. I proceed by briefly sketching two moral views, either

of which would yield the judgment that the owner's keeping the drug for his own (or his friend's) use is permissible. It shall be shown that neither of these views (one of which seems to be Taurek's) implies that the numbers should not count.

1. The Moral Permissibility of Partiality

One view that could produce Taurek's verdicts on cases 1 and 2 is this: morality allows individuals to be quite partial to their own interests, and to those of friends and relatives, when making certain decisions that will affect people's vital interests. Such a view is quite consistent with the widely held doctrine that morality is impartial between persons in the sense that (i) moral rules apply equally to all, and (ii) the system of moral rules is designed to protect and promote the interests of everyone. For there are at least two good reasons that a moral system that is impartial in this sense should allow individuals to be quite partial in their conduct in certain contexts. First, people are, for the most part, strongly psychologically disposed to be partial to themselves, their friends, and their loved ones, when very important interests are at stake. Hence, moral rules that require strict impartiality in such circumstances are likely to be generally disobeyed and costly to enforce, and may engender skeptical attitudes toward moral rules in general. Further, allowing partiality in individual conduct strengthens certain valuable personal relationships, such as love and friendship, and valuable social institutions such as the family. (One wonders, e.g., if love could exist between two persons, each of whom knows that the other would treat his interests only on a par with those of strangers.) Thus, it is plausible to suppose that a moral system whose rules allow considerable partiality in individual conduct will better serve the interests of the members of groups governed by those rules than would a moral system requiring strict impartiality.[2]

Suppose that we adopt this view of morality, and regard the giving of aid by individuals as one area in which partiality is allowed to operate. Then we can arrive at Taurek's verdicts about cases 1 and 2 without supposing that the numbers do not count in such cases. It is rather that, though the numbers do count, they do not count enough to override the owner's understandable partiality toward his own, or his friend's, interests. I suspect that this sort of reasoning is what underlies the intuitions of many who agree with Taurek's verdicts. Taurek, however, objects to this analysis on the grounds that we would not allow considerations of friendship to carry the day if the owner has contracted to deliver the drug to the five strangers. But, if true, this only goes to show that contractual obligations are, so to speak, higher on the list of moral priorities than considerations of friendship. That this should be so is understandable, given the vital importance of contracts in promoting effective social cooperation. In general, it seems that, in moral reasoning about giving aid, contracts take precedence over friendship, which in turn takes precedence over "the numbers" or considerations of total utility. If this is so, Taurek's verdicts on cases 1 and 2 would be correct, but the numbers would still count for something.

As our intuitions *are* affected by partiality considerations, Taurek's first two cases are not a good test of whether the numbers should count. To decide whether they should, it is best to consider only cases in which those needing aid are either all strangers (case 3) or all friends. What of the latter case? If the above explanation of our intuitions is correct, numbers should count for something, and one should save the five friends (assuming the one friend is not a much closer friend). I suspect, however, that Taurek would treat this case like case 3, and say that either alternative is permissible and there is no sound basis for choosing between them. For Taurek's arguments suggest that a more general view of the nature of moral obligation, and not simply the idea that partiality is permissible, may underlie his position.

2. A Libertarian Account of Moral Obligation

Some believe that there are only three sorts of moral obligations. First, duties of non-interference, that require one not to assault or kill others (except to repel or punish an attack), and not to interfere with their actions or chosen uses of their property (except insofar as such acts and uses violate the rights of others). Second, contractual or quasi-contractual obligations based on (i) explicit or tacit

agreements, or (ii) the duties of a social or institutional role that one has agreed to occupy. Third, duties of restitution that require one to compensate another if he has suffered harm as the result of one's unjust, reckless, or negligent acts. This belief may be conjoined with the further belief that there is a right to acquire property and use it as one chooses (so long as the rights of others are not violated), but there is no right to survive that would impose obligations on others to use their property to keep one alive. Let us call this conjunction of beliefs "the libertarian account of moral obligation."[3]

There are four pieces of evidence that, taken together, suggest that Taurek is presupposing some such libertarian account of obligation. First, he apparently regards the argument that the owner, in keeping the drug for himself or his friend, violates no one's rights, as being sufficient and conclusive. Second, he asserts that the owner would be obligated to give the drug to the five strangers if he had contracted to do so. Third, Taurek admits that our intuitions suggest that a Coast Guard captain ought to evacuate a larger rather than a smaller group of citizens off an island threatened by volcanic eruptions. But he contends that this is because we implicitly assume a quasi-contractual obligation on the part of the captain to do so. Fourth, Taurek's second argument in support of the claim that the owner acts permissibly when he keeps the drug for himself seems to reflect the libertarian view of the importance of property rights. This can be seen in the following way. While Taurek challenges us to give a reason *the owner* would accept for giving up the drug, he does not suppose we must be able to give a reason *the five* would accept for not seizing the drug. Now each of the five could come up with a justification for their seizing the drug that, like the justification offered by Taurek's owner, satisfies the Golden Rule. Each could claim that if *he* were the owner in such a case, he would give up the drug to save five people. (If one doubts the veracity of this claim on the grounds that people will do whatever they believe necessary to survive, one should also doubt the veracity of what Taurek's owner says when he claims he would not ask for or, presumably, steal the drug if he were one of the needy five.) The fact that Taurek considers it relevant whether a convincing argument could be offered to the owner, but not whether such an argument could be offered to the five, suggests that he holds the libertarian view that the retention of one's property requires no special justification, even when others need it to survive.[4]

If, as may well be the case, Taurek is presupposing something like the above described account of obligation, his verdicts about cases 1 and 2 follow without the issue of whether the numbers count being touched at all. To see this, we may consider the following Libertarian Aid Principle that states what is, on the above account, a necessary condition for one person being obligated to aid another.

(LAP)   Person A is obligated to aid person B *only* if either (i) A has contracted to do so (or is bound to do so in virtue of some quasi-contractual relationship) or (ii) A is responsible for B's needing aid or owes B compensation for other past harms.

Notice that (LAP) has some very counter-intuitive consequences. It implies, for example, that it is permissible for the owner in case 2 to simply pour the drug down a sewer, and save neither his friend nor the five strangers. Taurek, in a footnote, mentions this issue, but refuses to endorse the common sense view that the owner is obligated to save *someone*. This is a further indication that he may accept (LAP) or some principle much like it. For the sake of argument then, let us grant (LAP) and see if Taurek can extract from it the conclusion that the numbers should not count.

From (LAP) it follows directly that the owner (who is assumed to be neither responsible for the plight of the strangers nor contractually bound to deliver the drug) is not obligated to give the drug to the five. But this is only because, on the libertarian view, one who has not wronged others or contracted (or "quasi-contracted") to aid them is never obligated to give aid. Thus, the owner's lack of obligation in no way bears on the question of whether the numbers should count in moral decision making. The conclusion that the numbers should not count follows only if, in addition to (LAP), one accepts the following principle:

(O)   Moral reasoning and decision making about giving aid is concerned solely with determining one's moral obligations (in the libertarian sense).

But (LAP) and (O) should not both be accepted. Consider the case in which the owner does not need the drug to survive (though the five strangers do), but simply wants to drink it because it tastes good. According to (LAP), the owner is under no obligation to give the drug to the five. Applying (O) to this case then yields the absurd conclusion that the fact that human lives are at stake has no place in one's moral reasoning or decision making in this case. Clearly this is a conclusion that Taurek, given his reverence for individual human lives, would be loathe to accept. But then, if his verdicts on cases 1 and 2 are derived—as they appear to be—from (LAP), he must give up the claim that they in any way show that the numbers should not count.

The point may be put in the following way. If we use the very restrictive libertarian concept of moral obligation (as Taurek apparently thinks we should), then there is a lot more to morality than obligations, and more to moral reasoning than determining what one's obligations are. One may reason morally about which of several permissible (according to (LAP)) acts in aid situations one should or ought perform, all things considered. In such deliberations, the numbers of persons aided by each act would count for something. Or at least nothing Taurek says shows otherwise.

In summary, the conclusion that it is permissible for the owner to save himself or his friend rather than five strangers can be derived from a libertarian theory of obligation that Taurek never acknowledges or argues for, but which he appears to presuppose. However, this theory implies that the numbers should not count only if we assume the further principle, (O). But (O) in conjunction with the libertarian theory implies that human life should not count either. As Taurek's discussion of case 3 indicates that he cannot accept this last implication, consistency would require him to reject the assumption which implies that the numbers should not count. It is conceivable that Taurek could provide an alternate principled defense of his verdicts on cases 1 and 2, though none is offered in the paper or comes readily to mind. Until he does, we must conclude that insofar as Taurek's remarks on cases 1 and 2 are aimed at undermining the claim that the numbers should count, they miss the mark.

II.

In the latter part of his paper, Taurek turns to the case in which the owner can save either one stranger or five other strangers. His view is that the owner has "absolutely no reason for showing preference to them [the five] as against him [the one], and no reason for showing preference to him as against them." He recommends flipping a coin to decide to whom to give the drug. Using the concept of indifference, as decision theorists do, to signify the absence of a preference between two alternatives, we may state Taurek's view thus: one should be indifferent between saving the one stranger and the five.[5] Taurek offers three arguments in support of this view. The first is the now familiar claim that no one's rights are violated if the procedure he recommends is followed. As shown above, this argument does not bear on the numbers question, and I shall not consider it further. The other arguments are that the one stranger's life is as valuable to *him*self as are the lives of the others to *them*selves, and that the value of one person's life (or disvalue of his pains) cannot, as utilitarians suppose, simply be summed with the value of the lives (or disvalue of the pains) of others. Taurek has fastened on a valid and significant point in these arguments, and I shall allude to it later. But first I present an argument which shows that Taurek's conclusion about the case of the six strangers is mistaken.

Let us name the six strangers, calling the one who needs all the drug Sam, and the others Mel, Tim, Art, Cal, and Len. Let A_1 be the act of giving the whole dose to Sam, and A_2 be the act of giving one-fifth of it to each of the others. According to Taurek, we should be indifferent between A_1 and A_2. But note that there are other acts the owner could perform. He could, for example, give one-fifth of the drug to each of Mel, Tim, Art, and Cal, and pour the rest on the ground. Call this act A_3.[6] Compare A_3 and A_1. According to Taurek's analysis, one should be indifferent between them, between saving the four and saving the one. But it is a general presupposition of rational choice that indifference (i.e. the absence of preference) is a transitive relation. It follows, therefore, that we should also be indifferent between A_2 and A_3. But this is to be indifferent between saving Mel, Tim, Art, and Cal, on the one hand, and saving all four of them *plus Len*, on the other. None of us (especially Len) is likely to find this implication of Taurek's view acceptable.

Is there an adequate reply to this *reductio* [from *reductio ad absurdum*, the reduction of an argument to an absurdity] argument against Taurek's view? The argument cannot be set aside on the grounds that Taurek is not concerned with cases involving overlapping groups. For it shows that his analysis of choices that do not involve such groups already has implications regarding choices that do, and these implications are unacceptable. Could Taurek claim that one should prefer A_1 to A_3, that it would be *better* to give all the drug to Sam than to save Mel, Tim, Art, and Cal, while wasting some of the drug? No, for to prefer A_1 to A_3 because the latter involves wasting medicine that could be used to save an additional life would hardly be to show the equal concern for Mel, Tim, Art, and Cal's lives (in comparison with Sam's), that Taurek feels is appropriate in these aid situations. I conclude that consistency requires giving up either (i) the judgment that it is preferable to save Len's life in addition to Mel, Tim, Art, and Cal's lives, or (ii) the principle of transitivity of indifference, or (iii) Taurek's view about the case of the six strangers. I suggest that it is the last of these that should be abandoned.[7]

There are also more general reasons for doubting Taurek's contention that the numbers should not count *at all* in cases of this kind, reasons based on a plausible analogy between morality and prudence. Consider Taurek's claim that one party should not be forced to undergo a large pain (on the grounds that the total amount of pain suffered would be less) to save a large number of persons from each suffering smaller pains.[8] This seems correct in many cases. But the same principle applies to a rational person's choices between his own pains. Some pains are so awful that it may well be rational for a person to prefer to suffer several somewhat lesser pains than to suffer such a pain once, even if this increases the total amount of pain he will suffer.[9] Yet one can admit this without jumping to the absurd conclusion that a rational person will be indifferent between suffering one pain of a given intensity and many pains of that same intensity. The fact that pains should not be summed in the neat way utilitarians suggest does not mean their numbers do not count at all—for rational prudence or for morality.

The biggest challenge to one who would take Taurek's position is to explain why the numbers, which clearly count *so heavily* in rational prudence, should count for *absolutely nothing* in morality. Of course, there is this crucial difference, noted by Rawls and emphasized in Taurek's arguments: morality concerns distributions among distinct individuals.[10] This difference is a reason for being somewhat skeptical about utilitarianism. But it seems that some burden of proof must fall on the theorist who goes to the opposite extreme and fails to count the numbers at all, to explain how the distinctness of individuals leads to such a vast disparity between the principles of rational prudence and rational morality. As far as I can determine, Taurek has offered no such explanation, nor any hint of what one might look like.

It may be noted, in this regard, that there are proposals for dealing with life-saving cases that fall between the utilitarian prescription to save the larger number, and Taurek's recommendation to ignore the numbers and flip a coin. One compromise proposal that seems rather natural is to hold a lottery that proportions the probability of each group being saved to the size of the group. This proposal has the advantage of respecting each individual in the sense that no one is denied all chance of being saved solely on the grounds that he happens to be in the smaller group, yet it takes the relative size of the groups heavily into account. Perhaps this procedure will ultimately prove to be unsatisfactory, perhaps it places too much weight on the numbers. Yet it is surely superior to any procedure that does not in any way take account of the numbers.

Notes

[1]John Taurek: "Should the Numbers Count?" p. 214. I have benefited from having seen an earlier version of Taurek's paper, and having attended a discussion in which he defended some of the points contained therein. The criticisms of Taurek's paper presented here complement (and occasionally overlap) those offered by Derek in his paper "Innumerate Ethics," p. 227.

[2]There are, of course, overriding reasons for requiring *public officials* to act impartially in exercising their powers of office.

[3]The most influential philosophical exposition of such a view of moral obligation is Robert Nozick's *Anarchy, State, and Utopia* (New York, 1974). See especially pp. ix, 9-10, 28-34, 58, 90-95, 149-55, 167-82, and 238.

[4]I am not denying that with his life at stake, the owner is justified in keeping the drug. The point is that the assumption that acts leading to the owner's death (the surrender or theft of the drug) require justification, while acts leading to the death of the five (the owner's retention of the drug) do not, reflects the libertarian view of the relative importance of property rights and other considerations.

[5]Taurek is not recommending indifference to the plight of the strangers. It is equal concern for the plight of each, not lack of concern, that accounts for his recommendation that neither alternative be preferred to the other.

[6]Is A_3 a "genuine" alternative? It would save more lives than A_1. More important, as regards the question of what Taurek seems committed to, is the fact that A_3 is permissible according to (LAP). Philippa Foot has pointed out to me that, unless (O) is assumed as well, it does not follow that there are no moral reasons that rule out A_3 as a possible action. (See the text below for a comment on a proposed reason of this kind: that A_3 involves wasting some of the drug.) But here Taurek faces an apparent dilemma. If he rejects (O), he is, as argued in Section I, left without any argument for his conclusion that the numbers should not count. If, on the other hand, he accepts (O), he must treat A_3 as a genuine alternative and deal with the present argument.

[7]Taurek might well choose to reject transitivity. This would save him from endorsing the strongly counterintuitive view that it is alright to prefer to have a large number of strangers lose their lives than to have another stranger lose his arm. If transitivity of preference and indifference for rational agents is presupposed, this view follows from two others that Taurek endorses: (i) It is alright to prefer the loss of stranger C's life to the loss of stranger B's arm, and (ii) one should be indifferent between the loss of stranger C's life and the loss of the lives of a large number of other strangers.

[8]Marilyn M. Adams offers a similar argument in "Hell and the God of Justice," *Religious Studies* 11, (1975), p. 439.

[9]This point would be more widely recognized if people were not confused by the misguided idea that intensity of pain must be identified with levels of (negative) subjective utility, as measured by the subject's preference behavior.

[10]John Rawls: 1971, *A Theory of Justice* (Cambridge, Mass.), Secs. 5, 6, and 30.

Why I May Count the Numbers

KEN DICKEY ▪ University of California, Riverside
Unpublished

Ken Dickey argues that John Taurek's position in "Should the Numbers Count?" leads to inconsistent results when applied to certain "real-life" conflict cases. Specifically, Dickey shows that Taurek's claim that the numbers should not count conflicts with Taurek's emphasis on empathy for persons.

In the first section, Dickey characterizes Taurek's position by considering Taurek's judgments about three Drug cases. In sum, Taurek maintains that, other things being equal, it is permissible for the owner of the drug to give the drug to either the five (who each needs one-fifth of the drug) or the one (who needs all of the drug in order to survive), whether (i) the one is the owner of the drug, (ii) the one is someone the owner knows and likes, or (iii) all six persons are strangers to the owner. Taurek also maintains, however, that the owner should not act on this permission **arbitrarily**; rather, he should give each person an equal chance to survive unless he has some reason for acting to save *either* the one or the five. In the Drug case in which all six persons who need the drug are strangers, Taurek claims that he would flip a coin to decide what to do.

In the second section, Dickey suggests that the demand that the owner not act arbitrarily on his permission to dispense the drug is all the moral force there is to Taurek's claim that the numbers should not count. This demand to avoid acting arbitrarily also justifies Taurek's judgment that the owner should flip a coin (or use some other fair procedure) to decide what to do in the drug case in which all six persons are strangers.

Next, Dickey considers why Taurek is concerned about preventing harms to persons in the first place. He identifies Taurek's empathetic concern with losses to persons as the important factor. He notes, with Taurek, that losses to persons are not additive across persons; nevertheless, he suggests that, given Taurek's concern with losses to persons, it would not be arbitrary for the owner of the drug to minimize the amount of loss to any one person.

In the final section, Dickey argues that in certain real-life cases it would not be arbitrary to save the five, given Taurek's concern with minimizing the amount of loss to any one person. First, he suggests that given a certain type of harm, the amount of loss to a person varies across persons. (For example, losing a right arm results in a greater amount of loss to a right-handed pitcher in major league baseball than it does to most other persons.) Second, he notes that, given that the drug owner is ignorant about the amount of loss to be suffered by each of the six, there is a greater probability that the drug owner will prevent the greatest amount of loss to any one person if he gives the drug to the five than if he gives the drug to the one. Finally, he observes that acting on relative probabilities in this way is not objectionable, so Taurek appears to be committed to the view that acting so as to save the five in the drug case in which all six persons are strangers (*and* the drug owner is ignorant of the **relative harms**) is not arbitrary.

Dickey notes that his argument is limited to cases in which the type of harm results in variable amounts of losses to persons, and that death might not be properly considered such a harm. Furthermore, he is explicit about the importance to his argument of the restrictions on the knowledge available to the deciding agent; if the Drug case is described in such a way that the owner knows the potential amounts of loss to each of the six in advance, the argument does not apply. Finally, Dickey observes that since his argument does not presuppose the additivity of losses to persons across persons, it may provide a novel justification for acting so as to save the greater number in certain conflict cases.

---

*WHAT OUGHT I TO DO WHEN CONFRONTED WITH a conflict case fitting the following schema: I can either save one person from a certain harm x, or save five others from the same type of harm, but not both? John Taurek has raised considerable controversy in arguing that in such trade-off situations, the mere fact that

(A) Only one person will suffer harm x if one choice is made, whereas five people will suffer the same type of harm if another choice is made.

should be irrelevant in determining what to do. Taurek claims:

> The general question discussed here is whether we should, in such trade-off situations, consider the relative numbers of people involved as something in itself of significance in determining our course of action. The conclusion I reach here is that we should not.[1]

In this paper I shall present Taurek's position that the numbers should not count by considering three conflict cases fitting the schema above. These cases are from Taurek. The type of potential harm for each of the six persons involved, for all of these cases, is that of death. It is unfortunate that Taurek presents his position via these examples involving deaths, since this raises the question as to whether Taurek intends for his position to apply to other types of harms as well.[2] I shall argue in this paper that Taurek's position is inconsistent when extended to cases in which potential harms other than deaths are involved. Correcting for this inconsistency raises a novel justification of the moral relevance of fact (A) in determining what to do.

One preliminary note is in order here. It seems uncontroversial that Taurek's position that the numbers should not count is intended (among other things) to serve as a guide for private citizens in making decisions in real-life situations with features fitting the schema above. Such real-life situations, of course, involve various limitations on the knowledge available to the deciding agent. I shall assume throughout this paper that Taurek's position is indeed intended as an action-guiding principle, but I should perhaps make this assumption explicit by qualifying the thesis of this paper, thus: Taurek's position that the numbers should not count is inconsistent when applied to cases in which harms other than deaths are involved, *if interpreted as an action-guiding principle for private citizens in real-life situations.*

~

Case 1:

David has a supply of some life-saving drug. David is one of six people who will all certainly die if not treated with the drug. David requires all of the drug if he is to survive. Each of the other five requires only one-fifth of the drug. David has no special obligations to any of the other five. What ought David to do?[3]

Taurek holds ". . . it is morally permissible for David in this situation to give himself all of his drug." I shall not dispute Taurek's judgement.

Case 2:

I have a supply of some life-saving drug. David is one of six people who will all certainly die if not treated with the drug. David requires all of the drug if he is to survive. Each of the other five requires only one-fifth of the drug. David is someone I know and like, but I have no special obligations to him or any of the other five. What ought I to do?

Taurek believes I am permitted but not required to save David, since David is someone I know and like. In holding this belief, Taurek endorses the following principle regarding the non-agent-relativity of permissions in cases like this:

> (NAR) *If it would be morally permissible for B to choose to spare himself a certain loss H, instead of sparing another person, C, a loss H', in a situation where he cannot spare C and himself as well, then it must be permissible for someone else, not under any relevant special obligations to the contrary, to take B's perspective, that is, to choose to secure the outcome most favorable to B instead of the outcome most favorable to C, if he cannot secure what would be best for each.*

Derek Parfit disputes (NAR), thereby disagreeing with Taurek's judgement in Case 2, while agreeing with his judgement in Case 1. Specifically, Parfit believes David's permission to save the one (i.e., himself) in Case 1 is agent-relative.[4] Taurek believes David's permission to save the one in Case 1 is non-agent-relative. I shall not dispute Taurek's judgement.[5]

Case 3:

I have a supply of some life-saving drug. Six people will all certainly die if not treated with the drug. One requires all of the drug if he (or she) is to survive. Each of the other five requires only one-fifth of the drug. I do not know any of the six involved and have no special obligations to any of them. What ought I to do?

Clearly, given his judgement in Case 1, Taurek believes it would be permissible for the one who requires all of the drug to save himself, special obligations aside, were he in a position to do so. Also, it seems uncontroversial that, according to Taurek, it would be permissible for one of the five who requires only one-fifth of the drug to save himself

(and the other four who each requires only one-fifth of the drug), special obligations aside, were he in a position to do so.

Accordingly, given his acceptance of (NAR), Taurek should believe that, special obligations aside, it is permissible for me, in Case 3, to save either the one who requires all of the drug or one of the five who requires only one-fifth of the drug (and the other four who each requires only one-fifth of the drug). So if I decide in Case 3 to act on my non-agent-relative permission to save the five persons who each requires only one-fifth of the drug, simply because I like the idea of saving five strangers instead of just one, it seems I should, according to Taurek, be allowed to do so.

But to do so would be in violation of Taurek's claim that the relative numbers of people involved should not count in deciding what to do!

Taurek seems to be in a dilemma here. Either I really do have permission to save the five in Case 3 or I don't. If I don't, then it seems there must be something wrong with (NAR). If I do, then what can be the force of Taurek's claim that the numbers *should not* count?

I believe the best way of characterizing Taurek's position to avoid this dilemma is to say that, according to Taurek, while I have a non-agent-relative permission to save either the one or the five in Case 3, I *should not* act on this non-agent-relative permission in an arbitrary manner.

> In the trade-off situation as presently conceived, all six persons are strangers to me. I have no special affection for any one of them, no greater concern for one rather than any of the others. Further, by hypothesis, my situation will be made neither worse nor better by either outcome. Any preference I might show, therefore, if it is not to be thought arbitrary, would require grounding . . . [In] this situation I have absolutely no reason for showing preference to them as against him, and no reason for showing preference to him as against them.

Accordingly, we can summarize Taurek's position on Case 3 as follows. While I have a non-agent-relative permission to save either the five who each requires only one-fifth of the drug or the one who requires all of the drug, I should not save the five *simply because* I like the idea of saving five strangers instead of just one. To do so would be to act in an arbitrary manner, according to Taurek, and I should not act on my non-agent-relative permissions in an arbitrary manner.

So what *should* I do? Taurek says he would flip a coin to decide what to do, since this is one way to "treat each person equally by giving each an equal chance to survive."

~

Inferring from Taurek's position on Case 2 that the fact that

(B)   David is someone I know and like

suffices to make my acting so as to save him non-arbitrary, we can now explicate Taurek's claim that the numbers should not count in the following Arbitrariness Principle:

> (AP) *In conflict cases of the type under consideration, I should not act on non-agent-relative permissions in an arbitrary manner, where "arbitrary manner" (i) includes acting on the basis of the relative numbers of people involved, in itself, as a significant factor in making a decision, and (ii) does not include acting in order to save someone I know and like.*

Now, it can be argued from controversial premises that (AP) is both implausible[6] and irrelevant when considering what to do in Case 3.[7] But since I do not want to employ premises in this paper which Taurek can reasonably reject, I shall not object to the substantive elements of (AP) here.

Nevertheless, it is important to see that the "should not" of (AP) captures all of the moral force of the "should not" in Taurek's claim that the numbers should not count. This "should not" should not be interpreted as a moral restriction in any straight-forward sense, since we must keep in mind that it occurs within the context of a non-agent-relative permission. In particular, (AP) does not commit Taurek to the judgement that I am *required* to save David in Case 2. Rather, in this case, according to Taurek, I have a non-agent-relative permission to save either David or the five; (AP) merely declares that should I act in this case to save David, my doing so would not be arbitrary. In contrast, Taurek believes that should I act in Case 3 to save the one (or the five) without first flipping a

coin (or employing some other fair procedure), my doing so would be arbitrary.

~

Above, I stated that I would not object to the substantive elements of (AP). Nevertheless, I believe most of us find (AP) to be incomplete as an action-guiding principle, because the notion of "arbitrary manner" which it employs is not yet fully developed. Moreover, I shall provide strong textual evidence to suggest that Taurek himself has a more specific notion of "arbitrary manner" in mind.

To do this I should like to consider the reason Taurek gives for wanting to prevent harms to persons in the first place. Sanders has plausibly suggested that the real force of Taurek's argument is that "We must never consider the loss *of* persons, only the loss *to* persons."[8] Consider the following passage from Taurek:

> It seems to me that those who, in situations of the kind in question, would have me count the relative numbers of people involved as something in itself of significance, would have me attach importance to human beings and what happens to them in merely the way I would to objects which I valued. If six objects are threatened by fire and I am in a position to retrieve the five in this room or the one in that room, but unable to get out all six, I would decide what to do in just the way I am told I should when it is human beings who are threatened. Each object will have a certain value in my eyes. If it happens that all six are of equal value, I will naturally preserve the many rather than the one. Why? Because the five objects are together five times more valuable in my eyes than the one.
>
> But when I am moved to rescue human beings from harm in situations of the kind described, I cannot bring myself to think of them in just this way. I empathize with them. My concern for what happens to them is grounded chiefly in the realization that each of them is, as I would be in his place, terribly concerned about what happens to him. It is not my way to think of them as each having a certain objective value, determined however it is we determine the objective value of things, and then to make some estimate of the combined value of the five as against the one . . . It is the loss to this person *that I focus on.*

Given Taurek's view that only losses *to* persons (and not losses *of* persons) are morally relevant,[9] his claim that the relative numbers of people involved, in itself, should not count in deciding what to do is justified by observing that losses *to* persons, like headaches, are not additive across persons: "The discomfort of each of a large number of individuals experiencing a minor headache does not add up to anyone's experiencing a migraine." Or, as Taurek notes of his position on Cases 1–3, "This reflects a refusal to take seriously in these situations any notion of the sum of two persons' separate losses."[10]

Now consider Case 3. Since losses to persons are not additive across persons, according to Taurek, it is appropriate to consider the potential loss to the one person who needs all of the drug if he is to survive, and compare that to the potential loss to *each one* of the five, not to the group of five.

But this leads to a question as to whether the *amount* of loss to each of the persons is morally relevant, according to Taurek. In particular, does Taurek consider it arbitrary to act on non-agent-relative permissions so as to *prevent the greatest amount* of loss to any one person? I do not believe so:

> *My way of thinking about these trade-off situations consists, essentially, in seriously considering what will be lost or suffered by this one person if I do not prevent it, and in comparing the significance of that for him with what would be lost or suffered by anyone else if I do not prevent it. [emphasis added]*[11]

Taurek's position, then, actually amounts to the following Modified Arbitrariness Principle:

> (MAP) *In conflict cases of the type under consideration, I should not act on non-agent-relative permissions in an arbitrary manner, where "arbitrary manner" (i) includes acting on the basis of the relative numbers of people involved, in itself, as a significant factor in making a decision, (ii) does not include acting in order to save someone I know and like, and (iii) does not include acting so as to prevent the greatest amount of loss to any one person.*

Again, (MAP) does not commit Taurek to the view that I am *required* to act so as to prevent the greatest amount of loss to any one person. (In fact, he denies any such requirement.) Nevertheless, given that I

have a non-agent-relative permission to save either the one or the five in Cases 1–3, it would not be arbitrary for me to act so as to prevent the greatest amount of loss to any one person.

~

Given (MAP), we may now return to Taurek's judgement on what to do in Case 3. He believes I should flip a coin to decide what to do, because "in this situation I have absolutely no reason for showing preference to them as against him, and no reason for showing preference to him as against them." But is it true, given (MAP) clause (iii), that I have absolutely no reason for showing preference to them as against him?

In Case 3 we know that all six persons will potentially suffer the same *type of harm*, namely death. But does it follow that the potential *amount of loss to each person* is the same? Yes, if we accept the following thesis:

(T) The amount of loss to a person who dies is the same for all persons who die the same type of death.

I have doubts about (T), but I shall not raise them here.[12] Rather, I should like to consider whether (MAP) can be consistently extended to a case parallel to Case 3, but which involves a type of harm other than death.

Case 3':

I have a supply of some right-arm-saving drug. Six people will certainly lose their right arms if not treated with the drug. One requires all of the drug if he (or she) is to retain his (or her) right arm. Each of the other five requires only one-fifth of the drug. I do not know any of the six involved and have no special obligations to any of them. What ought I to do?

If we wish to extend Taurek's judgement on Case 3 to Case 3', we must presume that Taurek would say in Case 3': (1) I have a non-agent-relative permission to prevent the loss to either the one or the five, and (2) I should flip a coin (or use some similar procedure) to decide what to do, since (3) this is the only way to show an equal concern for all of the parties involved, given that (4) I have no (non-arbitrary) basis for preferring to prevent the loss to either the one or the five.

However: is (4) true, given clause (iii) of (MAP)? I do not believe so, for it is not only true in Case 3' that I do not *know* any of the six people involved. It is also true that I do not know everything there is to *know about* the six people involved. Perhaps I do not know, for example, whether any of the six is a right-handed pitcher in Major League Baseball.

But now, given my lack of knowledge about the six people involved, isn't there a probability greater than zero and less than one that at least one of them is, say, a right-handed pitcher in Major League Baseball? And surely it is true that the *amount of loss* to a right-handed pitcher in Major League Baseball, in losing his right arm, is greater than it is for most other people in the population, in suffering the same *type of harm*. But since in saving the group I would be saving five people instead of just one, I would, in saving the group, have a five-times-greater probability of saving a right-handed pitcher in Major League Baseball.[13]

Next, if I am, as Taurek seems to be, seriously concerned with preventing the greatest *amount of loss* to any one individual, it would be rational in Case 3' to act so as to *maximize the probability* that I am acting so as to prevent the greatest amount of loss to any one individual. Finally, since I can see nothing morally objectionable about acting on relative probabilities in this way, I conclude it would not be arbitrary, according to clause (iii) of (MAP), for me to act in Case 3' so as to save the five— *without* first flipping a coin.

This argument can, I believe, be generalized to cover any type of harm that results in variable amounts of losses to individuals.[14] But it is also highly plausible that all harms other than death[15] share this feature. Hence, it can be shown that Taurek's position (explicated here as (MAP)), if interpreted as an action-guiding principle for private citizens in real-life situations (where there are epistemic limits on one's knowledge about the individuals involved), cannot be consistently extended to types of harms other than death. In Case 3', (MAP) clause (i) holds that it *would* be arbitrary for me to act on my non-agent-relative permission to save the five without first flipping a coin, whereas a rational extension of (MAP) clause (iii) holds it *would not* be arbitrary for me to do so.

The mere fact that (MAP) cannot be consistently applied as an action-guiding principle in Case 3' does not tell us which clause is best to abandon. Most of us, however, would prefer to abandon clause (i). In doing so, we express our considered judgement that in cases like Case 3', I am permitted to save the greater number of persons, and it is not arbitrary for me to do so. Moreover, it is interesting to note that this considered judgment, because it does not require the additivity of harms to separate persons for its justification, is in fact consistent with Taurek's views on why it is that potential harms to persons are significant in determining our course of action.

Notes

*Research for this paper was supported by the University of California Toxic Substances Research and Teaching Program. A shortened version of this paper was presented at the Pacific Division Meeting of the American Philosophical Association, held in Oakland, March 1989. I am greatly indebted to Larry Alexander, Carl Cranor, John Fischer, Dwight Furrow, Alan Nelson, Alexander Rosenberg, and John Taurek for comments on previous drafts of this paper.

[1]All internal citations are to Taurek, p. 214. See also Taurek's claim: "The numbers, in themselves, simply do not count for me. I think they should not count for any of us." Quite a number of interesting articles have arisen in response to Taurek's initial paper. See Kagan, p. 252, Kamm, Kavka, p. 236, Parfit, p. 227, Sanders, Shaw, and Woodward. Of related interests are Thomson, p. 279, and Fischer, p. 308.

[2]In commenting on an earlier draft of this paper, John Taurek has indicated that he does not intend to restrict the applicability of his position to cases involving deaths. Nevertheless, I have not changed the text since one might reasonably maintain that death is significantly unlike other types of harms. See note 12, below.

[3]As Taurek notes, this case was previously described by Philippa Foot, p. 59.

[4]Parfit, p. 227.

[5]But see Woodward, p. 532. Woodward suggests that excuses for actions are agent-relative, whereas justifications are non-agent-relative.

[6]Here I have in mind Sanders's suggestion that in at least some cases, the relative numbers of people involved is not an arbitrary consideration. Still, one might object, in addition, to clause (ii) of (AP).

[7]Here I have in mind Parfit's view that the permissions of concern are agent-relative. See note 4, above.

[8]Sanders, p. 13.

[9] But note the qualifications in the passage cited, which suggest that Taurek may have some concern for losses *of* persons, in some circumstances at least. Sanders has argued that if one views the occurrence of many deaths as a loss *of* persons (even if one considers each death to be primarily a loss *to* a person), then the additivity of many separate deaths is reasonable.

[10] Parfit disagrees with Taurek by maintaining that only Taurek and C. S. Lewis accept the thesis "(M) If one person is harmed, that would be just as bad as if any number are each equally harmed."

[11] There is additional evidence to suggest that Taurek does not consider it arbitrary to act on non-agent-relative permissions so as to prevent the greatest amount of loss to any one person. This evidence arises from the consideration of a case which Taurek discusses by way of clarifying (NAR). In this case, I may either save one person, B, the loss of his arm, or some other person, C, the loss of his life, but not both.

Taurek claims it would be permissible for B to save himself, were he in a position to do so, and using (NAR), concludes it must be permissible for me to save B in this case as well, provided I have no special obligations to save C. Furthermore, Taurek claims that this is precisely what he would do if B's welfare were more important to him than C's.

What Taurek does not consider here is what he would do if B's welfare were *equally* important to him as C's, perhaps because he does not know either of them. Would he flip a coin in such a case to decide what to do? Or, even more relevant to the question at hand, suppose *I* am in the position to act, not Taurek; then would Taurek consider it arbitrary for me to act so as to prevent C's loss of life?

Taurek does not discuss this question, so we are left somewhat in the dark about his judgement. However, there is nothing in Taurek's justification of his judgement for Case 3 that commits him to flipping a coin in this case as well. It is safe to assume then, that Taurek believes, with most of us, that it would not be arbitrary in this case to act so as to prevent C's loss of his life (rather than B's loss of his arm) *without* first flipping a coin. The reason that it would not be arbitrary to prevent the harm to C in this case, I suggest, is simply that it is not arbitrary to act so as to prevent the greatest amount of loss to any one person.

[12] Sanders, in footnote 3, p. 5, questions whether death constitutes a loss to the individual who dies. Presumably, Sanders' doubt is implicit in the familiar Symmetry Argument, commonly attributed to Epicurus. For discussions of the Symmetry Argument, as well as worthwhile responses to the argument, see Brueckner and Fischer, as well as McMahan.

But even putting this first doubt aside, it seems clear to me that, looking at things from the third-person point of view, the value of life to an individual varies with the age and the level of completion of the life plans of that individual. (Taurek has agreed to this point in personal conversation. Also, see Quinn ["Abortion: Identity and Loss"], pp. 43–4, and McMahan, especially p. 58.) Moreover, if we look at things from the first-person point of view, it seems clear to me that the amount of loss to a suicidal person who dies is less than it is to others who die.

The upshot of all of this is that I believe (T) to be either trivial (if death does not constitute a loss to the individual who dies), or false (if it does).

[13] This is only approximately true, since we cannot strictly assume replacement in computing the probability of saving at least one right-handed pitcher in Major League Baseball for the group of five.

[14] A generalized form of the argument is as follows. We identify a type of harm by objectively specifiable characteristics. Associated with any such harm will be a distribution of losses to persons, which can be represented by plotting a graph with Number of People on the vertical axis, and Amount of Loss on the horizontal axis. Since we are concerned only with losses to persons in this argument, assume the Amount of Loss is always a positive number.

Assume any distribution of losses to persons you like (normal, or otherwise), so long as it is not represented by a "spike" on our graph—the case in which the entire population suffers the same amount of loss. Now randomly select each member of a group of five individuals in the population, and likewise for a group of one. My claim is that there is a greater probability that at least one individual from the group of five will suffer a greater amount of loss than the one individual than there is that the one individual (from the group of one) will suffer a greater amount of loss than each (and every) one of the group of five.

[15] But see note 12, above.

References

Brueckner, Anthony L., and Fischer, John Martin, "Why is Death Bad?" *Philosophical Studies*, 50 (1986), pp. 213–221.

Fischer, John Martin, "Thoughts on the Trolley Problem," p. 308.

Foot, Philippa, "Abortion and the Doctrine of Double Effect," in *Moral Problems: A Collection of Philosophical Essays*, Second Edition, James Rachels, ed., (Harper & Row: New York, 1975), pp. 59–70.

Kagan, Shelly, "The Additive Fallacy," *Ethics*, 99 (1988), pp. 5–31.

Kamm, Frances Myrna, "Equal Treatment and Equal Chances," *Philosophy & Public Affairs*, 14 (1985), pp. 177–94.

Kavka, Gregory S., "The Numbers Should Count," *Philosophical Studies*, 36 (1979), pp. 285-94.

McMahan, Jeff, "Death and the Value of Life," *Ethics*, 99 (1988), pp. 32-61.

Parfit, Derek, "Innumerate Ethics," *Philosophy & Public Affairs*, 7 (1978), pp. 285-301.

Quinn, Warren, "Abortion: Identity and Loss," *Philosophy & Public Affairs*, 13 (1984), pp. 24-54.

Sanders, John T., "Why the Numbers Should Sometimes Count," *Philosophy & Public Affairs*, 17 (1988), pp. 3-14.

Shaw, William H., "Elementary Lifesaving," *The Southern Journal of Philosophy*, 18 (1980), pp. 87-97.

Taurek, John M., "Should the Numbers Count?" *Philosophy & Public Affairs*, 6 (1977), pp. 293-316.

Thomson, Judith Jarvis, "The Trolley Problem," *The Yale Law Journal*, 94 (1985), pp. 1395-415.

Woodward, James F., "Why the Numbers Count," *The Southern Journal of Philosophy*, 19 (1981), pp. 531-40.

 *Part VI*

METHODOLOGY

The Additive Fallacy

SHELLY KAGAN ▪ University of Illinois, Chicago
Ethics, 1988

Kagan's essay is concerned with the methodology of moral philosophy. Philosophers often defend or attack the moral relevance of different distinctions. The problem is how one can defend or attack different claims concerning the moral relevance of different distinctions.

Kagan centers the essay on the strategy used by some moral philosophers of comparing two cases that differ only in terms of a particular factor. Factors that remain the same in each case are called **constant factors**, and those that are different (and are presumably being tested) are called **variable factors**. If the cases are deemed morally divergent, then this difference is attributed to the difference in the variable factor. Such arguments are called **contrast arguments**. Kagan argues that this strategy of resolving moral disputes is faulty because it makes a bad assumption about how different factors in such a case can be properly examined.

In discussing contrast arguments, both sides will agree on a correctly constructed pair of cases, and then argue whether a change in a given factor involved in these cases makes a difference in our overall moral assessment of the cases. Moral philosophers attacking an alleged pair of contrast cases try to show that the cases fail to support their conclusions. Kagan identifies four ways that this is done, all of which, he claims, presuppose the validity of the contrast strategy.

Kagan disagrees with the contrast strategy. At work in this strategy is an assumption that, if a factor has relevance, then for *any* pair of cases where the factor under scrutiny varies (and the rest of the factors are held constant), the cases will have a different moral status. So, appeal to such cases should determine whether the factor in question is of some moral significance. Kagan says that the assumption at work here is that if a factor makes a difference anywhere, it makes a difference everywhere. This is called the **ubiquity thesis**.

The ubiquity thesis, Kagan says, follows from the idea that moral principles are universal in a certain way. Kagan disagrees with this idea, however, arguing that moral factors that cause moral effects are not necessarily universal.

Kagan also finds that the model underlying this philosophical strategy is one that assumes that an act has its moral status based on the factors that are involved in a given moral situation. Theorists disagree, however, as to how the status of an act is affected by these factors. Such a relationship depends on the function that these factors are supposed to play for the theory. Kagan calls this function the **governing function**. This function determines how the factors in any given case act together to determine an act's moral status. Here Kagan argues that those who use contrast strategies presuppose a view about how this governing function operates—that such a function is additive.

"Additive" here means that the factors involved in any given case are added up. Some of them are positive factors and others are negative. The overall status of the act is derived by comparing the negative and positive factors and determining which side possesses a preponderance of effects. So, the overall status of an act is the net sum of these divergent factors. If the act is the sum of these positive and negative factors, then if one sees them all as fixed, except for the one, then the sum should vary with the change in the one factor.

With this approach, if a moral factor is genuinely relevant, then changing it will always make a difference in the moral status of the act. This universal property of such a factor makes it consistent with the ubiquity thesis. Kagan concludes that people who propose contrast strategies are accepting the additive assumption because it explains how the strategy is supposed to work.

Kagan next argues that the **additive assumption** should be rejected. His first argument involves cases where we examine the act of killing someone in self-defense. In one case, an agent defends himself against an aggressor by pushing him into a pit, and in another, the agent does not inform an aggressor that he is about to fall into a pit. Kagan asserts that most people want to argue that in such cases the distinction between doing harm and allowing harm makes no difference, even though in most cases we do see a distinction between doing harm and allowing harm.

Kagan argues that if the additive assumption is true then our claims about the above self-defense case must be false. The reason is that if the ubiquity thesis is true, then it cannot be the case that this example provides an exception to our moral intuition that there is a difference between doing harm and allowing harm. Self-defense cannot just be a factor that when added to such do/allow problems changes the overall moral status of the act. Kagan argues that instead self-defense may be more like a multiplier that when in place diffuses the do/allow distinction. Kagan argues that the additive model probably does not work for most moral views.

Other than contrast arguments, Kagan points out another form of argument that also relies on the additive assumption—**transport arguments**. Assuming some validity to the additive assumption, the transport argument isolates particular features of a case and determines their relative strengths. Next, the individual parts are transported into more complex cases. Given the additive assumption, such a move is seen as valid, and we infer that the relative strength of a factor will remain the same when it is transported into more complex arguments. If the assumption is false, then the strategy does not work, because we can see that what we derive from any particular factor cannot be fixed across different contexts.

In the final section of the paper, Kagan argues that we could do without the additive assumption. One of the possible alternatives offered is to analyze clusters of factors instead of individual factors, thus acknowledging that individual factors cannot be separated to determine their moral relevance. There are similar problems even here. Ultimately, arguments that appeal to our intuitions about constructed cases may need to be replaced with what Kagan calls more foundational moral theories.

I. CONTRAST ARGUMENTS

MUCH MORAL PHILOSOPHY IS CONCERNED WITH defending or attacking the moral relevance of various distinctions. Thus consequentialists disagree with deontologists, and deontologists disagree among themselves, over whether any moral weight should be given to such distinctions as that between what one does and what one merely allows, or to the distinction between what one intends as a means, and what one merely foresees as a side-effect, and so on. Similarly, there is disagreement over the moral relevance of such factors as the motive of the agent, the consequences of a given act, or the guilt of those who may be harmed. (On some matters, perhaps, there is widespread agreement: there seems to be a contemporary consensus, e.g., that skin color is of no intrinsic moral importance.)

Such discussions, of course, are of intrinsic theoretical interest, for as moral philosophers we would like to have adequate beliefs about which factors (and which distinctions) are morally relevant.[1] They are also, furthermore, of some practical importance, for we appeal to such factors in assessing the moral status of actions in difficult and controversial cases, and in order to explain and defend our judgments. Obviously, however, such practical applications are of limited value until we have determined whether or not a given distinction actually merits being given moral weight. But how are we to settle this? How can we defend, or attack, claims involving the moral relevance of different distinctions?

A very common form of argument proceeds by offering a pair of cases that differ only in terms of the factor in question.[2] If we judge the two cases to be morally different, it is argued, this difference must arise from the different values of the given factor[3] (everything else being held constant), and so the factor is shown to be morally relevant. If we judge the cases to be similar, on the other hand, despite the variation in the given factor, this shows that the factor is not actually morally relevant after all. Let us call the pair of cases offered for comparison contrast cases (since the argument turns on the presence or absence of a contrast in our judgments about the cases), and let us call arguments of this sort contrast arguments.

By way of example, consider the distinction between what I do and what I (merely) allow. If I take out my gun and shoot you, I have brought about your death, killed you: I have done harm. In contrast, if I merely come upon you drowning, and fail to throw you the life preserver, I have not done any harm to you, even if you drown: I have only allowed harm. Most of us not only draw this distinction, we give it moral weight, holding that doing harm is worse than merely allowing harm. Now it is not easy to make the do/allow distinction precise, but this need not concern us here. Assuming that we can make the distinction, we still need to ask: is it morally relevant?

A critic of the do/allow distinction might argue as follows: "The issue of whether I brought about a given harm or merely allowed it is not itself of intrinsic moral importance. No doubt the distinction is typically correlated with other factors which do make a difference morally, and this has perhaps blinded us to the irrelevance of the do/allow distinction itself. For example, cases of doing harm are typically also cases of harming as a means, or cases where the agent has a repugnant motive, or cases where the consequences would be better if the act in question were avoided, and so on; cases of allowing harm, on the other hand, typically do not display these features. [Different critics will, of course, offer different lists of factors.] For this reason, cases of doing harm typically are worse than cases of allowing harm. But this does not show that the distinction between doing and allowing itself affects the moral status of an act. For if the distinction were morally relevant, it should make a difference even when all of these other factors are held constant. We can see that this isn't so, however, by considering this pair of contrast cases:

(a) Gertrude pushes Bertrand into a deep pit, hoping that the fall will kill him so that she will inherit the family fortune;

(b) Seeing that Bertrand is about to fall into a deep pit, Gertrude deliberately refrains from warning him, hoping that the fall will kill him so that she will inherit the family fortune.

These cases display the same morally relevant features (e.g., motive, outcome, etc.); they differ only with regard to the doing or allowing of harm. If the do/allow distinction were itself of genuine moral importance, there should be some difference in the moral status of the two acts. But surely Gertrude's behavior in the second case is quite as bad as in the first, despite the fact that in the first case she kills Bertrand, while in the second she merely allows him to die. Since the difference between doing and allowing harm does not make a difference in this case, we can see that the do/allow distinction is not itself of any intrinsic moral importance."

Armed with this conclusion, the critic may go on to derive moral implications concerning other cases. He might, for example, argue that our failure to make significant contributions to famine relief is roughly the moral equivalent of murder. For although we are only allowing the starving to die, given the moral irrelevance of the do/allow distinction, our failure to aid is morally as bad as if we were killing them. (Other differences, of course, e.g., our lack of ill will toward the starving, may ameliorate the badness of our act somewhat in comparison with typical cases of murder.)

There are a number of ways in which a defender of the do/allow distinction might attempt to defuse the critic's argument, and I will discuss some in the next section. But first it is important to see that contrast arguments can be used to advocate as well as to criticize a distinction. Thus the advocate of the do/allow distinction might argue as follows: "Admittedly, cases of doing harm typically differ from cases of allowing harm in terms of *several* morally relevant factors. But of course this does not show that the do/allow distinction lacks moral importance in its own right. If it *were* morally irrelevant, then in contrast cases where the only difference was whether harm was done or merely allowed, all other features being held constant, no moral difference between the cases should remain. But we can see that this is not so, by considering the following pair of cases:

(c) Ludwig sees Sylvia drowning, but since the rocks beneath the water would do extensive damage to his boat, he decides not to rescue her;

(d) Ludwig sees that his boat is about to hit Sylvia, but since avoiding her would mean steering into the rocks, which would do extensive damage to his boat, he decides not to change course.

Certainly there is something morally unacceptable about Ludwig's behavior in the first case; but surely his action is even worse in the second. Yet how could there be this moral difference in the status of the two cases[4] if the do/allow distinction were morally irrelevant? After all, all of the other relevant features of the two cases are the same. So it must be that the do/allow distinction *is* of intrinsic moral importance, and what we have just established is that doing harm is morally more significant than merely allowing harm."

Armed with *this* conclusion, the advocate may go on to suggest that negative duties (not to do harm) are more strict than positive duties (to provide aid). Or she might use her conclusion in defense of the claim that an innocent person may not be harmed, even if this is the only way to save several other people from equivalent harms (see Sec. VI below). And so on.

This time it is the critic of the distinction who must try to disarm the contrast argument. But it should be clear that although the two sides may disagree about the use of particular instances of contrast arguments, they share a common belief in the general strategy behind such arguments. Both sides believe that with a properly constructed pair of contrast cases, the moral status of the cases will differ if and only if the do/allow distinction is morally relevant.

II. DIFFICULTIES IN USING CONTRAST ARGUMENTS

Obviously enough, additional contrast arguments concerning doing and allowing can be offered using other pairs of cases. It is equally obvious that contrast arguments can also be constructed (and have been constructed) concerning other disputed factors. It is worth noting, however, that contrast arguments can be used not only to test the relevance of various factors for the moral status of *acts*, but also to test the relevance of factors for *other* categories of moral concern, such as the moral character of the agent, or the moral value of states of affairs. (There is, as it were, more than one dependent variable in ethics.) In principle, a factor which is irrelevant for one category might well be relevant for some other category. For simplicity, however, I will limit our examples to arguments concerning the relevance of factors for the moral status of acts.

It should also be noted that in actual practice, contrast arguments are rarely spelled out as explicitly as in the examples I have given. Indeed, in many cases, we are not actually presented with a pair of contrast cases at all: the argument may simply draw our attention to the overall moral status of a single case with some salient feature; it may then conclude that the given feature has made a difference to the status of that case. Such arguments are apt to be unintelligible unless we assume that there is an implied reference to the missing member of the contrast pair: it is taken to be so obvious that the moral status would differ in the corresponding case in which all other features are held constant except for the given factor, that there is no need to explicitly state this fact.

Contrast arguments, then, are an important and widely used method of tackling questions about the relevance of disputed factors. Both advocates and critics of the factor in question propose appropriate contrast cases, in the shared belief that examination of such cases will indicate whether or not the given factor has genuine moral weight. And since both sides accept the validity of the general strategy behind contrast arguments, each side is troubled by the existence of the contrast cases that appear to support the other side. For example, as already noted, the advocate of the do/allow distinction must do something to impugn the negative argument based on cases *a* and *b*; and the critic of the distinction must do something to undermine the positive argument based on cases *c* and *d*. In such disputes, each side must attempt to disarm the contrast arguments offered by the other side.

There are several different approaches that have been commonly used to argue that—despite initial appearances—a given pair of contrast cases fails to support the desired conclusion concerning the relevance of some factor. This is because although the strategy of contrast arguments is generally accepted, it is not always an easy matter to apply the strategy properly. Here are some of the things that can go wrong:

i) Since contrast arguments are based on the idea that the effect (or lack of effect) of a given factor will be exposed when all other factors are held constant, a pair of contrast cases is useful only if all other things really *are* held constant. If some other factor is varied asymmetrically in the pair of cases (e.g., if the motive is worse in one case than in another), then the differential impact of this other factor may well mask the effect (or lack of effect) of the original factor being tested. (Critics, confronted with positive arguments, may then be able to claim that the difference in the moral status of the two cases is due entirely to the difference in the second factor. Advocates, confronted with negative arguments, may be able to claim that the similar overall moral status of the two cases is the net result of the two genuine factors cancelling out each other's individual effects.) Most criticisms of contrast arguments involve the charge that other things have not been kept equal in the contrast cases, that is, that some relevant factor (other than the one being examined) differs from one case to the other.

One might well wonder whether it is ever possible to apply the strategy adequately, for one might hold that we never *can* keep all the other morally relevant factors constant. (Perhaps differences in the factor we want to test are unavoidably correlated with differences in some other relevant factor.) This is an important worry, but I want to put it aside, noting only that this objection still seems to concede the theoretical validity of the contrast strategy: perhaps we cannot actually keep everything else equal, but if we *could* . . .

ii) Contrast arguments are based on the idea that when all factors are held constant except for the one being examined, if the factor in question is of genuine moral relevance, this will make a difference to the moral status of the contrast cases. Thus a pair of cases will only be of use if the two really do differ in terms of the factor being tested. Obviously, a contrast pair will not reveal anything about the importance of, for example, motive, or consequences, if both cases display the *same* motive, or the same consequences, and so on. Often it will be uncontroversial whether this condition has been satisfied, but not always. For example, a critic of the do/allow distinction might offer a pair of cases that differ only in terms of whether exotic life-support equipment for a terminal patient is turned off or merely allowed to malfunction, arguing that the moral status of these cases is the same. Such a contrast argument might be attacked by a defender of the distinction on the grounds that turning off life-support equipment in such a case is merely allowing the patient to die and is not actually a case of doing harm at all.

Criticisms of this sort may force us to specify, much more exactly than we have previously done, criteria for determining when we have instances of one or the other side of the given distinction (or of specific values of the factor in question, when more than two are possible, as in, e.g., motive). Such specifications may well be controversial, so there will remain room to criticize contrast arguments that rely on them.

iii) Contrast arguments turn on whether a pair of properly constructed cases differ in moral status. Inevitably, however, such arguments can only appeal to our intuitive judgments about the given cases. Since few would hold that our intuitions in such matters are infallibly accurate or completely precise, it is possible to question whether our intuition is sufficiently sensitive to detect moral differences in all cases in which they are present. In some cases, for example, it might be suggested that one or another of the factors that are being held constant is so forceful that the moral status of both cases is extreme—so extreme, in fact, that the remaining difference between the cases is relatively slight in comparison. In such situations, the difference between the cases—although genuine—is lost on our insufficiently sensitive intuitions. Thus both cases may be so horrible, or so wonderful (or even so obviously acceptable) that our failure to notice any difference in the moral status of the cases may not be accepted as sufficient evidence that such a difference is actually lacking. Such a challenge can be met by trying to construct contrast cases where the factors being held constant are "toned down," so that any possible difference resulting from the variation in the factor under examination will stand out better.

Even if the other factors are subdued, so that the impact of the given factor will have a better chance of being detected, it still might be the case that although the factor makes a genuine difference it is such a slight one that our intuition remains insufficiently sensitive to detect it. However, although critics of the given factor must admit that this remains a possibility, even the advocate of the factor will have to concede that if this is indeed the situation then the factor is of negligible importance, and for practical purposes can be overlooked.

iv) Since a contrast argument has persuasive force only for those who share the intuitive moral assessment of the contrast cases, it remains open for someone to reject a given argument on the grounds that he sincerely fails to make the judgments that the argument presupposes. It is in order to avoid such challenges, of course, that those who offer contrast arguments strive to find cases where the intuitive judgments are uncontroversial. Focusing on such uncontroversial cases has two advantages. First, this obviously allows the argument to retain potential persuasive force against some who might otherwise escape it. Second, since the presence of disagreements in intuitive judgments for a particular case calls into question, at the very least, the confidence that we can place in the *accuracy* of our intuition concerning that case, focusing on uncontroversial cases allows the argument to proceed where we have the greatest confidence in our intuitive judgments.

This last point, however, raises a much more radical objection: perhaps for some range of cases we should not trust our intuitions at all. It might be held that our intuitive moral judgments may well be wildly inaccurate (even when there is a consensus), telling us that one act is morally worse than another, when in fact the opposite is the case. Such skepticism about the accuracy of our intuitions might be held because our intuition is thought to be morally corrupt, or because it is thought that there is simply no reason to give our intuitions any particular credence, or for a variety of other reasons. Such worries should, I think, be taken more seriously by all who are not intuitionists, but once again I note the problem only to put it aside: *most* contemporary moral philosophy relies heavily on appeals to moral intuitions, and for better or for worse, contrast arguments are no different in this regard.

These, then, are some of the basic ways that particular contrast arguments have been criticized. Such arguments turn on comparing the moral status of well-constructed contrast cases. As such, they have been attacked on the ground that the cases described are not actually well contructed, whether because the factor under examination does not vary properly between the two cases (ii), or because all other factors are not held constant (i). Similarly, such arguments have been attacked on the ground that our assessment of the contrast cases is impaired, whether because of a lack of sufficient precision in our intuition (iii), or because of a more general lack of dependability and accuracy (iv). I want to emphasize, however, that although all of these criticisms can be used to attack particular contrast arguments, they share a theoretical acceptance of the general strategy behind such arguments: if we *were* to construct an adequate pair of contrast cases, and if we *did* accurately assess the moral status of those cases, then a moral difference in the cases would appear if and only if the given factor were of intrinsic moral relevance.

III. THE UBIQUITY THESIS

The account of contrast arguments I have just given normally lies mostly implicit in our use of such arguments; but I believe most will recognize it as a reasonable portrayal of the thinking that lies behind our common practice. I have spent a fair amount of space developing this account in order to draw attention both to the wide use of such arguments and to their plausibility. Contrast arguments are based on a clear and plausible strategy, and that strategy can be accompanied by a well-articulated set of considerations that must be met if the strategy is to be properly applied.

Nonetheless, I believe that our in-principle acceptance of contrast arguments must be mistaken. Despite its plausibility, the strategy relies on an underlying assumption concerning the role of factors—an assumption that is questionable and should probably be rejected. Yet without this assumption, contrast arguments cannot be used to derive the conclusions we draw from them. (A much more limited use for such arguments may remain; see Sec. VII below.)

The contrast strategy clearly assumes that if a factor has genuine moral relevance, then for *any* pair of cases, where the given factor varies while others are held constant, the cases in that pair will differ in moral status. (The difference, of course, need not be so extreme as to make, e.g., one act permissible and the other act impermissible; the point is simply that *some* difference in moral status

should exist.) That is, putting aside difficulties with proper construction and assessment, in principle *any one pair of cases* should be sufficient to settle the question of whether the given factor is of intrinsic moral relevance. In effect, the contrast strategy must be assuming that if variation in a given factor makes a difference *anywhere*, it makes a difference *everywhere*. Let us call this the *ubiquity thesis*.

Contrast arguments presuppose the ubiquity thesis. Without this assumption, after all, from the mere fact that some particular pair of contrast cases did not differ in moral status, critics of the given factor could not go on to conclude that the factor must lack intrinsic moral significance—for it might well make a difference in other cases, even though it did not make one here. Similarly, without this assumption, from the mere fact that some particular pair of contrast cases *did* differ in moral status, advocates of the given factor could not go on to conclude that the factor must make a difference in other cases where it is present—for it might well fail to do so someplace else even though it did make a difference here. Indeed, recognizing that the contrast argument makes this assumption—that if the factor makes a difference anywhere it must make one everywhere—helps to explain why both critics and advocates are at such pains to disarm the contrast cases offered by the other side: if the assumption is correct, a single well-constructed and properly assessed pair of cases from either side must be decisive.

The ubiquity thesis is in need of some defense. Why must a factor make a difference everywhere if it makes one anywhere? There is a strong temptation to think that this must follow (indeed, follow trivially) from the fact that the fundamental principles of morality are universal,[5] that is, that the basic principles that determine the moral status of an act do not vary from case to case. Admittedly, the applicability of derivative principles may change with the situation, but the underlying principles of morality do not. But this means that the role that a given genuine moral factor plays in determining the moral status of an act must be universal as well: it too cannot vary from case to case. Therefore—or so it seems to follow—if a factor makes a difference *somewhere* it must make a difference *everywhere*.

Despite the seductiveness of this line of thought, I believe it is mistaken. I do find it plausible to think that the universal nature of fundamental moral principles implies that the role a genuine factor plays must be universal as well. But I do not think that we can infer the ubiquity thesis from this. That thesis asserts that if a factor ever makes a difference to the overall moral status of an act, it must always do so. That is, it assets that a particular kind of *effect* must be universal. Obviously, however, the universality of that particular effect will only follow from the universality of the role that the factor plays, if it is part of that role that it have that effect. Once again, it may seem trivial to assert that every effect that a factor has is part of its role (or, at the very least, that this particular effect must be part of its role); but in fact this depends on substantive claims about the roles of genuine moral factors.

An analogy may be helpful here. The presence or absence of oxygen has a role in determining chemical reactions. This role is presumably universal—that is, the fundamental laws of chemistry do not vary from case to case. Yet, obviously enough, the particular effects of oxygen's presence or absence do vary: in some cases, for example, the presence of oxygen makes a difference to whether or not a compound burns; but it would be a mistake to think that it must make this difference in every case. This is because making a difference to whether compounds burn is not, strictly speaking, part of the role of oxygen in the laws of chemistry. Rather, it is a consequence of that role in particular cases. The mere fact that the role of oxygen in the laws of chemistry is universal does not imply that some particular kind of effect must be universal. Similarly, the mere fact that the role of some factor in the fundamental principles of morality must be universal does not automatically imply that some particular effect must be universal. Whether the ubiquity thesis is true depends on taking a substantive position on the role of genuine moral factors.

Talk of the role of moral factors seems to naturally suggest the following general model: the moral status of an act is a function of the various (genuinely relevant) factors that come into play in the given situation. Different moral theories will, of course, hold different views about which factors are of intrinsic moral importance; but whatever the particular list, all theories agree that the overall status of an act in a given situation depends on the values that the genuine factors (whatever they are) have in that situation. This agreement, however, is limited to the view that there is a function of *some* sort connecting the values of the factors to the overall status of the act. Exactly *how* the status of the act is thought to be affected by the factors depends on what *particular* function is accepted by the given moral theory.

Let us call the function (whatever it is) that is taken to determine the overall status of the act on the basis of the values of the factors the *governing function*. In principle, even theories that agree about the list of relevant factors might disagree about what the governing function is like, and thus disagree about how the factors combine and interact in determining the act's overall moral status.

When we say that the role of a given moral factor is universal, we are saying that the governing function remains the same from case to case. That is, the rules governing the interaction of the various moral factors in determining the moral status of an act remain constant.

But this does not yield the ubiquity thesis. Depending on the particular governing function accepted by a theory, it might well be that variation in a given factor would make a difference to the moral status of the act in certain situations, but not in others—because of differences in the interactions of the various moral factors arising from the differences in the values of the *other* factors. Only for particular kinds of governing functions will the ubiquity thesis hold true. What I want to suggest is that those who offer contrast arguments presuppose a particular view of the nature of the governing function.

IV. THE ADDITIVE ASSUMPTION

The view which underlies the use of contrast arguments seems to be this: the function that determines the overall status of the act given the values of the particular factors is an *additive* one. That is, the status of the act is the net balance or sum which is the result of adding up the separate positive and negative effects of the individual factors. On this view, each factor makes a contribution, whether positive or negative, to the moral status of the act. (The strength of the contribution will depend on the particular value of the factor in the given situation, e.g., how *much* good will be done by the act.)

The overall status is the sum of these positive and negative contributions.

In effect, each of the positive factors provides a reason *for* performing the act (the strength of the reason depending on the value of the factor), and each of the negative factors provides a reason for *not* performing the act. The moral status of the act depends on whether the combined weight of the reasons for performing the act is greater or less than the combined weight of the reasons for not performing the act—and by how much.

It is worth stressing that the view that the governing function is additive is more than the mere suggestion that the overall status is the sum of two amounts—that is, the joint positive contribution and the joint negative contribution. Rather, each of these amounts is in turn taken to be the sum of the individual contributions of the individual factors. Each factor makes its own contribution to the status of the act, and the overall status is the sum of these separate contributions.

It is certainly not obvious that the contrast argument assumes that the governing function is additive. Yet I think that something like this assumption must be made for there to be any reason to believe that a well-constructed pair of contrast cases will differ in moral status if and only if the given factor has intrinsic moral relevance.

It is easy to see why one will believe in the ubiquity thesis—and thus in the strategy behind contrast arguments—if one believes that the governing function is additive. For if the overall status of an act is the sum of the separate contributions made by the individual factors, then if one holds all but one of those contributions fixed (by holding all but one of the factors constant) and varies the remaining contribution (by varying the factor under examination), the sum will have to vary as well. The mathematical analogy should make this clear. If $S = x + y + z$, then if we hold x and y constant, but vary z, S will have to vary as well. *Any* genuine difference in z will have to make a difference to S, no matter *what* the values of x and y—provided only that x and y are kept constant. (The same is true, of course, for each of the other variables.) Similarly, then, if the governing moral function is additive, if we hold all but one factor constant, no matter what contributions those particular factors make, varying the remaining factor will have to vary the remaining contribution, and thus will have to make a difference to the sum.

Now for some purported factors, no doubt, variations in the factor will make no difference to the contribution the factor makes. But this is just to say that the factor is not of any genuine moral relevance. Since it will contribute equally to the moral status of all acts, it can just as easily—and less misleadingly—be dropped from consideration altogether. (Consider, e.g., the claim that being performed in time makes a positive contribution to the moral status of the act, a contribution whose size is constant, no matter what the time of performance.) For any genuine factor, variations will affect the contribution, and thus the sum.[6] And as we have just seen, variation will affect the sum no matter what the contributions of the other factors. Thus for a genuine factor, differences in that factor will always make a difference to the overall moral status of the act. But this, of course, is the ubiquity thesis.

Thus the assumption that the governing function is additive—the *additive assumption*—is sufficient to ground the strategy behind contrast arguments. Furthermore, the additive assumption seems plausible in its own right. The model of morally relevant factors making positive and negative contributions to the overall moral status of the act is a familiar and attractive one. As I have noted, the thought that typically there are reasons for and against an act naturally lends itself to the view that the governing function is additive. I suggest, therefore, that those who offer contrast arguments have been tacitly (or explicitly) presupposing the additive assumption.

It should be noted, however, that the ubiquity thesis does not itself entail the additive assumption. That is, there are logically possible governing functions which satisfy the ubiquity thesis although they are not themselves additive. Therefore, commitment to contrast arguments does not itself logically presuppose acceptance of the additive assumption.[7] However, despite this logical possibility, it is difficult to think of any other independently attractive views about the nature of the governing function which reject the additive assumption and yet nonetheless manage to provide plausible reason to believe that the ubiquity thesis will still be satisfied. Therefore I want to stick to my conjecture that contrast arguments are accepted because—and only because—of the belief that the governing function is additive.

I have, however, been somewhat inaccurate in my presentation of the additive assumption. To be more precise, I have smuggled in a second assumption concerning the nature of the governing function. In discussing the implications of the additive assumption, I have done more than assume that the overall status of the act is the sum of the separate contributions of the individual factors. I have also presupposed that the size of a given factor's contribution is determined solely by the value of that factor: variations in the given factor will affect the nature of its contribution; but variations in the *other* factors will *not* affect the contribution made by the factor in question. That is, I have assumed that the size of a factor's contribution is *independent* of everything other than the value of the factor itself.

Strictly speaking, the assumption that the governing function is additive does not entail that the contributions of the individual factors are independent. One might believe that the overall status of an act is the sum of the contributions made by individual factors, while at the same time holding that the size of the contribution of a given factor is determined in part by the values of other factors. Note that with such a view there would be no particular reason to assume that the ubiquity thesis was true, for it might well be the case that although variation in a given factor would make a difference to its contribution in most situations, in *certain* situations (because of the particular configuration of the other factors) such variation might make *no* difference to the contribution, and thus none to the overall sum. It is only by assuming that the contribution a factor makes is independent of the other factors that there is some reason to think that such a possibility is avoided.

It should also be noted that the assumption of independent contributions does not entail the additive assumption. One might hold, for example, that the overall moral status of an act is not the result of adding but rather of *multiplying* some of the separate, independent contributions of the individual factors—perhaps adding the rest. Once again, however, on such a view there would be no

particular reason to assume that the ubiquity thesis was true.

The mathematical analogy should make this clear. If $S = x \cdot y + z$, then although differences in y would normally make a difference to S when x and z are held constant, in those cases where x is equal to zero, differences in y would *not* affect S. Similarly, if the contributions of some of the moral factors are multiplied, then it might well be in certain cases that even variation in a genuine factor would make no difference to the overall moral status of the act. (No doubt it would be somewhat strained to speak of the factor's *contribution* in such a case.) It is only by assuming that the governing function is additive that there is any plausible reason to assume that this possibility is avoided.

Thus it would be more precise to say that those who offer contrast arguments appear to be presupposing both that the governing function is additive and that individual contributions are independent. Despite the logical separability of these two assumptions, however, they combine naturally in the view I have been describing. The very term "contribution" strongly suggests both assumptions. It would seem somewhat strained to speak of the contribution of an individual factor, if in fact that contribution was determined not only by the given factor but by the other factors as well. And as already noted, talk of contributions seems somewhat out of place in contexts which are not additive.

All of this suggests that it might be more accurate to speak of contrast arguments as presupposing "the model of independent, summed contributions"—or perhaps "the contribution assumption." Nonetheless, for purely mnemonic reasons (and possibly idiosyncratic ones, at that) I am going to continue referring to "the additive assumption"—hereafter understanding it to include independence, and not just additiveness per se. My reason is simply that I find this label effective in quickly conjuring up the entire model I have in mind, while other labels are less effective in this regard.

My claim, then, is that one should accept the strategy behind contrast arguments only if one accepts the additive assumption. It is not so much that contrast arguments *could* not be sound if the additive assumption is false, but rather that there is no plausible reason to think that they *are* sound if the additive assumption is false.

V. THE PLAUSIBILITY OF THE ADDITIVE ASSUMPTION

The view that the moral status of an act is the sum of individual positive and negative contributions— the particular reasons for and against performing the act—is, I have suggested, a familiar and attractive one. Nonetheless, I believe that the additive assumption should be rejected. More exactly, I believe that the assumption is a controversial one, likely to be false on most moral theories. To assume the truth of the additive model without defense, therefore, is unacceptable: it begs the question against most plausible theories, and it may well be incompatible with one's own considered views.

One or two examples should be sufficient to show that most theorists will need to reject the additive assumption. Consider, first, the issue of self-defense. Most of us believe that in some situations killing someone in self-defense can be morally permissible. Imagine such a situation, and compare these two cases:

(e) In order to defend myself against the aggressor, I push him into a pit, expecting the fall to kill him;

(f) In order to defend myself against the aggressor, I refrain from warning him about the pit into which he is about to fall, and I expect the fall to kill him.

Most of us will certainly want to claim that the moral status of these two cases is the same, even though, obviously enough, in the first case I do harm, while in the second case I merely allow it. Not everyone will accept this judgment: some may insist that there is a slight difference, but it is lost on our insufficiently sensitive intuitions; others (e.g., pacifists) may claim the difference is rather significant. Nonetheless, most of us will want to maintain that the distinction between doing harm and allowing harm makes *no* difference in such legitimate cases of self-defense. The crucial point to see is that even the *advocate* of the do/allow distinction may well want to make this claim, and surely it is coherent for her to do so. In fact, this view—that although the difference between doing harm and allowing it typically has a great effect on the moral status of an act, in cases of self-defense it makes no difference whatsoever—is

not only coherent: most of us want to claim that it is true.

Yet if the additive assumption is correct, then the view I have just described *must* be false, since it violates the ubiquity thesis to claim that although the do/allow distinction normally makes a difference, in cases of self-defense it does not. Thus, if we make the additive assumption (thereby justifying the ubiquity thesis), this view can be ruled out a priori. Obviously, however, such a move would simply beg the question. On the other hand, if we want at the very least to allow for the possibility of such views—we cannot simply presuppose that the governing function is additive. The example of self-defense suggests that most of us (unwittingly, perhaps) are committed to the rejection of the additive assumption.

It seems a mistake to treat the factor of self-defense as though it made an independent contribution to the overall moral status of the act—a contribution to be added to that made by other factors. A more natural interpretation, one closer to our intuitive understanding of the situation, would be to view the factor of self-defense as acting more like a zero multiplier.

Recall the earlier mathematical example where $S = x \cdot y + z$, and suppose for simplicity that x can equal only zero or one. When x is equal to one, differences in y will make a difference to S; but when x is equal to zero, differences in y will not matter at all. The self-defense/non-self-defense factor seems to act somewhat like x in this example: normally, with a value of one, it allows the do/allow distinction to make a difference; but in cases of self-defense, it takes on the value of zero, and so differences between doing and allowing harm do not affect the moral status of the act at all.

I would not want to put too much weight on this mathematical analogy; I certainly do not think it captures all that we intuitively want to say about the interaction of self-defense and the do/allow distinction. But it clearly comes closer than viewing the governing function in strictly additive terms. It seems reasonable to suspect that intuitively adequate representations of most views in this area would have to stray even further from the additive path. This does not prove, of course, that the correct governing function is nonadditive. But it does, I think, show that most will want to accept this conclusion, and that arguments that presuppose the opposite will tend to beg the question.

A second example suggests that even in some areas where we may initially seem able to give an additive formulation, we may nonetheless require a nonadditive one if we are to capture more of what we want to say. Most of us believe that the alleviation of suffering is a morally relevant factor: the fact that an act will relieve suffering provides a reason for performing that act (although the reason can, of course, be outweighed by other considerations). Thus, when all things are equal, if we can aid only one of two people in pain, there is greater reason to help the one whose suffering is greater. Suppose, however, that all things are not equal, and a second factor comes into play: imagine that the person whose pain is greater—Trixie—is partially responsible for the plight of both, while the other person—Fritz—is not responsible at all. Most of us want to say of such situations that there is somewhat less reason to aid Trixie than there would be were she free from responsibility; and if her responsibility is significant enough, we may judge it better to aid Fritz, even though he is in considerably less pain.

Now we could, I suppose, view this in an additive manner. The magnitude of Trixie's suffering makes an independent, positive contribution to the moral status of aiding her. This is offset by her partial responsibility, which makes an independent negative contribution—that is, provides a reason for not aiding her. The sum of these two contributions may well be less than the corresponding sum for aiding Fritz, where the admittedly smaller positive contribution is not offset by any negative factor.

Such a model may seem plausible so long as we imagine Trixie morally blameless, despite her partial responsibility. The problem is that the additive assumption requires this same model even when Trixie is morally to blame for having performed the act which created the situation. Perhaps, for example, Trixie had attempted to harm Fritz, but her scheme had gone awry, harming them both, and her more significantly. The additive model can point to her guilt as a reason for not helping Trixie, but it is forced to maintain that the magnitude of her suffering provides just as strong a reason to aid her as if she were innocent. Yet many would want to reject exactly this latter claim: the suffering of

the guilty simply does not count as much as the suffering of the innocent.

Obviously, not all will share this judgment; but those who do will find it plausible to reject the additive assumption. It will seem more appropriate to view the factor of innocence/guilt not as making an independent contribution, but rather as a multiplier—this one able to range from one to zero. Fritz is innocent, so the multiplier has the value of one, and his suffering can take on its full potential weight. Trixie is guilty, so the multiplier is less than one, and her suffering counts less. Potentially, with significant enough guilt, the multiplier would be equal to zero, and so one's suffering would not count at all. (A more pronounced version of this view might allow the multiplier to range between positive one and negative one. If the wicked deserve to be unhappy, then the presence of suffering and desert should together sometimes yield a positive contribution.)

Once again, I certainly would not want to claim that this alternative model captures all that we want to say about the interplay of desert and well-being. But it seems a more natural fit than the additive model,[8] and it suggests that those sympathetic to such views should reject the additive assumption.

One possible response to the examples I have given is that they merely show the difficulty of capturing certain moral views in an additive model using the *particular* factors I have described. Some might suggest, in the light of this, that the additive assumption could be preserved in a given case provided that we appeal instead to a different, more adequate list of the morally relevant factors. This possibility should certainly be conceded. Indeed, there is a sense in which it is trivially true.[9] The question, however, is whether one can describe an acceptable list of morally relevant factors that can be incorporated into an additive model across the board: moral views that escape one or two particular examples may fall prey to others. Since each example relies on substantive claims about moral theory, no one example will convince everyone that the additive assumption needs to be rejected. But I hope it is clear that examples such as the two I have given could easily be multiplied.

Reflection on such examples, I believe, should support two conclusions. First, since a great number of moral views are incompatible with the additive assumption, it is unacceptable to criticize such views through the use of arguments that simply presuppose that assumption: to do so merely begs the question. Second, since one's own moral views are likely to be incompatible with the additive assumption, it is dangerous to defend those views through the use of arguments that presuppose that assumption: to do so may render one's position incoherent.

I suspect, in fact, that for most views the additive model is grossly inadequate. It is not merely that the claim that the *entire* governing function is additive is false. Rather, on most views, *most* of the governing function will fail to be additive. For most factors, their role in determining the overall moral status of an act simply cannot be adequately captured in terms of separate and independent contributions that merely need to be added in.

If this is right—if the implausibility of the additive model is so easily seen—the question becomes: what draws us to the additive assumption in the first place? What explains the persistent temptation to assume an additive model? "Persistent temptation" seems exactly the right phrase here. In my own case, at least, I find myself naturally gravitating toward the additive assumption; despite my conscious intention to avoid simply assuming that factors should be treated in an additive fashion, I catch myself unwittingly making just this assumption nonetheless.

Part of the attraction may lie in the fact that the additive assumption seems a natural generalization from a plausible treatment of simple cases. Suppose that a young child is drowning, and I can save him at negligible cost (and there are no other morally relevant features to the case). There is an almost irresistible account of this case, which fairly seems to stare us in the face: the fact that the child can be saved from death provides a *reason* for taking steps to save him—a reason of a certain strength.

Imagine, next, that in order to rescue the child, I would have to tell a lie (e.g., to the owner of the boat). Intuitively, this provides a reason for *not* taking the necessary course of action—a reason of a certain strength. But this does not affect the fact that there is still a reason *for* taking the necessary steps—the fact that it would save the child's life. The correct account seems obvious: there is a

reason for and a reason against, and the permissibility of the act depends upon which reason is stronger. Furthermore, the strength of each individual reason seems independent of the presence or absence of the other reason. The need to lie provides a reason not to perform the act, which may or may not be outweighed on balance; but the strength of that reason in itself does not seem affected by the amount of good that will be done by the lie. Similarly, the reason for taking the boat—that it saves a life—may or may not be outweighed on balance; but it does not seem in itself any weaker than in the original case where it was the only relevant reason.

In short, the additive model suggests itself as the obvious account for the simple case I have just described: the two factors make their own independent contributions, and the status of the act is determined by adding—balancing—these separate contributions. And it is natural to assume that the extra complications caused by bringing in other factors can be handled in the same manner. For example, if the drowning child is *my* child, this seems to give me an extra reason for taking the boat—a reason to be added to the others. And so on.

Thinking about cases like these may tempt us into the general conclusion that the governing function is additive. Especially when the question is never consciously posed, such cases make it easy to tacitly assume that the additive model is correct. But the temptation should be resisted. It may well be that in isolated cases it is illuminating to think of the morally relevant factors as making individual positive or negative contributions to the moral status of the act; but there is no reason to assume that this model has any general applicability. As I have suggested, for most moral theories the interplay of moral factors is simply too complicated to be adequately captured in additive terms.

Yet the additive assumption remains attractive nonetheless. In fact, the very drive to understand moral judgments can pull us toward it. After all, it is hardly philosophically helpful to view such judgments as black boxes, the grounds of which cannot be analyzed. And if we want to understand the moral status of an act, no analytic tool could be more basic than the simple question: what reasons are there to perform the act, and what reasons are there not to perform it? But now the very language of reasons makes it easy to think in additive terms. If there are various reasons for and against an act, then moral judgment is a matter of evaluating and weighing the individual reasons, and balancing them. Indeed, the image of a balance scale immediately suggests itself: each reason falls like a coin with a certain weight into one or the other of the two pans in the scale; the greater the combined weight in a given pan, the more it tips the balance in its own favor. And since each reason must be grounded in some morally relevant feature of the situation, progress in understanding is gained by isolating the particular factor that generates the given individual reason.

Thus we arrive, once again, at the additive assumption. The view is a natural one to hold, and at times it feels almost irresistible. As we have seen, however, the additive model is questionable enough that there is certainly no reason to assume that it is true without argument. Indeed, on many views, there is actually reason to believe that it is false.[10]

VI. TRANSPORT ARGUMENTS

Given the seductiveness of the additive assumption, it is not surprising that most of us rely on it frequently and unwittingly. Once we make the assumption, some extremely attractive forms of argument become available to us. Throughout this paper, I have, of course, stressed the reliance of contrast arguments on the additive assumption. But an even more powerful—and quite common—form of argument relies on this assumption as well. I will call these arguments *transport arguments*.

Most cases are complex enough that, even if we can agree on the list of morally relevant factors, it is difficult to know how to proceed so as to arrive at and defend a judgment concerning the overall moral status of the act in question. But if the additive assumption is correct, a method naturally suggests itself, for we can isolate the individual contributions of particular factors. By constructing simple enough cases, we can isolate particular features and note the strength of the reason that a given feature grounds. We can then "transport" this information back into complex and more controversial cases: observing the presence of the same feature, we can infer that it grounds a reason of the same strength. Coupled with similar knowledge

concerning the other factors in the complex case, we can then justify a judgment about the overall status of the act by summing the individual positive and negative contributions.[11]

Actual applications of this strategy are, of course, subject to various practical difficulties, and this gives room for criticism of particular arguments. But in many cases, it should be noted, even fairly rough assessments of the individual contributions (or merely comparative orderings of their relative strengths) may be enough to support a given judgment.

Provided we are making the additive assumption, the strategy behind such transport arguments seems legitimate. For so long as we view factors as making separate and independent contributions, there is reason to think that when we "transport" a given feature from situation to situation it will continue to ground a reason of the same strength. Recall the image of coins in a balance: each individual coin always makes the same particular contribution, no matter what other coins are in the pans as well.

If the additive assumption is false, however, then the strategy behind transport arguments is illegitimate, for the "contribution" of a factor will not be fixed in this way. For example, if the contribution is dependent not only on the single feature, but on other factors as well, then despite the preservation of the feature considered in isolation, a changed context could easily result in a significantly altered contribution. Similarly, even if the contributions are independent, but are not simply to be summed, then a feature which in one context combines with the other factors so as to ground a reason for performing an act might, in other contexts, combine with the altered factors to ground a reason of a different strength, or even a reason which *opposes* the given act.

Thus, if the additive assumption is false, the sort of argument that straightforwardly combines the results concerning the impact of factors on simple cases into conclusions about more complex cases is called into question. (The same is true, of course, for arguments that transport results from particular complex cases to *different* complex cases.) For such arguments typically turn on attempts to isolate the separate contributions of individual factors, and without the additive assumption such attempts are ill-conceived.

Given the ease with which one can slip into making the additive assumption unwittingly, however, it is often difficult to recognize that a given transport argument is relying on a controversial and potentially question-begging premise. The assumption is rarely articulated, and even when one realizes the need to make it, it is readily agreed to. It may be helpful, therefore, to consider one or two examples carefully.

Do Numbers Matter?

Imagine that I have to choose between saving one innocent person, who will otherwise die, or saving five other innocent people, who will otherwise die. Which group should I save, the one or the five? Assuming there are no other morally relevant factors, almost all of us would say it is better to save the larger group. Given that—unfortunately—I cannot manage to get to both groups in time to save all six, it is better that five should live than one: there is greater reason to save the five than there is to save the one.

Not everyone, however, believes that the numbers matter in this way. Given that someone will be saved no matter which group I choose, these people claim that there is no more reason to save the five than the one.[12] Since it would be improper simply to dismiss this "anti-number" position dogmatically, various arguments have been offered in defense of the more common "pro-number" position.

One argument asks us to consider, first, a simple case where we must decide whether or not to save Claudia (as opposed to doing nothing). Obviously, if all other things are equal, there is a significant reason to save her: this is surely what we mean when we say that morally her life counts for something. Next, consider a different case where we must choose whether to save Albert or to save Bernard, for we cannot manage to save both. Here, if all other things are equal, there is surely no more reason to pick the one than the other: we are faced with a tie. Finally, consider the case where we must choose between saving only Albert, or saving both Bernard and Claudia. Since the choice between Albert and Bernard was a tie, and the opportunity to save Claudia's life counts for *something*, the tie

must now be broken: there is greater reason to save the two than there is to save only the one. (If $X = Y$, and $Z > 0$, then $X + Z > Y$.) Thus the numbers do count after all, and the anti-number position must be mistaken.[13]

For years, I found this argument persuasive. But now it seems clear to me that it simply presupposes the additive assumption, and thus begs the question. Admittedly, the possibility of saving Claudia's life is a morally relevant factor. But it is only by illegitimately making the additive assumption that the argument can infer that this feature makes an independent contribution that can simply be added to the contributions of the other factors, without regard to the changed context.

The advocate of the anti-number position readily admits that the possibility of saving a life—rather than doing nothing—grounds a reason—of a certain strength. But without the additive assumption, little can be inferred from this. For example, it does not follow that the possibility of saving two lives—rather than doing nothing—grounds a reason twice as strong. And even if this latter conclusion were accepted as well, it would not follow that there was more reason to save the two than the one. For without the additive assumption, there are no grounds for assuming that the reason generated by the possibility of saving two lives is as strong when the alternative is not that of merely doing *nothing*, but rather that of doing something of genuine moral *value*, namely, saving the one. Thus even if there is more reason to save two (rather than doing nothing) than to save one (rather than doing nothing), it does not follow that there is more reason to save two rather than saving one.

Since the advocate of the anti-number position denies that the relevance of human lives can be correctly captured in an additive manner, it is obvious that arguments against that position must not simply presuppose the additive model. It is because it is so easy to make the additive assumption without realizing it, that arguments that actually beg the question can be thought persuasive. None of this, of course, shows that the anti-number position is correct. It may well be that the factor of human lives *should* be treated in an additive manner; but it will take a stronger argument to prove this.

Do/Allow Again

For a second example, let us return to the controversy over the importance of the do/allow distinction. Imagine that the only way I can save the lives of Gustav and Emile is by killing Philippa, and suppose, for simplicity, that there are no other morally relevant factors. Despite the fact that my killing Philippa would result in there being two alive rather than only one, most of us would say that it is wrong to kill her. Many would appeal to the moral relevance of the do/allow distinction in defense of this judgment, noting that I face a choice between *doing* harm to Philippa and merely *allowing* harm to Gustav and Emile.

However, even if we grant the relevance of the distinction between doing and allowing harm, it is not obvious exactly how this justifies the prohibition against killing Philippa. To clarify this view, someone defending the prohibition might argue as follows:

"Consider a case in which I can save two lives, by donating $1,000. While it would be meritorious of me to make this sacrifice, I am not morally required to do so. However, since I *would* have to save the two lives if I could do so at negligible costs, presumably the size of the sacrifice is a morally relevant factor; in this case, it evidently grounds a reason for my not making the sacrifice of sufficient strength to counter the reason *for* making it (i.e., that it would save two lives). Now consider the different case in which I can save $1,000 by killing someone. This is clearly impermissible, despite the fact that the same size sacrifice is at stake as in the first case, and there are even fewer lives involved. If killing the one to save $1,000 is forbidden, while allowing two to die rather than spending $1,000 is permitted, this must be because the reason for not killing one is stronger than the reason for not allowing two to die. But this means that if the only way to save the lives of Gustav and Emile is by killing Philippa, there is greater reason to refrain from killing her. For killing Philippa is only supported by the reason for not allowing the other two to die, while refraining is supported by the reason for not killing someone—and we have just seen that the latter reason is stronger than the former reason."

Having worked through the earlier example, it should now be clear that despite the plausibility of this argument, it too relies on the additive assumption. Even if we grant the intuitive assessment of the two initial cases, the conclusion does not follow unless we assume an additive model. First of all, the argument clearly assumes that the overall moral status of each of these cases is the sum of two contributions: on the one hand, a reason in favor of killing/letting die, based on the cost to me of doing otherwise; and on the other hand, a reason which opposes that act, either on the grounds that it is a killing or on the grounds that it is a letting die. Second, it assumes that the strength of the reason based on the cost to me is the same in both cases, presumably on the grounds that the strength of this reason is determined solely by the size of the sacrifice. Without both of these assumptions, there is no reason to infer that the reason for not killing one is stronger than the reason for not allowing two to die. Yet without the additive assumption, there is no particular reason to believe either.

Furthermore, even if we accept the argument's conclusion so far, it still does not follow that there is greater reason not to kill Philippa in our original case. For without the additive assumption, there is no particular justification for assuming that the reason not to kill has the same strength, regardless of whether the reason for killing is merely that it will save $1,000 or that it will save two innocent lives. Thus, even if the reason for not killing some one person (when the only reason for doing so is that it will save $1,000) is stronger than the reason for not allowing two people to die (when the only reason for doing so is that it will save $1,000), it still does not follow that there is greater reason not to kill Philippa when the reason for doing so is that it will save the lives of both Gustav and Emile.

Had the argument under examination been successful, it would have been part of an illuminating account of why there is a prohibition against harming some so as to prevent harm to others. Since it relies on the dubious additive assumption, however, I believe the argument must be rejected—at least in the absence of a defense of that assumption. It is obvious, of course, that the rejection of this argument does not itself prove that the prohibition in question cannot be adequately supported. But still, it does deprive that prohibition of an intuitively plausible and attractive defense.

The two examples we have considered only begin to give one a sense of the variety of transport arguments that can be found. The use of such arguments is extremely widespread in moral philosophy, and the rejection of the underlying strategy calls into question many powerful and plausible arguments. Yet once we have abandoned the additive assumption, I can see no justification for accepting the general strategy behind such arguments. It remains a possibility, of course, that in some individual cases the application of the strategy will not lead to any false conclusions. But obviously enough, in the absence of a justification for the general strategy, arguments that simply rely on that strategy will have to be rejected as unsound.

Once we have recognized the illegitimacy of making the additive assumption, therefore, we can see the need to reconsider numerous arguments that we previously found persuasive. In this paper I have drawn attention to the way in which both contrast arguments and transport arguments rely on this assumption. The use of such arguments, I believe, is quite common. But I suspect that reliance on the additive assumption is even more widespread than this suggests, and that further forms of argument need to be questioned as well. Given the naturalness of making the additive assumption, it should not surprise us to find that it has crept unrecognized into many of the arguments offered in moral philosophy. Nor should it surprise us to find that identifying these arguments will often be difficult: many such arguments, after all, are quite silent about their (tacit) reliance on an assumption to which we readily—albeit illegitimately—agree.

VII. DOING WITHOUT THE ADDITIVE ASSUMPTION

As we have seen, the additive assumption naturally supports a project of trying to identify the separate and independent contributions of individual factors. When we reject the additive assumption, however, there is no particular reason to believe that this project can meet with any general success. At best, one might instead attempt to identify *clusters* of features which together always combine to generate a reason of a particular strength for or against performing an act. On such an alternative

approach, there would be no telling in advance how many factors would be involved in any given cluster (and perhaps in rare cases a "cluster" might actually be composed of a single factor), but once one had identified such a cluster, its contribution could be added to those of the other clusters present in a given case. Admittedly, one would still be weighing and balancing *reasons* on this approach, but a model of this sort would recognize that reasons are not the contributions of individual factors taken in isolation.

Such an approach does get beyond the simplicity of the additive assumption, but it reveals its seductive influence nonetheless. For this view still thinks in terms of separate contributions (of individual clusters, now, rather than individual factors) that are added in determining the overall moral status of the act. Now in some cases it may be possible to separate out individual clusters of factors, each of which makes its own independent contribution. But it should be stressed that, in the absence of an argument, there is no particular reason to assume that even this is possible.

Well, at the very least, can't we assume that the features of a case can be divided into two groups—that is, those which jointly ground reasons *for* performing the act, and those which jointly ground reasons for *not* performing the act? This seems modest enough, but even this can only be agreed to with care. For it may be that the strength of the case for performing the act is not independent of the factors that intuitively make up the case for *not* performing the act, and vice versa. (Put another way: we must not assume that membership in the two groups will be exclusive.) Indeed, in some cases it simply may not be illuminating to attempt to sort the features into groups of positive and negative factors.

I do not know if this last, gloomy possibility is ever actually realized. But I suspect that it is the lingering influence of the additive assumption that creates the mild temptation simply to dismiss it out of hand.

Abandoning the additive assumption obviously does not mean that it will no longer be possible to offer arguments concerning the relevance and particular roles of individual moral factors. But it does, I think, mean that it will be much more difficult to offer satisfactory arguments in this area.

For example, as we have seen, without the additive assumption contrast arguments simply cannot be used to support the general conclusions that are normally derived from them. Nonetheless, even without that assumption, I believe that one may be able to derive certain modest conclusions from arguments of this sort.

Imagine a pair of contrast cases that differ in overall moral status, apparently because of variation in some particular factor. Armed with the additive assumption, an advocate of that factor could have gone on to derive forceful conclusions about the importance of that factor in *other* cases. Having given up the additive assumption, however, those conclusions cannot be so readily demonstrated. Nonetheless, a more modest conclusion does still seem in order. Assuming that the contrast cases are well-constructed and properly assessed, if they differ in moral status it *does* seem to show that the factor in question is of genuine moral relevance. For surely *something* has to account for the difference in status of the two cases, and by hypothesis all other factors have been ruled out.

At this point, however, a pessimistic position suggests itself: even if it is true that a given factor can thus be shown to be morally relevant in some particular case, nothing of any general theoretical importance can be inferred from this. For without the additive assumption, we cannot conclude that the factor will make a similar difference in other cases; we can only conclude that it would do so in exactly similar cases. But this conclusion is so restricted in scope as to be of no use for theoretical purposes.

Such pessimism seems too hasty, however, for a somewhat more moderate conclusion may be possible. Even without the additive assumption, a demonstration that a factor does make a difference in one case may still create a *presumption* that it does so in other cases as well. After all, if the factor has a particular effect in one case, there will have to be some *reason* why it does not have the same effect in other cases. This shifts the burden of proof: those who wish to deny that the factor has the given effect in some particular case must point to an attending difference in some second feature (or group of features) and offer a plausible account of how that second feature interacts with the given factor so as to alter its effects. Similarly, if a factor is

shown to make no difference to a particular pair of contrast cases, one cannot infer that it makes no difference anyplace at all. But such a demonstration does create a presumption against that factor: those who claim that it does matter elsewhere will need to point to some second feature and offer a plausible account of why it affects the impact of the original factor.[14]

It would be equally mistaken, however, to replace our hasty pessimism with a hasty optimism. To believe that the additive assumption should be rejected is to believe that factors frequently do interact in such a way as to alter the particular effects of a given factor from case to case. Thus we should expect that it will be quite common for the presumptions I have just described to be appropriately overridden. But this means that we will have to enter into the detailed discussions of the roles of particular factors after all. There is no shortcut.

What we are forced to do is to start producing plausible theories of the interactions of the various morally relevant factors. And if such theories are not to be ad hoc, presumably they will have to be based on theoretical accounts of what makes the individual factors relevant in the first place. Mere examination of cases is not likely to be of much help in the production of such accounts.

Ultimately, then, the rejection of the additive assumption will force us to put less emphasis on the intuitive assessment of cases, and more emphasis on the construction of fundamental moral theory. But this, I believe, is all to the good.[15]

Notes

[1]I take it that if all values of a given factor have the same moral importance, then the factor is of no genuine moral relevance. (For example, skin color is morally irrelevant, for differences in skin color make no moral difference.) On the other hand, for a factor of genuine moral relevance, it will be important to distinguish between the relevantly different values of the factor. The *distinctions* that make up a classificatory scheme for a given factor are morally relevant if and only if they compartmentalize the values of that factor into groups whose differences are morally relevant.

[2]Some prominent and explicit examples of this sort of argument include: Michael Tooley, "Abortion and Infanticide," *Philosophy and Public Affairs* 2 (1972): 37–65, at pp. 58–60; Richard Trammell, "Saving Life and Taking Life," p. 116, and "Tooley's Moral Symmetry Principle,"

Philosophy and Public Affairs 5 (1976): 305–13; James Rachels, "Active and Passive Euthanasia," p. 111; Peter Singer, *Practical Ethics* (Cambridge: Cambridge University Press, 1979), pp. 149–52 (cf. pp. 162–68 and 195–97); and Jonathan Bennett, "Morality and Consequences," in *The Tanner Lectures on Human Values*, vol. 2, ed. Sterling McMurrin (Cambridge: Cambridge University Press, 1981), pp. 45–116, at pp. 72–95. Bennett is by far the fullest presentation.

[3]For some factors it will be important to distinguish several values: there may be, e.g., many relevantly different types of motive. For other factors, however, it may simply be a question of whether a certain feature is present or absent: e.g., do we have a case of causing harm, or don't we? In the latter situation, it will often be a matter of terminological convenience to speak of an always-present factor with two possible values (e.g., culpability, with the possible values of guilt or innocence), rather than of a one-valued factor (e.g., guilt) that may be either present or absent. It is also worth noting that in some cases we might treat a factor as having two values (e.g., guilt/innocence), while recognizing that in other cases a more fine-grained approach to the same factor may be appropriate (e.g., distinguishing between different levels of guilt).

[4]To be exact, of course, the question is not whether the cases themselves differ in moral status but, rather, whether the acts of the agents described in the particular cases differ in moral status. For simplicity of exposition, however, I will frequently use the imprecise formulation.

[5]Bennett is one of the few who explicitly recognizes that the contrast argument assumes the ubiquity thesis. He suggests that the assumption follows from the universal nature of basic reasons (pp. 73–74; cf. p. 92). Unfortunately, Bennett does little to explain this suggestion, but it may be that he is making what I will go on to call the "additive assumption."

[6]There might also be cases where variations in a genuine factor did not actually result in a variation in the contribution that the factor makes. But this would be tantamount to showing that the variation under consideration was morally irrelevant. (One might believe, e.g., that doing harm is worse than merely allowing it, and nonetheless hold that certain differences in how harm is done—e.g., with a gun or with a knife—are of no moral relevance.) To be precise, no doubt, one should speak of morally relevant variations in morally relevant factors, but for obvious reasons I have avoided this cumbersome locution.

[7]The ubiquity thesis actually assumes that for each genuine factor, whenever all other factors are kept constant, the governing function will be equal to a function of the given factor which is one-to-one. That is, with the values of other factors fixed, no two (relevantly different) values of the given factor will be mapped onto (i.e., determine) the same overall moral status. The assumption that the governing function is "one-to-one" in this way is weaker than the additive assumption. It is also worth noting in this regard that mere satisfaction of the ubiquity thesis does not itself guarantee that a given value of the factor will always make a contribution of the same size (nor even that the direction of the contribution will be constant—i.e., always positive or always negative). Contrast arguments do not require these stronger conditions, although many believe that they are satisfied as well. (See the discussion of transport arguments in Sec. VI; and cf. n. 11 below.) My thanks go to Peter Vallentyne and Ken Manders for discussion of these matters.

[8]This alternative model gives up the belief that contributions of the individual factors must be summed, but it continues to view those contributions as separate and independent. It might be suggested that it would be more natural still to give up the independence condition. One could avoid the need to talk of multiplying the separate contributions of the two factors, by holding that there is a single contribution here—that of the suffering—but that the nature of this contribution is not independent of the factor of desert. It is not altogether clear to me what turns on this disagreement, but what is important for our purposes is that this model, too, would entail rejecting the additive assumption.

[9]Provided that one is willing to accept unnatural and ad hoc factors, there will always be a way to save the additive assumption. After all, one could insist that there is only *one* genuine factor: the complete specification of the given act's place in the history of the world. The additive assumption would hold trivially on this view: the contribution made by this global factor would satisfy independence (for there are no other factors on which to be dependent); and the overall status of the act would be the "sum" of this single contribution. The interesting question is whether there is a satisfying way to specify factors below the global level and still maintain the additive assumption. For most views, I doubt it.

[10]G. E. Moore's defense, in *Principia Ethica*, of an organic theory of the good can be seen as a rejection of the additive assumption in a particular area of value theory. Indeed, my entire discussion of the additive assumption can be viewed, with hindsight, as a generalization of Moore's point to all of ethics, together with an application of this generalization to areas where its relevance has not been recognized. Something similar to the additive assumption has also been criticized by Michael Philips, in an article published after I had completed this essay ("Weighing Moral Reasons," *Mind* 96 [1987]: 367–76).

[11]Contrast arguments, it will be recalled, assume that if a given factor makes a difference somewhere, it will make a difference everywhere; but they do not necessarily

assume that it will make the *same* difference everywhere (see n. 7 above). Transport arguments, however, clearly make this bolder assumption as well. Obviously, if the bolder assumption is true, the more modest one will also be true.

[12]This position has been defended by John M. Taurek, "Should the Numbers Count?" p. 214; and, I believe, by G. E. M. Anscombe, "Who Is Wronged?" *Oxford Review,* vol. 5 (1967).

[13]I learned this argument from T. M. Scanlon (who, however, does not endorse it). More complicated versions of the argument can be found in Jonathan Glover, *Causing Death and Saving Lives* (New York: Penguin, 1977), pp. 207-9, and in Gregory S. Kavka, "The Numbers Should Count," p. 236; but I believe that both of these make mistakes similar to the ones I discuss below. Both Glover and Kavka offer additional arguments against the anti-number position, as does Derek Parfit in "Innumerate Ethics," p. 227.

[14]It might be suggested, however, that there is an important asymmetry in the power of positive and negative contrast arguments. For a successful positive argument can establish that the factor in question is of genuine moral relevance, and must appear in the governing function (even if the factor will not have a noticeable effect anywhere else). A negative argument, on the other hand, cannot establish that the given factor is *not* of genuine moral relevance and does *not* appear in the governing function—for the factor might still make a difference someplace else. I believe, however, that this apparent asymmetry is not a deep one. A positive argument tells us that variation in a particular factor makes a difference in a specific context. A negative argument tells us that variation in a particular factor makes *no* difference in a specific context. The information gained is symmetrical. I suspect that the appearance of asymmetry is actually an artifact of our preference for having our theories stated only in terms of what is of moral *relevance*, rather than what is of moral *irrelevance*.

[15]I owe a debt to Dan Brock, who offered the original contrast argument that set me wondering what was wrong with them.

In Defense of the Contrast Strategy

HEIDI MALM ▪ Loyola University of Chicago
Unpublished

In this paper, Malm responds to Kagan's "The Additive Fallacy." She focuses on the strategy of examining pairs of cases which are designed to examine one particular moral distinction. Such cases involve a division into constant and variable factors. In both cases the constant factors are the same, while the variable factor, representing the moral distinction being tested, is different. Such cases care called contrast cases and the strategy employing such cases is referred to as the **contrast strategy**.

Kagan argues that confidence in the contrast strategy is unjustified. The premises of the argument are: (1) that the strategy presupposes the ubiquity thesis (that if a variation in a factor makes a difference anywhere, it makes a difference everywhere); (2) that the ubiquity thesis presupposes the additive assumption (that a moral act is the sum of positive and negative factors involved in the act); and (3) that the additive assumption is false.

Malm defends the contrast strategy by arguing that the first premise is false. There are three parts to her argument: she maintains that Kagan's analysis of the strategy focuses on a particular type of moral claim that she believes is false; she believes that Kagan has erred by failing to characterize sufficiently the idea of **morally significant**; and she argues that if Kagan's third premise is true, then the first one must be false.

She begins her argument by pointing out that Kagan, by linking the contrast strategy to the ubiquity thesis, has erroneously limited the contrast strategy to "always-or-never" claims. Malm believes that Kagan must think that advocates of a contrast argument are trying to establish always-or-never claims, which would require the ubiquity thesis.

Against Kagan, Malm asserts that there are legitimate uses of the contrast strategy that do not aim to establish an always-or-never claim. First, *negative* uses of the contrast strategy to *refute* particular moral claims do not presuppose the ubiquity thesis; no inferences are being made to the moral status of acts in other pairs of cases. Second, contrast arguments can be used to *support* an always-or-never claim. An appropriate contrast can be evidence that the claim is correct, without regarding it as conclusive. Third, contrast arguments can be used to *establish* a morally significant difference between X and Y, without the aid of the ubiquity thesis. Malm suggests that Kagan fails to see this point because of the way he understands the notion of "morally significant."

According to Malm, Kagan's notion of "morally significant" involves the idea that "the difference between X and Y is morally significant if and only if the fact that act A has the property 'is an instance of X' and act B has the property 'is an instance of Y' *will* effect (as opposed to *can* effect) a difference in the moral status of A and B when other things are equal." Malm calls the entailments of this account the **"maximal entailments** of a moral significance claim." She claims this account has the following problems. First, the claim that there is a significant difference entails only that there is at least one pair of cases in which the difference makes a moral difference. Second, our intuitive judgments do not support maximal entailments. The judgments we make indicate that the status of acts differ in some cases and not in others. Third, the notion of *effecting* may be too strong. It seems possible that a given distinction is morally significant without that distinction being the *cause* of the difference in the status of the acts.

Since Kagan's account of "morally significant" does not seem to be adequate, Malm thinks it best to begin with a minimal definition: to say that the difference between X and Y is morally significant is to say, minimally, that "the fact that a given act has the property 'is an instance of X' rather than the property 'is an instance of Y' is *relevant* to determining the moral status of the act." Malm suggests that the difference in properties can be relevant without it always manifesting its relevance as a difference in moral status. If so, we can deny the maximal entailments and establish a morally significant difference between X and Y without the aid of the ubiquity thesis.

THE TYPICAL WAY TO TEST THE MORAL SIGNIFIcance of non-moral distinctions is to examine pairs of cases that differ only in that regard. For example, to test the significance of the killing-letting die distinction, we examine pairs of cases that differ only in that one case involves an act of killing, while the other case involves an act of letting die. If our considered moral judgments about the two cases tell us that they differ in moral status, then we have evidence that the killing-letting die distinction is morally significant. If they tell us that the cases do not differ in moral status, we have evidence that the distinction is not significant.

Let us call the matched pairs of cases *contrast cases*, and call the arguments that employ them in conjunction with our considered moral judgments *contrast arguments*. Let us also call the general strategy of using contrast cases and arguments to reach conclusions about the moral significance of various distinctions the *contrast strategy*. Shelly Kagan argues that while the contrast strategy is widely used, our confidence in it is unjustified.[1] His argument has three main premises. (1) The contrast strategy presupposes the *ubiquity thesis*—the view that "if a variation in a given factor makes a difference anywhere, it makes a difference everywhere."[2] (2) The ubiquity thesis presupposes the *additive assumption*—the view that the moral status of a given act is the *sum* of the contributions made by the various wrong-or-right making properties of the act.[3] And (3) the additive assumption is false. Thus if each of his premises is correct, we have little reason to trust the conclusions we draw via the contrast strategy.

My aim is to defend the contrast strategy against Kagan's argument. To do this I will concede the truth of premises 2 and 3 and argue that premise 1 is false. In more detail, I will argue that (a) Kagan has addressed the contrast strategy only as it is used to establish a particular sort of moral claim (a sort of claim which, I might add, we have good reason to believe is false), (b) he has failed to adequately characterize the notion of "morally significant"—yet that is the central notion in the claims that the contrast strategy is designed to test; and (c) if the third premise of Kagan's argument is correct, the first premise is false.

Let us focus, as does Kagan, on distinctions that concern act-types (e.g., killing and letting die, acting and refraining), and on the moral status of particular acts, as opposed to the moral status of agents. In order to provide a means for testing the moral significance of a given distinction the contrast strategy presupposes, at the very least, the following three claims. Suppose that X and Y are act-types.

(1)   If the difference between X and Y is morally significant, then there will be at least one pair of cases that differ only in that act A has the

property "is an instance of X" and act B has the property "is an instance of Y" and A and B differ in moral status.

This claim is entailed by the meaning of "morally significant," at least as that notion applies to distinction between act-types. I will have more to say about it later.

(2)   If there is at least one pair of cases that differ only in that act A has the property "is an instance of X" and act B has the property "is an instance of Y," and A and B differ in moral status, then the distinction between X and Y is morally significant.

This claim needs to be granted as an assumption of the contrast strategy. Though it is logically possible, I suppose, for the antecedent to be true and the conclusion false, it is difficult to see how this could be the case—especially if we grant that a difference in the moral status of two acts must be attributable to some difference in the properties of those acts.

(3)   Our considered moral judgments about particular cases (at least the judgments on which we rely), are correct.

This claim also needs to be granted as an assumption of the contrast strategy. If we reject it, then we reject many forms of moral argumentation along with the contrast strategy.

Let us refer to the above set of claims as the *minimal assumption* of the contrast strategy. It is this assumption that allows us to use our considered moral judgments about particular cases as *evidence* that a given distinction is, or is not, significant.

Kagan, however, maintains that the contrast strategy assumes more than the minimal assumption.

> *The contrast strategy clearly assumes that if a factor [distinction] has genuine moral relevance then for any pair of cases, where the given factor varies while others are held constant, the cases in that pair will differ in moral status. . . . In effect, the contrast strategy is assuming that if variation in a given factor makes a difference anywhere, it makes a difference everywhere. Let us call this the* ubiquity thesis.[4]

Before explaining *why* Kagan thinks that the contrast strategy presupposes the ubiquity thesis, it will be helpful to explain what the addition of this thesis entails. Consider the distinction between killing and letting die. Without the ubiquity thesis, if we find one pair of cases in which other things are equal and the acts of killing and letting die differ in moral status, we can infer only that the killing-letting die distinction is morally significant (via claim 2 of the minimal assumption). With the addition of the ubiquity thesis, we can also infer that acts of killing and letting die will differ in moral status in every pair of cases in which other things are equal. Similarly, with the ubiquity thesis in hand, if we find one pair of cases in which the acts of killing and letting die do *not* differ in moral status (other things equal), we can infer that they never do (other things equal). In short, the ubiquity thesis allows us to derive what I will call *always-or-never* claims from our considered moral judgments about individual pairs of cases. Always-or-never claims assert either that there always is, or that there never is, a difference in the moral status of the particular acts when other things are equal. (These claims are to be distinguished from claims about the moral significance of a given distinction in that the latter concern the distinction itself while the former concern the moral status of particular acts that differ with respect to the distinction when other things are equal.)[5]

The fact that the ubiquity thesis allows us to derive always-or-never claims from judgments about individual pairs of cases, exposes two grounds for holding it suspect. First, were the ubiquity thesis correct, it would exclude from consideration the logical possibility that a morally significant distinction only sometimes gives rise to a difference in the moral status of the acts when other things are equal. Second, were the ubiquity thesis correct, we could derive claims that we have reason to believe are false, from judgments we presume to be true. The judgments we take as evidence about, for example, the killing-letting die distinction or the doing-allowing distinction, indicate that there are some pairs of cases in which the acts differ in moral status (other things equal), and other pairs of cases in which they do not (other things equal).[6] Thus if these judgments are correct then the always-or-never claims are not.

Yet Kagan maintains that the ubiquity thesis is an important part of the contrast strategy. He writes:

Contrast arguments presuppose the ubiquity thesis. Without this assumption, after all, from the mere

fact that some particular pair of contrast cases did not differ in moral status, critics of the given factor could not go on to conclude that the factor must lack intrinsic moral significance—for it might well make a difference in other cases even though it did not make one here. Similarly, without this assumption, from the mere fact that some particular pair of contrast cases did differ in moral status, advocates of the given factor [emphasis added] could not go on to conclude that the factor must make a difference in other cases where it is present—for it might well fail to do so someplace even though it did make a difference here.[7]

This passage exposes two related assumptions. First, Kagan is assuming that "advocates" of a given distinction *need* (or at least want) to "go on to conclude" that the acts will differ in moral status whenever other things are equal. Only then would they need the ubiquity thesis. The motivation for this assumption seems to be Kagan's understanding of "morally significant." I will return to it later.

Second, and more generally, Kagan is assuming that the *goal* of a contrast argument is to establish an always-or-never claim. Achieving that goal would require the ubiquity thesis.[8] But clearly there are uses of the contrast strategy that lack that goal, and I will discuss some in a moment. Further, the conclusions Kagan draws seem directed against the contrast strategy itself—the general method of using contrast cases and arguments to "tackle questions about the moral relevance of disputed factors"—not merely against the use of that strategy to establish a particular sort of moral claim.[9] For example, after arguing that the contrast strategy presupposes the ubiquity thesis, and in turn the (false) additive assumption, he writes:

My claim, then, is that one should accept the strategy behind contrast arguments only if one accepts the additive assumption. . . . Since a great number of moral views are incompatible with the additive assumption it is unacceptable to criticize such views through the use of arguments that simply presuppose that assumption. . . . Once we have recognized the illegitimacy of making the additive assumption, therefore, we can see the need to reconsider numerous arguments that we previously found persuasive.[10]

To see that there are legitimate uses of the contrast strategy that do not aim to establish an always-or-never claim (and thus neither presuppose the ubiquity thesis nor the additive assumption) consider, first, *negative* uses of the contrast strategy—the use of contrast arguments to *refute* particular moral claims. In particular, consider any always-or-never claim. Since such a claim entails either that there always is, or that there never is a difference in the moral status of the particular acts when other things are equal, it can be refuted by showing that there is one pair of cases in which there is not a difference, or is a difference, in the moral status of the acts (other things equal). But these negative uses do not presuppose the ubiquity thesis because no inferences are being made to the moral status of acts in other pairs of cases.

Second, contrast arguments can be used to *support* an always-or-never claim. An advocate of a given claim may offer an appropriate contrast case as *evidence* that her claim is correct, without intending that evidence to be regarded as conclusive. She may hope that further investigation will uncover more evidence in support of her claim, and none against it, and thereby leave us *prima facie* justified in accepting that claim. Of course, the fact that this rarely seems to happen with respect to the distinctions that are typically tested with the contrast strategy, may lead us to discount this use of the strategy. But it is a use that does not presuppose the ubiquity thesis nonetheless.

Third, and most importantly, contrast arguments *can be used* to establish a morally significant difference between X and Y, without the aid of the ubiquity thesis. To develop this point I need to discuss the notion of "morally significant," as it applies to a distinction between act-types.

Though he does not explicitly tell us what he means by "morally significant," Kagan seems to be working with the following account: the difference between X and Y is morally significant if and only if the fact that act A has the property "is an instance of X" and act B has the property "is an instance of Y," will effect (as opposed to can effect) a difference in the moral status of A and B when other things are equal. (I will refer to the entailments of this account as the *maximal entailments* of a moral significance claim.) He writes, for example, that the "general strategy behind contrast arguments" assumes that "a moral difference in the cases would appear *if and only if* the given factor were of intrinsic moral relevance," and that "contrast arguments are based on the idea

that . . . if the factor in question is of genuine moral relevance, this *will* make a difference to the moral status of the contrast cases" (emphasis added).[11] Further, this definition accords with Kagan's focus on always-or-never claims, as well as his assumption that an "advocate" of a given distinction needs to be able to show that the particular acts will differ in moral status whenever other things are equal.

Yet there are a number of problems with this definition. First, the logic of the matter does not commit us to the maximal entailments. Since the claim that there is *not* a significant difference between X and Y entails that there are *no* cases in which other things are equal and the acts differ in moral status, the claim that there is a significant difference entails only that there is at least one. Second, our intuitive judgments do not support the maximal entailments. As I discussed in connection with the ubiquity thesis (and have argued in detail elsewhere),[12] the judgments we make with respect to many distinctions indicate that there are some pairs of cases in which the acts differ in moral status, and other pairs of cases in which they do not (other things equal).[13] Third, the notion of *effecting* a difference may be too strong. It seems possible that a given distinction can be morally significant without that distinction being *the cause* of the difference in the moral status of the acts. Finally, if this is how we define "morally significant," then advocates of a given distinction need the ubiquity thesis only if claim 2 of the minimal assumption is false. Yet that claim is at least as plausible, if not more so, as the ubiquity thesis.

In the absence of an argument defending the definition that Kagan appears to employ, it seems best to begin with a minimal definition. As I see it, to say that the difference between X and Y is morally significant is to say, minimally, the following: the fact that a given act has the property "is an instance of X" rather than the property "is an instance of Y" is *relevant* to determining the moral status of the act. "Relevant" is vague, but not unacceptably so, since it is possible that there are different types of significance. The important question is whether the difference in properties can be relevant without it always manifesting its relevance as a difference in moral status. If it can, then we can deny the maximal entailments and establish a morally significant difference between X and Y without the aid of the ubiquity thesis.

Consider the properties "performed in society S" and "performed in society T" and suppose that moral relativism is correct. (I will drop this assumption and return to traditional distinctions in a moment.) Now consider a given act, say, an act of eating meat on Friday. If the moral code of S prohibits the eating of meat on Fridays, while the moral code of T does not, then the difference between the properties is clearly morally relevant: the status of the act changes when we substitute the one property for the other. But this does not entail that the status of any act must change when we substitute the one property for the other. It may be the case that the moral codes of S and T both prohibit some types of acts and both permit others. Still, whether an act has one property or the other is relevant to determining the moral status of the act because it tells us which moral code to consult.[14] The difference between the properties "performed in society S" and "performed in society T" would be morally irrelevant only if we know that the moral codes of S and T are identical.

Returning to the traditional distinctions, can the fact that a given act has the property "is an instance of killing," for example, rather than the property "is an instance of letting die" be relevant to determining the moral status of the act without it being the case that a change in those properties always results in a change in moral status? The above discussion suggests that it can. To explain this point further I need to introduce two models of moral evaluation.

The first model will be called the *rulebook* model of evaluation. It presupposes that for each prima facie wrong act-type there is a corresponding rule-book that lists the grounds and circumstances under which acts of that type are permissible. The rule-books are, in other words, a complete statement of the general prohibition regarding that act-type (e.g., "Do not kill except in circumstances Q, R, or S"). To assert on this model that the difference between X and Y is morally significant is to assert that the rule-books for X and Y are not identical: one permits acts of its type in circumstances and (or) on grounds that the other does not. Thus whether an act has the property "is an instance of X" or the property "is an instance of Y" is relevant to determining the moral status of the act because it tells us which rule-book to consult. But since the rule-books may overlap in some places, the assertion of a

morally significant difference between X and Y does not commit us to the maximal entailments.

The second model, which I will call the *numerical model of evaluation,* is the one in which Kagan's argument seems to function. On this model, the moral status of a given act is a function of the contributions made by the various wrong-or-right making properties of the act. For example, while the property "resulted in a major harm" might contribute a −20 to the assessment of the act, the property "resulted in a minor harm" might contribute a −5. To assert on this model that the difference between X and Y is morally significant is to assert that the numerical value given to the property "is an instance of X" is different from the numerical value given to the property "is an instance Y" (e.g., "is an instance of killing" may contribute a −10 to the status of the act, while "is an instance of letting die" may contribute a −8).

By itself, even the numerical model of evaluation does not commit us to the maximal entailments of a moral significance claim. We encounter that problem only if we add the following two conditions: (1) the value of the contribution made by any given property is not altered by the presence or absence of any other property,[15] and (2) the values of the various contributions are to be added (rather than multiplied or another more complex function). Yet these two conditions are the conditions of Kagan's additive assumption—an assumption which he argues (and I agree) is false.[16]

Thus we are committed to the maximal entailments of a moral significance claim only if the additive assumption is correct. And thus if the additive assumption is false, then we can establish a morally significant difference between X and Y without the aid of the ubiquity thesis: one pair of cases in which the acts differ in moral status is enough. In short, if the third premise of Kagan's arguments is true, the first premise is false.

Notes

[1]Shelly Kagan, "The Additive Fallacy," p. 252.
[2]op. cit.
[3]Kagan does not speak of wrong- or right-making properties, but instead, of reasons for or against the act. These are equivalent for our purposes.
[4]op. cit. Kagan uses the terms "moral relevance," "moral significance," and "intrinsic moral significance" interchangeably. Also, though this statement of the ubiquity thesis is vague, because the notion of "making a

difference" is vague, the first part of the quoted passage shows that Kagan intends "making a difference" to mean making a difference to the moral status of the acts.

[5]A claim that a given distinction is *not* significant entails an always-or-never claim (*i.e.*, that there is never a difference in the moral status of the acts). It is an open question, however, whether a claim that a given distinction is significant entails an always-or-never claim. The answer depends on how we define "morally significant."

[6]For example, acts of killing and letting die seem to differ in status when the victim is innocent and the means for *not* killing or letting die would have resulted in a serious harm to the agent. The risk of harm to the agent permits, it seems, the failure to prevent an even greater harm to an innocent other but not the causing of an even greater harm. On the other hand, acts of killing and letting die seem equal in status when the victim is not innocent (*i.e.*, both acts are done in self-defense), and when the means of not killing or letting die would require only minimal effort or risk on the part of the agent.

[7]op. cit.

[8]However, we may not need to *add* the ubiquity thesis to the minimal assumption. If our definition of "morally significant" entails that there will always be a difference in the status of the acts (other things equal), then that definition, together with claim 2 of the minimal assumption, entails the ubiquity thesis. The main point is that if the goal of the contrast strategy is to establish an always-or-never claim, then that strategy needs it to be the case that the ubiquity thesis is correct.

[9]op. cit. Kagan's initial discussion is also focused on the contrast strategy itself.

[10]op. cit.

[11]op. cit.

[12]References omitted for blind reviewing. Philippa Foot makes this point, at least indirectly, when she defends the moral significance of the difference between killing and letting die while denying that there will always be a difference in the moral status of the acts when other things are equal. Foot, "Euthanasia," *Philosophy & Public Affairs* vol. 6, no. 2, 1977.

[13]Interestingly enough, Kagan uses our judgments about multiple pairs of contrast cases (see note 5) to show that the additive assumption is false. Thus if he is correct in maintaining that contrast arguments presuppose the ubiquity thesis and that the ubiquity thesis presupposes the additive assumption, then his method for showing that the additive assumption is false presupposes that the additive assumption is true.

[14]It may be tempting to say that the difference is not relevant in these cases, but that seems to put the cart before the horse. It entails that we can know whether a given property is relevant to determining the moral status of the act only after we know what that status is.

[15]In other words, if the property "is an instance of killing" has a value of -10, then it always contributes a -10. The presence of another property, say, "being done for personal gain" or "being done in self-defense" would contribute its own value, and would not alter the contribution of "is an instance of killing."

[16]Kagan's argument against the additive assumption seems to be directed more against the first condition than the second.

Part VII

THE TROLLEY PROBLEM REVISITED

The Trolley Problem

JUDITH JARVIS THOMSON · Massachusetts Institute of Technology
The Yale Law Journal, 1985

Thomson begins by reminding us of Philippa Foot's version of the Trolley Problem (see Foot, p. 59). In Trolley Driver it *is* permissible for the driver of a runaway trolley to divert the trolley and thereby kill an innocent person in order to save five people. In Transplant it *is not* permissible for a surgeon to kill an innocent visitor in order to save five patients each of whom needs a transplant to live. What explains the difference between these cases?

To answer this question, Foot appeals to the claim that killing is worse than letting die. According to this view, the surgeon may not kill the visitor; he must let the five patients die. By contrast, the trolley driver has a choice, not between killing and letting die, but between killing one person or killing five. Since killing five is worse than killing one, the driver may shunt the trolley away from the five people.

Thomson disagrees with this solution. To illustrate the difficulty with Foot's position, she introduces a new scenario, Bystander 1 (see Introduction). Bystander 1 is the same as Trolley Driver with the exception that the active agent is not the trolley driver but is instead an innocent bystander who is walking by the trolley tracks. Thomson thinks that it is still permissible for the agent to intervene so that the trolley kills the one instead of the five. Thus Thomson believes it is permissible for the bystander to kill the one rather than letting the five die. If this is so, Foot's proposal is inadequate.

In the course of discussing Foot's proposal, Thomson points out certain ambiguities in the claim, "Killing five is worse than killing one." She fixes upon the following as the appropriate interpretation: "(II′) If a person is faced with a choice between doing something *here and now* to five, by the doing of which he will kill them, and doing something else *here and now* to one, by the doing of which he will kill only the one, then (other things being equal) he ought to choose the second alternative rather than the first."

Thomson attempts to find a difference between the Bystander 1 and Transplant cases first by employing the Kantian argument that people should be treated as ends and never only as means. It appears, with this criterion, that in Transplant the one person is being treated as a means—it is through the loss of his life that the others are saved. This is not true of Bystander 1. This important difference between the two cases is explained thus: saving the five in Transplant requires the death of the one, but saving the five in Bystander 1 does not. If the one went out of existence right before the bystander pulled the switch, then the five would still be saved. The exact opposite is true of the Transplant case, where there is a direct relation between the one and the five. However, Thomson considers the loop variant of Bystander 1, Bystander 3. In this case, there is a bit of track that connects the spur and the main track; thus, but for the existence of the one, the shunted train would continue around the loop and run over the five. In this case, killing the one is a means to saving the five, and yet the case seems morally equivalent to Bystander 1.

Ultimately Thomson finds two important differences between Bystander 1 and Transplant. First, the bystander saves the five by making something that threatens them threaten the one instead. Second, the bystander does this without infringing a stringent right of the one.

So in Transplant it is impermissible to save the five: the surgeon would be introducing a new threat and also violating **stringent rights.** In contrast, in Bystander 1 the agent redirects an extant threat, and his means of doing so (shunting the train) does not in itself violate any stringent right.

Thomson next considers Fat Man (see Introduction). Thomson points out that an important difference between this case and Bystander 1 is that the agent in Fat Man actually violates a stringent right in the means he uses to make the threat threaten one rather than five. Pushing the fat man (the means of making the threat threaten fewer) infringes a stringent right of his, whereas the action of switching the trolley onto the other track in itself does not infringe anyone's rights.

What if the agent in Fat Man wobbles a hand rail causing the fat man to fall off the bridge, rather than directly pushing him off the bridge? Whereas it might seem that such an action is the equivalent of the agent throwing the switch in Bystander 1, Thomson points out that there is a significant difference in the means by which the five are saved in the two cases. In the new Fat Man case, saving the five requires that the fat man's body actually hit the trolley. In Bystander 1 all that is required is that the switch is thrown, not that the person is actually hit. Just getting the trolley on the side track does not necessarily constitute an infringement of rights.

I.

SOME YEARS AGO, PHILIPPA FOOT DREW ATTENTION to an extraordinarily interesting problem.[1] Suppose you are the driver of a trolley. The trolley rounds a bend, and there come into view ahead five track workmen, who have been repairing the track. The track goes through a bit of a valley at that point, and the sides are steep, so you must stop the trolley if you are to avoid running the five men down. You step on the brakes, but alas they don't work. Now you suddenly see a spur of track leading off to the right. You can turn the trolley onto it, and thus save the five men on the straight track ahead. Unfortunately, Mrs. Foot has arranged that there is one track workman on that spur of track. He can no more get off the track in time than the five can, so you will kill him if you turn the trolley onto

him. Is it morally permissible for you to turn the trolley?

Everybody to whom I have put this hypothetical case says, Yes, it is.[2] Some people say something stronger than that it is morally *permissible* for you to turn the trolley: They say that morally speaking, you *must* turn it—that morality requires you to do so. Others do not agree that morality requires you to turn the trolley, and even feel a certain discomfort at the idea of turning it. But everybody says that it is true, at a minimum, that you *may* turn it—that it would not be morally wrong in you [sic] to do so.

Now consider a second hypothetical case. This time you are to imagine yourself to be a surgeon, a truly great surgeon. Among other things you do, you transplant organs, and you are such a great surgeon that the organs you transplant always take. At the moment you have five patients who need organs. Two need one lung each, two need a kidney each, and the fifth needs a heart. If they do not get those organs today, they will all die; if you find organs for them today, you can transplant the organs and they will all live. But where to find the lungs, the kidneys, and the heart? The time is almost up when a report is brought to you that a young man who has just come into your clinic for his yearly check-up has exactly the right blood-type, and is in excellent health. Lo, you have a possible donor. All you need do is cut him up and distribute *his* parts among the five who need them. You ask, but he says, "Sorry. I deeply sympathize, but no." Would it be morally permissible for you to operate anyway? Everybody to whom I have put this second hypothetical case says, No, it would not be morally permissible for you to proceed.

Here then is Mrs. Foot's problem: *Why* is it that the trolley driver may turn his trolley, though the surgeon may not remove the young man's lungs, kidneys, and heart?[3] In both cases, one will die if the agent acts, but five will live who would otherwise die—a net saving of four lives. What difference in the other facts of these cases explains the moral difference between them? I fancy that the theorists of tort and criminal law will find this problem as interesting as the moral theorist does.

II.

Mrs. Foot's own solution to the problem she drew attention to is simple, straightforward, and very attractive. She would say: Look, the surgeon's choice is between operating, in which case he kills one, and not operating, in which case he lets five die; and killing is surely worse than letting die[4]—indeed, so much worse that we can even say

(I) Killing one is worse than letting five die.

So the surgeon must refrain from operating. By contrast, the trolley driver's choice is between turning the trolley, in which case he kills one, and not turning the trolley, in which case he does not *let five die*, he positively *kills* them. Now surely we can say

(II) Killing five is worse than killing one.

But then that is why the trolley driver may turn his trolley: He would be doing what is worse if he fails to turn it, since if he fails to turn it he kills five.

I do think that that is an attractive account of the matter. It seems to me that if the surgeon fails to operate, he does not kill his five patients who need parts; he merely lets them die. By contrast, if the driver fails to turn his trolley, he does not merely let the five track workmen die; he drives his trolley into them, and thereby kills them.

But there is good reason to think that this problem is not so easily solved as that.

Let us begin by looking at a case that is in some ways like Mrs. Foot's story of the trolley driver. I will call her case *Trolley Driver*; let us now consider a case I will call *Bystander at the Switch*. In that case you have been strolling by the trolley track, and you can see the situation at a glance: The driver saw the five on the track ahead, he stamped on the brakes, the brakes failed, so he fainted. What to do? Well, here is the switch, which you can throw, thereby turning the trolley yourself. Of course you will kill one if you do. But I should think you may turn it all the same.[5]

Some people may feel a difference between these two cases. In the first place, the trolley driver is, after all, captain of the trolley. He is charged by the trolley company with responsibility for the safety of his passengers and anyone else who might be harmed by the trolley he drives. The bystander at the switch, on the other hand, is a private person who just happens to be there.

Second, the driver would be driving a trolley into the five if he does not turn it, and the bystander would not—the bystander will do the five no harm at all if he does not throw the switch.

I think it right to feel these differences between the cases.

Nevertheless, my own feeling is that an ordinary person, a mere bystander, may intervene in such a case. If you see something, a trolley, a boulder, an avalanche, heading towards five, and you can deflect it onto one, it really does seem that—other things being equal—it would be permissible for you to *take* charge, *take* responsibility, and deflect the thing, whoever you may be. Of course you run a moral risk if you do, for it might be that, unbeknownst to you, other things are not equal. It might be, that is, that there is some relevant difference between the five on the one hand, and the one on the other, which would make it morally preferable that the five be hit by the trolley than that the one be hit by it. That would be so if, for example, the five are not track workmen at all, but Mafia members in workmen's clothing, and they have tied the one workman to the right-hand track in the hope that you would turn the trolley onto him. I won't canvass all the many kinds of possibilities, for in fact the moral risk is the same whether you are the trolley driver, or a bystander at the switch.

Moreover, second, we might well wish to ask ourselves what exactly is the difference between what the driver would be doing if he failed to turn the trolley and what the bystander would be doing if he failed to throw the switch. As I said, the driver would be driving a trolley into the five; but what exactly would his driving the trolley into the five consist in? Why, just sitting there, doing nothing! If the driver does just sit there, doing nothing, then that will have been how come he drove his trolley into the five.

I do not mean to make much of that fact about what the driver's driving his trolley into the five would consist in, for it seems to me to be right to say that if he does not turn the trolley, he does drive his trolley into them, and does thereby kill them. (Though this does seem to me to be right, it is not easy to say exactly what makes it so.) By contrast, if the bystander does not throw the switch, he drives no trolley into anybody, and he kills nobody.

But as I said, my own feeling is that the bystander *may* intervene. Perhaps it will seem to some even less clear that morality requires him to turn the trolley than that morality requires the driver to turn the trolley; perhaps some will feel even more discomfort at the idea of the bystander's turning the trolley than at the idea of the driver's turning the trolley. All the same, I shall take it that he *may*.

If he may, there is serious trouble for Mrs. Foot's thesis (I). It is plain that if the bystander throws the switch, he causes the trolley to hit the one, and thus he kills the one. It is equally plain that if the bystander does not throw the switch, he does not cause the trolley to hit the five, he does not kill the five, he merely fails to save them—he lets them die. His choice therefore is between throwing the switch, in which case he kills one, and not throwing the switch, in which case he lets five

die. If thesis (I) were true, it would follow that the bystander may not throw the switch, and that I am taking to be false.

III.

I have been arguing that

(I) Killing one is worse than letting five die

is false, and a fortiori that it cannot be appealed to to explain why the surgeon may not operate in the case I shall call *Transplant*.

I think it pays to take note of something interesting which comes out when we pay close attention to

(II) Killing five is worse than killing one.

For let us ask ourselves how we would feel about *Transplant* if we made a certain addition to it. In telling you that story, I did not tell you why the surgeon's patients are in need of parts. Let us imagine that the history of their ailments is as follows. The surgeon was badly overworked last fall—some of his assistants in the clinic were out sick, and the surgeon had to take over their duties dispensing drugs. While feeling particularly tired one day, he became careless, and made the terrible mistake of dispensing chemical X to five of the day's patients. Now chemical X works differently in different people. In some it causes lung failure, in others kidney failure, in others heart failure. So these five patients who now need parts need them because of the surgeon's carelessness. Indeed, if he does not get them the parts they need, so that they die, he will have killed them. Does that make a moral difference? That is, does the fact that he will have killed the five if he does nothing make it permissible for him to cut the young man up and distribute his parts to the five who need them?

We could imagine it to have been worse. Suppose what had happened was this: The surgeon was badly overextended last fall, he had known he was named a beneficiary in his five patients' wills, and it swept over him one day to give them chemical X to kill them. Now he repents, and would save them if he could. If he does not save them, he will positively have murdered them. Does *that* fact make it permissible for him to cut the young man up and distribute his parts to the five who need them?

I should think plainly not. The surgeon must not operate on the young man. If he can find no other way of saving his five patients, he will now have to let them die—despite the fact that if he now lets them die, he will have killed them.

We tend to forget that some killings themselves include lettings die and do include them where the act by which the agent kills takes time to cause death—time in which the agent can intervene but does not.

In face of these possibilities, the question arises what we should think of thesis (II), since it *looks* as if it tells us that the surgeon ought to operate, and thus that he may permissibly do so, since if he operates he kills only one instead of five.

There are two ways in which we can go here. First, we can say: (II) does tell us that the surgeon ought to operate, and that shows it is false. Second, we can say: (II) does not tell us that the surgeon ought to operate, and it is true.

For my own part, I prefer the second. If Alfred kills five and Bert kills only one, then questions of motive apart, and other things being equal, what Alfred did *is* worse than what Bert did. If the surgeon does not operate, so that he kills five, then it will later be true that he did something worse than he would have done if he had operated, killing only one—especially if his killing of the five was murder, committed out of a desire for money, and his killing of the one would have been, though misguided and wrongful, nevertheless a well-intentioned effort to save five lives. Taking this line would, of course, require saying that assessments of which acts are worse than which other acts do not by themselves settle the question what it is permissible for an agent to do.

But it might be said that we ought to by-pass (II), for perhaps what Mrs. Foot would have offered us as an explanation of why the driver may turn the trolley in *Trolley Driver* is not (II) itself, but something more complex, such as

(II') If a person is faced with a choice between doing something *here and now* to five, by the doing of which he will kill them, and doing something else *here and now* to one, by the doing of which he will kill only the one, then (other things being equal) he ought to choose the second alternative rather than the first.

We may presumably take (II') to tell us that the driver ought to, and hence permissibly may, turn the trolley in *Trolley Driver*, for we may presumably view the driver as confronted with a choice between here and now driving his trolley into five, and here and now driving his trolley into one. And at the same time, (II') tells us nothing at all about what the surgeon ought to do in *Transplant*, for he is not confronted with such a choice. If the surgeon operates, he does do something by the doing of which he will kill only one; but if the surgeon does not operate, he does not do something by the doing of which he kills five; he merely fails to do something by the doing of which he would make it be the case that he has not killed five.

I have no objection to this shift in attention from (II) to (II'). But we should not overlook an interesting question that lurks here. As it might be put: *Why* should the present tense matter so much? Why should a person prefer killing one to killing five if the alternatives are wholly in front of him, but not (or anyway, not in every case) where one of them is partly behind him? I shall come back to this question briefly later.

Meanwhile, however, even if (II') can be appealed to in order to explain why the trolley driver may turn his trolley, that would leave it entirely open why the bystander at the switch may turn *his* trolley. For he does not drive a trolley into each of five if he refrains from turning the trolley; he merely lets the trolley drive into each of them.

So I suggest we set *Trolley Driver* aside for the time being. What I shall be concerned with is a first cousin of Mrs. Foot's problem, viz.: Why is it that the bystander may turn his trolley, though the surgeon may not remove the young man's lungs, kidneys, and heart? Since *I* find it particularly puzzling that the bystander may turn his trolley, I am inclined to call this The Trolley Problem. Those who find it particularly puzzling that the surgeon may not operate are cordially invited to call it The Transplant Problem instead.

IV.

It should be clear, I think, that "kill" and "let die" are too blunt to be useful tools for the solving of this problem. We ought to be looking within killings and savings for the ways in which the agents would be carrying them out.

It would be no surprise, I think, if a Kantian idea occurred to us at this point. Kant said: "Act so that you treat humanity, whether in your own person or in that of another, always as an end and never as a means only." It is striking, after all, that the surgeon who proceeds in *Transplant* treats the young man he cuts up "as a means only": He literally uses the young man's body to save his five, and does so without the young man's consent. And perhaps we may say that the agent in *Bystander at the Switch* does not use his victim to save his five, or (more generally) treat his victim as a means only, and that that is why he (unlike the surgeon) may proceed.

But what exactly is it to treat a person as a means only, or to use a person? And why exactly is it wrong to do this? These questions do not have obvious answers.[6]

Suppose an agent is confronted with a choice between doing nothing, in which case five die, or engaging in a certain course of action, in which case the five live, but one dies. Then perhaps we can say: If the agent chooses to engage in the course of action, then he uses the one to save the five only if, had the one gone out of existence just before the agent started, the agent would have been unable to save the five. That is true of the surgeon in *Transplant*. He needs the young man if he is to save his five; if the young man goes wholly out of existence just before the surgeon starts to operate, then the surgeon cannot save his five. By contrast, the agent in *Bystander at the Switch* does not need the one track workman on the right-hand track if he is to save his five; if the one track workman goes wholly out of existence before the bystander starts to turn the trolley, then the bystander *can* all the same save his five. So here anyway is a striking difference between the cases.

It does seem to me right to think that solving this problem requires attending to the means by which the agent would be saving his five if he proceeded. But I am inclined to think that this is an overly simple way of taking account of the agent's means.

One reason for thinking so[7] comes out as follows. You have been thinking of the tracks in *Bystander at the Switch* as not merely diverging, but continuing to diverge, as in the following picture:

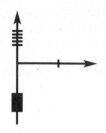

Consider now what I shall call "the loop variant" on this case, in which the tracks do not continue to diverge—they circle back, as in the following picture:

Let us now imagine that the five on the straight track are thin, but thick enough so that although all five will be killed if the trolley goes straight, the bodies of the five will stop it, and it will therefore not reach the one. On the other hand, the one on the right-hand track is fat, so fat that his body will by itself stop the trolley, and the trolley will therefore not reach the five. May the agent turn the trolley? Some people feel more discomfort at the idea of turning the trolley in the loop variant than in the original *Bystander at the Switch*. But we cannot really suppose that the presence or absence of that extra bit of track makes a major moral difference as to what an agent may do in these cases, and it really does seem right to think (despite the discomfort) that the agent may proceed.

On the other hand, we should notice that the agent here needs the one (fat) track workman on the right-hand track if he is to save his five. If the one goes wholly out of existence just before the agent starts to turn the trolley, then the agent cannot save his five[8]—just as the surgeon in *Transplant* cannot save his five if the young man goes wholly out of existence just before the surgeon starts to operate.

Indeed, I should think that there is no plausible account of what is involved in, or what is necessary for, the application of the notions "treating a person as a means only," or "using one to save five," under which the surgeon would be doing this whereas the agent in this variant of *Bystander at the Switch* would not be. If that is right, then appeals to these notions cannot do the work being required of them here.

V.

Suppose the bystander at the switch proceeds: He throws the switch thereby turning the trolley onto the right-hand track, thereby causing the one to be hit by the trolley, thereby killing him—but saving the five on the straight track. There are two facts about what he does which seem to me to explain the moral difference between what he does and what the agent in *Transplant* would be doing if *he* proceeded. In the first place, the bystander saves his five by making something that threatens them instead threaten one. Second, the bystander does not do that by means which themselves constitute an infringement of any right of the one's.

As is plain, then, my hypothesis as to the source of the moral difference between the cases makes appeal to the concept of a right. My own feeling is that solving this problem requires making appeal to that concept—or to some other concept that does the same kind of work.[9] Indeed, I think it is one of the many reasons why this problem is of such interest to moral theory that it does force us to appeal to that concept; and by the same token, that we learn something from it about that concept.

Let us begin with an idea, held by many friends of rights, which Ronald Dworkin expressed crisply in a metaphor from bridge: Rights "trump" utilities.[10] That is, if one would infringe a right in or by acting, then it is not sufficient justification for acting that one would thereby maximize utility. It seems to me that something like this must be correct.

Consideration of this idea suggests the possibility of a very simple solution to the problem. That is, it might be said (i) The reason why the surgeon may not proceed in *Transplant* is that if he proceeds, he maximizes utility, for he brings about

a net saving of four lives, but in so doing he would infringe a right of the young man's.

Which right? Well, we might say: The right the young man has against the surgeon that the surgeon not kill him—thus a right in the cluster of rights that the young man has in having a right to life.

Solving this problem requires being able to explain also why the bystander may proceed in *Bystander at the Switch*. So it might be said: (ii) The reason why the bystander may proceed is that if he proceeds, he maximizes utility, for he brings about a net saving of four lives, and in so doing he does *not* infringe any right of the one track workman's.

But I see no way—certainly there is no easy way—of establishing that these ideas are true.

Is it clear that the bystander would infringe no right of the one track workman's if he turned the trolley? Suppose there weren't anybody on the straight track, and the bystander turned the trolley onto the right-hand track, thereby killing the one, but not saving anybody, since nobody was at risk, and thus nobody needed saving. Wouldn't that infringe a right of the one workman's, a right in the cluster of rights that he has in having a right to life?

So should we suppose that the fact that there are five track workmen on the straight track who are in need of saving makes the one lack that right—which he would have had if that had not been a fact?

But then why doesn't the fact that the surgeon has five patients who are in need of saving make the young man also lack that right?

I think some people would say there is good (excellent, conclusive) reason for thinking that the one track workman lacks the right (given there are five on the straight track) lying in the fact that (given there are five on the straight track) it is morally permissible to turn the trolley onto him. But if your reason for thinking the one lacks the right is that it is permissible to turn the trolley onto him, then you can hardly go on to explain its being permissible to turn the trolley onto him by appeal to the fact that he lacks the right. It pays to stress this point: If you want to say, as (ii) does, that the bystander may proceed because he maximizes utility and infringes no right, then you need an independent account of what makes it be the case that he infringes no right—independent, that is, of its being the case that he may proceed.

There is *some* room for maneuver here. Any plausible theory of rights must make room for the possibility of waiving a right, and within that category, for the possibility of failing to have a right by virtue of assumption of risk; and it might be argued that that is what is involved here, i.e., that track workmen know of the risks of the job, and consent to run them when signing on for it.

But that is not really an attractive way of dealing with this difficulty. Track workmen certainly do not explicitly consent to being run down with trolleys when doing so will save five who are on some other track—certainly they are not asked to consent to this at the time of signing on for the job. And I doubt that they consciously assume the risk of it at that or any other time. And in any case, what if the six people involved had not been track workmen? What if they had been young children? What if they had been people who had been shoved out of helicopters? Wouldn't it all the same be permissible to turn the trolley?

So it is not clear what (independent) reason could be given for thinking that the bystander will infringe no right of the one's if he throws the switch.

I think, moreover, that there is *some* reason to think that the bystander will infringe a right of the one if he throws the switch, even though it is permissible for him to do so. What I have in mind issues simply from the fact that if the bystander throws the switch, then he does what will kill the one. Suppose the bystander proceeds, and that the one is now dead. The bystander's motives were, of course, excellent—he acted with a view to saving five. But the one did not volunteer his life so that the five might live; the bystander volunteered it for him. The bystander made him pay with his life for the bystander's saving of the five. This consideration seems to me to lend some weight to the idea that the bystander did do him a wrong—a wrong it was morally permissible to do him, since five were saved, but a wrong *to him* all the same.

Consider again that lingering feeling of discomfort (which, as I said, some people do feel) about what the bystander does if he turns the trolley. No doubt it is permissible to turn the trolley, but still . . . but still . . . . People who feel this discomfort also think that, although it is permissible to turn the trolley, it is not morally required to do so. My own view is that they are right to feel and think these things. We would be able to explain why this is so if we supposed that if the bystander turns the trolley, then he does do the one track workman a wrong—if we supposed, in particular, that he infringes a right of the one track workman's which is in that cluster of rights which the workman has in having a right to life.[11]

I do not for a moment take myself to have established that (ii) is false. I have wished only to draw attention to the difficulty that lies ahead of a person who thinks (ii) true, and also to suggest that there is some reason to think that the bystander would infringe a right of the one's if he proceeded, and thus some reason to think that (ii) is false. It can easily be seen that if there is some reason to think the bystander would infringe a right of the one's, then there is also some reason to think that (i) is false—since if the bystander does infringe a right of the one's if he proceeds, and may nevertheless proceed, then it cannot be the fact that the surgeon infringes a right of the young man's if *he* proceeds which makes it impermissible for *him* to do so.

Perhaps a friend of (i) and (ii) can establish that they are true. I propose that, just in case he can't, we do well to see if there isn't some other way of solving this problem than by appeal to them. In particular, I propose we grant that both the bystander and the surgeon would infringe a right of their ones, a right in the cluster of rights that the ones have in having a right to life, and that we look for some *other* difference between the cases which could be appealed to to explain the moral difference between them.

Notice that accepting this proposal does not commit us to rejecting the idea expressed in that crisp metaphor of Dworkin's. We can still say that rights trump utilities—if we can find a further feature of what the bystander does if he turns the trolley (beyond the fact that he maximizes utility) which itself trumps the right, and thus makes it permissible to proceed.

VI.

As I said, my own feeling is that the trolley problem can be solved only by appeal to the concept of a right—but not by appeal to it in as simple a way as that discussed in the preceding section. What we were attending to in the preceding section was only the fact that the agents would be killing and saving if they proceeded; what we should be attending to is the means by which they would kill and save.[12] (It is very tempting, because so much simpler, to regard a human act as a solid nugget, without internal structure, and to try to trace its moral value to the shape of its surface, as it were. The trolley problem seems to me to bring home that that will not do.)

I said earlier that there seem to me to be two crucial facts about what the bystander does if he proceeds in *Bystander at the Switch*. In the first place, he saves his five by making something that threatens them instead threaten the one. And second, he does not do that by means which themselves constitute infringements of any right of the one's.

Let us begin with the first.

If the surgeon proceeds in *Transplant*, he plainly does not save his five by making something that threatens them instead threaten one. It is organ-failure that threatens his five, and it is not *that* which he makes threaten the young man if he proceeds.

Consider another of Mrs. Foot's cases, which I shall call *Hospital*.

> Suppose [Mrs. Foot says] that there are five patients in a hospital whose lives could be saved by the manufacture of a certain gas, but that this will inevitably release lethal fumes into the room of another patient whom for some reason we are unable to move.[13]

Surely it would not be permissible for us to manufacture the gas.

In *Transplant* and *Hospital*, the five at risk are at risk from their ailments, and this might be thought to make a difference. Let us by-pass it. In a variant on *Hospital* —which I shall call *Hospital'* — all six patients are convalescing. The five at risk are at risk, not from their ailments, but from the ceiling of their room, which is about to fall on them. We can prevent this by pumping on a ceiling-support-mechanism; but doing so will inevitably release lethal fumes into the room of the sixth. Here too it is plain we may not proceed.

Contrast a case in which lethal fumes are being released by the heating system in the basement of a building next door to the hospital. They are headed towards the room of five. We can deflect them towards the room of one. Would that be permissible? I should think it would be—the case seems to be in all relevant respects like *Bystander at the Switch*.

In *Bystander at the Switch*, something threatens five, and if the agent proceeds, he saves the five by making that very thing threaten the one instead of the five. That is not true of the agents in *Hospital'* or *Hospital* or *Transplant*. In *Hospital'*, for example, what threatens the five is the ceiling, and the agent does not save them by making *it* threaten the one, he saves them by doing what will make something wholly different (some lethal fumes) threaten the one.

Why is this difference morally important? Other things being equal, to kill a man is to infringe his right to life, and we are therefore morally barred from killing. It is not enough to justify killing a person that if we do so, five others will be saved: To say that if we do so, five others will be saved is merely to say that utility will be maximized if we proceed, and that is not by itself sufficient to justify proceeding. Rights trump utilities. So if that is all that can be said in defense of killing a person, then killing that person is not permissible.

But that five others will be saved is not all that can be said in defense of killing in *Bystander at the Switch*. The bystander who proceeds does not merely minimize the number of deaths which get caused. He minimizes the number of deaths which get caused by something that already threatens people, and that will cause deaths whatever the bystander does.

The bystander who proceeds does not make something be a threat to people which would otherwise not be a threat to anyone; he makes be a threat to fewer what is already a threat to more. We might speak here of a "distributive exemption," which permits arranging that something that will do harm anyway shall be better distributed than it otherwise would be—shall (in *Bystander at the Switch*) do harm to fewer rather than more. Not just any distributive intervention is permissible: It is not in general morally open to us to make one die to save five. But other things being equal, it is not morally required of us that we let a burden descend out of the blue onto five when we can make it instead descend onto one.

I do not find it clear why there should be an exemption for, and only for, making a burden which is descending onto five descend, instead, onto one. That there is seems to me very plausible, however. On the one hand, the agent who acts under this exemption makes be a threat to one something that is *already* a threat to more, and thus something that will do harm *whatever* he does; on the other hand, the exemption seems to allow those acts which intuition tells us are clearly permissible, and to rule out those acts which intuition tells us are clearly impermissible.

VII.

More precisely, it is not morally required of us that we let a burden descend out of the blue onto five when we can make it instead descend onto one *if* we can make it descend onto the one by means which do not themselves constitute infringements of rights of the one.

Consider a case—which I shall call *Fat Man*—in which you are standing on a footbridge over the trolley track. You can see a trolley hurtling down the track, out of control. You turn around to see where the trolley is headed, and there are five workmen on the track where it exits from under the footbridge. What to do? Being an expert on trolleys, you know of one certain way to stop an out-of-control trolley: Drop a really heavy weight in its path. But where to find one? It just so happens that standing next to you on the footbridge is a fat man, a really fat man. He is leaning over the railing, watching the trolley; all you have to do is to give him a little shove, and over the railing he will go, onto the track in the path of the trolley. Would it be permissible for you to do this? Everybody to whom I have put this case says it would not be. But why?

Suppose the agent proceeds. He shoves the fat man, thereby toppling him off the footbridge into the path of the trolley, thereby causing him to be hit by the trolley, thereby killing him—but saving the five on the straight track. Then it is true of this agent, as it is true of the agent in *Bystander at the Switch*, that he saves his five by making something which threatens them instead threaten one.

But *this* agent does so by means which themselves constitute an infringement of a right of the one's. For shoving a person is infringing a right of his. So also is toppling a person off a footbridge.

I should stress that doing these things is infringing a person's rights even if doing them does not cause his death—even if doing them causes him no harm at all. As I shall put it, shoving a person, toppling a person off a footbridge, are *themselves* infringements of rights of his. A theory of rights ought to give an account of what makes it be the case that doing either of these things is itself an infringement of a right of his. But I think we may take it to be a datum that it is, the job which confronts the theorist of rights being, not to establish that it is, but rather to explain why it is.

Consider by contrast the agent in *Bystander at the Switch*. He too, if he proceeds, saves five by making something that threatens them instead threaten one. But the means he takes to make that be the case are these: Turn the trolley onto the right-hand track. And turning the trolley onto the right-hand track is not *itself* an infringement of a right of anybody's. The agent would do the one no wrong at all if he turned the trolley onto the right-hand track, and by some miracle the trolley did not hit him.

We might of course have imagined it not necessary to shove the fat man. We might have imagined that all you need do to get the trolley to threaten him instead of the five is to wobble the handrail, for the handrail is low, and he is leaning on it, and wobbling it will cause him to fall over and off. Wobbling the handrail would be impermissible, I should think—no less so than shoving. But then there is room for an objection to the idea that the contrast I point to will help explain the moral differences among these cases. For it might be said that if you wobble the handrail, thereby getting the trolley to threaten the one instead of the five, then the means you take to get this to be the case are just these: Wobble the handrail. But doing that is not *itself* an infringement of a right of anybody's. You would do the fat man no wrong at all if you wobbled the handrail and no harm came to him in consequence of your doing so. In this respect, then, your situation seems to be exactly like that of the agent in *Bystander at the Switch*. Just as the means he would be taking to make the trolley threaten one instead of five would not constitute an infringement of a right, so also would the means you would be taking to make the trolley threaten one instead of five not constitute an infringement of a right.

What I had in mind, however, is a rather tighter notion of "means" than shows itself in this objection. By hypothesis, wobbling the handrail will cause the fat man to topple onto the track in the path of the trolley, and thus will cause the trolley to threaten him instead of the five. But the trolley will not threaten him instead of the five unless wobbling the handrail does cause him to topple. Getting the trolley to threaten the fat man instead of the five *requires* getting him into its path. You get the trolley to threaten him instead of them by wobbling the handrail only if, and only because, by wobbling the handrail you topple him into the path of the trolley.

What I had in mind, then, is a notion of "means" which comes out as follows. Suppose you get a trolley to threaten one instead of five by wobbling a handrail. The means you take to get the trolley to threaten the one instead of the five include wobbling the handrail, *and* all those further things that you have to succeed in doing by wobbling the handrail if the trolley is to threaten the one instead of the five.

So the means by which the agent in *Fat Man* gets the trolley to threaten one instead of five include toppling the fat man off the footbridge; and doing that is itself an infringement of a right of the fat man's. By contrast, the means by which the agent in *Bystander at the Switch* gets the trolley to threaten one instead of five include no more than getting the trolley off the straight track onto the right-hand track; and doing that is not itself an infringement of a right of anybody's.

VIII.

It is arguable, however, that what is relevant is not that toppling the fat man off the footbridge is itself an infringement of *a* right of the fat man's but rather that toppling him off the footbridge is itself an infringement of a particularly stringent right of his.

What I have in mind comes out in yet another variant on *Bystander at the Switch*. Here the bystander must cross (without permission) a patch of land that belongs to the one in order to get to the switch; thus in order to get the trolley to threaten

the one instead of five, the bystander must infringe a right of the one's. May he proceed?

Or again, in order to get the switch thrown, the bystander must use a sharply pointed tool, and the only available sharply pointed tool is a nailfile that belongs to the one; here too the bystander must infringe a right of the one's in order to get the trolley to threaten the one instead of five. May he proceed?

For my own part, I do not find it obvious that he may. (Remember what the bystander will be doing to the one by throwing that switch.) But others tell me they think it clear the bystander may proceed in such a case. If they are right—and I guess we should agree that they are—then that must surely be because the rights which the bystander would have to infringe here are minor, trivial, non-stringent—property rights of no great importance. By contrast, the right to not be toppled off a footbridge onto a trolley track is on any view a stringent right. We shall therefore have to recognize that what is at work in these cases is a matter of degree: If the agent must infringe a stringent right of the one's in order to get something that threatens five to threaten the one (as in *Fat Man*), then he may not proceed, whereas if the agent need infringe no right of the one's (as in *Bystander at the Switch*), or only a more or less trivial right of the one's (as in these variants on *Bystander at the Switch*), in order to get something that threatens five to threaten the one, then he may proceed.

Where what is at work is a matter of degree, it should be no surprise that there are borderline cases, on which people disagree. I confess to having been greatly surprised, however, at the fact of disagreement on the following variant on *Bystander at the Switch*:

> The five on the straight track are regular track workmen. The right-hand track is a dead end, unused in ten years. The Mayor, representing the City, has set out picnic tables on it, and invited the convalescents at the nearby City Hospital to have their meals there, guaranteeing them that no trolleys will ever, for any reason, be turned onto that track. The one on the right-hand track is a convalescent having his lunch there; it would never have occurred to him to do so if the Mayor had not issued his invitation and guarantee. The Mayor was out for a walk; he now stands by the switch.[14]

For the Mayor to get the trolley to threaten the one instead of the five, he must turn the trolley onto the right-hand track; but the one has a right against the Mayor that he not turn the trolley onto the right-hand track—a right generated by an official promise, which was then relied on by the one. (Contrast the original *Bystander at the Switch*, in which the one had no such right.) My own feeling is that it is plain the Mayor may not proceed. To my great surprise, I find that some people think he may. I conclude they think the right less stringent than I do.

In any case, that distributive exemption that I spoke of earlier is very conservative. It permits intervention into the world to get an object that already threatens death to those many to instead threaten death to these few, but only by acts that are not themselves gross impingements on the few. That is, the intervenor must not use means that infringe stringent rights of the few in order to get his distributive intention carried out.

It could of course be argued that the fact that the bystander of the original *Bystander at the Switch* makes threaten the one what already threatens the five, and does so by means that do not themselves constitute infringements of any right of the one's (not even a trivial right of the one's), shows that the bystander in that case infringes no right of the one's at all. That is, it could be argued that we have here that independent ground for saying that the bystander does not infringe the one's right to life which I said would be needed by a friend of (ii).[15] But I see nothing to be gained by taking this line, for I see nothing to be gained by supposing it never permissible to infringe a right; and something is lost by taking this line, namely the possibility of viewing the bystander as doing the one a wrong if he proceeds—albeit a wrong it is permissible to do him.

IX.

What counts as "*an* object which threatens death"? What marks one threat off from another? I have no doubt that ingenious people can construct cases in which we shall be unclear whether to say that if the agent proceeds, he makes threaten the one the very same thing as already threatens the five.

Moreover, which are the interventions in which the agent gets a thing that threatens five to

instead threaten one by means that themselves constitute infringements of stringent rights of the one's? I have no doubt that ingenious people can construct cases in which we shall all be unclear whether to say that the agent's means do constitute infringements of stringent rights—and cases also in which we shall be unclear whether to say the agent's means constitute infringements of any rights at all.

But it is surely a mistake to look for precision in the concepts brought to bear to solve this problem: There isn't any to be had. It would be enough if cases in which it seems to us unclear whether to say "same threat," or unclear whether to say "non-right-infringing-means," also seemed to us to be cases in which it is unclear whether the agent may or may not proceed; and if also coming to see a case as one to which these expressions do (or do not) apply involves coming to see the case as one in which the agent may (or may not) proceed.

X.

If these ideas are correct, then we have a handle on anyway some of the troublesome cases in which people make threats. Suppose a villain says to us, "I will cause a ceiling to fall on five unless you send lethal fumes into the room of one." Most of us think it would not be permissible for us to accede to this threat. Why? We may think of the villain as part of the world around the people involved, a part which is going to drop a burden on the five if we do not act. On this way of thinking of him, nothing *yet* threatens the five (certainly no ceiling as yet threatens them) and a fortiori we cannot save the five by making what (already) threatens them instead threaten the one. Alternatively, we may think of the villain as himself a threat to the five. But sending the fumes in is not making *him* be a threat to the one instead of to the five. The hypothesis I proposed, then, yields what it should: We may not accede.

That is because the hypothesis I proposed says nothing at all about the source of the threat to the five. Whether the threat to the five is, or is caused by, a human being or anything else, it is not permissible to do what will kill one to save the five except by making what threatens the five itself threaten the one.

By contrast, it seems to me very plausible to think that if a villain has started a trolley towards five, we may deflect the trolley towards one—other things being equal, of course. If a trolley is headed towards five, and we can deflect it towards one, we *may*, no matter who or what caused it to head towards the five.

I think that these considerations help us in dealing with a question I drew attention to earlier. Suppose a villain says to us, "I will cause a ceiling to fall on five unless you send lethal fumes into the room of one." If we refuse, so that he does what he threatens to do, then he surely does something very much worse than we would be doing if we acceded to his threat and sent the fumes in. If we accede, we do something misguided and wrongful, but not nearly as bad as what he does if we refuse.

It should be stressed: The fact that he will do something worse if we do not send the fumes in does not entail that we ought to send them in, or even that it is permissible for us to do so.

How after all could that entail that we may send the fumes in? The fact that we would be saving five lives by sending the fumes in does not itself make it permissible for us to do so. (Rights trump utilities.) How could adding that the taker of those five lives would be doing what is worse than we would tip the balance? If we may not infringe a right of the one in order to save the five lives, it cannot possibly be thought that we may infringe the right of that one in order, not merely to save the five lives, but to make the villain's moral record better than it otherwise would be.

For my own part, I think that considerations of motives apart, and other things being equal, it does no harm to say that:

(II) Killing five is worse than killing one

is, after all, true. *Of course* we shall then have to say that assessments of which acts are worse than which do not by themselves settle the question of what is permissible for a person to do. For we shall have to say that, despite the truth of (II), it is not the case that we are required to kill one in order that another person shall not kill five, or even that it is everywhere permissible for us to do this.

What is of interest is that what holds inter-personally also holds intra-personally. I said earlier that we might imagine the surgeon of *Transplant* to have caused the ailments of his five patients. Let us imagine the worst: He gave them chemical X

precisely in order to cause their deaths, in order to inherit from them. Now he repents. But the fact that he would be saving five lives by operating on the one does not itself make it permissible for him to operate on the one. (Rights trump utilities.) And if he may not infringe a right of the one in order to save the five lives, it cannot possibly be thought that he may infringe the right of that one in order, not merely to save the five lives, but to make his own moral record better than it otherwise would be.

Another way to put the point is this: Assessments of which acts are worse than which have to be directly relevant to the agent's circumstances if they are to have a bearing on what he may do. If A threatens to kill five unless B kills one, then although killing five is worse than killing one, these are not the alternatives open to B. The alternatives open to B are: Kill one, thereby forestalling the deaths of five (and making A's moral record better than it otherwise would be), or let it be the case that A kills five. And the supposition that it would be worse for B to choose to kill the one is entirely compatible with the supposition that killing five is worse than killing one. Again, the alternatives open to the surgeon are: Operate on the one, thereby saving five (and making the surgeon's own moral record better than it otherwise would be), or let it be the case that he himself will have killed the five. And the supposition that it would be worse for the surgeon to choose to operate is entirely compatible with the supposition that killing five is worse than killing one.

On the other hand, suppose a second surgeon is faced with a choice between here and now giving chemical X to five, thereby killing them, and operating on, and thereby killing, only one. (It taxes the imagination to invent such a second surgeon, but let that pass. And compare *Trolley Driver*.) Then, other things being equal, it does seem he may choose to operate on the one. Some people would say something stronger, namely that he is required to make this choice. Perhaps they would say that

(II′) If a person is faced with a choice between doing something *here and now* to five, by the doing of which he will kill them, and doing something else *here and now* to one, by the doing of which he will kill only the one, then

(other things being equal) he ought to choose
the second alternative rather than the first

is a quite general moral truth. Whether or not the
second surgeon is morally required to make this
choice (and thus whether or not (II') is a general
moral truth), it does seem to be the case that he
may. But this did seem puzzling. As I put it: Why
should the present tense matter so much?

It is plausible to think that the present tense
matters because the question for the agent at the
time of acting is about the present, viz., "What may
I here and now do?," and because that question is
the same as the question, "Which of the alternatives here and now open to me may I choose?" The
alternatives now open to the second surgeon are:
kill five or kill one. If killing five is worse than
killing one, then perhaps he ought to, but at any
rate he may, kill the one.

Notes

[1] See P. Foot, "The Problem of Abortion and the
Doctrine of the Double Effect," p. 59.

[2] I think it possible (though by no means certain) that
John Taurek would say, "No, it is not permissible to (all
simply) turn the trolley; what you ought to do is flip a
coin." See Should the Numbers Count?, p. 214. (But he is
there concerned with a different kind of case, namely that
in which what is in question is not whether we may do
what harms one to avoid harming five, but whether we
may or ought to choose to save five in preference to
saving one.) For criticism of Taurek's article, see Innumerate Ethics, p. 227.

[3] I doubt that anyone would say, with any hope of
getting agreement from others, that the surgeon ought to
flip a coin. So even if you think that the trolley driver
ought to flip a coin, there would remain, for you, an
analogue of Mrs. Foot's problem, namely: Why ought the
trolley driver flip a coin, whereas the surgeon may not?

[4] Mrs. Foot speaks more generally of causing injury
and failing to provide aid; and her reason for thinking
that the former is worse than the latter is that the negative duty to refrain from causing injury is stricter than the
positive duty to provide aid. See P. Foot, supra note 1.

[5] A similar case (intended to make a point similar to
the one that I shall be making) is discussed in The Priority
of Avoiding Harm, in Killing and Letting Die 172, 194–95
(B. Steinbock ed. 1980).

[6] For a sensitive discussion of some of the difficulties,
see Davis, Using Persons and Common Sense, 94 Ethics
387 (1984). Among other things, she argues (I think
rightly) that the Kantian idea is not to be identified with
the common sense concept of "using a person." Id. at 402.

[7] For a second reason to think so, see . . . note 13.

[8] It is also true that if the five go wholly out of existence just before the agent starts to turn the trolley, then
the one will die whatever the agent does. Should we say,
then, that the agent uses one to save five if he acts, and uses
five to save one if he does not act? No. What follows and is
false. If the agent does not act, he uses nobody. (I doubt
that it can even be said that if he does not act, he lets them
be used. For what is the active for which this is passive?
Who or what would be using them if he does not act?).

[9] I strongly suspect that giving an account of what
makes it wrong to use a person would also require appeal
to the concept of a right.

[10] R. Dworkin, Taking Rights Seriously ix (1977).

[11] Many of the examples discussed by Bernard
Williams and Ruth Marcus plainly call out for this kind of
treatment. See B. Williams, Ethical Consistency, in Problems of the Self 166 (1973); Marcus, Moral Dilemmas and
Consistency, 77 J. Phil. 121 (1980).

[12] It may be worth stressing that what I suggest calls for
attention is not (as some construals of double effect would
have it) whether the agent's killing of the one is his means
to something, and not (as other construals of "double effect" would have it) whether the death of the one is the
agent's means to something, but rather what are the means
by which the agent both kills and saves. For a discussion of
"the Doctrine of the Double Effect," see P. Foot.

[13] Id. at 29. As Mrs. Foot says, we do not use the one
if we proceed in Hospital. Yet the impermissibility of proceeding in Hospital seems to have a common source with
the impermissibility of operating in Transplant, in which
the surgeon would be using the one whose parts he takes
for the five who need them. This is my second reason for
thinking that an appeal to the fact that the surgeon would
be using his victim is an over-simple way of taking account of the means he would be employing for the saving
of his five.

[14] Notice that in this case too the agent does not use
the one if he proceeds. (This case, along with a number of
other cases I have been discussing, comes from Thomson,
Killing, Letting Die, and the Trolley Problem, p. 67. Mrs.
Thomson seems to me to have been blundering around in
the dark in that paper, but the student of this problem
may possibly find some of the cases she discusses useful.)

[15] See supra text accompanying notes 9–11.

The Trolley Problem Revisited

MICHAEL J. COSTA ▪ University of South Carolina
The Southern Journal of Philosophy, 1987

Michael J. Costa sets out versions of Bystander 1 and Transplant. (See Introduction.) Costa explores some possible differences between the two cases. He deems the following irrelevant: the difference in the time that the decisions are made; the responsibilities of outside parties; the contributory responsibilities of the people involved; the special responsibility that the doctor may have by virtue of the fact that he is a medical professional (as opposed to the non-interested bystander in Trolley); preventing harm versus doing good; and direct versus indirect killing. Costa thinks that it is easy to manipulate the problem so that the relevance of each distinction is eliminated, while our intuition about the difference between the two problems remains.

Costa does see some difference, however, on the basis of the intentional structure of the cases. The doctor directly kills the one person visiting the hospital, while the bystander does something that just happens to result in the death of the one on the spur of track. Costa explains the relevance of this distinction by breaking it into two differences in the cases. The first difference is that the doctor in Transplant kills the one *in order* to save the five while the bystander does not. The second is that the doctor kills the one person intentionally while the bystander does not. (Contrast Quinn, p. 179.) Costa explains the latter difference by identifying a distinction in attitudes between the two agents. The doctor views the death of the one as the means of saving the five. The bystander does not see the death of the one as a means to saving the five, but only as a consequence of doing so.

As to the first difference, Costa argues that the death of the one in Transplant is part of a causal chain that saves the five. They will not be saved unless the organs of the one are transplanted into their bodies, and this will not occur unless the one visitor to the hospital dies. On the other hand, the death of the one in Trolley is just a causal consequence of throwing the switch. The death of the one is not required to save the five in the same way that it is in Transplant. All that is required to save the five in Trolley is that the trolley be directed onto the spur of track and away from the five. This difference in the significance of the causal structure of events in the two cases is explained by Costa through a **component theory of action.** By this he means the theory that all actions contain parts which are other actions and non-action events. Parts of actions are initiating events (that start things going) and other parts are terminating events (end-products of the action). Actions that stand in a means-relation to other actions are also considered parts of that action. So, Costa says, if a switch is flipped by moving a finger, then the moving of the finger is a component of the flipping of the switch.

By this analysis, the killing of the one by the doctor is directly related as an action-component to the saving of the five others. The death of the one and the saving of the five are connected in a means-relation along a causal chain of actions. Alternatively, the death of the one in Trolley is not directly in a causal chain with the saving of the five. The throwing of the switch by the bystander does cause the death of the one, but the death of the one does not cause the saving of the five in the same way that it did in Transplant. So, killing the one in Trolley is not a component of saving the five.

The moral significance of this difference between the two cases is explained through the Principle of the Double Effect (PDE). (See previous discussions of the DDE, particularly Nagel, Quinn, Thomson, and Davis.) According to this principle, it is all right for an agent to act in a way that produces some harm (in the aforementioned cases the harm is the death of the one), if the act produces some good, the agent has a good reason for committing the act, and the harm is neither a means of obtaining the good nor intended as an end. According to the PDE, it is not permissible for the doctor to kill the one to save the five. In that case, the doctor clearly uses the harm (killing the one) to do the good (saving the five), and does so intentionally. On the other hand, the bystander is permitted by the PDE to save the five, insofar as the death of the one is a mere side-effect here.

IN AN IMPORTANT PAPER,[1] JUDITH THOMSON discusses a set of examples that collectively present something she calls the "trolley problem." The central examples were adapted by Thomson from some presented in an earlier paper by Phillipa Foot.[2] The examples I use below to set the problem do not agree in detail with either those of Foot or Thomson; but the problem they present is essentially the same, I believe, as that discussed by Thomson. In any case my concern is not so much to evaluate critically what Thomson had to say (it will become apparent that I am roughly in agreement with Thomson's treatment), but to "milk" the problem to a greater extent than Thomson or others for its considerable interest for both action and moral theories. I will develop a connection between the problem and certain contemporary theories of action, and I will show how the problem seems to provide support for the controversial Principle of Double Effect.

I. THE TROLLEY PROBLEM

My version of the trolley problem involves comparing the following two cases:

The Transplant Case

Doctor Jones has five patients who are seriously ill. Patients A and B have lung disease, patient C has heart disease, and patients D and E have kidney disease. If extraordinary medical measures are not taken within the next few days all five patients will die. All five patients can be saved (we will suppose), if appropriate transplant operations are performed. The problem is that no suitable organ donors are currently available or likely to be available within the next few days. In the course of treating another patient, F, for a minor ailment, Doctor Jones discovers that he is a perfect tissue match for all five of her terminally ill cases. Furthermore, F has healthy heart, lungs, and kidneys; and he has antecedently signed a donor agreement to allow the use of his organs on his death. Dr. Jones believes that if she kills F she can use his heart, lungs, and kidneys to save the lives of A, B, C, D, and E. This belief motivates her to give F an injection that kills him painlessly and in a way that makes it appear that he has died of natural causes. She then uses his organs to save the lives of the other five patients. No one ever discovers that F did not die of natural causes.

The Trolley Case

Mr. Smith is walking along some trolley tracks one day when he is shocked to see a runaway trolley barreling out of control along the tracks. Quickly glancing down the tracks, Smith sees five people (call them A, B, C, D, and E) standing in the path of the runaway trolley and blissfully unaware of their danger. He realizes that if he were to try to warn them by yelling, they would not be able to react in time to clear the tracks before the car would hit them. Smith notices, however, that he is standing next to a switch. If he throws the switch, the runaway trolley will switch to a sidetrack and the five people will be saved. Unfortunately, there is another person, F, standing on the sidetrack. Smith sees that if he were to throw the switch, it would result in the death of F, but that the other five people would live. He further believes that if he refrains from acting, five of the people will die and only F will live. These considerations motivate Smith to throw the switch. F is killed by the trolley car and A, B, C, D, and E are saved.

The puzzle, put very briefly, is this. It seems that Dr. Jones' act is morally wrong, despite the utilitarian justification for it. On the other hand, it is not at all clear that Smith's act is morally wrong. It may even be that Smith's act is morally praiseworthy.[3] Yet the two cases appear to be exactly parallel to each other in the relevant respects. What is the nature of the differences between the two cases that explains this radical difference in moral intuitions?

Foot's original examples were presented in the context of a discussion of whether killing is morally worse than letting die. It may initially seem right to explain why Dr. Jones' act is morally wrong in terms of killing being worse than letting die, even at proportions of five to one. Dr. Jones should let her five patients die rather than kill F. But this explanation runs into conflict with the trolley case. For if it is wrong to kill one rather than let five die, then we should feel that Smith also did the wrong thing. But we don't. Whatever the significance of this for the question of whether there is an important moral difference between killing and letting die (see Thomson's paper for further discussion), it is clear that the difference in moral intuitions between these two cases cannot be explained in terms of the killing/letting die distinction. So we must look elsewhere for the morally relevant differences.

II. SUGGESTIONS ABOUT RELEVANT DIFFERENCES

The Time Factor

One factor that might be considered a relevant difference between the cases is that Smith has to act on the spur of the moment, whereas Dr. Jones has time to think things over and make plans. Now it seems to me that at best this difference would explain why we might be more forgiving toward Smith than toward Jones. Smith made the wrong choice, but he was rushed, after all. Any of us in the same position might have instinctively reacted in the same way. But the intuition claimed in the puzzle is that Smith did not *do* anything wrong, not just that he should be forgiven or his punishment mitigated by the circumstances. Moreover, one can change the cases so that the time difference is no longer present. We can make circumstances such that Doctor Jones must act instantly to kill F or forever miss her chance to save the five patients. Likewise, we can have Smith locked in an isolation booth with no contact at all to the outside world except to the switch and make it the case that he knows for several hours (or days) that the runaway trolley will imperil the five persons on the track. It seems to me that these changes will not significantly change the intuitions.

The Responsible Outside Party

Another suggestion is that in the trolley car case there is someone else to blame for the consequences—namely, the person responsible for the runaway trolley. Smith merely made the best of a bad situation. On the other hand, there is no one but Dr. Jones to blame in the other case.

In response to this, it doesn't seem to me to be a credible moral principle that someone is relieved of responsibility in case there is someone else who is more seriously to blame. Moreover, the trolley case can be changed so as to eliminate this difference without changing our intuitions. Suppose that instead of a runaway trolley we have an avalanche caused by some natural occurrence.[4] Smith can do something (perhaps push a plunger causing a preset charge to blast) that will divert the avalanche from its present course, thereby saving the lives of A, B, C, D, and E, but, unfortunately, causing the death of F. There is no one else to blame here, but this seems in no way to change our intuitions that Smith did nothing morally wrong.

Contributory Responsibility

Another suggestion is that F in the trolley case bears some contributory responsibility for the (for him) unhappy result. After all, F was putting his life in danger by standing on the trolley tracks. One who acts knowingly in this way must accept the risk of foreseeable dangers, such as, in this case, getting hit by a trolley. It is on the same principle that spectators attending a baseball game or golf match must accept the foreseeable risk of getting hit by a ball. F, himself, is (at least partially) to blame for the result in the trolley case. On the other hand, while F did accept some foreseeable risks in the transplant case, e.g., risks of mistaken diagnosis, treatment errors, etc., being murdered is not one of the foreseeable risks of placing oneself under the care of a doctor.

Whatever the significance of this difference between the cases, and I don't think that it can have much weight, the cases can be changed once again to eliminate the difference. Suppose that F did not realize that he was on trolley tracks, and this, not through carelessness, but because the tracks were not obvious to sight. Suppose that the sidetrack that F is on is one that is no longer in use, and that F knows this. There are various ways in which the case can be elaborated so as to eliminate any presumed risk-taking on the part of F without changing our moral intuitions.

Special Responsibility

Sometimes I hear the suggestion that the relevant difference between the cases is that Dr. Jones' act violates a special kind of responsibility that she has, given her position as a doctor. Doctors are charged with *healing*, not killing. Presumably, Dr. Jones took an oath to use her medical skills to save lives. Jones' act, in addition to causing a death, is a violation of her oath and her special position of responsibility. On the other hand, Smith has no such special position in the trolley car case. Thus, Jones' act is significantly worse than Smith's.

Again, I think that this difference cannot be the salient difference between the cases. For one thing we can change the trolley car case so that Smith also has a position of special responsibility. Suppose, for example, that Smith is the safety engineer for the trolley car lines. If anything, it seems to me that this change strengthens the intuition that Smith's act was not morally wrong. (It may, of course, be that Smith is liable for the accident because of *other* actions or omissions.) Alternatively, we could suppose that Jones is not a doctor in the transplant case. She is merely an interested bystander, who kills F knowing that his organs can be used by qualified doctors to save the lives of the other five patients. This doesn't at all change the intuition that what Jones did was morally wrong.

Preventing Harm Versus Doing Good

One suggestion I have heard is that there are three principles relevant to the problem: (1) Do not do harm, (2) Prevent harm, and (3) Do good. These stand in a hierarchy with (1) outweighing (2) and (2) outweighing (3). Both Jones and Smith seem to violate (1) insofar as they both cause harm to F. If the trolley case involves preventing harm and the transplant case doing good, however, then there is a morally significant difference between them on the basis of principles (2) and (3).

There are a number of things to observe about this suggestion. First, if the hierarchy is absolute, then the principles do not produce the *right* moral difference. Remember that our intuition was that Smith did not *do* anything wrong. According to this suggestion Smith *would* have done something wrong (in violating principle (1)); it merely would not have been as grave a wrong as what Jones did.

An alternative would be to hold that the hierarchy is weighted rather than absolute. This would make it possible that doing harm to *one* could be justified by preventing harm to *five*, but that it could not be justified by *doing good* to five.

There are problems, however, for even this alternative. For one thing, the difference between preventing harm and doing good is less than crystal clear with respect to the two cases. Wasn't Dr. Jones acting so as to prevent harm (the natural harm of disease and death) to her five patients? Even if a distinction between the cases can be drawn on this basis, the trolley case can be changed so as to change our moral intuitions without changing its status relative to the three principles. Suppose that there is no sidetrack or switch but that F is standing next to Smith beside the track. Smith reasons that he can prevent the trolley from striking the five people on the track only by pushing F, a huge, but clumsy, 300 pounder, onto the track in front of the runaway trolley. F's bulk will bring the trolley to a halt before it strikes the other five, at the cost, of course, of F's life.[5] In this case, it seems clear that Smith's act would be as bad as Dr. Jones' act in the transplant case even though their relative status with regard to the three principles would remain the same as in the original cases.

Direct Versus Indirect Killing

The way that some attempt to describe the relevant differences in the cases is to say that Dr. Jones directly killed her patient F, whereas Mr. Smith merely did something that happened to result in the death of F. I think, indeed, that there is *something* to this point; but it is difficult to make the truly salient difference clear.

It is clear that Dr. Jones killed (indeed, murdered) F. But isn't it just as clear that Smith killed (though not murdered) F? Dr. Jones did something that led directly to the death of F, namely, gave him the injection. But Smith also did something that directly led to the death of F, namely, pulled the switch. Now one could argue, I suppose, that Dr. Jones' act was more "directly" connected with F's death than was the act of Smith. But in both cases there is a causal chain of intervening events. It would be silly to say that the difference is the *number* of intervening events. For one thing, no one agrees about how to *count* events. Furthermore, it is hard to see how the mere number of intervening events would be *morally* relevant except insofar as it is related to epistemic issues about whether the consequence is forseen or foreseeable on the part of the agent. But in the problem cases, both Jones and Smith clearly foresee the outcomes of their actions. Smith knows that his pulling the switch will cause the death of F just as

clearly as Dr. Jones knows that her giving the injection will cause the death of F. Both Smith and Jones act knowingly. Moreover, both Smith and Jones have the same motivation for their acts—to save the lives of the five people at risk. What then is the *morally* relevant difference between the cases?

III. RESOLUTION OF THE PROBLEM

I believe that there are two morally relevant differences between the two cases. The first is that Jones killed F *in order* to save the lives of the others, whereas Smith did not. In the trolley case F's death is merely the causal consequence of the act (throwing the switch) that is the means by which Jones saves the lives of the others.[6] The second difference is that Jones killed F intentionally and Smith did not. This explains the intuition that Jones' killing of F was murder, but that Smith's killing of F was not. Before addressing the question of why these differences are morally relevant, I want to take a brief excursion into action theory to try to identify the facts of the cases that ground these two differences.

Let us consider the second difference first. Why is Jones' killing of F intentional and Smith's killing of F not? Both Jones and Smith acted with the knowledge that their respective actions would result in the death of F. So we cannot explain the difference in terms of one agent acting knowingly and the other not. Both killed F knowingly. Moreover, both agents had the same goal in mind, to save the lives of the five parties at risk. We are not forced to attribute to either a desire to kill F. We may suppose that Jones views F's death as a very bad thing and entirely regrettable. Of course, Jones knows that F's death is necessary in the circumstances if the lives of the other five patients are to be saved, and she acts nevertheless. This may allow us to attribute to Jones, if not a desire for F's death, perhaps (using Davidson's[7] term) a "pro attitude" toward it. But it seems that the same things can be said with respect to Smith. Smith knows that F's death is necessary in the circumstances if the lives of the others are to be saved, and he acts nevertheless. So perhaps Smith also has a "pro attitude" toward the death of F.

There just isn't any basis *here* for explaining why one killing was intentional and the other was not.

Of course, there is some difference in the attitudes that we can plausibly attribute to the two agents. Jones views her killing of F as the means to saving the lives of the others, and Smith does not. This is the only basis I can see on which we can call Jones' act intentional and Smith's not. This makes the second difference in the cases indirectly dependent upon the first. It is the respective agents' perception of their actions being or not being in certain means relations that explains the difference in intentionality of the actions.

Another example may help to confirm this point. Consider a doctor who is treating a cancer patient with chemotherapy. The doctor knows that the chemotherapy will produce nasty side-effects, such as nausea. But the doctor does not cause the patient's nausea intentionally. Causing the patient nausea is not viewed by the doctor as the means by which she tries to arrest the patient's cancer. Compare this to a case in which a doctor slaps a person's face in an effort to bring the person out of hysteria. Here the doctor is causing the person pain intentionally. And this is not because the doctor desires to cause the patient pain, but because causing pain in this case is viewed by the doctor as a means to doing something that the doctor does want to do, bring the person out of hysteria.

Let us now address the first difference. What are the facts of the case that justify the claim that killing F is the means by which Jones saves the lives of the others? I suggest it is that the death of F is actually a link in the causal chain that results in the continued life of the others. The death of F is a cause of the organs being available, and the organs being available is a cause of the continued life of the other patients. On the other hand, in Smith's case, the death of F is not a cause of the continued life of the other five. Smith's throwing the switch causes the car to go down the side-track, and the car's going down the sidetrack is the cause of the continued life of the other five. F's death does not appear in this causal chain at all. It is merely a causal consequence of one of the events that is in the causal chain, the throwing of the switch. Despite the fact that Smith kills F knowingly, F's death here is merely an epiphenomenon.

I can think of no other differences in the cases that could ground the claim that the killing of F is the means by which the lives are saved in Jones' case but not in Smith's. (It cannot be *grounded* in differences in attitude between Jones and Smith because, as shown above, the only relevant attitudinal difference is indirectly dependent upon the difference in means relations.) But why should a difference in the causal positions of events make a difference in the means relations between the relevant actions? A component theory of action provides the metaphysical perspective for a satisfying answer to this question.

By a "component theory" of action I mean a theory that claims that actions in general contain as components (proper parts) other actions and non-action events. Typically an action consists of the entire causal chain of events from the initiating intentional event (volition?, triggering desire?, triggering intention?) to the terminating event. The "terminating event" for an action of type A is the event of a type whose causation (in the right way) is necessary and sufficient for an action of type A to occur. The terminating event of a killing is a death, and the terminating event of a raising of an arm is the rising of the arm.[8] Under a component theory, the terminating event is also the terminal event of the causal chain of events comprising the action. When an action stands in a means relation to another action, it is in general a component of that other action. If I flip a switch by moving my finger, then my moving my finger is a component of my flipping the switch.[9]

As we have seen, the death of F plays a different causal role in the transplant as compared to the trolley case. In the transplant case, it is directly in the causal chain between Jones' action of giving F the injection and the lives of the others being saved. In terms of a component account, we can say that Jones' killing of F includes her giving F the injection as a component action and that her killing of F is itself an action component of her saving the lives of the others.[10] Jones killed F by giving him an injection, and she saved the lives of the others by killing F. The means relations are

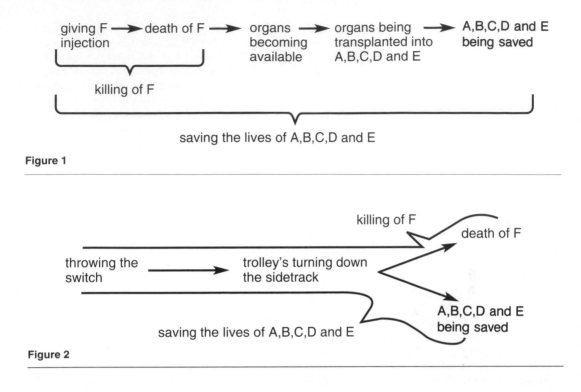

Figure 1

Figure 2

paralleled in the part relations among the relevant actions. See figure 1.

On the other hand, in the trolley case, the death of F is not directly in the causal chain between Smith's throwing the switch and the lives of the others being saved. Smith's throwing the switch does cause the death of F, and so there is an action of Smith's killing F that includes his throwing the switch as a component. Moreover, Smith killed F by throwing the switch; and this relationship is paralleled in the component relationship. But since the death of F does not cause the lives of the others being saved, Smith's killing of F is *not* a component of his saving the lives of the others (although it does overlap with it). This grounds the claim that Smith did not save the lives by means of killing F. Compare figure 2 to the diagram of the transplant case.

According to this view the differences in the causal relations of the death of F in the two cases mark a difference in the causal and mereological relations between the actions of killing F and saving the lives of the others in the two cases. The claim that Jones saved the lives by means of killing F, but that Smith did not, is grounded in these differences in causal and mereological relations. These differences also provide intuitions in support of the claim that Jones killed F intentionally and Smith did not. If an agent views an act as a means to an intended act and proceeds to act, then the agent intends the means as well. This is because to intend an act is to intend every (anticipated) part of that act. But an agent can recognize that doing a part of an intended act will result in some overlapping act without intending the overlapping act.

IV. RELATIONS TO THE PRINCIPLE OF DOUBLE EFFECT

We are now ready to address the question of why these properties of the respective actions are morally significant. The Principle of Double Effect (PDE) provides a ready explanation. According to PDE it is permissible for an agent to act in a way that results in some evil or harm provided that: (1) the act also involves or produces a good; (2) the agent has a proportionately grave reason for acting, and (3) evil or harm is neither intended nor the means to producing the good.[11] PDE justifies Smith's actions but not those of Jones, since her acts violate condition (3). Indeed, the trolley problem provides support for PDE, since we haven't found any other plausible explanation of our moral intuitions here.

Those who are critical of PDE, of course, are likely to be dubious about the proposed solution to the trolley problem. The most telling response for them would be to show that there is some *other* positive account of the difference in moral intuitions in the case. I have reviewed and argued above against all the other candidate accounts with which I am familiar; but, of course, that does not prove that no better alternative exists. Another response for opponents is simply to mount a negative attack against the PDE solution. It will be of interest to see what the bases of such an attack might be and what can be said in defense of PDE.

One basis for such an attack would be to use the same strategy that I used to dispose of a number of proposed solutions, namely, to argue that the cases can be changed in a way such that the proposed solution no longer applies even though there is no change in moral intuitions. For example, suppose that Dr. Jones injects F with something that merely renders him unconscious. While he is unconscious she removes the relevant organs, and F dies *as a result* of her removing the organs.[12] Here F's death is merely a causal consequence of the act that is the means to saving the lives (i.e., removing F's organs), but our moral assessment of Jones' acts is not improved one iota.

The objection supposes that by changing the transplant case in this way has made it exactly analogous to the trolley case as far as PDE is concerned. This is far from the case. It is true that in the revised scenario Jones does not save the lives of the others by means of *killing* F. But she still uses harm to F as a means to her end in a way that Smith does not, and this explains why our moral assessment of the cases does not change. The act which Smith uses as a means (i.e., throwing the switch) is itself morally neutral. But the act which Jones uses as a means certainly is not. It consists of violating

F's body and making use of his organs without his permission. Killing a person is only one way of using the person as a means to an end. Indeed, we can change the case so that F does not die. Suppose that all that Dr. Jones needs to save the others is one of F's kidneys. (She can dice this up and make from it a serum that will save the others from an otherwise fatal illness.) Dr. Jones' act is still wrong if she takes the kidney without permission, even if F should survive the operation with no ill effects. One cannot violate the body of another in *this* way as a means to doing some good.

As an alternative, the objector might try to change the circumstances of the trolley case so that harm to F is the means by which *Smith* saves the lives of the others. I take it that substantial support for PDE is provided by considering such changes. For, nearly every change I can think of that would have doing harm to F as the *means* by which Smith saves the lives (e.g., the change discussed above in which Smith stopped the trolley by pushing F onto the track) is a change in which Smith's act no longer appears to be morally permissible.

There are apparent exceptions, however. Suppose in the trolley case that *no one* is standing on the sidetrack. Smith can divert the trolley by throwing the switch without causing physical harm to anyone. F, however, owns the switch, and he has expressly forbidden anyone but himself to throw it. Surely, it is nevertheless permissible for Smith to throw the switch in order to save the lives of the others. Yet his act of throwing the switch is a violation of F's rights (for the sake of argument I will ignore the plausible claim that in these circumstances F does not have the right to deny the use of the switch, despite being the owner of it), and this act is the means by which he saves the lives of the others. So PDE does not explain why Smith's act is permissible here.

One can grant, however, that PDE does not explain why Smith's act is permissible in the revised case and still hold that it *does* explain why Smith's act is permissible in the original case. PDE, as I have presented it, is a principle that provides that certain acts are permissible in certain circumstances. It is compatible with PDE that there are *other* principles that would provide that acts are permissible in *other* circumstances. It may be that some people interpret PDE as saying that an act that involves or produces some harm is permissible *only if* the harm is neither intended nor used as a means to an end. But I do not interpret PDE in that way.[13]

It is compatible with my understanding of PDE that acts that involve or produce some evil can sometimes be justified by the fact that they are the means to some act that involves or produces some proportionately great good. *Sometimes* the end justifies the means. The end does not justify the means in the transplant case, however. Violating someone's body is a particularly nasty evil that is not to be justified by the fact that it is the means to saving five lives. The end does justify the means in the revised trolley case. Using someone's property against their wishes is an evil, but one that *can* be justified by its being the means to saving five lives. The killing of F in the original trolley case, however, is not justified as being the means to a proportionately good end. It is justified by the fact that it is merely the side effect of doing what is necessary to produce the proportionately good end. PDE can justify acts that could not be justified as being the means to an end.

There is one last kind of possible counterexample that we should consider. Suppose that the trolley case is changed in the following way. F is standing on the sidetrack, but no one is standing on the main line. Smith notices that F is on the sidetrack and that he will be killed if the switch is thrown, but Smith throws the switch anyway in order to see if it is working properly. Now it may be thought that PDE applies to this revised case. After all, Smith does not kill F intentionally nor as a means to what he intends to do. Once the trolley begins to go down the sidetrack, Smith's curiosity is satisfied; and F's death occurs subsequently as a mere side effect of the act that is the means to satisfying Smith's curiosity. Smith does not use harm to F as a means nor does he kill F intentionally. But surely his act is morally abhorrent.

The feature of PDE that this attempted counterexample overlooks is that PDE requires that the agent have a proportionately grave reason for the act.[14] Clearly, the reason of satisfying Smith's curiosity is not sufficiently grave to outweigh the evil involved in bringing about the death of F. PDE would not justify Smith's actions even though the evil was not brought about intentionally or as the means to some intended result.

We can recap the attempted challenges to PDE and the responses to them as follows:

(1) There are cases in which the agent's actions are morally wrong despite the fact that some of the evil caused is neither intended nor a means to some intended act. Response: There are two kinds of cases here. First, there is the case in which the means act violates PDE because it involves some independent evil (e.g., the case in which Jones removes F's organs, resulting in his death). Second, there is the case in which PDE is violated because there is not a proportionately grave reason for acting (e.g., the case in which Smith throws the switch out of curiosity).

(2) There are cases in which the agent does something involving or producing some evil intentionally or as a means to some end, yet the agent's actions are permissible (e.g., the case in which Smith throws the switch despite the fact that F has prohibited his doing so). Response: PDE should be interpreted as a principle of permissibility, not a principle of impermissibility. To show that an act conflicts with PDE is to show that it is not permissible *on the grounds of PDE*. It may be shown to be permissible on some *other* legitimate moral grounds. This does not have the result that PDE is dispensable: for there are cases, such as the original trolley case, in which only PDE can explain the permissibility of the action.

There is one further challenge to PDE that is worth noting. It is a request for the supporter of PDE to explain *why* acting intentionally has the moral significance bestowed upon it by PDE. Why is it that a person who acts knowingly but unintentionally may permissibly perform an act that would be wrong for a person acting intentionally, even though both persons act on the same motivation and neither acts on desire? A beginning of an answer is that a person who acts intentionally in such circumstances must be using the act as a means to her end, and that being willing to use certain kinds of evils as a means to an end is itself an additional evil. We have seen in our examples that this is often the case when the evil involved is violating the body of some person. Here we might suppose that the additional evil derives from the agent's treating a person as an *instrument*. This can be viewed as intrinsically evil, or it can be viewed as evil because it reveals a character trait in the agent that is likely to produce bad consequences in other circumstances.[15] Following out these suggestions, however, is too big a project to undertake here.[16]

Notes

[1]Judith Jarvis Thomson, "Killing, Letting Die, and the Trolley Problem," p. 67.

[2]Phillipa Foot, "The Problem of Abortion and the Doctrine of the Double Effect," p. 59.

[3]All that is needed to raise the problem is the claim that Smith's act is morally permissible whereas Jones' act is not. In a provocative article "Should the Numbers Count?" brought to my attention by a referee of this journal, John Taurek (p. 214) argues that morally the numbers don't count. His argument, which concerns centrally a different example from Foot's paper cited above, would not directly attack the claim that Smith's act was permissible. It would seem to imply, however, that Smith could not give the greater number of lives saved as a morally relevant reason for his action. I find Taurek's argument dubious for basically the reasons given by James Woodward in "Why the Numbers Count," *The Southern Journal of Philosophy*, vol. XIX (1981): 531–540.

[4]Thomson also discusses an avalanche case, but with respect to a different point. See "The Trolley Problem," p. 279.

[5]Thomson provides a similar example in "The Trolley Problem."

[6]This is the salient difference noted by Thomson. See "The Trolley Problem." I also think that Thomson would agree with my claim that Jones' killing of F was intentional and Smith's killing of F was not, though I'm not sure that she would agree that this is morally significant. See *Acts and Other Events*, (Ithaca: Cornell University Press, 1977), pp. 270–2.

[7]Donald Davidson, "Actions, Reasons, and Causes," reprinted as Essay 1 in *Essays on Actions and Events* (Oxford: Oxford University Press, 1980), pp. 3–4.

[8]Cf. Lawrence Davis' discussion of "doing-related events" in his *Theory of Action*, (New Jersey: Prentice-Hall, 1979), p. 6.

[9]Thomson's own theory of action is a component theory. See *Acts and Other Events*, Irving Thalberg, *Perception, Emotion, and Action* (New Haven: Yale University Press, 1977); John Searle, *Intentionality* (Cambridge: Cambridge University Press, 1983); and Myles Brand, *Acting and Intending* (Cambridge: M.I.T. Press, 1984) also hold, or are favorably inclined toward, component theories of action. This is not to say that they would agree

with everything I have said about a component theory in this paragraph.

[10]One may object to the claim that Jones' killing F is a part of her saving the lives of the others on the grounds that her saving the lives of the others does not begin until she begins to operate on *them*, and this is after she has killed F. This intuition can be accommodated by identifying the act that Jones accomplishes by killing F as her *putting herself in a position to save the lives of the others*. On this view Jones' killing of F is merely a preparatory act for her saving the lives. It would stand in a similar position to saving the lives as walking up to a door stands to subsequently opening the door. One does not open the door by walking up to it, but one does put oneself in a position to open the door by walking up to it. This change can be made throughout the argument without affecting its results.

[11]For a more precise statement of the PDE and a review of its history, see Joseph Boyle, "Toward Understanding the Principle of Double Effect," *Ethics*, vol. 90 (1980): 527–38.

[12]It may be that this is the way that Thomson intends her transplant case to go. She says the doctor "can take the healthy person's parts, killing him, and install them in his patients, saving them." ("The Trolley Problem.")

[13]It may be that my version of the PDE is a departure from tradition in this regard. In his own statement of the PDE ("Double Effect," p. 532) Boyle presents it as a necessary as well as a sufficient condition for permissibility, but the traditional version he cites (p. 528) is stated as a sufficient condition only. Boyle does not discuss this point.

[14]Boyle points out ("Double Effect," p. 528, n. 7) that deontological considerations may be all or part of the "grave reason." The grave reason clause also prevents the PDE from justifying an agent's actions in a case in which there was some *other* way to produce the same good without producing any evil or harm at all. In such a case, the agent would not have had a "grave reason" for performing the act he did, since he could have brought about the same good in another, less costly, way.

[15]For an account along the latter lines see Norvin Richards, "Double Effect and Moral Character," *Mind*, vol. XCIII (1984): 381–97. Richards reviews some of the typical criticisms of the PDE in his article.

[16]I am indebted to Randy Hickman, Barry Loewer, Richard Nunan, Ferdy Schoeman, Bob Strikwerda, and a referee of this journal for helpful comments on an earlier version of this paper.

Another Trip on the Trolley

MICHAEL J. COSTA ▪ University of South Carolina
The Southern Journal of Philosophy, 1987

Costa previously argued in "The Trolley Problem Revisited" that the Principle of the Double Effect (PDE), provides a solution to the trolley problem. In this essay, he argues against some of Thomson's counterexamples. His objective is to protect the PDE against these examples.

One of the examples that Thomson gives involves the scenario in which the tracks which diverge at the switch actually come back together in a loop. (See Bystander 3 in Introduction.) Thus, if the bystander does nothing, the trolley will kill the five but then will be halted so that the one is saved. If the switch is thrown, the one will be killed, but again this will stop the momentum of the trolley, and the five will be saved. The difference between this case and Bystander 1 is that if the one had not been on the track, and the bystander had thrown the switch, then the five would have been killed anyway. Thomson maintains that it is still morally permissible for the bystander to save the five in this case. The extra track does not make any difference.

Costa thinks there is a difference here, however. In this case, the life of the one is in danger from the start because if the five were not on the track then he would be killed. The mediating event by which the one's life is saved is the death of the five. The choice then facing the bystander is either to let the five die and thus let the one live, or to cause the death of the one so that the five are saved. Because some lives are used as the instrument to save other lives, the PDE is at work again in this case.

Costa tests this explanation by slightly changing the scenario so that now the main line continues and only the sidetrack loops around to where the five are seated. If the bystander does nothing, the five die, but if this is the case, it is not the reason why the one is saved. Here, Costa thinks, it is not all right to pull the switch. The life of the one would be used to save the lives of the others, and there is no other situation to consider in which the death of the five is the means by which the one is saved. On this basis, Costa asserts that Thomson's new case does not show that the explanation in his earlier essay is wrong.

The second example Costa cites is the Hospital scenario. In this case, a gas must be manufactured to save the lives of five hospital patients. However, if this gas is produced, fumes will leak out which will kill another patient who cannot be moved. Thomson says that it would be wrong to produce the gas in this case, and Costa agrees. But he does not see it as a counterexample to the PDE.

In order for the PDE to work, he explains, the act that produces the good and bad consequences must not be an evil. Costa thinks that in this case the production of the gas is an evil even though the consequences are unintended. Such a point of view seems to imply that in the original trolley problem, since there were foreseeable bad consequences, the act must have been an evil thing. To solve this dilemma, Costa incorporates a distinction that Thomson makes between redirecting an existing threat and creating an entirely new one, and applies this to the PDE. The bystander is only redirecting an existing threat; he did not cause the trolley to begin its runaway course, i.e., he is not doing something that is inherently evil. Someone who brings a new threat into the world, like the creation of the gas, is creating a *prima facie* evil. (Contrast Fischer's cases: Bad Man 1 and 2; and Flood 1 and 2.) Costa closes his article with a trio of examples, the missile examples, which illustrate the points he makes about originating an evil and diverting an extant threat.

IN MY ARTICLE "THE TROLLEY PROBLEM REVISited"[1] (hereafter "TPR") I argued that the answer given to the Trolley Problem by Judith Thomson in her 1976 article "Killing, Letting Die, and the Trolley Problem"[2] (hereafter "TP1") was substantially correct and I attempted to draw some consequences from this for both action theory and the controversial Principle of Double Effect (hereafter "PDE"). In her recently published collection of essays, *Rights, Restitution and Risk*, Thomson republishes the 1976 article and newly publishes a follow-up treatment entitled simply "The Trolley Problem" (hereafter "TP2").[3] In the latter Thomson largely disowns her earlier analysis (she says "Mrs. Thomson seems to me to have been blundering around in the dark in that essay") and offers a new solution in terms of "a 'distributive exemption' which permits arranging that something that will do harm anyway shall be better distributed than it otherwise would be." The reason why a bystander may throw a switch causing a runaway trolley to divert to a sidetrack and kill an innocent person (rather than continue down the main line and kill five innocent persons) is not that one may cause harm for the sake of an outweighing good provided that the means to the good is not itself an evil and the harm is not intended (roughly the answer provided by PDE and seemingly the one Thomson was inclined toward in TP1), but the distributive exemption principle noted above.

I shall not here engage in detailed examination of Thomson's new proposal. I do think that Thomson's discussion in TP2 contains valuable insights and sheds considerable new light on the problem. I also think that her proposal has weaknesses (a fact acknowledged by Thomson), and that it is unlikely to be the last word on the topic (which is testimony to the depth and interest of the problem). My primary objective here is to respond to some cases provided by Thomson in TP2 that she apparently takes to be counterexamples to her earlier analysis. I think that the PDE solution developed in my TPR can be defended against these examples. Readers who are not familiar with the problem may wish to refer to TP1, TP2 and TPR,[4] but I think that my discussion below can be followed without such background.

In the version of the Trolley Problem discussed in TPR the mainline and the sidetrack diverge. Here it seems that it is morally permissible for the bystander (Smith) to pull the switch in order to save the five (A, B, C, D, and E) who are at risk on the main line even though his action causes the trolley to divert to the sidetrack and kill an innocent person (F) who would have survived if Smith had done nothing. The solution endorsed in TPR maintains that it is important to the permissibility of Smith's act in this case that the killing of F not be the means by which the other five are saved. One of Thomson's examples in TP2 challenges this by changing the circumstances in the case so that the tracks which diverge at the switch come back together in a loop as depicted in the diagram below.

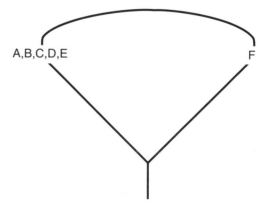

Here we are to assume that if Smith does nothing the trolley car will kill the five but be halted by their bodies so that F will be saved. If Smith throws the switch F will be killed, but again the trolley car will be halted by the body so that A, B, C, D, and E will be saved. Now if Smith should throw the switch it appears that he is saving the lives of the five by means of killing F. If F had not been on the track so that his body would stop the trolley, the other five would have been killed even if Smith had thrown the switch. And Smith is surely still causing the death of F, for if he had done nothing F would have lived. Thomson says that nevertheless Smith's act is permissible. ". . . we cannot really suppose that the presence or absence of that extra bit of track makes a major moral difference as to what an agent may do in these cases . . ."

Now it is not so clear to me that our intuitions are the same with respect to the revised case. That "extra bit of track" makes a substantial difference in the causal and counterfactual properties of the case (as it would not, for example, if it had simply been tacked on to one or the other of the ever further diverging tracks of the original case), and it is not obvious that this makes no moral difference. Let us suppose, however, that Thomson is right in her claim that Smith's act would still be morally permissible. I am further willing to admit that in this case (as opposed to the original case) Smith's killing of F is a means by which he saves the lives of the others. Therefore, I cannot explain his act's being permissible in the same way as for the original case. It does not follow, however, that the explanation given for the original case was wrong. For there may be something present in the revised case that provides some other means of justifying Smith's act. Indeed, I think this is so.

In the original case F's life is not at risk until the switch is pulled. But in the revised case F's life is endangered from the start. If the other five were not on the track, F would be hit by the trolley whether Smith pulled the switch or not. If Smith does not pull the switch, then the mediating event by which F's life is saved is the death of the other five. So the choice facing Smith is whether to let five die *thereby* letting F live, or to cause the death of F in order that the five may live. Whichever choice Smith makes some lives are the instrument by which another life or lives are saved. It seems to

me that this is the proper explanation as to why it is permissible for Smith to pull the switch in the revised scenario. PDE is presented in TPR as merely a sufficient condition for an act's being permissible. It is compatible with the fact that causing harm in order to do a good is sometimes permissible for other reasons.

We can test this explanation of the revised case by making one further change to the scenario. Suppose that the main line continues on and only the sidetrack loops around as depicted below:

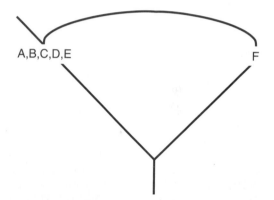

A,B,C,D,E   F

Now if Smith does nothing the five will still die: but their deaths would not be the means by which F's life is saved, since if they had not been there the trolley would have continued down the main track and F would have been perfectly safe. Here I think it is impermissible for Smith to pull the switch. His pulling the switch would constitute his using the death of F as a means of saving the lives of the others. And in this case there is no counterbalancing consideration of the lives of the others being the instrument by which F's life is saved. If Smith does not pull the switch F lives, but it is not the case that F's life is saved *by* the deaths of others. If I am correct in my claim that Smith's act is not permissible in this case, then Thomson's revised trolley case does not show that the explanation given in TPR is faulty. Moreover, my asymmetrical loop case would show that *Thomson's* explanation is faulty, since it would say that Smith's act is permissible.

Thomson has another example, however, which seems to create a different problem for the analysis given in TPR. She calls the example *Hospital* and describes it as follows:[5]

Suppose that there are five patients in a hospital whose lives could be saved by the manufacture of a certain gas, but that this will inevitably release lethal fumes into the room of another patient who for some reason we are unable to move.

Thomson says that it would be impermissible to manufacture the gas in this case even though the harm caused to the other patient would not be intended nor the means to saving the lives of the others. I agree, but I do not see that the case provides a counterexample to PDE. For PDE to be satisfied the act that produces the good and bad consequences must not itself be an evil.[6] Here it seems clear to me that the manufacture of the gas is *itself* an evil, even though the harmful consequences are not intended. If this is so, PDE is not satisfied by the gas manufacture case and no genuine counterexample has been presented.

But if this is true, then what about our original trolley case? Smith there knew that his action of throwing the switch would have harmful consequences (that it would lead to the death of F). So if an act that has foreseeable bad consequences is itself an evil, then Smith's throwing the switch is an evil and PDE is not satisfied even in the original trolley scenario.

Here an insight of Thomson's proves to be very helpful. Thomson draws a distinction between merely redirecting an existing threat or source of harm and creating a new one. Her "distributive exemption" provides that an agent's rights have not been violated if she is caused harm by the redirection of an already existing threat (to a sufficient number of others) provided that the means of redirecting the threat is not itself a substantial infringement of her rights.

Thomson does not find it "clear" why there should be such an exemption; and given the format in which she presents this consideration (i.e., as a special exemption to rights), it is hard to see what grounds it could have. But if we change to the standpoint of analyzing the case according to PDE, the grounds for such a consideration become apparent. Someone who is merely redirecting an existing threat for some good reason (e.g., Smith in the original Trolley Case) is not doing something that is evil in and of itself. On the other

hand, one who brings some *new* threat or source of foreseeable harm into the world is engaged in an act that is itself a *prima facie* evil and one that is more difficult to justify. This is so even if the end results are the same in terms of total harm caused versus total harm prevented. There is an important moral difference between redirecting an existing source of harm and creating a new one. One who does the latter is *originating* harm. That is itself a *prima facie* evil.

Now it may seem to be an *ad hoc* maneuver to make use of Thomson's own distinction to save PDE from her counterexamples, so some further comments are in order here. First, it appears clear to me that Thomson's distinction is both real and important. (This is not to say that it is easy to specify it precisely.) Further, I think it is very plausible that one who *originates* a source of foreseeable harm is engaged in a *prima facie* evil even if the harm is not intended. Given these two claims, the gas manufacture case is not a counterexample of PDE. However, one might feel that the cost of this maneuver is to remove all explanatory power from PDE. PDE no longer *explains* why Smith's actions in the Trolley Problem are permissible. All the real explanatory work is being done by Thomson's distinction. The reason why Smith's throwing of the switch is permissible and the manufacture of the gas is not is that Smith's act involves merely the redirection of an existing source of harm whereas the manufacture of the gas involves the creation of a new source of harm.

It does not seem to me, however, that *all* of the explanatory work is being done by Thomson's distinction. According to PDE the reason why Smith's act is permissible and the manufacture of the gas is not is that Smith's act involves doing something that is not itself an evil in order to produce a good, whereas the manufacture of the gas is itself an evil. In neither case is the harm produced intended or the means to the good. So the only part of PDE that comes into play in distinguishing these cases is the requirement that the act by means of which the good is produced not itself be an evil, and Thomson's distinction (and not PDE) is the thing that explains how the two cases differ with respect to this requirement. But two further points need to be noted. First, Thomson's distinction has to be wedded to an exemption principle for it to do any independent explanatory work. Why is it that a person's rights are not violated if harm to her is caused by a person's redirecting an existing threat rather than originating a new one? We have an explanatory gap here that does not exist in the PDE explanation. Second, Thomson's principle must itself incorporate consideration of *means*. The exemption does not apply if the means of redirecting the existing threat itself involves a serious violation of the person's rights. Why should this be the case? Again there is no such explanatory gap in the PDE explanation. It is of essence to PDE that the means not themselves be evil. In short, while Thomson's distinction is important and fills an explanatory gap that previously existed in the PDE account of the Trolley Problem, it is not clear that any more adequate alternative explanation has been offered.

Let me close by offering a trio of cases that display the various distinctions we have been discussing in an especially clear way.

Missile I

A runaway nuclear-armed missile is headed toward a major metropolitan area. If it should strike it, a million lives will be lost. Mr. Black sends a signal that diverts the missile from its path, and sends it to a sparsely populated area where its explosion takes only a dozen lives.

Missile II

This is like Missile I, except that in this case the only way that Black can keep the missile from striking the metropolitan area is to send up an antiballistic missile to intercept it. He does so. The antiballistic missile is successful and its destruction of the runaway missile costs no lives. However, a dozen people are killed by the exhaust of the antiballistic missile on its path to intercept.

Missile III

This is like Missile I, except that the only way that Black can keep the missile from striking the metropolitan area is to take remote control of a private plane without the permission of the plane's occupants. He directs the plane on a collision course with the runaway missile. The two collide and the collision costs no lives other than [those] of the dozen occupants of the private plane.

Now it may be that Black's acts are permissible in all three cases even if he foresees that the dozen lives will be lost. However, there is an important distinction. Black's act in Missile I is *clearly* permissible. Black's act in Missile II is less clearly permissible. And Black's act in Missile III is dubiously permissible and quite possibly impermissible (it would count as murder, wouldn't it?—or justifiable homicide?). Neither PDE nor Thomson's exemption principle would explain the (possible) permissibility of Black's acts in Missile II and III. If Black's acts here are permissible, they are so simply because of the vast disparity between number of lives saved and number of lives lost. But PDE does provide a basis for distinguishing among the three cases. In Missile I, Black's act satisfies PDE. In Missile II, Black's act does not satisfy PDE, but only because his act is itself a *prima facie* evil in that it originates a foreseeable harm. In Missile III, Black's act not only involves originating a foreseeable source of harm but also using that harm as a means to bringing about some good. Perhaps Thomson's approach could also distinguish between Missile II and III. It may say that Missile III involves a *double* violation of the rights of the harmed parties, or it may say that using harm to one as a means to something is a more serious violation of the person's rights than merely originating something that foreseeably causes harm to her. But it is dubious that any such explanation would be more natural than that offered by PDE.

Notes

[1]*The Southern Journal of Philosophy*, Vol. XXIV (1986), No. 4, pp. 437–49.

[2]*The Monist*, Vol. 59 (1976), pp. 204–17.

[3]Ed. William Parent, (Cambridge: Harvard University Press, 1986). TPI is Essay 6 and TP2 is Essay 7. All parenthetical page references in the text are to this book.

[4]They may also wish to refer to the source of many of Mrs. Thomson's examples, Phillipa Foot, "The Problem of Abortion and the Doctrine of Double Effect," pp. 59.

[5]TP2, p. 107. The example derives from Mrs. Foot, *op. cit.* Thomson also discusses a variant on the case (Hospital') which I shall ignore since it introduces no new relevant considerations.

[6]This is made clear in condition (3) of PDE as stated in TPR, p. 445. Use of this condition to handle other purported counterexamples is discussed on pp. 446-7 of TPR.

Thoughts on the Trolley Problem

JOHN MARTIN FISCHER ▪ University of California, Riverside
Unpublished

This article is in part a response to Thomson's "The Trolley Problem." Fischer criticizes Thomson's solution to the problem and provides discussion that generates a new version of the problem.

The discussion of what Fischer calls Thomson's Trolley Problem involves Bystander 1 and Transplant. (See Introduction.) The Extended Trolley Problem deals with Drug and Fat Man as well. The Extended Trolley Problem is, "What is it in virtue of which Bystander 1 and Drug are themselves similar but both different from Transplant and Fat Man?"

Fischer follows Thomson in rejecting the DDE on the basis of its distinction between such cases as Transplant and Hospital. (See Introduction; contrast Costa, p. 303.) Thomson's proposed solution to the Trolley Problem is as follows. First, one must distinguish: a) diverting an already existing threat so that it threatens one rather than five; and b) preventing a threat to five by introducing a new threat to one. Her point is that it is generally permissible to *divert* an existing threat, but not permissible to *introduce* a new one. Second, in order for one's acts to be permissible, the means one employs to get the threat to threaten one (rather than five) must not infringe a stringent right. In Drug it is permissible to save the five because a new threat is not introduced, and no one's rights are violated. In Fat Man the means of causing the threat to threaten one rather than five (pushing the Fat Man) infringes a stringent right of his; thus, it is not permissible to save the five. Thomson's proposed solution would rule out saving the five in *both* Transplant and Hospital, whereas the Doctrine of the Double Effect discriminates between the two cases. In this respect Thomson's approach is superior to the Doctrine of the Double Effect.

Fischer argues that the first ingredient in Thomson's solution generates problematic moral discriminations. Consider the following cases. In Bad Man I, unless you shoot an innocent person, the bad man will shoot five; however, if you shoot one, he will not shoot five. In Bad Man II, the bad man is about to shoot five. You can deflect the bullet, but this kills one. In these cases, it appears that it would be morally permissible to save the five in I just in case it would be permissible to save the five in II. The cases are morally on a par. Thomson's approach, however, would differentiate the two cases, because the first case involves the introduction of a new threat, whereas the second case involves the deflection of an already extant threat. In

Fischer's view, Thomson is committed to a moral distinction that does not comport with our considered moral judgments.

Thomson might indeed differentiate Bad Man I and Bad Man II, since she does differentiate the following parallel cases of Harry and Irving. The Russians have launched an atom bomb toward New York. Harry could deflect the bomb by pushing a button, but then the bomb would destroy Worcester. In the same scenario, Irving could launch an American bomb onto Worcester; this would destroy the Russian bomb and save New York. Thomson seems to claim that Harry may deflect the bomb, but Irving may not bomb Worcester. Fischer, on the other hand, claims that the Harry-Irving cases are also morally on a par: Harry may deflect the bomb onto Worcester if and only if Irving may bomb Worcester. Thus, Thomson's differentiation does not seem to hold.

Someone might attribute the symmetry Fischer finds between the Bad Man cases to the fact that a villain is involved in them. However, Fischer shows that the same point can be made without the evil component. Flood I (a new threat is introduced) and Flood II (an existing threat is deflected) are parallel cases to the Bad Man cases, except for the evil element. Fischer claims that the two Flood cases are morally on a par, but Thomson's method would have to distinguish them.

Fischer now examines the second ingredient in Thomson's solution, the claim requiring non-infringement of rights in the *means*. In Jiggle-the Tracks I, a trolley's direction is changed (by jiggling the track) to save five people, but the change kills an innocent man who happens to stand near the bifurcation. In Jiggle-the Tracks II, the case is the same except that the jiggling of the track causes the man to topple in front of the trolley. According to Fischer, there is no important moral difference between the two cases; however, Thomson's approach must distinguish them, since in the second case one's means of saving the five would be infringing stringent rights of the one. (A similar pair of examples is presented: Lethal Gas I and II.)

The final example is Ramp. The situation is similar to the Fat Man case, but in Ramp the only way to save the five would be by shoving the trolley onto the fat man (rather than the fat man onto the trolley as in Fat Man). Fat Man and Ramp are morally on a par, but again Thomson's approach would issue in an implausible differentiation. The fat man's stringent right is violated by the means of saving the five in Fat Man but not in Ramp. These considerations show that Thomson's solution is inadequate; it is not generalizable in a satisfactory way.

Ramp, however, is morally on a par with Bystander 1. If so, Fischer is committed to saying that Bystander 1 is morally on a par with Fat Man. He is willing to accept this assimilation for the following reasons. First, Bystander 1 is morally similar to Ramp, because the direction of the train (to the right or upward) is not morally significant. Second, Ramp is morally similar to Fat Man, because whether one "throws the man onto the train" or the "train onto the man" is not morally significant. Thus, it is hard to deny that Bystander 1 is morally on a par with Fat Man.

If this is correct, we must re-think our original intuition about Fat Man. Further, it would follow that the Extended Trolley Problem is no real problem, because one of its presuppositions—that it would obviously be impermissible to save the five in Fat Man—is incorrect.

We are now left with "Fischer's Trolley Problem:" in virtue of what are Bystander 1, and Fat Man, and Drug similar to each other but crucially different from Transplant? It might also be possible to conclude that it is impermissible to save the five in Bystander 1, because it is impermissible to do so in Fat Man. In this case, we are left with Your Trolley Problem: in virtue of what are Bystander 1, Transplant, and Fat Man similar to each other but crucially different from Drug?

I.

IN TWO FASCINATING AND PROVOCATIVE PAPERS, Judith Jarvis Thomson discusses the Trolley Problem.[1] In the more recent paper, Thomson suggests a solution to the problem. I shall first give a version of the Trolley Problem. Next, I shall criticize Thomson's purported solution to the problem. In the course of this criticism, it will become clear that I have my own Trolley Problem. That is, if my criticism of Thomson's putative solution is correct, then it is necessary to re-think the intuitive assumptions that generate the original problem (or, at least, a problem closely related to the original problem). Further, this will leave us with a new version of the "lovely, nasty problem."

II.

Let us follow Thomson in calling the first case, Bystander at the Switch. A trolley is hurtling down the tracks. There are five "innocent" persons on the track ahead of the trolley, and they will all be killed if the trolley continues going straight ahead.[2] There is a spur of track leading off to the right. Unfortunately, there is one innocent person on that spur of track. The brakes of the trolley have failed, and you are strolling by the track. You see that you could throw a switch that would cause the trolley to go onto the right spur. You are an "innocent bystander," i.e., not an employee of the railroad, and so forth. You can throw the switch, thus saving the five persons but causing the one to die, or you can do nothing, thus allowing the five to die. What should you do?

Well, it seems that it would at least be permissible for you to turn the trolley to the right, thus saving the five but killing the one. Perhaps it is also

obligatory to do this, but it is at least intuitively plausible that one *may* turn the trolley to the right.

Consider now a second case, Transplant. Thomson asks you to imagine that you are a surgeon, "a truly great surgeon." Now there are five persons in the hospital, each of whom needs an organ in order to survive. It just happens that an innocent visitor has arrived in the hospital, and you know that he is tissue-compatible with all the people who need organs, and that you could cut him up and distribute his parts among the five who need them. Would it be permissible for you to perform the operation (without his consent)?

Clearly, it would not be permissible for you to proceed. Why is it permissible for you to save the five in Bystander at the Switch but not in Transplant? This is what Thomson is inclined to call the Trolley Problem, and I shall call it, Thomson's Trolley Problem.[3]

I now wish to develop what I call the Extended Trolley Problem. It is obviously quite similar to (although slightly different from) Thomson's Trolley Problem. Consider a third case, Drug. You own a bottle of medicine. Five persons are dying, and each needs one-fifth of the medicine in order to survive. Another person is dying, but he needs all of the medicine in order to survive. What ought you to do?

Supposing that you have not promised the medicine to the one person, it seems that it is at least permissible for you to give the medicine to the five. Perhaps it is also obligatory to give the medicine to the five (given that you do not need it), but it is evidently at least permissible to do so.

But consider now a fourth case, Fat Man, which I again borrow from Thomson. You are standing on a bridge watching a trolley hurtling down the tracks toward five innocent persons. The brakes have failed, and the only way in which you can stop the train is by impeding its progress by throwing a heavy object in its path. There is a fat man standing on the bridge next to you, and you could push him over the railing and onto the tracks below. If you do so, the fat man will die, but the five will be saved.

What ought you to do? Whatever else is true about the situation, it seems that it would be impermissible for you to push the fat man over the railing. Thomson emphasizes this point, saying, "Everybody to whom I have put this case says it would not be [permissible]."[4] Now the question arises, why is it permissible to save the five in Drug but not in Fat Man? Obviously, this is parallel to the question about Bystander at the Switch and Transplant, which constitutes Thomson's Trolley Problem. The Extended Trolley Problem is this: what is it in virtue of which Bystander at the Switch and Drug are themselves similar but both different from Transplant and Fat Man?[5] Given what Thomson says about Fat Man, she should find the Extended Trolley Problem as pressing as Thomson's Trolley Problem.

III.

It might be useful briefly to consider whether the Doctrine of the Double Effect could be employed to solve the Extended Trolley Problem. The Doctrine of the Double Effect distinguishes between intended effects and foreseen but unintended effects, and it says that it is sometimes permissible to kill an innocent person as a foreseen but unintended effect of what one does, whereas it is impermissible to kill an innocent person either as an end or a means to some end one intends to bring about.

To apply the Doctrine to the Extended Trolley Problem, it could be said that in the cases, Transplant and Fat Man, one would in a clear sense be killing an innocent person as a means to some intended end, and thus one's actions would be impermissible. In contrast, in Bystander at the Switch and Drug, one would be killing as a mere side-effect of an action designed to achieve some intended end, and thus, one's action would be permissible.

It is notoriously difficult to explain exactly what the difference is between intending an outcome and merely foreseeing it in such a way as to allow us to classify various problematic cases uncontroversially. I shall not focus on this problem here. For my purposes it will be sufficient simply to assume that we have some method of distinguishing

between clear cases of intending (as either an end or means) and of merely foreseeing. The problem with the doctrine as a purported solution to the Extended Trolley Problem, as Thomson and others have pointed out, is that it is not generalizable; there are cases into which the Doctrine of the Double Effect introduces a moral differentiation that is antithetical to common sense.

To see this, consider an example which Thomson again borrows from Foot, Hospital.[6] There are five persons in a hospital whose lives could be saved by the manufacture of a certain gas. A side-effect of the process of manufacturing the gas is that lethal fumes will be released into the room of another patient (whom we are unable to move).

What is particularly odd about the Doctrine of the Double Effect is that it would prohibit us from saving the five in Transplant, whereas it would permit us to save the five in Hospital. This differentiation is too fine, however. Intuitively, I believe, we feel that it would be impermissible to save the five in either Transplant or Hospital. It is a constraint on any adequate solution to the Extended Trolley Problem that the solution be generalizable to other cases, and thus the Doctrine of the Double Effect is not a satisfactory solution: it generates a spurious, ungrounded discrimination. (This feature of the doctrine can be brought out by considering various other pairs of cases. For instance, the doctrine appears to prohibit an abortion performed by crushing the skull of the fetus, whereas it appears to allow a mother to take a fever-reducing drug that would, as a side-effect, kill the fetus.)

IV.

In her more recent paper, Thomson suggests a solution to the Trolley Problem (and, presumably, the Extended Trolley Problem). Thomson says:

> Suppose the bystander at the switch proceeds: He throws the switch, thereby turning the trolley onto the right-hand track, thereby causing the one to be hit by the trolley, thereby killing him —but saving the five on the straight track. There are two facts about what he does which seem to me to explain the moral difference between what he does and what the agent in Transplant would be doing if he proceeded. In the first place, the bystander saves his

five by making something that threatens them threaten one instead. Second, the bystander does not do that by means which themselves constitute an infringement of any right of the one's.[7]

So there are two basic ingredients in Thomson's suggestion for a solution. First, one must distinguish between (a) diverting a threat that already threatens five onto one; and (b) preventing something from threatening five by introducing a new threat to the one. Thomson's point is that it is sometimes permissible for one to divert an already extant threat in order to reduce the incidence of harm, whereas it is generally impermissible to reduce the incidence of harm by introducing a new threat. Second, in order for one's acts to be permissible, the means one employs to get the threat to threaten one rather than five must not infringe a stringent right.

Let us note how Thomson's solution would distinguish Drug from Fat Man. In Drug, one does not save the five by introducing a new threat to the one, and further, one's means of saving the five (giving them the medicine) does not in itself violate any of the one's rights. Thus, in Drug it is permissible to save the five. But in Fat Man one's means of getting the threat to threaten one rather than five (pushing the fat man over the railing) infringes a stringent right of the fat man—his right not to be pushed over a railing of a bridge. Thus, with Thomson's approach, it would not be permissible to save the five in Fat Man.

So Thomson's approach is a promising solution to the Extended Trolley Problem. Are there cases in which Thomson's approach differs from the Doctrine of the Double Effect? Yes, since Thomson's proposed solution would rule out saving the five in *both* Transplant and Hospital, whereas the Doctrine of the Double Effect (implausibly) discriminates between these cases. (In Transplant, one is introducing a new threat to the one and in so doing infringing a stringent right, and in Hospital one is impermissibly introducing a new threat to the one.) In this respect Thomson's approach is superior to the Doctrine of the Double Effect.

V.

I said above that there are two basic ingredients to Thomson's purported solution to the Trolley Problem. The first ingredient claims that there is an important distinction between diverting an already *extant* threat and introducing a *new* threat. I shall argue that this part of Thomson's approach appears to generate problematic moral discriminations.

Suppose that you are told by a bad man that if you do not shoot one innocent person, he will shoot five innocent persons, but that if you do shoot the one, he will refrain from shooting the five. Let us call this case, Bad Man I. We may here imagine that you cannot shoot the bad man, and that the only way to save the five is to shoot the one.

In Bad Man II the situation is slightly different. A bad man is about to shoot five innocent persons. You have a ray gun with which you could deflect the bullets and thus save the five. Unfortunately, the only way of deflecting the bullets would be onto one innocent person, which would cause his death.

I do not know exactly what to say about the two "Bad Man" cases. That is, I do not know whether it would be morally permissible to act in such a way as to save the five in both cases. It seems to me that it would be morally permissible to save the five in Bad Man I just in case it would be morally permissible to save the five in Bad Man II. I believe that the two cases, although factually different in certain respects, are morally on a par. However, since Bad Man I involves the introduction of a new threat, whereas Bad Man II involves the deflection of an already extant threat (*via* an apparently permissible means), Thomson's approach evidently must distinguish between the two cases. Here, in my view, Thomson is committed to a moral distinction that does not comport with our considered moral judgments.

Thomson might simply insist that there really is a moral difference between Bad Man I and Bad Man II. That she might take this tack is indicated by her discrimination of the cases of Harry and Irving:

(8)   Harry is President, and has just been told that the Russians have launched an atom bomb towards New York. The only way in which the bomb can be prevented from reaching New York is by deflecting it; but the only deflection-path available will take the bomb onto Worcester. Harry can do nothing, letting all of New York die; or he can press a button, deflecting the bomb, killing all of Worcester.

(9) Irving is President, and has just been told that the Russians have launched an atom bomb towards New York. The only way in which the bomb can be prevented from reaching New York is by dropping one of our own atom bombs on Worcester: the blast of the American bomb will pulverize the Russian bomb. Irving can do nothing, letting all of New York die; or he can press a button, which launches an American bomb on Worcester, killing all of Worcester.[8]

Thomson does not explicitly commit herself to the conjunctive claim that Harry may deflect the bomb but that Irving may not bomb Worcester, but she claims that "most people would agree" to this pattern of judgments about the cases.[9] Thomson might claim that since the cases of Harry and Irving are parallel to Bad Man II and Bad Man I, and that since Harry may deflect the bomb but Irving may not bomb Worcester, we should conclude that there really is an important moral difference between the two Bad Man cases. In contrast, I am inclined to believe that there is no moral difference between the two Bad Man cases, and in virtue of the parallel between the cases of Harry and Irving and the two Bad Man cases, that there is reason to believe that the alleged moral difference between the cases of Harry and Irving does not really exist. That is, I am inclined toward the view that, since you may save the five in Bad Man I if and only if you may save the five in Bad Man II, Harry may deflect the bomb onto Worcester if and only if Irving may bomb Worcester. For me, the Bad Man cases undermine the alleged judgments of "most people" in the cases of Harry and Irving.

Someone might attribute the symmetry that I find between the Bad Man cases to the fact that there is a villain involved in them. It might be claimed that the fact that we do not wish to be party to the projects of evil people has a tendency to swamp the asymmetry to which Thomson has pointed us, and distorts our intuitions concerning the cases.[10] But I believe that this is not the explanation for the symmetry which I find. Consider, for example, the following cases which are structurally similar to the Bad Man cases, except that they lack the "evil component."

Five people are in a very deep gorge toward which a flood is proceeding. If you do nothing, the flood will kill the five people. Under the circumstances, the only way to save the five is to yell very loudly to them; this will warn them so that they can climb to safety. But you know that if you were to do this, the sound waves would dislodge a rock, which would fall on (and kill) one innocent person (who is in a nearby gorge). Call this case Flood 1.

Flood 2 is similar: five people are in a very deep gorge toward which a flood is proceeding. In this case, however, you know that there is not enough time for the five people to climb to safety. Indeed, the only way that you can save the five is by yelling very loudly, thus dislodging a rock which would prevent the flood from killing the five. The only problem with this is that you realize that the rock would cause the flood to be diverted to a nearby gorge, thus killing one innocent person.

It is my view that the two Flood cases are morally on a par. One may save the five in Flood 1 just in case one may save the five in Flood 2. But in Flood 1 you would be introducing a new threat, whereas in Food 2 you would simply be deflecting an already extant threat. Thus, whereas I believe that the two cases ought to be treated as equivalent, Thomson's approach would distinguish them. And there is no evil person here to distort our intuitions; we can suppose that the floods are caused by natural disasters, and so forth. Thus the apparent symmetry in our considered opinions about certain cases cannot be explained by reference to the distorting effect of an evil person.

In this section, I have discussed some cases which are problematic for Thomson in virtue of the first ingredient of her putative solution to the Trolley Problem—the claim that there is an important moral difference between deflecting an already extant threat and introducing a new threat. Although I think that these cases are problematic for Thomson, I confess that some people may not agree with my judgments about the cases. Thus, I do not think that it is obvious that these cases are *decisive* against Thomson. Now I wish to turn to cases which are problematic for Thomson in virtue of the second ingredient: the claim that one's means of deflecting the already extant threat must not infringe a stringent right. Again, my claim will be that Thomson's approach issues in more nuanced moral discriminations than are justified by common sense, and thus that Thomson's approach suffers from a defect that is parallel to that of the Doctrine of the Double Effect. I believe that the cases which are problematic for Thomson in virtue of the second ingredient provide an even more convincing case against her approach than the cases pertinent to the first ingredient.

VI.

Consider the following case, Jiggle the Tracks I. A trolley is hurtling down a track toward five innocent persons. As before, the brakes have failed, and there is no way to stop the trolley. You are a bystander watching the scenario develop. You notice that there is a spur of track leading to the right on which (very close to the bifurcation of the tracks) stands one innocent person. You also notice that there is a button which you could push which would cause the tracks to "jiggle" in such a way as to cause the train to go onto the right fork. If you were to push the button, you would save the five persons but cause the death of the one.

What to do? Well, it seems intuitively permissible to push the button, and Thomson's approach would yield this result. You would be deflecting a threat which threatens five in such a way that it threatens one, and your means of doing so (pushing the button) would not violate anyone's rights.

Imagine now a related case, Jiggle the Tracks II. Everything is the same here except for the manner of track-jiggling which would result from your pushing the button. That is, there is a trolley hurtling down the tracks toward five persons, with a spur leading to the right on which there stands a man (very close to the point of track bifurcation). This time if you push the button, the tracks would be jiggled in such a way that the man would be toppled onto the track in front of the train. We can suppose that the man is large enough to stop the progress of the train, but that if this were to occur, he would be killed.

Now my view about this case is that it is "morally parallel" to Jiggle the Tracks I. I believe that it would be morally permissible to push the button in Jiggle the Tracks II if and only if it would be morally permissible to do so in Jiggle the Tracks I. Whereas it seems to me that there is no important moral difference between the two cases, Thomson's approach must distinguish them. She must say that although it is morally permissible to push the button in Jiggle

the Tracks I, it is not morally permissible to do so in Jiggle the Tracks II. In Thomson's proposed solution to the Extended Trolley Problem, one's means of causing the threat to threaten one rather than five must not infringe a serious right of the one person. But in Jiggle the Tracks II one's means of getting the train to threaten the one rather than the five involves toppling the one man onto the other track, which is presumably an infringement of a stringent right of his. (This is not less stringent a right than the right not to be pushed off a bridge, which Thomson takes to be stringent. Note that she must say that the right not to be pushed off a bridge is stringent, even if the bridge is extremely close to the ground, in order to secure her intended result in Fat Man.)

At this point someone might attempt to defend Thomson against my charge of inappropriate differentiation of the two cases by claiming that in Jiggle the Tracks II, the pushing of the button is the means whereby you cause the trolley to threaten the five rather than the one, and pushing the button does not in itself constitute an infringement of the one's rights. But Thomson cannot say this. Remember what Thomson says about Fat Man:

> . . . shoving a person is infringing a right of his. So also is toppling a person from a footbridge. I should stress that doing these things is infringing a person's rights even if doing them does not cause his death —even if doing them causes him no harm at all. As I shall put it, shoving a person, toppling a person off a footbridge, are themselves infringements of rights of his . . .
>
> We might of course have imagined it not necessary to shove the fat man. We might have imagined that all you need to do to get the trolley to threaten him instead of the five is to wobble the handrail . . . Wobbling the handrail would be impermissible, I should think —no less than shoving . . .
>
> What I had in mind, then, is a notion of "means" which comes out as follows. Suppose you get a trolley to threaten one instead of five by wobbling a handrail. The means you take to get the trolley to threaten the one instead of the five include wobbling the handrail and all those further things that you have to succeed in doing by wobbling the handrail if the trolley is to threaten the one instead of the five.[11]

Note that this interpretation of "means," within the context of Thomson's theory, is attractive. In contrast, it would be radically implausible to adopt an interpretation according to which a moral distinction would be drawn between a case in which you must topple the fat man by shoving him and a case in which you could topple the fat man by wobbling the handrail. But if one employs the interpretation of means sketched above, then one cannot say that toppling the man is not part of one's means of getting the trolley to threaten the one instead of the five in Jiggle the Tracks II. So Thomson seems to be committed to a rather unsettling differentiation of the two Jiggle cases.

Consider next a similar pair of cases. Let us call the first case, Lethal Gas I. In this case you can see that lethal gas is proceeding down a hallway toward a room in which there are five innocent persons. You know that there is a trap-door leading to a small room to the right. If you open the trap-door, the lethal gas will be directed to the right, killing an innocent man who is sitting in the room.

Lethal Gas II is similar except that you know that if you open the trap-door and do nothing else, the lethal gas will continue proceeding toward the end of the hallway. (Perhaps there is a different draft of air in Lethal Gas II than in Lethal Gas I.) You see, however, that if you open the trap-door and push the one man (who, again, is sitting in a small room to the right) into the main hallway, he will stop the lethal gas. Lamentably, if you push the man into the hallway, the lethal gas will kill him.

In Lethal Gas I, you divert the gas onto the man. In Lethal Gas II, you push the man into the gas. So Thomson must distinguish the two cases in virtue of the second ingredient of her purported solution to the Trolley Problem: her claim that the means one employs in causing the threat to threaten one instead of five must not infringe a stringent right. There is a clear factual difference between the two cases, but I do not think that this factual difference underwrites a moral difference. It seems to me that one may save the five in Lethal Gas I just in case one may save the five in Lethal Gas II. Independently of whether one believes that one *may* save the five in either case, it seems to me that the two cases are morally on a par.

I think that we can drive this point home as follows. Lethal Gas 1* is exactly like Lethal Gas 1 except that it is explicit that you open the trap-door by pushing some button in front of you (which initiates the appropriate mechanism). And Lethal

Gas 2* is just like Lethal Gas 2 except that you cause the man to topple into the main hallway by pushing some button in front of you (which initiates the appropriate mechanism). Certainly, Lethal Gas 1* is morally parallel to Lethal Gas 2.* Further, it seems to me that Lethal Gas 1* is morally parallel to Lethal Gas 2* if and only if Lethal Gas 1 is morally parallel to Lethal Gas 2. Hence, Lethal Gas 1 is morally parallel to Lethal Gas 2. Just as in the two Jiggle cases, in the two Lethal Gas cases, Thomson is committed to a finer set of moral discriminations than is licensed by our considered moral judgments.

I wish now to consider a final example, Ramp. Ramp is in many respects quite similar to Fat Man: there is a trolley hurtling down a track toward five innocent persons, and an innocent fat man standing on a bridge above the tracks. Let us suppose that the bridge is a railroad bridge (i.e., with railroad tracks on it). And let us imagine that you could push a button that would cause a ramp to go up underneath the train. Further, if you were to push the button and thus cause the ramp to go up, you would thereby cause the train to jump up to the tracks on the bridge and to continue along those tracks. If you were to push the button, you would save the five, but regrettably, the train would run over the fat man. In Fat Man the only way in which you could save the five would be by shoving the fat man onto the train. In Ramp the only way in which you could save the five would be by "shoving the train onto the fat man." In all other respects the cases are the same, and I have a strong inclination to say that Fat Man and Ramp are morally on a par. If so, we again have a case where Thomson's approach issues in an implausible differentiation. This is because in Fat Man, one's means of causing the threat to threaten one rather than five involves an infringement of a stringent right of the fat man, whereas in Ramp it does not.

To strengthen my point, consider Fat Man.* In Fat Man* the situation is exactly as it is in Fat Man, except that you can push a button which would cause the bridge's handrailing to wobble, which would cause the fat man to topple in front of the train. Although there is a factual difference, I think that it is clear that there is no moral difference between Fat Man and Fat Man.* And it seems to me quite evident that there is no moral difference between Fat Man* and Ramp. I do not find it normatively plausible to suppose that the factual difference between these two cases really underwrites a moral difference between them. How can it make a difference whether one pushes the button that causes the fat man to fall into the path of the train or the button that causes the train to "jump" toward the fat man? Thus, because there is no reason to think that the pertinent judgments are not transitive, it should be evident that there is no moral difference between Fat Man and Ramp.

If this is correct, then it is evident that Thomson's approach to providing a solution to the Trolley Problem is inadequate; it is not generalizable in a satisfactory way.

VII.

Perhaps the reader will not have failed to notice a rather disconcerting implication of the above remarks. I claim that Fat Man* and Ramp are morally on a par, and thus that Fat Man and Ramp are as well. But Ramp is clearly morally on a par with Bystander at the Switch. Thus it would seem that I am committed to saying that Bystander at the Switch is morally on a par with Fat Man, and this result is rather alarming indeed. After all, it is a presupposition of the Extended Trolley Problem that it would be permissible to save the five in Bystander at the Switch but *not* in Fat Man.

One might take the apparent implication of my criticism of Thomson—that Bystander at the Switch and Fat Man are morally parallel—as a *reductio* of the criticism of Thomson. But I am rather inclined to persist in my claim that Fat Man and Ramp are on a par, and thus that the second ingredient of Thomson's approach is problematic. Remember that the two Jiggle the Tracks cases and the two Lethal Gas cases *independently* motivate the claim that the second ingredient is problematic. Thus I believe that it is more reasonable to accept the implication of the criticism of Thomson—that the cases of Bystander at the Switch and Fat Man are morally similar—than to take it to be a *reductio* of the criticism. And because I believe that it would be permissible for you to save the five in Bystander at the Switch, obviously I must accept that it is permissible to save the five in Fat Man, even though this is rather surprising, and it is the result with which everybody to whom Thomson has put this case disagrees.

I am willing to accept this result because there is a plausibility argument for it which is implicit in

what I've said above, and I do not see how I could challenge this argument. There are two steps, each of which is seemingly unassailable. First, Bystander at the Switch is morally similar to Ramp, because whether the train is shunted to the right or upward cannot be morally significant. Second, Ramp is morally similar to Fat Man, because whether one "throws the train onto the fat man" or "throws the fat man onto the train" cannot be morally significant. Thus, it is hard to deny that Bystander at the Switch is morally on a par with Fat Man.

Where does all this leave us? I have argued that Thomson's proposed solution to Thomson's Trolley

Problem (and presumably to the Extended Trolley Problem) is inadequate in a way which is parallel to the inadequacy of the Doctrine of the Double Effect. Although the two approaches depart from common sense in different ways, they both posit moral discriminations that do not match the contours of common sense. If my criticism of Thomson is correct, then I must ask that we re-think our unreflective intuition about Fat Man. Furthermore, if the criticism is correct, it would follow that the Extended Trolley Problem is no real problem, because one of its presuppositions—that it would be impermissible to save the five in Fat Man—is incorrect. Of course this still leaves us with Thomson's Trolley Problem, to which I have not presented a solution. Regrettably, we are also left with a new problem, which I might (immodestly) call Fischer's Trolley Problem: how are Bystander at the Switch, Fat Man, and Drug similar to each other but crucially different from Transplant?

You might resist my conclusion about Fat Man by insisting that all that I have established by introducing Ramp, *if* I have established anything at all, is that Fat Man and Bystander at the Switch are morally on a par. I have gone on to conclude that it is permissible to save the five in Fat Man, because it is permissible to save the five in Bystander at the Switch. But you might say that one might as well conclude that it is impermissible to save the five in Bystander at the Switch, because it is impermissible to do so in Fat Man.

I agree that I have not argued that one must come to my conclusion rather than the alternative conclusion (your conclusion), and I do not know how I could provide such an argument. However, it is useful to see that there is a residual problem "either way." If one agrees with me about the cases, then one is faced with Fischer's Trolley Problem. If one comes to the conclusion that it is impermissible to save the five in Bystander at the Switch, then one is faced with Your Trolley Problem: how are Bystander at the Switch, Transplant, and Fat Man similar to each other but crucially different from Drug?[12,13]

Notes

[1]"Killing, Letting Die, and the Trolley Problem," p. 67, and "The Trolley Problem," p. 279. Thomson attributes the original formulation and discussion of the

problem to Philippa Foot, "The Problem of Abortion and the Doctrine of the Double Effect," p. 59.

[2]I shall use "innocent" in a rather broad sense to mean that the persons have not done anything morally wrong in virtue of which they "deserve" to die or have forfeited their right to life, etc. Furthermore, I shall assume throughout this paper that no "special" facts distinguish the persons involved in the cases. For instance, none of the six persons involved in Bystander at the Switch is a mass-murderer, great scientist, and so forth; furthermore, one has not made special arrangements with any of them. Of course, I shall be engaging in schematic and partial descriptions of the various cases, and the reader needs to keep in mind that certain ways of filling in the details of the cases will affect the moral judgments appropriate to the cases.

[3]Sometimes I shall simply use the term, Trolley Problem, to refer to either of the two problems that I shall distinguish as Thomson's Trolley Problem and the Extended Trolley Problem.

[4]Thomson, in *Rights, Restitution, and Risk: Essays in Moral Theory*, William Parent (ed.), Cambridge: Harvard University Press, 1986, p. 109.

[5]I take the point asserting parallelism to be compatible with the fact that in Bystander at the Switch you might be killing five, whereas in Drug you might be failing to save five.

[6]*Ibid.*

[7]*Ibid.*

[8]*Ibid.*

[9]*Ibid.*

[10]I am grateful to correspondence with Judith Thomson for this point.

[11]*Ibid.*

[12]One might take the existence of these residual problems to be evidence that the methodology that places weight on intuitive judgments about cases is not worthwhile. But whereas I believe that we must be extremely careful in the consideration of examples, I do not see how we can avoid it. Furthermore, it might be thought that the arguments employed in this paper are problematic in virtue of being **sorites**-type arguments. Now I do not have a general theory of the distinction between specious arguments of the sorites sort and acceptable arguments employing transitivity. I can only point out that the arguments employed above do not make use of extremely large numbers of applications of some very small change, as one finds in the obviously fallacious sorites-type arguments. Furthermore, it is clear that it does not follow from the existence of some fallacious sorites-type arguments that *any* argument employing transitivity is unacceptable.

[13]I have benefited from discussing the issues dealt with in this paper with: Robert Hanna, Jonathan Harwitz, and Mark Ravizza. I am very grateful for comments on a previous version of this paper from Judith Jarvis Thomson.

Morality *De Re*: Reflections on the Trolley Problem

ROBERT HANNA ▪ University of Colorado, Boulder
                      Unpublished

Traditional moral theory might lead us to think that moral principles are determined exclusively from the internal, rational standpoint of the moral agent and strictly in advance of actual experience (**a priori**). The main thesis of this paper is that moral principles are sometimes determined from a standpoint which is both external to the moral agent and experiential (**a posteriori**). Hanna calls this approach to moral principles **morality *de re*** ("of things"). Several other recent moral theorists, such as Thomas Nagel and Bernard Williams, have brought similar externalistic and a posteriori moral phenomena under the term-of-art "moral luck," but have *not* argued for a significant role for these phenomena in the determination of moral principles.

Hanna begins by setting up the classic Trolley Problem. Various standard solutions to the problem are then discussed in some detail: (1) the distinction between killing and letting die; (2) the distinction between negative and positive duties; (3) the Doctrine of Double Effect; and (4) Judith Thomson's solution. After having laid out and criticized each putative solution, Hanna goes on to suggest his own solution which he calls the Principle of Moral Inertia. The solution turns on being able to distinguish between **participants** and **bystanders** with respect to a given moral situation. In the penultimate section, this approach is extended to the problem of telling the moral difference between Good and Bad Samaritans. Hanna concludes by frankly admitting that he is not in possession of an effective decision procedure or criterion for distinguishing between moral participants and bystanders, although he does not think that this harms his argument for his main thesis.

The familiar construal of the killing/letting die distinction in terms of active vs. passive bringings-about of death does not seem in and of itself to carry any moral weight. Hanna suggests, however, that the distinction is intuitively related to moral integrity: it is a greater violation of a person's integrity actively to bring about a death than passively to do so. (He thinks that this rationale also underwrites the distinction between negative and positive duties and the Doctrine of Double Effect.) Even with this underpinning, however, the moral principle embodying killing/letting die is implausible in cases in which an evil person has intentionally set up a choice between killing one and letting five die. Both seem intuitively impermissible, but the killing/letting die distinction entails that only the killing option is impermissible, while the letting die option is permissible.

The distinction between negative and positive duties implies that there is a more stringent moral demand on us to refrain from harming other persons than to preserve their well-being. Two arguments are presented by Hanna against this principle. The upshot of both arguments is that the principle rather unintuitively rules out the permissibility of turning the trolley onto the one in cases such as the one called Bystander 1 (as opposed to Bystander 2) in the Introduction.

Converted into a **moral principle** applicable to trolley cases, the Doctrine of Double Effect says that while it is impermissible to kill a person as the necessary means or intended result of an action, it is permissible to kill someone as a foreseen side-effect of that action. Hanna dispatches this principle by means of what amounts to two variants on Bystander 1. In the first, the one is standing directly in front of the switch in such a way that the bystander will have to push him in front of the trolley if he is to save the five. In the second, the one is standing right beside the switch in such a way that when the bystander turns the switch in order the save the five, the one will be knocked by the switch into the path of the trolley. The Doctrine of Double Effect makes the first of these cases impermissible and the second permissible. Hanna argues that the two cases are morally equivalent, however, because the structural difference between them (the minute difference in where the one is standing) seems morally negligible: either both are permissible or both impermissible. Hanna also argues against Thomson's proposal.

Having demonstrated the downfall of the four standard solutions to the Trolley Problem, Hanna then turns to his own proposal. He begins by defining a **moral situation**: the main idea is that of a causal process in the physical world that also involves moral agents in such a way that they can be harmed or benefited by the process. A participant is then said to be a moral agent actually *in* one of these situations, while a bystander is said to be a moral agent *outside* one of these situations. The moral principle based on these notions holds that while it is at least sometimes permissible to kill a participant in order to save five, it is impermissible to kill a bystander in order to save five. According to this principle, then, in Bystander 1 (just as in the Introduction's Bystander 2, Bystander 3, Drug, Boat, and Random Mechanism cases), the one is a participant and may be killed in order to save the five, while in Fat Man (just as in the Introduction's Transplant, Shark, Scan, and Hospital cases), the one is a mere bystander and may not be so killed. Hanna calls this the Principle of Moral Inertia because—as against a claim made by Judith Thomson to the effect that there is no such principle—sometimes moral difference seems to turn primarily on whether a person just happens to *be* part of an ongoing causal process, or just happens *not to be* part of an ongoing causal process. It should be noted that an important virtue of the Principle of Moral Inertia, as opposed to the other proposed solutions, is that it generates intuitively plausible results in *all* the central trolley-type cases.

Hanna goes on to extend his principle to another range of related cases, those involving the question of intervention or non-intervention in moral situations. Who is the Good or Bad Samaritan, and why? Hanna claims that the issue of Good and Bad Samaritanhood is best understood in terms of the **participant/bystander distinction** developed in the trolley cases.

I.

HOW DO EXTERNAL, CONTINGENT, ACTUAL STATES of affairs in the world play a role in morality? It might ordinarily be thought that such phenomena are morally irrelevant, and that what counts morally is what can be rationally, impersonally, derived *a priori* from insight into natural law, following the categorical imperative, intuition of rights and duties, fair choice behind the veil of ignorance, or from a projection of possible good or bad consequences. Doubtless, these things are each very important in moral life; but they by no means exhaust it. The world[1] is a totality of states of affairs in which things, acts, values, and meanings at least partially transcend the human moral agent, and as Heidegger [1889–1976] points out, the agent is simply "thrown" into this world.[2] As a consequence, there are moral occasions on which the actual, brute condition of the world—its purely existential, inertial character—simply overrides or at least constrains other kinds of moral claims. On such occasions, strange as it may seem, the "ought" is in some sense derivable from the "is." Morality is to this extent unavoidably *de re*. To modify Sartre's famous slogan slightly, here moral existence precedes moral essence.

There are in truth quite a variety of ways in which brute facticity plays a morally significant role in human affairs. This variety may be collected together under the more general category of "moral luck," a current term-of-art which is somewhat loosely defined, but nevertheless very important.[3] "Moral luck" means, roughly, those aspects of moral experience which (1) are somehow beyond rational, human control; (2) are given *a posteriori* as opposed to *a priori*; and (3) are in some sense external, contingent, and conditioned. Although these terms are not themselves uncontroversial, the general sense of moral luck is, I think, clear. It is the idea of a moral fate or necessity which is not a fatalism; it involves a worldly givenness which is consistent with the existence of responsible action.[4] In any case, what I want to focus on is an aspect of moral luck not much mentioned in current discussions, namely the accidental, "thrown" place or direction of movement of the human body[5] with respect to moral situations

already underway in the world. The dimension of moral life which depends on these locative and directional considerations I dub "moral inertia."[6] It makes a moral difference sometimes just *where* the moral agent happens to find himself relatively to ongoing moral situations, and just what he already happens to be "up to."

II.

Perhaps the best way to illustrate the relevance of moral inertia for morality is to see how it shows itself in a fairly restricted range of cases. I shall focus on cases having to do with how a death comes about, because (1) philosophers have already spilled a certain amount of ink for the sake of this topic, thus giving my account a certain dialectical force; and (2) it provides a particularly clear set of examples in which the manifest structures of moral inertia seem likely to agree with our intuitive or "phenomenological" assessment of the moral variations across the cases.

Judith Jarvis Thomson, in an important pair of papers[7] which play variations on a theme provided originally by Philippa Foot,[8] considers a range of cases which center on the moral significance of the way in which death comes about. Given current discussions about euthanasia, abortion, and the conduct of war, the moral importance of this topic is obvious.[9] Thomson's analysis focuses on what she calls the "Trolley Problem." I will present this problem in a way which is in part similar to, but in part different from, Thomson's account. (Nevertheless it must be understood that the general style of these examples is entirely due to Thomson.) We will begin with two basic cases.

The Trolley Driver

Edmund is the driver of a trolley which has lost its brakes, and is running away out of control. There is a "Y"-shaped intersection on the tracks ahead of the trolley; at the end of one branch of the "Y" stands one person unable to get out of the way, while at the end of the other branch stand five people in the same predicament. The "Y" intersection is constructed so that Edmund has no way of knowing which way the trolley will turn if left alone, but he can by means of a control button in the trolley turn it deliberately onto one or another of the two branches.

The Spectator on the Bridge

Edgar is walking on the bridge which crosses above some trolley tracks, and sees what is to all appearances a runaway trolley speeding towards five people standing on the tracks on the far side of the bridge. The five have no way of getting off the tracks in time to save themselves. There is an Enormous Individual standing on the bridge, looking down onto the tracks. Edgar quickly realizes that the only way to stop the trolley before it gets to the five is to push the Enormous Individual off the bridge so that the great weight falls squarely in front of the trolley.

The Trolley Problem, as I see it, is this. Our third-person moral judgments[10] tell us that it is permissible for Edmund in *The Trolley Driver* either to turn his trolley onto the one, thereby saving the five, or simply to let the trolley take its own course; while it seems quite impermissible for Edgar in *The Spectator on the Bridge* to push the Enormous Individual off the bridge in order to save the five. Why is it that Edmund can save his five, but Edgar cannot save his?[11]

What does seem clear about the two cases is that in *The Trolley Driver* we can adopt a utilitarian form of moral reasoning which makes human worth additive and the goal to bring about the greatest good for the greatest number—thereby telling us that Edmund can permissibly save the five and sacrifice the one. Or else we can opt for an "innumerate" form of moral reasoning which takes each life threatened as equally, non-additively, valuable from its own point of view—thereby telling us that Edmund can permissibly let the trolley go on as it will, just as if he had decided to flip a coin.[12] There is of course room for discussion on these options; some will think, for instance, that it is not only permissible but obligatory to sacrifice the one in *The Trolley Driver* in order to save the five; and these people will find the innumerate "coin toss" strategy objectionable. I do think, however, that given the structure of the case, the universal (strong) disjunction of the two strategies holds. *Everyone* would seem to agree either on the utilitarian or on the innumerate approach; but not everyone, of course, on both.

What I am particularly keen on discovering, in any event, is why in *The Spectator on the Bridge* neither the utilitarian nor the innumerate form of moral reasoning has any force. It is simply impermissible for Edgar to push the Enormous Individual down onto the tracks, even though utilitarian reasoning extrapolated from *The Trolley Driver* seems to say that one can or must sacrifice the one to save the five. The innumerate approach just does not seem relevant in this case. So clearly what is at work in the moral difference between the two cases is something other than straightforward utilitarian or innumerate principles. In short, what we are looking for is some sort of non-utilitarian or non-consequentialist constraint on utilitarian or consequentialist principles.

I have so far neglected to mention that it is an intrinsic feature of these two cases (and also of the other I will mention) that there are no special obligations in effect for, or binding claims made upon, either Edmund or Edgar; that none of the threatened persons' identities is known and so far as anyone can tell, these persons do not differ in any morally relevant way from the ordinary run of adult human beings; and that none of the threatened persons took any special risks, or broke any promises, or violated anyone's rights, in order to get where he is now. In short then, in all of these cases, unless otherwise specified, "all other things remain equal." Thus it is very likely that whatever it is that is making the moral difference here is a more or less undiluted essential moral structure of the cases.

There have been a variety of attempts to articulate the nature of this moral structure by stating moral principles by which we can divide the two cases, and come up with answers which at once conform to our third-person judgments and leave no moral remainders. As a way of setting the stage for my own suggestion, I will run through four of the most important candidates.

(1.)

The well-known distinction between killing and letting-die can be brought to bear on these two cases. For all its familiarity, however, the distinction is not as clear as one would like it to be. "Killing" seems to mean roughly "actively, deliberately, determining a death directly," while "letting-die" means "passively, deliberately, allowing a death to be determined."[13] The distinction, as is obvious, has to do with whether a person who stands in a morally significant relation to another's death has a deliberate, direct, influence on the causal sequence terminating in another person's death; or whether by contrast the first person deliberately refrains from a direct influence on the causal sequence, where this influence would have saved the second person who is in any case sure to die.[14] (Naturally there are many other ways of bringing about deaths besides these.)

Conceptually, the distinction remains troublesome pending fuller clarification of the notions of "bringing about," "influence on a causal sequence," "active," "passive," "refraining," and so on. But at a macroscopic, phenomenological level what the distinction is driving at seems clear enough. The badness of the bad thing (i.e., the death) seems to attach itself to the "active agent" (the one who kills) in a way distinct from the way in which it attaches to the "passive agent" (the one who lets-die). Owing simply to the nature of the causal chain, the death is traceable directly back to the "active agent," but not to the "passive agent." On the whole (and it is hard to say precisely why) it seems better morally not to have bad things attach directly to the moral agent by way of his causality (other things being equal). This moral judgment would seem to be based on the on-the-whole-preferable inviolability of moral integrity—and not on the "moral self-indulgence" which is involved in the squeamishness about "dirty hands."[15]

Applying this distinction between killing and letting-die to our cases, we come up with the following:

(KLD) **In pairs of cases in which there is respectively the option of either (a) killing one, or (b) letting one or five die, it is impermissible to do (a) but permissible to do (b).**

(By a "pair of cases," I will mean two cases which differ only with respect to the relevant options, and for which all other things remain equal.) It seems initially that we are on to something here. Edmund in *The Trolley Driver* is certainly permitted by (KLD) at least to let the trolley do what it may, and therefore not actually to steer it onto one of the branches. For steering it onto one of the branches would be deliberate, direct action determining the death of some of the persons, and therefore killing.

Obviously, killing five is worse than killing one, and thus killing one is the only morally conceivable option for Edmund here. But by (KLD), this is impermissible. By contrast, simply letting the trolley run on would mean letting one or five die, and this is permissible by (KLD). (KLD) therefore satisfies at least the disjunction of intuitively permissible options with respect to the *The Trolley Driver*, although it utilizes neither the utilitarian nor the innumerate forms of reasoning.

In *The Spectator on the Bridge,* on the other hand, Edgar kills the one if he pushes him off the bridge in front of the speeding trolley. Even if Edgar were only to wobble the handrail a little, causing the Enormous Individual to fall,[16] it would still be killing insofar as Edgar would play a determining, direct, deliberate, causal role in the sequence leading to the Enormous Individual's death. Since Edgar obviously has the option of simply letting the five die—merely by doing nothing—by (KLD) Edgar's pushing the one off the bridge is impermissible. So (KLD) seems to comport with our judgments about the two cases.

(KLD), however, does not seem to be ultimately plausible as the principle behind the moral difference in the two cases. Why? In the first place, most people who hear about the Trolley Problem agree that it is permissible for Edmund in *The Trolley Driver* to turn the trolley deliberately onto the one, thereby saving five. In fact, it seems likely that a vast majority of moral judgers (assuming that they would be inclined to grant the permissibility of either option) would say that it is "*more* permissible" to do this than simply to "toss the coin" and let the trolley go on, thereby risking the deaths of five. As we have noted, some even say that it is obligatory for Edmund to turn the trolley onto the one. Certainly (KLD) does not allow for either of these intuitions, and therefore would seem to be importantly flawed.

Besides that argument (which flirts with the fallacy of *ad populum*), we can consider a variant on *The Trolley Driver* in which Edmund$_2$ is a cruel torturer who has brought it about that the six innocent people are on the tracks, and he can either simply let the trolley go on or decide which of the two branches to choose. Whatever Edmund$_2$ does in this variant seems impermissible and equally bad; yet one option involves a killing, and the other only a letting die. (KLD), which says that where there is an option of killing one or letting one or five die, killing one is impermissible and letting one or five die is permissible, cannot therefore be correct.

(2.)

Another distinction which seems to cast light on the Trolley Problem is that between "negative duties" and "positive duties." This distinction points out that in general there are more stringent demands on the moral agent to refrain from actively harming other persons than to preserve their well-being. In the case of deaths, this means that there is a more stringent demand not to kill than to save lives. The refraining-type duties are negative, while the preserving-type duties are positive. This distinction is a close relative of killing *versus* letting-die. In killing *versus* letting-die, the crucial thing seems to be not to violate the moral integrity of the good agent by transitivity of badness along causal chains. In the distinction between negative and positive duties, the idea is that we are simply obliged never deliberately to harm actively where the option of refraining is possible, and this overrides the *prima facie* duty to save innocent persons about to die. All the cases of killing will be cases proscribed by negative duties, and all the cases where letting die is permissible will be cases in which positive duties are overridden by negative duties. Thus killing *versus* letting-die and negative duties *versus* positive duties will line up appropriately, while nevertheless the latter distinction seems to articulate more clearly the essential structure of the moral judgment.

Returning to our trolley cases, we can now try out a new principle:

(NP) **In pairs of cases in which there is respectively the option of either (a) violating a negative duty to refrain from actively harming one, or (b) violating a positive duty to save one or five, it is impermissible to do (a) but permissible to do (b).**

Here (NP) seems to have isolated the difference between *The Trolley Driver* and *The Spectator on the Bridge* in a way superior to that of (KLD), while still comprehending the central moral insight motivating (KLD). The first option of *The Trolley Driver* in which Edmund decides to run the trolley is rendered impermissible by (NP). Since killing five is

obviously impermissible where killing one is impermissible, and since killing one (thus violating a negative duty) is impermissible where there is the option of violating only a positive duty to save one or five, both parts of the first option are impermissible. Consequently, by (NP) the second option of *The Trolley Driver* is permissible, since in neither case does Edmund actively harm anyone. By contrast, when we apply (NP) to *The Spectator on the Bridge*, the principle clearly dictates that we refrain from killing the one (which would violate a negative duty), even if it will save five. So like (KLD), (NP) seems to have satisfied the disjunction of options in *The Trolley Driver* as well as the third-person judgment about *The Spectator on the Bridge*.

Nevertheless, (NP) too has some important flaws. Like (KLD), (NP) unintuitively rules out the first option of *The Trolley Driver*, so long as there is also the option of simply letting the trolley run on. The apparent greater plausibility of (NP) over (KLD) is usually displayed by means of cases in which the *only* options are killing one or killing five, such as another variant on *The Trolley Driver* in which Edmund₃ *must* turn the trolley and cannot refrain.[17] In such cases, the moral agent faces the violation of two negative duties (not a negative as against a positive), and, obviously where two negative duties will be violated, the right thing to do is to minimize the violation and kill the one. But that this case is somewhat special and not general is shown by the result of the application of (NP) to the original *Trolley Driver*. It simply seems permissible to minimize deaths in *Edmund* even if there is the option of refraining from turning the trolley altogether. So (NP) would seem to be false.

Perhaps more important than this argument, however, is the objection arising from the following case:

The Good Samaritan at the Switch

Cordelia is walking along beside some trolley tracks, and comes to a branch in the tracks at which there is a spur leading off to the right. There is a manual switch at the intersection. Suddenly she sees a driverless runaway trolley racing towards the intersection; she notices at the same time that there are five people straight ahead on the tracks, and one person on the right-hand spur. None of the persons will be able to get out of the way in time. Cordelia is able to operate the manual switch.

Obviously, Cordelia can either switch the trolley onto the right-hand spur, killing the one, or she may refrain from direct action, thus letting the five die. Even though Cordelia is not the driver of the trolley, but only a passerby, nevertheless the array of options available to her is quite analogous to that of Edmund in *The Trolley Driver*. If she decides to switch, then she violates a negative duty to refrain from actively harming. And if she stands there and does nothing, she violates at worst a positive duty to save five. So by (NP) she must do nothing. But remember now that in the second variant on *The Trolley Driver* in which Edmund$_3$ *must* turn the trolley, it is permissible to do so, so long as the driver *must* kill no matter what he does. Is it plausible to hold that Edmund$_3$ can save his five, but Cordelia in *The Good Samaritan at the Switch* cannot, simply because she did not have the bad luck to be caught in the runaway trolley? Thus (NP) seems to counsel moral passivity where the possibility of moral activism does certainly seem permissible. If Cordelia's action is permissible, then (NP) is false.

(3.)

The next candidate goes under the somewhat ponderous name of the "doctrine of the double effect." This doctrine has to do with the difference between bringing something about as the means or the end of a given action, as against bringing it about as a foreseen side-effect of that action. This distinction also falls into the family of which (KLD) and (NP) are members. For the most part, the classes of killings, violations of the negative duty to refrain from actively bringing about deaths, and active bringings-about of deaths as the means or end of an action, will be coextensive. Nevertheless, while the classes of lettings-die and violations of the positive duty to save lives will be strictly coextensive, the class of determining deaths as a foreseen side-effect will not—some of the deaths foreseen as side-effects will be killings and also violations of a negative duty. For example, innocent victims of military target-bombing are killed as a foreseen side-effect of destroying the target. So there will be some cases of killings which are also violations of a negative duty, and which are not active bringings-about of death as the means or end of an action. Nevertheless, (DE) too will enable the

moral agent to protect his integrity by permissibly avoiding actions which will involve badness transitively attaching to the agent along the line of causal influence. How does it do this? Side-effects, even foreseen ones, are at best "extrinsically" brought about by a given action, so therefore to bring about something—say, a death—in this way is quite different from bringing it about in the "intrinsic" way required for means and ends. The notion of "the means" is troublesome, but it becomes a little clearer if we say that some state-of-affairs x is the means of some state-of-affairs y if and only if x must occur in order for y to occur.[18] We do not require that x be the *only* thing to occur in order that y occur, only that it *has to* occur. The "must" and "has to" we are using here indicate a necessity which is stronger than causal necessity, but weaker than logical necessity. It could perhaps, following Kripke, be called a "metaphysical necessity." This will involve that the state-of-affairs which is the means be somehow intrinsic or essential to the state-of-affairs which is the end. Willing the end, or intending it, therefore wills or intends the means. The moral idea behind the doctrine of the double effect is that in general it seems morally worse to be essentially or intrinsically involved with bad states of affairs, than it is to be only contingently or extrinsically involved with them. The distinction involved in the doctrine of the double effect is therefore a *modal* distinction.

Converting the doctrine of the double effect into a principle relevant to the Trolley Problem, we get:

(DE)   In pairs of cases in which there is respectively the option of either (a) actively harming one as the means or end of an action, or (b) actively or passively harming one or five as a foreseen side-effect of an action, it is impermissible to do (a) but permissible to do (b).

What this new principle allows is not only that we can now take the agent's intentions into account in a fuller way, but also that we can utilize the internal structure of the action more fruitfully than before. Thus in *The Trolley Driver*, in the first option, we can say that the end of Edmund's action is to save the five people, and the means is turning the trolley. Turning the trolley is something that *has to* come about if Edmund is to save the five. The harming of the one is not intrinsically required by Edmund's saving the five, and if by a miracle it happened that the one escaped the collision with the trolley, the end and means of the action would remain exactly the same. Consequently, we see that the death of the one becomes the foreseen, extrinsic side-effect of the action. In the second option in *The Trolley Driver*, since Edmund refrains from taking direct action and merely lets the trolley run on, any deaths resulting are obviously neither the means nor end of his action, but only foreseen side-effects. The "coin-toss" strategy ensures intentional neutrality. Thus either of the disjuncts of the options in *The Trolley Driver* could be satisfied by (DE): both actions are permissible. This gives (DE) an immediate advantage over both (KLD) and (NP).

On the other hand, if we switch over to *The Spectator on the Bridge*, the harming of the Enormous Individual is clearly the means to saving the five. If the trolley by some miracle does not hit the Enormous Individual, then the five cannot be saved. It is, in short, essential to the saving of the five that the Enormous Individual be hit by the trolley. The killing of the Enormous Individual *constitutes* the saving of the five in this context. Trivially, Edgar, if he refrains from acting, passively brings about the deaths of the five as a foreseen side-effect of his action. Thus by (DE) Edgar's action in *The Spectator on the Bridge* is impermissible, which agrees with our moral judgments.

(DE), however, is not wholly without flaw. In the first place, there is the often-noted factual difficulty that every case in which someone apparently harms as the means or end of an action can be redescribed so that the harm becomes a foreseen side-effect.[19] Thus in *The Spectator on the Bridge* we can apparently redescribe Edgar's pushing the Enormous Individual off the bridge in order to save the five, as Edgar's exercise of the strength of his arms against a large mass in order to save the five.

More importantly, however, there is another line of objection to (DE) which can be seen if we consider the following two cases:

The Victim in Front of the Switch

Kent is walking along beside some trolley tracks, and comes to a branch in the tracks at which there is a spur leading off to the right. There is a manual switch at the intersection which he knows how to operate. Suddenly

he sees a driverless trolley racing towards the intersection; he notices at the same time that there are five people straight ahead on the tracks beyond the intersection, and no one on the right-hand spur. None of the five will be able to get off the tracks in time to avoid the trolley. Unfortunately, there is another person standing directly in front of the switch who clearly sees what is happening, but who is doing nothing about it. Kent sees that the only way to get to the switch in time to divert the trolley onto the right-hand spur will be to push the one onto the tracks in front of the speeding trolley.

The Victim Beside the Switch

Gloucester is walking along beside some trolley tracks, and comes to a branch in the tracks at which there is a spur leading off to the right. There is a manual switch at the intersection which he knows how to operate. Suddenly he sees a driverless trolley racing towards the intersection; he notices at the same time that there are five people straight ahead on the tracks beyond the intersection, and no one on the right-hand spur. None of the five will be able to get off the tracks in time to avoid the trolley. Unfortunately, there is another person standing right beside the switch, who clearly sees what is happening, but who is doing nothing about it. Gloucester sees that when he pulls the switch in order to divert the trolley onto the right-hand spur, the arm will swing around and knock the one directly into the path of the oncoming trolley. There is no time to warn the one.

Now according to (DE), Kent's action in *The Victim in Front of the Switch* is clearly impermissible, insofar as pushing the one out in front of the trolley is intrinsically required in order to get to the switch in time to save the five. So the pushing and therefore the harming is the means to saving the five. On the other hand, Gloucester's action in *The Victim Beside the Switch* is clearly permissible by (DE), since the means to saving the five is pulling the switch; the arm's swinging-around to knock the one in front of the trolley is a mere foreseen side-effect of the action.

Is it really plausible, however, to see a moral difference between Kent's action and Gloucester's? It seems obvious to me that if Gloucester's action in *The Victim Beside the Switch* is permissible, then so is Kent's in *The Victim in Front of the Switch*. For suppose we granted the difference that (DE) would have us see here. Then all Kent would have to do in order to avoid the blame attaching to his action would be to shove the person over *beside* the switch, and then throw the switch—thereby bringing about the one's death (he is knocked in front of the trolley by the swinging arm) as a foreseen side-effect and not the means or end of the action. (Let us call this the "sideways-shoving variant" on *The Victim in Front of the Switch*.) But this two-step approach to saving the five does not seem to me to be significantly different in any moral way from the one-step approach in the original *The Victim in Front of the Switch*—or, for that matter, from the no-step approach in *The Victim Beside the Switch*. How could the moral difference between *The Victim in Front of the Switch* and its sideways-shoving variant turn merely on having shoved the one a little sideways in the variant instead of just a little harder in the original? Thus *The Victim in Front of the Switch* does not differ morally from its sideways-shoving variant. And we will grant, I think, that the variant on *The Victim in Front of the Switch* does not differ morally from *The Victim Beside the Switch*. We can conclude, therefore, that (DE) is false.

(4.)

A sharp-witted reader of the preceding may have balked at something I said about the sideways-shoving variant on *The Victim in Front of the Switch*, namely that a person was pushed (even though just a little sideways) without his consent. This seems to violate a right of the person not to be pushed around without his consent, and thus we might want to say that the sideways-shoving variant becomes impermissible just like *The Victim in Front of the Switch*, hence giving us something very like (DE)'s resolution of the cases. There does seem to be something worth exploring in this suggestion. We have been concentrating so far mainly on the difference between doing something directly and indirectly allowing something, as the key to the moral difference in the Trolley Problem. But the appeal to rights gets us away from this perhaps misleading concentration. Both *The Victim in Front of the Switch* and *The Spectator on the Bridge* seem to involve violations of person's rights not to be pushed or thrown in front of speeding trolleys without their consent.

We will have to be careful about this talk of rights for two reasons, however. In the first place, assuming that we still want to defend both of Edmund's options in *The Trolley Driver*, and Cordelia's action in *The Good Samaritan at the Switch*, then clearly not just any rights violation involved in the case will be sufficient to make an action impermissible. For in *The Trolley Driver*, both permissible options involve violating a right of the one killed, namely the right to life; similarly, in *The Good Samaritan at the Switch*. So we will have to be careful to say that we cannot permissibly violate the rights of a person in the action itself (i.e., in the means) by which we bring it about that one dies while five are saved. In *The Spectator on the Bridge*, the action which is the means to saving the five (i.e., pushing the one off the bridge, or even just wobbling the handrail so that he falls) involves a violation of the one person's rights, while the action in *The Trolley Driver* and *The Good Samaritan at the Switch* (i.e., turning the trolley, letting it run on, or throwing the switch) do not.

Secondly, moreover, it is not at all clear that any type of rights violation, even if involved in the action itself, will be sufficient to make that action impermissible. For suppose in a variant on *The Good Samaritan at the Switch* Cordelia₂ also has to push a bicycle belonging to the one out of the way of the switch, thereby pushing it in front of the trolley. This minor rights violation would not, clearly, make the action of turning the trolley onto the one impermissible, if we have previously agreed that Cordelia's action in *The Good Samaritan at the Switch* is permissible. Property rights (at least where the property is not very valuable) just are not so very important in life-and-death cases. Thus we should apparently say that only stringent rights violations in the action itself (i.e., in the means) will be sufficient to make the action impermissible.

Something else we might notice about the permissible actions in *The Trolley Driver* and *The Good Samaritan at the Switch*, as against the impermissible action in *The Spectator on the Bridge*, is that while in *The Trolley Driver* and *The Good Samaritan at the Switch* Edmund and Cordelia merely redirect the original threat onto the one, in *The Spectator on the Bridge* a new threat is introduced by Edgar onto the one—namely, pushing him off the bridge onto the tracks. So perhaps it also makes a moral difference whether the old threat is being redirected, as against whether a new threat is being introduced, in the very action which brings about the death.

Putting this thought about rights together with the thought about old and new threats, we may come up with another principle, due to Judith Jarvis Thomson:[20]

(T)   In pairs of cases in which there is respectively the option of either (a) harming one by means of a new threat which in the action itself violates the stringent rights of the one, or (b) harming one or five by deflecting the original threat or simply allowing the original threat to take its course, without stringent rights violations in the action itself, it is impermissible to do (a) but permissible to do (b).

It is worth noticing that it is only the conjunction of the thought about rights and the thought about deflecting threats which makes (T) plausible. For there are cases involving the introduction of new threats which are permissible, and also cases involving stringent rights violations which are permissible. It would take us too far afield to go into these precisions at the moment.[21] What is important for now is that their conjunction seems to yield a rather strong new principle which does not seem to depend on the violation-of-integrity principle implicit in the doing/allowing distinction involved in (KLD), (NP), and (DE), and which nevertheless gives us the right results.

Or seems to. Both Edmund's action in *The Trolley Driver* and Cordelia's action *The Good Samaritan at the Switch* are permissible by (T), as required, since neither involves stringent rights violations in the action itself, and both involve deflections of the original threat onto the one, not the introduction of a new threat. And Edgar's action in *The Spectator on the Bridge* is impermissible on both counts, since it involves the stringent rights violation of hurling the one onto the tracks from the bridge and also introducing the new threat which is that self-same hurling. Let us now go on to *The Victim in Front of the Switch*, its sideways-shoving variant, and *The Victim Beside the Switch* for a moment, however, and see what the new principle gives us. On the face of it, according to (T), Kent's action in *The Victim in Front of the Switch* must be permissible and Gloucester's

in *The Victim Beside the Switch* permissible. For the action in *The Victim in Front of the Switch* involves the stringent rights violation of Kent's pushing the one in front of the trolley, and the same action introduces a new threat as opposed to deflecting the original one. In *The Victim Beside the Switch*, on the other hand—like the actions in *The Trolley Driver* and *The Good Samaritan at the Switch*—the action of throwing the switch is neither in itself a stringent rights violation, nor the introduction of a new threat.

The kicker in all of this, however, as in our argument against (DE) comes with the intermediate case of the sideways-shoving variant on *The Victim in Front of the Switch*. As defenders of (T), we would naturally want to assimilate the variant to the original, thereby making Kent$_2$'s action impermissible, since it seems objectionable that we could move from impermissibility to permissibility merely by arranging to shove the one sideways first, then knocking him in front of the trolley with the swinging arm of the switch. If (T) has any force, it must comprehend both cases. But if the action in the sideways-shoving variant is impermissible by (T), it is by no means obvious why. For in the variant, if we consider the action which itself brings about the death of the one (i.e., the throwing of the switch which swings the arm about), that action is identical with the action in *The Victim Beside the Switch* which brings about the death of the one—and that action is permissible by (T). What then is supposed to make Kent$_2$'s action in the variant impermissible? We might turn to the preceding "first-step" of shoving the one sideways. But this is neither a stringent rights violation, nor is it itself the introduction of a new threat. Neither of the two steps, and hence not the two steps together, introduces a new threat or involves a stringent rights violation. So it follows that the two-step action in the sideways-shoving variant on *The Victim in Front of the Switch* is not impermissible by (T) if the action in *The Victim Beside the Switch* is not impermissible. But if we have assimilated the moral upshot of the variant to that of the original, it also follows that the action in the original is not impermissible. The non-impermissibility of the action in *The Victim in Front of the Switch*, however, clearly entails the falsity of (T), since Kent obviously has the option of permissibly doing nothing and letting the trolley run onto the five. Thus the last of our four candidate principles goes the way of the others.

III.

Having run through our "short-list" of applicants for explicating our intuitive moral assessment of the Trolley Problem, and having rejected all the candidates, we may plausibly ask: Which moral principle really is at work in the moral difference between *The Trolley Driver* and *The Spectator on the Bridge?* As might have been guessed, I want to say that there is something morally significant about the way of the world and the way agents find themselves "thrown" into that world, which is making the difference between the two cases. What is essential is "how things stand" when the situations are just getting underway, where this includes "where the situation is heading," "who is involved and who is not involved," and "what those involved or uninvolved persons are 'up to.'" All of this is undoubtedly very vague, and I hope to make it slightly clearer; but at the moment what I want to emphasize is the point that we explicitly or implicitly assess *all* moral situations with respect to the three features just mentioned. Insofar as a third-person moral judgment with respect to a moral situation is possible, we are already working with a rough but guiding interpretation of "how things stand" with respect to that situation.

Granting this idea of moral interpretation[22] for the moment, the moral principle I want to propose with respect to the range of cases already considered is roughly the following: we cannot permissibly cause persons not already implicated or involved in the ongoing threatening situation to be placed in the situation in order either to harm or to benefit them, or in order that they will cause harm or benefit to somebody else. It will be a corollary of this descriptive principle that people not implicated or involved in the situation already underway have no obligation to enter into or intervene in the situation, all other things being equal. In fact, it seems plausible to say that uninvolved persons have a kind of *existential* right to remain uninvolved, a right which stems entirely from the physico-intentional inertial frame or moral field established by the ongoing situation.

Thus my point is that in general, and other things being equal, being involved or implicated in a threatening or benefitting situation creates a necessity of response or reaction *not* binding on those not already implicated in the situation. For those outside the situation, response or reaction (or at least response or reaction in the same way) is not morally necessary. To compel the uninvolved to become involved is impermissible as a consequence. I will want to say, then, that the moral difference between *The Trolley Driver* and *The Spectator on the Bridge* consists in the fact that the one in *The Trolley Driver* is involved in the situation, while the one in *The Spectator on the Bridge* is not; that Edmund, the trolley driver, when he acts or refrains violates no existential right to uninvolvement belonging to the one; and Edgar, the spectator on the bridge, when he acts, *does* violate such a right.

The basis for this moral principle is a rather obvious ontological point about how constituents of states-of-affairs relate to the state-of-affairs of which they are constituents, and how other entities relate to the original state-of-affairs. Those involved in or implicated in a situation, are, by way of their bodies and intentionalit[ies],[23] constituents of the situation. The idea of a "situation" or "state-of-affairs," as I am using it, means a partly physical, partly ideal[24] whole made up of persons and physical entities, but also values, meanings, possibilia, and other correlates of human intentionality.[25] There could be several distinct "situations" containing the same physical event as a part. For those persons involved in the situation, therefore, whatever is done constitutes a response or reaction to the *total situation* and not merely to the physical event which is a constituent part. Every embedded, first-person response or reaction to the situation, regardless of whether it involves a physico-causal motion, makes a difference to the situation; similarly, every change in the situation constitutes at least a possible influence on those persons involved in the situation. These contingent features of the situation make up an existential or ontological constraint which, other things being equal, has moral force.

As a way of making these ideas a little clearer, I would like to state a few definitions, and make a few distinctions. By a "moral situation," or "moral state-of-affairs" I mean a complex whole containing ordinary physical objects, intentional correlates which are ideal objects, and persons, such that:

(1) Part of the whole is a physico-causal event.

(2) The bodies of the persons are among the physical constituents of the physical event.

(3) The event has an isolable beginning and an end.

(4) The moral situation is spatio-temporally coextensive with the event, but not reducible to it.

(5) At the beginning of the situation it is the case that some harm or benefit will come to some of the persons in the situation as a direct result of the current course of the situation.

(6) There is a **bivalence principle** of harms or benefits for persons in the situation, such that if someone would be harmed as a result of the current direction of the situation, but is not, that counts as a benefit; and if someone would be benefited as a result of the current direction of the situation, but is not, that counts as a harm. Some persons in the situation may be neither harmed nor benefited.

(7) The current course of the situation is interpreted, judged, charted, or tracked by some of the persons whose bodies are in the physical event, and these interpretations are a part of the complex physico-ideal situation.

(8) The first-person interpretations or judgments are, in part, assessments of the values borne by the possible harms and benefits for persons.[26]

(9) Part of what is meant by the "course of the situation" is that the array of values borne by persons and things changes from the beginning to the end of the situation.

(10) Of those persons making value-assessments, at least some have it in their power to modify the current course of the situation.

Now in what follows, I shall focus on moral situations in which some harm, but not necessarily some benefit, will come to persons involved in the situation if the situation continues on in the same way. I call these "threat-situations." It should be noticed that there is an important distinction to be made between the moral situation in its initial and terminal stages. When the state-of-affairs is just getting underway, there are still a number of possible pathways open to prospective outcomes, although there is still a central directional focus. As the situation progresses, naturally these pathways are either selected or rejected until finally at the terminal stage, one pathway has been selected out

[sic] as the actual pathway of the event. This idea is important, because the persons who are involved in the situation are not only involved in it at the end, as actual receivers of harms or benefits, or as actual possessors of values, but also are involved at the beginning as possible receivers or determiners of harms or benefits. Because there are persons who are possible receivers, and because there are persons who are both assessors and possible determiners, there is moral agency with respect to that situation. Where there are no persons who are assessors and possible determiners of harms or benefits, the situation is not moral.

The total moral situation includes not only the actual physico-causal event, but also all the relevantly possible pathways which are parts of its ideal structure. I imagine the total situation to be a kind of finite branch structure roughly analogous to the "Y"-structure and its variants that we have been using in the Trolley Problem. The branches are the possible pathways to the possible outcomes, and the course of the actual situation is a kind of trolley moving along the branches. I am further assuming that in its initial and later stages every moral situation can be at least roughly expressed as a diagram of one of these branch-structures—a kind of moral flow-chart. If the situation cannot be even very roughly so expressed by anyone in it, then this will generally be because things are just too overwhelming and muddled to be able to interpret just what the situation is, or how it will go. Where this massive first-person interpretive muddling occurs, even if the person is a possible determiner of harms or benefits, the role of moral agency in assessing and determining harms or benefits will begin to reduce to zero. As it does so, the situation becomes vanishingly moral. It seems likely, for example, that certain terrifying situations of natural disaster, or in wartime, bear this structure.[27]

In order to understand "implication" or "involvement" in a moral situation better, it seems necessary to distinguish between *participants* and *bystanders* with respect to a given moral situation. By a participant in a moral situation I mean any person whose body is or becomes a constituent part of the physico-causal event or possible events which are contained within the total situation. A bystander, by contrast, is any person whose body is not a part of the physical event or possible events, and whose current ordinary business will not bring him into the situation. That is: it is *inconsistent* with a bystander's current ordinary business that he shall be brought into the situation. The idea of "current ordinary business" is somewhat vague but crucial. It is obviously a certain pattern of intentions, value-assessments, dispositions, and context, and not merely of simple bodily behavior. It is what a person is presently "up to." "Ordinary" in "current ordinary business" is meant to imply that no special obligations or contracts or other binding claims are in effect other than those intrinsic to the "business" itself. Someone who is "up to" something has a rough plan which he can articulate, and can also reasonably expect to be able to carry out. Current ordinary business does not determine what a person *will* do, but it does indicate what is excluded by, or inconsistent with, itself. Something is inconsistent with a person's current ordinary business if it is something that he cannot reasonably expect to do or suffer in the course of his affairs.

Another distinction needs to be made, namely that between "controlling" and "non-controlling" participants in a moral situation. A controlling participant is a participant who can determine harms or benefits within the situation, either for himself or for others; a non-controlling participant can at best receive harms or benefits, not determine them. More specifically, a controlling participant is a person whose deliberate action or deliberate refraining from action can determine the distribution of harms or benefits which come about in the course of the situation. A non-controlling participant cannot determine the distribution of harms or benefits, no matter what he does, although of course he can receive harm or benefit. A participant who receives only harm is called a "victim."

On the basis of this little battery of ideas, I would like to restate the rough moral essence or principle I mentioned above (I will return to its corollary later). I dub this descriptive principle the "Principle of Moral Inertia," alluding to an offhand observation made by Thomson:

> There is no Principle of Moral Inertia: there is no prima facie *duty to refrain from interfering with existing states of affairs just because they are existing states of affairs.* [28]

Thomson is absolutely correct in what she says here. There is no Principle of Moral Inertia as she has expressed it. But, I want to say, embedded in our existing moral practices and judgments there *is* a *prima facie* duty to refrain from forcing those persons not already implicated (or on their way to being implicated) in a moral situation to become implicated in that situation. And the reason for this seems to stem simply from the brute existential fact that there is a moral situation underway already which *just happens* not to involve that person. So there is a Principle of Moral Inertia:

(MI)   It is impermissible for anyone to force a bystander to become a participant in a moral situation, in particular, to become a victim.

Compatibly with this general principle, other things being equal, it is sometimes permissible for controlling participants to harm non-controlling participants in order to bring about a good distribution of a threat. By contrast, it is impermissible to make bystanders into victims for the same reasons. Why is this so? Why is it that bystanders have a legitimate complaint against those who force them into situations in order to bring about good consequences, but non-controlling or controlling participants have no such grounds for complaint? I think that it is simply because although we can have morally justifiable complaints against other persons, we cannot have morally justifiable complaints against the world. The world is just not accessible to complaint; it is in some sense simply given to us—or we to it. "Railing against fate," although it is certainly relevant to morality,[29] is not *in itself* the expression of a moral claim against a bad person. The structure of the world, not a villain, makes participants into possible victims, and those participants simply have to accept that it is therefore sometimes permissible (other things being equal) for something very bad to be prevented by making them actual victims.

Applying (MI) back now to the cases discussed in section II, we can come up with the following restricted principle:

(MI$_R$)   In cases in which there is the option of either (a) harming one bystander by forcing him into the threat-situation, or (b) harming one or five participants in the same threat-situation only

in order to bring about the best possible distribu-tion of the threat, it is impermissible to do (a) but sometimes permissible to do (b).[30]

This obviously allows us to account for the cases of *The Trolley Driver* and *The Spectator on the Bridge*. The one in *The Trolley Driver* is clearly a participant, since one of the pathways of the ongoing trolley-event will make him a victim. The mere existence of the possible pathway, as physically represented by the switching mechanism and spur, is sufficient to implicate the one. By contrast, the Enormous Indi-vidual on the bridge in *The Spectator on the Bridge* is neither a physico-causal part of the trolley-event, nor is it consistent with his ordinary business that he shall be brought into the moral situation. The Enor-mous Individual is a bystander, if anyone is. Thus it is permissible to bring about the death of the one in order to save the five in *The Trolley Driver*, but not in *The Spectator on the Bridge*. For the purposes of (MI$_R$) *The Good Samaritan at the Switch* is just like *The Trolley Driver*. Again, the mere existence of the switching mechanism and spur in *The Good Samari-tan at the Switch* is sufficient to implicate the one along one of the possible pathways of the developing moral situation.[31] The only difference between *The Trolley Driver* and *The Good Samaritan at the Switch* is that the agent in the latter, Cordelia, is someone who has moved herself from being a bystander to being a beneficent controlling participant, unlike Edmund in the former. But this is certainly not im-permissible by my Principle of Moral Inertia. Agents *can* permissibly be Good Samaritans; the Principle of Moral Inertia is by no means fatalistic, unlike Thomson's rejected "Principle of Moral Inertia."

Things get more difficult when we turn to *The Victim in Front of the Switch*, its sideways-shoving variant, and *The Victim Beside the Switch*, although not intolerably so. The one in *The Victim in Front of the Switch* is a participant, because his body is involved in the physical event to the extent that by merely reaching out he can determine a different distribution of harms and benefits than is projected by the current course of the situation. This is cer-tainly consistent with his current ordinary busi-ness. Thus the current ordinary business of the one will bring him into the situation. So what makes *The Victim in Front of the Switch* different from *The Trolley Driver* and *The Good Samaritan*

at the Switch is that in *The Victim in Front of the Switch* the one is a controlling participant, and not merely a non-controlling participant as in the latter two cases. But the one in *The Victim in Front of the Switch* is nevertheless still a participant, and hence by (MI$_R$) it is sometimes permissible to push him in front of the trolley as a means to saving the five. If Kent's action in *The Victim in Front of the Switch* is permissible, then I take it that Kent$_2$'s action in the sideways-shoving variant is permissible, although a little more circuitous. And finally, Gloucester's ac-tion in *The Victim Beside the Switch* is permissible, on the sheer strength of the fact that Kent's and Kent$_2$'s actions are permissible by (MI$_R$).

To summarize, then. All of the proposed prin-ciples, the four mentioned in section II and (MI$_R$), agree with our third-person moral judgments about *The Trolley Driver* and *The Spectator on the Bridge*, namely, that the proposed action in the first is per-missible, while the proposed action in the second is impermissible. (KLD) and (NP) fall away with respect to *The Good Samaritan at the Switch*, by making Cordelia's action impermissible; but it is generally agreed that this is proof of their falsity. (MI$_R$) distin-guishes itself from (DE) and (T) by claiming that Kent's action in *The Victim in Front of the Switch* is permissible, while the other two claim that it is impermissible. All three principles agree about Gloucester's action in *The Victim Beside the Switch*. My point is that if Gloucester's action is permissible, so should Kent's action be, and the proof lies in the intermediate case, the sideways-shoving variant on *The Victim in Front of the Switch*. Both (DE) and (T) will have to agree that Kent's action in the original is permissible. Furthermore, there are no good moral reasons provided by either (DE) or (T) to distinguish the original from the variant, or the variant from *The Victim Beside the Switch*. By sim-ple transitivity, then, *The Victim in Front of the Switch* is morally indistinguishable from *The Vic-tim Beside the Switch*, and must be permissible. Explained in the terms I have been using, if a con-trolling participant can consistently with the pur-suit of his current ordinary business do something to defuse a threatening situation—as is the case with the one in *The Victim in Front of the Switch*, its sideways-shoving variant, and *The Victim Beside the Switch* —but is *not* acting, then it seems permis-sible for another well-intentioned agent to sacrifice the first participant in order to defuse the threatening situation, and benefit the five.[32] It would seem to be a virtue of the Principle of Moral Inertia that it preserves this intuitively plausible result, even independently of the more general ideas which lie behind it.

IV.

An issue lurking in the preceding account, but which has not yet been dealt with, is the problem of *intervention*, that is, the choosing-to-be-involved by a bystander. In the present jargon, an "intervener" is a bystander who deliberately makes himself a controlling participant. It is crucial to distinguish interveners such as Edgar, Cordelia, Kent, Kent$_2$, and Gloucester from those who are *already* controlling participants, such as Edmund in *The Trolley Driver* and the one in *The Victim in Front of the Switch*, its sideways-shoving variant, and *The Victim Beside the Switch*. The moral situation forces the necessity of response or reaction on the latter four, but not upon the preceding four.

An intervener who intends to bring about benefits or to prevent harms is called a "Good Samaritan"; an intervener who intends to bring about harms or reduce benefits is a "Bad Samaritan." Most treatments of this issue say that a Bad Samaritan is a person who simply fails to respond in the way a Good Samaritan would.[33] But I think that this is a confusion based on failing to distinguish between bystanders and participants in moral situations. A controlling, involved person who acts in the way he ought to is a *good participant*; a controlling participant who fails so to act is a *bad participant*. If I am correct, the moral inertial frame is different for participants and bystanders. What this means is that many persons who are presently being called Bad Samaritans are in fact bad participants; the intuitive wrongness we feel in the action of the man who will not lean over to give a hand to his drowning wife[34] has nothing to do with intervention or Samaritanhood, but only with the basic claims binding on *any* participant in a moral situation. (I have not actually said what these basic, binding claims are; this would require an entirely different sort of investigation.)

I will now restate the general corollary to (MI):

(MI$_C$) Intervention is never obligatory for bystanders—all other things being equal—but rather is always supererogatory.

Why is this the case? Why do our actual practices and judgments make it manifest that we are not obliged to be Good Samaritans? Various justifications of non-interventionism have been attempted, most of them having to do with consequences (too much effort is required, or too much threat of harm or loss) and some of them having to do with rights (say, of self-determination or self-preservation). My descriptive justification falls on the side of rights, roughly speaking, but gives a rather different source for that right. The right is the right of a bystander to remain a bystander, and its source is this: the parameters of a moral situation determine the moral field or inertial frame in any given set of moral circumstances, dividing everyone into participants and bystanders (there will also generally be borderline cases). To become a participant willingly is a way of creasing the moral field of force which goes beyond that established by the inertial frame of the moral situation. There is nothing, morally speaking, to prevent someone from entering the situation so long as his intentions are good, but on the other hand there is nothing to compel him either. And this lack of compulsion stems purely from the fact that the structure of the world has not made him a participant in the moral situation.

It is of paramount importance to see, however, that this particular absence of obligation to intervene does not entail *either* that people are never, as bystanders, obliged to intervene, *or* that all obligation with respect to the moral situation is suspended. If other things are not equal, that is, if special contracts, promises, or personal relationships obtain, or if a person somehow helped to bring about the threatening situation in the first place, then he will be obligated even as a bystander to intervene.

Moreover, even where all other things are equal, there are a set of weak but important obligations on bystanders which may be collected under the category of what Judith Thomson calls "Minimally Decent Samaritanhood."[35] Minimally Decent Samaritanhood, as I understand it, involves only that one cannot go out of one's way to harm people or to prevent benefits from accruing to other people. So one must refrain from maleficent action of this kind. Failure to meet this minimal requirement is what I am calling Bad Samaritanhood. But another obligation should be added to Minimally Decent Samaritanhood, namely the requirement that short of intervention, further indirect action of a certain type is required of nearby bystanders in order to prevent harm. By "further indirect action" I mean trivial changes in bodily position or direction and consistent with the pursuit of one's own current ordinary business, which have no direct physico-causal impact on the moral situation, but which may have an indirect intentional effect upon participants in the situation.

The only kind of indirect, intentional action required of bystanders, it seems, is to *report*. Reports are uses of signals (voice, handwave, telephone, flag, etc.) to alert the proper authorities, whose instituted duty it is to intervene in the appropriate situations. For instance, firemen, policemen, rescue specialists, nurses, doctors, and ship-captains are instituted interveners—official Good Samaritans, as it were—in a fairly well specified, limited range of situations. No one is an instituted intervener in *every* type of threat-situation.[36] Thus bystanders are obligated only to give reports, not to become participants. One's right to avoid entering the situation in any direct way seems certainly to be compatible with contacting (or at least trying to contact) those who are delegated to intervene in the appropriate type of situation.

Failure to meet this fairly weak requirement as a nearby bystander is what might be called "Wretched Samaritanhood." This idea seems to capture our intuitions about the Kitty Genovese case, in which thirty-eight bystanders did nothing while a woman was stabbed to death in the streets of New York City. We are particularly outraged in this case not so much because those bystanders did not rush out and try to overpower the attacker, but because none of them even reported. This moral fact has nothing in particular to do with utility or ease of effort. Minimally Decent Samaritanhood requires all reasonable effort for reports, quite independently of utility. The reasonableness of the effort has everything to do with the inertial frame of the moral situation, that is, with whether and how the appropriate persons are participants and bystanders. Someone who happens to be standing close enough to be able to reach out and touch Kitty Genovese or her attacker could quite possibly be obligated to try to overpower him. On the other hand, persons living in upstate New York would not in all likelihood be obligated even to report, even if they somehow were instantaneously aware of the attack. Everything depends on the structure of the actual or developing situation, and the contingent location of its participants and bystanders.

V.

It will be quite obvious that the biggest difficulty in the account just given is how we can limit the shape of moral situations and thereby be able to say who is a participant and who is a bystander. I have given a few hints as to how we might go about doing this, but obviously I am not in possession of a special decision-procedure for participanthood or bystanderhood. I have stressed already that the account is meant to be intuitive or phenomenological which means that it reads distinctions and structures directly off [sic] fairly clear cases, given the ordinary assessment of moral differences and identities among them. In the concrete moral "lifeworld," there will certainly be borderline cases, and frequently enough the shape of moral situations in the making will be largely indiscernible. The borderline cases will remain open for third-person moral discussion, and the indiscernible cases will approach the very limits of moral assessment. Nevertheless, in a wide variety of cases moral judgers (be they third-persons or first-persons) simply do see how participants and bystanders may be divided up, and this division expresses certain implicit constraints on moral judgment and action.[37]

Notes

[1] By "the world" I do not mean merely physico-causal nature, nor do I mean what Putnam calls the metaphysically real "WORLD" (see *Meaning and the Moral Sciences* [London: Routledge and Kegan Paul, 1978], p. 125). Rather, I have in mind the phenomenological concept of the world: the total network of states-of-affairs possessing possible or actual human significance. See M. Heidegger, *Being and Time*, trans. J. Macquarrie and E. Robinson (New York: Harper and Row, 1962), p. 93, third signification.

[2] Heidegger, *Being and Time*, pp. 174, 219–224.

[3]See B. Williams, "Moral Luck," in *Moral Luck* (Cambridge: Cambridge University Press, 1981), pp. 20–39; T. Nagel, "Moral Luck," in *Mortal Questions* (Cambridge: Cambridge University Press, 1979), pp. 24–38; and M. C. Nussbaum, *The Fragility of Goodness: Luck and Ethics in Greek Tragedy and Philosophy* (Cambridge: Cambridge University Press, 1986), pp. 1–21.

[4]Aristotle discusses many aspects of moral action in the face of luck (*tuche*), but especially important for my purposes are the actions included under the rubric of "mixed actions." Mixed actions are voluntary, chosen actions carried out under conditions of duress. There is an involuntary aspect to such acts, but they are on the whole considered to be voluntary and also chosen as the result of deliberation. See Aristotle, *Nicomachean Ethics*, trans. T. Irwin (Indianapolis: Hackett, 1985), II, 9, 1110a4-b9, pp. 53–55. As we will see, the Trolley Problem involves a range of particularly extreme cases of "mixed actions."

[5]By the "human body" I have in mind the "lived body" as discussed by M. Merleau-Ponty in the *Phenomenology of Perception*, trans. C. Smith (London: Routledge and Kegan Paul, 1962), pp. 67–365 especially. This means that "place" and "direction of movement" will have not merely a physico-causal sense, but also an intentional sense. Intentional description involves reference to values, meanings, persons, and acts. In ethics, intentional description obviously takes precedence over physicocausal description.

[6]I borrow this term from Judith Jarvis Thomson, who uses it in a slightly different way. See Section III below, note 28.

[7]Judith Jarvis Thomson, "Killing, Letting Die, and the Trolley Problem," p. 67; "The Trolley Problem," p. 279.

[8]P. Foot, "The Problem of Abortion and the Doctrine of the Double Effect," p. 59. See also G. E. M. Anscombe's brief reply to Foot's paper: "Who is Wronged?," *The Oxford Review*, 5 (1967): 16–17.

[9]For a general overview of the issues, and several central recent articles, see B. Steinbock, ed., *Killing and Letting Die* (Englewood Cliffs, N.J.: Prentice-Hall, 1980). Among the articles collected here, I have found two particularly helpful: Nancy Davis, "The Priority of Avoiding Harm" (pp. 172–214); and John Harris, "The Survival Lottery" (pp. 149–155).

[10]I distinguish throughout this essay between "first-person moral judgments" and "third-person moral judgments." By a first-person moral judgment I mean a judgment made by a person in a moral situation, as a result of moral deliberation, leading directly to moral action. By a third-person moral judgment I mean a judgment made by a person outside a moral situation, about first-person moral judgments and actions in that situation, embodying a moral assessment of those first-person judgments and actions.

Failure to distinguish between these quite disparate points of view on the same moral situation can lead to serious confusions in philosophical ethics. For instance, first-person moral judging is frequently analyzed as if it were occurring from a third-person standpoint.

[11]Both Thomson and Foot have proposed a pair of cases that are supposed to run relevantly parallel to the Trolley Problem. The first case is one in which a doctor has six terminally ill patients and one vial of medicine which is a cure for the illness afflicting the patients. One patient needs all of the medicine, however, while the other five need only one-fifth each. Who should get the medicine, the one or the five? The second case is one in which a surgeon has five terminally ill patients, each of whom needs a different organ transplant in order to be saved. A healthy person visits the hospital, and the question arises as to whether the doctor can permissibly seize that person and vivisect him for the five organs in order to safe the other five people. Our third-person moral judgment apparently tells us that in the first case it is permissible *either* simply to give the medicine to the five, thereby saving them but bringing about the death of the one, or to flip a coin. This case would then apparently run parallel to The Trolley Driver. And our moral judgment apparently also tells us that in the second case it is clearly impermissible to seize the one for purposes of organ transplants, even if it would save five. This case would then apparently run parallel to The Spectator on the Bridge.

In my opinion, the hospital cases do not actually run parallel to the trolley cases. The hospital cases do not in fact satisfy the constraint that all other things remain equal. In the hospital cases there is an implicit assumption at work to the effect that doctors by virtue of the socially-instituted roles they play in the practice of healthcare in our culture, simply do not operate on healthy people without their consent. And it is *that* assumption which is making the moral difference between the two cases.

[12]See J. Taurek, "Should the Numbers Count?" p. 214. See also D. Parfit, "Innumerate Ethics," p. 227. I am extending Taurek's argument here, since his cases involve only "trade-off" situations in which harm is certainly coming to six people if nothing is done, and the moral agent can save one or save five, but not both.

[13]I use "determined" here as a causal term that is neutral between doing and refraining. Determination is at least a sufficient condition of a result's occurring, though perhaps not a necessary condition.

[14]Some analysts of this distinction speak of "passive killings" and "active lettings-die," but this simply seems to confuse the issue. I have defined the two terms so that all killings are active, and all lettings-die are passive. All active determinations of death are killings; all passive determinations of death are lettings-die.

[15]On integrity and moral self-indulgence, see B. Williams, "Utilitarianism and Moral Self-Indulgence," in *Moral Luck*, pp. 40–53; and "A Critique of Utilitarianism," in J. J. C. Smart and B. Williams, *Utilitariansim: For and Against* (Cambridge: Cambridge University Press, 1973), pp. 77–150.

[16]Thomson discusses this variant in "The Trolley Problem."

[17]Foot's use of this sort of example for the defense of (NP) actually turns on the rather specious idea that simply because the driver is a driver, he kills no matter what he does. This seems doubtful. Captains of naval vessels take on special responsibilities merely by becoming captains, but trolley drivers very likely do not take on the same rich set of responsibilities. See Foot, "The Problem of Abortion and the Doctrine of the Doctrine Effect." Thomson also speaks of the trolley driver as the "captain of the trolley" ("The Trolley Problem"). Is not the trolley driver more like a custodian than a captain? Do custodians have the same responsibilities as captains? The phenomenological differences are important for the structures of third-person moral judgments.

[18]This analysis of "the means" is indebted to Thomson; see "The Trolley Problem." Thomson uses this analysis in a somewhat different connection, however.

[19]This sort of objection to the Doctrine of Double Effect is noted by Foot, "The Problem of Abortion and the Doctrine of the Double Effect"; and by T. Nagel, "War and Massacre," in *War and Moral Responsibility*, ed. M. Cohen, T. Nagel, and T. Scanlon (Princeton: Princeton University Press, 1974), p. 11.

[20]This full principle comes out only in "The Trolley Problem." Thomson's original account in "Killing, Letting Die, and the Trolley Problem" focuses mainly on the idea of deflecting the original threat as against introducing a new one.

[21](A) Here is a case involving a new threat, which is nevertheless permissible. Suppose that the only way to get medicine to save five people in an emergency is to take a swipe at a bellicose druggist. This is a new threat which is not a stringent rights violation, and it seems to be permissible in the circumstances. (B) Here is a case involving a stringent rights violation, which is still permissible. Suppose (as Thomson does in an analogous way in "The Trolley Problem") a variant on The Good Samaritan at the Switch in which the right-hand spur loops back to join the main track, and the one is the Enormous Individual. It still seems permissible for Cordelia to deflect the trolley onto the one, as Thomson admits, but since the trolley *must* hit the Enormous Individual in order to save the five, this action is the means, and therefore a stringent rights violation intrinsic to the action itself.

[22]"Moral interpretation" is the process of understanding that results in third-person moral judgments. It has significant parallels with literary hermeneutics. I hope to develop this idea further elsewhere.

[23]I say "intentionality" and not merely "intentions" because the former is the genus of which the latter is but one species. "Intentionality" means "directedness toward the world," and this happens in many ways, while "intentions" generally refer to the aiming toward explicit ends, involving plans of action.

[24]I am using "ideal" as Husserl uses "ideell." *Ideell* for Husserl contrasts importantly with both real and *reell*. Something which is *real* is concrete and spatio-temporally fixed; something which is *reell* is a non-independent or immanent part of a whole, normally a psychological whole. An ideal object is abstract, repeatable over space and time, and non-psychological. See E. Husserl, *Logical Investigations*, trans. J. N. Findlay (London: Routledge 1970), vol. 1, pp. 110, 174, 327–328; vol. 2, pp. 576–577.

[25]I use "intentional correlate" rather than "intentional object" because of the unfortunate tendency to construe the latter as implying a purely *mental* object. Intentional correlates (or, as they are sometimes called, "contents") to coin a phrase, "just ain't in the head." I use this Putnamian phrase with apologies, since Putnam takes a rather dim view of the concept of intentionality in general, and of phenomenology in particular—perhaps precisely because of the unfortunate tendency just mentioned. See H. Putnam, *Reason, Truth, and History* (Cambridge: Cambridge University Press, 1981), pp. 2, 28, and 41–43. For a more appreciative view of intentionality and phenomenology, see the papers in *Husserl, Intentionality, and Cognitive Science*, H. Dreyfus and H. Hall, (eds.) (Cambridge, MA: M.I.T. Press, 1982).

[26]For a theory of values relevant to morality and ethics, see M. Scheler, *Formalism in Ethics and Non-Formal Ethics of Values*, trans. M. S. Frings and R. L. Funk (Evanston: Northwestern University Press, 1973). Scheler distinguishes carefully between values and bearers of values in the emotive realm, just as in the logical realm we distinguish between meaning and reference.

[27]But we will have to be careful here. War may be hell, yet it is not necessarily chaos. There will be room frequently for moral response even under great duress. Our commendation of wartime courage and excoriation of wartime crime proves this. The vanishing point of morality is a *limit* of threat-situations, not an internal feature of them.

[28]Thomson, "Killing, Letting Die, and the Trolley Problem."

[29]"Railing against fate" is an essential aspect of tragedy, which is an important ethical phenomenon. On tragedy and ethics, see Nussbaum, *The Fragility of Goodness*, pp. 23–84, 378–421.

[30]The main class of apparent counterexamples to (MI_R) would be pairs of cases in which the first is obviously

impermissible because it involves harming a bystander by forcing him in to a moral situation, and the second is obviously impermissible as well even though it would involve harming one or five participants in accordance with good intentions. An example of this type of pair is: Case (A), in which a terrorist demands the life of one person in order to appease him so that he will not kill five, and you offer to select one arbitrarily and then to kill that one yourself; as against Case (B), in which a terrorist tells you that unless you shoot one of his five prisoners, he will shoot all five. Both the action in Case (A) and the two options in Case (B) seem impermissible, yet (MI_R) would seem to entail that one of the options in Case (B) is permissible. This is only an apparent counterexample, for two reasons. First, (MI_R) says only that it is *sometimes* permissible to harm one or five participants, not that it is *always* permissible; this is a case where it is impermissible. Secondly, Case (B) is in fact unlike the cases we have been considering, since the moral situation has been artificially created by a villain. All of the five participants in Case (B), as well as "you," are bystanders who have been forced into the situation. This forcing is in *general* impermissible by (MI), and so Case (B) is morally tainted. Case (B) is in fact a moral dilemma for "you:" to shoot the one is to be a willing tool of the terrorist, and thus wrongful according to the "doctrine of the intervening agent" (see Davis, "The Priority of Avoiding Harm," pp. 202–204); and to refrain from saving the five is to fail to do the beneficent thing, and thus wrongful. (MI) is therefore compatible with the existence of moral dilemmas.

[31]In an interesting variant on The Good Samaritan at the Switch, John M. Fischer proposes that instead of the switching mechanism, $Cordelia_2$ would be supplied with a magic wand that could switch the trolley from the main track to the spur; without the magic wand, the trolley could not be shunted onto the spur. Fischer's query is: would the one on the spur now become a bystander rather than a participant? If so, it would appear to introduce an unjustifiable difference between The Good Samaritan at the Switch and The Trolley Driver, because by (MIR) the former would now become impermissible. My answer is that even with only a "magical" switching mechanism in existence, the mechanism is still in existence; and therefore the one is still implicated as a participant along a relevantly possible pathway. Just because the magic wand's functioning would be a [strange] . . . state of affairs, that does not make it any the less a state of affairs. If there is such a wand in $Cordelia_2$'s possession, then that is a component part of the total situation. This brings out the important point that not all constituents of a moral situation will be obvious to the first-person agents and judgers in the situation; it is the more comprehensive third-person perspective that is determining for moral assessment.

[32]This particular explanation is not entailed directly by (MI_R), but does seem to be compatible with it. The utilitarian imperative to save the five and sacrifice the one, in conjunction with (MI_R), seems to entail it. The utilitarian doctrine of "negative responsibility" (see Williams, "A Critique of Utilitarianism," pp. 93–100) seems to hold sometimes for participants in threat-situations, but never for bystanders.

[33]See J. Kleinig, "Good Samaritanism," *Philosophy and Public Affairs*, 5, 4 (Summer 1976): 382–407.

[34]This example, an actual one, is mentioned in Kleinig, "Good Samaritanism," p. 384.

[35]J. Thomson, "A Defense of Abortion," in *The Rights and Wrongs of Abortion*, ed. M. Cohen, T. Nagel, and T. Scanlon (Princeton: Princeton University Press, 1974), pp. 18–21.

[36]It is telling that in the comic strips only superhumans are obligated to intervene in *every* type of threat-situation.

[37]I would like to thank John M. Fischer both for introducing me to the Trolley Problem and for detailed comments on an early version of this paper. In addition, I would especially like to thank Martha Hanna for her fine moral discrimination in many discussions of these issues.

BIBLIOGRAPHY

Abbreviations

A	*Analysis*
AER	*American Economic Review*
CJP	*Canadian Journal of Philosophy*
E	*Ethics*
JMP	*Journal of Medicine and Philosophy*
JP	*Journal of Philosophy*
L	*The Listener*
M	*Mind*
NYTM	*The New York Times Magazine*
OR	*Oxford Review*
P	*Philosophy*
PAS	*Proceedings of the Aristotelian Society*
PPA	*Philosophy & Public Affairs*
PPQ	*Pacific Philosophical Quarterly*
PR	*The Philosophical Review*
PS	*Philosophical Studies*
PT	*Psychology Today*
RS	*Religious Studies*
SJP	*The Southern Journal of Philosophy*
TS	*Theological Studies*
WLR	*Washington Law Review*

Abelson, Raziel, and Friquegnon, Marie-Louise. 1982. *Ethics for Modern Life*. 2nd edition. New York: St. Martin's Press.

Adams, Marilyn. 1975. "Hell and the God of Justice." RS, 11, 433–447.

Adams, Robert. 1976. "Motive Utilitarianism." JP, 73, 467–481.

Anscombe, G. Elizabeth M. 1957. "Does Oxford Moral Philosophy Corrupt the Youth?" L, LVII (February, 14), 267–271.

———. 1958. "Modern Moral Philosophy." P 33 (January), 1–19. Reprinted in Thomson and Dworkin,* eds. 1968.

———. 1963. *Intention*, 2nd ed. Oxford: Blackwell.

———. 1966. "A Note on Mr. Bennett." A, 26, 208.

———. 1967. "Who is Wronged?" OR, 5, 16–17.

———. 1970. "War and Murder." In Wasserstrom,* ed. 1970.

Aquinas, Thomas. 1970. *Summa Theologiae*. Cambridge: Blackfriars.

Austin, John. 1863. *Lectures on Jurisprudence*. London: Murray.

Beauchamp, Tom and James Childress. 1979. *Principles of Biomedical Ethics*. Oxford: Oxford University Press.

Bennett, Jonathan. 1981. "Morality and Consequences." In McMurrin,* ed. 1981.

Bentham, Jeremy. 1789. *An Introduction to the Principles of Morals and Legislation*.

Boyle, Joseph M. Jr. 1980. "Toward Understanding the Principle of Double Effect." E, 90, 527–538.

Brand, Myles. 1984. *Intending and Acting*. Cambridge, MA: MIT Press.

Brant, R. B. 1959. *Ethical Theory*. Englewood Cliffs, NJ: Prentice-Hall.

Bratman, Michael. 1987. *Intentions, Plans, and Practical Reason*. Cambridge, MA: Harvard University Press.

Brink, David. 1986. "Utilitarianism and the Personal Point of View." JP, 417–438.

Brody, Baruch. 1972. "Thomson on Abortion." PPA 1, no. 3 (Spring), 335–340.

Brueckner, Anthony. 1986. "Brains in a Vat." JP, LXXXIII, 148–167.

Brueckner, Anthony and John Martin Fischer. 1986. "Why is Death Bad?" PS, 50, 213–221.

Casey, John. 1971. "Actions and Consequences." In Casey,* ed. 1971.

——— ed. 1971. *Morality and Moral Reasoning*. London: Methuen.

The Catholic Encyclopedia. 1907. Entry on abortion. New York: Appleton.

Copp, David. 1984. "Considered Judgments and Moral Justification: Conservatism in Moral Theory." In Copp and Zimmerman,* ed. 1984.

Copp, David and David Zimmerman. 1984. *Morality, Reason, and Truth*. Totowa, NJ: Rowman and Allanheld.

Daniels, Norman. 1984. "Two Approaches to Theory Acceptance in Ethics." In Copp and Zimmerman,* ed. 1984.

Daniels, Norman, ed. 1989. *Reading Rawls*. Stanford, CA: Stanford University Press.

Davidson, Donald. 1963. "Actions, Reasons, and Causes." Reprinted in Davidson,* 1980.

———. 1967. "The Logical Form of Action Sentences." Reprinted in Davidson 1980.

———. 1969. "The Individuation of Events." Reprinted in Davidson 1980.

———. 1970. "Criticism, Comment, and Defence." Reprinted in Davidson 1980.

———. 1980. *Essays on Actions and Events*. Oxford: Oxford University Press.

Davis, Lawrence. 1979. *Theory of Action*. Englewood Cliffs, NJ: Prentice-Hall.

Davis, Nancy. 1980. "The Priority of Avoiding Harm." In Steinbock,* ed. 1980.

———. 1984. "Using Persons and Common Sense." E, 94, 382–406.

Delmer, Sefton. 1971. *The Counterfeit Spy*. New York: Harper & Row.

Devine, Philip E. 1978. *The Ethics of Homicide*. Ithaca, NY: Cornell University Press.

Dietrichson, Paul. 1969. "Kant's Criteria of Universalizability." In Wolff,* ed. 1969.

Dinello, Daniel. 1971. "On Killing and Letting Die." A, 31, 83–86.

Donagan, Alan. 1977. *The Theory of Morality*. Chicago, IL: University of Chicago Press.

Downing, A. B., ed. 1969. *Euthanasia and the Right to Death.* Los Angeles, CA: Nash Publishing Co.

Duff, R. A. 1973. "Intentionally Killing the Innocent." A, 33, 16–19.

———. 1976. "Absolute Principles and Double Effect." A, 36, 68–80.

Dworkin, Ronald. 1977. *Taking Rights Seriously.* Cambridge, MA: Harvard University Press.

———. 1989. "The Original Position." In Daniels,* ed. 1989.

Feinberg, Joel, ed. 1973. *The Problem of Abortion.* Belmont, CA: Wadsworth.

———. 1984. *Harm to Others.* Oxford: Oxford University Press. Volume 1 of Feinberg, 1984–1988.

———. 1984-1988. *The Moral Limits of the Criminal Law.* Oxford: Oxford University Press. In four volumes.

Finnis, John. 1973. "The Rights and Wrongs of Abortion." PPA, 2, no. 2 (Winter), 117–145.

Fischer, John Martin. Forthcoming, 1991. "Tooley and the Trolley." PS.

Fitzgerald, P. J. 1967. "Acting and Refraining." A, 27, 133–139.

Fletcher, George. 1967. "Prolonging Life: Some Legal Considerations." WLR, XLII, 999–1016.

———. 1978. *Rethinking Criminal Law.* Boston, MA: Little Brown.

Foot, Philippa. 1977. "Euthanasia." PPA, 6, no. 2 (Winter), 85–112. Reprinted in Foot* 1978.

———. 1978. *Virtues and Vices and Other Essays.* Berkeley, CA: University of California Press.

———. 1984. "Killing and Letting Die." In Garfield,* ed. 1984.

———. 1985. "Morality, Action and Outcome." In Honderich,* ed. 1985.

Frankena, William. 1973. *Ethics.* Englewood Cliffs, NJ: Prentice-Hall.

Frey, R. G. 1975. "Some Aspects to the Doctrine of Double Effect." CJP, 5, 259–283.

Fried, Charles. 1978. *Right and Wrong.* Cambridge, MA: Harvard University Press.

———. 1979. "Correspondence." PPA, 8, no. 4 (Summer), 393–395.

Garfield, Jay, ed. 1984. *Abortion: Moral and Legal Perspectives.* Amherst, MA: University of Massachusetts Press.

Geddes, Leonard. 1973. "On the Intrinsic Wrongness of Killing Innocent People." A, 33, 93–97.

Gillon, Raanan. 1969. "Suicide and Voluntary Euthanasia: Historical Perspective." In Downing,* ed. 1969.

Glover, Jonathan. 1975. "It Makes No Difference Whether Or Not I Do It." PAS, Supp., 49, 172–76.

———. 1977. *Causing Death and Saving Lives.* Harmondsworth, England: Penguin.

Grassian, Victor. 1981. *Moral Reasoning.* Englewood Cliffs, NJ: Prentice-Hall.

Griffin, James. 1977. "Are There Incommensurable Values?" PPA, 7, no. 1 (Fall), 44–47.

Grisez, Germain. 1970. *Abortion: The Myths, the Realities, and the Arguments.* New York: Corpus Books.

Hall, Jerome. 1960. *General Principles of Criminal Law,* 2nd Edition. Indianapolis, IN: Bobbs-Merrill.

Hampshire, Stuart, ed. 1978. *Public and Private Morality.* Cambridge: Cambridge University Press.

Hanik, James. 1975. "Some Light on Double Effect." A, 35, 147–151.

———. 1976. "On 'The Survival Lottery.'" P, 51, 223–25.

Hardin, Garrett. 1974. "Lifeboat Ethics: The Case Against Helping the Poor." PT (September), 38–43 & 123–126.

Hardin, Russell. 1988. *Morality Within the Limits of Reason*. Chicago, IL: University of Chicago Press.

Hare, R. M. 1981. *Moral Thinking*. Oxford: Clarendon Press.

Harman, Gilbert. 1975. "Moral Relativism Defended." PR, 84, 3–22.

Harris, John. 1975. "The Survival Lottery." P, 50, 81–87.

Hart, H. L. A. 1967. "Intention and Punishment." Reprinted in Hart* 1968.

———. 1968. *Punishment and Responsibility*. Oxford: Oxford University Press.

Hart, H. L. A. and A. M. Honore. 1985. *Causation and the Law*, 2nd Edition. New York: Oxford University Press.

Hodgson, D. H. 1967. *Consequences of Utilitarianism: A Study in Normative Ethics & Legal Theory*. New York: Oxford University Press.

Holmes, Oliver Wendell. 1881. *The Common Law*. Boston, MA: Little, Brown.

Honderich, Ted, ed. 1985. *Morality and Objectivity*. London: Routledge and Kegan Paul.

Isenberg, Arnold. 1979. "Critical Communication." In Kennick,* ed. 1979.

Kagan, Shelly. 1989. *The Limits of Morality*. Oxford: Oxford University Press.

Kamisar, Yale. 1969. "Euthanasia Legislation: Some Non-Religious Objections." In Downing,* ed. 1969.

Kamm, Myrna Frances. 1982. "Abortion: A Philosophical Analysis." In Abelson and Friquegnon,* 1982.

———. 1982. "The Problem of Abortion." In Abelson and Friquegnon,* 1982.

———. 1983. "Killing and Letting Die: Methodological and Substantive Issues." PPQ, 64, 297–312.

———. 1985. "Supererogation and Obligation." JP, LXXXII, 118–138.

———. 1985. "Equal Treatment and Equal Chances." PPA, 14, 177–194.

———. 1986. "Harming, Not Aiding, and Positive Rights." PPA, 15, 3–32.

———. Forthcoming. *Morality, Mortality*. Oxford: Oxford University Press.

Kant, Immanuel. 1964. *Groundwork of the Metaphysics of Morals*. Translated by H. J. Paton. New York: Harper & Row.

Kelly, Gerald. 1958. *Medico-Moral Problems*. St. Louis, MO: Catholic Hospital Association.

Kennick, W. E., ed. 1979. *Art and Philosophy*. 3rd edition. New York: St. Martin's Press.

LaFave, Wayne R. and Austin W. Scott, Jr. 1972. *Handbook on Criminal Law*. St. Paul, MN: West.

Lewis, C. S. 1944. *The Problem of Pain*. New York: Macmillan.

Luce, R. Duncan and Howard Raifa. 1957. *Games and Decisions*. New York: John Wiley and Sons.

Lyons, David. 1965. *The Forms and Limits of Utilitarianism*. Oxford: Clarendon Press.

Mackie, John. 1977. *Ethics*. Harmondsworth, England: Penguin.

Manngan, Joseph. 1949. "An Historical Analysis of the Principle of Double Effect." TS, 10, 41–61.

Marcus, Ruth. 1980. "Moral Dilemmas and Consistency." JP, 77, 121–136.

McFadden, Charles. 1961. *Medical Ethics*. 5th edition. Philadelphia, PA: F. A. Davis.

McMahan, Jeff. 1988. "Death and the Value of Life." E, 99, 32–61.

McMurrin, Sterling, ed. 1980. *The Tanner Lectures on Human Values*, vol. 1. Cambridge: Cambridge University Press.

———. 1981. *The Tanner Lectures on Human Values*, vol. 2. Cambridge: Cambridge University Press.

Mill, John Stuart. 1863. *Utilitarianism*.

Montmarquet, James. 1982. *"Doing Good: The Right and the Wrong Way."* JP, LXXIX, 439–455.

Moore, G. E. 1903. *Principia Ethica*. Cambridge: Cambridge University Press.

Nagel, Thomas. 1972. "War and Massacre." PPA, 1, no. 2 (Winter), 123–144. Reprinted in Nagel* 1979 b.

———. 1979 b. "Equality." Reprinted in Nagel* 1979 b.

———. 1979 b. *Mortal Questions*. Cambridge: Cambridge University Press.

———. 1980. "The Limits of Objectivity." In McMurrin* 1980.

———. 1986. *The View From Nowhere*. Oxford: Oxford University Press.

The New Catholic Encyclopedia. 1967. "The Principle of Double Effect." New York: McGraw-Hill.

Nicholson, Susan Teft. 1978. *Abortion and the Roman Catholic Church*. Knoxville, TN: Journal of Religious Ethics Monograph.

Nozick, Robert. 1974. *Anarchy, State, and Utopia*. New York: Basic Books.

O'Donnell, Thomas. 1957. *Morals in Medicine*. Westminister, MD: Newman Press.

———. 1976. *Medicine and Christian Morality*. New York: Alba House.

O'Neill, Onora. 1975. *Acting on Principle: An Essay on Kantian Ethics*. New York: Columbia University Press.

Parfit, Derek. 1979. "Correspondence." PPA, 8, no. 4 (Summer), 395–397.

———. 1984. *Reasons and Persons*. Oxford: Clarendon Press.

Perkins, Rollin M. and Ronald N. Boyce. 1982. *Criminal Law*. Mineola, NY: Foundation Press.

Prosser, William L. 1971. *Handbook of the Law of Torts*, 4th edition. St. Paul, MN: West.

Quinn, Warren. 1984. "Abortion: Identity and Loss." PPA, 13, 1 (Winter), 24–54.

Rachels, James, ed. 1971. *Moral Problems*. New York: Harper & Row.

———. 1981. "Reasoning About Killing and Letting Die." SJP, 19, 465–473.

———. 1986. *The End of Life: Euthanasia and Morality*. Oxford: Oxford University Press.

———. 1988. "Euthanasia, Killing, and Letting Die." In Sterba,* ed. 1988.

Railton, Peter. 1984. "Alienation, Consequentialism, and the Demands of Morality." PPA, 13, no. 2 (Spring), 134–171.

Rawls, John. 1971. *A Theory of Justice*. Cambridge, MA: Harvard University Press.

———. 1974. "Some Reasons for the Maximin Criterion." AER, 64, Papers & Proc., (May), 141–146.

———. 1982. "Social Unity and Primary Goods." In Sen and Williams,* eds. 1982.

————. 1980. "Kantian Constructivism in Moral Theory." JP, 515–572. The Dewey Lectures.

Richards, Norvin. 1984. "Double Effect and Moral Character." M, XCIII, 381–397.

Robinson, Paul H. 1984. *Criminal Law Defenses*, vol. 1, St. Paul, MN: West.

Russell, Bruce. "Presumption, Intrinsic Relevance, and Equivalence." JMP, 4, 263–268.

St. John-Stevas, Norman. 1964. *The Right to Life*. New York: Holt, Rinehart and Winston.

Salmond, John. *Jurisprudence*, 11th ed. London: Sweet & Maxwell.

Sanders, J. T. 1988. "Why the Numbers Should Sometimes Count." PPA, 17, 3–14.

Scanlon, T. M. 1975. "Preference and Urgency." JP, LXXII, 655–669.

————. 1978. "Rights, Goals, and Fairness." In Hampshire,* ed. 1978.

Scheffler, Samuel. 1982. *The Rejection of Consequentialism*. Oxford: Clarendon Press.

Searle, John. 1983. *Intentionality*. Cambridge: Cambridge University Press.

Sen, Amartya. 1982. "Rights and Agency." PPA, 11, no. 1, 3–39.

Sen, Amartya and Bernard Williams, eds. 1982. *Utilitarianism and Beyond*. Cambridge: Cambridge University Press.

Shaw, William. 1980. "Elementary Lifesaving." SJP, 18, 87–97.

Sidgwick, Henry. *The Method of Ethics*, 7th edition. London: Macmillan.

Singer, Peter. 1979. *Practical Ethics*. New York: Cambridge University Press.

Slote, Michael. 1985. *Common-sense Morality and Utilitarianism*. Boston, MA: Routledge & Kegan Paul.

Smart, J. J. C. and Bernard Williams. 1973. *Utilitarianism: For and Against*. Cambridge: Cambridge University Press.

Steinbock, Bonnie, ed. 1980. *Killing and Letting Die*. Englewood Cliffs, NJ: Prentice-Hall.

Sterba, James, ed. 1988. *Morality in Practice*. Belmont, CA: Wadsworth.

Tanner, Michael. 1964–5. "Examples in Moral Philosophy." PAS, 65, 61–76.

Thalberg, Irving. 1977. *Perception, Emotion, and Action*. New Haven, CN: Yale University Press.

Thomson, Judith Jarvis. 1971. "A Defense of Abortion." PPA, 1, no. 1 (Fall), 47–66.

————. 1977. *Actions and Other Events*. Ithaca, NY: Cornell University Press.

————. 1986. *Rights, Restitution, and Risk: Essays in Moral Theory*. William Parent, ed. Cambridge, MA: Harvard University Press.

————. 1990. *The Realm of Rights*. Cambridge, MA: Harvard University Press.

Thomson, Judith Jarvis and Dworkin, Gerald, eds. 1968. *Ethics*. New York: Harper & Row.

Tooley, Michael. 1972. "Abortion and Infanticide." PPA, 2, no. 1 (Fall), 37–65.

————. 1973. "A Defense of Abortion and Infanticide." In Feinberg* 1973.

————. 1983. *Abortion and Infanticide*. Oxford: Clarendon Press.

Veatch, Robert. 1977. *Case Studies in Medical Ethics*. Cambridge, MA: Harvard University Press.

Wallace, James. 1978. *Virtues and Vices*. Ithaca, NY: Cornell University Press.

Walzer, Michael. 1977. *Just and Unjust Wars*. New York: Basic Books.

Wasserstrom, Richard, ed. 1970. *War and Morality*. Belmont, CA: Wadsworth.

Williams, Bernard. 1973a. "Ethical Consistency." In Williams* 1973 b.

————. 1973 b. *Problems of the Self*. Cambridge: Cambridge University Press.

Williams, Glanville. 1957. *The Sanctity of Life and the Criminal Law*. New York: Knopf.

————. 1961. *Criminal Law: The General Part*. 2nd edition. London: Stevens.

Wolff, Robert Paul, ed. 1969. *Foundations of the Metaphysics of Morals with Critical Essays*. Indianapolis, IN: Bobbs-Merrill.

Woodward, James F. 1981. "Why Numbers Count." SJP, 19, 531–40.

Index

Credits

Arisaka, Yoko - cartoons
Used with the permission of the artist.

Bennett, Jonathan - "Whatever the Consequences . . ."
By permission of the author. This article first appeared in *Analysis*, 1966.

Boorse, Christopher & Roy A. Sorensen - "Ducking Harm"
Christopher Boorse & Roy Sorensen, "Ducking Harm," *The Journal of Philosophy*, LXXXV, 3 (March 1988), p. 115–134. Reprinted by permission of *The Journal of Philosophy* and the authors.

Costa, Michael J. - "The Trolley Problem Revisited" and "Another Trip on the Trolley"
Reprinted by permission of the author and *Southern Journal of Philosophy*, 1987.

Davis, Nancy (Ann) - "The Doctrine of Double Effect . . ."
Davis, Nancy ("Ann"), "The Doctrine of Double Effect: Problems of Interpretation," *Pacific Philosophical Quarterly*, 1984, Vol. 65, No. 2, pp. 107–123. Reprinted by permission of *Pacific Philosophical Quarterly* and the author.

Dickey, Ken - "Why I May Count the Numbers"
Reprinted by permission of the author.

Fischer, John Martin - "Thoughts on the Trolley Problem"
Reprinted by permission of the author.

Foot, Philippa - "The Problem of Abortion . . ."
By permission of the author.

Hanna, Robert - "Morality *De Re*: Reflections on the Trolley Problem"
Reprinted by permission of the author.

Kagan, Shelly - "The Additive Fallacy"
Kagan, Shelly, "The Additive Fallacy," *Ethics*, 1988. Reprinted by permission of The University of Chicago Press and the author.

Kavka, Gregory S. - "The Numbers Should Count"
Kavka, Gregory, "The Numbers Should Count," *Philosophical Studies*, 1979. Reprinted by permission of Kluwer Academic Publishers.

Malm, Heidi - "Killing, Letting Die and Simple Conflicts"
Malm, H. M., "Killing, Letting Die and Simple Conflicts," *Philosophy and Public Affairs*, Vol. 18, N. 3. Copyright (c) 1989 by Princeton University Press. pp. 238–258 reprinted by permission of Princeton University Press.